Proceedings of the 2015 International Conference on

Software Engineering and Information Technology

(SEIT2015)

Proceedings of the 2015 International Conference on

Software Engineering and Information Technology (SEIT2015)

Guilin, Guangxi, China 26 – 28 June 2015

Editor

Xiaolong Li

Indiana State University, USA

World Scientific

NEW JERSEY • LONDON • SINGAPORE • BEIJING • SHANGHAI • HONG KONG • TAIPEI • CHENNAI • TOKYO

Published by

World Scientific Publishing Co. Pte. Ltd.
5 Toh Tuck Link, Singapore 596224
USA office: 27 Warren Street, Suite 401-402, Hackensack, NJ 07601
UK office: 57 Shelton Street, Covent Garden, London WC2H 9HE

British Library Cataloguing-in-Publication Data
A catalogue record for this book is available from the British Library.

SOFTWARE ENGINEERING AND INFORMATION TECHNOLOGY (SEIT2015)
Proceedings of the 2015 International Conference on Software Engineering and Information Technology

ISBN 978-981-4740-09-8

Printed in Singapore

Editorial

On behalf of the organizing committee of the 2015 International Conference on Software Engineering and Information Technology (SEIT2015), I would like to welcome all of you to participate in this wonderful conference held in Guilin, Guangxi, China during June 26-28, 2015. The SEIT2015 aims to provide an excellent international academic forum for sharing knowledge and results in theory, methodology and applications on information technology, computing intelligence and computer applications, algorithm and simulation, signal and image processing, electrical engineering and software engineering. The conference looks for significant contributions to all above fields.

The SEIT2015 has so far been an important event and has attracted many scientists, engineers and researchers from academia, government laboratories and industry internationally. This year, we received more than two hundred submissions and after rigorous review, sixty seven papers were accepted. The participants come from nine countries. There were two keynote presentations, six oral sessions and one poster session.

The SEIT2015 organizing committee would like to express our sincere appreciation to all authors for their contributions to this book. We would like to extend our thanks to all the referees for their constructive comments on all papers; especially, we would like to thank to organizing committee for their hard work that allowed the success of the SEIT2015.

Contents

Chapter 1

Information Technology

An Access Control Protocol for Wireless Sensor Networks

X. Zheng*
College of Information Science and Technology, Gannan Medical University, Ganzhou Jiangxi

L.Z. Chen
College of Information Science and Technology, Gannan Medical University, Ganzhou Jiangxi

Z.B. Xie
College of Information Science and Technology, Gannan Medical University, Ganzhou Jiangxi

**Email: smile_335@126.com*

ABSTRACT: Nodes in a sensor networks may be lost because of power exhaustion or malicious attacks. Therefore it's necessary for new nodes' deployment. Using Bloom Filter, we propose an access control protocol including the mutual authentication procedure and common key generation. It's efficient for the nodes' addition, deletion and authentication. At last, the paper makes an analysis of the performance and safety about the proposed protocol.

KEYWORDS: Sensor network; Mutual authentication; Access control; Bloom Filter.

1. INTRODUCTION

Currently, wireless sensor networks are threatened by internal malicious nodes which inject illegal information, manipulate data, replicate nodes and forge nodes. Therefore, puts forward a kind of security, high efficiency, low energy consumption of the authentication protocol is a hot research in wireless sensor networks. Due to the nodes' characteristics of limited storage capacity, computing power and limited battery power, it's needed to consider the situation of the old nodes' energy depletion and the new nodes addition in the safe authentication, etc.

In 2007, Yun Zhou et al. proposed an access control protocol based on ECC public key algorithm. During the authentication, by comparing the new nodes' boot time of joining the network, and then verify the signature to realize a new node' authentication, and can complete the establishment of shared keys between neighboring nodes at the same time. However, malicious nodes can use the short interval of new node starts time to implement a malicious attack. On the other hand, public key digital signature algorithm consumes a lot of energy. In this paper, using ideas from the article [3] by Bloom Filter and Counting Bloom Filter, Use symmetric encryption algorithm to achieve mutual authentication, and use Diffie-Hellman algorithm to establish a shared key between nodes. Without using the start time of the new node, this agreement also can complete the mutual authentication. During the authentication process, nodes only need to store the filter data generated by the base and use the Bloom Filter to verify each other's public key, without transmission of digital certificates and thus improves the authentication efficiency, reduces the communication cost.

2. PROPAEDEUTICS

2.1. *Concepts of bloom filter*

Bloom filter [4] is a kind of random data structure of high spatial efficiency, it can be used to judge whether an element is belong to a collection. When the initial state, Bloom Filter is an array containing M digits, and each set to 0. Suppose there is a such set $S=\{s_1,s_2,\cdots,s_n\}$, and $\{h_i\}_{i=1}^{k}$ is k mutually independent hash function, in which $h_i: S \mapsto \{0,\cdots,m-1\}$. In order to decide whether "s" is an elements of set "S" for each calculation, and calculate h_i using $h_i\left(s_j\right)$. If all the position of $h_i\left(s_j\right)$ is 1 (1≤i≤k), then $s_j \in S$, otherwise $s_j \notin S$ $s_j \notin S$. But sometimes it will mistakenly consider the elements belonging to this which accurately do not (false positive). The error rate can be estimated, now we assume that the $kn < m$ and each hash function is completely random. When all the elements which are in this collection $S=\{s_1,s_2,\cdots,s_n\}$ are mapping to the m digits array by k hash functions, the probability that one digit of this array is a zero is $\left(1-\frac{1}{m}\right)^{kn} \approx e^{-kn/m}$, so the error rate $f=\left(1-\left(1-\frac{1}{m}\right)^{kn}\right)^{k} \approx \left(1-e^{-kn/m}\right)^{k}$.

2.2. *To minimize the error rate [4,5]*

Since the Bloom Filter need multiple hash function which can map set to the array, so how many hash function should choose to reduce the error rate when it query elements? There are two mutually exclusive reason: If the number of hash function is a lot, the ratio of getting the result of 0 is grate for an element do not belong to the set; But on the other hand, if the number of hash function is a few, then there will be more 0 in the array. Note that, if $f=\left(1-\left(1-\frac{1}{m}\right)^{kn}\right)^{k} \approx \left(1-e^{-kn/m}\right)^{k}$, then $f=e^{k\ln(1-e^{-kn/m})}$.

We define $g=k\ln(1-e^{-kn/m})$, as long as the g get the minimum, f will get the minimum. Due to $\frac{dg}{dk}=\ln(1-e^{-kn/m})+\frac{kn}{m}\frac{e^{-kn/m}}{1-e^{-kn/m}}$, when $\frac{dg}{dk}=0$, g will get the minimum, in the same times of $k=\frac{m}{n}\ln 2$. At this time, $f_{\min}=\left(\frac{1}{2}\right)^{\frac{m}{n}\ln 2}=(0.6185)^{\frac{m}{n}}$.

3. THE ACCESS CONTROL PROTOCOL

The access control protocol contains three phases: system initialization, mutual authentication and key negotiation process and the addition and revocation of node. Based on the elliptic curve digital signature have the advantages of key short, fast processing speed, and low bandwidth requirements, in the key negotiation process we choose Diffie-Hellman algorithm.

Set F_q is a finite field, q is a prime number. The base to choose the appropriate elliptic curve constructed the point set $E(F_q)$, G is the element with n steps of $E(F_q)$, FR is one of the elements of F_q. Select safe hash function $h(\cdot)$, and get the system parameters $D=(q,E(F_q),FR,G,n,h)$.

3.1. *System initialization*

Proposed there are r nodes in a fixed region adjacent, denoted as $\{N_1,N_2,\cdots,N_r\}$. Set a (pk_i,sk_i) s the public key and private key for node N_i. Install a Bloom Filter and a Counting Bloom Filter in the base station, which assign different key pair (pk_i,sk_i) for each node $N_i\,[i\in r]$ and use a one-way hash function to calculate sk_i z times (z is the maximum number of nodes of the fixed network), generates a hash chain of length $z+1$: $h^0(sk_i), h(sk_i), h^2(sk_i),\cdots, h^i(sk_i),\cdots h^z(sk_i)$, exist $h^m(sk_i)=h(h^{m-1}(sk_i))$. Then construct the set: $S_N=\{<N_1,pk_1>,<N_2,pk_2>,\cdots\}$, #{ } represents the cardinality, where #{ S_N }$=r$. Using the system to provide k independent hash function (e.g., SHA - 1) that provided by the system, base station application of Bloom Filter technology calculate a m - bit vector v_N, denoted as $v_N=v_N^0 v_N^1\cdots v_N^{m-1}$. And every v_N^i, $i\in[0,m-1]$, content that $v_N^i=\begin{cases}1, if\ \exists l\in[1,k], j\in[1,r], s.t. h_l(N_j\|pk_j)=i\\ 0, otherwise\end{cases}$. This way, $<N_j,pk_j>\in S_N$, if and only if the components all the hash function $h_l(N_j\parallel pk_j)=i$ meet that $v_N^i=1$. The base station calculate the vector $\overline{v_N}=\overline{v_N^0}\,\overline{v_N^1}\cdots\overline{v_N^{m-1}}$ to v_N in Counting Bloom Filter, and every $\overline{v_N^i}$, $i\in[0,m-1]$, meeting that $\overline{v_N^i}=\#\{(N_i\parallel pk_i)\,|\,h(N_i\parallel pk_i)i, for\exists l\in[1,k], j\in[1,r]\ \}$. Finally, the base station preload the key pair (pk_i,sk_i), a one-way hash chain $h(\cdot)$ and vector v_N to each node side, and keep $\overline{v_N}$ secretly. The base station also broadcast the parameters $D, h^z(sk_i), i\in[1,r], z, \{h_l(\cdot)\}_{l=1}^k$.

3.2. *Two-way authentication key negotiation process*

In the mutual authentication process of the protocol, each node once successfully verified, the base station update their hash values once broadcasted. That is, if a node N_i has been successfully verified m times, the station broadcast $h^{z-m}(sk_i)$. Here, assuming that node N_i has been successfully verified u times, node N_j has been successfully verified w times, the base broadcast $h^{z-u}(sk_i)$ and $h^{z-w}(sk_j)$ firstly. So the mutual authentication and key negotiation process is as follows:

(a) N_i send $N_i\parallel pk_i$ to N_j, start the two-way authentication.

(b) N_j send $N_j\parallel pk_j$ to the legally registered node N_i.

- Verify the N_i is a legally registered node;
- N_j use the k independent hash function $\{h_l(\cdot)\}_{l=1}^k$ to calculate $v_N[h_l(N_i\parallel pk_i)]=?1$. If and only if all the $l\in[1,k]$, meeting $v_N[h_l(N_i\parallel pk_i)]=1$, then pk_i is the real public key

of N_i. If verified pk_i is true, then continue to the next step; if it is false, then cancel the connection.

- send $N_j \| pk_j$ to N_i.
- (c) N_i s N_j end $C_i = E_{\sigma_{ij}}(h^{z-u-1}(sk_i))$ to the legally registered node N_j.
- Verify the N_j is a legally registered node; In the similar method, N_i calculate $v_N[h_l(N_j \| pk_j)] = ?1$. If and only if all the $l \in [1,k]$, meeting $v_N[h_l(N_j \| pk_j)] = 1$, then pk_j is the real public key of N_j. If verified pk_j is true, then continue to the next step; If it is false, then cancel the connection.
- N_i calculate $\sigma_{ij} = sk_i \cdot pk_j$ and $C_i = E_{\sigma_{ij}}(h^{z-u-1}(sk_i))$.
- N_i sends $C_i = E_{\sigma_{ij}}(h^{z-u-1}(sk_i))$ to N_j.
- (d) N_j sends $C_j = E_{\sigma_{ij}}(h^{z-w-1}(sk_j))$ to N_i.
- N_j calculate $\sigma_{ij} = sk_j \cdot pk_i$, verify $h(D_{\sigma_{ij}}(C_i)) = ?\, h^{z-u}(sk_i)$. If equal, then N_i is a trusted node, continue to the next step; if not equal, then cancel the connection.
- N_j calculate $C_j = E_{\sigma_{ij}}(h^{z-w-1}(sk_j))$ and send C_j to N_i.

(e) N_i verify that $h(D_{\sigma_{ij}}(C_j)) = ?\, h^{z-w}(sk_j)$. If equal, for N_j is a trusted node, you can continue to communicate with the shared key; if not equal, then cancel the connection.

In this way, the node N_i and the node N_j show their legal status to each other, realize the mutual authentication and key agreement. Specifically as shown:

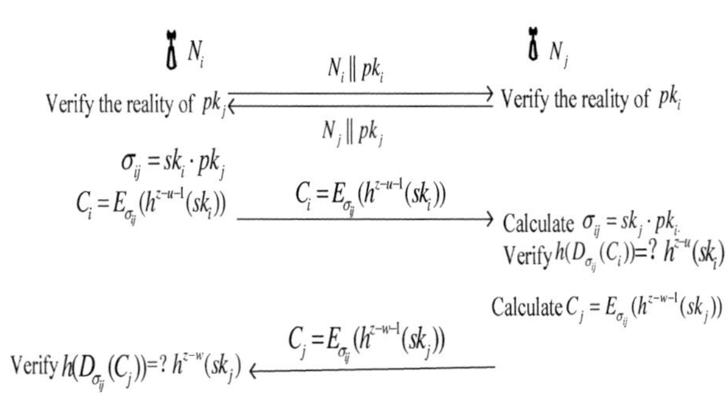

Figure 1. Mutual authentication key negotiation process.

3.3. *The revocation and addition of nodes*

When there is a malicious forgery sensor node, etc., you need to revoke the node; when the sensor node energy depletion, etc., need to add new nodes. The base station use Counting Bloom Filter technology to realize revocation and join nodes.

3.3.1. *The revocation of nodes*

Assuming revoked node N_j, the base station performs the following actions:

(a) Firstly checks the hash value $\{h_l(N_j \| pk_j)\}_{l=1}^{k}$ of N_j. If $h_l(N_j \| pk_j) = i$, then $\overline{v_N^i}$ of base station do the operation to minus 1.

(b) According to the updated vector $\overline{v_N}$, a new vector v_N' can be obtained by base, remember to $v_N' = v_N^{0'} v_N^{1'} \cdots v_N^{m-1'}$. This moment $v_N' = 1$, if and only if $\overline{v_N^i} \geq 1$, otherwise $v_N' = 0$.

(c) Calculated $v_{\Delta N} = v_N \oplus v_N'$ ($\oplus$ show xor or operation), then delete vector v_N. Obviously $v_{\Delta N}$ is also a m-bit vector, with up to k bits to 1.

(d) The base station broadcasts the vector $v_{\Delta N}$ in the region.

(e) The sensor nodes according vector $v_{\Delta N}$ to the updated vector v_N. If $v_{\Delta N}^i = 1$, then $v_{\Delta N}^i = 0$, $i \in [0, m-1]$.

This completes the revocation of a sensor node. After the node revocation, will also destroy its corresponding key pair pk_j / sk_j.

3.3.2. *The addition of nodes*

Suppose there is a new node N_{r+1} requires join the network, firstly N_{r+1} need to register in the base station, obtain a key pair (pk_{r+1}, sk_{r+1}). The base make use of Bloom Filter technology, to map $< N_{r+1}, pk_{r+1} >$ to the range of $\{0 \cdots m-1\}$, getting updated vector v_N, and using Counting Bloom Filter technology to obtain updated vector $\overline{v_N}$. Revocation node using the same method, the base station calculates vector $v_{\Delta N}$ according to the updated vector v_N, $\overline{v_N}$, then broadcast vector $v_{\Delta N}$.

After registering a new node N_{r+1}, the base station calculates the node's one-way hash chain $h(sk_{r+1})$, and preloads it to the node side N_{r+1}. With the node N_{r+1} for the initial certification, the base station broadcast $h^z(sk_{r+1})$, and so, other nodes in the region know when a new node is added. Next, the same steps to certification.

4. SECURITY ANALYSIS AND PERFORMANCE ANALYSIS

4.1. *Security analysis*

The agreement based on the base station is absolutely credible, malicious node can't get the private key. During the authentication process, a malicious node can obtain the public key by eavesdropping network traffic, but it can't calculate the correct shared key which is used to verify the hash values are bound to fail, so as to cancel the connection.

The security of this agreement depends on Diffie-Hellman algorithm for discrete logarithm difficulty, the safety of the hash function and the confidentiality of the node's private key. Safe assumption based on only the real node know the private key, once the node's private key leak, the agreement will not work.

4.2. *Performance analysis*

In the mutual authentication and key agreement process, the main calculation of a node is needed to finish is that: a plot point is calculated based on ECC, a symmetric encryption and hashing calculation. In the article [2], the main computing node is a dot product calculations, once ECDSA signature and ECDSA solution to sign out. Therefore, this protocol has a smaller amount of calculation, without having to carry a digital certificate of merit. On the other hand, the node only needs to store the filter data generated of base side, hash value chain and node key pair.

5. CONCLUSION

This paper presents a wireless sensor network access control protocol that can achieve mutual authentication and key agreement between nodes, when a new node is added, this agreement also play a role. In addition, the agreement also facilitates the dynamic management of nodes.

REFERENCES

- [1] Zhou. Y, Fang. Y, Zhang. Y. Securing wireless sensor networks: a survey [J], IEEE Communications Surveys, 2008, v10, 6-28.
- [2] Zhou. Y, Zhang. Y, Fang. Y. Access control in wireless sensor networks [J], Security issues in Sensor and Ad Hoc Networks, 2007, v5, 3-13.
- [3] Ren K, Lou W, Zhang Y. Multi-user broadcast authentication in wireless sensor networks [C]. 4th Annual IEEE Communications Society Conference, San Diego, CA, United States, 2007, 223-232.
- [4] Mitzenmacher M. Compressed Bloom Filters [J], IEEE/ACM Transactions on Networks, 2002, v10, 613-620.

Stochastic Analysis of Sleep Mode Based on Mobile Traffic in Heterogeneous Cellular Network

Y. Chen* & Q. Zhu
Jiangsu Key Lab of Wireless Communications, Key Lab on Wideband Wireless Communications and Sensor Network Technology of Ministry of Education Nanjing University of Posts and Telecommunications, Jiangsu Nanjing, 210003, China
**Email: 1173133649@qq.com*

ABSTRACT: Due to the exponential growth of mobile data traffic, Heterogeneous Cellular Network (HCN) has been a long-term trend of mobile communications, which will also bring rapid increase of energy consumption. In this paper, the average achievable capacity of users in a cell and the throughput of users at the Macro cell-edge are derived by using a stochastic geometry based model. With consideration of mobile traffic model, a technical approach of Pico base station (PBS) sleep mode is introduced in order to achieve the lowest energy consumption. An energy consumption minimization problem is formulated and the optimal sleeping probability for PBS is determined. Numerical results confirm the achieved energy savings performance of proposed sleep mode without damaging the system performance.

KEYWORDS: Heterogeneous cellular network; Sleep mode; Energy savings.

1. INTRODUCTION

With the growing demand for mobile data traffic, the fifth generation (5G) system will be composed of heterogeneous cellular network (HCN) which can not only improve the system capacity, but also make cell deployment more flexible. However, the Energy Efficiency (EE) is becoming pretty hot due to the sharp rise in energy consumption in HCN [1].

A novel analytical and practical network model using stochastic geometry is proposed in this paper. Under this model, the positions of all base stations (BSs) are drawn from a Poisson Point Process (PPP). It is proved that the PPP model is more idealized and tractable than the traditional grid model. Also, it can describe the dense and complex mobile communication network better than the traditional one [2].

There have been many studies on sleeping methods in order to solve the problem of energy consumption caused by the rapid development of communication and information technology. In [3], the energy savings is studied in an Orthogonal Frequency Division Multiple Access (OFDMA) network by using the PPP model. With consideration of outage probability and BS transmission power, the BS sleep modes are discussed respectively under two path loss models. The same problem is considered in [4] and the authors' aim is to investigate the EE with sleep mode in HCN. A BS power consumption minimization problem is formulated with consideration of outage probability and users' uplink power constraint. And the technical approach of BS sleep mode is proved to reduce energy consumption effectively. The authors in [5] raise questions on energy-spectral efficiency trade off in HCN with sleep control and analyze the relationship between EE and spectrum efficiency. How the threshold affects the energy efficiency is also analyzed with the aid of stochastic geometry and markov chain theory. However, the sleep modes in the above papers are investigated without consideration of mobile traffic.

In this paper, a system model is proposed base on the PPP model and the PBS sleep mode is analyzed in order to reduce energy consumption in HCN. According to the proposed sleep mode, the PBS will enter into sleep mode when the traffic load in Pico cell is below a given threshold and its users are handed off to the neighboring Macro cells. Since the Quality of Service (QoS) will be deteriorated as a result of turning off some Pico base stations (PBSs), the average achievable capacity of users in a cell and the throughput of users at the Macro cell-edge will be analyzed in this paper and the given QoS requirement is certain to be met while minimizing the energy consumption. Finally, the energy consumption minimization problem is constructed based on the mathematical analysis and then the optimal sleeping probability for PBS is determined.

The remainder of the paper is organized as follows. Section 2 describes the system model. In Section 3, the mathematical model, including the analysis of average achievable capacity of users in a cell, the throughput of users at the Macro cell-edge, mobile traffic model and the BS power consumption model are discussed. Then, the PBS sleep mode of HCN is proposed in Section 4. The numerical results are presented in Section 5 and finally, the conclusion is drawn in Section 6.

2. SYSTEM MODEL

2.1. *Heterogeneous cellular network model*

As seen in Figure 1, the two-tier HCN model consists of Macro base stations (MBSs) and PBSs deployed according to homogeneous PPP. Under this model, the positions of MBSs and PBSs are modeled as independent homogeneous PPPs Φ_1, Φ_2 with density λ_1, λ_2. No inter-tier interference is considered and the orthogonal multiple access is employed within a cell, i.e. there are no intra-cell interference.

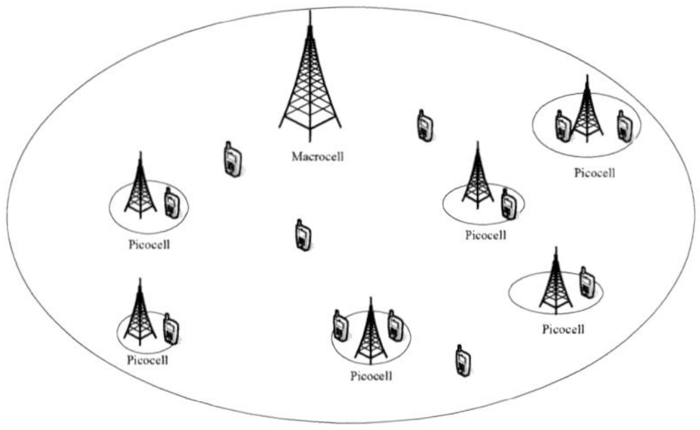

Figure 1. Downlink HCN with MBSs and PBSs.

2.2. *Signal-to-interference-plus-noise ratio model*

In this paper, the power loss propagation model is used with the same path loss exponent $\alpha (\alpha > 2)$ for each tier. The Rayleigh fading is also assumed here. It is assumed that the mobile user under consideration is located at the origin and its SINR from the nearest BS in each tier is

$$SINR_i(\mathrm{r}_i) = \frac{P_i h_i |r_i|^{-\alpha}}{\sum_{k \in \Phi_{i\backslash o}} P_{i,k} h_{i,k} |r_{i,k}|^{-\alpha} + W} \tag{1}$$

where P_i is the BSs' transmission power in tier i, $|r_i|$ is the distance of the typical user from the nearest BS in the i th tier, $k \in \Phi_{i\backslash o}$ denotes BSs except the serving BS in tier i, $|r_{i,k}|$ is the distance from BSs $k \in \Phi_{i\backslash o}$ to the origin, h_i and $h_{i,k}$ are all the exponentially distributed channel power with unit mean, and W is the noise power.

3. MATHEMATICAL MODEL

3.1. *Average achievable rate*

According to [2], the probability density function (PDF) $f(\mathrm{r}_i)$ of r_i for each tier is

$$f(\mathrm{r}_i) = 2\pi\lambda_i r_i \exp\left(-\lambda_i \pi r_i^2\right) \tag{2}$$

The average achievable capacity of users in the cell of tier i is

$$\begin{aligned} \overline{C}_i &= \int_0^\infty \mathrm{E}\left[B_i \log_2(1+\mathrm{SINR}_i)\right] f(r_i)\, dr_i \\ &= 2\lambda_i \pi \int_0^\infty \mathrm{E}\left[B_i \log_2(1+\mathrm{SINR}_i)\right] r_i \exp\left(-\lambda_i \pi r_i^2\right) \end{aligned} \tag{3}$$

where B_i is the bandwidth available in the cell of tier i.

According to [2], in the particular case of $\alpha = 4$ and $I = \sum_{k \in \Phi_{i\backslash o}} P_{i,k} h_{i,k} |r_{i,k}|^{-\alpha} \gg W$, the average achievable capacity of users in the cell of tier i can be further simplified as

$$\begin{aligned} \overline{C}_i &= \int_0^\infty \frac{1}{1+\sqrt{2^{\zeta/B_i}-1}\arctan\left(\sqrt{2^{\zeta/B_i}-1}\right)} d\zeta \\ &= 2.14 B_i \ \ bits/s \end{aligned} \tag{4}$$

Assuming the available bandwidth of each cell is shared among all its users, so the average achievable capacity of each user in the cell of tier i is obtained

$$\overline{C}_{i,p} = 2.14 B_{i,p} \ \ bits/s \tag{5}$$

where $B_{i,p}$ is the bandwidth available of each user in the cell of tier i.

3.2. *Throughput of users at the macro cell-edge*

The throughput of users at the Macro cell-edge is defined as the capacity achieved by the user which is at a distance R from its serving MBS. If an area A is covered with N Macro cells with a circular coverage area of radius R, then $kA = N\pi R^2$ for k is a geometry constant and $k \le 1$. Also, it can be derived that $\gamma_1 = \frac{N}{A} = \frac{k}{\pi R^2}$.

According to [2], in the particular case of $\alpha = 4$ and $W \to 0$, the capacity achieved by the user which is at a distance R from its serving MBS is

$$\begin{aligned} \tau_{1,R} &= \int_0^\infty \exp\left(-\gamma_1 \pi R^2 \sqrt{2^{\zeta/B_{1,p}}-1}\arctan\left(\sqrt{2^{\zeta/B_{1,p}}-1}\right)\right) d\zeta \\ &= \int_0^\infty \exp\left(-k\sqrt{2^{\zeta/B_{1,p}}-1}\arctan\left(\sqrt{2^{\zeta/B_{1,p}}-1}\right)\right) d\zeta \end{aligned} \tag{6}$$

The probability that the throughput of users at the Macro cell-edge is above a threshold ζ is formed as

$$P\left(\tau_{1,R} > \zeta\right) = \exp\left(-k\sqrt{2^{\zeta/B_{i,p}}-1}\arctan\left(\sqrt{2^{\zeta/B_{i,p}}-1}\right)\right). \quad (7)$$

3.3. *Mobile traffic model*

According to [6], the number of active users in a cell at time t for each tier $M_{i,t}$ follows Poisson distribution as

$$f_{M_{i,t}}(x_i;\Upsilon_i) = \frac{\Upsilon_i^{x_i}\exp(-\Upsilon_i)}{x_i!} \quad (8)$$

where $\Upsilon_i = 0.0031\exp\left(1.085\lg\left(\overline{C}_i\right)\right)$.

The mean traffic throughput demand per user is denoted as $R_{i,t} = 10^{\Omega}$ where Ω follows log-normal distribution. So, the PDF for the mean traffic throughput demand per user is

$$f_{R_{i,t}}(y_i;\mu,\sigma) = \frac{\exp\left(-\left(\left(\ln\left(\lg(y_i)\right)-\mu\right)^2/2\sigma^2\right)\right)}{y_i\lg(y_i)\sigma\sqrt{2\pi}\ln 10} \quad (9)$$

where $\mu = 1.35$ and $\sigma^2 = 0.2$.

The traffic throughput demand per cell in each tier can be derived as $R_{i,t} = M_{i,t}R_{i,t}$ and the PDF $f_{R_{i,t}}(z)$ for it can be expressed as

$$f_{R_{i,t}}(z_i) = \sum_{x_i=1}^{\lfloor z_i \rfloor}\frac{\exp\left(-\left(\left(\ln\left(\lg(z_i/x_i)\right)-\mu\right)^2/2\sigma^2\right)\right)}{z_i\lg(z_i/x_i)\sigma\sqrt{2\pi}\ln 10}\frac{\Upsilon_i^{x_i}\exp(-\Upsilon_i)}{x_i!} \quad (10)$$

It's known that the expected value of the traffic date per user in each tier at time t is

$$E\left(R_{i,t}\right) = 10^{\exp\left(\mu+\frac{\sigma^2}{2}\right)}. \quad (11)$$

Therefore, the expected value of the traffic date per cell in each tier at time t can be expressed as

$$E\left(R_{i,t}\right) \simeq 0.0031\times 10^{\exp\left(\mu+\frac{\sigma^2}{2}\right)}\exp\left(1.085\lg\left(\overline{C}_i\right)\right). \quad (12)$$

Given the average achievable capacity of users per cell in each tier, the expected traffic load is defined as

$$E\left(L_{i,t}\right) = \frac{E\left(R_{i,t}\right)}{\overline{C}_i} = \frac{54.98\exp\left(1.085\lg\left(\overline{C}_i\right)\right)}{\overline{C}_i}. \quad (13)$$

3.4. *Base station power consumption model*

Generally, the BS power consumption consists of two fundamental parts. One is the static power consumption of all circuit elements. Another one is the power consumption that scales with the radio frequency (RF) output power of the BS. Therefore, the mean power consumption of the BS in tier i over time period T can be expressed as [7]

$$E\left(E_i\right) = T\left(\frac{P_i}{v_i}E\left(L_{i,t}\right) + P_{i,s}\right) = T\left(\frac{P_i}{v_i}\frac{54.98\exp\left(1.1\lg\left(\overline{C}_i\right)\right)}{\overline{C}_i} + P_{i,s}\right) \quad (14)$$

where v_i is the radio head efficiency, $P_{i,s}$ is the static power consumption of the BS.

4. SLEEP MODE

The main content of this paper is the research on the energy savings when the sleep mode is applied in PBSs. As mentioned before, a PBS sleep mode is applied here. When the traffic load in Pico cell is below a given threshold Ξ at time t, the PBS will enter into sleep mode and its users will be handed off to the neighboring Macro cells while ensuring that the average achievable capacity of each user in a Macro cell $\overline{C}_{1,p}^{'}$ is no less than the given threshold Λ. It shall also be ensured that the probability that the throughput of users at the Macro cell-edge maintained above the threshold Θ is larger than θ. The implementation of PBS sleep mode is random that PBSs are turned off with probability $\beta\ (0 \le \beta \le 1)$ and the remaining active PBSs follow a new PPP with density $\lambda_2^{'} = (1-\beta)\lambda_2$ according to the PPP thinning property. Meanwhile, the expected number of active users in a Macro cell is expressed as $\Upsilon_1^{'} = \Upsilon_1 + \frac{\lambda_2}{\lambda_1}\Upsilon_2\beta$.

The probability that the traffic load in a Pico cell is below certain threshold Ξ is given by

$$P\left(L_{2,t} < \Xi\right) = \int_{\overline{C}_2 L_{2,0}}^{\overline{C}_2\Xi} f_{r_{2,t}}(z_2)dz_2 = \int_{\overline{C}_2 L_{2,0}}^{\overline{C}_2\Xi}\sum_{x_2=1}^{\lfloor z_2 \rfloor}\frac{\Upsilon_2^{x_2}\exp(-\Upsilon_2)}{x_2!}\frac{\exp\left(-\left(\left(\ln\left(\lg(z_2/x_2)\right)-\mu\right)^2/2\sigma^2\right)\right)}{z_2\lg(z_2/x_2)\sigma\sqrt{2\pi}\ln 10}dz_2 \quad (15)$$

According to the expected number of active users in a Macro cell after implementing the sleep mode, the average achievable capacity of each user in a Macro cell is obtained as

$$\overline{C}_{1,p}^{'} = 2.14B_{1,p}^{'} = 2.14\frac{B_1}{\gamma_1^{'}} = 2.14\frac{B_1}{\Upsilon_1 + \frac{\lambda_2}{\lambda_1}\Upsilon_2\beta}. \quad (16)$$

Given a certain Macro cell-edge requirement (Θ,θ), the probability that the throughput of users at the Macro cell-edge maintained above the threshold Θ is

$$\mathrm{P}\left(\tau_{1,R}^{'} > \Theta\right) = \exp\left(-k\Delta(\Theta,\Xi)\arctan\Delta(\Theta,\Xi)\right) \quad (17)$$

where $\Delta(\Theta,\Xi) = \sqrt{2^{\frac{\Theta\Upsilon_1^{'}}{B_1}} - 1} = \sqrt{2^{\frac{\Theta\left(\Upsilon_1 + \frac{\lambda_2}{\lambda_1}\Upsilon_2\beta\right)}{B_1}} - 1}$.

Based on the foregoing analysis, the energy consumption problem considering the PBS sleep mode is discussed. Since the energy consumption of whole network is dominated by the BSs, it will be reduced with the gradual turning off of PBSs. Therefore, the purpose of this paper is to obtain the optimal energy savings by determining the sleeping probability for PBS. And the sleeping probability for PBS optimization problem is formulated as

$$\begin{aligned} &Max \quad \beta \\ &s.t. \quad \beta \le \mathrm{P}\left(L_{2,t} < \Xi\right) \\ &\qquad\ \theta \le \exp\left(-k\Delta(\Theta,\Xi)\arctan\Delta(\Theta,\Xi)\right). \\ &\qquad\ \Lambda \le 2.14\frac{B_1}{\Upsilon_1 + \frac{\lambda_2}{\lambda_1}\Upsilon_2\beta} \end{aligned}$$

The solution of this problem is achieved for

$$\beta = \min\left(\mathrm{P}\left(L_{2,t} < \Xi\right), \beta_{\Theta,\theta}, \frac{\left(\frac{2.14B_1}{\Lambda} - \gamma_1\right)\lambda_1}{\lambda_2\gamma_2}\right)$$

where $\mathrm{P}\left(L_{2,t} < \Xi\right)$ can be solved by using the "Gauss-Kronrod" technique. If the solution of $\theta = \exp\left(-k\Delta(\Theta,\Xi)\arctan\Delta(\Theta,\Xi)\right)$ in $[0,1]$ can be obtained by dichotomy, it is written as $\beta_{\Theta,\theta}$. Otherwise, $\beta_{\Theta,\theta} = 0$.

5. NUMERICAL RESULTS AND DISCUSSIONS

The numerical results and discussions for the proposed PBS sleep mode are presented in this section. Here the HCN is modeled, the initial density of MBS is $\lambda_1 = 10^{-6}m^{-2}$ and the density of PBS is $\lambda_2 = 10\times10^{-6}m^{-2}$.

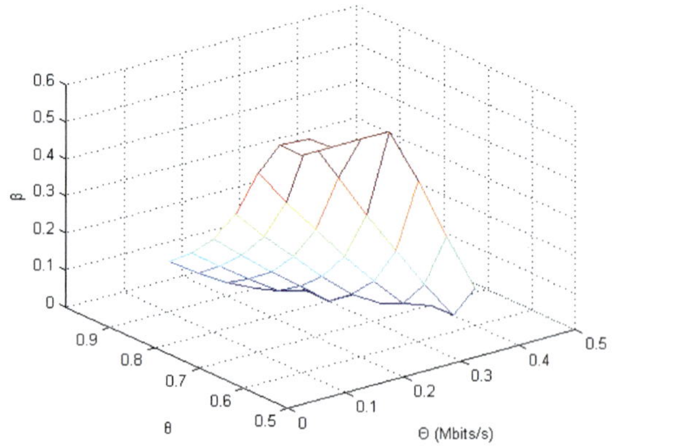

Figure 2. Sleeping probability for PBS with proposed sleep mode as a function of (Θ,θ).

Figure 2 demonstrates the sleeping probability for PBS as a function of (Θ,θ) given the condition of $B_1 = 5MHz$, $B_2 = 1MHz$, $\Xi = 0.1$ and $\Lambda = 0.8\times10^6\ bits/s$. As seen from the plot, the sleeping probability for PBS increases with the decrement of Macro cell-edge requirement (Θ,θ), i.e. it is more energy efficient. Since PBSs are gradually turned off, more users are handed off to the neighboring Macro cells. It will inevitably lead to a decline in the performance of the throughput at Macro cell-edge. Hence, it takes only a decline in Macro cell-edge requirement to ensure the sleeping probability for PBS. In addition, there is no change in the sleeping probability when the Macro cell-edge requirement (Θ,θ) is below a certain value. This is because the average achievable capacity of each user in Macro cell has been equal to the given threshold, i.e. the maximum sleeping probability has been reached.

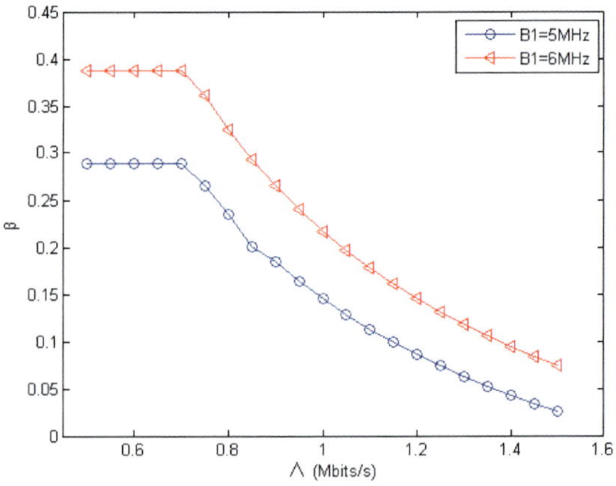

Figure 3. Sleeping probability for PBS with proposed sleep mode as a function of Λ.

Figure 3 presents the sleeping probability for PBS with respect to Λ for different values of B_1 with $B_2 = 1MHz$, $\Xi = 0.1$, $(\Theta, \theta) = (0.2\, Mbits/s, 0.7)$. In this figure, the sleeping probability for PBS decreases with the increment of the average achievable capacity requirement Λ, i.e. the energy savings performance becomes worse. In this paper, it's assumed that the available bandwidth is divided equally between all users in a cell, so the expected number of active users in Macro cell will increase along with more and more PBSs being turned off. That's the reason why the sleeping probability is affected by the average achievable capacity of each user in Macro cell. However, there is no increment in the sleeping probability when the average achievable capacity requirement Λ is below a certain value. That's because the Macro cell-edge performance (Θ, θ) has been equal to the given threshold, i.e. the maximum sleeping probability has been reached. As can also been observed from the plot, higher sleeping probability is achieved for greater available bandwidth B_1, which is based on that bandwidth has a decisive role in the average achievable capacity of users in a cell and the throughput of users at the Macro cell-edge.

6. CONCLUSIONS

In this paper, the energy savings of HCN with PBS sleep mode is investigated. Using stochastic geometry, the closed-form expressions of average achievable capacity of users in a cell and throughput of users at the Macro cell-edge are derived. With consideration of mobile traffic model, the energy consumption problem is constructed and the optimal sleeping probability for PBS is obtained. The numerical results validate the energy savings performance of the proposed sleep mode.

Future work may include different cases of mobile traffic models. In addition, the open access which means the user is allowed to access any tier's BSs will be considered in HCN.

REFERENCES

- [1] Hossain, E. et al. 2014. Evolution toward 5G multi-tire cellular wireless networks: an interference management perspective. IEEE Wireless Communication Magazine 21(3):118-127.
- [2] Andrews, J.G. et al. 2011. A tractable approach to coverage and rate in cellular networks. IEEE Transactions on Communications 59(11):3122-3134.
- [3] Tsilimantos, D. et al. 2013. Stochastic analysis of energy savings with sleep mode in OFDMA wireless networks. IEEE INFOCOM Proceedings: 1097-1105. Turin: IEEE CS.
- [4] Peng, J.L. et al. 2014. Stochastic Analysis of Optimal Base Station Energy Saving in Cellular Networks with Sleep Mode. IEEE Communications Letters 18(4):612-615.
- [5] Peng, J.L. et al. 2013. Stochastic Geometry Analysis of Energy Efficiency in Heterogeneous Network with Sleep Mode. IEEE Wireless Communications Letters 2(6): 615-618.
- [6] Laner, M. et al. 2012. Users in cells: a data traffic analysis. IEEE Wireless Communications and Networking Conference: 3063–3068. Paris: IEEE CS.
- [7] Wang, S.Y. & Guo, W.S. 2013. Energy and cost implications of a traffic aware and quality-of-service constrained sleep mode mechanism. IET Communications 7(18): 2092-2101.

Design and Implementation of a Library Management System Based on RFID

Y. Liu
Library of Changsha University of Science & Technology, Changsha, Hunan, P.R. China, 410114
Email: 540988542@qq.com

ABSTRACT: The explosive increasing books puzzle the librarians in managing, sorting, circulating and inventing them efficiently and accurately. The widely used bar codes technology in the libraries is unable to meet the requirements. Considering the advantages of RFID technology such as contactless penetrating tag identification, large information capacity of tag, The paper developed a library management system using the RFID technology under the Qt Creator integrated development environment, which uses RFID tags and readers to realize the library information inputting, lending and return and library information management, etc.

KEYWORDS: Library management system, RFID, Bar code, Qt Creator.

1. INTRODUCTION

Due to the rapid development of science and technology in modern society, all kinds of literature resources are growing explosively, which puzzle the librarians in managing, sorting, borrowing and inventorying them efficiently and accurately.

At present, the bar code identification technology is widely used in the management of libraries in our country [1]. This technology has the characteristics of low cost and simple, but there are numerous limitations, such as needing manual operation. The work to borrow or return the books using bar code technology is tedious and time consuming to the readers and the librarians. Furthermore, a lot of mistakes will produce when the bar codes were damaged or stained, so seriously affected the borrowing efficiency and service quality [2].

With the maturity and popularity of the RFID technology, using the RFID technology can not only solve the contradiction between the librarians and the readers, also can improve the work efficiency of the librarians. So the paper introduced a library management system developed under using the RFID technology under the Qt Creator integrated development environment, which uses RFID tags and readers to realize the library information inputting, lending and return and library information management, etc.

2. RFID AND SYSTEM DEVELOPMENT PLATFORM

Radio Frequency Identification (RFID) technology, which was developed in the 1990s, is a non-contact automatic identification technology using RF signal through space coupling (alternating magnetic field or electromagnetic field) and transmit information through non-contacting message to static or moving objects [3,4,5]. RFID is often referred to as induction electronic chip or induction card, contactless card, electronic tag, electronic bar code, etc. A simple RFID system consists of read/write device, transponder or an electronic tag, its working principle is launched by reading and writing a certain frequency of radio wave energy to the transponder, used to drive the transponder circuit, read the inside of the transponder ID code [3,4,6,7].

RFID has some superiorities to bar code. For example, RFID can be made into smaller size and/or into different shapes, it has resistance to water and oil, reusable, longevity, penetrating and safer. So, the RFID technology has been widely used in various industries [5], such as in automatic charging system, entrance guard system, identity card and so on.

The Qt Creator 2.8.1 under Windows operation system was utilized to develop the book management system. The QT Creator is a multi-platform C++ graphical user interface application framework. It provides developers all the necessary functions to build a state-of-the-art graphic user interface (GUI). It is fully object-oriented and easy to be expanded in programming. Qt Creator can view, edit the code, and view the interface, and design, modify, compile, and so on in graphical form, and even debug the application under the PC environment. At the same time, Qt Creator is a cross-platform tools, it supports a variety of operating system platforms, including Linux, MacOS, Windows [8].

3. OVERALL DESIGN OF THE SYSTEM

A book management system, using the contactless IC card and RFID reader, was developed to realize the borrowing, returning of books, and managing the personnel information. It has specific functions as following:

(1) The librarian can manage the books information and personnel information. The librarian can add, delete, or modify the information of books and the borrowers. And the borrowers also can query the relevant information of books.

(2) The borrowers can identify themselves by swiping theirs Identification cards and borrow the books by swiping the IC cards of the book. The librarians can see which books were borrowed by someone through building the relations between the books and the borrowers.

(3) The borrowers can return the books by swiping his ID card, and the system can display the information of the returned books. The librarians can know which books were returned by whom at the same time.

There are four modules in the system: the Borrowing module is functioned to the books borrowing and establishing the relation between the borrowers and the books. The Returning module is functioned to release the relations after the borrowers returned the books. The Books management module is functioned to add, delete, or modify the information, to query the information of the borrowed books. And the borrower personnel information management module is functioned to record the information of the borrowers.

4. THE DESIGN OF THE SYSTEM

4.1. *The design of the main system interface*

Because the system consists of four modules, namely the borrowing module, returning module, books management module and the borrower personnel information management module, so these four parts should be displayed in the main interface. One can understand the functions of every module clearly through the main interface. The designed main interface of the system was shown in Figure 1.

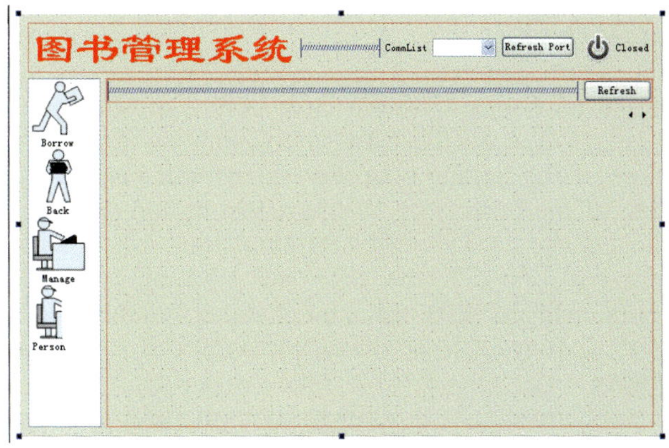

Figure 1. The main interface of the system.

As shown in figure 2, the icons of the four modules of the system were set on the left side of the main interface. And there are three more buttons were added into the main interface, the function of the Closed button is to switch off the books management system, the Refresh Port button is to Refresh the serial interface, and the function of Refresh button is to read the card. The function of CommList is to choose the serial port.

4.2. *The design of borrow module*

The main function of this module is to borrow books. To borrow books successfully, the borrower should swipe his ID card firstly, then swipe the IC cards of the books, and finally click the borrow button. The system will build relations between the borrower and the borrowed books. And the books were displayed as Borrowed, and they can not be borrowed anymore. The interface of the borrow module was designed as shown in Figure 2.

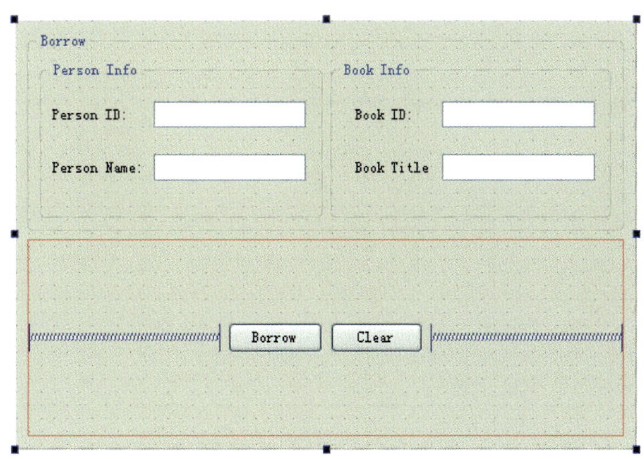

Figure 2. The interface of the Borrow module.

The functions of the Borrow and Clear buttons was borrowing the books or clearing the borrowing information respectively.

4.3. *The design of the Return book module*

The main function of this module is to return the borrowed books. To return the books, the borrower should swipe his ID card firstly, then swipe the IC cards of the books, then the system will display the time of the borrowing. If the return button was then clicked, the books will be returned successfully. The relations between the borrower and the returned books will be relieved, and statuses of the books were displayed as In store, and they can be reborrowed.

The interface of Return book module was designed as shown in Figure 3.

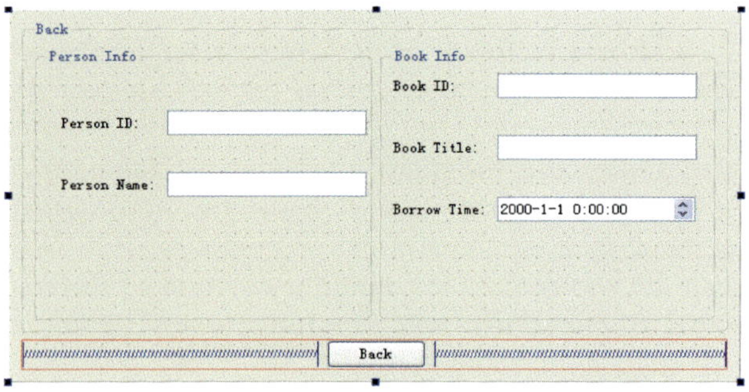

Figure 3. The interface of the Return module.

4.4. *The design of Books management module*

The main function of this module is to manage the books, including add, delete or modify the information of books, display the status, inquiry the time of borrowed or returned of the books. The interface of the Books management module was designed as shown in Figure 4.

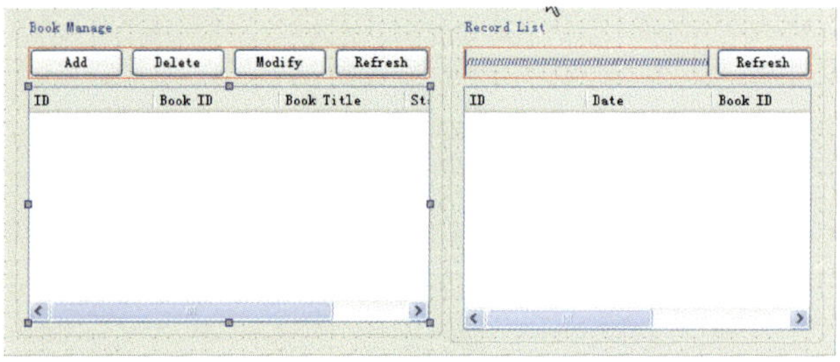

Figure 4. The interface of the Books management module.

The functions of five buttons were adding, deleting, modifying and refreshing the information of books respectively.

5. TESTS OF THE SYSTEM

This system was tested after composed, and it was found that the four function modules of the system can be operated successfully. As to the limited space, the detailed test process and test results were not listed in this paper.

6. CONCLUSIONS

This paper developed a book management system using Qt Creator software platform under the Windows operating system, based on the fully understand of the current status and development trend of books management system management system and RFID technology.

The system makes full use of the technical advantage of RFID and contactless IC card. It can realize self-service in borrowing or return books by the borrowers, reduce the workload of the librarians, and solve the contradiction between the readers and the library.

REFERENCES

- [1] Cai Meng-xin. RFID in Library [M]. Beijing: Beijing Library Press. 2010.2
- [2] Chen Jin, Deng Jing-kang, Jing Xiang-gu. RFID technology and application in Library [M]. Shanghai: Profile of Shanghai Jiao Tong University Press. 2013.1
- [3] Zhang Xiao-hui. Present and future of library RFID technology [M]. Beijing: World Book Inc. 2011.12
- [4] Gao Jian-liang, He Jian-biao. Principle and Technology of RFID in Internet of Things [M]. Beijing: Publishing House of Electronics Industry. 2013.7
- [5] Tian Xian-long. Advanced tutorial of High frequency RFID technology [M]. Beijing: Metallurgical Industry Press. 2012.4
- [6] http://www.bainuosoft.com/tiaoma/81.html
- [7] Stephen Prata. C++ Primer Plus [M]. Beijing: Posts & Telecom Press. 2012.7.
- [8] Lu Wen-zhou. The development and instance of QT [M]. Beijing: Publishing House of Electronics Industry. 2013.6.
- [9] Hanson A, Levin B L. Building a Virtual Library. Hershey: Information Science Publishing. 2003.2.

The Application of Advanced Clock Synchronization Technology in Intelligent Substation System

F. Zhai [1], Y.F. Cao[2], W. Cen[3], Z.Q. Sun[4] & X.B. Liang[5]
China Electric Power Research Institute, Beijing, 100192, China

Email: [1]zhaifeng@epri.sgcc.com.cn, [2]caoyongfeng@epri.sgcc.com.cn, [3]cenwei@epri.sgcc.com.cn, [4]sunzhiqiang@epri.sgcc.com.cn, [5]liangxiaobing@epri.sgcc.com.cn

ABSTRACT: According to the different requirements of clock synchronization's precision for intelligent substation system at all layers, this paper has applied the GPS clock synchronization technology and PTP clock synchronization technology to intelligent substation system's simulation platform. It has designed a clock synchronization scheme which can reach to microsecond precision by using substation control layer, bay layer and process layers three layers hierarchical clock synchronization mechanism, so as to ensure the equipment's clock being accurate, reliable, and unified at all layers of the intelligent substation system.

KEYWORDS: Intelligent substation system; GPS clock synchronization; PTP clock synchronization; Timestamp.

1. INTRODUCTION

With the high growth of electric power demand, digital economy's development and the adjustment of national energy policy, the relationship among the power grid, electric power market and the electricity customers is more and more close, customer's demand for power quality has been improved continually. In order to satisfy the power supply's energy saving, environmental protection, high efficient, reliable, stable and sustainable development requirements, the construction of the smart grid is imperative. The intelligent substation is the important base and support for the construction of the strong smart grid, which is the source of power grid operation data collection and the command's execution units. It uses advanced, reliable, integrated, low carbon and environmental intelligent equipment, makes total station information digitalization, communication platform networked, information sharing standardization as basic requirements, not only can automatically complete such basic functions as data collection, measurement, control, protection, monitoring and so on, but also can support such advanced functions as grid's real-time automatic control, intelligent adjustment, online analysis and decision, collaborative interaction and so on [1-2]. The realization of these functions need to further improve the accuracy and efficiency for intelligent substation's information interaction and data processing, so a variety of master station and equipment's time synchronization problem is particularly important, especially the clock synchronization's accuracy plays a vital role for such functions as the data sampling, fault recording, automatic control and so on in intelligent substation system's process layer. It is imminent to solve the problems of intelligent substation clock synchronization, design a more precise, economic, simple, efficient, standardized clock synchronization system [3]. In order to solve above problems, it applies the GPS clock synchronization technology and PTP clock synchronization technology to intelligent substation system's simulation platform, using substation control layer, bay layer and process layers three layers hierarchical clock synchronization mechanism to design a clock synchronization scheme which can reach microsecond precision, which ensured the accuracy, reliability and unity of the intelligent substation's station control layer, spacer layer and process layer's host and device clock, laid a solid foundation for smart grid's reliable and stable operation.

2. THE LOGICAL ARCHITECTURE OF INTELLIGENT SUBSTATION COMMUNICATION SYSTEM

So far, most of the intelligent substation systems are constructed based on IEC61850 standard. The intelligent substation systems are divided into three layers from the function, those are the station control layer, spacer layer and process layer, see figure 1. The station control layer is composed of background monitoring system, remote control device, information protection substation system, message monitoring system, video monitoring system and other subsystems, which understand and master the real-time running status of the whole substation, control the substation, realize the functions of information collection, calculation, analysis, storage and contact with the remote dispatching center through interval layer device. The interval layer device generally refers to such secondary equipment as relay protection devices, measurement and control device and so on, which are composed of different voltage grade of protection device, measurement and control device, monitoring device, metering device, wave record device, ac/dc power supply and so on, to realize such functions as collecting real-time data and information, protection and controlling for primary equipment, implement operation atresia, making priority control to set out commands of collecting data, statistical calculations and control, and transiting the executing data etc. The process layer is composed of such collecting and executing units as merging unit and intelligent terminals to complete the functions as electricity energy distribution, conversion, transmission and measurement, control, protection, metering, condition monitoring and other related functions [4-5].

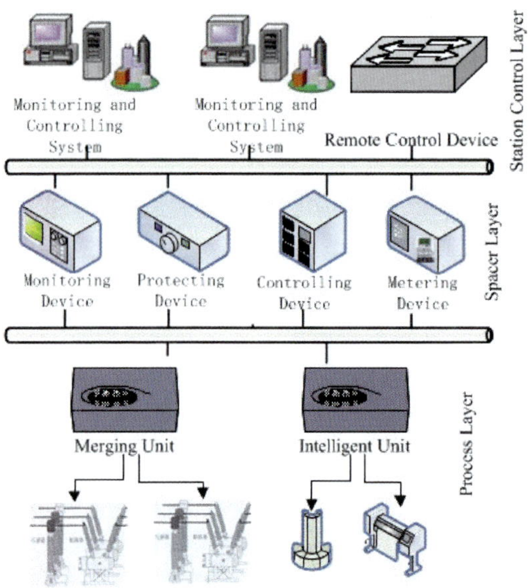

Figure 1. The Logical Architecture of Intelligent Substation.

3. THE APPLICATION OF CLOCK SYNCHRONIZATION TECHNOLOGY IN INTELLIGENT SUBSTATION SYSTEM

So far, the commonly used clock synchronization technology are GPS clock synchronization clock synchronization technology and network clock synchronization technology, etc. GPS (Global Positioning System) is the second generation satellite positioning, navigation and timing system, which can globally coverage, all-weather real-timely provide the user with highly synchronous time to international standard time (UTC), as well as the longitude, latitude and other information, so it can be widely used in electric power system [6-7]. However, in the intelligent substation system, the station control layer, spacer layer and process layer' measuring and monitoring equipment number is large, and they are distributed dispersedly, if each terminal or device is equipped with GPS clock synchronization device, the cost is huge, and the maintenance is also very difficult. PTP high accuracy network clock synchronization protocol based on IEEE1588 can achieve sub-microsecond synchronization precision and all kinds of the synchronous message can be divided into many messages to transmit based on the network protocol and user datagram protocol, which is more suitable for distributed deployment data acquisition terminal, metering and controlling devices to synchronize clock [8]. Therefore, in order to ensure intelligent substation system clock is accurate, efficient and consistent, it can adopt a hybrid hierarchical clock synchronization mechanism, which is deploying GPS satellite clock synchronization device at the station control layer master station side so as to make the station control layer clock consistent with GPS satellite clock, the spacer layer device's clock is consistent with the station control layer clock, and the process layer device's clock is consistent with the spacer layer device's clock though PTP high accuracy network clock synchronization protocol, the clock synchronization system's structure is shown in Figure 2.

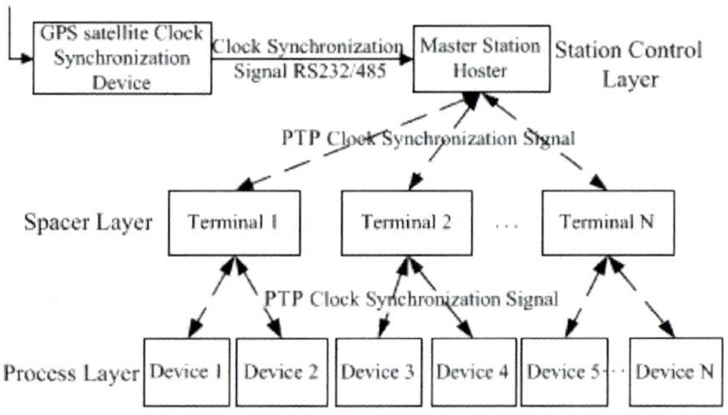

Figure 2. Clock synchronization system structure diagram.

3.1. *Application of GPS clock synchronization technology in station control layer*

GPS clock synchronization system includes three parts, which are the ground monitoring center, space satellites and clock synchronization device, see Figure 3. Among them, the ground monitoring center mainly includes GPS control station, monitoring station and communication auxiliary system, which can track and maintain the satellites in the outer space, monitor satellite's operation situation and signal's performance, updated satellite clock's correction volume and the ephemeris, determine the user's position and time, etc. The space satellites include 24 on-orbit satellites mainly distributed in 6 orbital planes, which rotate the earth 1 cycle every 12 hours, mainly used to provide distance signal and the time data message to the user. The clock synchronization device mainly includes GPS timing clock and satellite antenna. The GPS timing clock can simultaneously receive 4 to 8 satellite signals at any moment by satellite antenna in its view range, then make protocol conversion, the local time conversion and error correction by the signal processing unit, decode the clock signal which can meet all kinds of demands for devices time setting. In the GPS clock synchronization system, as long as the satellite orbit distribution being designed rationally, the user can observe at least three satellites at any point on the earth, and measure the distance between the satellite and them, they can accurately calculate the position and time, the time accuracy can reach nanosecond [9].

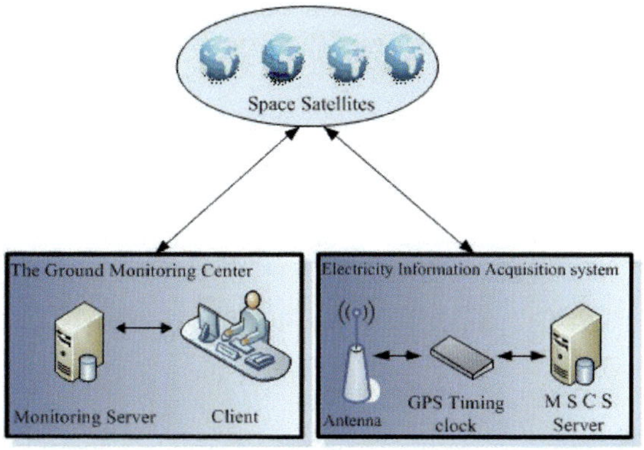

Figure 3. GPS clock synchronization system.

In the intelligent substation station control layer clock synchronization system, the ground control center monitor the satellite's operating status and signal's performance within the scope of vision first, if the signal is in good condition, GPS timing clock will receive satellite's UTC time information, then process it by the signal processing unit, to correct the station control layer clock synchronization server's internal clock, and put this time as the standard time to correct device's time in spacer layer and process layer.

The key component in intelligent substation station control layer clock synchronization system is the GPS timing clock, which is composed of GPS satellite single receiving unit, electricity level conversion unit, central processing unit, displaying unit, clock control unit and clock information output unit, the specific structure see Figure 4. The GPS signal receiving unit acquaints the standard clock information to transmit to electricity level conversion unit, then, converts it to the TTL level signal which can be recognized by the central processing unit, the central processing unit make protocol conversion, local time conversion, error correction and decoding to the received information, then display the effectively posited GPS clock information on LCD screen. If it is difficult to locate accurately, the clock control unit controls the display unit to display GPS timing clock's inner time, at the same time, the GPS timing clock will transmit the processed standard clock information to the master station clock synchronization server to correct its internal clock by clock information output unit [10].

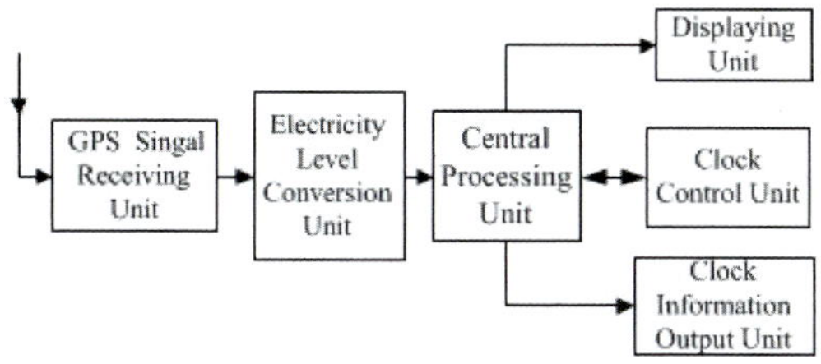

Figure 4. GPS timing clock's structure.

3.2. *Application of PTP Clock Synchronization Technology in spacer layer and process layer*

PTP protocol (Precision Time Protocol) is a kind of precision clock synchronization protocol defined by the IEEE-1588 standard. It is easy to implement, occupies less network and computing resources, the cost is relatively low, whose hardware clock synchronization precision can reach ns level, software clock synchronization precision can reach ms level, therefor it can be widely used in more dispersal terminals and measuring monitoring equipment's clock synchronization system [11]. PTP protocol mainly use the Ethernet as transmission medium, though timestamp mechanism to realize the time's synchronization between master clock and slave clock by calculating the clock deviation between the master clock and slave clock and the information packets' transmission delay time in the network [12]. It defines four message types, those are synchronization information message (Sync), following information message (Follow_Up), delay request information message (Delay_Req) and delay response information message (Delay_Resp), the basic principle see Figure 5.

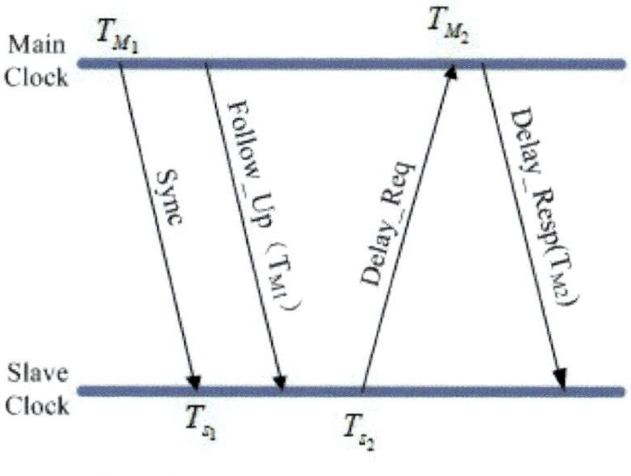

Figure 5. PTP protocol's basic principle.

(1) At first, the master clock send Sync to the slave clock and record the Sync's real send time T_{M_1}, then send the (Follow_Up) to the slave clock. The Follow_Up packet contains the time information T_{M_1}.

(2) The slave clock receives the Sync message and records its arrival time T_{s_1}, calculate the clock deviation between master clock and slave clock by T_{s_1}, T_{M_1} and the network delay time T_{delay}, The clock deviation is:

$$T_{\text{offset}} = T_{s_1} - T_{M_1} - T_{\text{delay}} \quad (1)$$

(3) The slave clock send the Delay_Req to master clock and record the real delay request message's send out time T_{s_2}.

(4) The master clock receives Delay_Req, and record the message's real arrival time T_{M_2}, then send the delay response information message (Delay_Resp) to the slave clock, in which, the Delay_Resp includes time information T_{M_2}. It can calculate the message's transmission delay time between the master clock and the slave clock by T_{s_1}, T_{M_1}, T_{s_2} and T_{M_2}, which is:

$$T_{\text{delay}} = \frac{(T_{s_1} - T_{M_1}) + (T_{M_2} - T_{s_2})}{2} \quad (2)$$

Though above calculation, the slave clock can get the clock deviation and the network transmission delay time to correct the current slave clock's time to synchronized with the master clock. In the intelligent substation spacing layer and process layer's network system, the master clock and the slave clock can realize the clock synchronization by periodically exchanging the clock synchronization message with timestamp.

4. THE CLOCK SYNCHRONIZATION PERFORMANCE TESTING IN THE INTELLIGENT SUBSTATION SYSTEM

In order to verify the intelligent substation system's clock synchronization accuracy, it has set a clock synchronization test system on intelligent substation simulation platform, the test system see Figure 6. In order to ensure the test data's fairness and reliability, this test system has introduced clock synchronization test device which can acquaint GPS satellite standard clock signal directly. In the process of clock synchronization, the test device first sent TEST_REQ test request message to the station control layer host clock, spacer layer device clock and the process layer device clock by group broadcasting mode. When they have received the test requests message, they record the current time, and send TEST_RESP test response message to the test host at predetermined time, the test host records the arrival time of each response message to judge the clock synchronization effect by comparing the timestamps with the message received and response time.

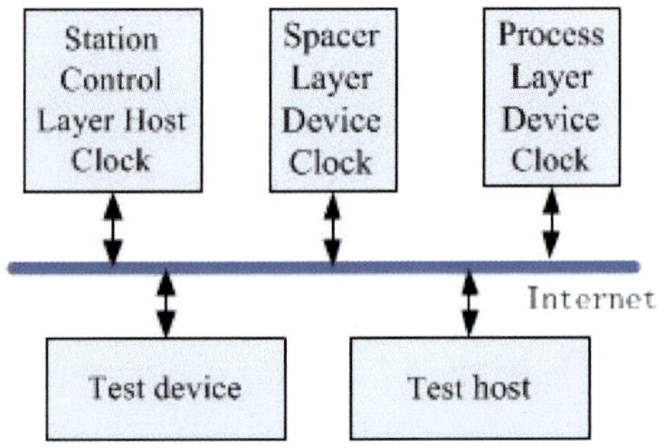

Figure 6. Clock synchronization test system.

The entire test sustained 12 h, the test cycle is20 ms, test results are shown in Table 1.

Table 1. Clock synchronization system test results.

test item	Master	Terminal	Device
test number	2160000	2160000	2160000
test frequency (1/ms)	15	15	15
average deviation (μs)	0.025	0.48	0.98
max positive deviation (μs)	0.039	4.583	7.945
max negative deviation (μs)	-0.041	-2.167	-5.618

Since the intelligent substation system's station control layer host clock is directly timed from the GPS satellite clock synchronization device, the synchronization error primarily depends on the accuracy of GPS time clock, whose clock accuracy can reach to ±50ns or less. The spacer layer and process layer device use high precision PTP clock synchronization technology to carrying out clock synchronization, whose clock accuracy can reach to 5μs and 8μs or less respectively. It can fully meet the intelligent substation system's clock synchronization requirements.

5. CONCLUSIONS

In order to ensure all levels of the intelligent substation system's clock synchronization, this paper has applied the GPS clock synchronization technology and PTP clock synchronization technology to intelligent substation system's simulation platform. It has designed a clock synchronization scheme which can reach to microsecond precision by using substation control layer, bay layer and process layers three layers hierarchical clock synchronization mechanism. From the testing result, the system's clock synchronization accuracy can satisfy the requirements of IEC61850 standard, the scheme is feasible, and can effectively solve the problems about master station, terminal and monitor and measure equipment's real-time requirements in intelligent substation system, so it has high application value.

REFERENCES

- [1] Gao Xiang. The Application Technology of Digitized Substation [M] Beijing: China Electric Power Press, 2008: 53-156.
- [2] Gao Xiang. The Application Propect of Digitized Substation [J] East China Electric Power, 2006, 34(8) 47-53.
- [3] Zhang Yanhui. Research on an Optimized Time Synehronism Scheme for Smart Substation [D]. Thesis for the Master Degree in North China Electric Power University 2011.
- [4] Liu Ting. The Research on Information Security Management of Intelligent Power Substation [D]. Thesis for the Master Degree in North China Electric Power University 2013.
- [5] Xu Yonggang, Feng Yang, Wang Shuang. Information Security of Smart Substation Protection System Research [J] Electronic Measurement Technology. 2014, 37(6) 135-142.
- [6] Wu Peitao. Application Of GPS Clock Syntion [J]. Scientific Innovation and Application, 2012, 11, 56-57.
- [7] Jin Xiangli. Application Of GPS Clock Synchronizing Technology in Electric Automation [C]. Electric Industry Information Conference in 2009, 482-484.
- [8] Yin Zhi-liang, Liu Wan-shun, Yang Qi-xun, Qin Yin-li. A New IEEE 1 588 Based Technology for Realizing the Sampled Values Synchronization on the Substation Process Bus [J]. Automation of Electric Power Systems, 2005, 29(13) 60-63.
- [9] Dong Jian-li, Zhou Dan. Design and implementation of general timing monitored control system based on GPS [J]. Computer Engineering and Design, 2007, 28(12) 3006-3012.
- [10] Huang Jingyao, Zhang Chao, He Mingchuan, Zhao Hui jie Yang Shuang. Design and Application of Power System GPS Synchronous Clock Device [J]. Computer Measurement & Control, 2012, 20(12) 3355-3358.
- [11] Song Bo, Sun Chao, Jiang Shou-da. A High-Precision Local Area Network Clock Synchronization Method Based on PTP Protocol [J]. Techniques Of Automation And Applications, 2010, 1 67-70.
- [12] Yang Li, Zhao Jian guo, Peter A Crossley, Chen Da chao. Application of IEEE1588 V2 in pure digital protection system [J]. Electric Power Automation Equipment, 2010, 10, 98-102.

Research of Transmission Scheduling Algorithms in Mobile Wireless Networks

B. Zeng*, L. Yao & G. Yang
Department of Management Engineering, Naval University of Engineering, Wuhan, Hubei, China
Email: zbtrulice@163.com

ABSTRACT: In this paper, we are interested in designing a transmission scheduling algorithms in a packet radio network which can satisfy the requirements of such ad-hoc, mobile multimedia applications. Firstly the impact factors of packet collision are analyzed from two viewpoints of broadcast and point to point. Secondly a complete characterization of the link and broadcast scheduling problems is given, including a full analysis of the interference environment proper to each. Furthermore, a comprehensive comparison of link and broadcast scheduling is presented, including a simulation to demonstrate the throughput characteristics of each algorithm.

KEYWORDS: Channel access algorithms; TDMA; Adhoc networks; Scheduling algorithms.

1. INTRODUCTION

The radio channel access problem is of utmost importance in all types of radio communication systems. The problem can be simply stated: given a specific and common radio channel of fixed bandwidth, how do we distribute channel resources in frequency and time such that any two nodes may reliably communicate? This problem is the problem of multiple accesses. With the proliferation of data networks, and, more recently, of cellular radio communication systems, many multiple access methods have been designed and studied.

Multiple access schemes are largely categorized in the literature as being of the fixed assignment or random types (Xin et al. 2007). Fixed assignment multiple access refers to a broad class of multiple access techniques where each user is assigned some, or all, of the system resources for its exclusive use. The three principal methods for sharing this bandwidth are frequency division multiple access (FDMA); time division multiple access (TDMA); and code division multiple access (CDMA). Fixed assignment multiple access schemes are relatively efficient when each user has continuous, steady information to transmit. When the information is inherently bursty, however, these mechanisms can prove to be inefficient because assigned resources may sit idle for prolonged periods of time while others may be fully loaded (Lichun et al., 2003; Arora al., 2012). Random multiple access schemes have been developed to resolve this efficiency issue. Random multiple access provides a more efficient and flexible approach to sharing channel access in the context of short, spurious communications.

In contrast with fixed-assignment access schemes where no contention exists for channel resources, random multiple access are based on the idea that users must compete for use of the system resources. Thus, contention, and how to manage it, is the primary concern of random multiple access techniques. Depending on how rigorous the contention management mechanisms are, we say that the random access scheme is more or less disciplined. Of the two broad, principal types of random multiple access schemes, ALOHA and carrier sense multiple access (CSMA), ALOHA is the least disciplined.

We see that fixed-assignment and random multiple access schemes offer very different solutions to the problem of sharing a common communication channel. Fixed-assignment multiple access schemes are best suited for continuous, real-time multimedia traffic where throughput and associated delay are of primary importance, whereas random multiple access schemes are effective in bursty traffic environments (Huang et al. 2007). Hybrid multiple access schemes, such as reservation ALOHA and its close cousin, packet reservation multiple access, aim at integrating elements of these two broad approaches into a single access method capable of supporting mixed traffic types. Because the network must carry multimedia traffic, it must be capable of carrying both continuous, real-time traffic in addition to short, bursty data. Those applications which generate real-time traffic, typically voice and video, require certain bandwidth and delay guarantees which are best provided by fixed-assignment multiple access schemes.

2. THE SCHEDULING PROBLEM

Our discussion and analysis of the scheduling problem begins with an understanding of collision mechanisms in packet radio networks. Specifically, depending on the type of transmission scheduling scheme used in the packet radio network, transmissions may be subject to two types of collisions: primary and secondary interference. Primary interference occurs when any single node is expected to do more than a single activity in one time slot. For example, a node might be scheduled to receive and transmit at the same time; or a node might be scheduled to simultaneously receive from two different transmitters. Secondary interference refers to the situation where a certain receiver *R*, listening for transmissions from transmitter T_1, is within range of a second transmitter T_2 whose transmissions, though not intended for R, interfere with the transmissions of T_1 (Gore et al. 2007).

The problem of assigning transmission rights to the nodes of the radio network can be approached in two different ways: broadcast (node) scheduling, and link (point-to-point) scheduling (Nguyen et al. 2009). For broadcast scheduling, it is the nodes which are assigned time slots during which they may transmit to any of their neighbors. In the case of link scheduling, time slots are allocated to the directed links between pairs of nodes.

2.1. *Broadcast scheduling*

Let us be given a packet radio network represented by the directed graph $G=(V, E)$. Here, *V* represents the set of all nodes in the network ($|V|=N$) while *E* represents the set of all directed links (u, v) between all neighbor nodes $u, v \in V$. The broadcast scheduling problem consists in associating a slot with each node subject to the following constraints:

- Each node is assigned to a single slot;
- Any pair of nodes which are directly linked or which share a common neighbor cannot be assigned to the same slot; and
- The number of slots is minimized.

The problem as detailed above consists of the optimal broadcast scheduling problem. This problem is closely related to the classic graph theoretic vertex coloring problem and has been shown to be NP-complete [2], and thus the optimal solution can only be determined from an exhaustive search of all possible solutions. In the context of static networks where the network topology is constant in time, such a computational effort might be justifiable. In the context of mobile packet radio networks, however, reevaluating the optimal schedule after each topology change is clearly infeasible. Furthermore, the optimal solution requires global connectivity information [3]. Collecting such information to a central location for computational purposes could prove to be very inefficient and is inconsistent with our initial objective that the network be distributed. For these reasons, we dismiss the optimal broadcast scheduling problem and instead reformulate the scheduling problem as follows:

- Each node is assigned to at least one slot; and
- Any pair of nodes which are directly linked or which share a common neighbor cannot be assigned to the same slot.

This constrained broadcast scheduling problem consists of the maximal broadcast scheduling problem. Here, maximal means that for any given slot in the schedule, no additional node can be allowed to transmit without interfering with the transmission of at least one node already scheduled in that slot.

Let V_m denote the subset of all nodes in *V* scheduled to transmit in slot *m*. We call V_m the *m*-th broadcast mode. For each node, $u \in V_m$, we let $C^m{}_u$ denote the broadcast zone of *u* as the union of nodes a and its one-hop and two-hop neighbors. The non-interference condition of the problem can then be expressed as follows:

$$\forall u, v \in v_m, v \notin C_u^m \tag{1}$$

This condition guarantees that no primary interference will occur in any given slot. By blocking the broadcasting node's one-hop neighbors, we guarantee that this node will not have to both transmit and receive in the same slot. Similarly, by blocking the broadcasting node's two-hop neighbors, we guarantee that its one-hop neighbors will not be scheduled to receive from two different nodes in the same slot.

Clearly, it is desirable, though it is not essential, that any node be allowed to transmit as often as possible, subject to the initial conditions set in the problem statement. In terms of efficiency, it is desirable that for each broadcasting mode V_m,

$$V = \bigcup_{u \in V_m} C_u^m \tag{2}$$

In short, we wish that, for each broadcast mode in the cycle, each node be either transmitting or receiving. If this condition holds for a given broadcast mode, then this mode is said to be maximal. When the condition fails, the broadcast mode is not maximal and at least one node may be added to that slot without causing interference.

The maximal broadcast schedule is determined as follows. Begin with the lowest numbered node not already scheduled and assign it to the current slot, then block its one-hop and two-hop neighbors from transmitting in this slot. Next, evaluate if the current broadcast mode is maximal. If it is not, schedule in the current slot the lowest numbered node not included in the broadcast mode; reevaluate the mode; and repeat until the mode is maximal. If all nodes have not been scheduled to transmit at least once, then designate a new slot and repeat the process. This algorithm is illustrated in Fig. 1.

We have so far discussed and analyzed both the optimal and maximal broadcast scheduling problems. We have seen that in the context of mobile packet radio networks, it is unrealistic if not impossible to consider solutions to the optimal scheduling problem and must thus limit ourselves to the maximal scheduling problem.

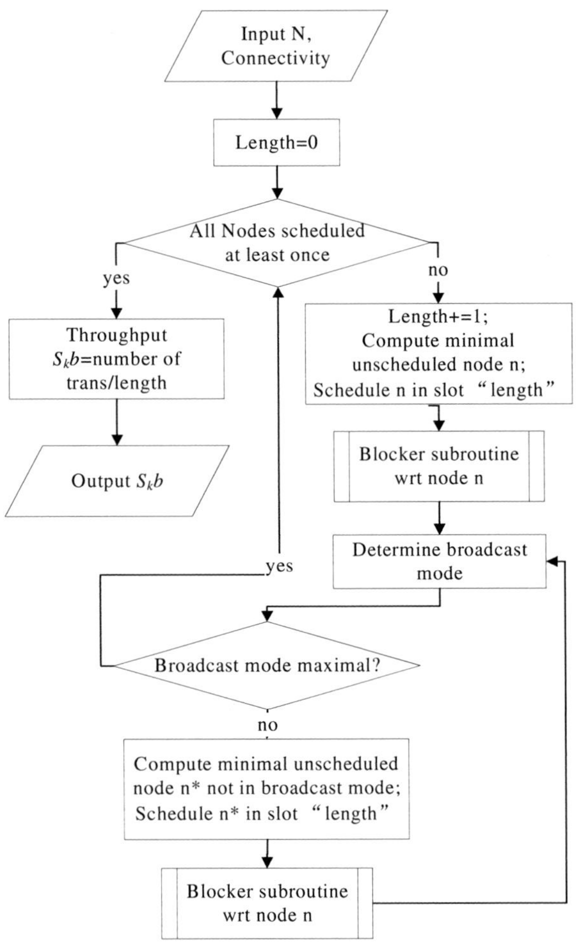

Figure 1. Algorithm for determining a maximal broadcast schedule.

2.2. *Link scheduling*

As was the case for the broadcast scheduling problem, let us be given a packet radio network represented by the directed graph $G=(V, E)$. Each directed link (u, v) can be represented by its sending node u and its receiving node v. The optimal link scheduling problem consists in associating a slot with each directed link subject to the following constraints:

- Each directed link is assigned to a single slot;
- Links (α,u) and (u, γ) cannot be assigned to the same slot, where α and γ represent neighbors, different or identical, of u, i.e. any single node cannot be both a sending and receiving node at the same time;
- Links (u, v) and (w, z) must be assigned to different slots if link $(w, v)\in E$, i.e. for any single sending node, its associated receiving node's neighbors cannot also be sending nodes in the same slot; and
- The number of slots is minimal.

In much the same manner as in the case for the optimal broadcast scheduling problem, the optimal link scheduling problem is closely related to the classic graph theoretic vertex coloring problem and has been shown to be NP-complete. For this reason, we choose to dismiss solving this problem and instead reformulate it as the following maximal link scheduling problem:

- Each directed link is assigned to at least one slot;
- Links (α, u) and (u, γ) cannot be assigned to the same slot, where α and γ represent neighbors, different or identical, of u, i.e. any single node cannot be both a sending and receiving node at the same time; and
- Links (u, v) and (w, z) must be assigned to different slots if link $(w, v)\in E$, i.e. for any single sending node, its associated receiving node's neighbors cannot also be sending nodes in the same slot.

Let E_m denote the subset of all links in E scheduled for activation in slot m. Associated with E_m are the two subsets of all nodes in V, S_m and R_m, representing respectively the sending nodes and receiving nodes of slot m. We call V, S_m and R_m, the m-th link activation, sending, and receiving modes, respectively. For each link $(u, v) \in E_m$, let $C^m_{(u,v)}$ denote the link activation zone of (u, v) consisting of all links incident on sending node u; all links incident on receiving node v; all links incoming to the neighbors of u; and all links outgoing from the neighbors of v. Thus, the non-interference condition of the problem can be expressed as follows:

$$\forall(u,v),(w,z)\in v_m,(w,z)\notin C^m_u \tag{3}$$

This condition guarantees that neither primary or secondary interference will occur in any given slot. More specifically, by blocking all links incident on the sending node and receiving nodes, we guarantee that both the sending and receiving nodes will not be subject to primary interference, be it either having to transmit to more than a single node; having to transmit and receive in the same slot; or having to receive from more than one transmitting node. By blocking all links incoming to the neighbors of the sending node, we guarantee that these neighbors will not be subject to secondary interference. Similarly, secondary interference at the receiving node is eliminated by blocking all links outgoing from its neighbors.

As was the case for broadcast scheduling, we do not wish to construct schedules which, though they might be maximal, do not allow all links to be activated at least once in the TDMA cycle. Furthermore, in order to maximize point-to-point throughput, it is desirable that links be activated as often as possible in each cycle, subject to meeting the constraints imposed by the non-interference criteria.

It is desirable, though not essential, that any link be activated as often as possible, subject to meeting the initial conditions set in the problem statement. In terms of efficiency, it is desirable, that for each link activation mode,

$$E = \bigcup_{(u,v)\in E_m} C^{m}_{(u,v)} \tag{4}$$

In other words, we wish that all links, for any link activation mode, be either active or blocked. The link activation mode is maximal when this condition holds. When the condition fails, at least one node may be added to the link activation mode without causing interference.

The maximal link schedule is similarly determined as maximal broadcast schedule. The algorithm begins by associating each link with a unique identifier. Consider any link (u,v).This link is labelled with the unique number $linkid=(u\text{-}1)N+v$. Begin with the lowest numbered link not already scheduled and assign it to the current slot. Block all links incident on the transmitting and receiving nodes; all links incoming to the transmitting node's neighbors; and all links outgoing from the receiving node's neighbors. Evaluate if the current link activation mode is maximal. If it is not, schedule in the current slot the lowest numbered link not included in the link activation mode; reevaluate the mode; and repeat until the mode is maximal. If all links have not been scheduled for activation at least once, then designate a new slot, and repeat the process.

3. CHOICE OF SCHEDULING ALGORITHM

Our evaluation process begins with a determination of design objectives which must be met by the scheduling algorithm. In our case, we establish the essential design objectives as follows:

- The algorithm must not rely on global connectivity information to produce a schedule;
- In the case of broadcast scheduling, the algorithm must produce schedules which allow each node to successfully broadcast at least once in the TDMA cycle; and
- In the case of link scheduling, the algorithm must produce schedules which allow each link to be successfully activated at least once in the TDMA cycle.

Some general observations can be made about each scheduling approach which may be helpful in making our selection. Link scheduling is better suited for point-to-point traffic. In link scheduling, every node can transmit at least one distinct packet to each of its neighbors in at most one cycle since each directed link is activated at least once per cycle. On the other hand, consider a packet radio network, its associated broadcast schedule and one of its nodes u of order n. Assume that u has been allocated s slots per cycle for transmission. Then node u requires $k=\lceil n/s \rceil$ cycles to transmit one distinct packet to each of its neighbors. Only in the best scenario where a node is allocated at least as many slots as it has neighbors will it be able to distinctly communicate with each neighbor in a single cycle.

Broadcast scheduling is better suited for broadcast traffic. The advantage is easy to see: in the case of broadcast scheduling, only a single transmission is required for all of a node's neighbors to receive a broadcast packet, while in the case of link scheduling, broadcast packets must be routed as separate packets to each neighbor, i.e. the number of transmissions required by the sending node equals its order.

The object of this paper was to examine the delay experienced by both point-to-point and broadcast traffic in packet radio networks using link and broadcast scheduling strategies. In the case of point-to-point traffic only, results indicate that the average delays experienced is shorter for networks employing broadcast scheduling. Results are similar when 10 and 20 percent of total traffic is broadcast traffic. Thus, we see that despite the apparent superiority of link scheduling, broadcast scheduling translates in lower average delay for both point-to-point and broadcast types of traffic.

We are left, then, with determining the advantages of broadcast scheduling over link scheduling, or vice-versa, in terms of throughput. At this point, we define throughput simply as the average number of successful point-to-point transmissions which may occur per unit time.

Consider any packet radio network and its associated link and broadcast schedules. The broadcast and link schedules are L_b and L_l slots long, respectively. Let t_s, denote the slot duration, and let s_b and s_l denote the total number of transmissions allowed over the lengths of the broadcast and link schedules, respectively. Broadcast and link scheduling throughputs are then given as:

$$s_b = \overline{\left(\frac{s_b}{t_s L_b}\right)}, s_l = \overline{\left(\frac{s_l}{t_l L_l}\right)} \tag{4}$$

4. SIMULATION RESULTS

The precise, mathematical analysis of arbitrary networks is not feasible, and thus we choose to evaluate and compare throughputs of both scheduling strategies by simulation. A general depiction of the simulation which we implemented can be found in Fig. 2. Broadly described, this simulation evaluates the throughputs of broadcast and link scheduling by averaging over a large set of random network configurations.

In the simulation, N nodes are randomly (uniformly) distributed in a $d \times d$ square area. For a given radio range:, the connectivity map of the distribution is determined, where it is assumed that bidirectional links exist between any two nodes if the distance between them is less than or equal to r. Given the network topology, both maximal broadcast and link schedules are determined, allowing us to calculate both schedule lengths and the numbers of successful transmissions which can occur over the entire schedules. The link and broadcast throughput is then calculated for this one specific distribution. For each radio range, the throughput figures thus obtained are averaged over *runs* random placements. It is important to note at this point that in the case of broadcast scheduling, any node which is isolated, i.e. any node which has no neighbors, is not scheduled for transmission.

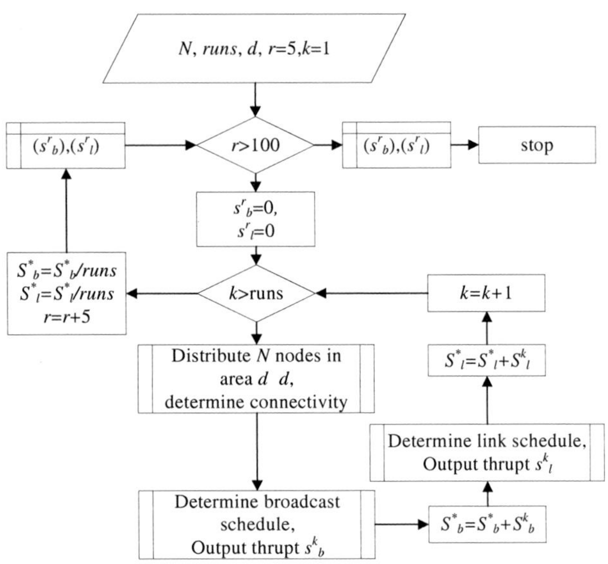

Figure 2. Simulation for throughput evaluation of broadcast and link scheduling.

We carried out simulations for 10 and 25 nodes, each distributed in areas of 100×100 and 250×250. For the case of 10 nodes, averages were computed over 10,000 *runs* for radio ranges between 5 and 100 units, in steps of five units. For the case of 25 nodes, averages were computed over 2,500 runs for radio ranges between 10 and 60 units for the case of d=100, and between 10 and 100 units for the case of d=250 units, both in steps of 10 units. Results for N=10 and 25 nodes are presented in Fig. 3 and Fig. 4 respectively.

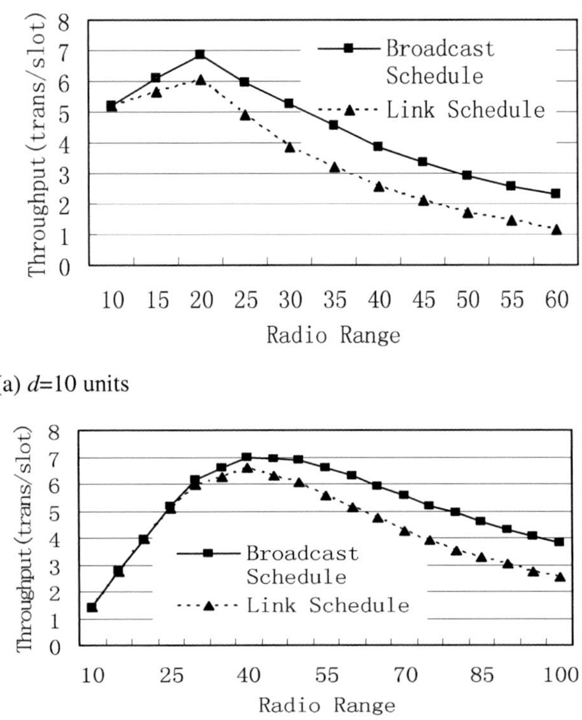

(a) d=10 units

(b) d=25 units

Figure 3. Throughput simulation results for 25 nodes.

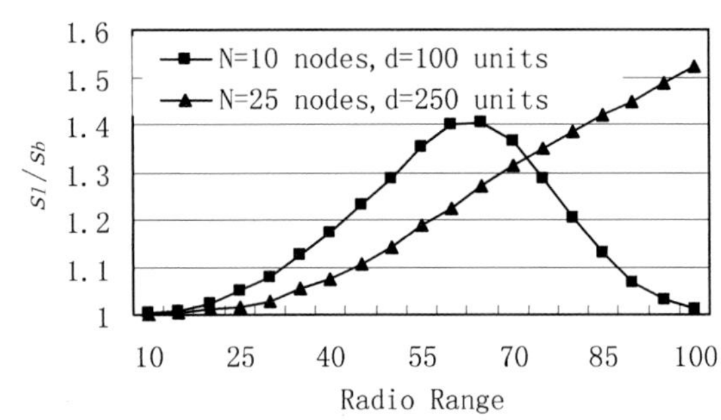

Figure 4. s_l/s_b as a function of radio range.

The general behavior of the throughput curves can be easily explained. At the low end of radio range values, nodes tend to be disconnected. The degree of connectivity will of course vary as a function of the distribution area, but it remains true that for a given distribution range, low radio ranges translate into low connectivity. Thus, at low radio range, few connections exist between nodes, resulting in poor throughput. Similarly, high radio ranges result in highly connected networks. It is therefore more difficult for nodes to simultaneously transmit since every node is within radio range of every other node. Thus, only a single node may transmit in any given slot, i.e. the cycle length equals the number of nodes, and throughput diminishes to a value of one transmission per slot.

We plotted the difference between broadcast and link scheduling in Figure 3. In this figure, the ratio s_l/s_b is plotted as a function of radio range for the cases of 10 nodes distributed in an area of 100×100 nodes and 25 nodes distributed in an area of 250×250. In the case of the 10 nodes, we see that the maximum difference between scheduling types is of the order of 40% of broadcast scheduling throughput with a peak throughput difference lower than 10%. In the plot of 25 nodes, we see that the maximum difference is not within the range of simulated radio range values and that the peak throughput difference is also of the order of 10%.

We see, then, that the advantage of link scheduling over broadcast scheduling is of the order of 10%. This advantage is quickly lost when we consider that for the case of link scheduling, half of throughput is used for acknowledgments. In effect, effective throughput for link scheduling is only half of that throughput plotted in Fig. 4. On the other hand, effective throughput for broadcast scheduling is only slightly lower than its simple throughput since it may use a passive ack scheme, and active acknowledgments are required in only a small fraction of all transmissions.

5. CONCLUSION

The problem of how to scheduling the packet transmission in a multiple access channel is studied in this paper. The key characteristics about the multiple access methods are analyzed and the three principal methods for sharing this bandwidth in multimedia communication are justified. Furthermore, the collision mechanism for each node of the network is characterized. Based on the studies, the two widely adopted methods which can be used to schedule the TDMA transmissions are focused: broadcast and link scheduling. By designing and implementing the two scheduling algorithms with the description of collision, the broadcast and link scheduling problems are fully analyzed. Lastly the advantages and shortcomings of two specific broadcast scheduling algorithms are discussed through simulation experiments.

ACKNOWLEDGMENT

This research is supported by the Natural Science Foundation of China under grant no. 71201172.

REFERENCES

- [1] Arora, A. & Krunz, M. 2012. The design of a channel-access protocol for a wireless ad hoc network with sectored directional antennas. *Ad Hoc Networks* 10(5): 284-298.
- [2] Gore, A.D., Karandikar, A. & Jagabathula, S. 2007. On High Spatial Reuse Link Scheduling in STDMA Wireless Ad Hoc Networks. in *Proceedings of Global Telecommunications Conference*: 736-741. Washington, USA.
- [3] Huang, S.C., Jun, W.P., & Hua J.2007. Minimum-Latency Broadcast Scheduling in Wireless Ad Hoc Networks. in *Proceeding of 26th IEEE International Conference on Computer Communications*: 733-739. Anchorage: AK.
- [4] Lichun, B. & Garcia-Luna-Aceves, J. J. 2003. Distributed dynamic channel access scheduling for ad hoc networks. *Journal of Parallel and Distributed Computing* 63(1): 3-14.
- [5] Nguyen, D., Garcia-Luna-Aceves, J.J. & Obraczka, K. 2009. Collision-Free Asynchronous Multi-Channel Access in Ad Hoc Networks. in *Proceedings of Global Telecommunications Conference*: 1-6. Honolulu, HI.
- [6] Xin, W., Garcia-Luna-Aceves, J.J. & Sadjadpour, H.R. 2007. Distributed Channel Access Scheduling for Ad Hoc Networks using Virtual MIMO. in *Proceedings of 16th International Conference on Computer Communications and Networks*: 203–20. Honolulu: HI.

Multi-feature Joint MSE Criterion Method for the Classification of U/V

Z.C. Jiang*, X.H. Li & C.H. Tian
Physics Department of Qinghai Normal University, Xining, Qinghai, 810008, China
E-mail: 738410992@qq.com

ABSTRACT: Single feature unvoiced / voiced classification algorithm usually not only fails to provide more accurate unvoiced / voiced information, but also the robustness to noise is low, which easily results in the speech quality of vocoder decoding become poor. To overcome this problem, one kind of linear discriminant algorithm of minimum square error criterion based on multi-feature joint is put forward. The classification of unvoiced / voiced is seen as two categories of mode recognition problems in the algorithm, sample vector of short-time speech is made up of three features of short-time amplitude, short-time zero-crossing rate and short-time self- correlation maximum value of speech; normalized augmented sample matrix is constructed by normalized augmented sample vectors of current frame and former four frames, and classification labels of unvoiced / voiced of sample vectors are added automatically; special margin vectors are constructed by constant that is matched with sample matrix; average vector of overall sample is calculated by sample matrix and classification labels; gradient descent algorithm of minimum square error criterion function is adopted, and optimal augmented weight vector of short-time speech is obtained; therefore, the classification of unvoiced / voiced is judged. The minimum memory and automatic update with the frame of all parameters are realized in the study, thus achieving inter-frame self-adaption of study and judgment. Simulation experiment shows: both the accuracy of classification of unvoiced / voiced and the robustness to noise have prominent enhancement than classical single feature method.

KEYWORDS: Minimum square error criterion; Weight vector; Sample (feature) vector; Gradient decent algorithm; Classification of U/V.

1. INTRODUCTION

The judgment of U/V is one of the most basic problems of speech signal processing, most speech processing systems such as low bit-rate speech coding, speech synthesis, speech recognition all depends on the judgment results of U/V. Classical and widely applied algorithms adopt single short-time features such as short-time amplitude (energy), short-time zero-crossing rate (threshold zero-crossing rate) and threshold [1-3]. With the rapid development of wireless communication technology of satellite communication and mobile communication, higher requirements for the analysis and extraction of speech incentive information are put forward in low bit-rate speech coding technology, in order to depict speech incentive ingredients in detail, thus providing more accurate incentive information for decoding speech, researchers put up with U/V description method of speech sub-band, and achieve great performance [4-6]. To increase the accuracy of the judgment of U/V and the robustness to noise of algorithm, the theory and method of statistic mode recognition are introduced into the judgment of voiced / unvoiced speech by researchers, and support vector machine classification method of speech with noise [7], cepstrum statistic classification method [8], recurrence quantification analysis [9], phase space reconstruction method [10], combined magnitude difference function [11], U/V decision without threshold method [12], three-order cumulants method [13] are raised.

In practice, the judgment of U/V is one problem of two categories mode recognition, the rationality and novelty of thought of U/V judgment can be solved by the theory and method of mode recognition, and meanwhile, optimal judgment can be realized using many short-time features of speech. Literature [4] adopts Fisher judgment method, and makes use of feature vector that is made up of many eigenvalues as criterion, which makes the misjudgment rate of U/V greatly reduce; literature [7] adopts support vector machine method for speech with noise to judge the classification, which increases the accuracy of judgment and the robustness to noise greatly. In the paper, one kind of statistics mode recognition method of U/V judgment is put forward: 3D feature vector of short-time speech is made up of short-time amplitude M_n, short-time zero-crossing rate Z_n, and short-time self-correlation maximum value r_m; normalized augmented sample matrix is constructed by normalized augmented sample vectors of current frame and former four frames, and classification labels of U/V of sample vectors are added automatically; special margin vectors are constructed by constant that is matched with sample matrix; average vector of overall sample is calculated by entries of sample matrix and classification labels; gradient descent algorithm of minimum square error (MSE) criterion function is adopted, and optimal augmented weight vector $\vec{a}^*$ of short-time speech is obtained; Update with the frame of all parameters is realized, thus realizing inter-frame self-adaption of optimal weight vector $\vec{a}^*$. Simulation experiment shows: compared with classical algorithm, both the accuracy of classification of U/V and the robustness to noise have prominent enhancement.

2. MINIMUM SQUARE ERROR CRITERION CLASSIFICATION PRINCIPLE

2.1. *Linear discriminant function and homogenous simplification*

General expression of linear discriminant function of two categories is as follows:

$$g(\vec{x}) = \vec{w}^T\vec{x} + w_0 \tag{1}$$

$\vec{x}$ is feature vector of d-dimension space X in the equation, it is also called sample vector, $\vec{w}$ is weight vector, $\vec{x}$ and $\vec{w}$ are expressed as follows separately:

$\vec{x} = [x_1, x_2, ...x_d]^T$ $\quad\quad$ $\vec{w} = [w_1, w_2, ...w_d]^T$

w_0 is a constant, it is called threshold weight. For linear classification problem of two categories, the following decision rule can be adopted:

Ordering $g(\vec{x}) = g(\vec{x}_1) - g(\vec{x}_2)$

If

$$\begin{cases} g(\vec{x}) > 0, \text{ then decision is } \vec{x} \in \omega_1 \\ g(\vec{x}) < 0, \text{ then decision is } \vec{x} \in \omega_2 \\ g(\vec{x}) = 0, \ \vec{x} \text{ is any or refuse} \end{cases} \tag{2}$$

Equation $g(\vec{x}) = 0$ defines one decision surface, which divides the points that belongs to ω_1 category and the points that belongs to ω_2 category. When $g(\vec{x})$ is linear function, the decision surface is hyperplane H.

Linear discriminant function defined by equation (1) is expressed as follows:

$$g(\vec{x}) = w_0 + \sum_{i=1}^{d} w_i x_i = \sum_{i=1}^{d} a_i y_i = \vec{a}^T\vec{y} \tag{3}$$

It is called homogenous simplification of linear discriminant function, wherein $\vec{y} = [1, \vec{x}]^T$, which is vector of $\hat{d} = d+1$ dimension space Y, and is called augmented sample vector; $\vec{a} = [w_0, \vec{w}]^T$, which is called augmented weight vector (generalized weight vector), its dimension is also $\hat{d} = d+1$ dimension.

Not hard to see, augmented sample vector $\vec{y}$ is compared with sample vector $\vec{x}$, although the dimension increases one dimension, Euclidean distance among samples keeps constant, sample vectors after transformation are still located in original X space. Equation $\vec{a}^T\vec{y} = 0$ confirms one hyperplane $\hat{H}$ that passes through original point in Y space, the division of d-dimension subspace of $\hat{H}$ is the same as the division of X space of original decision surface $\vec{w}^T\vec{x} + w_0 = 0$.

2.2. *Linearly detachable and linearly undetachable*

For sample set { $\vec{y}_1, \vec{y}_2, ...\vec{y}_n, ...\vec{y}_N$ } whose capacity is N (it is a constant), if existing one weight vector $\vec{a}$, which makes $\vec{a}^T\vec{y} > 0$ for any $\vec{y} \in \omega_1$ and $\vec{a}^T\vec{y} < 0$ for any $\vec{y} \in \omega_2$, then this group of sample set is linearly detachable; otherwise, it is called linearly undetachable. In return, if sample set is linearly detachable, then existing one weight vector $\vec{a}$, which can classify each sample correctly.

However, for sample set whose capacity is N, linearly undetachable sample may exist, namely, the probability of linearly detachable sample is not always 1.

2.3. *Sample normalization*

If sample set $\{\vec{y}_1, \vec{y}_2, ...\vec{y}_N\}$ is linearly detachable, then certain or some weight vector $\vec{a}$ must exist, thus enabling the following expression to establish.

$$\begin{cases} \vec{a}^T\vec{y}_i > 0, \text{ for any } \vec{y}_i \in \omega_1 \\ \vec{a}^T\vec{y}_j < 0, \text{ for any } \vec{y}_j \in \omega_2 \end{cases} \tag{4}$$

All weight vectors $\vec{a}$ that meets above expression can classify all N samples correctly. If one negative signal is added before sample $\vec{y}_j$ that is from ω_2 category, namely, ordering $\vec{y}'_j = -\vec{y}_j$, wherein $\vec{y}_j \in \omega_2$, then $\vec{a}^T\vec{y}'_j > 0$. Therefore, if ordering

$$\vec{y}'_n = \begin{cases} \vec{y}_i \ , \text{ for any } \vec{y}_i \in \omega_1 \\ \vec{y}_j \ , \text{ for any } \vec{y}_j \in \omega_2 \end{cases}$$

Then the original classification sign of samples can be ignored, as long as one weight vector $\vec{a}$ is found, wherein $\vec{a}^T\vec{y}'_n > 0$ can be satisfied for all sample $\vec{y}'_n$, $n = 1,2,...N$. The above process is called the normalization of sample, $\vec{y}'_n$ is called normalized augmented sample vector, it is still expressed using $\vec{y}$.

2.4. *Solution vector and solution area*

Solution vector is defined as the weight vector that meets $\vec{a}^T\vec{y}_n > 0$ in the situation of linearly detachable, wherein $n = 0,1,2,...N$, and it is denoted by $\vec{a}^*$. Weight vector is one point of sample space, each sample imposes restriction on weight vector according to $\vec{a}^T\vec{y}_n > 0$. Equation $\vec{a}^T\vec{y}_n = 0$ confirms one hyperplane $\hat{H}_n$ that goes through original point of sample space, $\vec{y}_n$ is its normal vector. If solution vector exists, then it must be positive side of $\hat{H}_n$, because only when it is positive side, $\vec{a}^T\vec{y}_n > 0$ can be met. N samples will generate N hyperplanes, which divides sample space into two half-space. If solution vector exists, then it must be in the overlapping area of N positive half-space, any vector in this area is solution vector $\vec{a}^*$. Solution vector is often more than one, but one area that is made up of an infinite number of solution vectors, this area is called solution area.

2.5. *The restriction for solution vector- margin vector*

To make solution vector more reliable, solution vector can be restricted. The solution vectors that are more closer to the middle of solution area can classify new sample more correctly. Therefore, margin $b > 0$ is introduced, and solution vector $\vec{a}^*$ that meets $\vec{a}^T\vec{y}_n \geq b$ is looked for. Obviously, the overlapping area (new solution area) of authorized edition that is generated by $\vec{a}^T\vec{y}_n \geq b > 0$ is located in original solution area, the distance of boundary of new solution area from the boundary of original solution area is $b/\|\vec{y}_n\|$.

As long as solution area $\vec{a}^*$ is located in solution area strictly, then requirements can be met. Obviously, after margin $b > 0$ is introduced, the possibility that algorithm of solution vector $\vec{a}^*$ converges on certain point of the boundary of solution area can be avoided.

2.6. *Square error criterion function and pseudo-inverse solution*

For normalized segmented sample vector, linear discriminant function can be written as $g(\vec{x}) = \vec{a}^T\vec{y}$. If existing one weight vector $\vec{a}$, the following expression can be established.

$$\vec{a}^T\vec{y}_n > 0, n = 1,2,...N \quad (5)$$

Then sample $\vec{y}_n$ can be classified correctly. The task of designing one linear classifier is to solve the solution of one group of N linear inequality (5). To make the solution more reliable, margin $b > 0$ is introduced, then expression (5) is as follows:

$$\vec{a}^T\vec{y}_n \geq b_n > 0, n = 1,2,...N \quad (6)$$

If inequality group has solution, namely, inequality group is consistent, which indicates that sample is linearly detachable, and solution vector can be found. If inequality group doesn't have solution, namely, inequality group is not consistent, which indicates sample is linearly undetachable, for any weight vector a, some sample must be classified falsely, at the moment, the solution vector that makes the number of false classified sample least can be looked for, it is still denoted by $\vec{a}^*$. Therefore, the inequality group (6) can be written as follows:

$$\vec{a}^T\vec{y}_n = b_n > 0, n = 1,2,...N \quad (7)$$

Wherein b_n is any given positive constant. Expression (7) is written as the form of simultaneous equations, it is as follows:

$$\vec{Y}\vec{a} = \vec{b} \quad (8)$$

In the equation, $\vec{Y}$ is normalized augmented sample vector matrix of $N \times \hat{d}$ dimension.

$$\vec{Y} = \begin{bmatrix} \vec{y}_1^T \\ \vec{y}_2^T \\ \vdots \\ \vec{y}_N^T \end{bmatrix} = \begin{bmatrix} y_{11} & y_{12} & \cdots & y_{1\hat{d}} \\ y_{21} & y_{22} & \cdots & y_{2\hat{d}} \\ \cdots & \cdots & \cdots & \cdots \\ y_{N1} & y_{N2} & \cdots & y_{N\hat{d}} \end{bmatrix} \quad (9)$$

$\vec{b}$ is N-dimension margin vector, $b_n > 0, n = 1,2,\cdots,N$

$$\vec{b} = [b_1, b_2, \cdots, b_N]^T \quad (10)$$

In general, sample number N is always larger than dimension $\hat{d}$, so $\vec{Y}$ is long matrix, and generally is column full rank matrix. The number of equations is greater than the number of unknown, so it is one contradictory equation group, and has no exact solution generally. Defining an error vector:

$$\vec{e} = \vec{Y}\vec{a} - \vec{b} \quad (11)$$

And defining square error criterion function $\vec{J}_s(\vec{a})$ is as follows:

$$\vec{J}_s(\vec{a}) = \|\vec{e}\|^2 = \|\vec{Y}\vec{a} - \vec{b}\|^2 = \sum_{n=1}^{N}(\vec{a}^T\vec{y}_n - b_n)^2 \quad (12)$$

Looking for $\vec{a}$ that makes $\vec{J}_s(\vec{a})$ minimization as the solution of problem, this is least square approximate solution of contradictory equation group, it is also called pseudo-inverse solution or MSE solution, and still denoted by $\vec{a}^*$. Criterion function defined by equation (12) is called MSE criterion function.

Solving gradient $\nabla\vec{J}_s(\vec{a})$ of $\vec{J}_s(\vec{a})$ in equation (12), and ordering $\nabla\vec{J}_s(\vec{a})$ equal to zero, thus getting $\vec{Y}^T\vec{Y}\vec{a}^* = \vec{Y}\vec{b}$. Therefore, solving the problem of $\vec{Y}\vec{a} = \vec{b}$ is translated into solving the problem of $\vec{Y}^T\vec{Y}\vec{a}^* = \vec{Y}\vec{b}$. The biggest feature of this equation is as follows: matrix $\vec{Y}^T\vec{Y}$ is square matrix of $\hat{d} \times \hat{d}$ dimension, and it is nonsingular generally, so one unique solution can be solved:

$$\vec{a}^* = \vec{Y}^+\vec{b} \quad (13)$$

In the equation, $\vec{Y}^{+}$ is matrix of $\hat{d}\times N$ dimension, it is called left pseudo-inverse matrix.

$$\vec{Y}^{+}=(\vec{Y}^{T}\vec{Y})^{-1}\vec{Y}^{T} \quad (14)$$

$\vec{a}^{*}$ is MSE solution of equation (8) (it is also called pseudo-inverse solution).

2.7. *Gradient decent algorithm of square error criterion function*

Pseudo-inverse equation (13) of MSE solution of equation (8) needs to calculate pseudo-inverse equation (14), calculating pseudo-inverse matrix $\vec{Y}^{+}$ of $\vec{Y}$ matrix generates many problems: square matrix $\vec{Y}^{T}\vec{Y}$ is required to be nonsingular; the calculated amount of solving $\vec{Y}^{+}$ is large; calculating pseudo-inverse matrix may introduce larger calculated error; margin vector $\vec{b}$ is not easily updating with the frame. Therefore, it is not suitable to adopt pseudo-inverse method to solve MSE solution, $\vec{a}^{*}$ can be solved using gradient decent algorithm of optimal technology.

Solving gradient of $J_s(\vec{a})$ in equation (12), the following equation can be obtained:

$\nabla J_s(\vec{a})=2\vec{Y}^{T}(\vec{Y}\vec{a}-\vec{b})$

Therefore, gradient decent algorithm can be written as follows:

$$\begin{cases}\vec{a}(1), \text{ any} \\ \vec{a}(k+1)=\vec{a}(k)-\rho_k\vec{Y}^{T}(\vec{Y}\vec{a}-\vec{b})\end{cases} \quad (15)$$

Wherein $\rho_k=\rho_1/k$, ρ_1 is step length, ρ_1 is any constant; k is iterations. At the moment, weight vector sequence obtained by this algorithm converges on weight vector that makes $\nabla J_s(\vec{a}) = 2\vec{Y}^{T}(\vec{Y}\vec{a}-\vec{b})$ equal to zero, that is MSE solution.

2.8. *Square error function and the equivalence property of fisher criterion*

It can be proved that when sample capacity is N, the number of two categories of sample is N_1 and N_2 separately, former N_1 components of margin vector $\vec{b}=[b_1,b_2,\cdots,b_N]^T$ are N/N_1, latter N_2 components are N/N_2, MSE solution $\vec{a}^{*}$ is equivalent to Fisher solution. Meanwhile, $w_0^{*}=-\vec{m}^{T}\vec{w}^{*}$ and the following judgment rule are obtained:

$$\begin{cases}\text{If } \vec{w}^{*T}(\vec{x}-\vec{m})>0, \text{ then decision is } \vec{x}\in\omega_1 \\ \text{If } \vec{w}^{*T}(\vec{x}-\vec{m})<0, \text{ then decision is } \vec{x}\in\omega_2\end{cases} \quad (16)$$

Wherein $\vec{m}$ is average value of overall sample.

$$\vec{m}=(N_1\vec{m}_1+N_2\vec{m}_2)/N \quad (17)$$

In the equation, $\vec{m}_1,\vec{m}_2$ is average value of sample of two categories ω_1, ω_2 separately [14].

3. ALGORITHM PRINCIPLE OF MSE CRITERION FOR VOICED / UNVOICED SPEECH JUDGMENT

According to two categories classification principle of MSE criterion, on kind of multi-feature joint U/V judgment algorithm based on minimum square error criterion $J_s(\vec{a})$ is designed, it is shown as Figure 1. The algorithm is constituted by seven functional modules, the working principle and function of each module is described as follows separately.

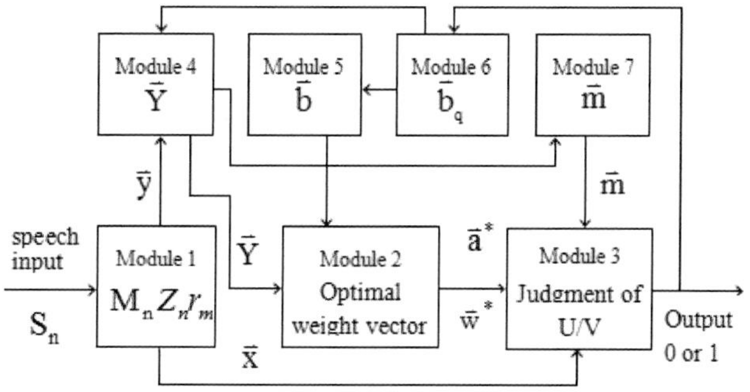

Figure 1. Flow diagram of algorithm principle.

Module 1: extracting short-time features of speech, and constituting normalized augmented sample vector $\vec{y}$. For short-time speech (frame) that is input, extracting short-time amplitude M_n, short-time zero-crossing rate Z_n, short-time normalization maximum self-correlation r_m separately, constituting normalized augmented sample vector $\vec{y}$.

$$\vec{y}=[1,\vec{x}]^T \quad (18)$$

Wherein, $\vec{x}=[M_n,Z_n,r_m]$ (19)

$$M_n=\sum_{m=n}^{n+L-1}|x_w(m)| \quad (20)$$

$$Z_n=\frac{1}{2}\sum_{m=n}^{n+L-1}|\text{sgn}[x_w(m)-\text{sgn}[x_w(m-1)]]| \quad (21)$$

$$r_m=\frac{\sum_{m=n}^{n+L-1-p}x_w(m)x_w(m+p)}{\sum_{m=n}^{n+L-1-p}(x_w(m))^2} \quad (22)$$

L is the frame length of speech (the window length), p is pitch period. The dimension d of feature vector (sample) $\vec{x}$ is three; the dimension $\hat{d}$ of normalized augmented sample vector $\vec{y}$ is four. Module one has two outputs: one is $\vec{y}$, it is used to update sample matrix $\vec{Y}$ (module four), another one is $\vec{x}$, it participates in the judgment of U/V in module three.

Module four: normalized augmented sample matrix (it is called sample matrix for short) $\vec{Y}$, the dimension is $N \times \hat{d}$, line number N is the number of sample vector $\vec{y}$, N is five. Sample vectors of former five-frame speech are prestored in the matrix of $\vec{Y}$, and each line is arranged according to the time sequence, it is shown as equation (9).

Sample matrix $\vec{Y}$, margin vector $\vec{b}$, any initial weigh vector $\vec{a}$ (1) and any step parameter ρ_1 solves optimal weight vector $\vec{a}^*$ using iteration method according to equation (15). For current frame, $\vec{Y}$ updates first, then solving $\vec{a}^*$. Update is conducted according to the principle of first in first out, namely, sample vector $\vec{y}$ of current frame that is output by module one is input into the last line of sample matrix $\vec{Y}$, then the first line is extruded, thus keeping the dimension $N \times \hat{d}$ of $\vec{Y}$ constant.

After operating five frames, all prestored $\vec{Y}$ has been updated; later, in the iteration process of solving optimal weight vector $\vec{a}^*$ of each frame, sample vectors of current frame and former four frame are applied, which can bring three aspects of advantages: the first one is current frame $\vec{a}^*$ is solved using sample vector $\vec{y}$ of current frame, making $\vec{a}^*$ realize inter-frame self-correlation, thus enabling the judgment of U/V realize self-correlation; the second one is $\vec{a}^*$ has smooth property in frame, this is because current frame $\vec{a}^*$ not only is decided by sample vector of current frame, but also sample vector of former four frames; the third one is that due to the dimension of sample matrix $\vec{Y}$ is low (5×4 dimension), which makes the data quantity of iteration operation of module 2 small, thus making the rate of convergence accelerate.

Module six: classification label vector $\vec{b}_q$, whose dimension is $N \times 1$, storing the corresponding classification label of each sample vector (each line) of sample matrix. There are two aspects of function: the first one is margin vector is updated using classification label of former five frames; the second one is mobilizing sample matrix that has been updated to update overall average vector, thus preparing for the judgment of current frame. Update method is simple, the judgment results of current frame feed back to itself, and update is conducted according to the principle of first in first out.

Module seven: the average vector $\vec{m}$ of overall sample, whose dimension is $d \times 1$, and update is conducted in each frame. The function of $\vec{m}$ is to judge the U for the current frame with optimal weight vector $\vec{a}^*$ and sample vector $\vec{x}$ according to equation (16).

The update method of $\vec{m}$ is as follows: for current frame, according to the indication of classification vector, voiced sample and unvoiced sample are added separately in $\vec{Y}$ that has been updated, then the sum divides sample number N, namely, $\vec{m}$ of corresponding current frame is got according to the calculation of equation (17). The update of $\vec{m}$ realizes inter-frame self-correlation.

Module five: margin vector $\vec{b}$, whose dimension is $N \times 1$. The function is to ensure segmented optimal weight vector $\vec{a}^*$ not converge on the boundary of solution area, that is the restriction of weight vector optimal algorithm. Margin vector $\vec{b}$ is updated according to the indication of classification vector, when the judgment results of current frame are output, classification vector is updated first, then reading the number N_2 of "1", namely, the frame number of unvoiced speech, and solving the frame number of voiced speech, that is $N_1 = N - N_2$, then the number N_1 of N/N_1 and the number N_2 of N/N_2 are stored into former N_1 location and latter N_2 location of column vector $\vec{b}$ whose dimension is $N \times 1$ separately, the update of $\vec{b}$ is finished ($N = 5$).

Module two: solving optimal augmented weight vector $\vec{a}^*$ using gradient decent algorithm. $\vec{a}(1)$ is 4D column vector whose components are any constant; ρ_1 of iteration step length $\rho_k = \rho_1 / k$ is any constant, step length ρ_k becomes small as iteration time increases, so the iteration is varied step length iteration. For current frame, using normalized augmented sample matrix $\vec{Y}$ that has been updated and margin vector $\vec{b}$ that corresponds to former five frames, optimal augmented weight vector $\vec{a}^* = [\vec{w}_0^*, \vec{w}^*]^T$ can be solved through limited times iteration according to equation (15). The dimension of $\vec{a}^*$ is 4×1, latter 3D is optimal weight vector $\vec{w}^*$.

Module three: the judgment of U/V. For current frame, using output $\vec{w}^*$ of module 2 and average vector $\vec{m}$ of overall sample that has been updated, the judgment of U/V for current frame is got according to equation (16). When the judgment is output, using the output judgment results (U/V label 0 or 1)to update classification label vector according to the principle of first in first out, thus updating margin vector.

To sum up the function and principle of each module, algorithm function module can be divided into three categories. The first one is the category of short-time feature extraction, only including module one; the second one is the category of memory and memory update, it is constituted by module four, module five ,module six and module seven; the third one is the category of study and judgment, it is made up of module two and module three.

The study process is one process of solving optimal weight vector through iteration using gradient decent algorithm. Study depends on feature vectors of current frame speech that is input just now and several frames speech that have been passed (memory), when next frame comes, memory is updated. The judgment is the same, it depends on optimal weight vector of current frame, updated average vector of overall sample is obtained in the guidance of classification label. Memory and the update of memory plays a crucial function role in study and judgment output. In this algorithm, not only the memory quantity of memory and memory update is small, but also inter-frame update is simple, thus not only study algorithm convergence and judgment algorithm speed are enhanced effectively, but also many performance objectives such as inter-frame self-correlation and inter-frame smooth are realized conveniently.

4. SIMULATION EXPERIMENTS

4.1. *Direct simulation experiments of algorithm*

4.1.1. *Speech sample and sample label of experiments*

Experiments speech takes from two samples of voice library yyk2.wav that is established by the author, named YB1 and YB2 separately, and they are linear PCM digital speech of 8 kHz sampling, 8 bit quantization, without noise.

Due to the universality and uncertainty of many factors such as sayer and what to say, the classification of U/V does not have objective standard, which brings many difficulties for the correct judgment of classification of U/V. Therefore, experiment speech sample can be labeled manually in advance, and this can be temporary or reference standard. Labeling method is as follows: framing and numbering the sample; amplitude and the change trend of amplitude of each frame sample points are observed successively. For sample points of frame which has period distribution, it is labeled as voiced, and expressed by "1"; for sample points of frame which has random distribution, it is labeled as unvoiced, and expressed by "0"; for frame which has mixed distribution of periodicity and randomness, it is labeled as voiced when periodicity is dominant, and it is labeled as unvoiced when randomness is dominant; each frame label corresponds to frame number. Label parameter is as follows: YB1: the length is 7.94 seconds, sample points number is 63520, frame number is 397; YB2: the length is 9.83 seconds, sample points number is 78640, frame number is 419; frame length of 20 milliseconds is 160 points.

4.1.2. *Experiment system (procedure) and experiment method*

For algorithm in this paper (multi-feature MSE classification method of U/V, which is called DFMSE method for short), which is programmed using high-level language, and is saved in the hardware using document name DFMSE.m.

Choosing the classical algorithm of U/V classification – Rabiner algorithm (it is called Rab algorithm for short) as the basis of judging algorithm in this paper. Rabiner algorithm is one classification algorithm of U/V that depends on single feature of short-time speech, and is one outstanding algorithm of classical algorithms. It has been widely applied. When finishing Rabiner algorithm programming, it is saved in the hardware using document name Rab.m.

Experiment one: the comparison experiment of YB1 under different SNR;

Experiment two: the comparison experiment of YB2 under different SNR.

4.1.3. *Experiment results*

Sample label results are as follows: YB1: frame number of voiced is 247, frame rate of voiced is 62.97%; frame number of unvoiced is 172, frame rate of unvoiced is 37.03%. YB2: frame number of voiced is 250, frame rate of voiced is 58.95%; frame number of unvoiced is 147, frame rate of unvoiced is 41.05%.

The results of experiment one: for YB1, when the SNR of speech and background noise is 30 dB, the rate of U/V of Rab method is 62.46%, 37.53% separately; DFMSE method is 62.72%, 37.28% separately; the deviation of labeled value of both algorithms is very small. When SNR reduces to 10 dB, the rate of voiced and unvoiced of Rab method is 54.16%, 45.84% separately, the deviation of labeled value is 8.81%; DFMSE method is 60.45%, 39.55% separately, the deviation of labeled value is 2.52%, which reduces 6.29% than the deviation of Rab method.

The results of experiment two: for YB2, when SNR is 30 dB, the deviation of labeled value of both algorithms is small; when SNE reduces to 10 dB, the deviation of labeled value of Rab method and DFMSE method is 9.06%, 2.63% separately, the latter reduces 6.43% than the former.

4.2. *Application simulation experiment of algorithm*

4.2.1. *Experiment method and experiment system (procedure)*

The accuracy degree of the classification of U/V is directly reflected in output speech of speech processing system. It will influence the accuracy of recognition in speech recognition system directly, and it will influence the quality of synthetic speech of decoding terminal in speech coding system.

Standard LPC-10 vocoder (software) is chosen, the classification portions of U/V are replaced by Rab algorithm and DFMSE algorithm of this paper separately, other portions keep the same, then two experiment used vocoders (software) are obtained, programming them, and they are stored in the hardware using document name R-LPC.m and DF-LPC.m separately.

Experiment three: YB1 and YB2 are output two vocoders of R-LPC and DF-LPC separately, testing decoding speech under different SNR, and evaluating the equality of decoding speech, thus indirectly evaluating the property of classification algorithm of U/V in this paper.

4.2.2. *Experiment results*

R-LPC: when SNR is 30 dB, speech intelligibility is 98%, MOS score is 1.98, DRT is 87.6%; when SNR is 10 dB, three indexes are 97%, 1.82, 81.4% separately.

DF-LPC: when SNR is 30 dB, three indexes are 97%, 1.96, 88.7%; when SNR is 10 dB, three indexes are 97%, 1.91, 87.2%.

Experiment results show: when SNR is 30 dB, decoding speech quality of two vocoders is very close, which indicates that classification algorithm of U/V in this paper is consistent with single feature algorithm; but with the increasing of environment (background) noise, SNR declines; when SNR reduces to 10 dB (mobile communication is often in such environment), MOS score and DRT of R-LPC decoding speech (Diagnostic Rhyme Score) are superior to R-LPC obviously, this is performance brought by DFMSE algorithm.

For the same input speech, coding and decoding time of DF-LPC is one-sixth longer than R-LPC, which indicates that the processing time of DFMSE algorithm is longer.

5. CONCLUSIONS

The algorithm of classification of U/V based on multi-feature joint MSE criterion put forward in this paper, which makes full use of many strong relevant short-time features of speech signal, and combined with memory, optimal classification objective is realized through study; update with the frame of all parameters is realized, thus achieving inter-frame self-adaption. Simulation experiments show: compared with classical algorithm that depends on single feature, both the accuracy of U/V classification of the algorithm and the robustness in the noise environment have prominent enhancement.

REFERENCES

- [1] Boersma P. Accurate short-term analysis of the fundamental frequency and the harmonics-to-noise ratio of a sampled sound [J]. *Proc. of the Institute of Phonetic Sciences of the University of Amsterdam*, 1993, 17:97-110.
- [2] Kobayashi H, Shimamura T. A modified cepstrum method for pitch extraction [A]. *The 1998 IEEE Asia-Pacific Conference on Circuits and Systems [C]*.1998. 299-302.
- [3] Li Zhao. *Speech Signal Processing* [M]. Beijing: China Machine Press, 2010: 37-39.
- [4] Xiao-yan Dang, Xuan Wei, Hui-juan Cui, Kun Tang. Improvement of voiced-unvoiced classification vocoders [J]. *Journal of Tsinghua University (Science and Technology)*, 2008, 48(7): 1119-1122.
- [5] Kan Hong, Ye Li, Hui-juan Cui, Kun Tang. Bandpass-voicing mode-based error resilience scheme for vocoder gains [J]. *Journal of Tsinghua University (Science and Technology)*, 2008, 48(10): 1621-1624.
- [6] Ye Li, Kan Hong, Tong Wang, Hui-juan Cui, Kun Tang. Fuzzy unvoiced/voiced decision-making for sub-bands for SELP vocoder [J]. *Journal of Tsinghua University (Science and Technology)*, 2008, 48(7): 1101-1103.
- [7] Feng-yan Qi, Chang-chun Bao. A method for voiced/unvoiced/silence classification of speech with noise using SVM [J]. *Acta Electronica Sinica*, 2006, 34(4): 605-611.
- [8] Ahmadi S, Spanias A S. Cepstrum-based pitch detection using a new statistical V/UV classification algorithm [J]. *IEEE Trans. on Speech and Audio Processing*, 1999, 7(3): 333-338.
- [9] Run-qiang Yan, Yi-sheng Zhu. U/V decision based on recurrence quantification analysis [J]. *Journal of Electronics and Information Technology*, 2007, 29(7): 1703-1706.
- [10] Liang Chen, Xiong-wei Zhang. Nonlinear voiced/unvoiced decision based on phase space reconstruction [J]. *Journal of China Institute of Communications*, 2003, 24(6): 16-22.
- [11] Jian Liu, Fang Zheng, Jing Deng, Wen-biao Wu. Combined magnitude difference function based pitch tracking algorithm [J]. *Acta Electronica Sinica*, 2006, 34(10): 1925-1928.
- [12] Zhan-cai Jiang, Gang Yao. Algorithm of U/V decision without threshold and pitch detection [J]. *Computer Engineering and Applications*, 2011, 47(25): 135-139.
- [13] Na Ying, Xiao-hui Zhao. A speech unvoiced/voiced classification and voiced harmonic extraction algorithm—using third-order cumulant based on sinusoidal speech model [J]. *Computer Engineering and Applications*, 2006, 42(1): 66-68.
- [14] Zhao-qi Bian, Xue-gong Zhang. *Pattern Recognition* [M]. Beijing: Tsinghua University Press, 2005:101-106.

A Self-Adaptation Learning iBeacon High Precision Indoor Positioning System

S.H. Cao[1,*], Q.H. Wang[1], L.D. Wang[1], H.X. Zhang[1] & Y.F. Lou[2]
[1] *College of Qianjiang, Hangzhou Normal University, Hangzhou, 310036, China*
[2] *Zhuhai College of Jilin University, Zhuhai, 519 041, China.*
[*] *Email: caoshihu@126.com*

ABSTRACT: This paper constructs frame design and work process of indoor positioning system for iBeacon Bluetooth, it puts forward system method with high-precision indoor positioning of self-adaptation learning and algorithm. It makes analysis and points out that DSK-SVR algorithm positioning method design can extract the judgment ability of positioning characteristic from the perspective of enhancing generalization of learning machine.

KEYWORDS: iBeacon Bluetooth; Self-adaptation learning; High-precision positioning.

1. INTRODUCTION

Bluetooth positioning is one kind of wireless transmission technology [1, 2] with short distance and low consumption; it is the language from point to point and data business. Bluetooth technology has universal application in the field of wireless communication in short distance; meanwhile, it plays an important effect in field of short-distance detection. When Bluetooth technology is used in indoor positioning, it needs to be firstly install access point of Bluetooth signal, configures network into network connection model of motile users, and set bluetooth equipment as the main equipment of this micro-net, then we can make positioning on users.

This paper makes discussion of using Bluetooth technology and machine learning method to solve identification problem of high-precision positioning and user behavior model. It uses regression method to make modeling for signal intensity to realize self-adaptation free-calibration positioning, the positioning effect is superior to the past research work.

2. FRAME DESIGN ON BLUETOOTH INDOOR POSITIONING SYSTEM

2.1. *System frame of Bluetooth sensor network*

Bluetooth signal intensity is usually sent and controlled by module power of wireless radio frequency, the usual unit is dBm. Bluetooth standard provides 2 kinds of inquiry models: Inquiry Standard and Inquiry Result with RSSI.

This paper collects sensor data by establishing complete Bluetooth sensor network, the whole system frame is indicated by Figure 1, it adopts positioning frame based on infrastructure-based, Bluetooth sensor node will automatically scan Bluetooth module on mobile of user, and the backstage server will complete positioning and calculation work. On the contrast, the positioning frame based on client-based generally needs user terminal to install software, the terminal will forwardly scan each sensor node (or AP node), this needs to complete positioning and calculation process in the terminal, while in fact, the calculation resources and power are limited to user terminal.

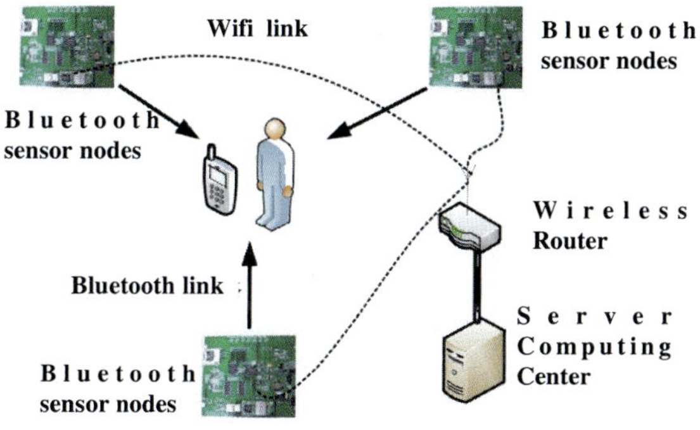

Figure 1. System frame of Bluetooth sensor network.

2.2. *Work process of Bluetooth sensor network*

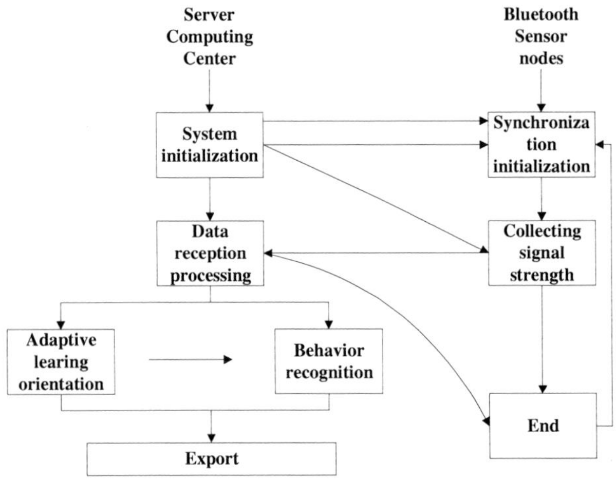

Figure 2. System work flow chart.

The flow of system work is coordinate work by calculation center of server and node, which is indicated by Figure 2, the communication interaction of both parts make communication by frame form indicated, the number lab corresponds to the frame lab. Server calculation center firstly controls each Bluetooth node to complete synchronization if each Bluetooth node and master, which will allocate length of inquiry cycle and interval, Bluetooth anchor node will feed back to server for the first time, server will choose user equipment of collecting data according to user terminal equipment appeared in the coverage range of signal, then start collection process of data, it will make inquiry loss disposal and filtration disposal for the original signal transmitted by anchor node of Bluetooth, respectively input into positioning module and behavior identification module to make positioning analysis and identification analysis, and gets the test result.

3. BLUETOOTH HIGH-PRECISION POSITIONING BASED ON SELF-ADAPTATION LEARNING ALGORITHM

3.1. *Establishment of positioning function based on SVR (DSK-SVR algorithm)*

SVR-based has special advantages [5] in solving non-linear regression problem of finite sample, by integrating SVR learning and establishing reflection relations between positioning characteristic and physical characteristic. SVR learning algorithm uses VC [6] dimension in statistics learning and minimization theory of structure and risk as base, the upper bound on real risk of learning machine and confidence range is composed of 2 parts. This paper adopts DSK-SVR (Direct Sparse Kernel Support Vector Regression) to study and construct non-linear reflection relations of positioning characteristic and physical position. DSK-SVR learning algorithm is the improvement method of standard and insensitive SVR algorithm. DSK-SVR can effectively reduce number of support vector and reduce calculation complication of SVR learning machine under condition of guaranteeing generalization ability of SVR learning.

Using the KDDA [6] method into the DSK-SVR algorithm sample space data through a nonlinear transformation into high-dimensional feature space so that the original data, not by linear regression modeling data in the sample space, can be in high dimensional feature space using the method of linear regression modeling. Aiming at the characteristics of nonlinear transform Bluetooth signal strength, the introduction of KDDA estimation method to solve the problem in this position, will convert the Bluetooth signal samples into a high dimensional feature space, and then the linear regression, the mapping relationship between the establishment of direct signal space and physical space.

3.2. *Learning algorithm process of self-adaptation*

The detailed algorithm process is as follows:

Step 1: Radio N; after data collection on the whole Bluetooth correlation, and gets the original data of Radio Map, and then makes clustering, it is respectively RadioMap 1, ... ,

Step 2: Classify user terminal to certain sub Radio Map by clustering block;

Step 3: Through the corresponding AP choice strategy of Radio Map and KDDA change matrix to extract the positioning characteristic with judgment ability.

Step 4: Input real-time characteristic into the corresponding SVR positioning function, and gets the final positioning result.

Offline period, firstly choose several referential points in the target positioning area, and collect RSS signal of each AP in each referential point and store in Radio Map. Secondly, divide Radio Map into several sub-Radio Map by clustering algorithm, moreover, it gives the optimal AP choice strategy in each Radio Map and extracts positioning characteristic by KDDA change, gets corresponding sub Radio Map after transformation. Finally, it makes SVR learning on the Radio Map after transformation to construct reflection relations between positioning characteristic and physical position.

4. SIMULATION OF TEST EXAMPLE

The typical positioning ML (SNR estimation algorithm), WKNN (Machine learning classification algorithm), SVR (The regression algorithm of support vector machine), also combine with clustering and AP choice algorithm (DSK-SVR) proposed by this paper. As it is indicated by Figure 3, average positioning bias of DSK-SVR and positioning bias is minimum, they are respectively 1.53 meters and 1.31 meters, reduces 18.2% and 16.6% than ML algorithm, reduces 28.5% and 27.6% than SVR algorithm. Therefore, the positioning precision of DSK-SVR characteristic extraction algorithm is obviously higher than the other characteristic extraction algorithm.

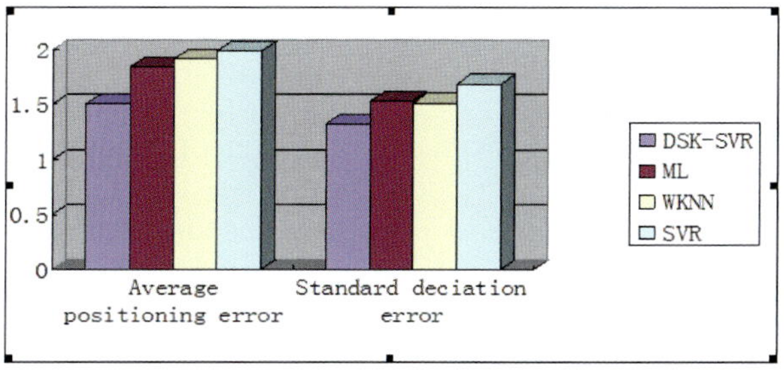

Figure 3. Comparison of different positioning characteristic extraction algorithm.

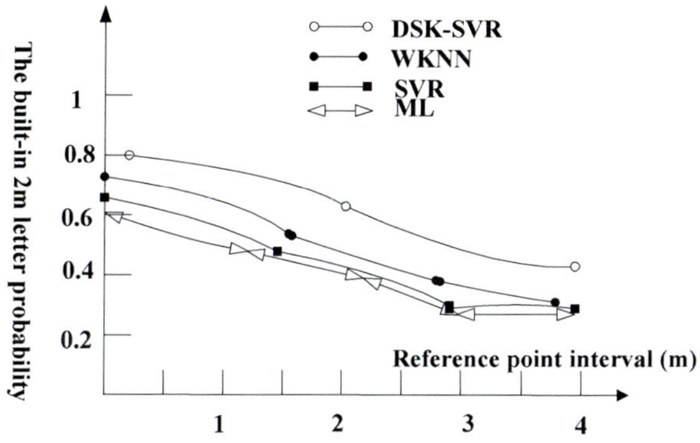

Figure 4. Effect of confidence probability of referential node within 2 meters.

Figure 4 compares the confidence probability of each positioning algorithm with internal of referential point is respectively 1, 2, 3 and 4, we can see that with density increase in referential point, positioning precision also increases, the DSK-SVR algorithm has higher calculation accuracy, increase the density of the reference point will directly add to the off-line phase reference point acquisition workload, and reference point acquisition workload reduced by at least one times above. In contrast, the reference point interval by reducing the workload of the reference point acquisition as far as possible, this paper experiment scene reference point interval is set to 2 meters.

5. CONCLUSION

In this paper, we proposed a self-adaptation learning iBeacon indoor positioning system which adopted DSK-SVR algorithm, simulation shows that DSK-SVR proved effective for the positioning accuracy, modeling process in the use of samples of the signal, signal information content more, as the effect is more ideal. DSK-SVR prevents noise signal introducing into positioning algorithm, and reduces dimension of input characteristic to certain extent. Cluster partitioning algorithm limits positioning model in the sub-area of positioning, avoids RSS causing suboptimum problem of model due to changes in physical position, and it also simplifies positioning function model of SVR.

ACKNOWLEDGMENT

This work is supported by the Natural Science foundation of Zhejiang (LQ14F020008), China; Hangzhou Science and Technology Committee (20140633B34), China; Key disciplines project and Fondation for the returned overseas Chinese schloar of Hangzhou Education Bureau, Qian Jiang College, Hangzhou Normal University (2015QJJL01), and Project of Zhuhai College of Jilin University, China.

REFERENCES

- [1] Jonathan Raper, Georg Gartner, Hassan Karimi and Chris Rizos. A critical evaluation of location based services and their potential. *Journal of Location Based Services*, 2007, 1(1): 5-45.
- [2] Ma Yuqiu, Long Chengzhi, Shen Shuqun. Long-distance Portable Positioning Technology and Indoor Positioning Technology. *Data Communication*, 2004, 5: 2-5.
- [3] Chang Yongyu, Yang Ning. CDMA Wireless Positioning Technology and Application, *Communication Technology*, 2003, 6: 1-5.
- [4] Zhang Hao, Zhao Qianchuan. Indoor Positioning System of Bluetooth Mobile Phone. *Computer Application*, 2007, 31 (11): 77-79.
- [5] Z. Zhuang, K.-H. Kim and J. P. Singh. Improving energy efficiency of location sensing on smartphones. *In ACM MobiSys*, 2010.
- [6] Xie Quanying, Liu Ming, Zhang Xing. Study and Overview on Mobile Wireless Sensor Network Positioning. *Computer Science and Engineering Institute Forum of University of Electronic Science and Technology of China*, 2012, 20(1).
- [7] Dinh Phung, Brett Adams, Svetha Venkatesh and Mohan Kumar. Unsupervised context detection using wireless signals. *Pervasive and Mobile Computing*, 5(2009) 714-733.
- [8] Hung H. Bui, Ding Phung, Svetha Venkatesh and Hai Phan. The Hidden Permutation Model and Location-Based *Activity Recognition*. AAAI, 2008.
- [9] Tim van Kasteren, Athanasios Noulas, Gwenn Englebienne and Ben Krose. Accurate Activity Recognition in a Home Setting. Ubicomp 2008.

Front-end Website Performance Optimization Based on Web Storage in Html5

P.P. Wang*, Z.Q. Wei & Z. Li
Department of Computer Science and Technology, Ocean University of China, Qingdao, China
*Email: wangpeipei0816@126.com

ABSTRACT: Web storage is an important technique to scale the performance optimizing of front-end website. Due to the limited space in web storage, exceptions would occur and nothing can be stored when the space is full. A low overhead and adaptive method based on Least Recently Used-Threshold (LRU-Threshold) algorithm is proposed in this paper to solve the problems. It generally considers recency as the main factor and chooses the threshold on the basic of the reading rate of items. Some items would be replaced with a new one according to the location of reference seen in the web storage streams and some will not be stored over the threshold. Through the experiments, the data in web storage can be replaced automatically and exceptions would not occur.

KEYWORDS: Performance optimization; Web storage; LRU-Threshold.

1. INTRODUCTION

According to the online graduate programs, if the page response time is more than 4 seconds, about a quarter of the people will give up on opening it; and if people wait it for more than 8 seconds, 70 percent will never visit it again [1]. Obviously, the website response time plays an important part of all website's users experience.

The performance golden rule [2] indicates that 80-90 percent of the website response time is spent on the web front-end program. As shown in Figure 1, the process of a page loading fully from an http request is listed below:

(1) Establishing a http link and sending http request.

(2) Server responding, then packaging html document and returning.

(3) Browser downloading the html document that packaged by server.

(4) Browser downloading components, such as css files.

(5) Page rendering

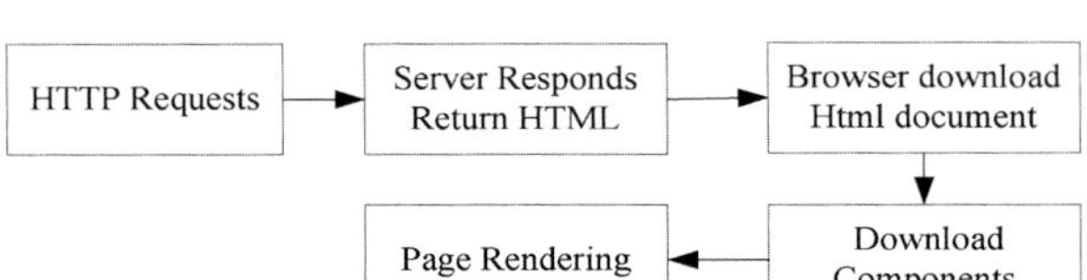

Figure1. The process of a page loading fully from an http request.

Some optimization strategies are proposed and applied to programs, like reducing http requests, using a content delivery network, adding an expires header, putting style sheets at the top etc.[3]. They achieve by reducing the transmission time at step (2), or html download time at step (3) and (4), which is worth exporting the occupancy rate.

Steve Souders points out that if the browser's cache is empty, the html document spends only 5 percent of the total response time, while 95 percent is waiting for the components [3], which means that caches have an important effect on the process.

In the early 1990s, cookies technology was put forward at RFC2965 [4] of W3C, which is earliest to store resources in the client. The history of local caches technology [5] is shown in Figure 2.

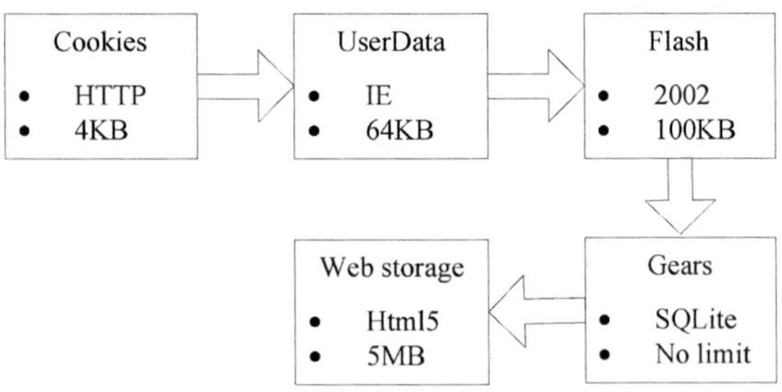

Figure 2. The history of local caches technology.

Cookies provide too small space to meet the need and it contains a number of security and privacy infelicities [6]. UserData has compatibility problem that it is only supported by Internet Explorer on the windows operating system. Flash is not supported by Apple at mobile terminal, although Apple has a strong share at the mobile market. SQLite has enough space but it needs the plugin to be installed, so it is not popular with people. Web storage in html5 is preferred by the users without these problems.

Web storage has adventages compared with other technology:

1) Web application can be used offline with using web storage.
2) It can monitoring events of the browser to make corresponding response, such as offline, online, storage change and so on.
3) It is more manageable without additional request header data.

Web storage in html5 provides a way to store key-value pairs, which are sometimes called items [7]. And it is widely supported by almost all the browsers, even Internet Explorer, showed in Figure 3.

Terminal	PC					Phone		
Browsers's Version	IE	FireFox	Chrome	Safari	Opera	iOS	Opera	Android
	8.0+	3.5+	4.0+	10.5+	10.5+	3.2+	11.0+	2.1+

Figure 3. Browsers that supports web storage in html5.

Web storage offers two storage objects: local storage and session storage, which stores the data as a string. The storage object allows for some simple functions, including setting, getting, removing, and clearing [8].

The session storage is for users to perform a single transaction of plan and design, and being validify on one single page. It means that when the page is closed, the data in session storage will be deleted. The local storage is across multiple windows, and the valid range can be more than the current session. After a window is closed, the data in local storage still can be used when the window is open again.

However, it has the limited space of about 5 million bytes at computer terminal and half of which at mobile terminal. When the space is full, no resource can be stored any more unless all the resources is cleared. This is a potential exception, which is solved can optimize the front-end website performance.

2. METHOD

2.1. *Website performance optimization based on web storage*

Web storage is widely used in web application and smartphone browser, and it provides enough space to store caches, including some files of css or javascript, even images. The effects of web storage on website performance optimization are listed below.

1) Reducing http request. Web storage stores much data, including resoures which can touch off http request. Due to the limited concurrency of browser, once the number of concurrent requests reaches boundary, others can only wait these requests for more time. Therefore, less response time by using web storage can impress up-on users.
2) Reducing size of download data from server. Web page download time is related to the page size, while more size the page is, more time it needs. There is no need to download the resources stored in web storage, and the page size is smaller than the one without using caches.
3) Using web storage is faster than http caches. According to Modify, a mobile e-commerce platform that helps optimizing websites, if web developers could choose the way of data caching, critical resources can be stored or updated in a more efficient way than http cache. And it points out that the web storage outperforms http cache performance by a factor of 5 in iOS5 and iOS6 [9].

2.2. *LRU-Threshold*

LRU-Threshold algorithm is extensions of the well-known LRU (Least Recently Used) algorithm. And it is widely used in different areas, such as disk buffers, database buffer management, paging etc. [10].

This strategy use recency as the main factor, and an object is not stored when size of the object exceeds a given threshold, which is the main difference with LRU [10]. It generally gives each object a field to record the time *t* from last visiting, and the object with the largest *t* will fall into disuse quickly when there is a need.

In this paper, items is stored as a string by using web storage, with the default form of an array. The location of items means the recency that they are visited without the field recording the time *t*. And it adds an item named *useSize* to record the size of user used in web storage.

Before inserting an item, the size of the item must be calculated, which is used at the item *useSize*. The flowchart of the proposed method is also given in the Figure 4. It is showed from the Figure 4 that the method of website performance optimization includes:

(1) Caching nothing if the size of the item exceeds the threshold.
(2) Clearing some items to release more space and store a new item.
(3) Changing the location of the item when it is visited.

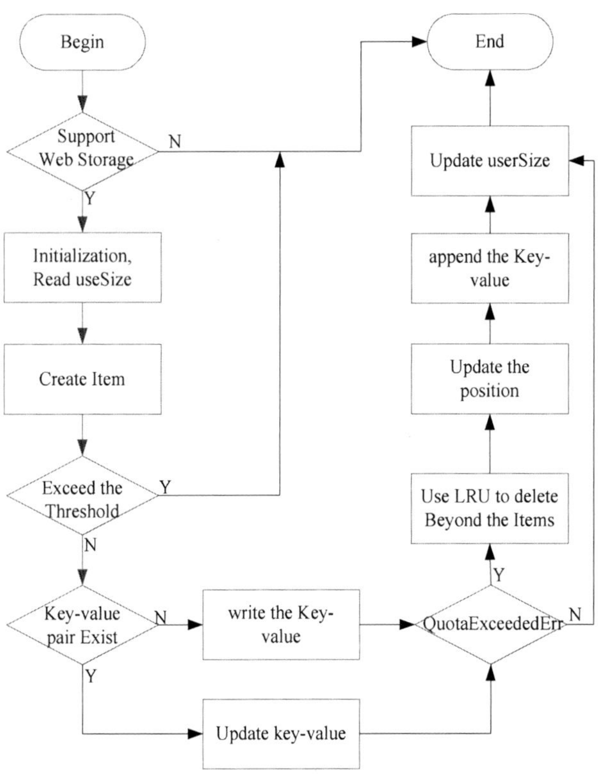

Figure 4. The flowchart of the proposed method.

3. EXPERIMENTS AND RESULTS

The experiment runs on Internet Explorer 11 in consideration of that different browsers have different performances.

3.1. *The selection and validation of the threshold*

To visit the data on the disk, the size of the data and the time visiting is in a positive correlation in theory. However, when the amount of data to visit is fixed, what relationship between one time visiting size of the data and reading rate?

Because of the total size of the web storage on smartphone terminal, this experiment supposes to visit the total amount of 2.5 million bytes. It sets the size of item that to be read be a variable value, as X axis shown in figure 5, to research on the curve trend of the reading rate. Due to the value of the reading rate is too small, this experiment records the number of times in half of one minute, as Y axis shown in Figure 5.

As shown in figure 5, when the total is fixed, with the increasing of the size of one time visiting data, the number of times increases firstly and then decreases, which means that the ralationship between the size of item and the reading rate decreases firstly and then increases. So, the reading rate is low if the size of item is too large after the peak. Therefore, the threshold in this experiment is selected as 15000 bytes.

Local storage and session storage in web storage is similar in use. This experiment use local storage to complete the validation. First, it checks the environment, initializes and creates some items. And the data of local storage is shown in Table 1 at column 1.

Table 1. The result in local storage.

useSize	index	key	
		1	2
148475	0	Item1	Item1
	1	Item2	Item2
	2	Item3	Item3
	3	Item4	Item4
	4	Item5	Item5
	5	Item6	Item6
	6	Item7	Item7

Then the new item with the key *itemNew* is inserted, and the value exceeds the threshold. The data in local storage is shown in Table 1 at column 2 after inserting.

Comparing column 1 with column 2 in Table 1, the new item with the key *itemNew* is fail to be stored into local storage and the value of *useSize* is unchanged. It is validated that an item *i* can not be stored when the size exceeds the given threshold.

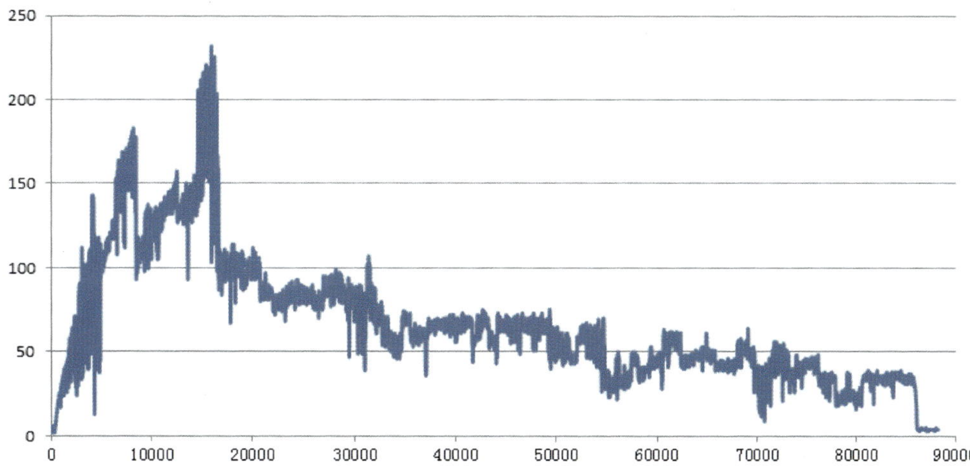

Figure 5. The relationship between the size of item and reading rate.

3.2. *The positional change of items with the thought of LRU-Threshold*

Combining the thought of LRU-Threshold, the applitation of the algorithm in this experiment is following:

(1) Adding the item at the end of the local storage array when it is created,

(2) Modifying the positon of the item at the end of the array when it is updated or visited

(3) Deleting the item at the head of the array for the new one when the size of the data reaches the limit.

In the experiment, the item with the key *Item5* is visited again without value changing. Then checking the locality of items in local storage, and it is shown in Table 2 after the key *Item5* being visited.

Table 2. The result in local storage after the item with the key *Item5* is visited.

useSize	index	key
148475	0	Item1
	1	Item2
	2	Item3
	3	Item4
	4	Item6
	5	Item7
	6	Item5

As shown in Table 2, the location of items is changed and the item with the key *Item5* is at the last position of the local storage array. Though time is spent when LRU-Threshold algorithm is executed, but it can be ignored compared with the time of getting or setting items in web storage.

3.3. *The validation of replacing automatically*

The replacement of items happens automatically when the space is full or the exception *QuotaExceededError* occurs. To solve the potential problem, the size of remain place can be calculated, and technological process includes:

(1) Calculating the size of the item and checking that whether the size is large than the threshold before it is inserted.

(2) Getting the item and recalculating the *useSize* if the item is to be modified.

(3) Calculating the remaining size and checking whether it is enough or not.

(4) Using the algorithm to delete an item and turning to the step (3) if the remaining size is not enough.

(5) Inserting the item at the end of the local storage array.

When the configuration items is stored, the data of local storage is shown in Table 3.

Table 3. The result in local storage after configuration.

useSize	index	key
4998248	0	key1
	1	key2
	2	key3
	3	key4
	4	key5
	5	key6
	6	key7

There are as many as more than 300 items that would be stored if this configuration items by the threshod of 15000 bytes. So in this part of experiment, the threshold is ignored in these configuration items.

The item with the key *keyNew* is created, and the size is 10000 bytes, which is obviously meet the condition in step (3). And the data in local storage is shown in Table 4.

Table 4. The result of after the item with the key *keyNew* is inserted.

useSize	index	key
3375207	0	key2
	1	key3
	2	key4
	3	key5
	4	key6
	5	key7
	6	keyNew

The item with key *key1* disappears and the value of *useSize* is changed as shown in Table 4 compared with Table 3. And the new item is at the last position of local storage array. It is validated that some items in web storage can be replaced automatically when the place is full but a new item should be inserted.

4. CONCLUSION

In this paper, a method based on LRU-Threshold algorithm is proposed to sovle the problems that exceptions occur and data would not be stored when the space is full, which are caused by the limitation of space in web storage. And the relationship between the size of the item and reading rate is investigated, which produces the number of the threshold. It is validated that the website performance is optimized by cofiguring the item *useSize* to monitor the remaining size in web storage, controlling the size of the item with the threshold and replacing the items automatically.

ACKNOWLEDGEMENT

This work is supported by Self Innovation and Achievements Transformation of Shandong Province (No. 2014CGZH0708) and International Cooperation in Science and Technology project (No. 2013DFA10490).

REFERENCES

— [1] Online Graduate Programs. 2012. Instant America Network Search. *http://www.onlinegraduateprograms.com/instant-america/.*

— [2] Brutlag J, Abrams Z, Meenan P. 2011. Above-the-fold time: measuring Web page performance visually. *Velocity: Web Performance and Operations Conference.*

— [3] Souders S. 2008. High-performance web sites. *Communications of the ACM* 51(12): 36-41.

— [4] Montulli, L., & Kristol, D. 1997. HTTP State Management Mechanism. *Internet Engineering Task Force.*

— [5] Park J S, Sandhu R. 2000. Secure cookies on the Web. *IEEE internet computing* 4(4): 36-44.

— [6] Pilgrim M. 2011. The past, present and future of local storage for Web applications. *Dive into HTML5.*

— [7] Hickson I. 2011. Web storage. *Draft, W3C, October 4th 2011, http://dev.w3.org/html5/webstorage/ accessed on* 4(11).

— [8] West W, Pulimood S M. 2012. Analysis of privacy and security in HTML5 web storage. *Journal of Computing Sciences in Colleges* 27(3): 80-87.

— [9] Perter Mclachlan. 2013. Smartphone Browser Local Storage is up to 5x Faster than Native Cache. *http://www.mobify.com/blog/smartphone-localstorage-outperforms-browser-cache/.*

— [10] Podlipnig S, Böszörmenyi L. 2003. A survey of web cache replacement strategies. *ACM Computing Surveys (CSUR)* 35(4): 374-398.

— [11] Williams, Stephen, and Edward A. Fox. 1995. Caching proxies: Limitations and potentials. *Proceedings of the Fourth International World Wide Web Conference.*

— [12] Cherkasova, L. 1998. *Improving www proxies performance with greedy-dual-size-frequency caching policy.* Hewlett-Packard Laboratories.

— [13] Kristol, D. M. 2001. HTTP Cookies: Standards, privacy, and politics. *ACM Transactions on Internet Technology (TOIT)* 1(2): 151-198.

— [14] Stefanov, Stoyan. 2012. *Web Performance Daybook. Vol. 2.* O'Reilly Media, Inc.

A Channel Availability Prediction Method Suitable for HF ALE System

G. Lin*
Postgraduate Team 3 CCE, PLAUST, Nanjing, China

Y.P. Cheng & H. Jiang
College of Communications Engineering, PLAUST, Nanjing, China
**Email: lingang910104@163.com*

ABSTRACT: Considering the deficiency of traditional HF ALE system on frequency usage, integrating the concept of cognitive radio technology, this paper puts forward a channel availability prediction method for HF communications based on Hidden Markov Model (HMM). We set up a three-state HMM prediction model of channel availability according to the principle of channel usage in HF communication, and give out the corresponding specific prediction process. The simulation results show that the model can well predict the changes of channel with accuracy above 89%.

KEYWORDS: HF ALE; Hidden Markov model; Spectrum prediction.

1. INTRODUCTION

HF communication works on the band ranging from 1.5 to 30 MHZ through the atmosphere by the ionosphere reflection. It is the earliest appeared and widely used way of wireless communication, and till now is still a significant means at middle-long distance. Due to the serious frequency-selective fading caused by the change of the ionosphere, how to choose the suitable frequency to improve the reliability of HF communication has been one tough problem waiting to be solved. Traditional automatic link establishment (ALE) [1] choosing the communication frequency to be used from the frequency sets granted by the frequency planning department, whose accuracy based on a long-term statistical analysis and forecast has been not able to realize the reliable HF communication in the increasingly crowded electromagnetic environment of the ionosphere.

In the next generation of automatic link establishment standard MIL-STD-188-141C, The US Dept. of Defense explicitly puts forward the idea of applying the concepts of cognitive radio to HF spectrum sensing, forecast and choosing. So the combination of cognitive radio and HF communication [2] is widely studied nowadays, which is also a key technology of the next generation of HF communication. The prediction method based on hidden Markov model [3]-[6] is a typical representative.

For the deficiency of traditional HF ALE system on frequency utilization, this paper raises a new kind of channel availability prediction method based on hidden Markov model (HMM) for HF communication. By the division of HF channel availability, this method can not only predict the channel state (free or occupied), but also roughly predict the duration of the channel state. It can reduce the channel switching cost of commonly used single timeslot spectrum prediction, which has more practical significance for HF communication whose transmission delay is large.

The rest of this paper is organized as follows: section 2 provides the basic theory of HMM [7] and spectrum sensing, section 3 provides the prediction method of this paper, section 4 provides the simulation and the results, section 5 provides the conclusions.

2. THE THEORY OF HMM AND SPECTRUM SENSING

2.1. *Hidden Markov model*

As shown in Fig. 1, the HMM is a doubly stochastic process consisting of two parts. The first one is the hidden Markov chain that describes the transition of the hidden states i.e. the true states with the states transition probability matrix A. π is the initial probability matrix for system. The second one is a general stochastic process describing the relationship between hidden states and observation states O with the observation probability matrix B.

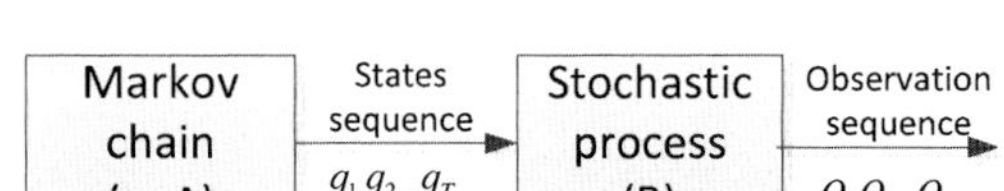

Figure 1. HMM structure diagram.

The mathematical definition of HMM is as follows:

1) States transition probability matrix: $A = \{a_{ij}\}$ of size N^2 where N is the number of states and $a_{ij} = P(q_{t+1} = S_j \mid q_t = S_i)$, $1 \le i, j \le N$. The set of hidden states is $S = \{S_1, S_2, ..., S_N\}$ and the state at time t is denoted as q_t.

2) Observation probability matrix: $B = \{b_i(k)\} = \{b_{ik}\}$ of size $N \times M$ where $b_i(k) = P(o_t = V_k \mid q_t = S_i)$ $1 \le i \le N; 1 \le k \le M$, o_t is the observation at time t and the set of the observation symbols is $V = \{V_1, V_2, ..., V_M\}$. The observation sequence is $O = o_1 o_2 ... o_T$ where $o_t \in V$ and T is the number of observations in an observed sequence.

3) Initial probability matrix:

$\pi = \{\pi_i\}, \pi_i = P(q_1 = S_i), 1 \le i \le N$

For convenience, the compact notation used for an HMM will be $\lambda = (A, B, \pi)$. The precondition of Using the HMM to solve the problem of spectrum prediction is to get the observation sequence as the basis of model training and state prediction, which mainly relies on the spectrum sensing.

2.2. *Spectrum power quantization*

The spectrum sensing process works as follows: listening on the specified channel with spectrum monitoring and acquisition device to get the sensing sequence of L time slots expressed as

$O = o_1 o_2 ... o_L$, $o_l \in \{0,1\}$, $l \in \{1, 2..., L\}$, preprocessing the sensing sequence, getting the classification result(seen in 2.3) of channel availability by analysis of channel occupancy state as the inputting training sequence for HMM.

In order to observe the HF channel state more clearly, [8] analyzed the duty ratio of received power and found two obvious peaks, as shown in Fig. 2. We set a threshold between the two peaks γ, the left of which means there's no user on the channel with state '0' and the right of which means there existing some user on the channel with state '1'.

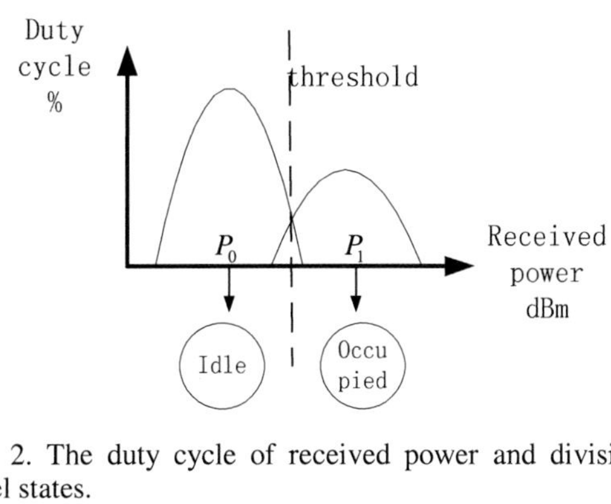

Figure 2. The duty cycle of received power and division of channel states.

After the quantitative process above we can get the binary observation sequence $O = o_1 o_2 ... o_L$ showing the channel changes of some bandwidth in a certain time. '0' and '1' respectively represent the channel states of 'idle' and 'occupied'. The mapping relationship is as follows:

$O = o_1 o_2 ... o_L$,

$$o_l = \begin{cases} =1 & P_l > \gamma \\ =0 & P_l < \gamma \end{cases}, l \in \{1, 2..., \mathrm{L}\} \tag{1}$$

2.3. *Classification of channel availability*

Channel occupancy state can only tell whether there exists some user on the channel or not in a short time such as 2 seconds. If we want to find out the regulation of the channel usage and predict the channel availability, we need to analyze the channel occupancy state for longer time. Here, based on the channel states we get in part B of 2 seconds, we define the set of channel availability of 1 minute.

The dividing standard of channel availability [1], [8] depends on the longest time that the HF user takes to transmit its data frames. Taking the most typical protocol STANAG5066 as an example, it defines frames called D-PDU, which have 46 bytes of overhead and up to 1023 bytes of user data. Most HF data communications use a data rate of 600bps or 1200bps, under which the longest transmitting time would last for 14.25s (1069 bytes at 600bps).

Then we can give out the dividing standard of channel availability used for HF communication. Supposing a user occupying the channel for ζ s, the channel availability can expressed as follows:

$$U = \begin{cases} U_1 & \text{available} & \zeta < 15\text{s} \\ U_2 & \text{unavailable} & \zeta > 45\text{s} \\ U_3 & \text{partially available} & 15\text{s} < \zeta < 45\text{s} \end{cases} \tag{2}$$

As for U_1, there is at most 15 s in 1 min during which the channel is occupied, so the waiting user outside can use this channel. As for U_2, there is at least 45 s in 1 min during which the channel is occupied, so the waiting user outside cannot transmit the longest frame in the remaining 15s. As for U_3, the channel is partially available, the waiting user outside could make a choice to use it.

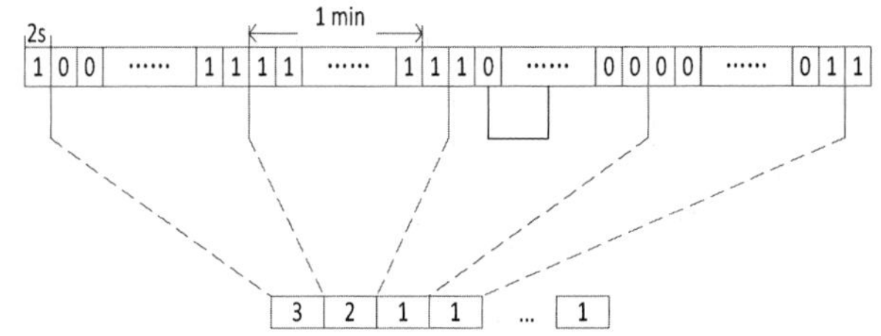

Figure 3. Division of HF channel availability.

Now we can get the channel availability sequence $U = \{u_1, u_i ... u_T\}, i = 1...\mathrm{T}, u_i \in V = \{$1: available, 2: unavailable, 3: partially available$\}$ from sensing sequence O shown as Fig. 3. Sequence U will be used as the inputting observation sequence (training sequence) of HMM.

3. PREDICTION METHOD BASED ON HMM

3.1. *States transition of HF channel availability*

Combined with the definition about the state of the channel availability, we can give out the transition process of HF channel availability shown as Fig. 4 where $Q = \{q_1, q_i ... q_T\}, i = 1...\mathrm{T}, q_i \in S = \{1,2,3\} = V$

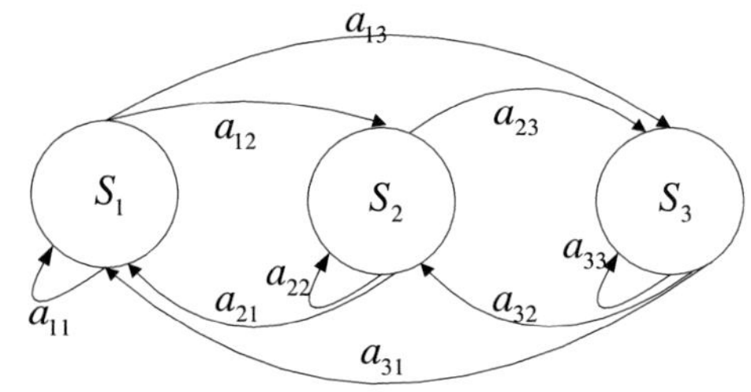

Figure 4. Transition of HF channel availability.

3.2. *Prediction procedure*

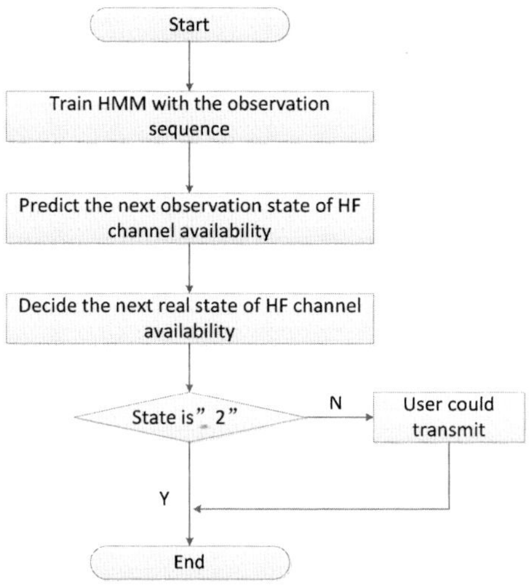

Figure 5. Prediction procedure of HF channel availability.

Fig. 5 shows the prediction process of HF channel availability based on HMM, which consists of three main procedures.

1) Taking $U = \{u_1, u_i ... u_T\}$ as the inputting sequence of the model and training the HMM with Baum-Welch algorithm to get $\lambda_{ML} = \arg\max_{\lambda} f(U \mid \lambda)$, $\lambda_{ML} = \{A, B, \pi\}$

To describe the algorithm conveniently, we import the forward variable

$$\alpha_t(i) = P(u_1, u_2, ..., u_t, q_t = i \mid \lambda) \tag{3}$$

Which means the partial probability that under the given HMM, when time comes to t, the observation sequence is $u_1, u_2, ..., u_t$ and the state at t is S_i. Its recursive relationship is as follows:

$$\alpha_{t+1}(j) = \sum_{j=1}^{N} \alpha_t(i)\ a_{ij} b_j(u_{t+1}), 1 \le j \le N, 1 \le t \le T-1 \tag{4}$$

Where $\alpha_1(j) = \pi_j b_j(u_1), 1 \le j \le N$

Similarly we can define the backward variable

$$\beta_t(i) = P(u_{t+1}, u_{t+2,...,} u_T \mid q_t = i, \lambda) \tag{5}$$

$$\beta_t(i) = \sum_{j=1}^{N} \beta_{t+1}(j)\ a_{ij} b_j(u_{t+1}), 1 \le i \le N, 1 \le t \le T-1 \tag{6}$$

Where $\beta_T(i) = 1, 1 \le i \le N$

Defining the middle variable

$$\gamma_t(i) = p(q_t = i \mid U, \lambda) \tag{7}$$

$$\xi_t(i, j) = p(q_t = i, q_{t+1} = j \mid \mathrm{U}, \lambda) \tag{8}$$

We can see that $\gamma_t(i) = \sum_{j=1}^{N} \xi_t(i, j)$.

Further we can get

$$\xi(i, j) = \frac{\alpha_t(i) \mathrm{a}_{ij}\ \beta_{t+1}(j)\ b_j(u_{t+1})}{\sum_{i=1}^{N} \sum_{j=1}^{N} \alpha_t(i) \mathrm{a}_{ij}\ \beta_{t+1}(j)\ b_j(u_{t+1})} \tag{9}$$

With U and the initial model $\lambda_0 = (A_0, B_0, \pi_0)$ known, the Baum-Welch algorithm works as follows:

Step 1: Using (4) and (6) to calculate $\alpha_t(i)$ and $\beta_t(i)$.

Step 2: Calculating $\xi_t(i, j)$ and $\gamma_t(i)$.

Step 3: Updating λ with the following formulas.

$\overline{\pi}_i = \gamma_1(i), 1 \le i \le N$

$$\overline{a}_{ij} = \frac{\sum_{t=1}^{T-1} \xi_t(i, j)}{\sum_{t=1}^{T-1} \gamma_t(i)}, 1 \le i \le N, 1 \le j \le N$$

$$\overline{b}_j(k) = \frac{\sum_{t=1,\ u_t = v_k}^{T} \gamma_t(j)}{\sum_{t=1}^{T} \gamma_t(i)}, 1 \le j \le N, 1 \le k \le M$$

2) Using the training results $\hat{\lambda}_{ML} = \{\hat{A}, \hat{B}, \hat{\pi}\}$ and the observation sequence we have, we compare $P(U^T, 1 \mid \lambda)$, $P(U^T, 2 \mid \lambda)$ and $P(U^T, 3 \mid \lambda)$ by Forward algorithm, we choose the state corresponding to the maximum probability as the next state. The algorithm works as follows:

Step 1: Initialization, $\alpha_1(j) = \pi_j b_j(u_1), 1 \le j \le N$

Step 2: Iteration,

$$\alpha_{t+1}(j) = b_j(u_{t+1}) \sum_{i=1}^{N} \alpha_t(i) a_{ij}, 1 \le j \le N, 1 \le t \le T$$

Step 3: When $t = T$, the iteration ends.

$$P(U^{T+1} \mid \lambda) = \sum_{i=1}^{N} \alpha_{T+1}(i)$$

Step 4: $u_{T+1} = u_i \mid_{\arg\{\max[P(U^T,1|\lambda), P(U^T,2|\lambda), P(U^T,3|\lambda)]\}}$

3) Combing the next observation state predicted above with the history observation sequence, we a get a new observation sequence. By Viterbi algorithm, the real next channel availability state can be predicted from the new observation sequence.

Here we define $\delta_t(i) = \max_j(\delta_{t-1}(j)\ a_{ji} b_{ik_t}), t \geq 2$

$\phi_t(i) = \arg\max_j(\delta_{t-1}(j)\ a_{ji})$

The algorithm works as follows:

Step1: Initialization, $\begin{cases} \delta_1(i) = \pi_i b_i(u_1) \\ \phi_1(i) = 0 \end{cases} 1 \leq i \leq N$

Step 2: Iteration,

$$\begin{cases} \delta_t(i) = \max_j(\delta_{t-1}(j)\ a_{ji} b_{ik_t}) \\ \phi_t(i) = \arg\max_j(\delta_{t-1}(j)\ a_{ji}) \end{cases} 1 \leq i \leq N, 2 \leq t \leq T$$

Step 3: Iteration ends $\begin{cases} p^* = \max_{1\leq i\leq N}(\delta_T(i)) \\ q^* = \arg\max_{1\leq i\leq N}(\delta_T(i)) \end{cases}$

4. SIMULATIONS AND RESULTS

The simulation contains two parts. The first one is the simulation for HMM with known λ to verify the reliability of the model. The second one assumes the channel occupancy follows a Poisson distribution and calculates the prediction accuracy of channel availability on this model.

4.1. *Reliability demonstration*

According to the parameter values given in table 1, the Matlab software generates a sequence of 500 elements and the corresponding hidden states sequence. Then we can carry out our first simulation with the two sequences.

Table 1. The estimation results of parameter for HMM.

Parameters	True value	Estimated value
π	0,0	0,0
A	$\begin{bmatrix} 0.90 & 0.03 & 0.06 \\ 0.04 & 0.92 & 0.04 \\ 0.04 & 0.04 & 0.92 \end{bmatrix}$	$\begin{bmatrix} 0.9017 & 0.0345 & 0.0638 \\ 0.0451 & 0.9138 & 0.0411 \\ 0.0397 & 0.0422 & 0.9181 \end{bmatrix}$
B	$\begin{bmatrix} 0.95 & 0.02 & 0.03 \\ 0.02 & 0.91 & 0.07 \\ 0.10 & 0.05 & 0.85 \end{bmatrix}$	$\begin{bmatrix} 0.9437 & 0.0211 & 0.0352 \\ 0.0186 & 0.9209 & 0.0605 \\ 0.1012 & 0.0535 & 0.8453 \end{bmatrix}$

Fig. 6 shows the training curve of the parameter $A(2,2)$ in states transition probability matrix A and the parameter $B(2,2)$ in observation probability matrix B. We can see that, with the increase of training sequence length, the training result finally converges and approaches the real value of the model. Fig. 7 shows the prediction results of HMM with parameters known, we can see with the increase of training sequence length, the prediction result finally converges and approaches 94%. The simulation can well verify the reliability of the model.

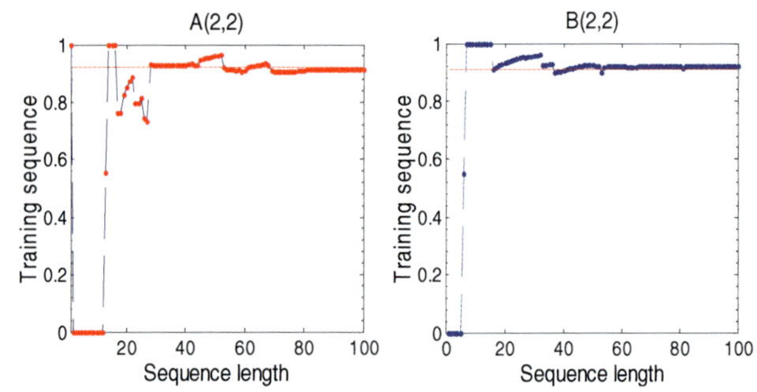

Figure 6. Training curve of HMM.

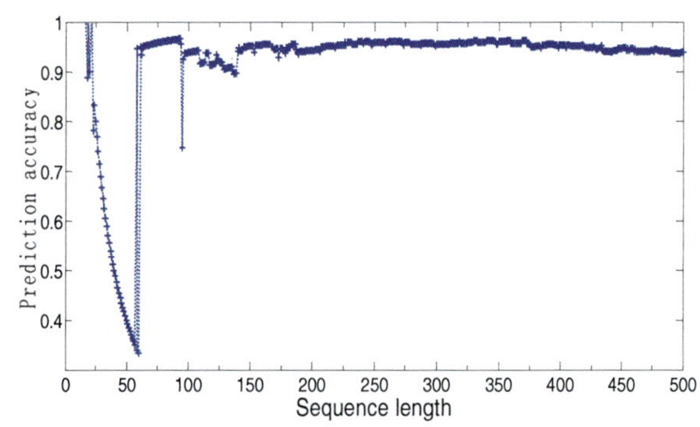

Figure 7. Prediction accuracy curve of HMM.

4.2. *Prediction accuracy*

The simulation emulates the channel occupancy with data following Poisson distribution and maps it to hidden states sequence. Then we add AWGN to the data and get the emulated observation sequence of HF channel. The length of the training sequence is 500. The values of SNR are 5dB, 10dB, 15dB, 20dB and 25dB respectively.

Fig. 8 shows the curve of prediction accuracy with 25dB SNR, we can see with the increase of training sequence length, the prediction result finally converges and reaches 73%.

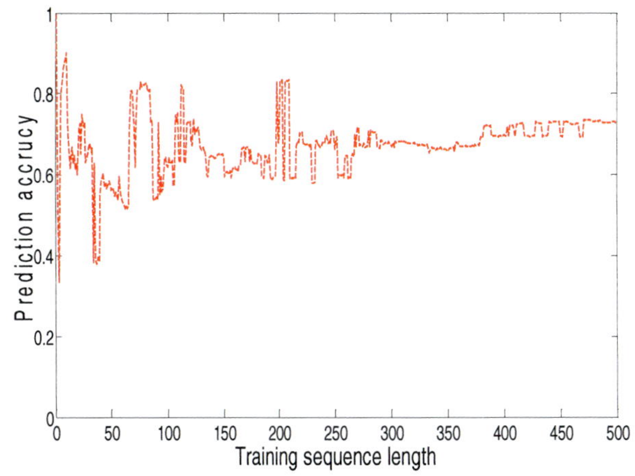

Figure 8. Prediction accuracy curve of HMM.

According to the division standard of channel availability in this paper, we define channel access rate $\phi = \varphi + (a + b) / 500$, where a represents the situation that the "available" is predicted to be "partial available" and b represents the situation that the "partial available" is predicted to be "available". Compared with φ, since channel can choose access under the both situations, ϕ can better tells the actual channel usages. Fig. 9 shows the curves of prediction accuracy and access rate, we can see with the increase of SNR, both φ and ϕ increase and converge gradually and the channel access rate approaches 89% when SNR is 25dB, which can well meet the need of channel access of HF.

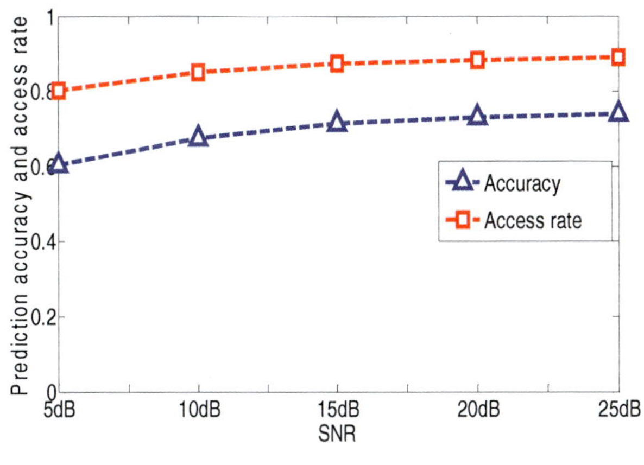

Figure 9. Curves of prediction accuracy and access rate.

5. CONCLUSIONS

Considering the deficiency of traditional HF ALE system on frequency usage, integrating the concept of cognitive radio technology, this paper puts forward a channel availability prediction method for HF based on Hidden Markov Model. We set up a three-state HMM prediction model of channel availability according to the principle of channel usage in HF communication and gives out the concrete prediction process. The simulation results show that when the observation sequence increases to a certain length, the model can well predict channel changes, whose accuracy can reach above 89%.

All of the simulations in this article are done by hypothetical data, which still have certain differences with actual characteristics of HF channel. In future study, we will consider to use real data measured from HF frequencies to further test the performance of the model.

REFERENCES

— [1] MIL-STD-188-141B[S], Military Standard, Interoperability and Performance Standards for Medium and High Frequency Radio Systems, US Dept. of Defense, March 1999.

— [2] E. Koski, W. Furman. Applying cognitive radio concepts to HF communications [C] 11th International Conference on Ionospheric Radio Systems and Techniques, IRST09, 2009.

— [3] I. A. Akbar, W. H. Tranter. Dynamic spectrum allocation in cognitive radio using hidden Markov models: Poisson distributed case [C] IEEE Southeast Conference, 2007: 196-201.

— [4] S. D. Barnes, B. T. Maharaj. Performance of a hidden Markov channel occupancy model for cognitive radio [C]. AFRICON, IEEE, 2011: 1-6.

— [5] T. Nguyeny, B. L. Mark, Y. Ephraim. Hidden Markov process based dynamic spectrum access for cognitive radio [C] Information Sciences and Systems (CISS). Baltimore, USA, 2011 45th Annual Conference on IEEE, 2011: 1-6.

— [6] K. W. Choi, E. Hossain. Estimation of primary user parameters in cognitive radio systems via hidden Markov model [J]. Signal Processing, IEEE Transactions on, 2013, 61(3): 782-795.

— [7] L. Rabiner. A tutorial on hidden Markov models and selected applications in speech recognition [J]. Proceedings of the IEEE, 1989, 77(2): 257-286.

— [8] L. Melián-Gutiérrez, HF spectrum activity prediction model based on HMM for cognitive radio applications [J], Physical Communication, 2013.

The Competition Dynamics of Information Propagation in Complex Network

J. Y. Lin*
School of Computer and Communication Engineering, University of Science and Technology, Beijing

M. Li
School of Mathematics and Systems Science, Beihang University
**Email: linjunyi_hi@126.com*

ABSTRACT: The "non-consensus" opinions pervade all patterns of human's interactive activities. In this paper, we study the phenomenon of the information competition dynamics induced by messages with opposite meaning. We construct a new information competition model which could perfectly match the reality in complex networks. It is shown that the k-shell value of nodes plays an important role in reflecting its competitive power in the information competition processes, classifying the nodes in the network with the k-shell decomposition technique. In particular, by varying the variables in our model different cases of information competition phenomena can be successfully explained. Our findings indicate that this new information competition model should be useful to the study on network information dissemination.

KEYWORDS: Information competition; K-shell decomposition; Complex network.

1. INTRODUCTION

The topological characteristics of complex networks such as the degree distribution, clustering, shortest path length, and modularity have been widely studied [1-3]. After BA model [4] was proposed by Barabási and Albert, BA was widely used in the models studying the dynamics in complex networks because almost all of the natural networks are scale-free networks which follow a power-law degree distribution. In recent years, a variety of techniques and models have been developed to help understanding the dynamic processes occurred in complex networks: the typical SIR and SIS model [5] to describe the disease diffusion in biological networks, the cascade failure model [6] to characterize the interaction among multiple networks and partially interdependent networks under attack, and the information dissemination model [7] to reveal the phase transition in social networks.

The mechanism of information propagation has attracted lots of attention from physicists. Social networks capture a multitude of relationships through which individuals could share ideas, change opinions, and make communications. M. Kitsak et al. have studied the influential spreaders in complex networks [8], while J. B. H. et al. have observed the absence of influential spreaders in rumor dynamics [9]. The crucial role of strong links in information cascading networks has been revealed [10] and the subtle role of weak links in information transmission in online social networks has been found by K. Xu et al. [11]. The controllability of complex network has been widely studied as well [12-13].

More recently, with the rapid development of communication technology, news and opinions can be easily exchanged or spread among large amounts of individuals. The online social networks, such as Facebook, Twitter, have provided a large open platform for everyone to exhibit his own personality and characteristic. People's perspectives about a new idea might be distinct. In this case, one may persuade or argue with the others trying to make his perspective accepted. Meanwhile, one might also be influenced by others who hold the opposite perspectives. This constructs a new form of information propagation, the information competition dynamics in social communicating networks, which has barely been involved in recent works [14-15].

In this paper, we focus on the information dynamics processes in the new form described above. We proposed a new information competition dynamics model that matches the phenomena of real world and can be used to capture the key features of mechanisms in these information dynamics processes. We carry out extensive numerical simulations according to the model, and the results show that both the k-shell value [16] (which will be explained in the 4th section) of nodes and the variables in the model play a vital role in information dissemination.

This paper is organized as follows. In section 2, we introduce the datasets used in this paper, and the definition of k-shell decomposition method. In section 3, we study the information competition processes in complex network. The information competition dynamics model is proposed. In section 4, the results and discussion of extensive numerical simulations are summarized.

2. THE NETWORK, DATESETS AND K-SHELL DECOMPOSITION

A network is a collection of nodes (which represent the individuals or users) with some correlated edges (which represent the relationship between two terminal nodes). We consider the undirected, connected network with N nodes and E correlated edges.

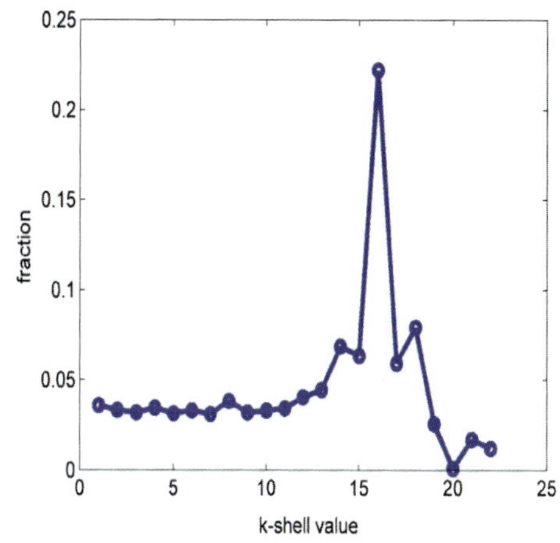

Figure 1. The k-shell value distribution of the BA network.

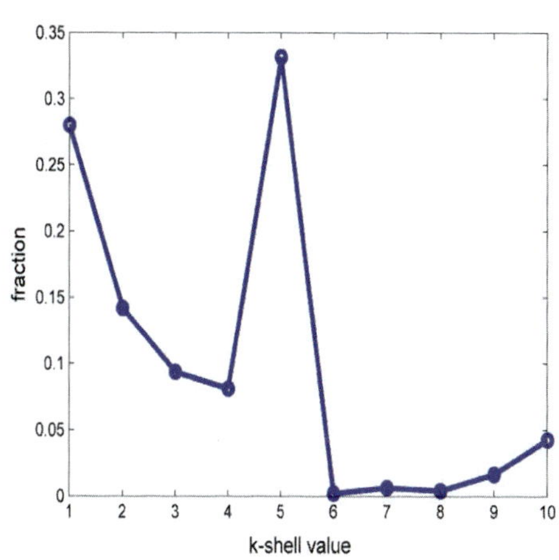

Figure 2. The k-shell value distribution of the P2P network.

We consider complex networks with two different structures. One is a random graph with power-law degree distribution (BA) with exponent 2.5, i.e. degree distribution $p(k) \propto k^{-\gamma}$, $\gamma = 2.5$. And the other is a real network based on the snapshots of the Gnutella peer-to-peer (P2P) file sharing network [17] with nodes representing hosts in the Gnutella network topology and edges representing connections between the Gnutella hosts. The detail information about the two networks is shown as below in Table 1.

Table 1. Information of the datasets used in this paper.

Name	N	E
BA	5000	115496
P2P	6301	20777

The k-shell [16] is a node index, which can be obtained in the following way: by recursively removing all the nodes of degree less than k, until the nodes in the remaining network have degree at least k, we call nodes in this sub-network k-core. And k-shell is the nodes in k-core but not in (k+1)-core. Figures 1 and 2 are the k-shell distribution for the BA and P2P respectively.

3. THE INFORMATION COMPETITION DYNAMICS MODEL

The model of information competition in a network can be defined in the following way. To simplify the problem we only consider the simplest case, i.e. there are just two opposite opinions and every node has to hold only one of them. Every individual (represented by vertex in the network) of total N has three probably states, and the state set is {sensitive (S), influencer (I), receiver (R)}. And a signal flag which represented by 1 or -1 will be used to characterize the trend that an individual believes the information or believes the opposite, and 0 represents the initial signal flag. So the state set can be easily extended as $\{S^1, S^{-1}, I^1, I^{-1}, R^1, R^{-1}, S^0\}$. The processes of the information competition dynamics can be briefly described as following:

1) At first, set all the nodes' states as sensitive, and all the signal flags as 0 (the initial signal flag). (We call these initial nodes S^0 for short)

2) Choose two vertices, set their states as influencer, and their signal flag as 1 and -1 respectively. (We call these two nodes I^1 and I^{-1} for short)

3) Among each time step, we search all of the target nodes with state S. For every target node:

i) If the target node is I^1, the target node connects with one (or more) his neighbors to spread the information. When I^1 encounters S^0, S^0 will become

I^1 with rate α_1; when I^1 encounters I^1 or R^1, the target node itself becomes R^1 with rate β_1; when I^1 encounters I^{-1}, I^{-1} will become I^{-1} with rate γ_1.

ii) If the target node is I^{-1}, the target node connects with one (or more) his neighbors to spread the information. When I^{-1} encounters S^0, S^0 will become I^{-1} with rate α_{-1}; when I^{-1} encounters I^{-1} or R^{-1}, the target node becomes R^{-1} with rate β_{-1}; when I^{-1} encounters I^1, I^1 will become I^{-1} with rate γ_{-1}.

4) Exclude (3) recursively until there are no nodes with state I (I^1 or I^{-1}) in the network.

5) Count the number of nodes with state R^1 and R^{-1}, and calculate the ratio of them.

This model is a composition of the typical disease diffusion model SIR[5] and the mechanism of information propagation in social communicating networks[11]. In the end of the processes, there is no node with state I, so we can make a conclusion that $\Phi_S(T)+\Psi_I^{\,1}(T)+\Psi_I^{\,-1}(T)=1$ where $\Phi_S(T)$ is the density of nodes with state S, $\Psi_I^{\,1}(T)$ and $\Psi_I^{\,-1}(T)$ are the density of I^1 and I^{-1}, respectively. In the following numerical simulations, we set $\beta_1=\beta_2=\gamma_1=\gamma_2=1$ because it just affects the time costs in our simulation, and our main results do not depend on the choice of these variables.

4. SIMULATION RESULTS

At first, we assume that for the given information, an individual only has two choices: accept it or accept the opposite, when encountering with one of his neighbors who hold the information, so we can simplify the model only to consider the case when $\alpha_1+\alpha_{-1}=1$, i.e. one individual will accept the information coming from his neighbors with rate α_1 and accept the opposite with rate $\alpha_{-1}=1-\alpha_1$. In Figures 3 and 4 we explore the relationship between the variable α_1 and the information competition processes. X-axis is the value of α_1 ranging from 0 to 1, and the Y-axis is the ratio R(1,-1) of R^1 and R^{-1} in the end of the processes.

Secondly, we use the k-shell decomposition to classify the nodes, and characterize the relationship between k-shell value and the information competition processes deeply. We use Υ_{kg} to represent the node set which each node in it has k-shell value k_g. For two sets Υ_{kg} and Υ_{kt}, we select each node i in Υ_{kg} and each node j in Υ_{kt} as the initial nodes in 2th step in the information competition dynamics model, and in the end we got a ratio, we executed this process 100 times (considering the computing costs) and average the ratio to get the mean ratio r_{ij}. And at last, we average all the r_{ij} to get the ratio $M(k_g, k_t)$ between two k-shell sets Υ_{kg} and Υ_{kt}, i.e.

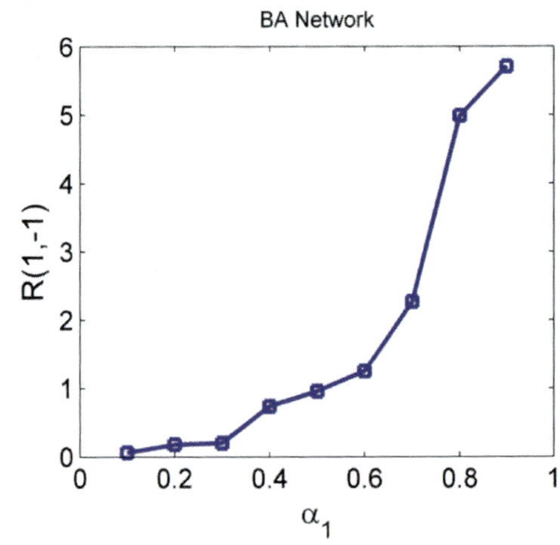

Figure 3. The relationship between variable α_1 and R(1,-1) in BA network by randomly choosing 1000 pairs of nodes as the initial nodes and calculating the average.

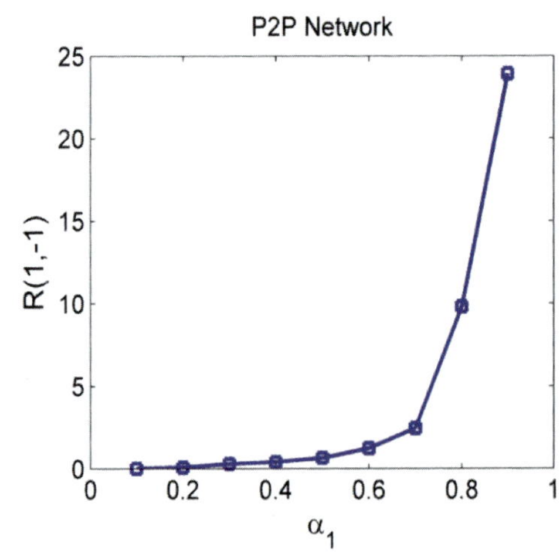

Figure 4. The relationship between variable α_1 and R(1,-1) in P2P network by randomly choosing 1000 pairs of nodes as the initial nodes and calculating the average.

$$M(k_s,k_t)=\frac{1}{|\gamma_{k_s}|\times|\gamma_{k_t}|}\sum_{i\in\gamma_{k_s},\,j\in\gamma_{k_t}}\gamma_{ij}$$

We plot the 2D graph where X-axis and Y-axis are both k-shell values and the value of $M(k_g, k_t)$ is described by the color of the rectangles in the graph shown in Figure 5 for the BA network and Figure 6 for the P2P network respectively. It shows that the nodes of high k-shell value have a stronger competitive power in the information competition processes than the nodes with low k-shell value. For the strategy to optimize the information transmission in the competition activities, we should locate the initial information at the nodes with high k-shell value to expanse the area of influence, on the contrary, to reduce the scale by keeping the information away with the nodes with high k-shell value.

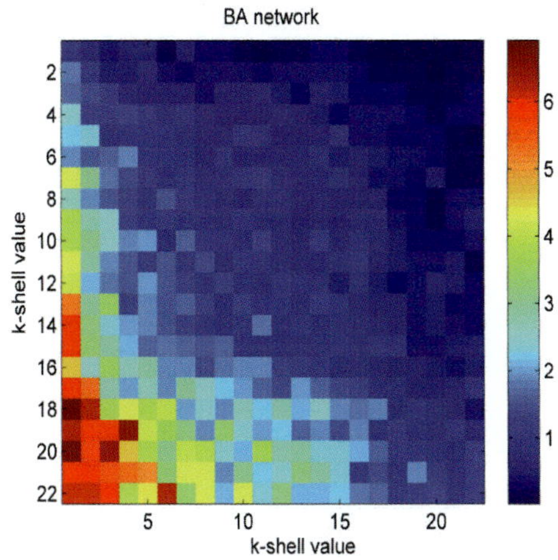

Figure 5. The relationship between k-shell value and the information competition processes in BA network, and the color of the rectangle represents the value of $M(k_g, kt)$.

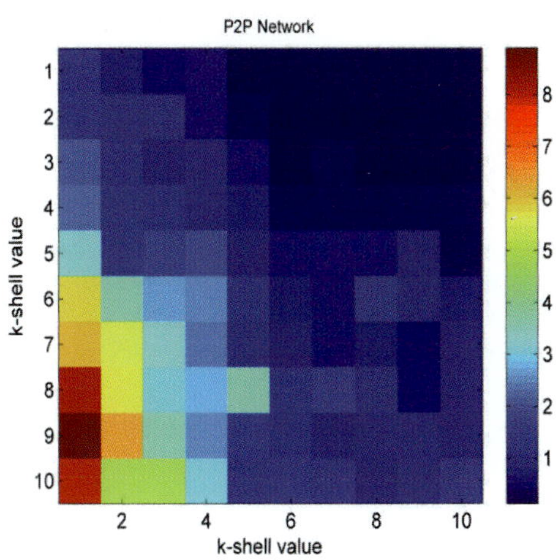

Figure 6. The relationship between k-shell value and the information competition processes in P2P network, and the color of the rectangle represents the value of $M(k_g, kt)$.

5. CONCLUSIONS

In this paper, we construct a new model to give a reasonable explanation to the spread of information occurring in social communicating networks. Considering a new popular form of information competition dynamics and the k-shell decomposition technique, we have shown that the nodes with high k-shell value have a stronger competitive power in the information competition processes. We argue that these findings could provide a useful framework to acquire detailed understanding of the information competition on network dynamics. We can assertively make sure that this model can be used to optimize the information transmission in complex networks.

ACKNOWLEDGEMENT

This work is supported by the Cultivation Project of National Natural Science Foundation of China (91130019) and the International Cooperation Project of Ministry of Science and Technology of China (2010DFR00700).

REFERENCES

- [1] Strogatz, S.H., Exploring complex networks. Nature, 2001. 410(6825): p. 268-276.
- [2] Boccaletti, S., et al., Complex networks: Structure and dynamics. Physics reports, 2006. 424(4): p. 175-308.
- [3] Wang X. F. and Chen G., Complex networks: small-world, scale-free and beyond. Circuits and Systems Magazine, IEEE, 2003. 3(1): p. 6-20.
- [4] Kleinberg, J.M., Navigation in a small world. Nature, 2000. 406(6798): p. 845-845.
- [5] Dorogovtsev, S.N., A.V. Goltsev, and J.F.F. Mendes, Critical phenomena in complex networks. Reviews of Modern Physics, 2008. 80(4): p. 1275.
- [6] G. Dong, et al., Percolation of partially interdependent networks under targeted attack. Phys Rev E, 2012. 85(1): p. 016112.
- [7] Newman, M.E.J. and D.J. Watts, Scaling and percolation in the small-world network model. Physical Review E, 1999. 60(6): p. 7332.
- [8] Kitsak, M., et al., Identification of influential spreaders in complex networks. Nature Physics, 2010. 6(11): p. 888-893.
- [9] Borge-Holthoefer, J. and Y. Moreno, Absence of influential spreaders in rumor dynamics. Phys Rev E, 2012. 85: p. 026116.
- [10] Pajevic, S. and D. Plenz, The organization of strong links in complex networks. Arxiv preprint arXiv: 1109.2577, 2011.
- [11] K. Xu, Zhao, J., and, J. Wu. Weak ties: Subtle role of information diffusion in online social networks. Physical Review E, 2010. 82(1): p. 016105.
- [12] Liu, Y.Y., J.J. Slotine, and A.L. Barabási, Controllability of complex networks. Nature, 2011. 473(7346): p. 167-173.
- [13] Bollobas, B. Graph Theory and Combinatorics: Proceedings of the Cambridge Combinatorial Conference in honor of P Erdos, 35 (Academic, New York, 1984).
- [14] L. P. Chi, Binary opinion dynamics with noise on random networks, Chinese Science Bulletin 56, 3630 (2011).
- [15] D. ben-Avraham, Exact solution of the nonconsensus opinion model on the line. Phys. Rev. E 83, 050101 (2011).
- [16] Carmi, S. Havlin, S. Kirkpatrick, S. Shavitt, Y. & Shir E. A model of Internet topology using k-shell decomposition. Proc. Natl. Acad. Sci. USA 104, 11150-11154 (2007).
- [17] Stanford Large Network Dataset Collection.

Resource Demand Predicting Based on Cluster Analysis in Cloud Computing Networks

N. Zhang, R.Y. Li* & N. Huang
**School of Reliability and Systems Engineering, Beihang University, Beijing 100191, P.R. China*
Email: liruiying@buaa.edu.cn

ABSTRACT: On-demand service is a new technology in cloud computing. The resource demand, which is changing dynamically, is the input of the optimal reliability design. So predicting the resource demand becomes very important in cloud computing. In this paper, we propose a resource demand predicting method based on cluster analysis and neural network, which divides the demand into several groups, and provides detailed prediction for different data group. This method is verified through data collected from ClarkNet. The results show that our proposed method is more effective and accuracy.

KEYWORDS: Cluster analysis; Predicting RBF; BP, Neural network; Cloud computing.

1. INTRODUCTION

With the rapid development of Internet technology, cloud computing is getting more and more attention and widely used. It has been applied in the new creative industries of mobile Internet, Internet of Things and so on [1]. Our demand for the diverse and massive cloud computing resource is dynamically changing. If the allocation of the resource cannot be changed with the its demand, it would lead to disastrous results, cause unpredictable delays and even encounter a surge in demand [2]. So predicting the dynamic resource demand is necessary. It can obtain information of the demands in advance for a period of time in the future and provide decision supports for reasonable and systemic configuration of cloud computing resources. So how to predict the cloud computing resource accurately and effectively directly impacts the optimal configuration (optimal reliability design), stable running of cloud computing and the profits of cloud computing providers.

Pioneers did a lot of work to predict the demand for cloud computing resource. Ardagna et al. [3] predicted the website request access rate using the exponential smoothing (ES) method, in which the proper ES model is estimated the smoothing factor. Huang et al. [4] developed a resource prediction model by double exponential smoothing method, and compared it with the results obtained by simple average and weighted moving average methods. However, the prediction results obtained from exponential smoothing method can be easily affected by the smoothing factor. Padala et al. [5] proposed a virtual resource control system named AutoControl. AutoControl could predict future information by the historical resource allocation message. Yang et al. [6] presented a novel service cloud architecture and used a linear regression model to predict the workload. However, the linear model can't reflect the dynamic characteristics of data.

In order to solve these problems and reflect the nonlinear feature of the cloud computing resource demand, many machine-learning algorithms, e.g., neural network [7-8], fuzzy inference [9] and Bayesian inferences [10], have also been used to support their prediction.

The cloud computing resource demand prediction model should be established based on complex, unknown, and non-linear relationships between user demands, time series and other factors. Artificial neural network (ANN) is a type of mathematical model and computational model which imitates biological neural network structure and function [11]. ANN has good ability to approximate intense dynamic data. Moreover, a neural network does not require assumptions about the input variable distribution and it can learn the non-linear relationships between the input and output functions. Usually, ANN provides better prediction result than ES and linear models. There are different types of data in the resource demand. Clustering analysis (CA) is a fundamental data analysis method. As an unsupervised classification technique, CA divides the resource demand into groups by similarity degree. Those data in the same group are with high similarity, while those between groups are with low similarity [12].

The combination of the ANNs and CA may bring detailed prediction for cloud computing resources.

In this paper, we propose a method combing the ANN and CA algorithms to predict the resource demand of cloud computing. It is useful to reduce the complexity and shorten the elapsed time substantially. Moreover, the method can improve the accuracy of the prediction.

2. BASIC CONCEPTS

2.1. *K-means clustering analysis*

Clustering analysis is a process to group the physical and abstract collection into multiple groups of similar objects, which aims at maximizing the degree of similarity between objects in the same group while minimizing that between objects of different groups [13]. K-means clustering analysis is a classical clustering analysis method. It aims to partition n observations into k clusters in which each observation belongs to the cluster with the nearest mean, serving as a prototype of the cluster. The algorithm flowchart of k-means clustering is shown in Fig. 1.

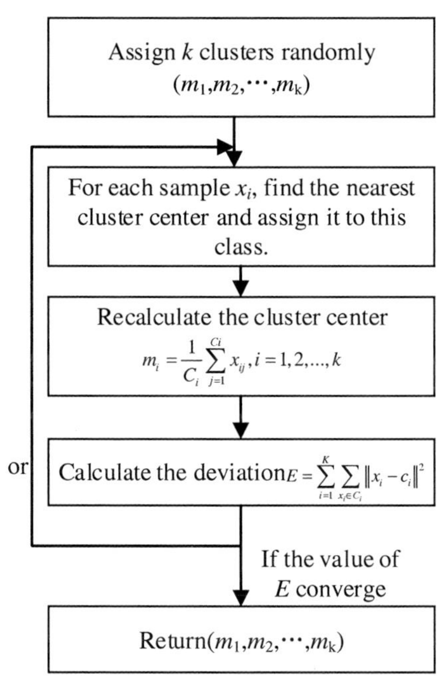

Figure 1. The algorithm flowchart of k-means clustering.

2.2. *Artificial neural network*

Artificial neural networks (ANNs) are a family of statistical learning algorithms inspired by biological neural networks, and they are used to estimate or approximate functions that can depend on a large number of inputs which are generally unknown. A neural network is an interconnected group of nodes and analogous to the vast network of neurons in a brain. The neural networks structure is shown in the Fig. 2. Here, each circular node represents an artificial neuron and an arrow represents a connection from the output of one neuron to the input of another. The RBF neural network model and the BP neural network model are the commonly used models. This paper is studied based on these two models.

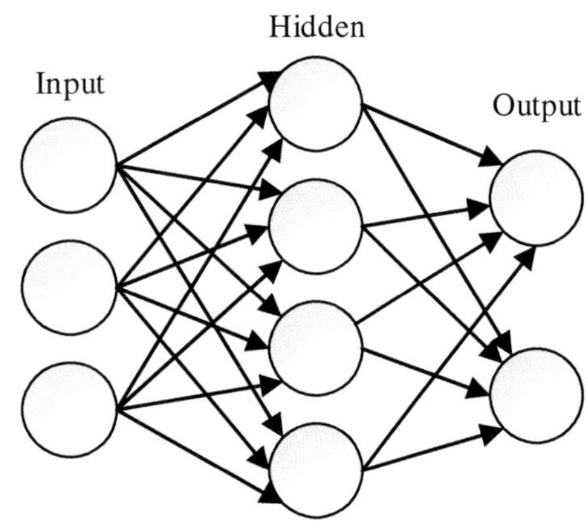

Figure 2. Artificial neural network structure.

3. PREDICTION METHOD BASED ON ANN AND CA

Firstly, our prediction method adopts k-means clustering algorithm to divide the resource demand data into different groups, and then adds the data in the same group of per time unit. Secondly, we use RBF neural network and BP neural network to train the data in different groups separately, generate the corresponding predicted value, and add the predicted results of per minute in different groups. The flow chart of the prediction method is shown in Fig. 3.

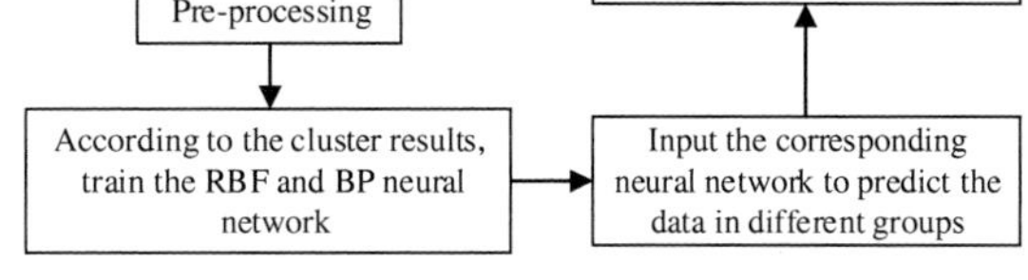

Figure 3. Flow chart of our prediction method.

The steps of our prediction method are as follows:

(1) Adopt the K-means cluster method to divide the resource demand data (in seconds) into k groups $\{C_1, C_2, \ldots, C_k\}$.

(2) Add the data of per time unit in the same group in order to take the time unit as time granularity to analysis the data.

(3) Data preprocessing, i.e, resource demand data normalization (see details in Section 3.1).

(4) Determine the number of data which is needed to predict the resource demand in the future. For example, a day's data (Data 1 to 1440) can be used to predict an incoming data (the 1441th data). Then we can use the Data 2-1441 to predict the 1442th data and so on. Please see details in Section 3.2.

(5) According to the resource demand data groups $\{C_1, C_2, \ldots, C_k\}$, use RBF and BP neural network to train and predict the next data.

(6) Use the corresponding RBF neural network or BP neural network to train the C_m.

(7) Post-processing (see Section 3.1), and then we can get the prediction results.

(8) Add the predicting results of pre time unit in different groups to get the total predicting results.

3.1. *Data pre-processing and post-processing*

Data normalization method is often used in the data pre-processing before the neural network prediction. Data normalization processing puts all data into the interval [0, 1], aiming at eliminating differences in magnitudes between the dimensional data and avoid the big errors in network predictions because of the differences in magnitudes between the input and output data. In this paper, the data normalization is realized using Eq. (1).

$$x_m = (x_k - x_{\min}) / (x_{\max} - x_{\min}) \tag{1}$$

where x_m is the data after the normalization processing, x_k is the data value in the data series, $x_{\min}$ is the minimum value in the data series, and $x_{\max}$ is the maximum value in the data series.

After the resource demand prediction, the predicted value should be renormalized, namely post processing. The renormalized formula is like Eq. (2)

$$y_k = y_m \times ((x_{\max} - x_{\min}) + x_{\min}) \tag{2}$$

where y_k is the predicting result after the renormalization processing, y_m is the predicting result before the renormalization processing.

3.2. *The procedures of the prediction*

This paper use rolling prediction method to predict. A rolling prediction is an add/drop process for predicting the future over a set period of time. Firstly, it executes one-step prediction, then feedbacks the network prediction output values to the network input layer and takes the prediction results as a part of the input data. If the initial input data are the actually observed data x_n, $x_{n+1} \ldots x_{n+m}$ (m is the cycle of the series values), the output data is the prediction value x^*_{n+m+1} at the next time. Then x_{n+1}, $x_{n+2} \ldots x_{n+m}$ and x^*_{n+m+1} would be as the input values to predict the next data x^*_{n+m+2}. Then x_{n+2}, $x_{n+3} \ldots x_{n+m}$, x^*_{n+m+1} and x^*_{n+m+2} would be as the input values to predict the next data x^*_{n+m+3}. Repeat iteration above, we can get the prediction results for a period time in the future. The k values can be predicted as the table 1.

Table 1. Rolling prediction.

Procedures	*The neural network input data*	*Output data (prediction value)*
1	$x_n, x_{n+1} \ldots x_{n+m},$	x^*_{n+m+1}
2	$x_{n+1}, x_{n+2} \ldots x_{n+m}, x^*_{n+m+1}$	x^*_{n+m+2}
…	…	…
k	$x_{n+k-1}, x_{n+k} \ldots x_{n+m+k-1}$	x^*_{n+m+k}

4. CASE STUDY

This paper uses the historical access information as input dataset from an actual running website [14], which contains two weeks' worth of all HTTP requests to the ClarkNet WWW server. ClarkNet is a full Internet access provider for the Metro Baltimore-Washington DC area. The dataset mainly records the requested information of users visited the website from 00:00:00 August 28, 1995 through 23:59:59 September 10, 1995, a total of 14 days. In this two week period there were 3,328,587 requests. We choose two days' data from 0:00:00 September 4, 1995 to 0:00:00 September 6, 1995 to analysis and test (see Fig. 4).

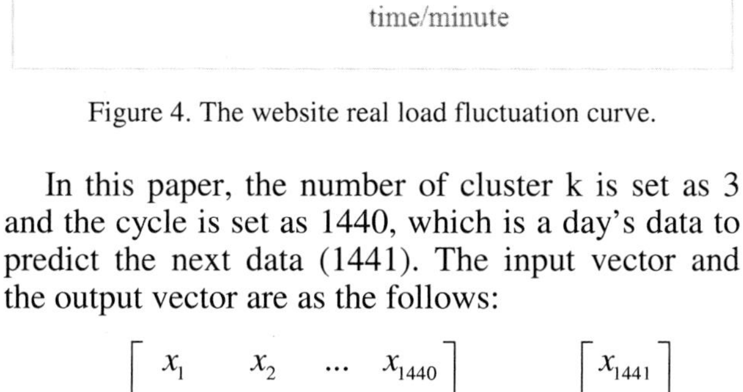

Figure 4. The website real load fluctuation curve.

In this paper, the number of cluster k is set as 3 and the cycle is set as 1440, which is a day's data to predict the next data (1441). The input vector and the output vector are as the follows:

$$P = \begin{bmatrix} x_1 & x_2 & \cdots & x_{1440} \\ x_2 & x_3 & \cdots & x_{1441} \\ \cdots & \cdots & \cdots & \cdots \\ x_{1440} & x_{1441} & \cdots & x_{2879} \end{bmatrix} \qquad T = \begin{bmatrix} x_{1441} \\ x_{1442} \\ \cdots \\ x_{2880} \end{bmatrix}$$

Base on the Section 3, we use the data to predict the resource demand in cloud computing.

To verify the effectiveness of our proposed method, we use BP and RBF method to do the comparison. The test results are shown as Fig. 5. In Fig. 5, the red lines are observation values and the blue lines are prediction values. In this figure, (a) is the prediction curve obtained based on RBF network using original data, (b) is that obtained based on RBF network using cluster results, (c) is the prediction curve obtained based on BP network using original data, (d) is that obtained based on BP network using cluster results.

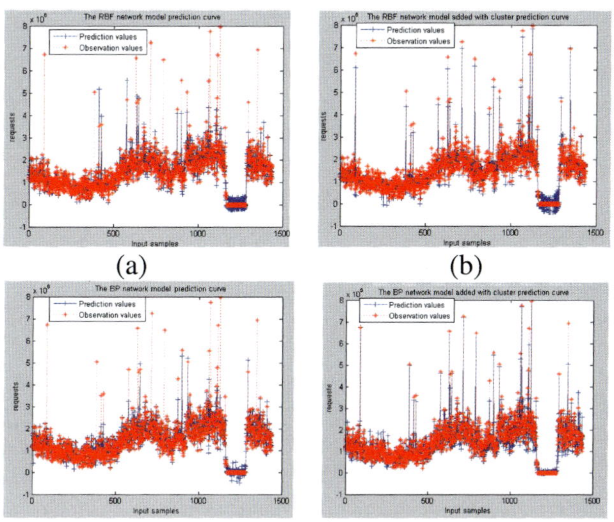

(a) (b) (c) (d)

Figure 5. Prediction results compared with the original data.

We use the the mean square error MSE to evaluate the system results. The computational formula of MSE is like Eq. (3), where n is the number of the data, w_i is the weight of the data, y_i is the actual value and $\hat{y}_i$ is the predicted value. The smaller the MSE, the more accurate the prediction.

$$MSE = \frac{1}{n}\sum_{i=1}^{n} w_i (y_i - \hat{y}_i)^2 \quad (3)$$

The Table 2 shows the prediction results obtained based on RBF and BP network using original data and using cluster results.

From the results, we can know that the neural network added with clustering is faster and more accuracy than traditional neural network algorithms.

The large data set are divided into several categories of similar data sets while added with the clustering method. At the same time in each category, data have high similarity. The training times must be reduced because of the decreased data sets. The convergence rate is improved because the data in small datasets have high similarity. Thus the training times reduce more.

Table 2. Results of the test.

Indictors	RBF	RBF using cluster	BP	BP using cluster
MSE	0.2910	0.1099	0.1778	0.0828
Time-consuming(s)	412	373	305	248

5. CONCLUSION

This paper proposes a resource demand predicting method which combines cluster analysis and neutral network together in cloud computing networks. Our case study shows that our proposed method is more accuracy; it also reduces the time consumption and decreases the complexity of the model in cloud computing resource demand predicting.

ACKNOWLEDGEMENTS

This work was supported by the National Natural Science Foundation of China (61304220) and the Beijing Natural Science Foundation (4143064).

REFERENCES

- [1] Deng Lei-lei, Yu Hang. Research on cloud-based data mining and its prospect [J]. Computer and modernization, 2012, (5): 93-95. DOI:10.3969/j.issn.1006-2475.2012.05.027.
- [2] Xu Da-yu, Yang Shan-lin, Luo He. Multi-source information resources management in cloud computing environment [J]. Computer Integrated Manufacturing System, 2012, 18(9): 2028-2039.
- [3] Ardagna D, Casolari S, Panicucci B. Flexible distributed capacity allocation and load redirect algorithms for cloud systems [C] C loud Computing (CLOUD), 2011 IEEE International Conference on. IEEE, 2011: 163-170.
- [4] Huang J, Li C, Yu J. Resource prediction based on double exponential smoothing in cloud computing [C] Consumer Electronics, Communications and Networks (CECNet), 2012 2nd International Conference on. IEEE, 2012: 2056-2060.
- [5] Padala P, Hou K Y, Shin K G, et al. Automated control of multiple virtualized resources [C] Proceedings of the 4th ACM European conference on Computer systems. ACM, 2009: 13-26.
- [6] Yang J, Liu C, Shang Y, et al. A cost-aware auto-scaling approach using the workload prediction in service clouds [J]. Information Systems Frontiers, 2014, 16(1): 7-18.
- [7] Prevost J J, Nagothu K M, Kelley B, et al. Prediction of cloud data center networks loads using stochastic and neural models [C] System of Systems Engineering (SoSE), 2011 6th International Conference on. IEEE, 2011: 276-281.
- [8] Wallace R M, Turchenko V, Sheikhalishahi M, et al. Applications of neural-based spot market prediction for cloud computing [J]. IEEE International Conference on Intelligent Data Acquisition & Advanced Computing Systems, 2013, 02:710-716.

— [9] Beghdad Bey K, Benhammadi F, Sebbak F. Fuzzy Subtractive Clustering Based Prediction Approach for CPU Load Availability [C] CLOUD COMPUTING 2013, The Fourth International Conference on Cloud Computing, GRIDs, and Virtualization. 2013: 215-220.
— [10] Islam S, Keung J, Lee K, et al. Empirical prediction models for adaptive resource provisioning in the cloud [J]. Future Generation Computer Systems, 2012, 28(1): 155-162.
— [11] Melchiorre C, Matteucci M, Azzoni A, et al. Artificial neural networks and cluster analysis in landslide susceptibility zonation [J]. Geomorphology, 2008, 94(3): 379–400.
— [12] Lu J S, Zhang B, Zhang X. Using Clustering Analysis to Predict Outflowing Water Quality of Selectively Drawn Water from Water Sources and Reservoirs [J]. Applied Mechanics & Materials, 2013, 409-410.
— [13] Qi Xinzhan, Liu Bingjie, Ji Haiyan. An Integrated neural network ensemble algorithm based on clustering technology [J]. Computer Simulation, 2010, 27(1): 166-169. DOI:10.3969/j.issn.1006-9348.2010.01.049.
— [14] http://ita.ee.lbl.gov/html/contrib/ClarkNet-HTTP.html

Traffic Light Remote Control System Based on DF Data Transceiver Module

C.Y. Liu*, M.F. Peng & S.Y. Yu
School of Electrical and Electronic Engineering, Harbin University of Science and Technology, Harbin, China
Email: liuchangyuan@hrbust.edu.cn

X.H. Wang
School of Information Engineering, Wuhan University of Technology, Wuhan, China

ABSTRACT: We propose a remote control using radio waves of new traffic lights traffic command mode, to solve the irrational problem of traffic congestion crossing when the vehicle from different directions. In the paper, we propose the traffic lights remote control system based on the use of DF data transceiver module, using PT2262 / PT2272 as codec chip for long distance control of traffic signals. Traffic police could change the traffic lights countdown time timely using their remote controls based on the changes in traffic flows at different times. This approach can replace the sign directing traffic, but more simple and convenient. It uses a micro control unit MCU, and the DF data transceiver module to transmit and receive instruction. This is a kind of radio wave communication in the 100m range farther than the infrared remote control, which could satisfy the actual needs. This system enables automatic operation and temporary intervention of traffic lights combined with stable and reliable. This system can drive lights and timing display circuit directly, it has a strong practical value.

KEYWORDS: DF data transceiver; Traffic light; Wireless remote control; Single chip microcomputer.

1. INTRODUCTION

With the further development of China's urbanization, city size continues to expand, increasing household incomes, a growing number of vehicles, but the urban transport system has not been able to keep up with growth in the number of motor vehicles, urban transport systems under increasing pressure. this makes the presence of traffic crossing the road is very scarce resources become more strained [1], the existing traffic light control system is provided fixed cycle time, the control does not achieve a reasonable distribution of resources, serious waste of road resources of the city, while crossing the traffic congestion also affects the efficiency in dealing with an emergency vehicle responding to an emergency when, fire, ambulance, police cars and other special vehicles in the course of duty blocked the road things happen, so urgently needed Looking for a new flexible traffic light control system.

Intelligent Transportation System at home and abroad has been a period of research [2,3], but most are still in the theoretical stage, the proposed traffic light control system based on DF wireless data transceiver module as part of the intelligent transportation system can have independent and simple, can be achieved and so on. the system can be easily flexible depending on how much of each intersection traffic traffic artificially change the state of the traffic lights, and green channels for the special vehicles and emergency situations.

Currently works for the automatic cycle of traffic lights, at the peak of traffic will always be greater in the case of a certain direction, so there will always be at the peak of the traffic police on duty appeared in some major intersections, coordination and command [1,2], in order to improve the utilization of transportation resources, but this approach requires at least two traffic police, to pay a lot of human capital.

SCM control system as a core, to propose solutions to bring a lot of flexibility, and because the system functions designed in this paper is simple, so choose the 51 microcontroller as master core difficulty of this system is a wireless communication Since this system is less traffic, while a one-way communication system, a communication within 100m, so the use of the DF data transceiver module as a communication module, the technology is mature, while the DF data transceiver module used 315Mhz 2ASK modulation, simple, easy to implement, 315Mhz band where the band is open, free use without approval. communication codec chip chose PT2262 / PT2272, the chips have been widely used in various fields, simple to use and can provide a larger number of address code, there is no need to consider the same frequency band interference and some other remote control [4].

2. SYSTEM STRUCTURE

The wireless remote control traffic light system consists of two parts, 1) Send module, 2) the receiving end of the transmission side and the core control section DF consists of microcontroller and wireless transmitter modules. Receiving end MCU control module, the data receiver module, LED three color control module and digital control module, the system structure shown in Figure 1.

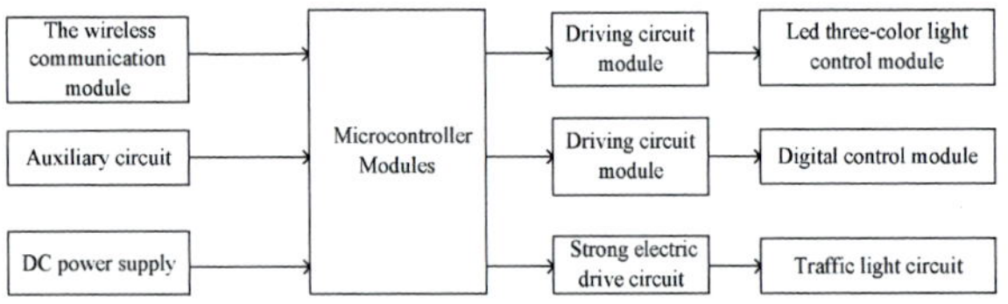

Figure 1. Traffic light system configuration diagram.

The traffic light control system designed for vehicular and pedestrian traffic intersection management four corners of the intersection traffic lights and junctions with a digital display to convert the remainder of the passage, according to the specific information for each traffic intersection, the control officer can send module sends data to a receiver module in real time to change the display status of the traffic lights, convenience, flexibility, high reliability [5].

3. THE WIRELESS COMMUNICATION MODULE

The wireless communication module contains DF data transmission module, data encoding chips and control chip. Data encoding chips use the PT2262 [6]. The control chips use the 51 microcontroller. Data transmission module is 315 Mhz 2ASK modulated DF data transmission module. SCM is used to collect key information, computing and processing the key information, sending the signal to the encoder chip PT2262 by pin, transmitted out by the information encoded modulation chip through DF data transmission module.

3.1. *Coding and control of realization*

PT2262 encoder chip has 18 pins, it provides up to 12 tri-state address code, and up to six data pin. Address code as the header of the data frame, it is used to distinguish between hosts. In the design of this system requires less than 8 signal communication. Meanwhile, in order to ensure the communication quality, the system selects four data pins of the program, and the address code is 8. Coding addresses will have hardware connection and achieved. Since the chip has an enable pin, in order to reduce system power consumption, the enable pin is connected to the microcontroller 51 and the MCU can control the emitter to control signals. 51 microcontrollers as part of the main chip of wireless transmitter, each pin MCU control functions and connections shown in Figure 2.

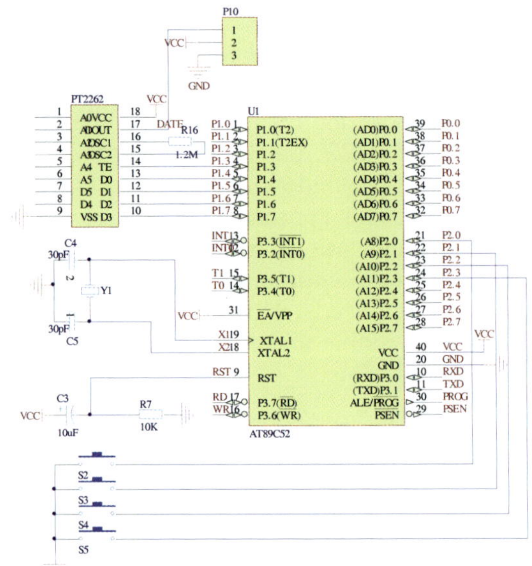

Figure 2. Encoding transmitter module circuit design.

The MCU's part of P3.4 ~ P3.7 are as key-sense pin, P1.0 ~ P1.3 are as an output data, P2.0 to enable pin. When the MCU internal procedures detects the button is pressed, the enable pin is set low first and output the corresponding level of the four output pins in accordance with the corresponding code.

The chip will transmit a continuous signal at the pin level is set high time, therefore high time longer count information is sent to is more. Not only after a long period of electromagnetic emission increases power consumption of the circuit, but also reduce the stability of the remote control and real-time systems. Therefore high time require precise control has reached the optimum working condition of the system. High time set by the program. After testing, high time MCU output at 200 milliseconds communicates is the best. However, if the time is too short, signal radiation may be affected by outside interference and noise. Thereby increasing the high-level output time is an effective means of interference.

3.2. *DF data transmission module*

This part is made up by the DF data transmission modules. By configure the codec chip external oscillation resistor to reach a good match. After several tests, we found that the transmitting terminal 1.2M, received a termination resistor 200k, communication distance can meet the requirements. Because the system uses the 315Mhz DF data transmission module, using SAW surface acoustic resonator frequency stabilization, frequency stability. When the ambient temperature changes in -25 ~ + 85 °C. The frequency drifts of only 3 × 10-6Hz / °C and DF data transmission module has a wide operating voltage range of 3 ~ 12V. When the voltage changes, transmission frequency is essentially the same, transmitter module receiver module supporting without any adjustment can be stably received, DF data module using 2-ASK modulated, low power consumption. When the data signal to stop the emission current is reduced to 0, DF transmitter module and a data signal input terminal can be resistor or connected directly. This system uses the operating current 20 ~ 28mA, transmit power is 40mW of DF data transmission module, transmitting distance farther, and higher reliability.

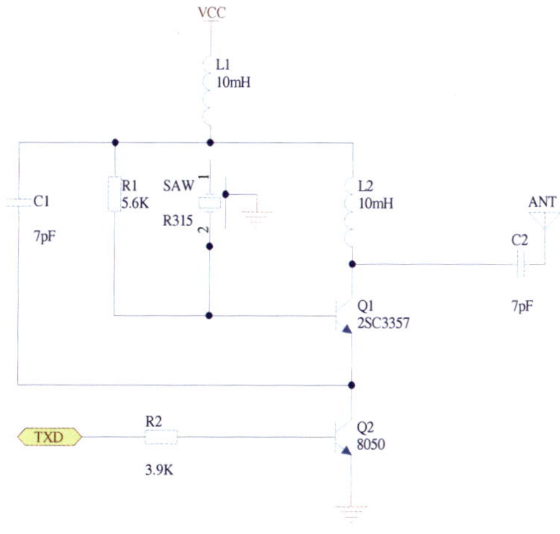

Figure 3. DF data transmission module circuit diagram.

3.3. *Transmission module programming*

Transmit coded chip is directly controlled by the MCU, the key is detected by the MCU. Which can eliminated interfere with the keys in the transmitter. At the same time data parameters transmitted after each keystroke standardized setting. So that we could avoiding interference may be caused by a number of human factors to improve system stability.

Since the chip used in the system of launch enable pin valid, transmitter chip will encode and transmitted data continuously that means enable pin high longer, then transmit the data out is more and the chance of receiving is much greater. However, if the time is too long will increase the power consumed by the transmission data. It can not accept the remote control of product size and battery life. Therefore, the chip enable pin high duration needs to be tested and analyzed, and set a reasonable value. The section from the microcontroller program is shown in Figure 4.

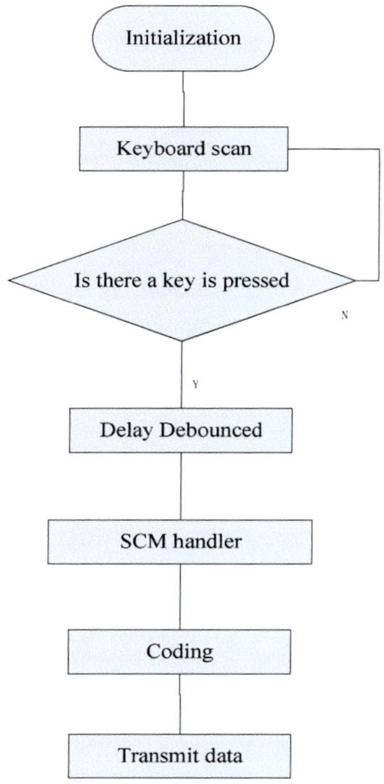

Figure 4. Transmitter module SCM process flow chart.

The system uses a wireless communication system is a binary amplitude shift keying (2-ASK) [7], the carrier frequency is315Mhz. Chip requires each codeword address code, data code, synchronization code, 12 data to form a complete codeword at least. With an oscilloscope measurement, each codeword requires approximately 3.4ms emission, not including the time interval between two adjacent codewords. And the communication between the chip requires at least twice comparison the address code. That means, every launch need to set the enable pin high 8ms, the time required to transmit the data once it is about8ms. So set high enable pin microcontroller time is more than8ms. During testing, in the case ofdistant50mstransmission time does not provide good stability. Therefore, we need further improvement in the case of longer distance transmission time. The system uses enable time is 200 milliseconds at last.

4. DATA RECEIVING AND MOTHERBOARD SECTION

This part is the core of this system. The motherboard contains the data receiver module, MCU, strong electric drive circuit and used to simulate traffic lights and LED digital tube lights. It also includes a peripheral circuit of said module.

4.1. *Data receiving module*

Define abbreviations and acronyms the first time they are used in the text, even after they have been defined in the abstract. Abbreviations such as IEEE, SI, MKS, CGS, sc, dc, and rms do not have to be defined. Do not use abbreviations in the title or heads unless they are unavoidable.

Data receiving module composed by DF data receiving module, 51 microcontroller micro control unit, decoder chip pt2272, peripheral circuit interference. Signals in which the data output pin decoder chip through interference by the voltage comparator consisting of filter portion.

Specific design is four-inverting input terminal of the four data terminal lm339 decoder chips are connected in sequence, four-inverting input terminal of the input signal is a lower voltage, four voltage comparator outputs are connected in sequence with the microcontroller P3.4 ~ P3.7. When no data is received to decoder chip, the output low 0, after a voltage comparator output is high. When the decoder chip receives the data, data output high, after a voltage comparator output is low. That is, when no data is received, the MCU P3.4 ~ P3.7 mouth is high, upon receipt of the data is low.

This system uses pt2272's non-latching mode, data output level is instantaneous, and whether the transmitter and launch the corresponding [8]. It's similar to the jog control, such a manner consistent with the characteristics of the remote control buttons.

Decoder chip pulled low the corresponding MCU pin by the voltage comparator when data is received. After release the transmitter button. MCU corresponding pin also goes high, thus simulating the independent press operation.

4.2. *DF data receiving module*

DF data receiving module use the super-regenerative receiver module that match the transmit section. The module normally appears in pairs with the DF data transmission module. Because of using the super-regenerative operating mode, this module has a strong anti-jamming capability. And the main way to interfere is pulse which is less affected. And the module has its own frequency selective network, filtered interference in free space antenna again with the selected frequency.

4.3. *MCU control module and program description*

This module includes MCU and peripheral circuits, traffic lights simulation section that the circuit diagram shown in Figure 5.

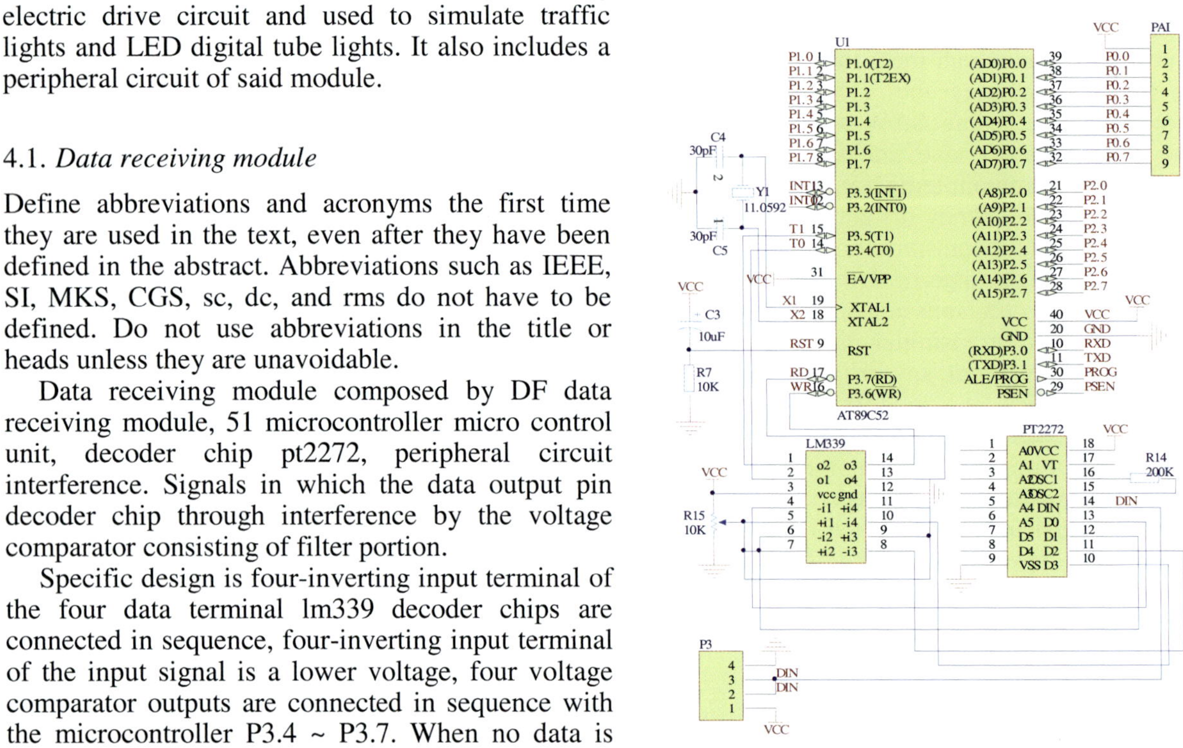

Figure 5. System motherboard microcontroller circuit diagram.

Program description: This module of MCU to complete the main work is detecting the received signal receiving module, judgment the signal and operating the traffic lights system set in accordance with changes.

The main loop of the program includes the key detection [9] control and traffic lights. Key detects detection and decoding chip pin level falling edge of the chip. That operating after detected the level changes. Due to emitting portion has a long transmission time. If the signal is interrupted, the main control MCU is likely to receive the two levels falling. Therefore, it needs to shield part of the key detection code in a period of time after MCU receives a valid data. It is completed by the timer in the program design. When the device detects the falling edge open the switch of timer 0. Start timing of 200ms, and close the key scan detection bit. That ensuring a data communication process will only be collected once.

After receiving module receives a signal, and determined the signal. If the S1 key is pressed, then the two red light are all bright, the time is shown as 30s. When dealing with emergencies or special vehicles to provide effective assistance, the S1 key is pressed again, traffic lights back to normal, cars are all normal driving. When S2 or S3 key is pressed, digital control timing is stopped, the display time is increased or decrease 1s to 60s and cycle becomes 0. When the S4 key is pressed, the digital timer restart, traffic lights goes to normal.

The part of the program flow chart in motherboard shown in Figure 6.

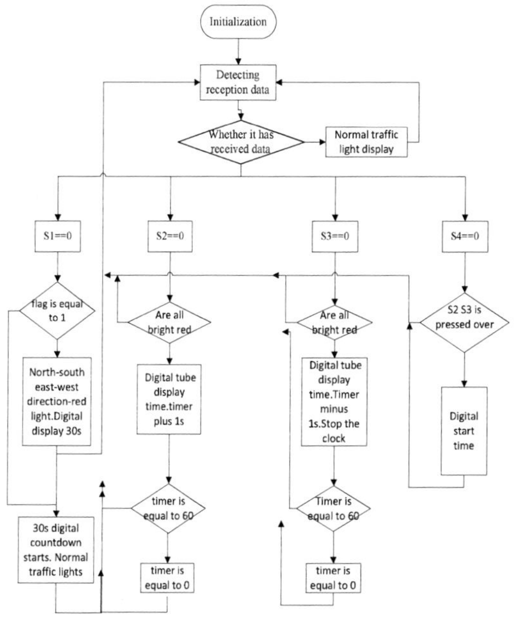

Figure 6. Motherboard module program flow chart.

5. STRONG ELECTRIC DRIVE MODULE

In the design and test system, MCU control module output to the diode system demonstration, in order to improve the portability of the system, while making the system more close to the actual use. This system design also includes an output portion of the drive module.

The traffic lights are actual used frequency alternating current, so the structures of drive module may have more sophisticated solutions. Here we use solid state relays (SSR) solution. SSR is a non-contact power semiconductor devices, the input can be very good with the TTL and the CMOS compatible numbers, input and output achieved through the optocoupler, isolation insulation more than 2kv, while avoiding the electromagnetic interference between the strong electrical systems and weak electrical systems, to help improve the stability of the system. Strong electric drive module of this system are shown below.

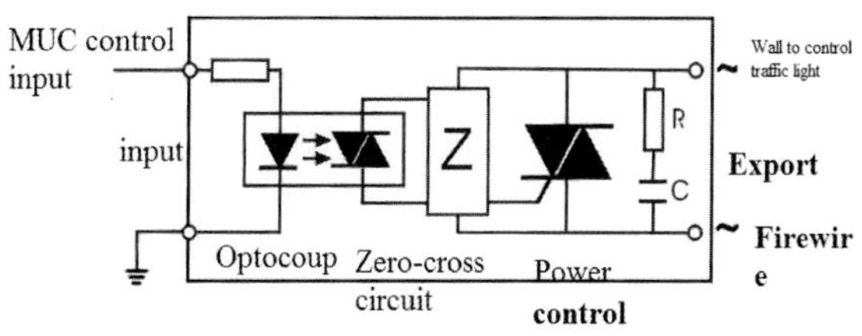

Figure 7. High voltage driver module principle diagram.

6. COMMUNICATION EXPERIMENT

The communication distance that traffic police from the lights are not more than 50m as usual, and there will be no cover. To verify the reliability of the system, this system does a few experiments at different distances without cover, sending and receiving communication signals 10 times under different conditions, respectively. The test results are shown in Table 1.

Table 1. Wireless transceiver module communication experiment.

Communication distance	Weather Conditions	Accuracy	Communication distance	Weather Conditions	Accuracy
m		%	m		%
60	Sunny & Fine	100	60	Cloudy & Rainy	100
70	Sunny & Fine	100	70	Cloudy & Rainy	90
80	Sunny & Fine	90	80	Cloudy & Rainy	90
90	Sunny & Fine	90	90	Cloudy & Rainy	80
100	Sunny & Fine	80	100	Cloudy & Rainy	70

The results showed like that the stability of the final system satisfies the design requirements. Under 60m it can achieve 100% accuracy of communication in different weather conditions. In 100m it can achieve 80% accuracy of communication without precipitation conditions. MCU stable, crash situation does not appear in the test.

7. CONCLUSION

The circuit of this system is easy to implement circuit, flexible control, low-power, wireless signal send and receive stable, reliable, has a strong practical value. It could assist traffic police in rush hour to divert traffic effectively [10]. To some extent, It could alleviate the problem of traffic congestion in the current period of the intersection that exist in the big cities [11,12], which could satisfy the actual needs. The design of traffic light system would play an important role of being used as part of the future of intelligent transportation systems. It can alleviate ease the traffic pressure and improve the role of social resources.

REFERENCES

- [1] Wang, G.F. et al. 2012, 5: 217-222. Intelligent Transportation System Development and Prospect Highway.
- [2] Jin, M.J. 2012, 5(30): 1-5. Intelligent Transport Systems Technology Status and Prospects of Development of China [J]. Journal of Transport Information and Safety.
- [3] Bian, K. et al. 2005:1664-1666. GSM Location Technique Using in Intelligent Traffic Control [C]. Guangzhou: P.R. China.
- [4] Wen, Z.D. et al. 2009, 28(6): 115-118. The Traffic Signal Control Based on the Flow Rate of Vehicles [J]. Exchange of experience.
- [5] Gong, R.X. et al. 2008, 29(4):385-388. Communications between Kingview and Intelligent Instruments Based on 51-Family Microcontrollers. Instrument Technology.
- [6] Liu, Y. et al. 2007, 26(9): 37-41. The design of the robot remote control system based on PT2262 / PT2272 [J]. Research and development.
- [7] Zhang, H. & Cao, L.N. 2008. Modern communication principle and technology (second edition) [M]. Xi'an: Xi'an University of Electronic Science and Technology Press.
- [8] Xie, J.X. 2011, 24(3):127-128,120. 51 MCU-based Smart Pressure Sensor as the Core. Development & Innovation of Machinery & Electrical Products.
- [9] Wu, G.W. 2011, 24(3):117-120. Design and simulation of traffic light control system based on AT89C51 single-chip processor, Mechanical and electrical product development and innovation.
- [10] Wu, G.W. 2012, 35(5):144-146. Design and simulation of traffic light control system based on AT89C51 single-chip processor. The modern electronic technology.
- [11] Lu´ıs C.B. et al. 2013:726-731. Traffic Management at Intersections: Legacy Mode for Vehicles not Equipped with V2V and V2I Communications [C]. ITSC 2013.
- [12] ZHANG, K.S. et al. 2010:165-168. Study on Urban Traffic Intelligent Guidance System [C].

Analysis and Simulation of Visibility Relationship in MEO Satellite Constellation

Y. Liu
Beijing Institute of Tracking and Telecommunications and Technology, Beijing, China
Email: liuyibittt@163.com

ABSTRACT: The satellite network is composed of several satellite and ground stations pointing to the satellite. The satellite constellation network plays an increasingly important role in the development of space. The inter satellite link technology which can guarantee the satellite network is a new trend of development. In this paper, a method of mutual visibility analysis of constellation internal satellites is established, and the validity of the method is demonstrated by simulation.

KEYWORDS: Satellite Constellation; MEO Satellite; Inter-satellite Link; Visibility.

1. INTRODUCTION

Since October 4, 1957, the Soviet Union launched Sputnik-1 Sputnik 1, the first satellite from the Baikonur, space technology has a rapid development. With the rapid development of science and technology, single satellite capabilities continue improving, satellite platform technology has a great development. Links between satellites are increasingly becoming development trend, which obtains the national science and technology workers' more and more concern and attention, also in the satellite countries construction more and more with application.

Satellite constellation network is a new research field, the national science and technology workers, more and more concern and attention, also in the satellite countries construction more and more with application. Such as in the field of navigation, start from the beginning of the sixties of the 20th century American transit system, countries of navigation satellite system attention more and more high. At present, the world has mainly the United States GPS, Russia GLONASS, the EU Galileo and the Beidou (COMPASS) four satellite navigation system [1]. Among them, the United States GPS and Russia GLONASS have been built in the global constellation, the European Galileo system and China's Beidou satellite navigation system in the process of building a global satellite network. Become a real network in order to make the satellite constellation, GPS and GLONASS constellation satellites with inter satellite link (Inter-Satellite link, ISL) equipment, to complete the data information in the ground and space segments of efficient and accurate delivery. In the future Navigation Satellite (Global System GNSS) should also be designed to join the ISL system, so that it constitutes a similar ground like network connectivity. Based on constellation networking, wireless links, in consideration of multiple access, frequency, network multi class problems. Use of the empty time division duplex (spatial time division, STD) inter satellite link system.

To achieve satellite networking, we must first solve the problem of mutual communication between satellites. The basis of communication between satellites is mutual visible between satellites. In this paper, the mutual visibility of a MEO satellite constellation is analyzed, and the simulation is carried out.

2. BASIC CONCEPTS

2.1. *Inter-satellite link*

The so-called inter satellite link, that is between the satellite and satellite transmission channel, by radio waves or is laser were established, can put all the satellites in the constellation connection as a organic whole, any user in the system are no need the support of ground communication network will be able to achieve the establishment of communication link, can greatly expand the coverage of constellation system, composition and management of seamless worldwide network. The inter satellite link can replace the relay work done by ground station.

2.2. *Time division ISL system*

Time division system of inter satellite link system between any visible satellites and establish multiple point to point of single frequency time-division two-way measuring wireless communication link, achieve inter satellite high accuracy dual one-way pseudo range measurement and high-speed time division duplex data transmission. In the inter satellite link satellite networks, the relationship decides the link establishment and time slot planning.

2.3. *MEO satellite*

MEO satellite orbit altitude of more than 5000km, was divided into two segments by Van Allen band. The MEO satellite has a moderate viewing time and coverage, and has a large selection range. The high stability of MEO satellite orbit can be the ideal choice for the deployment of the satellite navigation system. The information transfer delay between the MEO satellite and the earth is 100-130ms.

2.4. *Visibility*

As referred to in this paper between satellites are visible in consideration of the satellite under the shadow of the earth and satellite antenna angle constraint conditions between mutual visibility.

3. SATELLITE NETWORK MODEL

In this paper, a satellite constellation containing 24 MEO satellites with configuration of Walker 24/3/1 constellation is established. Each satellite is equipped with an antenna for a Ka frequency phased array antenna, beam scanning angle is ±β. Since the satellite is equipped with a satellite antenna, the total number of satellites in the constellation must be an even number in order to maintain the inter satellite link at any time. The satellite constellation is illustrated in Fig.1.

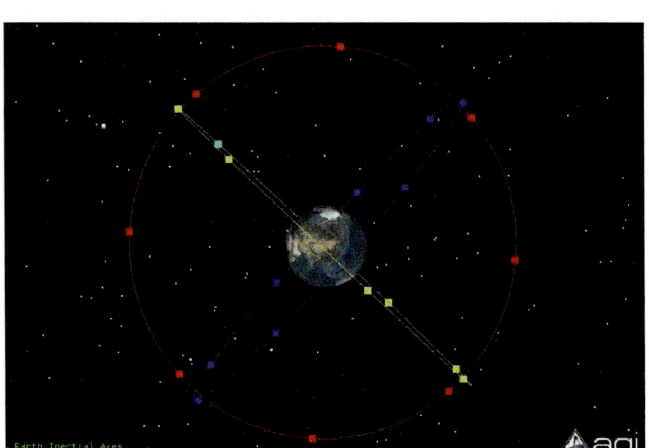

Figure 1. Satellite constellation model.

In time division system, the constellation of the entire running time is divided into a plurality of time slots, the "face to face", single satellite choosing in different time slots to complete all the visible satellites observation, observation data on more than one star. Each time slot division before to measure the communication frame and to measure the communication frame, each one-way measurement frame communication is further divided into several sub frames and measurement functions and communication in the two orthogonal channels at the same time. Time inter satellite link system transmitting and receiving share a Ka band frequency, 1.5 seconds time is defined as a time slot, in each time slot, between the satellite inter-satellite link only, do not interfere with each other. The communication time between a pair of nodes is a time slice, and a time slice includes two slots.

4. ANALYSIS OF VISIBILITY

Any satellite constellation can establish a physical premise of the inter satellite link is inter satellite inter visual. The two factor that affects the visibility of the stars is the earth shielding and the beam width of the satellite antenna (scan angle). Because of the above two constraints, the visible relationship between satellites is: permanent visible, discontinuous visible and never visible.

The average radius of the earth is R_E, the tangent of the satellite to earth and the angle between the satellite and the earth centroid is alpha, the tangent of the satellite and the angle between the tangent of the satellite and the satellite and the angle of the satellite antenna are shown in Fig. 2.

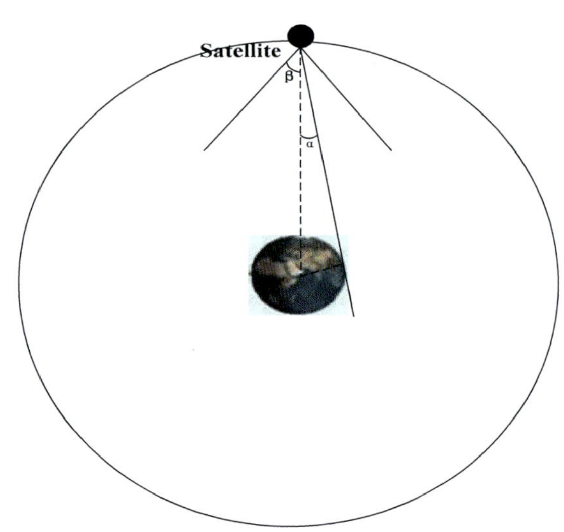

Figure 2. Angle of satellite antenna.

Relationship of α, h and R_E :

$$\sin\alpha = R_E / (R_E + h)$$

Assuming the height of source satellite is h_1, the distance to earth is d_1 and the height of destination satellite is h_2, the distance to earth is d_2. The radius of earth is R_E, the distance of two satellites is d, and the angle is γ. Then the relationship of above parameters is:

$$d_1 = h_1 + R_E$$

$$d_2 = h_2 + R_E$$

$$d_2^2 = d^2 + d_1^2 - 2dd_1 \cos\gamma$$

According to above relationships, the visibility between two satellites is illustrated in Fig. 3.

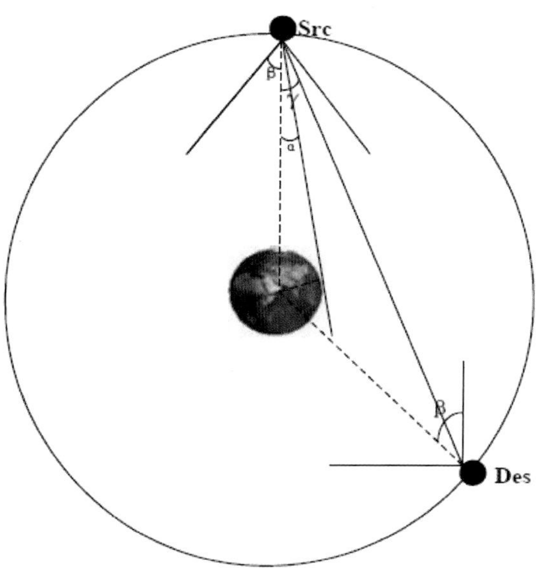

Figure 3. Visibility between two satellites.

According to above formula and diagram, we can find that, when $\gamma<\alpha$ between two satellites because in the shadow of the earth and not visible; when $\gamma>\beta$due to source satellite antenna, the coverage and invisible; two satellites between permanent and visible condition is, in the whole running cycle of the meet relation as follows:

$$\alpha < \gamma < \beta$$

5. SIMULATION

Due to the symmetry of Walker Constellation of satellites using STK software to 24 MEO satellite configuration for the first orbit of the walker 24/3/1 first satellites M_{11} the visibility simulation analysis can represent the state of the whole network of any satellite. 55 degrees in MEO satellite orbit inclination, orbital altitude of 21000km, satellite antenna angle is 60 degrees simulation, get visibility relations such as shown in Fig. 4.

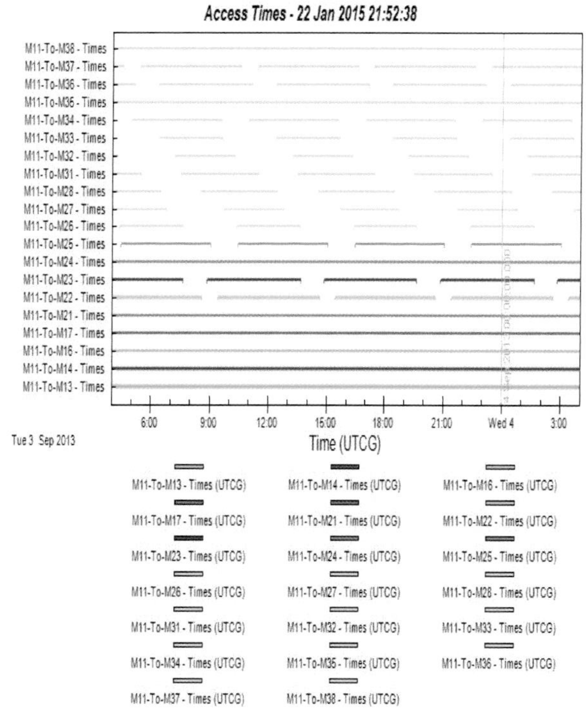

Figure 4. Visibility of Satellite M_{11}.

From the figure can be seen, 8 satellite in the M_{11} satellite and M_{13} and M_{14}, M_{16} and M_{17}, M_{21}, M_{24}, M_{35}, M_{38}, permanent and visible, and M_{12}, M_{15}, M_{18} never visible, and the rest of the other satellite intermittently visible. In the same way, other satellites in the constellation can be seen in the entire operating cycle of permanent visible satellites. From this, there are permanent visible satellites and discontinuous visible satellites in the constellation within 3 orbits, but the satellite is never visible in the same orbit. Because of the symmetry of Walker constellation, the visible relationship between M11 and other satellites can be extended to other MEO satellites.

In the inter satellite link system, the narrow beam antenna is used to establish directional link, so there are many points for the point link in any time slots.. Based on the above visibility relations, the link between different satellite nodes is chosen, which is divided into different time slots and link planning.

6. CONCLUSION

In this paper, the characteristics of the inter satellite link is analyzed, and a Walker constellation with 24 MEO satellites is designed. The relationship between the satellites is analyzed by using the mathematical method, and the simulation is the basis for the following design.

REFERENCES

- [1] Ricardo, Martin-Peiro Belen and Romay-Merino Miguel. The Galileo Constellation Design: A systematic approach. In Proceedings of the 18th International Technical Meeting of the Satellite Division of The Institute of Navigation, ION GNSS 2005, Long Beach, CA, United States, Sep 13-16 2005.1296-1301.
- [2] Ollie L, Larry B, Art G, et al. GPS III System Operations Concepts [J]. IEEE Aerospace and Electronic Systems Magazine, 2005, 20(1): 10-18.
- [3] Kulkarni S S. TDMA service for sensor networks [J]. In ICDCSW'04: Proceedings of the 24th International Conference on Distributed Computing Systems Workshops - W7: EC (ICDCSW'04, 2004:604 - 609.
- [4] Pavon-Marino P, Aparicio-Pardo R, Garcia-Manrubia B, et al. Virtual topology design and flow routing in optical networks under multihour traffic demand [J]. Photonic Network Communication, 2010, 19(1):42-54.
- [5] Akyildiz I F, Pelech J I, Yener B. A Virtual Topology Based Routing Protocol for Multihop Dynamic Wireless Networks [J]. Wireless Networks, 2001, 7(4):413-424.
- [6] Wicker S B. A Combined Localization and Geographic Routing Algorithm for Rapidly-Deployed Wireless Sensor Networks [J]. International Journal of Distributed Sensor Networks, 2008, 4(1):44-63.

Application Research on IPv6/GPRS-based Engineering Safety Quality Management System

C.X. Zhang
CITIC Investment Co. Beijing, China
S. Qian*
The College of Traffic Management Cadres, Department of Computer Science Institute, Beijing, China
J.H. Li
CCCC Fourth Highway Engineering Co., Ltd, Beijing, China
**Email: qs250@qq.com*

ABSTRACT: A kind of safety quality management system of the engineering construction enterprise is designed, including site Smartphone terminal and the background safety quality management information system. The Smartphone terminal is applied with ARM9 core MCU to control as well as IPv6 wireless self-organized network and GPRS technology for communication. The Smartphone terminal sends collected safety quality text and media information in the construction site to the aggregation node through wireless network and then the aggregation node sends data to the background safety quality management information system through GPRS network. The safety management personnel of the bureau forms the statistical data according to the declared safety and quality management data of the engineering project as well as issue it to the corresponding site terminal equipment according to the early warning level.

KEYWORDS: Engineering construction; Safety quality management; IPv6; GPRS.

1. INTRODUCTION

With the constant reform of construction modes of domestic engineering projects, projects become more and more, engineering becomes larger and larger, time limit becomes more and more urgent, and technical process demand becomes stricter and stricter. In addition, more and more technical personnel play multiple roles; many areas can't be supervised, inspection of some processes is neglected, process inspection and control can't be fully covered. And, potential hazards appear constantly and safety and quality risk control becomes more and more difficult. As the construction safety and quality management inspection and review results are filled in artificially in paper, they can't be timely obtained by the project department supervisor, competent department and leader of the company and competent department and leader of the bureau, thus the main managers can't understand the enterprise's production safety and quality problems during construction from a macro level.

In the paper, a kind of engineering safety quality management system based on Smartphone terminal is designed, the Smartphone terminal is used for safety quality management data collection, and IPv6 technology of the building enterprise headquarters is also used to establish the self-organized wireless communication network. During construction management of the enterprise, as construction of some areas has no mobile base station signal, the site terminal can be connected with adjacent brother nodes with mobile phone signals for ad-hoc network communication. The terminal around the mobile phone signal base station will be connected to GPRS network to serve as the aggregation node and send data of its own and other nodes to data center of the enterprise headquarters. The system can ensure that the front-line construction technical management personnel can timely collect safety quality data of the engineering construction site even the area with poor engineering geological conditions while without GPRS network to lay a basic informatization management channel for the safety quality management of the engineering.

2. SAFETY QUALITY MANAGEMENT SYSTEM ARCHITECTURE OF THE ENGINEERING

The IPv6/GPRS-based engineering safety quality management system is mainly composed of two parts: Smartphone terminal and rear safety quality management system. Every Smartphone terminal can form IPv6ad hoc network together with adjacent nodes IPv6ad and can also be connected with GPRS base station based on site conditions to become an aggregation node. The Smartphone terminal sends collected construction quality data and construction safety data and information in the construction site to the aggregation node through wireless self-organized network and then the aggregation node sends data to the rear safety quality management information system through GPRS network. The safety quality management system will form safety quality statistical analysis data according to the site safety quality management data and form early warning data and information according to the actual safety quality management level as well as utilize the Smartphone terminal to notify the personnel fully in charge of front-line safety quality management. The topological structure of the system is shown in Figure 1.

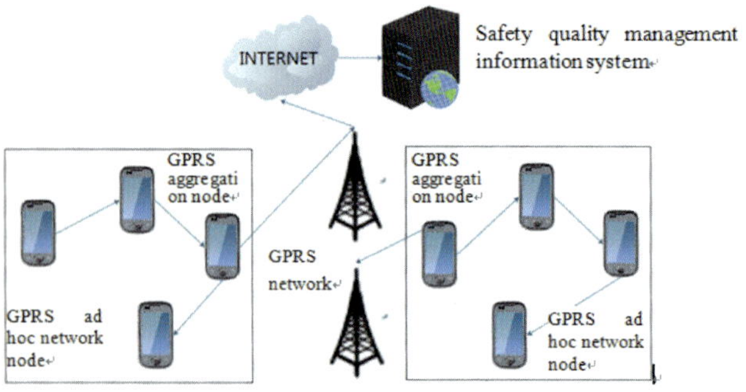

Figure 1. Topological structure of safety quality management system.

3. DESIGN OF THE SAFETY QUALITY MANAGEMENT SYSTEM

3.1. *Design principles of the Smartphone terminal*

The Smartphone terminal is a critical part of the whole system, which is used to collect safety quality management information through GPRS network as well as asynchronously send data to the background safety quality management server through the self-organization network/GPRS network. The site staff can also collect site safety quality data information through the Smartphone terminal equipment, and the background system will store data in the database, which can be used for data analysis and study of the safety quality management.

The terminal hardware part of the Smartphone is composed of ARM embedded development board and the peripheral modules. The development board mainly includes SAMSUNG ARM920T core processor S3C2410 and relevant FLASH memorizer, RAM memory and processor peripheral interface chip DM9000, etc. The peripheral modules mainly include SIMCOM GPRS module SIM900A, U-blox GPS receiving module Neo-6M, LCD touch screen, and GPS receiving antenna. The handheld terminal is adopted with lithium battery for power supply, with the rated capacity of 3100mAh and DC charging voltage of 5V. The hardware design is shown in Figure 2.

The core board and motherboard constitute a minimal complete application system, and the system can load and run the embedded Linux operating system, which is featured by small volume, low power consumption, strong processing capacity, etc. The core board is integrated with S3C2410 processor, 64MB SDRAM, 64M NAND FLASH and 1M BOOT FLASH. The motherboard provides the following peripheral interface: One four-wire RS-232 serial port, one USB HOST interface, one 10M/100M self-adapting Ethernet interface, one TFT LCD interface, and one JTAG interface. With the serial port, the user can conveniently debug the program in the laboratory; in addition, as S3C2410 supports JTAG debugging, ICE debugging can be neglected, thus reducing the project development cost.

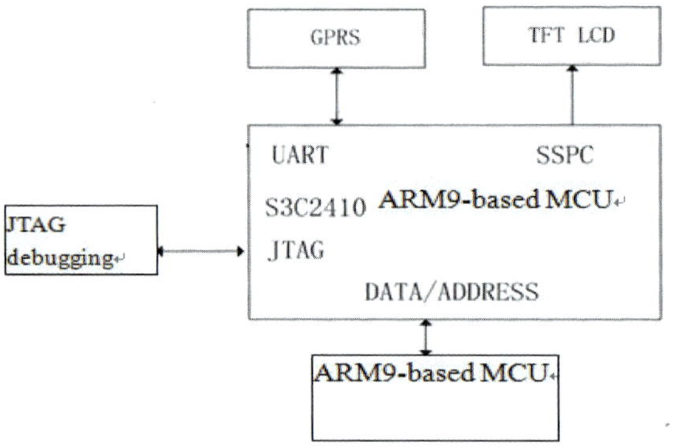

Figure 2. Composition principles of smartphone terminal hardware.

Generally, ARM embedded system's own operating system has Linux 2.4 core, it is necessary to recompile the operating system core and upgrade it to 2.6.11.7 version to support IPv6. As the version core is added with support to S3C2410 chip, no any patch is needed. Import S3C2410 default configuration file of the core source, and then select to support MTD equipment drive and NAND FLASH drive, and finally select the target file system and network equipment and protocol. The core source is added with the network chip CS8900A drive programs drivers/net/arm/cs89001h and cs89001c and configured with the network device drive make file and kconfig files. In addition, add CS8900A configuration option and adding rt2x00 drive program into the core of system. The Smartphone terminal system shall also be loaded with Frame buffer to support LCD display function.

3.2. *Design of Smartphone terminal software*

In the area without GPRS signal, the Smartphone terminal can realize IPv6 ad hoc network communication. When there are normal base stations nearby, the Smartphone terminal can perform data interaction with the background system through GPRS network and can serve as the aggregation node to become a bridge for communication between other nodes in ad hoc network and the command center. The first step of realization of the handheld terminal software shall be realization of mobile IPv6 and wireless ad hoc network integration on the existing hardware platform [4,5].

(1) Technical realization of IPv6ad hoc network

The realization of IPv6ad hoc network is mainly composed of routing module, NDP protocol modification and mobile IPv6 module. The routing module is used for multi-hop communication in wireless ad hoc network; NDP agreement modification is used to guarantee NDP work in multi-hop network, and mobile IPv6 module is used for roaming management in the mobile node. As AODV routing protocol is a kind of commonly-used on-demand driven routing protocol and it can be conveniently combined with the automatic configuration scheme of the wireless ad hoc network address, it is selected in the realization scheme.

The core version of Linux operating system of the handheld terminal is 2.6.11.7. The overall functions are as shown in Figure 3. The extension routing module (E-AODVD) is a kind of network routing module, which is integrated with extension AODV routing protocol (adding normal AODV routing protocol discovering wireless ad hoc network gateway function) and automatic configuration scheme of the wireless ad hoc network, network address, thus providing the wireless ad hoc network node with routing and address configuration function.

The module is extended and realized on aodv-uu-0.5-ipv6 version. RADVD module is a kind of router declaration module, it is a background program, which runs RS messages processed and received on the gateway and sends uncast or multicast RA message. This module is based on open source radvd-0.7.2 base, which modifies RS, RA message format and process. The above two modules are realized in the user mode of the system, which uses RAW Socket to receive and process IPv6 message. MIPL module is the mobile IPv6 module of Linux system. This module is based on mipv6-0.9.5-v2.4.2 version, which modifies MIPL mobile detection and automatic address configuration process. MIPL module invokes IPv6 tunnel module of the protocol stack and IPv6 network filtration module to build tunnels and processing messages and invokes the modified NDP protocol to complete the mobile detection process. The module is realized in the core mode in the protocol stack.

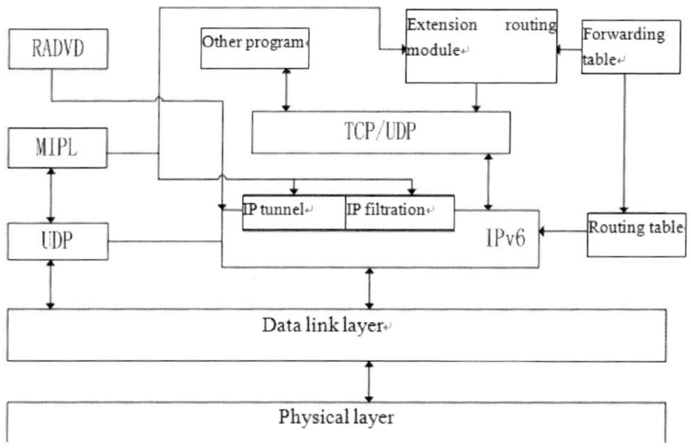

Figure 3. Realization of mobile IPv6 ad hoc network.

(2) Gateway effect of aggregation node

The aggregation node refers to the handheld terminal connected with GPRS network of ad hoc network, in addition to its own data collection operation, it also plays a key role in communication between other nodes in ad hoc network and the rear server. Viewing from IPv6 routing neighbor relations, other nodes in ad hoc network can think next hop of the aggregation node is the server of the background bureau data center. With position moving of the handheld terminal, each node may become the aggregation node.

Data transmission of the system is based on IPv6. Currently, INTERNET completely supports IPv6, but GPRS network doesn't support IPv6. To make IPv6 data packet passes through IPv4 network of GPRS, this system selects to realize OpenVPN tunnel, as OpenVPN is featured by flexible configuration, supporting NAT, supporting multiple operating systems, etc. The aggregation node is configured with OpenVPN Client. The OpenVPN Server runs in CERNET2, which can be configured on the server of the command center. The aggregation node packages IPv6 message in IPv4 message through OpenVPN tunnel to realize IPv6 transparent communication with the command center [6].

(3) Realization of handheld terminal software

The application layer software design mainly includes UI design, GPRS data protocol analysis, and data communication with the bureau data center. The main program of the handheld terminals is mainly composed of main data processing and display program and ad hoc network communication thread. The structure is as shown in Figure 4.

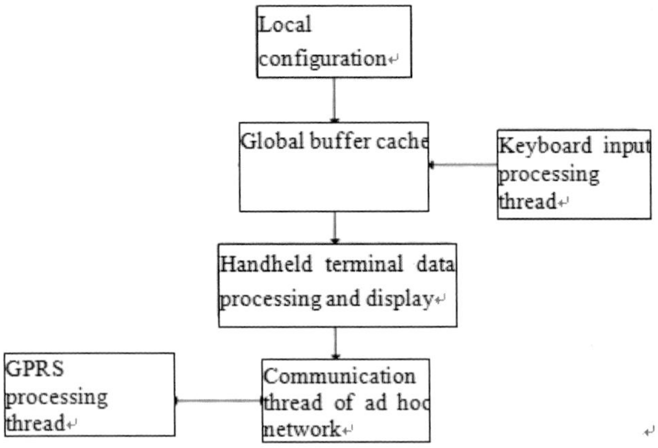

Figure 4. Handheld terminal software structure.

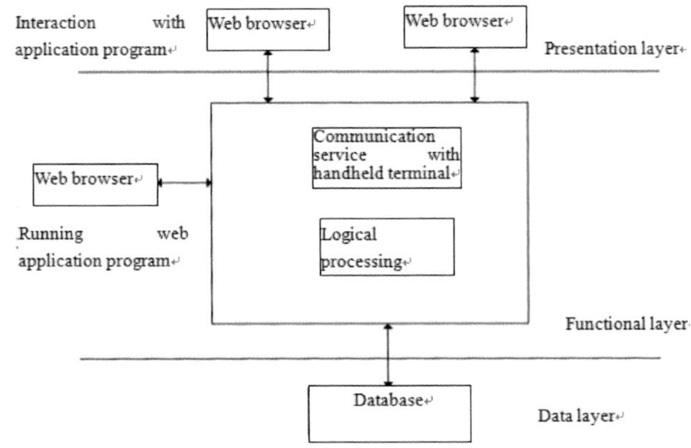

Figure 5. Software architecture of background safety quality management system.

The ad hoc network communication thread is the network interface of the program, which is used for communication between brother node and GPRS thread, and main data processing and display program will communicate with the bureau data center through the interface. GPRS processing thread will judge whether the current connection with base station is available, which is mainly used for receiving data from GPRS network interface and sending data.

The part between the bureau data center server and the Smartphone terminal is applied with the self-defined application layer data protocol, and the frame format domain is frame head, frame length, type, data, checksum, frame end in turn. The type domain is used to point out material demand information, scheduling command, etc.

3.3. *Design of background safety quality management system*

The background safety quality system management system is the application system based on B/S structure, which runs the supporting platform based on J2EE. The hardware includes PC server and working PC. The three-layer architecture using B/S mode is composed of the data layer, business logic function supporting layer and presentation layer (Figure 5). The system uses SPRING framework, HTML 5 and CSS3 for programming development as well as utilizes Ajax for interaction with the server. The communication service is used for coordinating communication with the remote handheld terminal; the logic processing server is used for processing the received Smartphone terminal data; saving it in the database, and sending the safety quality management command from the browser side.

The scheduling command center mainly includes 13 basic modules, including the standardized management, project management, quality inspection application management, safety inspection application management, statistical statement early warning, system management, quality inspection, inspection application review, safety inspection, affairs to be dealt with, etc. (Figure 6).

Figure 6. Functional module of command center.

4. CONCLUSION

The safety quality management of the engineering construction unit is an important work related to safety of the engineering unit staff and quality of building. The safety quality management difficulties during construction can't be precisely controlled only by the current artificial methods. In some construction area, as the mountains and other complex regions can't realize timely interaction of engineering data information, the informatization management system can't support the communication channel management of the site working face. In the paper, the designed IPv6/GPRS-based engineering safety quality management system can be used for data collection task in of the complex regional environment to ensure that the bureau or counterpart company can rationally control safety problems. In the system, one set of IPv6/GPRS-based Smartphone terminal equipment is mainly developed and the hardware part is adopted with ARM9-based core S3C2410 processor. In actual deployment, in order to control the cost, GPRS module of some Smartphone can e cut, and it is only necessary to ensure that there are sufficient aggregation nodes near GPRS base station. In addition, in order to deal with the site complex situation, vehicle-mounted GPRS base station can be properly used.

The engineering safety quality management system is realized based on IPv6 technology, which can adapt to wide application and popularization of IPv6 network in the future, thus having perspectiveness. As supplementation to GSM network, GPRS's low rate makes system function upgrading and extension limited. With the development of technology, 3G or 4G module can substitute GPRS module in the current handheld terminal in the future.

REFERENCES

— [1] Li Weiqin, Yang Yaping, Role-based Visit Control System [J], Electronic Engineer, 2000(26):16-21.

— [2] Zhang Bing, Xing Lili, Li Jun, Yang Fan. Study on Application of Wireless Self-organized Network in Earthquake Relief [J]. Journal of Natural Disasters, 2013, 02:191-196.

— [3] Liu Xin, Hu Guangwu, Chen Wenlong, Xu Ke. IPv6 Protocol Simplification Facing to the Internet of Things [J]. Journal of Tsinghua University (Natural Science Edition), 2013, 52(5):699-703.

— [4] Wang Guohui, Zhou Jihua, Shi Jinglin. Design and Realization of Integration of Ad Hoc Network and Mobile IPv6 Integration [J]. Computer Engineering, 2005, 18:127-129+182.

— [5] Wen Zhankao, Zhang Jinkui, Liu Jun, Wang Yu, Wang Xingwei. Open VPN-based IPv6 over IPv4 Tunnel Technology [J]. Journal of Xiamen University (Natural Science Edition), 2007, S2:50-53.

— [6] Su Ming, Wei Da, Qu Liangdong, Wang Munan, Kuai Wenbo. IPv6/CDMA-based Vehicle-mounted Information System Design [J]. Microcomputer Information, 2009, 10:188–189+ 269.

— [7] Li Jun, Zhang Bing, Xing Lili. Design of IPv6-based Embedded Video Monitoring System [J]. Computer Measurement & Control, 2010, 18(5):1014-1016.

Function P-sets and the Dynamic Hiding of P-information Law

C.X. Fan*
School of Control Science and Engineering, Shandong University, Jinan, Shandong, 250061 China
School of Electrical Engineering, Shandong University, Jinan, 250061 China
F.L. Chang
School of Control Science and Engineering, Shandong University, Jinan, Shandong, 250061 China
H. Zhong
School of Electrical Engineering, Shandong University, Jinan, 250061 China
**Email: fcxmar@sdu.edu.cn*

ABSTRACT: Function P-sets (packet sets) is a novel model with law and dynamic characteristics, which is composed of function internal P-set $S^{\bar{F}}$ and function outer P-set S^F. Using the structure, law and dynamic characteristic of function P-sets, the band information law and their generation as well as the hiding and hiding theorem of P-information in band information law and the recovery theorem of information law are given. Using the above theory results, an application example of information law hiding is given.

KEYWORDS: Function P-sets; Band information; Law hiding; Recovery theorem.

1. INTRODUCTION

Using the discrete values, the function $w(x) = a_{n-1}x^{n-1} + a_{n-2}x^{n-2} + \cdots + a_1x + a_0$ is generated by interpolation method [1] (for example, Lagrange's interpolation, piecewise interpolation and so on), which is an information law on the interval [*a*, *b*]. Here there are two questions to need to be solved: what kind of mathematical method is used to hide information law $w(x)$ to prevent from being stolen and distorted by others? In the paper, a novel mathematical theory and method will be used to give the answers about the question, which is function P-sets [1] and has been applied in many researches [2-5]. Function P-sets is the function form of P-sets (packet sets) [6-9].

2. BAND INFORMATION LAW AND THE HIDING THEOREM OF INFORMATION LAW

Definition 1 $w(x)$ is called information law generated by limited general function set $S = \{s_1, s_2, \cdots, s_q\}$ with the attribute set $\alpha = \{\alpha_1, \alpha_2, \cdots, \alpha_k\}$.

Definition 2 $w(x)^{\bar{F}}$ is called internal P-information law generated by function internal P-set $S^{\bar{F}} = \{s_1, s_2, \cdots, s_p\}$ with the attribute set $\alpha^F = \{\alpha_1, \alpha_2, \cdots, \alpha_\lambda\}$. $w(x)^F$ is called outer P-information law generated by function outer P-set $S^F = \{s_1, s_2, \cdots, s_r\}$ with the attribute set $\alpha^{\bar{F}} = \{\alpha_1, \alpha_2, \cdots, \alpha_t\}$.

Definition 3 The information law pair consisted of $w(x)^{\bar{F}}$ and $w(x)^F$ is called P-information law generated by function P-sets $(S^{\bar{F}}, S^F)$, and

$$(w(x)^{\bar{F}}, w(x)^F) \tag{1}$$

Definition 4 $< a, w(x)^{\bar{F}}, b, w(x)^F >$ is called band information law generated by P-information law $(w(x)^{\bar{F}}, w(x)^F)$, if $w(x)^{\bar{F}}$ and $w(x)^F$ are up-boundary and down-boundary of $< a, w(x)^{\bar{F}}, b, w(x)^F >$, respectively. *a* and *b* are its two different common points.

Theorem 1 If $w(x)_\lambda^{\bar{F}}$ is the internal P-information law generated by function internal P-set $S_\lambda^{\bar{F}}$, then there exists attribute set $\Delta\alpha \neq \varnothing$ to make $\Delta\alpha$, attribute set α_λ^F of $w(x)_\lambda^{\bar{F}}$ and attribute set α of $w(x)$ satisfy the following equation.

$$(\alpha_\lambda^F - \Delta\alpha) - \alpha = \varnothing \tag{2}$$

Theorem 2 If $w(x)_\lambda^F$ is the outer P-information law generated by function outer P-set S_λ^F, then there exists attribute set $\nabla\alpha \neq \varnothing$ to make $\nabla\alpha$, attribute set $\alpha_\lambda^{\bar{F}}$ of $w(x)_\lambda^F$ and attribute set α of $w(x)$ satisfy the following equation.

$$(\alpha_\lambda^{\bar{F}} \cup \nabla\alpha) - \alpha = \varnothing \tag{3}$$

Theorem 3 If $(w(x)_\lambda^{\bar{F}}, w(x)_\lambda^F)$ is P-information law generated by function P-sets $(S_\lambda^{\bar{F}}, S_\lambda^F)$, then there exists attribute set $(\Delta\alpha, \nabla\alpha) \neq \varnothing$ to make $(\Delta\alpha, \nabla\alpha)$, attribute set $(\alpha_\lambda^F, \alpha_\lambda^{\bar{F}})$ of $(w(x)_\lambda^{\bar{F}}, w(x)_\lambda^F)$ and attribute set α of $w(x)$ satisfy the following equation.

$$(\alpha_\lambda^F, \alpha_\lambda^{\bar{F}}) - ((\alpha \cup \Delta\alpha), (\alpha - \nabla\alpha)) = \varnothing \tag{4}$$

Theorem 4 If $< a, w(x)_\lambda^{\bar{F}}, b, w(x)_\lambda^F >$ is the band information law generated by P-information law $(w(x)_\lambda^{\bar{F}}, w(x)_\lambda^F)$, the sufficient and necessary condition of information law hidden in $< a, w(x)_\lambda^{\bar{F}}, b, w(x)_\lambda^F >$ is that the attribute set α_λ^F of $w(x)_\lambda^{\bar{F}}$ and the attribute set α of $w(x)$, the attribute set $\alpha_\lambda^{\bar{F}}$ of $w(x)_\lambda^F$ and the attribute set α of $w(x)$ satisfy equations (5) and (6), respectively.

$$\alpha_\lambda^F = \alpha \cup \Delta\alpha \tag{5}$$

$$\alpha_\lambda^{\bar{F}} = \alpha - \nabla\alpha \tag{6}$$

3. THE APPLICATION OF P-INFORMATION LAW IN BAND INFORMATION LAW HIDING

3.1. *The generation of band information law* $< a, w(x)^{\bar{F}}, b, w(x)^F >$

Given function set $S = \{s_1, s_2, \cdots, s_q\}$, and $\alpha = \{\alpha_1, \alpha_2, \cdots, \alpha_k\}$ is attribute set of *S*. y_i is the discrete distribution data set of $\forall s_i \in S$, $i = 1, 2, \cdots, q$, and

$$y_i = \{y_{i,1}, y_{i,2}, \cdots, y_{i,n}\} \tag{7}$$

Using y_i to get the discrete data set *y* of *S*, and

$$y = \{y_1, y_2, \cdots, y_n\} = \{\sum_{i=1}^{q} y_{i,1}, \sum_{i=1}^{q} y_{i,2}, \cdots, \sum_{i=1}^{q} y_{i,n}\} \tag{8}$$

After supplementing some attributes into α, general function set *S* becomes function internal P-set $S^{\bar{F}}$, and

$$S^{\bar{F}} = \{s_1, s_2, \cdots, s_p\} \tag{9}$$

Using the similar method to equations (7) and (8) to get the discrete data set $y^{\bar{F}}$ of $S^{\bar{F}}$, and

$$y^{\bar{F}} = \{y_1^{\bar{f}}, y_2^{\bar{f}}, \cdots, y_n^{\bar{f}}\} = \{\sum_{i=1}^{p} y_{i,1}, \sum_{i=1}^{p} y_{i,2}, \cdots, \sum_{i=1}^{p} y_{i,n}\} \tag{10}$$

After deleting some attributes from α, general function set *S* becomes function outer P-set S^F, and

$$S^F = \{s_1, s_2, \cdots, s_r\} \tag{11}$$

Using the similar method to equations (7) and (8) to get the discrete data set y^F of S^F, and

$$y^F = \{y_1^f, y_2^f, \cdots, y_n^f\} = \{\sum_{i=1}^{r} y_{i,1}, \sum_{i=1}^{r} y_{i,2}, \cdots, \sum_{i=1}^{r} y_{i,n}\} \tag{12}$$

3.2. *The hiding-reduction of* $w(x)$ *in* $< a, w(x)^{\bar{F}}, b, w(x)^F >$ *and its application*

Given discrete data set *y*, which are the discrete values at $t = 1, 2, 3, 4, 5, 6$ about important information law $w(x)$, and α is the attribute set of $w(x)$.

$$\begin{aligned} y &= \{y_1, y_2, y_3, y_4, y_5, y_6\} \\ &= \{1.100, 1.260, 1.630, 1.400, 1.310, 1.580\} \end{aligned} \tag{13}$$

$$\alpha = \{\alpha_1, \alpha_2, \alpha_3, \alpha_4\} \tag{14}$$

Given $\eta_i \in (0,1)$, $i = 1, 2, 3, 4$, and $\sum_{i=1}^{4} \eta_i = 1$. η_i is the separation coefficient, and $\eta_1 = 0.18$, $\eta_2 = 0.27$, $\eta_3 = 0.35$, $\eta_4 = 0.20$. Using $\eta_1 \sim \eta_4$ to separate $y_i \in y$ into $y_{i,1} = \eta_1 y_i$, $y_{i,2} = \eta_2 y_i$, $y_{i,3} = \eta_3 y_i$, $y_{i,4} = \eta_4 y_i$, $i = 1, 2, 3, 4, 5, 6$. The separation of y_i about η_i is listed in the Table 1.

Table 1. The separation of discrete value y_i about η_i of information law $w(x)$ with attribute set α.

k	1	2	3	4	5	6
$y_{i,1}$	0.188	0.233	0.293	0.253	0.233	0.284
$y_{i,2}$	0.296	0.340	0.440	0.377	0.351	0.427
$y_{i,3}$	0.386	0.438	0.571	0.490	0.466	0.553
$y_{i,4}$	0.230	0.249	0.326	0.280	0.260	0.316

The data in the table 1 and y_i in equation (13) satisfy $y_i = y_{i,1} + y_{i,3} + y_{i,4} + y_{i,4} = \sum_{j=1}^{4} y_{i,j}$.

α_5, α_6 are supplemented into α, or α_1, α_3 are deleted from α, then α becomes α_i^F or $\alpha_j^{\bar{F}}$,

$$\alpha_i^F = \alpha \cup \{\alpha_5, \alpha_6\} = \{\alpha_1, \alpha_2, \alpha_3, \alpha_4, \alpha_5, \alpha_6\} \tag{15}$$

$$\alpha_j^F = \alpha - \{\alpha_1, \alpha_3\} = \{\alpha_2, \alpha_4\} \tag{16}$$

Using the definition of function internal P-set[2], $y_{i,3}, y_{i,4}$ are deleted from table 1, then *y* becomes $y_i^{\bar{F}}$, and Table 2 is obtained.

Table 2. The separation of discrete value y_i about η_i of internal P-information law $w(x)_i^{\bar{F}}$ with attribute set α_i^F.

k	1	2	3	4	5	6
$y_{i,1}$	0189	0.236	0.293	0.253	0.236	0.284
$y_{i,2}$	0.297	0.340	0.441	0.378	0.354	0.427

From table 2 and equation (10), $y_i^{\bar{F}}$ is obtained, and

$$\begin{aligned} y_i^{\bar{F}} &= \{y_1^{\bar{f}}, y_2^{\bar{f}}, y_3^{\bar{f}}, y_4^{\bar{f}}, y_5^{\bar{f}}, y_6^{\bar{f}}\} \\ &= \{0.486, 0.576, 0.734, 0.631, 0.590, 0.711\} \end{aligned} \tag{17}$$

Using the definition of function outer P-set [2], $y_{i,5}, y_{i,6}$ are supplemented into table 1, then y becomes y_j^F, and Table 3 is obtained.

Table 3. The separation of discrete value y_i about η_i of outer P-information law $w(x)_j^F$ with attribute set α_j^F

k	1	2	3	4	5	6
$y_{i,1}$	0.189	0.236	0.293	0.253	0.236	0.284
$y_{i,2}$	0.297	0.340	0.441	0.378	0.354	0.427
$y_{i,3}$	0.386	0.441	0.571	0.490	0.468	0.553
$y_{i,4}$	0.230	0.252	0.326	0.280	0.262	0.316
$y_{i,5}$	0.312	0.121	0.271	0.167	0.139	0.230
$y_{i,6}$	0.127	0.240	0.193	0.270	0.283	0.378

From table 3 and equation (12), y_j^F is obtained, and

$$\begin{aligned} y_j^F &= \{y_1^f, y_2^f, y_3^f, y_4^f, y_5^f, y_6^f\} \\ &= \{1.541, 1.630, 2.095, 1.838, 1.742, 2.188\} \end{aligned} \tag{18}$$

$w(x)$ generated by y, $w(x)_i^{\overline{F}}$ generated by $y_i^{\overline{F}}$ and $w(x)_j^F$ generated by y_j^F are obtained by Lagrange interpolation function method and satisfy $w(x)_i^{\overline{F}} < w(x) < w(x)_j^F$, which are shown in figure 1.

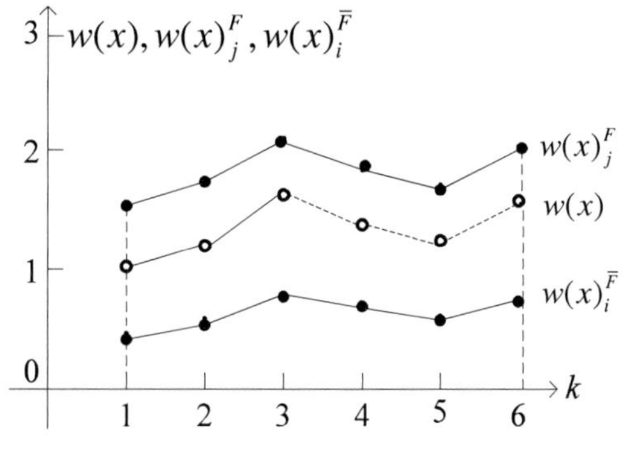

Figure 1. $< a, w(x)_i^{\overline{F}}, b, w(x)_j^F >$ is the band information law generated by P-information law $(w(x)_i^{\overline{F}}, w(x)_j^F)$, a=1, b=6. $w(x)$ is hidden in $< a, w(x)_i^{\overline{F}}, b, w(x)_j^F >$.

4. CONCLUSION

$w(x)$ is hidden in band information law $< a, w(x)^{\overline{F}}, b, w(x)^F >$, and $< a, w(x)^{\overline{F}}, b, w(x)^F >$ is not single, so it is difficult to steal $w(x)$ from $< a, w(x)^{\overline{F}}, b, w(x)^F >$. This is because people do not known the attributes supplemented into or deleted from α, even the definition form and structure of α_i. It is of no avail to steal $w(x)$ from $< a, w(x)^{\overline{F}}, b, w(x)^F >$ by classical mathematical methods, which is verified by many experiments. The study given in the paper is a novel application of function P-sets in dynamic information system.

ACKNOWLEDGEMENT

In the paper, the research was supported by the National Natural Science Foundation of China (Project No. 51307100).

REFERENCES

- [1] Kaiquan Shi. 2011. Function P-sets. International *Journal of Machine Learning and Cybernetics*, 2(4): 281-288.
- [2] Kaiquan Shi. 2014. P-information law intelligent fusion and soft information image intelligent generation. *Journal of Shandong University (Natural Science)*, 49(4): 1-17 (in Chinese).
- [3] Rong Lin, Chengxian Fan. 2012. Function P-sets and dynamic characteristics of information regularity. *Journal of Shandong University (Natural Science)*, 47(1): 121-126 (in Chinese).
- [4] Jingxiao Zhang, Xinhua Liu. 2012. Function P-sets and discovery of structure-physical properties law in analogues system. *Journal of Shandong University (Natural Science)*, 47(8): 98-102 (in Chinese).
- [5] Wenju Zhao, Chengxian Fan. 2011. Attribute dependence of function P-sets and its application. *Journal of Shandong University (Natural Science)*, 46(6): 115-120 (in Chinese).
- [6] Kaiquan Shi. 2009. P-sets and its applications. *An International Journal Advances in Systems Science and Applications*, 9(2): 209-219.
- [7] Kaiquan Shi. 2008. P-sets. *International Journal of Shandong University (Natural Science)*, 43(11): 78-84 (in Chinese).
- [8] Chengxian Fan, Hongkang Lin. 2012. P-sets and the reasoning-identification of disaster information. *International Journal of Convergence Information Technology*, 7(1): 337-345.
- [9] Hongkang Lin, Chengxian Fan. 2012. The dual form of P-reasoning and identification of unknown attribute. *International Journal of Digital Content Technology and its Application*, 6(1): 121-131.

Beijing Agricultural Scientific Technical Information Counseling Service Status and Countermeasure on the New Situations

C.S. Luo[1,2], Q.F. Wei[1,2*], Z.M. Li[1,2], C.Z. Cao[1,2] ,Y.M. Zheng[1,2] & Q. Guo[1,2]

1. Institute of Information on Science and Technology of Agriculture, Beijing Academy of Agriculture and Forestry Sciences, Beijing, 100097, China

2. Beijing Research Center of Engineering Technology on Rural Distance Information Service, Beijing, 100097, China

Email: weiqingfeng201@163.com

ABSTRACT: Agricultural scientific technical information service is an important bridge between agricultural technology achievement information and agricultural production. By the investigation of the current situation of agricultural scientific technical information consulting services in Beijing, and the analysis of restricting factors of the service, the technical countermeasures of its development under the new situation are provided in this paper to give the reverence for the construction of new agricultural scientific technical information counseling service system.

KEYWORDS: Agricultural scientific technical information; Counseling service; Situation; Countermeasure, Beijing.

1. INTRODUCTION

With the rapid development of Internet and the wide application of information technology in the field of agricultural scientific technical service, the information resources are more and more rich, information dissemination channels have risen steadily, but the service effect is still need to improve [1]. Based on the current situation, analyze the restriction factors on user access service, it is the key to solve the problem to upgrade the quality of service. The study analyzes the agricultural scientific technical information acquisition cost, the quality of information, and the user's own factors, and puts forward some countermeasures that how to use information technology and resources to provide farmer with diversification and full range services in the modern network environment. It is important to fully meet the farmer's demand of agricultural scientific technical information and solve their difficult problem of production.

2. SITUATION ANALYSIS ON AGRICULTURAL SCIENTIFIC TECHNICAL INFORMATION COUNSELING SERVICE

Fully understand the farmer's demand of agricultural scientific technical counseling service is the base that aiming to provide services and improve the service effect. Through field interviews, telephone interview and questionnaire, survey the general farmers, farming households with large scale, agricultural works, professional cooperative organizations in Miyun, Tongzhou, Daxing, Changping, Pinggu, Huairou and other counties. The main content of the investigation includes information equipment, information demand, the ways of information acquisition.

2.1. *Service equipment*

Information counseling equipment is the basic condition to obtain the agricultural scientific technical information. The use and popularity are bound to affect the consulting service work. The result of the survey is show in Fig. 1:

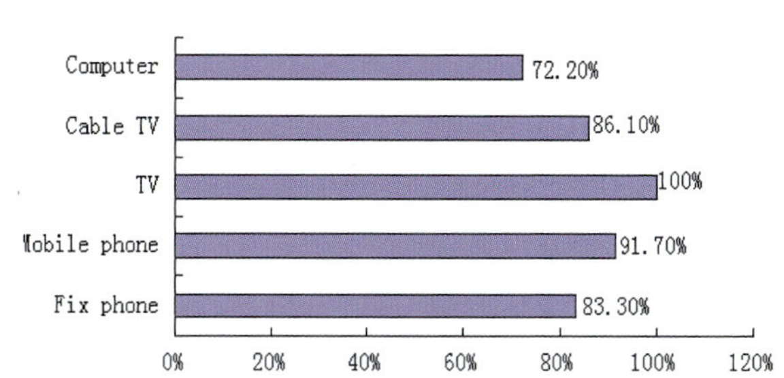

Figure 1. Equipment owning rate.

It can be found on the Fig. 1, the equipment owning rate has reached a higher level. Among them, television is the highest, it is 100%. Followed by mobile phone, it is 91.7%. Finally is the cable TV, fixed telephone, VCD or DVD, computer, respectively, they are 86.1%, 83.3%, 80.6%, 72.2%. The data is shown that the popularity of TV, mobile phone, fixed telephone, computer of Beijing agricultural users are higher. They are able to access information by information equipment. So, fully use the high frequency equipment and make the additional equipment as a supplement, integrate a variety of information channels, to carry out information consulting services, is an optimal choice.

2.2. *Counseling service demand*

Through the information demand investigation, it can provide individualized service for different user groups. The results of the investigation are as showed in Fig. 2:

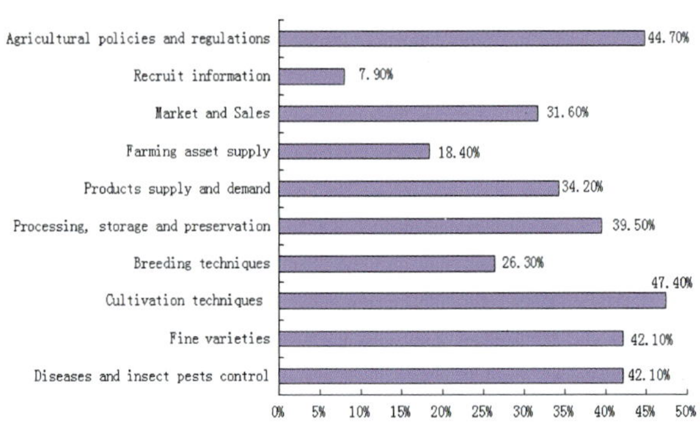

Figure 2. The statistic of consultation service demand.

It can be seen from the Fig. 2, more than 42% of the users are interested in the techniques of cultivation, the information of agricultural policies and regulations, the information of superior varieties, the control techniques of diseases and insect pests. More than 31% of the users are interested in the technology of processing, storage and preservation, the products supply and demand, sales. The least attention is on the information of breeding technicians, farming asset supply, recruit information. On the whole, the information required is widely. Among them, practical technicians, planting varieties, product price and national policy are the focus for farmers. For the agricultural science and technology information with a strong timeliness, meanwhile, their cultural level uneven, the ability to receive knowledge inconsistencies. If want to obtain better consulting service effect, large investment is required on information service resources development.

2.3. *Counseling service way*

It can be seen from the Fig. 3, users access information mainly concentrated on three channels: farming asset supply stores, the agricultural technology extension department and the village neighbor exchange. Provide technology and service are the main duty of agricultural technology extension department. Its service is authoritative and professional. It is a popular channel for farmers, accounts for 30%. Farming asset supply stores sales fertilizer and pesticide, and at the same time, also teaches the customers operating method. Obtain guidance service by this way accounted for 34%. Friends and relatives of farmers are with strong sense of trust, they often communicate planting and breeding experience with each other. Access to technical information through this way accounted for 20%. In other ways, such as bringing science and technology to the countryside, on-site training, technology demonstration and so on, accounts for 2%.

The analysis above shows that, although there is a strong demand of science and technology information of users, and with modern information equipment, but the acquisition channel is mainly on the traditional face-to-face communication. The farmer advisory information by means of modern information technology is scarce.

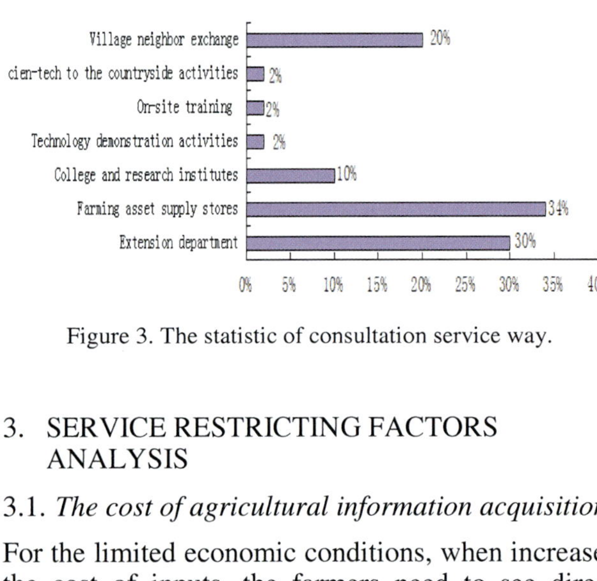

Figure 3. The statistic of consultation service way.

3. SERVICE RESTRICTING FACTORS ANALYSIS

3.1. *The cost of agricultural information acquisition*

For the limited economic conditions, when increases the cost of inputs, the farmers need to see direct benefits. So the cost is an important factor affecting the rural science and technology information service. Investigating on the farmer's investment in information services, it can help to know the farmer's attitude to charging service. It can provide the basic information for the services market operation. The results of the investigation show that (Fig. 4), the farmers who are willing to spend money to buy the information ratio are very low, only accounts for 12.8%. The farmers who will not spend money to buy services account for 30.9%. The majority of farmers that whether to buy or not depend on the role of information and the cost. 59% of the cooperatives are willing to spend money to buy services now. 30% of them can accept paid service later. Cooperation organization is whether to buy information firstly depends on the service role, then the cost of service. Overall, In view of the present situation of our agriculture is decentralized management, counseling services for public welfare continue to be the mainstream. For the part of cooperation organization, can provide for personalized service to explore the paid service.

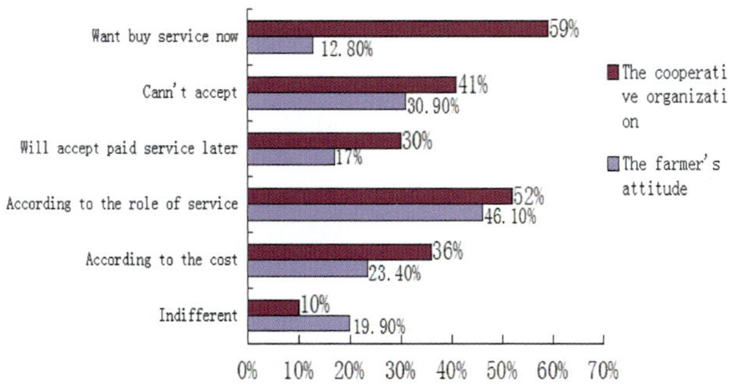

Figure 4. The statistic of paid service attitude.

3.2. *Agricultural scientific technical information quality*

It can be seen from the Fig. 5, the farmer of 24.8% thinks the information from website is timeliness and pertinence, the farmer of 34% thinks that information quality is not high. The agricultural cooperative organization of 21% thinks it is timeliness and pertinence, the agricultural cooperative organizations of 38% think the information quality is not high. Because of the applicability and timeliness of agricultural scientific technical information is affected by varieties, climate, soil, cultivation technology and so on, editing and processing of high quality information is very difficult. It also leads to homogenization easily. So, it must accord to user' personalized demand to provide information in time in season with high quality, in order to meet the needs of agricultural production.

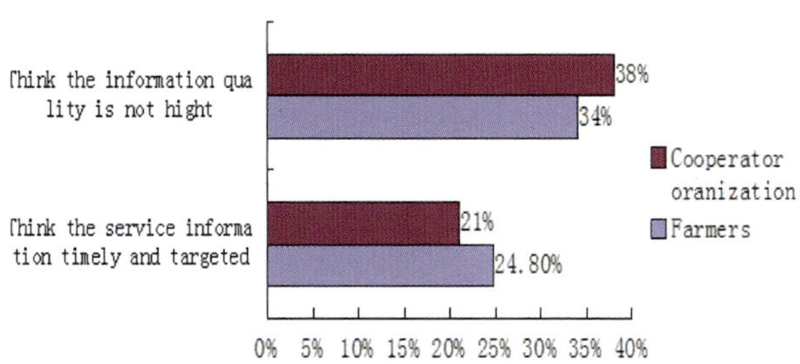

Figure 5. Agricultural scientific technical information.

3.3. *The restricting factor of users himself*

From the Fig. 6, the farmers of 11% think that their ability of information discrimination is poor, 22% of farmers do not know where to find information, 27% of them think their low level cultural lead to the difficult use of information, 65% of them think that the government lacks of full-time information service unit or department. The agricultural cooperative organization of 35.2% thinks their ability of information discrimination is poor, 46.1% don't know where to find information, 47.8% think their low level cultural lead to the difficult use of information,78.3% of them that the government lacks of full-time information service unit or department.

The result show that, on the one hand, for users quality of science and technology, in the face of the large amount of information, they often feel puzzled, it is difficult to find the information they really needed. On the other hand, though lots of agricultural information service site has been set up, farmers still don't know how to find the service to solve their problem. Relevant countermeasures include: firstly, full play the advantages of modern information technology, construct a convenient service system which can access to agricultural science and technology information at any time and any place by users' any terminal equipment. Secondly, develop intelligent agricultural scientific technical information service system to provide automation, convenient and flexible service for them.

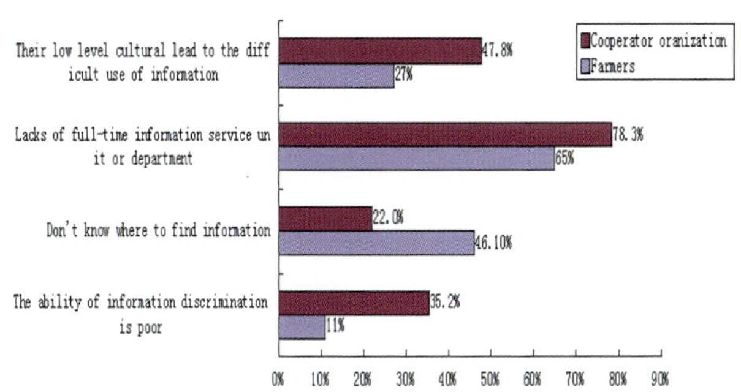

Figure 6. The statistic of the user's own factors effect.

4. STRATEGIES FOR THE SCIENTIFIC TECHNICAL INFORMATION CONSULTING SERVICE DEVELOPMENT ON NEW SITUATION

With the rapid development of information technology and the mobile network, and wide application of big data, cloud computing, internet of things and other emerging technologies, agricultural information service means will be more intelligent [2-3]. It has brought new opportunities and new method for agricultural scientific technical information consulting service.

4.1. *Develop intelligent service by variety of mobile terminal*

Currently, the variety and quantity of the mobile terminal increase rapidly, the mobile network transmission speed is faster, it has promoted the development of many applications, panel computer and mobile phone is no longer merely entertainment tool. They will be applied in the field of education and service in a large scale. Compared with the traditional PC, the panel computer and mobile phone price is lower, and the operation interface is more intuitive and more suitable for farmers to use. Those terminals will gradually penetrate into most of the farmers' hand obviously. So, based on the mobile terminal to develop agricultural scientific technical information consulting service, will promote a new service mode.

4.2. *Provide new service based on agricultural big data*

Agricultural big data are the practice of big data concepts, techniques and methods in the field of agriculture. Agricultural data relate to each link of land turning up, sowing, fertilization, plant protection, harvesting, storage, processing, sales etc. It is the data analysis and mining of cross domain. These data integration, mining and using will play a very important role in the development for modern agriculture [4]. Many current issues in the field of agriculture, such as food security, soil remediation, plant diseases and insect pests forecast and prevention, the adjustment of agricultural structure, agricultural prices, can be provided assist decision-making by the research and application of large data. By analyzing and application of agriculture big data, it can supply a new idea for the agricultural scientific technical information service, and also can provide scientific and technological information support for the development of the agricultural industry.

4.3. *Reduce the cost of counseling service using cloud services*

By the support of cloud computing, schedule and utilize the hardware resource of large capacity storage and computation comprehensively, and massive information resources of text, picture, voice, video, by the way of platform upward movement and service extends downward, Cloud service provides network take and use in time, convenience, low cost service for users. According to agricultural information demand, construct and apply agricultural cloud services platform, and provide public service for users. It can reduce the cost of consulting services, but also greatly enhance the ability of service.

4.4. *Develop standards to improve service quality*

In the process of service, if lack of applicable specifications, it is difficult to guarantee the service effect. Especially, some information is not scientific. Its application will result in agricultural production and farmers suffered losses. According to the demand of agricultural scientific technical information, develop service standards, such as the requirement of information quality, the regulation of counseling service organization, the regulation of service providing process, etc. Establishing a set of scientific, reasonable, level clarity and coordination service standard system, it will promote the healthy development of agricultural scientific technical information counseling services.

4.5. *Explore the service mechanism to promote long-term development*

In view of the weakness of agriculture, most of the information counseling services are public welfare. From the survey above, whether or not will spend money to buy the service, it depends on the function and cost of the service. Therefore, to some users with better economic conditions, provide pertinence, timeliness, personalized information service, and charge service fee through the establishment of membership. For example, can try this way at agricultural stores. Explore the service mechanism to promote long-term development of agricultural scientific technical information consulting service. It will eventually enhance the quality of services by playing the role of the market.

5. ACKNOWLEDGMENTS

The research work was supported by the National Sci-Tech Support Plan "Construction and application of provincial rural information service platform in developed area" (NO. 2014BAD10B02), the young scientist fund of BAAFS: Research on agricultural scientific technical online counseling system based on the knowledge map (NO. QNJJ201534), the innovation fund of BAAFS: Agricultural water-saving technology training and counseling service demonstration project (NO. KJCX20151409). The innovation fund of BAAFS: Development and application of "zhinongtong" APP. The corresponding author is Qingfeng Wei (weiqingfeng201@163.com).

REFERENCES

— [1] Y.S. Shi. Study on modern agricultural information technology and agricultural information counseling services [J]. Jiangsu rural economy. 2011(5):68-69.

— [2] Liu Yuan, Wang Rui-zhi, Yang Ze-lin. Research on development and applications of agricultural internet of things [J]. Guangdong Agricultural Sciences. 2013(23): 174-179.
— [3] Zhao Xing, Liao Guiping, Shi Xiaohui, Chen Cheng, et al. The construction of agricultural information service system which combines the technology of the internet of things and cloud computing [J]. Journal of agricultural mechanization research, 2012(4):142-147.
— [4] Sun Zhong-fu, Du Ke-ming, Zheng Fei-xiang, etc. Perspectives of Research and Application of Big Data on Smart Agriculture [J]. Journal of Agricultural Science and technology. 2013(6):63-71.

Analysis and Improvement of Certificateless Partially Blind Signature Scheme

E.G. Liu*
School of Science, East China Jiaotong University, Nanchang, Jiangxi, China.

X. Wang & H.J. Zhou
School of Science, East China Jiaotong University, Nanchang, Jiangxi, China
**Email: leg_eg@sina.com*

ABSTRACT: The security of the partially blind signature scheme without certificates proposed by He Junjie et al is analyzed, it is found that the scheme can not resist tampering attack on negotiated information. Therefore, proposed a partially blind signature scheme which can resist tampering attack on negotiated information, and the new scheme is proved to be existentially unforgeable against adaptive chosen message in the random oracle model and inv-CDH assumption difficulties.

KEYWORDS: Partially blind signature; Tampering attack on negotiated information; Random oracle model; Existentially unforgeable.

1. INTRODUCTION

The concept of blind signature was proposed in 1982 by Chaum (Chaum, 1983). The so-called blind signa- tures, that is, the signer sign the news or file while he dose not know the content of the file or message. Because of this feature, blind signatures are widely used in electronic payments and electronic voting. However, due to the blind signature is completely blind, the signers did not know the final signature completely, may cause the signature to be used illegally. To solve this problem, in 1996, the concept of partially blind signature was proposed by Abe et al (Abe, M. & Fujisaki E., 1996). The partially blind signature is, the signer and users negotiate the common information in advance, the signer sign the message while the content of message is unknown, and the request can not be illegally tampering with the common information.

The certificateless public key cryptography in 2003 proposed by Al-Riyami et al (Al-Riyami, S. & Paterson, K., 2003), there also a number of signature and encryption schemes appeared (Choi, 2007; Zhang, 2006; Zhang, 2008). In the certificateless cryptography, the private key generation center only generates partially private key, do not know the long-term private key, so this cryptography overcome the problem of certificate management in cryptography with certificate and key escrow in ID-based cryptosystem system. Combined certificateless cryptography with partially blind signature can generate certificateless partially blind signature scheme, in 2008 by Rong's (Rong, 2008) a certificateless partially blind signature was presented, but Yu's (Yu, 2010) pointed out that the signature does not have partial blindness, many certificateless partially blind signature schemes have appeared (Li, 2010; Tang, 2013), He Junjie et al (He, 2014) proposed a certificateless partially blind signature scheme, by analyzing the scheme can not resist tampering attack on common information. An improved certificateless partially blind signature scheme was proposed there, the scheme is proved to be existentially unforgeable against adaptive chosen message.

2. PRELIMINARIES

2.1. *Bilinear pairing*

Step 1: Define: Let G_1 be a cyclic additive group generated by P, whose order is a prime q and G_2 be a cyclic multiplicative group of the same order q.

The bilinear pairing which satisfies the properties: $e: G_1 \times G_1 \to G_2$

(1) Bilinear: $e(aP, bQ) = e(P,Q)^{ab}$, $\forall P,Q \in G_1$, $a,b \in Z_q^*$.

(2) Non-degenerate: There exists $P,Q \in G_1$, such that $e(P,Q) \neq 1$.

(3) Computable: any $P,Q \in G_1$, there is an efficient algorithm to compute $e(P,Q)$.

2.2. *Inverse Diffie-Hellman problem*

Given $aP, P \in G$, a is unknown, computes $a^{-1}P$.

2.3. *Malicious attackers model*

In certificateless signature scheme, there are two types of attackers:

(1) Type 1 attacker: can not know system master key, but you can replace the user's public key;

(2) Type 2 attacker: know the master key system, but can not replace the user's public key.

3. SECURITY ANALYSIS OF HE JUNJIE'S CERTIFICATELESS PARTIALLY BLIND SIGNATURE

3.1. *He Junjie's certificateless partially blind signature*

Step 1: Initialization: Choose bilinear pairing: $G_1 \times G_1 \to G_2$, G_1 be a cyclic additive group generated by P, whose order is a prime q and G_2 be a cyclic multiplicative group of the same order q, computes $g = e(P,P)$; select system master key $s \in_R Z_p^*$, systems public key $P_{pub} = sP$, select secure hash functions $H_1: \{0,1\}^* \to Z_q^*$, $H_2: \{0,1\}^* \times G_1 \to Z_q^*$, $H_3: \{0,1\}^* \to Z_q^*$, system public key P_{pub}, the system parameters $params = \{G_1, G_2, e, q, P, P_{pub}, g, H_1, H_2, H_3\}$, public the system parameters, the system master key is kept secret by the KGC.

Step 2: Secret key generation algorithm: the signer randomly chooses a secret value $x_A \in Z_q^*$.

Step 3: Public key generation: the public key is calculated $X_A = x_A P$, $Y_A = x_A P_{pub}$, $PK_A = (X_A, Y_A)$. Any person can verify whether the public is valid by verifying the equation $e(X_A, P_{pub}) = e(Y_A, P)$.

Step 4: Partial private key generation: the identity ID_A of the signer's and public key (X_A, Y_A) send to the KGC, computes $D_A' = (H_1(ID_A, PK_A) + s)^{-1}P + s(kP)$ and sent to the signer by open channel, the signer computes:

$D_A = D_A' - kP_{pub} = D_A' - s(kP) = (H_1(ID_A, PK_A) + s)^{-1}P$ and verify whether the partial secret key is valid by verifying the equation $e(D_A, H_1(ID_A, PK_A)P + P_{pub}) = g$.

Step 5: Signed protocol: For the message m to be signed, the signer and the user discussion the common information c in advance.

The signer random choose $x \in Z_q^*$, computes $r' = g^x$, sends r' to user B;

The user random choose two elements $\alpha, \beta \in Z_q^*$, computes $\eta = \alpha H_3(c) + \beta$, $r = r'^{\alpha} g^{\eta}$, $h = \alpha^{-1}(\beta + h) \bmod q$, $h' = H_2(m, c, U)$, and sends h to the signer A;

The signer computes $S' = (H_3(c) + x + h)SK_A$, and sends S' to the user B;

The user computes $S = \alpha S'$. This way, the valid signature is (r, S, m, c).

Verifier can verify whether (r, S, m, c) satisfy that the equation $e(S, H_1(ID_A, PK_A)X_A + Y_A) = r^{H_3(c)} g^{h'}$, if satisfy accept the partially blind signature, otherwise rejected.

3.2. *Security analysis*

This scheme was proposed by improving Tang's scheme(Tang, 2013), but it was analyzed to be not safe, the scheme can not resist tampering attack on negotiated information, a requester can change illegally pre-agree common information c into c_1 under the signer does not know circumstances, the specific steps as follows:

The signer random choose $x \in Z_q^*$, and computes $r' = g^x$, sends r' to user;

The user random choose two elements $\alpha, \beta \in Z_q^*$, compute $r = r'^{\alpha H_3(c)} g^{\beta}$, $h = \alpha^{-1}(H_3(c_1)^{-1}h' + \beta)$, and sends h to the signer, $h' = H_2(m, c_1, r)$;

The signer computes $S' = (xH_3(c) + h)SK_A$, and sends S' to the user;

The user computes $S = \alpha H_3(c_1)S'$.

This way, the $\sigma = (S, r, m, c_1)$ is a valid signature. In fact,

$$\begin{aligned}
e(S, H_1(ID_A, PK_A)X_A + Y_A) &= e(\alpha H_3(c_1)S', H_1(ID_A, PK_A)X_A + Y_A) \\
&= e(\alpha H_3(c_1)(xH_3(c) + h)SK_A, H_1(ID_A, PK_A)x_A P + x_A sP) \\
&= e(\alpha H_3(c_1)(xH_3(c) + \alpha^{-1}(H_3(c_1)^{-1}h' + \beta))P, P) \\
&= e((\alpha x H_3(c_1)H_3(c) + h' + H_3(c_1)\beta)P, P) \\
&= g^{\alpha x H_3(c_1)H_3(c) + h' + H_3(c_1)\beta} = r^{H_3(c_1)} g^{h'}
\end{aligned}$$

4. THE NEW CERTIFICATELESS PARTIALLY BLIND SIGNATURE

4.1. *The new scheme*

Step 1: Initialization: Choose bilinear pairing: $G_1 \times G_1 \to G_2$, G_1 be a cyclic additive group generated by P, whose order is a prime q and G_2 be a cyclic multiplicative group of the same order q, computes $g = e(P,P)$; select system master key $s \in_R Z_p^*$, systems public key $P_{pub} = sP$, select secure hash functions

$H_1: \{0,1\}^* \to Z_q^*$, $H_2: \{0,1\}^* \times G_1 \to Z_q^*$, $H_3: \{0,1\}^* \to Z_q^*$, the system public parameters $params = \{G_1, G_2, e, q, P, P_{pub}, g, H_1, H_2\}$, system public key P_{pub}, public the system parameters, the system master key is kept secret by the KGC. A is the signer, B is the user.

Step 2: Secret key generation algorithm: the signer randomly chooses a secret value $x_A \in Z_q^*$ as its long-term private key, the public key is calculated $X_A = x_A P$, $Y_A = x_A P_{pub}$. Any person can verify whether the public is valid by verifying the equation $e(X_A, P_{pub}) = e(Y_A, P)$. The identity ID_A of the signer's and public key (X_A, Y_A) send to the KGC, KGC generation signer's private key $D_A = sH_1(ID_A, X_A, Y_A)$ and sent to the signer, the signer can verify whether the partial secret key is valid by verifying the equation $D_A P = H_1(ID_A, X_A, Y_A)P_{pub}$.

Step 3: Signed protocol: For the message m to be signed, the signer and the user discussion the common information c in advance.

The signer random choose $r_1, r_2 \in Z_q^*$, computes $R_1 = g^{r_1}$, $R_2 = g^{r_2}$, sends (R_1, R_2) to user B;

The user random choose two elements $\alpha, \beta \in Z_q^*$, $U = R_1^{\alpha} R_2^{\alpha} g^{\beta}$, $h' = \alpha^{-1}(\beta + h) \bmod q$, $h = H_2(m, c, U)$, and sends h' to the signer A;

The signer computes $S' = (r_1 + r_2 + h')((H_3(ID_A, c, R_1, R_2) + D_A)x_A)^{-1}P$, and sends S' to the user B;

The user computes $S = \alpha S'$. This way, the (R_1, R_2, U, S, m, c) is a valid signature.

Verification:

verifier can verify whether (R_1, R_2, U, S, m, c) satisfy equation $e(S, H_3(ID_A, c, R_1, R_2)X_A + H_1(ID_A, X_A, Y_A)Y_A) = Ug^h$,

if satisfy accept the partially blind signature, otherwise rejected.

4.2. *Security analysis*

4.2.1. *The new scheme is valid*

$$\begin{aligned}
&e(S, H_3(ID_A, c, R_1, R_2)X_A + H_1(ID_A, X_A, Y_A)Y_A)\\
&= e(\alpha(r_1 + r_2 + \alpha^{-1}(\beta + h))(H_3(ID_A, c, R_1, R_2) + D_A)x_A)^{-1}P,\\
&H_3(ID_A, c, R_1, R_2)x_A P + H_1(ID_A, X_A, Y_A)x_A sP)\\
&= e(\alpha(r_1 + r_2 + h')((H_3(ID_A, c, R_1, R_2) + sH_1(ID_A, X_A, Y_A))x_A)^{-1}P,\\
&H_3(ID_A, c, R_1, R_2)x_A P + H_1(ID_A, X_A, Y_A)x_A sP)\\
&= e(\alpha(r_1 + r_2 + \alpha^{-1}(\beta + h))P, P) = g^{\alpha r_1 + \alpha r_2 + \beta + h} = R_1^{\alpha} R_2^{\alpha} g^{\beta} g^{h}\\
&= Ug^{h}
\end{aligned}$$

4.2.2. Blindness

Given a valid signature (m, c, R_1, R_2, U, S) and any group of partially blind signature signer publishing process retained intermediate variables (r_1, r_2, h', S'), have the following equation:

$$U = R_1^{\alpha} R_2^{\alpha} g^{\beta} \tag{1}$$

$$h' = \alpha^{-1}(\beta + h) \bmod q \tag{2}$$

$$S = \alpha S' \tag{3}$$

By (2) and (3) we can know α, β, $\alpha = \log_{S'} S$, $\beta = h' \log_{S'} S - h$, α, β is uniquely determined. Proved α, β which is determined by the following equation (2) and (3) satisfy the formula (1). Because (m, c, R_1, R_2, U, S) is a valid signature, it is verified to meet the equation:

$$e(S, H_3(ID_A, c, R_1, R_2)X_A + H_1(ID_A, X_A, Y_A)Y_A) = Ug^h,$$
$$h = H_2(m, c, U)$$

also

$$\begin{aligned}
&U = e(S, H_3(ID_A, c, R_1, R_2)X_A + H_1(ID_A, X_A, Y_A)Y_A)g^{-h}\\
&= e(\alpha(r_1 + r_2 + \alpha^{-1}(\beta + h))(H_3(ID_A, c, R_1, R_2) + D_A)x_A)^{-1}P,\\
&H_3(ID_A, c, R_1, R_2)x_A P + H_1(ID_A, X_A, Y_A)x_A sP)g^{-h}\\
&= e(\alpha(r_1 + r_2 + h')((H_3(ID_A, c, R_1, R_2) + sH_1(ID_A, X_A, Y_A))x_A)^{-1}P,\\
&H_3(ID_A, c, R_1, R_2)x_A P + H_1(ID_A, X_A, Y_A)x_A sP)g^{-h}\\
&= e(\alpha(r_1 + r_2 + \alpha^{-1}(\beta + h))P, P)g^{-h} = g^{\alpha r_1 + \alpha r_2 + \beta} = R_1^{\alpha} R_2^{\alpha} g^{\beta}
\end{aligned}$$

So $U = R_1^{\alpha} R_2^{\alpha} g^{\beta}$, proved that α, β which is determined by the following equation (2) and (3) satisfy the formula (1).

Therefore, between the valid signature and an arbitrary set of intermediate variables exist only blind factor α, β. So, even there is an infinite capacity of the signer can not link partially blind signature and signature, so the scheme has partially blinded.

4.2.3. *The new scheme can resist public key replaced attack*

Proof:

Because partial private key $D_A = sH_1(ID_A, X_A, Y_A)$, D_A is the signature for long-term public key X_A, the partial private key is essentially a Schnorr signature, Pointcheval and Stern has proven Schnorr signature scheme is unforgeable in the random oracle model. Therefore, if the replace long-term public key, D_A will change, so the new scheme can resist the public key replace attack.

Because the type two attack are more destructive, we only prove the scheme is not forged under type 2 attack.

4.2.4. *The new scheme is proved to be existentially unforgeable against adaptive chosen message in the random oracle model and inv-CDH assumption difficulties for the type 2 attacker M_2.*

Proof: Suppose M_2 have a non-negligible advantage break this scheme, the following construct an algorithm to solve the inv-CDH problem in probabilistic polynomial time.

For known $P, aP \in G_1$, $a \in Z_p^*$, in order to compute $a^{-1}P$, the algorithm B and M_2 interact, answer the attacker M_2, and asking H_1, H_2, H_3 random oracle, partial secret key inquiry, private inquiry, public inquiry. Interaction is as follows:

(1) System initialization: the algorithm generating parameters $params = \{G_1, G_2, e, p, P, P_{pub}, g, H_1, H_2\}$, the system public key $P_{pub} = sP$, and sends the master secret key s and system public parameters to the attacker M_2. Lists $L_1, L_2, L_3, L_{PK}, L_P, L_S$ are used to deal with the attacker M_2, H_1, H_2, H_3 random oracle inquiry, public key inquiry, partial secret key inquiry, signature inquiry. The table structure of list L_1 is (ID_i, X_i, Y_i, h_{1i}), algorithms B to answer H_1 inquiry by attackers to maintain list L_1; the table structure of list L_2 is (m, c, U, h_{2i}), algorithms B to answer H_2 inquiry by attackers to maintain list L_2; the table structure of list L_3 is $(ID_i, c, R_1, R_2, h_{3i})$, algorithms B to answer H_3 inquiry by attackers to maintain list L_3; the table structure of list L_{PK} is (ID_i, x_i, X_i, Y_i), algorithms B to answer public key queries and secret key queries by attackers to maintain list L_{PK}; the table structure of list L_P is (ID_i, D_i), algorithms B to answer partial private key queries by attackers to maintain list L_P; the table structure of

list L_S is $(ID_i,m,c,R_1,R_2,U,S,h_{2i})$, algorithms B to answer signature queries by attackers to maintain list L_S. Initialize all the tables are empty, assuming targets ID is ID^* for attackers, you can not ask the long-term private key of ID^*, a is used to simulate the long-term private key, corresponding to the public key $X_{ID^*}=aP$, $Y_{ID^*}=aP_{pub}$.

(2) H_1 inquiry: When $H_1(ID_i,X_i,Y_i)$ were asked, if (ID_i,X_i,Y_i,h_{1i}) in the list L_1, then returned h_{1i} to M_2, otherwise B randomly choose $h_{1i}\in Z_q^*$, returned h_{1i} to M_2 and added to the list L_1.

(3) H_2 inquiry: When $H_2(m,c,U)$ were asked, if (m,c,U,h_{2i}) in the list L_2, then returned h_{2i} to M_2, otherwise B randomly choose $h_{2i}\in Z_q^*$, returned h_{2i} to M_2 and added to the list L_2.

(4) H_3 inquiry: When $H_3(ID_i,c,R_1,R_2)$ were asked, if (ID_i,c,R_1,R_2,h_{3i}) in the list L_3, then returned h_{3i} to M_2, otherwise B randomly choose $h_{3i}\in Z_q^*$,returned h_{3i} to M_2 and added to the list L_3.

(5) Public key inquiry: When B receive about the public key inquiry:

(a) when $ID_i\neq ID^*$, if (ID_i,x_i,X_i,Y_i) in the list L_{PK}, send the corresponding value $(X_i Y_i)$ to M_2; otherwise B randomly choose $x_i\in Z_q^*$, computes $X_i=x_iP$, $Y_i=x_iP_{pub}$, added (ID_i,x_i,X_i,Y_i) to the list L_{PK}.

(b) when $ID_i=ID^*$, a is used to simulate the long-term private key, corresponding to the public key $X_{ID^*}=aP$, $Y_{ID^*}=aP_{pub}$, added $(ID^*,\perp,X_{ID^*},Y_{ID^*})$ to the list L_{PK} and return (X_{ID^*},Y_{ID^*}) to M_2.

(6) Partial private key inquiry: When B receive about the partial private key inquiry of ID_i, if (ID_i,D_i) in the list L_P, return D_i to M_2; otherwise B check list L_1 extract h_{1i}, computes $D_i=sH_1(ID_i,X_i,Y_i)$, add (ID_i,D_i) to the list L_P and return D_i to M_2.

(7) Private key inquiry: When B receive about the private key inquiry of ID_i:

(a) when $ID_i\neq ID^*$, if (ID_i,x_i,X_i,Y_i) in the list L_{SK}, return x_i to M_2 ;otherwise, B randomly choose $x_i\in Z_q^*$, computes $X_i=x_iP$, $Y_i=x_iP_{pub}$, then added (ID_i,x_i,X_i,Y_i) to the list L_{PK} and return x_i to M_2.

(b) when $ID_i=ID^*$, the algorithm terminate.

(8) Signature inquiry: When B receive about the signature inquiry of (ID_i,m,c):

(a) when $ID_i\neq ID^*$, algorithm B check list L_{PK}, L_1, L_P, randomly choose $r_1,r_2\in Z_q^*$, computes $R_1=g^{r_1}$, $R_2=g^{r_2}$, return (R_1,R_2) and public (X_i,Y_i) to M_2. M_2 choose blind factor $\alpha,\beta\in_R Z_q^*$, computes $U=R_1^{\alpha}R_2^{\alpha}g^{\beta}$, check list L_2 get $h=H_2(m,c,U)$, computes $h'=\alpha^{-1}(\beta+h)\bmod q$. Then B computes $S'=(r_1+r_2+h')((H_3(ID_A,c,R_1,R_2)+D_A)x_A)^{-1}P$, send S' to M_2. M_2 computes $S=\alpha S'$, so get the partially blind signature (R_1,R_2,U,S) of (ID_i,m,c), added $(ID_i,m,c,R_1,R_2,U,S,h_{2i})$ to the list L_s and return the (R_1,R_2,U,S) to M_2.

(b) when $ID_i=ID^*$, algorithm B check list L_{PK} get $(ID^*,\perp,X_{ID^*},Y_{ID^*})$, and check list L_1 get $H_1(ID^*,X_{ID^*},Y_{ID^*})$, check list L_3 get $H_3(ID^*,c,R_1,R_2,h_{3i})$, randomly choose $h'\in Z_q^*$ and $S\in_R G$, computes $U=e(S,H_3(ID^*,c,R_1,R_2)X_{ID^*}+H_1(ID^*,X_{ID^*},Y_{ID^*})Y_{ID^*})g^{-h'}$, if (m,c,U,h') in the list L_2, choose h',S again, computes U, return (R_1,R_2,U,S) to M_2.

If the algorithm does not terminate, then the attackers M_2 have not been ask for the target user's private key and asks for a signature, M_2 can have non-negligible advantage to produce a valid partially blind signature. According forking lemma, to hash replay M_2, can get two valid partially blind signature $(ID^*,m,c,R_1,R_2,U,S_1,h_1)$ and $(ID^*,m,c,R_1,R_2,U,S_2,h_2)$ on the message m, $h_1\neq h_2$. So :

$e(S_1,H_3(ID^*,c,R_1,R_2)X_{ID^*}+H_1(ID^*,X_{ID^*},Y_{ID^*})Y_{ID^*})=Ug^{h_1}$,

$e(S_2,H_3(ID^*,c,R_1,R_2)X_{ID^*}+H_1(ID^*,X_{ID^*},Y_{ID^*})Y_{ID^*})=Ug^{h_2}$,

have

$e(S_1-S_2,H_3(ID^*,c,R_1,R_2)X_{ID^*}+H_1(ID^*,X_{ID^*},Y_{ID^*})Y_{ID^*})=g^{h_1-h_2}$

where $X_{ID^*}=aP$, $Y_{ID^*}=aP_{pub}$,

$e(S_1-S_2,H_3(ID^*,c,R_1,R_2)aP+H_1(ID^*,aP,aP_{pub})aP_{pub})=g^{h_1-h_2}$

$(S_1-S_2)(H_3(ID^*,c,R_1,R_2)a+H_1(ID^*,aP,aP_{pub})as)=(h_1-h_2)P$

$a^{-1}P=(S_1-S_2)(H_3(ID^*,c,R_1,R_2)+sH_1(ID^*,aP,aP_{pub}))(h_1-h_2)^{-1}$

Therefore, given P and aP, $a\in Z_p^*$ is unknown, algorithm B successfully calculated $a^{-1}P$, inv-CDH problem has been resolved. The new scheme was proved to be existentially unforgeable against adaptive chosen message attack in random oracle model, and its security was reduced to inv-CDH assumption.

5. CONCLUSION

The security of a partially blind signature scheme proposed by He Junjie was analyzed, found that the scheme can not resist tampering common information attack. Thus proposed a new partially blind signature scheme, the signer's public key is bound to the hash function, can resist the public key replace attack, can resist tampering common information attack, and proved that the new scheme was existentially unforgeable against adaptive chosen message attack in random oracle model. The scheme is certificateless partially blind signature, overcome the problem of certificate management in cryptography with certificate and key escrow in ID-based cryptosystem system.

REFERENCES

- [1] Abe, M. & Fujisaki E. 1996. How to date blind signatures. Advances in Cryptology-ASIACRYPT'96: 244-251.
- [2] Al-Riyami, S. & Paterson, K. 2003. Certificateless public key cryptography. Advances in Cryptology- ASIACRYPT 2003. 2894: 452-473.
- [3] Chaum, D. 1983. Blind signatures for untraceable payments. Advance in Cryptology-Crypto'82: 199-203.
- [4] Choi, K. et al. 2007. Efficient certificateless signature schemes. Applied Cryptography and Network Security. 4521: 443-458.
- [5] He, J.J. et al. 2014. Cryptanalysis and improvement of a certificateless partially blind signature scheme. Journal of Xinyang Normal University. 27(2): 439-446.

- [6] Li, M.X. et al. 2010. Efficient certificateless partially blind signature scheme. Computer Engineering and Design. 31(22): 4817-4819.
- [7] Rong, W. J. 2008. Certificateless partially blind signature schemes. Journal of Zhangzhou Normal University (Nat Sci). 21(4): 44-47.
- [8] Yu, D. et al. 2010. New certificateless partially blind signature scheme. Application Research of Computers. 27(11): 4319-4321.
- [9] Tang, P.Z. et al. 2013. Efficient certificateless partially blind signature. Computer Engineering and Design. 34(2): 439-446.
- [10] Zhang, Z.F. et al. 2006. Certificateless public key signature: Security model and efficient construction. Applied Cryptography and Network Security. 3989: 293-308.
- [11] Zhang, L. & Zhang, F.T. 2008. Certificateless signature and blind signature. Journal of Electronics (China): 25(5): 629-635.

A Certificateless Partially Blind Signature Scheme

P.Z. Tang
1. School of Science, East China Jiaotong University, Nanchang 330013, Jiangxi
2. SEC Institute, East China Jiaotong University, Nanchang 330013, Jiangxi

J.F. Yang* & Q.L. Zhang
1. School of Science, East China Jiaotong University, Nanchang 330013, Jiangxi
2. SEC Institute, East China Jiaotong University, Nanchang 330013, Jiangxi
**Email: 909333782@qq.com*

ABSTRACT: The partially blind signature is an extension of the blind signature, which allows signer to include some common information negotiated by signer and the user of requesting signature. An efficient certificateless partially blind signature scheme is constructed. It is based on identity-based signature scheme proposed by Shim .The analysis of its correctness, partial blindness are subsequently presented. The new scheme based on the Computational Diffie-Hellman Problem (CDHP) and CDHP assumption. The new scheme based on the CDHP assumption is proved to be existentially unforgeable for adaptive chosen message and identity attacks in random oracle model. To analyze the performance of the scheme, indicating that the new scheme have more advantage than the majority of the existing partially blind signature scheme.

KEYWORDS: Partially blind signature; bilinear pairing; certificateless; random oracle model; Computational Diffie-Hellman Problem (CDHP);

1. INTRODUTION

The concept of blind signature was first proposed in 1982, the author is the Chaum D (Chaum D. 1983), blind signature is a signature of the signer must meet the property of blindness in the signing process, blindness refers not only to the signer does not know the contents of the information in the process, and the signature can not be traced after the signing by the signer, this feature makes the blind signature has been widely used, especially in the occasions which needs for anonymity, for example, e-cash and e-voting. However, the characteristic of blind signature can not be traced signature has a dual nature, because this advantages of the blindness has become precisely a fatal flaw, and led to the phenomenon of criminal misuse of signatures. 1996, Abe et al (Abe, M. & Fujisaki E. 1996) proposed the concept of the partially blind signature. For the partially blind signature, firstly, it keeps the blindness of the blind signature. Secondly, there is a pre-negotiated public information between the signer and the user, and it allows the signer embedded in the public information in the signing process, such as the time of signature and expiration date information, besides, the public information can not be allowed to deleted or modified illegally. In 2003, Ai-Riyami et al (Al-Riyami, S. & Paterson, K. 2003) proposed a certificateless public key cryptography, so the problem of key escrow in identity-based public key cryptosystem is solved. Subsequently, the certificateless partially blind signature became a very hot topic in public, because the certificateless partially blind signature not only inherited the partially blind signature features, but also maintained the more advantages of the certificateless public key cryptography system. In that case, it has a important role in our practice life. In 2008, the first certifcateless partially blind signature schem e was proposed by Rong weijian (Rong, 2008). Then, Su Wanli et al. (Su & Tan et al. 2009) proposed a provably secure certificateless partially blind signature scheme, In 2009. However, Rong and Su didn't proved strictly about the signature is existentially unforgeable. In 2009, zhang et al. (Zhang) proposed a provably secure certificateless partially blind signature scheme under their defined security model. In recent years, a variety of certificateless partially blind signature scheme (Li & Du, 2010; Yu & Yang et al. 2010; Tang & Li et al. 2013) have been proposed, but most of the papers are based on bilinear pairings cryptosystem, and there exist a problem of public information has been tampered. However, due to the large expenses of the bilinear pairing operation, which is difficult to achieve in real life application of the process. Therefore it is an effective way to reduce the use of bilinear pairings.

On the basis of the identity-based signature scheme which is proposed by Shim (SHIM, 2010), we construct a certificateless partially blind signature scheme. The new scheme only used the bilinear pairing in the verification phase, and computing efficiency relatively have more advantage.

2. PRELIMINARIES

2.1. *Bilinear pairing*

Assuming G_1 is a cyclic additive group, and G_2 is a cyclic multiplicative group, and they have the same order q. The map $e: G_1 \times G_1 \to G_2$ will be called bilinear pairing if it can satisfy the properties as follows:

(1) Bilinear: For any $A, B \in G_1, a, b \in Z_q^*$, such that $e(aA, bB) = e(A, B)^{ab}$.

(2) Non-degenerate: existing $A, B \in G_1$, such that $e(A, B) \neq 1$.

(3) Computability: For all $A, B \in G_1$, there is always an efficient algorithm that can calculate the value of $e(A, B)$.

2.2. *Computational Diffie-Hellman problem*

(1) Computational Diffie-Hellman problem (CDH problem): Given any $P \in G_1$, $x, y \in Z_q^*$, and given xP, yP, computes xyP.

3. A CERTIFICATELESS PARTIALLY BLIND SIGNATURE SCHEME

3.1. *Initialization*

In put the system security parameters 1^k, KGC select the cyclic additive group G_1 and order cyclic multiplicative group G_2, and they have the same order q, and P is a generator of G_1, bilinear pairing $e: G_1 \times G_1 \to G_2$, setting $g = e(P, P)$. KGC selects $s \in Z_q^*$ randomly as the system master key, and the system public key $P_{pub} = sP$, select a strong hash function: $H_1: \{0,1\}^* \to G_1$, $H_2: \{0,1\}^* \times G_1 \to Z_q^*$, $H_3: \{0,1\}^* \to Z_q^*$. The public system parameters: $Params = \{G_1, G_2, q, e, P, P_{pub}, g, H_1, H_2, H_3\}$.

3.2. *Key generation*

(1) Secret value selection: The signer A selects $x_A \in Z_q^*$ as his secret value.

(2) Partial public key generation: The signer A use his secret value to compute $P_A = x_A P$ as his partial public key.

(3) Partial private key generation: The signer A sends his identity ID_A and his partial public key P_A to KGC. And KGC computes $Q_A = H_1(ID_A, P_A)$, $D_A = sQ_A$ after receiving ID_A and P_A, and selects D_A as the signer's partial private key, then sends it to A.

(4) Whole private key generation: The signer receives the partial private key from KGC, then he can compute $S_A = x_A D_A$ based on his secret value x_A and the partial private key D_A, and regard S_A as the whole private key.

(5) Whole public key generation: The signer A computes $Q_A = H_1(ID_A, P_A)$ firstly, and let $PK_A = (P_A, R_A)$, and regard PK_A as his whole public key, where, $R_A = x_A Q_A$.

3.3. *Signature protocol*

Let us suppose the message m will be signed, regarding $share$ as the pre-negotiated public information, the signer A and user B are interaction for the message m to be signed, the signature process is as follows:

(1) Commitment: The signer A selects $r \in Z_q^*$ randomly, computing $K = rP$, sending K to the user B.

(2) Blindness: After the user B receiving K from A, he selects $\alpha, \beta \in Z_q^*$ randomly, computing $K_1 = \alpha K + \beta P$, $h = H_2(ID_B, m, share)$, $h_1 = \alpha h$, and sending h_1 to the signer A.

(3)Signing: After the signer A receiving h_1 from B, computing $V = (h_1 r + H_3(share))P_{pub} + S_A$, and sending V to the user B.

(4) Stripping: After the user B receiving V from A, computing $V_1 = V + \beta h P_{pub}$, such that get the partially blind signature $\sigma = (K_1, V_1)$ for the message $(m, share)$.

(5) Verification: After the verifier receiving the partially blind signature $\sigma = (K_1, V_1)$, computing $h = H_2(ID_B, m, share)$ firstly, then verifying whether the equation $e(V_1, P) = e(hK_1 + H_3(share)P + R_A, P_{pub})$ is established, if set up, accept the signature, or refuse.

4. SECURITY ANALYSIS

4.1. *The correctness and general safety of the scheme*

Theorem 1: The correctness of the proposed certificateless partially blind signature scheme can be verified.

Prove:

$$\begin{aligned} e(V_1, P) &= e(V + \beta h P_{pub}, P) \\ &= e((h_1 r + H_3(share))P_{pub} + S_A + \beta h P_{pub}, P) \\ &= e(h_1 rsP + H_3(share)sP + x_A D_A + \beta h P_{pub}, P) \\ &= e(\alpha hrsP + H_3(share)sP + x_A sQ_A + \beta hsP, P) \\ &= e(\alpha hrP + H_3(share)P + x_A Q_A + \beta hP, P_{pub}) \\ &= e(\alpha hrP + H_3(share)P + x_A Q_A + \beta hP, P_{pub}) \\ &= e(\alpha hK + H_3(share)P + R_A + \beta hP, P_{pub}) \\ &= e(h(\alpha K + \beta P) + H_3(share)P + R_A, P_{pub}) \\ &= e(hK_1 + H_3(share)P + R_A, P_{pub}) \end{aligned}$$

As is show above, the correctness of the proposed certificateless partially blind signature scheme can be verified.

Theorem 2: The proposed certificateless partially blind signature scheme meets partially blindness.

Prove: Given a valid signature $(m, share, K_1, V_1)$, and every group intermediate variables (r, K, h_1, V) retained in the partially blind signature process, next, only need to prove the existence of the unique blind factor (α,β), such that, $(m, share, K_1, V_1)$ map to (r, K, h_1, V). Because of:

$$K_1 = \alpha K + \beta P \quad (1)$$

$$h_1 = \alpha h \quad (2)$$

$$V_1 = V + \beta h P_{pub} \quad (3)$$

By equation (2) can be calculated only $\alpha = h_1 h^{-1}$, and Into (1) can be calculated and obtained only $\beta = \log_P(K_1 - \alpha K)$, next, verifying the unique blind factor (α,β) can determine equation (3).

Because a valid signature must satisfy the verified equation: $e(V_1, P) = e(hK_1 + H_3(share)P + R_A, P_{pub})$, where, $h = H_2(ID_B, m, share)$, and meeting $V = (h_1 r + H_3(share))P_{pub} + S_A$, So:

$$\begin{aligned}
& e(V + \beta h P_{pub}, P) \\
&= e((h_1 r + H_3(share))P_{pub} + S_A + \beta h P_{pub}, P) \\
&= e(h_1 rsP + H_3(share)sP + x_A D_A + \beta h P_{pub}, P) \\
&= e(\alpha hrsP + H_3(share)sP + x_A sQ_A + \beta hsP, P) \\
&= e(\alpha hrP + H_3(share)P + x_A Q_A + \beta hP, P_{pub}) \\
&= e(\alpha hrP + H_3(share)P + x_A Q_A + \beta hP, P_{pub}) \\
&= e(\alpha hK + H_3(share)P + R_A + \beta hP, P_{pub}) \\
&= e(h(\alpha K + \beta P) + H_3(share)P + R_A, P_{pub}) \\
&= e(hK_1 + H_3(share)P + R_A, P_{pub}) \\
&= e(V_1, P)
\end{aligned}$$

As is show above: $V_1 = V + \beta h P_{pub}$, I.e. only blind factor obtained from (1) and (2) by the simultaneous equation can determine (3). Therefore, even if the signer has unlimited computing power, nor make his signature and the signature process get linked, that is, the proposed certificateless partially blind signature scheme meets partially blindness.

4.2. *Provably secure under the random oracle model*

The paper (Al-Riyami, S. & Paterson, K. 2003) has defined two types of attackers in certificateless cryptography:

Type 1 (A_I): A_I can replace the user's public key, but can not know system master key;

(2) Type 2 (A_{II}): A_{II} can get the master key system, but can not replace the user's public key.

Because A_{II} has more attack power, only to prove that the certificateless partially blind signature scheme is existentially unforgeable for adaptive chosen message and identity attacks proposed under A_{II} attack, the method of this prove is similar to lemma 2 in the security model (Tang & Li et al. 2013).

Theorem 3: For type 2 A_{II}, the new scheme is proved to be existentially unforgeable for adaptive chosen message and identity attacks in random oracle model.

Prove: Assuming the existence of probabilistic polynomial time algorithm attacker A_{II}, C is a challenger to solve the CDH problem, an example is given, any known $P, xP, yP \in G_1$, unknown $x, y \in Z_q^*$, calculating $xyP \in G_1$, C can successfully forge a valid signature with a non-negligible probability ε, the following construct a challenge algorithm C to solve the CDH problem.

Challenger algorithm C and attacker algorithm A_{II} interact with the game, in the process, attacker A_{II} can ask H_1, H_2, H_3, the public key, secret key and signature polynomial limited many times. Where, H_1, H_2, H_3 is the random oracle, C can maintain the appropriate list $L_1, L_2, L_3, L_{PK}, L_{SK}$, L_{sig} to respond to the inquiry of A_{II}, and initialize all maintenance list is empty before the game starts. Game interaction is as follows:

(1) System Setup: the algorithm C generates system parameters: $Params = \{G_1, G_2, q, e, P, P_{pub}, g, H_1, H_2, H_3\}$, and sends them to the attacker A_{II}, the system public key $P_{pub} = yP$, where, y is used to simulate the system master key.

(2) H_1 inquiry: C selects k, $0 \le k \le q_{PK}$ randomly, identity $ID^* = ID_k$, and the corresponding user's public key is $PK_k = a_k P$, a_k is used to simulate the user's secret value. When C receives the $H_1(ID_i, P_i)$ inquiry from A_{II}, if (ID_i, P_i) has already exists in the list L_1, simply returns the corresponding value Q_{ID_i}, otherwise:

(a) If $i = k$, C choose $a_k \in Z_q^*$, let $a_k = b$; $Q_{ID^*} = bP$.

(b) if $i \ne k$, C choose $a_i \in Z_q^*$, let $Q_{ID_i} = a_i P$. Returns Q_{ID_i} to A_{II}, and adds (ID_i, P_i, Q_{ID_i}) to the list L_1.

(3) H_2 inquiry: When C receives $H_2(ID_i, m_i, share_i, K_{1i})$ inquiry from A_{II}, if $(ID_i, m_i, share_i, K_{1i})$ has already exists in the list L_2, simply return the corresponding value h_i to A_{II}, otherwise, selects $h_i \in Z_q^*$ randomly and returns to A_{II}, and adds $(ID_i, m_i, share_i, K_{1i})$ to the L_2.

(4) H_3 inquiry: When C receives $H_3(share_i)$ inquiry about the identity (ID_i, PK_i). if $(share_i)$ has already exists in the list L_3, then make $h_{3i} = H_3(share_i)$ directly return to A_{II}, otherwise, selects $h_{3i} \in Z_q^*$ randomly and return it to A_{II}, and adds to the list L_3.

(5) Public key inquiry: When C receives the public inquiry about the identity (ID_i, PK_i) from A_{II}:

(a) If $i \ne k$, C retrieves the list L_{PK} for the existence of (ID_i, P_i, R_i, x_i) firstly, if not exist, selects x_i randomly (provided that the H_1 inquiry about identity ID_i has been conducted), getting Q_{ID_i}, then calculates $P_i = x_i P, R_i = x_i Q_{IDi}$ and adds (ID_i, P_i, R_i, x_i) to L_{PK}, then returns (P_i, R_i) to A_{II}.

(b). If $i = k$, let $x_k = x$, such that $P_{ID^*} = xP, R_{ID^*} = xQ_{ID^*}$, C make (P_k, R_k) return directly to A_{II}.

(6) Secret key inquiry: When C receives the secret key inquiry about the identity ID_i from A_{II} (provided that the H_1 inquiry about identity ID_i has been conducted):

(a) If $i \ne k$, C searches for the list L_{PK}, if find appropriate (ID_i, P_i, R_i, x_i), takes advantage of x_i and calculate $S_i = x_i y Q_{ID_i}$, and returns it to A_{II}, otherwise, selects x_i, such that $P_i = x_i P, R_i = x_i Q_{ID_i}$, and adds (ID_i, P_i, R_i, x_i) to the list L_{PK}, and computing $S_i = x_i y Q_{ID_i}$, and returns S_i to A_{II}.

(b). If $i = k$, the algorithm terminates immediately.

(7) Signature inquiry: When C receives the signature inquiry about the identity $(ID_i, m_i, share_i)$ from A_{II}, C responds to the signature inquiry from A_{II} by maintaining the list L_{sig}.

(a) If $i \neq k$, C searches for the list L_1 firstly, getting Q_{ID_i}. Searches for the list L_3, getting h_{3i}. Searches for the list L_{PK}, getting (P_i, R_i, x_i). The challenger C selects $r_i, h_i \in_R Z_q^*$ randomly, calculating $K_{1i} = r_i P - (h_{3i} P + R_i) h_i^{-1}$, if $(m_i, share_i, K_{1i}, h_i)$ has already existed in the list L_2, then re-selects $r_i, h_i \in_R Z_q^*$ randomly, and calculates K_{1i}. Calculates $V_{1i} = r_i h_i P_{pub}$, and finally, transmits $\sigma(ID_i, m_i, share_i) = (K_{1i}, V_{1i})$ to A_{II} and adds it to the list L_{sig}.

All of the signature query response from C is valid, in fact:

$$\begin{aligned} e(V_{1i}, P) &= e(r_i h_i P_{pub}, P) \\ &= e(r_i h_i P, P_{pub}) \\ &= e(h_i (K_{1i} + (h_{3i} P + R_i) h_i^{-1}), P_{pub}) \\ &= e(h_i K_{1i} + h_{3i} P + R_i, P_{pub}) \end{aligned}$$

(b) If $i = k$, the algorithm terminates immediately.

(8) Signature forgery: If the challenger algorithm C does not terminate, then the attacker A_{II}, in the conditions of being absence of secret key inquiry about ID^* and signature inquiry about $(ID^*, m^*, share^*)$, through a limited inquiries many times, can output a valid forged signature $\sigma = (ID^*, m^*, share^*, K_1, V_1)$ for a input message $(m^*, share^*)$ with a non-negligible probability ε. According forking lemma (D. Pointcheval, J.Stern), H_2 inquiry is going to be forked (specific method in Ref. (D. Pointcheval, J.Stern)), by making A_{II} hash replay, C can get two valid signatures of the message $(m^*, share^*)$, respectively $(ID^*, m^*, share^*, K_1, V_{11}, h_1)$ and $(ID^*, m^*, share^*, K_1, V_{12}, h_2)$. Where, h_1, h_2 is the answering inquiries about the random oracle H_2, where $h_1 \neq h_2$, the answer of the random oracle H_1 inquiry about identity ID^* is: $Q_{ID^*} = bP$, h_3 is the answering inquiries about the random oracle H_3, Then:

$$e(V_{11}, P) = e(h_1 K_1 + h_3 P + R_{ID^*}, P_{pub}) \tag{4}$$

$$e(V_{12}, P) = e(h_2 K_1 + h_3 P + R_{ID^*}, P_{pub}) \tag{5}$$

By (4):

$$V_{11} = y(h_1 K_1 + h_3 P + x Q_{ID^*}) \tag{6}$$

By (5):

$$V_{12} = y(h_2 K_1 + h_3 P + x Q_{ID^*}) \tag{7}$$

Simultaneous (6) (7):

$$h_2 V_{11} - h_1 V_{12} = (h_3 P_{pub}(h_2 - h_1) + xybP(h_2 - h_1)),$$ where, $R_{ID^*} = xP, Q_* = bP, P_{pub} = yP$, get: $xyP = (h_2 V_{11} - h_1 V_{12}) b^{-1} (h_2 - h_1)^{-1} - h_3 b^{-1} P_{pub}$.

In summary, given any $P \in G_1, x, y \in Z_q^*$, known xP, yP, calculating and getting xyP, so the CDH problem is solved, so the scheme based on the $CDHP$ assumption is proved to be existentially unforgeable for adaptive chosen message and identity attacks in random oracle model.

5. PEFORMANCE ANALYSIS

In the general scheme, the relatively high amount of computation: bilinear pairing operation, the scalar multiplication operation in G_1, and special hash function "MapToPoint". In this paper, ing P, M and H to represent them in the calculation. Other computational negligible. In the following table, Su (Su &Tan et al. 2009) and Zhang (Zhang & Zhong, 2011) compared with the scheme in the amount of calculation, the results show that this scheme relative have more advantage.

Table 1. This scheme compared to other scheme in computation.

Scheme	Signing	Verifying	Total computation
this scheme	$5M$	$2M + 2P$	$7M + 2P$
Su	$10M$	$2M + 3P$	$12M + 3P$
Zhang	$3M + 2P + 2H$	$2P + 2H$	$3M + 4P + 4H$

6. CONCLUSION

An efficient certificateless partially blind signature scheme is constructed. It is based on identity-based signature scheme proposed by Shim. And the analysis of its correctness, partial blindness are subsequently presented. The new scheme based on the CDHP assumption is proved to be existentially unforgeable for adaptive chosen message and identity attacks in random oracle model. Analyze the performance of the scheme, from the Table 1 to know that our scheme relative have more advantage than the existing majority partially blind signature scheme.

REFERENCES

- [1] Chaum D. 1983. Blind signatures for untraceable payment [J]. Advances in Cryptology Proceedings of Crypto, (3): 199-203.
- [2] Abe, M. & Fujisaki E. 1996. How to date blind signatures [C]. LNCS1163: ASIACRYPT'96 Springer-Verlag, 244-251.

- [3] Al-Riyami, S. & Paterson, K. 2003. Certificateless public key cryptography. Advances in Cryptology - ASIACRYPT 2003. 2894: 452-473.
- [4] Rong, W. J. 2008. Certificateless partially blind signature schemes. Journal of Zhangzhou Normal University (Nat Sci). 21(4): 44-47.
- [5] Su W.L. & Tan S. C et al. 2009. Certificateless partially blind signature [J]. Jilin University (Engineering Science), 39 (4): 1094-1098.
- [6] Zhang L. & Zhang F.T. Certificateless partially blind signatures [C], Proc of the 1st International Conference on Information Science and Engineering. Washington DC:IEEE Computer Society: 2883-2886.
- [7] Li M. X. & Du G. H. 2010. Efficient certificateless partially blind signature scheme [J] Computer Engineering and Design, 31 (22): 4817-4819.
- [8] Yu D. & Yang Y. et al. 2010. New certificateless partially blind signature scheme [J]. Application Research of Computers, 27 (11): 4319-4321.
- [9] Tang P. Z. & Li X. X et al. 2013. Efficient and safe certificateless partially blind signature [J] Computer Engineering and Design, 34 (2): 439-446.
- [10] SHIM K A. 2010. An ID-based aggregate signature scheme with constant pairing computations [J]. The journal of Systems and Software, 83(10): 1873-1880.
- [11] D. Pointcheval, J. Stern. Security Proofs for Signatures, LNCS 1070, Advances in Cryptology: Proc. Eurocrypt'96, Spring, pp. 387-398.
- [12] Zhang X. P. & Zhong C., 2011. Efficient without trusted private key generator partially blind signature scheme [J] Computer Applications, 31 (4): 992-995.

An Improved User Anonymity-Preserving Biometric-based Multi-server Authenticated Key Agreement Scheme Using Mobile Device

Q. Jing
Department of Computing, Liaoning Petrochemical College, Liaoning Province, China
Email: quanjing198009@163.com

ABSTRACT: Authentication in multi-server environment plays an important role in distributed systems. Multi-server authenticated key agreement scheme allows users to register only once, and then access multiple services with session key establishment. However, security and privacy are crucial issues to guarantee identity authentication, data confidentiality and participant privacy. In this paper, we cryptanalyze Mishra et al.'s 'A secure user anonymity-preserving biometric-based multi-server authenticated key agreement scheme using smart cards', and point out that their scheme is vulnerable to session key compromised attack by insider curious service servers, and user behavior traced attack by common malicious attackers. In order to remedy the above weaknesses, we propose an improved scheme to enhance the security guarantee and privacy protection. Our improvement introduces public key for service servers to safeguard user identity and session key freshness. It not only remains the merits of the original scheme, but also achieves more security and privacy requirements. Finally the analysis shows that our improved scheme is more practical, but there is a tradeoff between security/privacy and performance.

KEYWORDS: Authentication; Security; Privacy; Multi-server; Mobile device.

1. INTRODUCTION

With the fast development of distributed computing and networks, it is more and more convenient to access multi-servers anytime and anywhere to obtain subscribed services with mobile device. However, security and privacy issues are concerned with the participants in distributed systems. As a common example, when a user wants to access multi-servers, the identity of the user must be authenticated by the remote server at first, and then the server grants specific access permissions according to his/her roles. It is expected that the user can be authenticated securely and authorized appropriately, while users' privacy can be preserved without compromising. In order to resolve these problems, access control mechanism, which is responsible for data assets and access privileges, is employed to guarantee system security and protect user privacy. In the access control mechanism, authentication is the first and most important defense line to detect illegal access and prevent hostile attack. Therefore, authentication method in multi-server environment becomes an important research subject.

Authentication in multi-server environment [1,2] has been studied for last decades, but there are still several security and privacy drawbacks [3-6]. In 2014, Chuang and Chen [7] proposed an anonymous multi-server authenticating key agreement scheme based on trust computing using smart cards, password, and biometrics. Their scheme is lightweight using only the nonce and a hash function. They claimed that their scheme not just supports multi-server environments but also achieves many security requirements. Nevertheless, Mishra et al. [8] pointed out that the scheme in [7] fails to protect denial-of-service attack, and cannot resist stolen smart card attack which causes the user's impersonation attack and server spoofing attack. In order to overcome these security flaws, Mishra et al. also proposed a secure user anonymity-preserving biometric-based multi-server authenticated key agreement scheme using smart cards. They claimed that their scheme is secure against carious attacks including the attacks found in [7]. In addition, the AVISPA simulation shows that their scheme is secure against replay and man-in-the-middle attacks.

However in both schemes [7] and [8], they assume that the multiple authorized servers fully trust each other. They also explained this assumption from two aspects: business (Cooperation Agreements, CA) and hardware (Trusted Computing, TC). Whereas the cooperated multiple servers can honestly execute the protocol details and never deceive the other participants in the system, but they are indeed curious about the contents of communication between users and the other servers. In details, a curious server can recover the session keys shared between users and the other servers, and decrypt their communication messages. In this paper, we consider the insider servers are honest but curious, and then cryptanalyze the scheme in [8] to show that curious servers can obtain the messages encrypted by session keys. Moreover, the scheme [8] provides only identity anonymity but cannot achieve untraceability. The adversaries can track the static information in the login messages, and then analyze specific user's behavioral habits and historical records of his/her location to compromise user privacy. In order to prevent such situations from happening, we also propose an improved scheme based upon the schemes in [7] and [8] to enhance the security guarantee and privacy protection.

2. CRYPTANALYSIS

This section describes the security risks in Mishra et al.'s scheme [8]. The detailed description of their scheme can be referred to the original literature [8], we omit its review in this paper due to space limitation.

2.1. *Session key compromised attack*

In this section, we introduce a more secure requirement about session key. The session key should be kept secure between the participants, and any other unauthorized parties cannot reveal it. Assume that the application servers are honest but curious, although Mishra et al.'s [8] scheme inherits the assumption of authorized servers fully trust each other in [7]. Our assumption is reasonable because all the service providers are greedy, and they always want to get more and more benefits and try to do everything without being detected.

According to server registration phase, the authorized application servers S_j and S_k share a common key PSK using the Key Exchange Protocol (IKEv2) [10], where $j \neq k$ and S_k is a curious server. Then S_k can compromise the session key $SK_{ji} = SK_{ij}$ shared between U_i and S_j by executing the following steps, and further decrypts the subsequent communication messages.

1. S_k eavesdrops the communication flows between U_i and S_j, and obtains the messages $Z_i = PSK \oplus A_i$, $M_1 = h(PSK) \oplus n_1$, $M_2 = ID_i \oplus h(n_1 \| B_i)$, $M_3 = h(ID_i \| n_1 \| B_i)$, SID_j, $M_4 = n_2 \oplus h(ID_i \| n_1)$, $M_5 = h(SK_{ji} \| n_1 \| n_2)$, $M_6 = h(SK_{ij} \| n_2 \| n_1)$.
2. S_k computes $B_i^* = h(A_i) = h(Z_i \oplus PSK)$, $n_1^* = M_1 \oplus h(PSK)$, $ID_i^* = M_2 \oplus h(n_1^* \| B_i^*)$, $n_2^* = M_4 \oplus h(ID_i^* \| n_1^*)$, $SK = h(ID_i^* \| SID_j \| B_i^* \| n_1^* \| n_2^*)$.
3. S_k verifies whether the following equations $M_3 \stackrel{?}{=} h(ID_i^* \| n_1^* \| B_i^*)$, $M_5 \stackrel{?}{=} h(SK \| n_1^* \| n_2^*)$, $M_6 \stackrel{?}{=} h(SK \| n_2^* \| n_1^*)$ hold. If the equations hold, then S_k confirms the session key $SK = SK_{ij} = SK_{ji}$ between U_i and S_j.

Furthermore, S_k can leak more secure communication credentials, e.g., ID_i, n_1, n_2, SK, to the attackers who want to pay for them and acquire more sensitive information by data mining. However, it is difficult to distinguish the one who compromisesthe sensitive information exactly. Because every service server has the ability (PSK) to obtain the same information as S_j and S_k, all the authorized servers have the same possibility to be the curious server. Therefore, S_k could be a malicious attack to compromise sensitive data (not only the session key, but also user identity and the contexts of communications) in the system without being detected.

2.2. *User behavior traced attack*

In this section, we discuss a higher privacy level: untraceability. In Mishra et al.'s scheme [8], user identity can be hidden in M_2, but Z_i as an alias is always the same in the login phase. Although their scheme achieves user anonymity, the curious servers and malicious attackers can still leak users' privacy (e.g., behavioral habits and historical movements) by data mining or network tracing. For instance, the curious server S_k can recover ID_i in step 2 of section 2.1, and acquire the contents of their communications. Then S_k can further analyze user's interests, health, businesses and officials. For another case, the malicious attackers could trace back some private information about user's location, tendency, and service provider's advantages. Therefore, Z_i is the only tag identifier which can help to erode privacy by the malicious attackers.

3. IMPROVEMENT

In this section, we present an improved scheme to enhance security and privacy protection mentioned in section 2. There are also five phases in our improvement: server registration phase, user registration phase, login phase, authentication phase, and password change phase. For the sake of simplicity, we are only going to describe our modified phases which are different from Mishra et al.'s scheme [8], including server registration phase, login phase, authentication phase. In other words, user registration phase and password change phase are as the same as the original scheme in [8], and we omit repeating their descriptions.

3.1. *Server registration phase*

S_j sends the RC an application server registration request if it would like to become an authorized service server. Then, RC replies with the key PSK to S_j via the Internet Key Exchange Protocol version 2 (IKEv2) [10]. Moreover, S_j should also make its public key $Y_j = g^{y_j}$ available for all users, and keep its secret key y_j private by itself. In this phase, S_j's public key is our modification, which is different from the original scheme.

3.2. *Login phase*

When U_i wants to login S_j, he/she first inputs ID_i and PW_i, and also imprints biometric BIO_i at the sensor of mobile device. Then MD_i performs the following steps to generate login request.

1. MD_i computes $N_i = N \oplus H(BIO_i)$, and then verifies whether the condition $V = h(ID_i \| N_i \| PW_i)$ holds. If the verification does not hold, MD_i terminates this procedure.
2. MD_i recovers $W_1 = h(PW_i \| N_i), W_2 = h(ID_i \oplus N_i), B_i = X_i \oplus W_1$, $h(PSK) = Y_i \oplus W_2$.
3. MD_i generates a random nonce $n_1 \in Z_p^*$, and computes $M_0 = g^{n_1}$, $M_1 = Y_j^{n_1} \oplus Z_i \oplus h(PSK)$, $M_2 = ID_i \oplus h(Y_j^{n_1} \| B_i)$, $M_3 = h(ID_i \| Y_j^{n_1} \| B_i)$.
4. MD_i finally sends the login request $\{M_0, M_1, M_2, M_3\}$ to S_j via a public channel.

3.3. *Authentication phase*

Upon receiving the login request, MD_i and S_j executes the following interaction steps to authenticate each other and exchange a session key.

1. S_j computes $Z_i = M_1 \oplus M_0^{y_j} \oplus h(PSK), B_i = h(A_i) = h(Z_i \oplus PSK), ID_i = M_2 \oplus h(M_0^{y_j} \| B_i)$.
2. S_j verifies whether the equation $M_3 \overset{?}{=} h(ID_i \| M_0^{y_j} \| B_i)$ holds. If it is valid, S_j authenticates U_i successfully, them generates a random nonce $n_2 \in Z_p^*$, and computes the session key $SK_{ji} = h(ID_i \| SID_j \| B_i \| M_0^{n_2})$.
3. S_j computes $M_4 = g^{n_2}, M_5 = h(SK_{ji} \| M_0 \| M_4)$, and sends $\{SID_j, M_4, M_5\}$ to U_i for mutual authentication.
4. After receiving the authentication request, U_i computes $SK_{ij} = h(ID_i \| SID_j \| B_i \| M_4^{n_1})$, and them verifies whether the condition $M_5 = ?h(SK_{ij} \| M_0 \| M_4)$ holds. If it holds, U_i successfully authenticates S_j.
5. U_i computes $M_6 = h(SK_{ij} \| M_4 \| M_0)$ and sends back $\{M_6\}$ to S_j.
6. Upon receiving M_6, S_j verifies whether it is valid through comparing $M_6 = ?h(SK_{ji} \| M_4 \| M_0)$. If it is invalid, S_j terminates the current communication session; otherwise, authentication with key agreement scheme is successfully finished.

Finally, U_i and S_j share a session key $SK_{ij} = SK_{ji}$ without compromising it to any others.

4. ANALYSIS

In this section, we analyze our modification in the aspects of security and performance.

4.1. *Security analysis*

Our lightweight modification introduce application server's private/public key and discrete logarithm problem to enhance the security and privacy protection. The detailed effects of our introductions are embodied in the following roles.

(1) User behavior traced attack can be resisted in our scheme, because there is not static information in the transactions any more. In details, all the transmitted messages $M_0 = g^{n_1}$, $M_1 = Y_j^{n_1} \oplus Z_i \oplus h(PSK)$, $M_2 = ID_i \oplus h(Y_j^{n_1} \| B_i)$, $M_3 = h(ID_i \| Y_j^{n_1} \| B_i)$, $M_4 = g^{n_2}$, $M_5 = h(SK_{ji} \| M_0 \| M_4)$, $M_6 = h(SK_{ij} \| M_4 \| M_0)$ are dynamic due to nonce n_1 and n_2. Two random numbers are private for their generators respectively, and they are unknown to any others because of discrete logarithm problem. In addition, discrete logarithm problem helps to hidden user identity ID_i in M_2, only the specific participant who knows n_1, B_i or y_j, B_i can recover it. Moreover, B_i is protected by n_1, PSK or y_j, PSk, that is to say nobody but U_i or S_j can recover it. As a result, user behavior

cannot be traced by insider curious service servers or common malicious attackers.

(2) Session key compromised attack can be resisted in our scheme. In our scheme, the session key shared between S_j and U_i is computed as $SK = h(ID_i \| SID_j \| B_i \| g^{n_1 n_2})$, it is secure under the following reasons. First, the identity of U_i is protected by n_1, B_i or y_j, B_i, thus anybody who does not know these secret values cannot reveal ID_i from M_2. Secondly, $B_i = X_i \oplus W_1 = h(A_i) = h(M_1 \oplus M_0^{y_j} \oplus h(PSK) \oplus PSK)$ can be recovered by the participants who knows $W_1 = h(PW_i \| N_i)$, A_i or y_j, PSK. In fact, only U_i, RC and S_j could compute B_i with their private information respectively. More important, our scheme can protect session key with forward secrecy, because authenticated Diffie-Hellman is introduced and discrete logarithm problem helps to guarantee the security of session key form being compromising by any other unauthorized parties. Therefore, our scheme protects the session key with forward secrecy, and avoids session key compromised attack.

4.2. *Performance analysis*

In this section, we analyze the performance of our scheme through comparing it with related schemes [7,8,11] in the aspects of security, computation, storage and communication.

Table 1. Comparison of security feature.

F	[7]	[8]	[11]	Ours	F	[7]	[8]	[11]	Ours
S1	●	●	●	●	S7	●	●	●	●
S2	●	●	●	●	S8	●	●	●	●
S3	○	●	●	●	S9	○	○	●	●
S4	○	●	●	●	S10	○	○	●	●
S5	○	●	●	●	S11	○	○	●	●
S6	○	●	●	●					

- S1: Mutual Authentication
- S2: Session Key Exchange
- S3: Three Factor Security
- S4: User Impersonation Attack Resistance
- S5: Server Spoofing Attack Resistance
- S6: Man-in-the-Middle Attack Resistance
- S7: Anonymity
- S8: Privileged Insider Attack Resistance
- S9: Untraceability
- S10: Session Key Compromising Attack Resistance
- S11: Forward Secrecy of Session Key

Table 1 shows that the scheme in [11] and our modification achieve the same security requirements, which are more secure than the schemes in [7] and [8]. Our scheme not only achieves the common security requirements, but also provides the following features: untraceability, session key compromising attack resistance and forward secrecy. It enhances the security of session key by Diffie-Hellman key exchange mechanism, and protects user privacy through dynamic login request without static login identity.

Table 2. Comparison of Computation Cost

Participant	[7]	[8]	[11]	Ours
U_i	$7T_h$	$9T_h$	$7T_h+3T_{me}$	$8T_h+3T_{me}$
S_j	$8T_h$	$7T_h$	$6T_h+3T_{me}$	$5T_h+3T_{me}$
RC	-	-	$9T_h+2T_{me}$	-
Total	$15T_h$	$16T_h$	$22T_h+8T_{me}$	$13T_h+6T_{me}$

$*T_h$: complexity of time consuming of hash operation

$*T_{me}$: complexity of time consuming of modular exponentiation

Table 2 shows the comparisons of computation cost in the schemes [7,8,11] and ours. We note that the biometric operations in these schemes are omitted in our comparisons because they all cost only one in login phase without considering the differences between biohash function and fuzzy extractor. Our scheme costs the fewest hash functions (13 times) than the others (rep. 15, 16, 22 times). However, the scheme in [11] and our improvement cost 8 and 6 times of modular exponentiation operation respectively, where $T_{me} \gg T_h$.

Table 3. Comparison of storage and communication cost.

Requirement	[7]	[8]	[11]	Ours
Storage	512bit	512bit	320bit	512bit
Communication	1152bit	1152bit	3520bit	1632bit

Table 3 shows the storage and communication cost analysis. We define the length of the identity, the output of hash function and the group element in $G(p,\cdot)$ are 32bit, 160bit and 320bit, respectively. The storage requirements for authentication information in the schemes [7,8] and ours are 512bits, but He and Wang's scheme in [11] only needs 320bits storage space. However, the schemes in [7,8] and our modification cost half communication resource comparing with the scheme in [11].

5. SUMMARY

In this paper, we point out the security weaknesses in Mishra et al.'s scheme and present a lightweight modification to enhance the security and privacy protection. The security analysis shows that our improvement can resist more security attacks and provides the most security features. In addition, the performance analysis shows that our scheme costs more computation resources to remedy the security weaknesses than the original schemes, while maintaining the communication cost as well as the originals. However, our modification achieves the most security requirements while costing less computation and communication resources than the scheme which provides the same security. Finally, we are looking forward to focusing on the tradeoff between security and performance in our future research.

REFERENCES

- [1] Li, Li-Hua, Iuon-Chang Lin, and Min-Shiang Hwang. "A remote password authentication scheme for multiserver architecture using neural networks". Neural Networks, IEEE Transactions on 12.6 (2001): 1498-1504.
- [2] Liao, Yi-Pin, and Shuenn-Shyang Wang. "A secure dynamic ID based remote user authentication scheme for multi-server environment." Computer Standards & Interfaces 31.1 (2009): 24-29.
- [3] Li, Xiong, et al. "An Enhancement of a Smart Card Authentication Scheme for Multi-server Architecture." Wireless Personal Communications (2014): 1-18.
- [4] Li, Xiong, et al. "A novel smart card and dynamic ID based remote user authentication scheme for multi-server environments." Mathematical and Computer Modelling 58.1 (2013): 85-95.
- [5] Li, Xiong, et al. "An efficient and security dynamic identity based authentication protocol for multi-server architecture using smart cards." Journal of Network and Computer Applications 35.2 (2012): 763-769.
- [6] Guo, Dianli, and Fengtong Wen. "Analysis and Improvement of a Robust Smart Card Based-Authentication Scheme for Multi-Server Architecture." Wireless Personal Communications (1762): 1-16.
- [7] Chuang, Ming-Chin, and Meng Chang Chen. "An anonymous multi-server authenticated key agreement scheme based on trust computing using smart cards and biometrics." Expert Systems with Applications 41.4 (2014): 1411-1418.
- [8] Mishra, Dheerendra, Ashok Kumar Das, and Sourav Mukhopadhyay. "A secure user anonymity-preserving biometric-based multi-server authenticated key agreement scheme using smart cards." Expert Systems with Applications 41.18 (2014): 8129-8143.
- [9] Jin, Andrew Teoh Beng, David Ngo Chek Ling, and Alwyn Goh. "Biohashing: two factor authentication featuring fingerprint data and tokenised random number." Pattern Recognition 37.11 (2004): 2245-2255.
- [10] Kaufman, Charlie. "Internet key exchange (IKEv2) protocol." (2005). https://tools.ietf.org/html/rfc5996
- [11] He, Debiao, and Ding Wang. "Robust Biometrics-Based Authentication Scheme for Multiserver Environment." Systems Journal, IEEE PP.99 (2013): 1-8. 10.1109/JSYST.2014.2301517

Performance Optimization of Teaching Web Application Based SSH Framework

J.C. Meng*, C.D. Shi & L.M. Luo
Capital Normal University, Beijing, China
Email: mengjc2014@126.com, 75834009@qq.com

ABSTRACT: Because Web applications hold the feature of cross-platform and others, so more and more applications use this form, so that its development environment is gradually maturing and variety of stable and rapid development framework have also appeared, such as SSH framework, but Web application performance issue has been always a problem occurs during operation. This paper took the teaching Web application as the background, described and researched for the potential problems, proposed solutions, and finally tested it to the desire to provide reference for similar studies.

KEYWORDS: SSH framework; WEB Applications; Performance Optimization.

1. INTRODUCTION

With the deepening integration of technology and education, educational Web applications become increasingly important. Web technology maturing and its cross-platformmake it run smoothly either in a desktop computer or on a mobile device. It also reduces the cost which cross-system development brings, and therefore Web application has a great development space.

With the rapid development of Web technology, some development framework with a friendly design concepts have also appeared, such as Struts, Hibernate, Spring, ibatis, JFinal, Play Framework and the like. The more popular, free and open source Java Web application framework is SSH framework, it is integration framework of Struts + Spring + Hibernate framework. SSH-based applications use a hierarchical framework design pattern, respectively, three major frameworks package Presentation layer, Logical layer and Data persistence layer, effectively reduce the coupling between the three layers, easy to transplant and modification, greatly improving the efficiency of the development.

However, SSH-based Java Web application may have a lot of performance problems in the actual operation. Primary and secondary school teaching Web application, for example, its biggest feature is the need for a large number of static resources into the page, such as static pictures, animation, Longman audio and video materials, etc., in order to provide assisted learning materials for teachers to teachtextbook knowledge in the classroom, while provide learning material to students out of class. So during server architecture, if the server software selected is only Tomcat application server, due to its low efficiency handling static resource, while high concurrent user access to the server, the server is prone to delaying responses, severe cases may be down. Therefore, these static resources need to a dedicated server tomanage and provide the necessary services, for the non-static resources such as JSP, Servlet, Class and number of the application's configuration files need to use server software like Tomcat to manage and support to achieve the purpose of separation resources from Static to dynamic, to improve server response time and the user experience. Another problem is the data cache. Caching technology can effectively improve server response time. Li Zhihui [1] (2013) said, "the first law of site performance optimization: Optimizing consider using caching to optimize performance," that is, when the site comes to performance bottlenecks, the first solution is to use cache. In the more complex software design, the cache is almost everywhere, and a large site architecture have used cache in many ways. In Primary and Secondary Web applications, its audience as students need more shorter response time than adults, so it need to use the appropriate caching techniques. In the database connection, the two sides were connected applications and databases, if not configure a database connection, it is easy to take up a lot of resources while concurrent fall in, resulting in a request response delay or failure, so it is necessary for both sides to configure the database connection pool.

This study took Englishintelligent E-Book System (hereinafter referred to as "eBook System") as the project background, for the issues raised above, improve the application and server, to improve the performance of the server.

2. PROJECT BACKGROUND

EBook system as the project background of this paper is committed to providing students 1:1 personalized digital classroom learning environment, but also to meeting the needs of independent learning after school. It is a self-learning tool software for primary which is able to tailor a personalized English learning resource, with resource miniaturization, Personalized Learning, Activities related resources and social activities and other characteristics. As the system for primary audience, it places on the display page a lot of pictures, text and other static resources to replace the text display. In the system all learning resources are uploaded and attached by teachers and other teachers and students can share the resources, which have been constructed rich online English learning environment.

3. FACTORS AND OPTIMIZATION MEASURES

3.1. *The main affect factors of web application performance*

(1) Because the system implants a lot of static resources, such as still pictures, video resources, audio resources, Doc documents, PDF documents, PPT documents, etc., so the movement of resources separationcan effectively reduce server response time.

(2) Since J2EE is a multilayer distributed architecture, so a lot of data communication between levels is a major factor affecting performance.

(3) Frequently establishing and closing connections can greatly reduce the performance of the system, so the use of connections often become the bottleneck in system performance.

3.2. *Optimization measures*

3.2.1. *Separation between static and dynamic resource*

The separation is a thinking for server framework, the core idea is to deploy static resources (Html, CSS, Javascript, images, videos, documents, etc.) and dynamic resource (Jsp, Servlet, Class, application configuration files, etc.) to different software on the server, when a user sends a request, the server judge resource type based on URL requested, then the task is distributed to the corresponding server software or program to perform a series of operations, the final response to the client. The separation contributes to the rational use of server resources, its configuration requires two types of software: Http servers and application servers. As used herein, it is free and open source software: Apache Http Server and Tomcat server under the Apache Software Foundation (hereinafter referred to as "ASF").

Apache Http Server (referred to as apache) under the ASF is an open source HTTP server which can run on most computer operating systems. With fast and reliable features, it is one of the most popular HTTP server software, but also it can be used as a load balancing server software. ASF Tomcat is a free open-source Web application server, a lightweight application server software. Compared with the apache, the difference is that Tomcat is the Servlet and JSP container, which is its default mode. In addition Tomcat also has the ability to deal with static HTML pages, however, compared with apache, Tomcat has lower power processing static HTML pages and otherstatic resources, so in a production environment, it often usesapache and Tomcat to improve the efficiency of the server response. The following describes how to configure it in the project.

Firstly, install Tomcat and apache software. Download the latest version of the Tomcat software from ASF official website and correctly installed on the server, open the browser and enter http: // localhost: 8080 /, if it displays "If you're seeing this, you've successfully installed Tomcat. Congratulations!" on the page, then it proofs that Tomcat has been installed successfully. Similarly, download the latest version of apache software and install it, point your browser to http: // localhost: 81 /, if the page is displayed "It works!", then it proves apache has been successfully installed.

Secondly, configure apache and Tomcat. Many characteristics ofapache is achieved by compiled module, the same to connecting apache and Tomcat. So download module mod_jk.so (mod_jk is connector of apache and Tomcat, which is maintained by the ASF.In its official website you can get the source code and binary code), copy the file to the "modules" folder underthe root directory of apache, and then configure conf / httpd.conf, load jk module, as the following code:

LoadModule jk_module modules\mod_jk.so

Although it is declared to load mod_jk module at server startup, but does not specify which Tomcat server(s) to connect, so it is necessary to introduce in the conf / httpd.conf the following code:

JkWorkersFile "conf\workers.properties"

Loading workers. properties under "conf" folder (code below) is to set the number of Tomcat and connecting each worker (In the apache, each Tomcat server is called a worker) configuration.

```
worker.list = controller
worker.tomcat1.port=8009
worker.tomcat1.host=localhost
worker.tomcat1.type=ajp13
worker.tomcat1.lbfactor = 1
worker.controller.type=lb
worker.controller.balanced_workers=tomcat1
worker.controller.sticky_session=false
worker.controller.sticky_session_force=1
```

If you configure multiple workers, through the use of load balancing, when the total load in certain circumstances, the requests are balanced to workers, which makes the number of requests per worker obtained relative to the total load to reduce.It can greatly reduce the system response time, but the focus of this study is concerned the software itself performance problems, and therefore only a worker is configured. Tomcat1 is marked corresponding Tomcat server, which is connected to a Tomcat by the specified label, so Tomcat in the corresponding configuration file% CALALINA_HOME% \ conf \ server.xml need to specify the same label, as follows:

```
<Engine name="Catalina" defaultHost="localhost" jvmRoute="tomcat1" >
```

Thirdly, we need to configure apache virtual hosts. The role of virtual host configuration tells apache server which requests to processing, as well as how to deal with and so on. According to the original directory structure, all static resources web project needed will be copied under "E: \ Apache2.2 \ webroot" (specific path may to set up depending on the situation). Then open the apache \ conf \ httpd.conf, add the following code in the file:

```
<VirtualHost *:81>
    ServerAdmin administer@126.com
    DocumentRoot E:\Apache2.2\webroot
    <Directory "E:\Apache2.2\webroot">
     Allow from all
    </Directory>
    ServerName cnu.com
    ServerAlias www.cnu.com
    DirectoryIndex index.html index.htm index.jsp
    index.action
    JkMount /*.jsp controller
    JkMount /*.cnu controller
</VirtualHost>
```

All requests apache server receives which takes HTTP as the transport protocol, 81 as the port number are referred to the virtual host: requests which URL extension is jsp or cnu are referred to the controller (previously configured load balancing worker) to deal with, namely dynamic resources request Tomcat server; otherwise, apache server request resources under "E \ Apache2.2 \ webroot" path, which is handled by the apache server. Then the word is over.

3.2.2. *Hibernate caching mechanism*

Hibernate is a facing Java environment, O / R Mapping database mapping tool, in essence, it packages JDBC for database operations. It not only managers the mapping from Java classes to database tables, but also provides data query and retrieval methods, and can greatly reduce processing time used to SQL and JDBC [2][3].

Hibernate provides two caching mechanism, the first one is the Session level cache or the first levelcache. Hibernate Session object is the basic channel that applications to exchange data with the database, usually corresponds to a transaction. After the transaction is closed, then the Session. In applications using Hibernate, Seesion cache is required, by default, it is turned on, also not be uninstalled. The second cache is a SessionFactory cache, application-level cache or the second level cache, It contains built-in cache and external cache. The built-in caches some data SessionFactory object collection attributes contain, which is read-only. SessionFactory external cache is a configurable plug-in, by default, SessionFactory will not enable this plug-in. SessionFactory survival range is the entire project, during the data exchange, all Session instances share the same SessionFactory configuration information and data. The advantage of this configuration is to save frequently accessed and little change data in cache of a local application server when the first query, when accessing the same data again, you can directly obtain from the local cache to improve query efficiency, shorten response time, while reducing the pressure on the database server.

While configuring a secondary cache helps to improve application performance, reduce database resources waste, but it needs to consider depending on the circumstances whether to use the secondary cache, and the cache can be configured to their specific cache policy for a certain persistent object. The cases suitable for use second-level cache are:

(1) Data update frequency is not too high

(2) Individual data is not too large

(3) Non-private information

The following will take eBook system for example, and configure Hibernate second level cache for Java Web system. There are many implementations of secondary cache, such as Ehcache, OSCache, JBoss Cache 1.x, JBoss Cache 2 and the secondary cache Hibernate itself to achieve. They have advantages and disadvantages (for detailed description you can referto Hibernate Reference Documentation).With rapid lean, etc., Ehcache is a framework within a process which is written in pure Java language, which mainly caches the database data and is the default secondary cache provider of Hibernate. It is suitable for this system.

First you need to import the necessary jar package under the path of WEB-INF \ lib, and then configure Ehcache profile,

```
<diskStore path="java.io.tmpdir"/>
<defaultCache
        maxElementsInMemory="3000"
        eternal="false"
        timeToIdleSeconds="120"
        timeToLiveSeconds="1200"
        overflowToDisk="true"
/>
```

Explicitly declare enable Hibernate second-level cache in Hibernate configuration file hibernate.cfg.xml, the code is as follows.

```
<property
   name="hibernate.cache.use_second_level_cache
   ">true </property>
<property name="cache.provider_class">
org.hibernate.cache.EhCacheProvider</property>
<property
   name="hibernate.cache.use_query_cache">
true   </property>
```

The first two <property> is the configuration of Ehcache, the third <property> is the configuration of query cache. Query caching is a query mechanism that based on the secondary cache. That is, if secondary cache opened, when the requests with the same query conditions and using the specified query method, the application server will first search data from local memory. If the query hits and the data is valid, then it returns the data directly, or from a database query, and cache to the application server. Thus, the only explicitly configure the query cache, the secondary cache can really play a role. While opening the query cache, but you did not specify the cache policy, and therefore also need to specify the cache policy in the configuration file of entity class. There are four optional caching strategy: transactional, read-write, nonstrict-read-write, read-only. Because Ehcache not support transactional cache types, it is possible to modify the cache data in eBook system, and it is strictly enforced transaction isolation, so read-write strategy is the best selection. Finally, when querying the data you need to use the query cache Query.setCacheable (true), then the secondary cache really take effect.

```
Query query = super.createQuery(hql);
query.setFirstResult(0);
query.setCacheable(true);
List<Keyword> list = query.list();
```

3.2.3. *Database connection pool*

MySQL is a free open source relational database management system and use standard SQL language for data access. Because of its small size, high speed, low cost, reliable, mature technology and other advantages, many small and medium sites in the development process choose MySQL as the site database. MySQL currently belongs to Oracle Corporation, containing the community and commercial version. There is a database connection pool (Thread _pool) plug-in configuration in a commercial version, but in the community edition, although not have this configuration, but you can use the thread cache (Threads_cached) tocache free connections. In applications, it also tend to configure the database connection pool. The more popular database connection pool technologies are Proxool, C3p0, DBCP, but because of too much bugsDBCP connection pool hold, Hibernate officials have announced that DBCP connection pool is no longer supported, and recommend Proxool and C3p0, but the specific choice needs to be applied depending on the characteristics of the program itself [4][5][6].

To select an appropriate database connection pool foreBook system, the author configure two connection pools, and test the efficiency of the two pools through comparing the average time by 10 tests each, a total of five times the average (Table 1). As can be seen from the table, two configurations are comparable in response time. Proxool is slightly faster than C3P0, so we choose Proxool as the database connection pool of the system.

Table 1. The average time of two connection pool.

A Fixed Request	Averate Time (ms)	
	C3P0	Proxool
1	814.3	811
2	836.1	825.4
3	814.7	822.5
4	859.8	813
5	824.8	840.4
Totle Average	829.94	822.46

But in the actual operation it may appear Http Status 500errors: Could not open Hibernate Session for Transaction (already configured minimum -connection-count = 10, maximum-connection-count = 100, house-keeping-sleep-time = 5000 and autoReconnect = true). This phenomenon is a direct result of the number of connections is insufficient due to Hibernate Session cannot be created. After testing, when clicking on a link, the connection application server and the database has not been turned off, then if the same client makes the same request again, application server and database server will re-establish a connection, but first requested connection is not disconnect, after a number of iterations the connection number reach the maximum database connection number, and then the error appears as described above, and therefore it needs to manually disconnect connection after the response. In proxool configuration, there is an attribute named maximum-active-time, the official described as: If the housekeeper comes across a thread that has been active for longer than this then it will kill it So make sure you set this to a number bigger than your slowest expected response! Default is 5 minutes. In the eBook system, slowest response in all the requests also within 5s, so in proxool set the maximum-active-time = 5000 (ms), that is, after five seconds the link is broken, you can solve the problem.

4. PERFORMANCE TESTING

4.1. *Static and dynamic separation test*

Test environment:

Operating System: Windows 7 Ultimate Edition Service Pack 1

Memory: 8GB (7.84GB available)

Processor: Intel Core 2 CPU Q9550 @ 2.83GHz

JDK version: 1.8.0_31

Myeclipse: 10.0

Database: MySQL 5.5.20

Tomcat: 7.0.59

Apache: 2.2

HP Loadrunner: 11.00.0.0

Test procedure:

Using Performance testing software Loadrunner 11.00.0.0 records test script referred to student status login operations, sets the virtual number of concurrent as 30, after running five minutes stop it. Record the number of Tomcat server threadsrunning in the run up to 2.5 minutes both cases Tomcat and Tomcat + apache, the test results are shown in Table 2.

Analysis:

When only configure Tomcat, client requests are forwarded to port 8080, so you can see the number of threads which run 105.When Tomcat + apache server, because the apache configured connection port number with Tomcat is 8009, so you can see run number of threads 4, a large number of client requests for static documents are processed by the apache server, Tomcat server is significantly reduced pressure.

Table 2. Application connection.

	Connection Number at 8009		Connection Number at 8080	
	Max	Current	Max	Current
Tomcat	200	1	200	105
Tomcat+apache	200	4	200	10

4.2. *Use cache test*

Test environment:

Operating System: Windows 7 Ultimate Edition Service Pack 1

Memory: 8GB (7.84GB available)

Processor: Intel Core 2 CPU Q9550 @ 2.83GHz

JDK version: 1.8.0_31

Myeclipse: 10.0

Database: MySQL 5.5.20

Test procedure:

Use a student status login to the system, test a fixed connection, then time and statistics it. In order to ensure the authenticity of the test results, statistics the time separately for the use of cache and not used, in each case after five times recording, each recorded average time for each 10 requests, and finally averaged. The test results are shown in Table 3.

Analysis:

From the test results, before the secondary cache is not configured, the total average response time of 4.85s or more. After 2-level cache, the total average response time is less than 0.85s, its query is nearly six times faster than before, which significantly improve the performance of the system.

Table 3. Click on the average time of a fixed link.

A Fixed Request	Averate Time (ms)	
	No Cache	Cache
1	4939.3	811
2	4911.8	825.4
3	4868.9	822.5
4	4862.6	813
5	4955.8	840.4

5. CONCLUSION

Currently, the feature of Web applications' cross-platform access enables application developers to develop once, run anywhere. It is easy to making server maintenance. For the users, it is widely accepted by customers that no need to install additional software access applications fast. However, during operation, sometimes there will be some problems, such as dealing with the problem of static resources, database connection problems, this time it needs for the system to specify a set of strategies to optimize performance for specific applications. This article takes eBook system as the background to optimize Web applications and makes some recommendations for improvement.

ACKNOWLEDGEMENT

This article is the result of "Building Strategies and application research of intelligent English learning resources", which is the key issue of Beijing Education Science Twelfth Five Year Plan.

REFERENCES

— [1] Zhihui Li. (2013). Large Web Site Technology Framework: Core Principles and Case Studies [M]. Electronic Industry Press. (In Chinese)

— [2] Hongbin Dong, & Yanping Dou. (2005).The solutions of the use of J2EE Hibernate data persistence layer [J]. 30 (B12), 17-18. (In Chinese)

— [3] Xuedao Cai. (2006). Hibernate development and integration application / Java development tool. Tsinghua University Press. (In Chinese)
— [4] Lei Ji, Li Li, Wei Zhou. (2006). J2EE- a proficient Eclipse Struts Hibernate Spring Integration Applications [J]. People Post Press. (In Chinese)
— [5] Dongbo Zhao, & Yuanyuan He. (2007). The research and application of query efficiency based on Hibernate. Science Technology and Engineering, 7(5), 883-885. (In Chinese)
— [6] HIBERNATE - Relational Persistence for Idiomatic Java [EB/OL].http://docs.jboss.org/hibernate/orm/5.0/manual/en-US/html_single/

Research of Crop Breeding Information Intelligent Collaborative System

Y. E[1], Y.P. Zhu[2]

[1,2]*Research Institute of Agriculture Information, Chinese Academy of Agricultural Science, Key Laboratory of Agri-information Service Technology, Ministry of Agriculture, Beijing, China, 100081*

[1]*Email: eyue@caas.cn*

ABSTRACT: In this paper, using the modern information technology, on the one hand, establish crop breeding information intelligent collaborative system, and provides a technical support and general tool for all kinds of data obtained from the process of crop breeding information integration and analysis; on the other hand, as a kind of key technology research and exploration, using the multi-agent technology in the field of distributed artificial intelligence, puts forward a kind of intelligent, collaborative and sharing method about big data of crop breeding control and management, for the big data of crop breeding research provides a new research method and train of thought.

KEYWORDS: Crop breeding information; Collaborative; Multi-agent.

1. INTRODUCTION

Improve the efficiency of crop breeding and seed cultivation is the key of the agricultural science and technology in our country. In our country, traditional crop breeding technology is still in the majority cases, at the same time, molecular breeding technology, transgenic breeding technology, genomic breeding techniques and crop simulation model technology and so on, these technology also got rapid development in the process of crop breeding application, and a lot of technology and method had been applied to crop breeding in preliminary such as genotype data and phenotypic data management systems, big data analysis systems and so on [1-5]. However, in the crop breeding target and technical route of uncertain situation, each additional uncertainty factors in crop breeding system, the randomness will multiply, resulting in increased difficulties of crop breeding. Therefore, this is necessary research to development of intelligent crop breeding data analysis tools, to provide auxiliary analysis and decision method for crop breeding expert.

In recent years, more and more of the Artificial Intelligence technology is applied to the research and development of decision support System, in order to improve the process and mechanism of problem solving, especially from the Distributed Artificial Intelligence of multi-Agent System (Multi Agent System, MAS) is becoming more and more attention. MAS involving a group of autonomous Agent, these Agents coordinate the intelligent behavior, knowledge, goal and plan so as to unite together to take action or to solve complex problems between them. Although based on the application of MAS in economic management, strategic planning and electronic commerce has a lot of progress [6-8], however, our country the application of Agent technology in the field of agricultural crops breeding research was less.

In this paper, aiming at the limitations of existing in the process of crop breeding and crop breeding of the complexity of the decision making problems, and discusses the establish of crop breeding intelligent collaborative decision support system based on Agent theory and method.

2. SYSTEM ARCHITECTURE

2.1. *The multi-agent technology*

Most researchers agree that the Agent is an entity, it could be continuously and independently operated, it has the ability to learn and with other Agent coexist and interact. In general, the Agent needs to have certain features, including the activity, autonomy, interaction, sociality, responsiveness, durative and adaptability and so on [9-10]. Some scholars have put forward the Agent should also have real-time performance, especially for artificial intelligence researchers, in addition to the above characteristics of the Agent, also should have some more personification features, such as knowledge, belief, intention, commitment and even emotional state of mind. Of course, any Agent is unlikely to have the nature of all of the above, the researchers usually according to the research purpose or the need of practical application, the design and implementation of the corresponding function.

Multi Agent system (MAS) is a loosely coupled network composed of multiple Agent, and often involve more than one Agent cooperation, coordination, negotiation analyzed and discussed, and the related problems such as complex interaction patterns. Compared with a single Agent, MAS has the following features: each member of the Agent only have incomplete information and problem solving ability, there is no global control, data is scattered or distribution, calculation is asynchronous, concurrent, or parallel. These Agents had different knowledge, goal and ability, they could be achieved information and solve the problem through communication and coordination each other.

2.2. *System architecture*

At present, in the process of crop breeding, both conventional crop breeding process, at the same time, with genetic breeding, molecular biological breeding aspects of a breakthrough, appear the molecular breeding and so on. Then, how to make full use of modern information technology, reasonable and organic integration these various crop breeding tools and relevant information and data, analysis and prediction system, improve the efficiency of crop breeding, has become a pressing need to solve the problem.

Parents of combination breeding, test design, test data record, sum up and the final selection breeding decisions, these involves to the mass crop breeding data collection, management and analysis, and cost crop breeders a lot of time and energy. At present, these mostly rely on the expert's experience in seed selection choices, so subjective influence is big, and lack standardization and normalization. At the same time, formed varieties, intermediate materials and imported materials lack of system, effective management and utilization in the process of crop breeding, these limited opportunities for found excellent quality of crop [11-12]. Therefore, the use of information technology to realize the data to the process of crop breeding and effective management and analysis of germplasm resources, reduce crop breeders dependence on experience, improve the crop germplasm innovation and utilization, it is the key of advance crop breeding information.

At present, there were some countries (such as The United States, Canada, the Netherlands and so on) have developed breeding experimental design and data management software, realize the mass breeding data management and sharing, breeding information level is greatly increased. But, in China, the breeding of auxiliary software and hardware products was still in its infancy, there are varieties of single, specific evaluation algorithm. Therefore, we urgently needs key technologies to strengthen research such as the crop breeding data management, analysis, comprehensive utilization, so as to realize the information management of crop breeding.

System architecture which is divided into four parts (Fig. 1):

1 Task interaction layer: To be responsible for the management of the man-machine interface, and undertake the user's communication, consultation and the results show interactive tasks, etc.

2 Information and resources layer: including the phenotypic data analysis and evaluation Agent, genotype data predict Agent, crop breeding knowledge Agent, crop simulation model Agent and so on. These Agents respectively to supply all kinds of function in the aspects of data, model and knowledge needs. It mainly responsible for according to the parameters set by the user, mainly to complete the information collection and processing, the specific elements that monitoring objects, monitoring the relevant information data acquisition and evaluation.

3 Task solving and decision making layer: To be responsible for implementing the system of decision support functions, including gene-environment interactions Agent, traits associated Agent, QTL identification analysis Agent and crop growth simulation Agent and so on, The layer included all kinds of functions Agents. It mainly responsible for accept the corresponding task information according to collaborative Agent and communication Agent in the task decomposition and distribution layer, and then establish the corresponding contact with information and resources layer, extract the relevant data, and according to the types and properties of the data, analysis, evaluation, and a relevant link in crop breeding (or critical control point) data analysis and detection of specific measures.

4 Task decomposition and distribution layer: Including the collaborative Agent, communication Agent, the layer is the core component of system scheduling and coordination. Specific tasks include: the determination of disposal scheme of crop breeding, task decomposition, coordination strategy formulation, monitoring the executive condition of function Agent, etc.

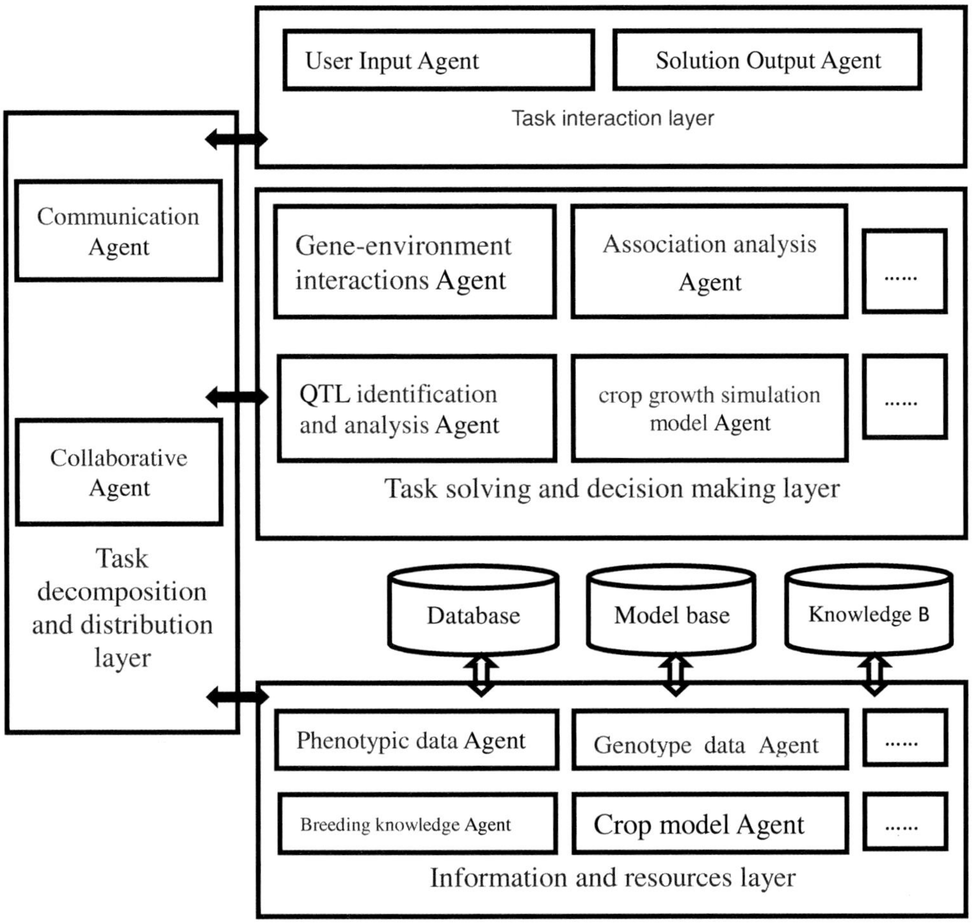

Figure 1. Crop breeding information intelligent collaborative system.

2.3. *Based on the communication of information sharing*

Through the research, in the process of information disposal of crop breeding, need each link (i.e., each functional Agent) between real-time, sufficient information resources sharing. The blackboard sharing interactive mechanism has this ability in the Agent technology, it is through the mutual information of the blackboard, prompting anyone Agent find useful information reasoning to solve problem and inference. Information sharing mechanism based on the blackboard, requires effective support of database technology, network technology, and communication technology. Based on the communication of information sharing mainly includes: task sharing, results sharing. At the same time, convenient to express, communication Agent to represent the blackboard sharing mechanism in the process of data disposal of crop breeding.

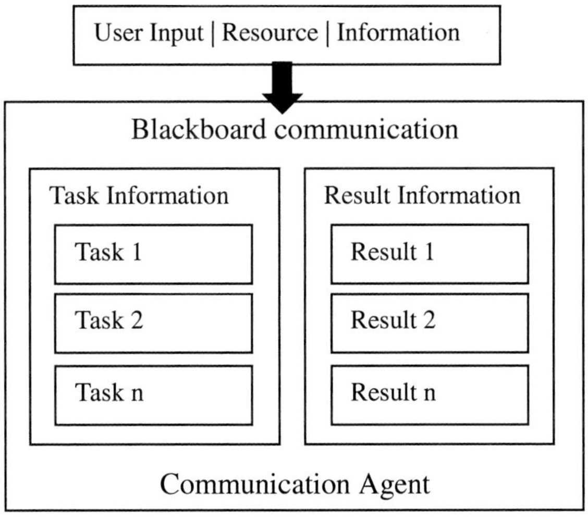

Figure 2. Information sharing based on the communication.

(1) Task sharing

Task sharing refers to through task decomposition, crop breeding reasoning decision rules, and the corresponding analysis process (each task of the relationship between each other) uploaded to the blackboard, these become a criterion to function Agent execute task. Execution Agent through establishing communications with the blackboard, according to their own mission behavior ability, coordinating with other Agent, prevent conflict, cooperative execute crop breeding data statistics, analysis task. Task shared purpose is to prevent at runtime resource conflict, goal conflict and other problems between Agent. Execution Agent through establishing communications with the blackboard, accept their own task, and provide crop breeding according to user's data analysis process, independently or with other Agent to complete the task.

(2) Results Shared

Results sharing refers to many functions agent participate different decision-making tasks in the process of crop breeding data analysis and disposal, the results will produce large amounts of data. According to the analysis of crop breeding scheme, each execution Agent in the system can be fully shared or part of shared these other Agent run results of data. For example, when an Agent execution ability and knowledge was limited, and it has any problem when independently complete the task, then it could be shared results of other Agent by using the blackboard in whole or in part result, the shortage of the supplement itself, achieve data and information of problem solving from other agent. In the process of crop breeding information disposal, need through the sharing of information resources and effective communication between different Agent to complete the work together, through the use of the mechanism of the blackboard, can realize the Agent to participate in together, realizes the resource sharing, to make up for the inadequacy of ability of a single agent's own behavior, improve the effective cooperation of each emergency department is important.

2.4. *Based on tasks of the collaborative decision-making*

The main function of task allocation is based on user set up the analysis of parameter, crop breeding conditions, and system function of actual situation, in accordance with the crop breeding rules, aimed at these different information of users provide, produce different subtasks, to facilitate different agent executed these missions. The distribution of the decision task of crop breeding played an importance role in reasonable distribution of tasks and coordination work in crop breeding. In crop information collaborative mode, the user input the crop breeding of analysis parameters is the foundation and basis of decision-making behavior main body, what kinds of parameters, it had what kind of parameters used to generate the method of decision scheme.

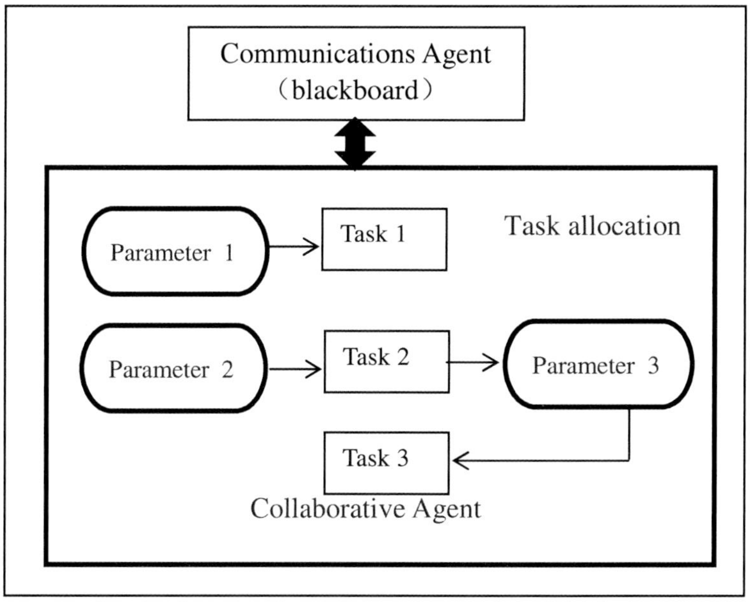

Figure 3. The collaborative decision-making based on tasks.

The main functions of the task coordination is according to the specific content of subtasks, these subtasks assigned to each function Agent, and determine which specific functions Agent (gene-environment interactions Agent, Agent QTL identification analysis, etc.) perform related subtasks, and when the Agent perform a task, and the Agent order (priority) when executing subtasks, the required resources, and the relationships between the subtasks and so on. In the process of information disposal of crop breeding, each function Agent corresponding to a specific mission goals (such as: character analysis and QTL mapping, association analysis, etc.). All kinds of subtask form by communication Agent and collaborative Agent to complete together.

3. WORKING PRINCIPLE

After decades of development, on the one hand, traditional crop breeding still occupies the dominant position; on the other hand, molecular breeding has been rapid development. How to be effective integration and cohesion between traditional breeding and modern molecular breeding data, and how to coordinate the traditional breeding and modern molecular breeding experts, thus achieve the crop breeding of high efficiency, these become some key problem in the crop breeding. The multi-agent technology, due to the characteristics of its own technology, crop breeding in all areas of the existing analysis tools can be encapsulated into functional Agent (such as Gene-environment interactions, QTL identification and analysis and so on). As each user, can need according to its own characteristics and research area, only need a simple parameter input or the conditions of input by the user Agent, as a result, concrete operation and analysis, a variety of software tools to the call, all of these operation get through Agent independent, parallel, collaborative perform, and realize intelligent, collaborative work in crop breeding data analysis.

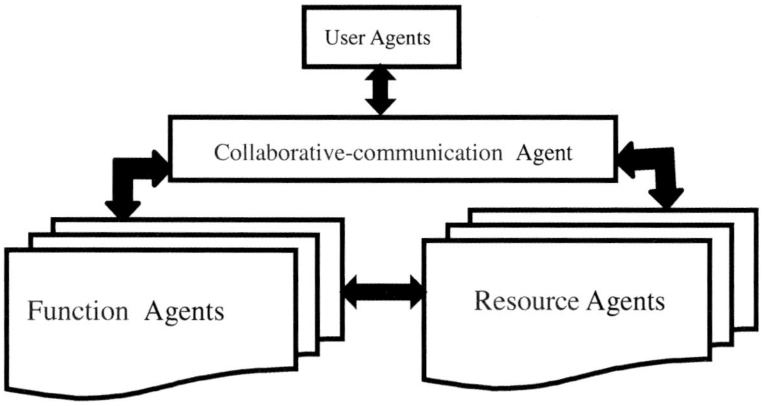

Figure 4. Work based on multi-agent.

Concrete implementation method:

(1) The user sign in a user Agent;

(2) Through the user Agent, input the relevant query conditions (or parameters);

(3) The user Agent establish a new connection state between collaborative Agent and communi -cation Agent;

(4) collaborative Agent and communication Agent according to the information, being finish task decomposition; Then, according to the result of decomposition to get each subtasks, and distribute these tasks to each Agent of solving this task (i.e., the various functional Agent);

(5) These functional Agent receives the task information, long-distance, parallel and separate (or cooperation) complete the relevant calculation, comparison, analysis, and so on;

(6) Each functional Agent to deliver the results to collaborative Agent and communication Agent;

(7) Collaborative Agent and communication Agent according to the function of each Agent back to the information (including: to complete the task information, unfinished task information, request the other Agent finish task information), determine the next step of work

(A) When finished task, to collect information and pass the user Agent;

(B) When did not complete the task, other functional Agent will decide whether to assign to the job; Turn to (4), and to continue;

(8) In the end, show the results by the user Agent.

While in crop breeding information analysis, a large amount of resources (data) distributed in different storage locations, through the use of Agent technology, it could be defined or design information gathering role, it could extraction and integration different types of data exists in different regions, and it could be according to the demand of the task, automatic requests data form different locations, realized data sharing. The user does not care about the location of the relevant data, only through the communication, coordination between Agent, realized data search, processing, and integration.

Crop breeding involves a lot of field experiments, laboratory experiments, and related data analysis and test work, often by different departments, different personnel (experts) separate implement-tation. Using Agent technology, the Agent can be defined as a variety of analysis/forecasting tool carrying device, users only need to define a breeding process planning, the process of concrete would be different functions Agent independence, autonomy complete related mission, through information sharing between Agents and task coordination, perform complex data analysis about crop breeding. The conventional breeding and modern molecular breeding and crop simulation model and so on realized organic together, the various and multi-level complete various stages or key link crop breeding data information analysis and arrangement work.

4. SUMMARY

Crop breeding information intelligent collaborative decision-making system provide important theoretical basis and the means of modern information technology to solve the crop breeding large data control and analysis of problems in our country.

Crop breeding is a heavy scientific research work, aim at backward technology about character parameter acquisition, analysis and utilization in the process of crop breeding in China, this paper used modern information technology closely with these key link in the process of crop breeding work, puts forward the concept of collaborative strategy based on Multi-Agent, this method organic combination of various types of data in the process of crop breeding, and improve the efficiency of crop breeding, provides a large-scale, commercial crop breeding needs technical means.

Crop seed industry is a national strategic, fundamental core industry, it is to promote long-term stable development of agriculture and the root of national food security. Practice has proved that cultivate good varieties was the basic way to realization of grain production, ensure food security, improving agricultural output, eased the contradiction between population and land. Therefore, the application of modern information technology, combined with the existing various crop breeding means, could further improve the level of crop breeding techniques, to speed up the process of our modern agricultural science and technology, improve the ability of the sustainable development of agriculture in our country.

ACKNOWLEDGEMENTS

This research was supported by research and application technology of commercialized breeding big data analysis by the Beijing municipal science and technology plan (D151100004215003). National 863 Programs Funded by Ministry of Science and Technology of China (2013AA102305). Agricultural system intelligent control and virtual technology team (CAAS-ASTIP-2015-AII-03).

REFERENCES

— [1] Qi Changhan, Liu Taoju, Tang Jianjun, Li Hui. Combining Crop Modeling and QTL Mapping into an Integral Plant Breeding Strategy, Scientia Agricultura Sinica 2004, 37(9):1390-1395.

— [2] Wang Jian-kang, Wolfgang H. Pfeiffer. Simulation Approach and Its Applications in Plant Breeding. Scientia Agricultura Sinica 2007, 40(1):1-12.

— [3] Li Dong, Ding Xin-quan, Wang Jun-min, Zhou Bin, Yan Cui-xiang. Application of Plant Modeling on Rice Breeding Cultivation: a Brief Review, China Rice, 2014, 20(2):35-39.

— [4] Yang Xiaodong, Yu Xueke, Huang Weilin, Jiao Guangjing. The Status and Development Strategies of Commercial Breeding Crops in China, Journal of Agriculture 2014, 4(2):117-120.

— [5] E Zhi-guo, Zhuang Jie-yun, Wang Lei, Information Platform of Rice Molecular Breeding Based on .net Framework, Hybrd rice, 2008 23(2):73-75.

— [6] Loor PD, Chevaillier P. Real-time retrieval for case-based reasoning in interactive multi-agent-based simulations. Expert Systems with Applications; 2011, 38, 5145-5153.

— [7] Javier Oscar, Lopez Romero, Self-organized and Evolvable Cognitive Architecture for Intelligent Agents and Multi-Agent Systems, 2010 Second International Conference On Computer Engineering and Applications: ICCEA 2010, Proceedings, 2010, page:417-421.

— [8] Shanu Guang an, Jiang Zheyuan, Cloud Federation Service Composition Model Based on Multi-Agent, Microelectronics & Computer, 2014, 9(31), 22-26.

— [9] Zhou Hao, Xie Xin, Modeling Research of Multi-Agent Interaction Based on Cognitive Emotion, Software Engineer, 2014, 12(17), 7-11.

— [10] Liu Dan, Cao Jiantong, Chen Jianming, Application of Agent-based Modeling: Literature Review, Technology Economics, 2014, 11(23), 96-101.

— [11] Vos J, Evers J, Buck-Sorlin G, et a1. Functional-structural plant modelling: a new versatile tool in crop science [J]. J Exp Bot, 2010, 61(8):2101-2115.

— [12] Cai Bin1, Ma Yu-fang, Qiu Xiu-rong, Application Research on Internet of Things in Intelligent Agriculture[c], Modern Agricultural Science and Technology, 2013, 14:23-31.

— [13] Zhang Lian-ping, Zhao Zhong-liang,Yan Jing-feng, Application of Intelligent System for Rice Bud Seed Production in Other Crops[c], Modern Agricultural Science and Technology, 2013, 17:77-84.

— [14] Pan Zongjin, Wang Wei, Pan Qunbin, Molecular Breeding Should Combine with Conventional Breeding Closely in Plants, Jiangxi Cotton, 2010, 5(32), 10-14.

— [15] Li Hui, Liu Taoju, Tang Jianjun, Qi Changhan, Crop Modeling, QTL Mapping and Their Complementary Role in Crop Breeding, Acta Agriculturae Universitatis Jiangxiensis, 2003, 25(1), 6-10.

— [16] Yang Xiaodong, Yu Xueke, Huang Weilin, Jiao Guangjing, The Status and Development Strategies of Commercial Breeding Crops in China, Journal of Agriculture, 2014, 4(2):117-120.

— [17] Li Yu, Wang Jian Kang, Qiu Li Juan, Ma You Zhi, Li Xin Hai, and Wan Jian Min, Crop Molecular Breeding in China: Current Status and Perspectives, Acta Agronomica Sinica 2010, 36(9): 1425-1430.

— [18] Zhang Wenying, Xu Haiming, Zhu Jun, Index Selection in Multi-environments Based an Additive-dominance and Additive x Additive Model with Environment Interaction, Cotton Science 2010, 22(1):89-95.
— [19] Shi ML, Sun QX, Chen XH, et al. Genetic Analysis on Yield-related Traits and Its Application for Breeding of Zea mays L. Fujian Journal of Agricultural Sciences, 2012, 27(12):1292-1297.
— [20] Li Xiaofang, Liu Yanzhuo, Liu Zhixia, Lu Dongbo, Mao Xingxue, Probe into Analysis Method of Plant Trait Series Data Models, Chinese Agricultural Science Bulletin, 2010, 26(5):55-62.
— [21] Luo H, Hu X J, Hu X X. Multi-agent negotiation model for distributed task allocation [C] IEEE International Conference on Information Management and Engineering. 2010;54-57.
— [22] Gutierrez Garcia J O, Sim K M, Agent-based cloud service composition [J]. Journal of Applied Intelligence, 2013, 38(3):436-464.
— [23] Gutierrez Garcia J O, Sim K M, Self-organizing agents for service composition in cloud computing [C], Proc of Cloud Computing Technology and Science. New York, IEEE Computer Society, 2010:56-66.

Research on Personalized Anonymity in Big Data Set

X.M. Ren
School of Software, Harbin University, Harbin, China
H.L. Lu
School of Internet of Things Technology, Wuxi Institute of Commerce, Wuxi, China
K.C. Wang, X.J. Qi & Q.Y. Gu
School of Software, Harbin University, Harbin, China
Email: min0070@sina.com

ABSTRACT: Nowadays a new big data era has begun. Blogs, Microblog, the Social Network and Internet of Things have made a wide variety of big data, there are great value in big data, but privacy protection is one of the major challenges of big data. In this paper, based on the personalized service demand of privacy protection data publishing, the latest progress of personalized privacy anonymity technology were reviewed. We analyzed and summarized the anonymous models according to the different forms of personalized needs such as CBK(L,K)-Anonymity and (k,l,p)-anonymity, and then we summarized the full paper and further research direction on personalized privacy anonymous technology was prospected.

KEYWORDS: Personalized anonymity; CBK(L,K)-Anonymity; (k,l,p)-anonymity.

1. INTRODUCTION

Nowadays Internet has become a very important part in our daily life. New services such as Blogs, Microblog, the Social Network and Internet of Things have made a wide variety of data, at the same time, Cloud computing provides a foundation platform for data storage, all of those lead to the arrival of the era of big data. There are great value in big data, and big data becomes the most valuable wealth of the enterprise, but big data also brings us great challenges. Privacy protection is one of the major challenges of big data.

People leave many trace data on the internet every day, our privacy information can be found by trace data analysis, cybercriminals use our privacy information which got by trace data analysis for fraud and deception, privacy disclosure makes the serious menace to our safety of lives and wealth. For example, taobao Websit, JD Websit monitor our purchases. Baidu Websit, Biying Websit monitor our queries. QQ, Microblog tapped our social relationship. Our e-mail record, chat record, Flash cookies leaked our habits and position information. So, individual data, even the enterprise data are possibly leaked at any moments, the big data security has become nowadays the main topic of information security.

K-anonymity [1], a model put forward by Samarati P and Sweeney L in 1998 to avoid privacy leaks, requests existence of a certain amount of unrecognizable individuals in the published data which cannot make the aggressor distinguish the concrete individual of privacy, and prevent the leak of individual privacy. K-anonymity got the universal concern of the academic circles, and a lot of scholars research and develop the technology on different levels.

2. RELATED CONCEPTS OF ANONYMITY

The research of this part uses two-dimensional table of data sets.

2.1. *k-anonymity*

Definition 1: Attributes.

Let $B(A_1,\ldots,A_n)$ be a table with a finite number of tuples. The finite set of attributes of B are $\{A_1,\ldots,A_n\}$.

Given a table $B(A_1,\ldots,A_n)$, $\{A_i,\ldots,A_j\} \subseteq \{A_1,\ldots,A_n\}$, and a tuple $t \in B$, use $t[A_i,\ldots,A_j]$ to denote the sequence of the values, $v_i,\ldots,v_j$, of $A_i,\ldots,A_j$ in t. Use $B[A_i,\ldots,A_j]$ to denote the projection, maintaining duplicate tuples, of attributes $A_i,\ldots A_j$ in B [1].

Attribute in table can be classified as four categories according to the role it plays.

- Explicit-identifier, refers to the attribute which can identify individual explicitly, such as name and social insurance number etc.

- Quasi-identifier(QI), existed in private table and external table, refers to a group of attributes that can recognize personal information by using link.
- Sensitive Attribute. The attribute has included individual sensitive information, such as salary, religion etc.
- Non-sensitive attribute. The attribute has included non-sensitive information.

Definition 2: Quasi-identifier.

Given a population of entities U, an entity-specific table $T(A_1,...,A_n)$, f_c: $U \rightarrow T$ and f_g:$T \rightarrow U'$, where $U \subseteq U'$. A quasi-identifier of T, written Q_T, is a set of attributes $\{A_i,...,A_j\} \subseteq \{A_1,...,A_n\}$ where: $\exists p_i \in U$ such that $f_g(f_c(p_i)[Q_T]) = p_i$.

Definition 3: k-anonymity.

Let $RT(A_1,...,A_n)$ be a table and QI_{RT} be the quasi-identifier associated with it. RT is said to satisfy k-anonymity if and only if each sequence of values in $RT[QI_{RT}]$ appears with at least k occurrences in $RT[QI_{RT}]$.

Table 1. Example of k-anonymity, where $k = 2$ and QI={Race,Birth,Sex,ZIP}.

Num	Race	Birth	Sex	ZIP	Disease
t1	asian	1974	F	3115**	hypertension
t2	asian	1974	F	3115**	short breath
t3	asian	1974	M	3114**	chest pain
t4	asian	1974	M	3114**	obesity
t5	black	1973	F	3114**	flu
t6	black	1973	F	3114**	short breath
t7	black	1973	F	3114**	obesity
t8	white	1973	F	3114**	chest pain
t9	white	1973	F	3114**	cancer

Table 1 adheres to k-anonymity, the quasi-identifier is $QI_T = \{Race, Birth, Sex, ZIP\}$ and $k = 2$. In particular, $t1[QI_T] = t2[QI_T]$, $t3[QI_T] = t4[QI_T]$, $t5[QI_T] = t6[QI_T] = t7[QI_T]$, $t8[QI_T] = t9[QI_T]$.

2.2. *Personalized anonymity*

Personalized privacy anonymous technology is anonymous method to meet the demand of personalized service based on the traditional anonymity technology. More specifically, pay more attention to providing different granularities of privacy protection needs of each record or sensitive attributes in data table, instead of traditional anonymous strategy which provides only the protection granularity of the entire data table.

Definition 4: personalized k-anonymity.

Let $RT(A_1,...,A_n)$ be a table and QI_{RT} be the quasi-identifier associated with it. RT is said to satisfy k-anonymity, RT is said to satisfy αk-anonymity too, α is granularity of each record or sensitive attribute.

3. CATEGORIES OF PERSONALIZED ANONYMITY

From the perspective of personalized service object, there are two types of personalized privacy anonymity methods, one is geared to the needs of the individual, the other is sensitive attribute value oriented [2].

3.1. *The individual oriented*

Personalized privacy anonymity is that tuple (individual) is personalized service object, personalized characteristic of sensitive attribute of each tuple was designed in order to meet the needs of personalized anonymity [2].

We build a classification tree of sensitive attribute according to Table 2, Figure 1 shows the sensitive attribue *Disease* classification tree.

Table 2. Original personal health data.

Num	Name	Age	Sex	ZIP	Disease
t1	Vanessa	28	F	311500	flu
t2	Winnie	32	F	311501	pneumonia
t3	Ken	46	M	311400	lung cancer
t4	Mars	45	M	311401	gastritis
t5	Pauline	49	F	311402	lung cancer
t6	Phoebe	47	F	311405	stomach cancer
t7	Rachel	47	F	311408	hepatitis
t8	Sarah	69	F	311403	liver cancer
t9	Teresa	68	F	311404	liver cancer

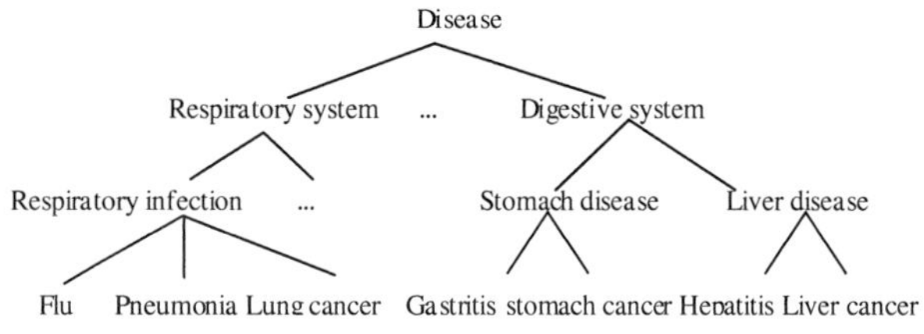

Figure 1. Classification tree of sensitive attribute.

So, we can create a generalization table (Table 3.) based on Figure 1.

Table 3. Generalized personal health information with guarding attributes according to Figure 1.

Num	Name	Age	Sex	ZIP	Disease
t1	Vanessa	28	F	311500	flu
t2	Winnie	32	F	311501	pneumonia
t3	Ken	46	M	311400	respiratory infection
t4	Mars	45	M	311401	gastritis
t5	Pauline	49	F	311402	respiratory infection
t6	Phoebe	47	F	311405	stomach disease
t7	Rachel	47	F	311408	hepatitis
t8	Sarah	69	F	311403	liver disease
t9	Teresa	68	F	311404	liver disease

We replace sensitive attribute value *lung cancer* of tuple *t3* in Table 3 with *respiratory infection* by generalization, so do *t5*, *t6*, *t8*, *t9*. The privacies of *t3*, *t5*, *t6*, *t8*, *t9* have been preserved, this shows personalized service of privacy protection.

3.2. *Sensitive attribute value oriented*

Personalized anonymity technology of sensitive attribute value-oriented puts sensitive attribute value in sensitive information as the research object, the domain of values were personalized constraints in order to meet the needs of personalized anonymity.

3.3. *Personalized (alp, dif)-anonymity*

Personalized (*alp*, *dif*)-anonymity [3] satisfies *k*-anonymity, the average leak probability of sensitive attribute value $\leq alp$ at the same time, difference value between the leak probability of sensitive attribute value and $alp \leq dif$ in equivalence class (the set of tuples whose attribute values are same), we can set different *alp* and *dif*, according to the degree of privacy protection in order to realize the personalized anonymity. Here *alp* denotes the degree of privacy protection as a whole, *dif* denotes the close degree between the leak probability of sensitive attribute value and *alp*.

Table 4. Example of personalized (alp,dif)-anonymity.

Age	Education	Sex	Disease
(40,50]	Masters	M	AIDS
(40,50]	Masters	M	AIDS
(40,50]	Masters	M	cancer
(40,50]	Masters	M	flu
[20,30)	Bachelors	F	fever
[20,30)	Bachelors	F	fever

In Table 4, we set *alp* threshold value of *AIDS* sensitive attribute value to 0.5, set *dif* to 0.2, set *alp* threshold value of *cancer* to 0.4, set *dif* to 0.3, set *alp* threshold value of *flu* and *fever* to 1.0, if the value is 1.0, we do not do privacy protection, *alp* and *dif* are specified by expert or experience value, table 4 is the example of personalized (*alp*, *dif*)-anonymity.

3.3.1. *Complete (α,k)-anonymity*

Complete (α,*k*)-anonymity model realizes personalized sensitive attribute protection by setting the frequency of occurences of sensitive attribute.

Definition 5. Complete (α,*k*)-anonymity.

T is a table, *QI* is Quasi-identifier, $SI(s_1,s_2,\ldots,s_m)$ is sensitive attribute, $QIgroup$ ($QIgroup_1$, $QIgroup_2,\ldots,QIgroup_n$) is the collection of equivalence class, the constraint frequency α_i ($0 \leq \alpha_i \leq 1$, $1 \leq i \leq m$) is specified for each s_i, if $\forall s_j$ ($s_j \in SI$) is satisfied $p(QIgroup_i, s_j) \leq \alpha$, here $p(QIgroup_i, s_j)$ denotes the frequency of occurrence of s_j in $QIgroup_i$, and $|QIgroup_i| \geq k$, so, *T* is satisfied complete (α,*k*)-anonymity.

For example, $\alpha_{AIDS} = 0.4$, $\alpha_{Cancer} = 0.4$, $\alpha_{Flu} = 0.9$, $\alpha_{Fever} = 0.9$, Table 5 satisfies complete (α,*k*)-anonymity.

Table 5. Example of complete (α, k)-anonymity.

Job	Birthday	ZIP	Disease
*	1974.*.*	3114**	AIDS
*	1974.*.*	3114**	Flu
*	1974.*.*	3114**	Fever
*	1974.*.*	3114**	Cancer
*	1974.1.*	311501	Cancer
*	1974.1.*	311501	Flu
*	1974.1.*	311501	AIDS

3.3.2. *CBK(L,K)-anonymity*

CBK (L,K)-Anonymity model [4] realizes personalized anonymity by setting up an influence matrix based on background knowledge.

Background knowledge can be acquired from domain expert, and also can be acquired by analyzing basic data directly. Background knowledge describes the influence degree of a variety of sensitive attribute produced by *QI* attributes, the sample matrix is as follows:

$$M|S = (t_{ij}|b_i)_{m\times(n+1)} = \left[\begin{array}{cccccc|c} QI_1 & QI_2 & QI_3 & QI_4 & \cdots & QI_n & S \\ t_{11} & t_{12} & t_{13} & t_{14} & \cdots & t_{1n} & b_1 \\ \cdots & \cdots & \cdots & \cdots & \cdots & \cdots & \cdots \\ t_{i1} & t_{i2} & t_{i3} & t_{i4} & \cdots & t_{in} & b_i \\ \cdots & \cdots & \cdots & \cdots & \cdots & \cdots & \cdots \\ t_{m1} & t_{m2} & t_{m3} & t_{m4} & \cdots & t_{mn} & b_m \end{array}\right] \quad (1)$$

Here, t_{ij} : the influence degree of NO. *j* sensitive attribute produced by NO. *i* QI attribute, b_i :the weight of sensitive attribute value of NO. *i*.

For example, the *flu* is common ailments, disease weight can use 0.11, because of the characteristic of local outbreaks of flu, *ZIP* weight uses 0.8, *Sex* weight uses 0.2 etc. The major diseases weight of *lung cancer*, *mammary cancer* and *AIDS* use 0.91, 0.92 and 0.93, but *mammary cancer* is associated with sex, So *Sex* weight uses 1.0, different disease must have different disease weight value.

Table 6. Example of CBK(L,K)-anonymity, *k*=2, *l*=2.

Num	Sex	ZIP	Disease
t1	F	311558	flu
t2	F	311568	flu
t3	*	3114**	lung cancer
t4	*	3114**	mammary cancer
t5	F	3114**	lung cancer
t6	F	3114**	lung cancer
t7	F	3114**	flu
t8	*	3114**	mammary cancer
t9	*	3114**	AIDS

Table 6 satisfies CBK(L,K)-anonymity, we choose $l \geq 2$, $\forall b_i < 0.5$, *t1* and *t2* are published directly because the weight of flu is 0.11, the data distortion is 0. *T3* and *t4*, *t8* and *t9*, *Sex* must be replaced with the generalization value of sex with "*" because the weight of *sex* of *t4* and *t8* is 1.

4. PERSONALIZED ANONYMITY OF SOCIAL NETWORK

The original research area of privacy protection in publishing data could be applied to relational data. So, the privacy protection models applied in relational database cannot be used directly in social network, which makes anonymous social network data more challenging than anonymous relation data.

Personalized (*k*,*l*,*p*)-anonymity [5] realizes the needs of individuals privacy. It protect individuals from three aspects. (1)Attacker can identify the sensitive relationship probability between individual and others less than p. (2) Attacker can reidentify individual no more than 1/*k*. (3) Individual sensitive label has been associated with *l* different sensitive values, and if individual privacy attribute is H, the probability of reidentify of individual is no more than 1/*k*, the probability of individual associated with sensitive label is no more than 1/*l* at the same time. In addition, if individual privacy attribute is M, the probability that individual is concluded no more than 1/*k*. Here, S (supreme), H (high), M (middle) and L (low) denote individuals personalized privacy needs.

For example, Figure 2 is a original social network graph, Figure 3 is the example of personalized (*k*,*l*,*p*)-anonymity. Here, "1" denotes sensitive edge relationship between any two nodes, "0" denotes non sensitive edge relationship between any two nodes in Figure 2 and Figure 3.

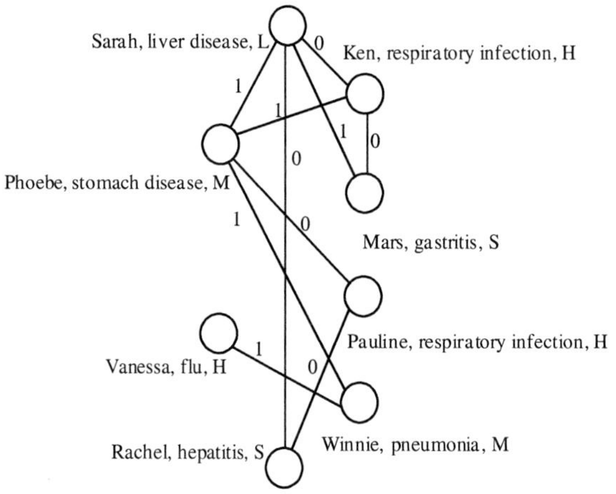

Figure 2. Original social network.

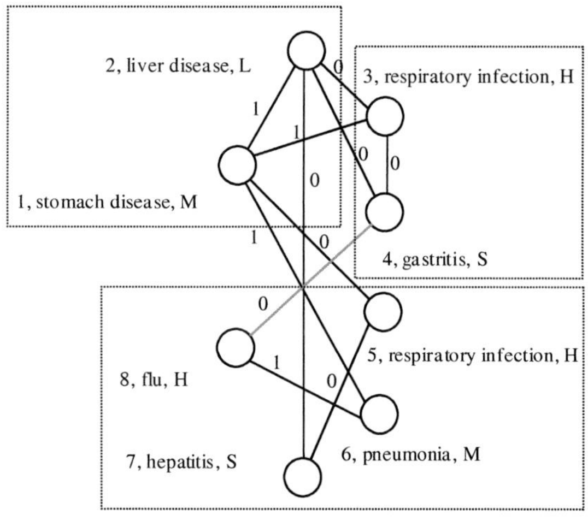

Figure 3. Example of personalized (2,2,0.4)-anonymity.

5. CONCLUSIONS

Personalized anonymity technology can improve the utility of anonymous data, and can protect users privacy better at the same time, but it is also confronted with much challenge, such as how to update the dynamic anonymity data, how to protect data of graph structure or network structure with personalized anonymity technology. The adaptive mechanism of personalized anonymity data publishing is the research area in the future.

ACKNOWLEDGEMENTS

The authors want to thank the helpful comments and suggestions from the anonymous reviewers. This work was supported by the project "Application Technology Research and Development of Harbin" (Grant No. 2014RFQXJ062), the project "Youth Academic Backbone of Ordinary Higher School of Heilongjiang Province" (Grant No. 1254G037).

REFERENCES

— [1] Samarati P, Sweeney L. 1998. Generalizing data to provide anonymity when disclosing information, *Proceedings of the Seventeenth ACM SIGACT-SIGMOD-SIGART Symposium on Principles of Database Systems, PODS, Seattle, WA, USA*. 188.

— [2] Wang Bo, Yang Jing. 2012. Research on Anonymity Technique for Personalization Privacy-preserving Data Publishing. *Computer Science,* 39(4):168-171.

— [3] Wang Qian, Qu Shengzhi, Shixiang Lin. 2009. Anonymity model based on expectation of sensitive attribute value. *Application Research of Computer.* l26(3):1109-1111.

— [4] Xiangmin Ren, Yang Jing et al., 2011. Research on CBK (L,K)-Anonymity Algorithm. *International Journal of Advancements in Computing Technology.* 3(4):165-173.

— [5] Jia Jiao, Peng Liu, and Xianxian Li. 2014. A Personalized Privacy Preserving Method for Publishing Social Network Data. *11th Annual Conference on Theory and Applications of Models of Computation. Springer International Publishing.*141-157.

Chapter 2

Computing Intelligence and Computer Applications

Innovative Research on O2O Marketing Mode Based on Social Networks

W.X. Xue
Management School, Beijing Union University, Beijing, China
Email: xuewanxin@126.com

*D.D. Li
Management School, Beijing Union University; Business School, University of International Business and Economics; Beijing, China
**Email: lidandanhdj@163.com*

ABSTRACT: With the rapid development of social networking and mobile e-commerce, a new e-commerce model of O2O mode quickly grows up. This mode is based on interactive of online and offline. And it is focuses on the experience of the model. Furthermore, this model expands a new way for marketing. This study aims to do the deep research on O2O mode, seeks to carry out innovative way and effect of O2O marketing model based on social networks.

KEYWORDS: Social network; O2O marketing mode; Innovative research.

1. RELATED CONCEPT

1.1. *O2O*

O2O (online 2 offline) is proposed by Alex Rampell who was the CEO and founder on August 7, 2010 (Lei Zhang, 2013). It means that we could combine the internet and the offline opportunity together, so the internet becomes the foreground of the offline transactions. The consumers could try goods and services offline, and then buy them online [1].

1.2. *The role, process and profit of O2O mode*

In O2O mode, you need to know clearly what the role of participation first. There are four participations including consumers, suppliers, third-party service providers, O2O operators. Secondly, there are four steps of transaction process. That is the online matchmaking, online payments, offline consumption, and message back indispensable. Third, the profit of O2O model is including price differences of products or services, the experience of consumer; revenue of online advertising; consumer payment by businesses; membership fees; other sources of income.

1.3. *Advantages impact and operational capacity of O2O mode*

By O2O mode, we can enrich products, enhance brand value, improve service quality, improve performance, integrate supply chain, and control drainage. Trough operating O2O, online and offline should be flowed together. The information capabilities, marketing capabilities, service capabilities and logistics capabilities can represent O2O operational capability of a company. We can understand O2O deeper from three angles. The first angle refers to we can online inquiry and buy goods or services of offline, and then go on to enjoy the service offline. The second angle is to achieve information and cash flow online without logistics flow. The third angle refers to strengthen consumer experience end to end of mobile Internet era. In this process, there are large number and variety of segments business models.

1.4. *About innovation*

Economics guru Joseph Alois Schumpeter said: Innovation is an economic category rather than the technical areas, it is not only refers to the creation of technological invention, but also refers to bring the technology that has been invented into the enterprise, in order to form new productivity. Management guru Peter Drucker said: Innovation is the ability to give the resources to create new wealth of resources into real resources. Hongqiao Zhou said: Innovation is a human instinct, is the people's needs. The ability to innovate is to protect them and inspired them out. Innovation is also an art. Internet thinking is innovation and there is no set formula. We have to integrate online and offline, and to consumption interactive and fused. The Chinese market is a very attractive market and developing rapidly. Technological innovation and progress are more quickly than in the past. The innovation of a year is over the past decade to produce. The development of artificial intelligence has brought us many new opportunities, including O2O. Internet technology could make people's lives more efficient, intelligent, efficient and creative. It is a very good attempt. Smart parking, smart visits and cultural industry projects, can use the Internet to make the service more intelligent than before. There are a lot of opportunity of O2O, not just retail and cultural, but also including financial, telecommunications and other industries. Innovation applies innovation diffusion theory. Innovation diffusion theory is proposed by Rogers. It is one of the most important theoretical results to accept new things, and it concerned about the impact of mass media on society and culture. There are five factors in innovation: convenience, compatibility, complexity, reliability and perceived sex. There are five types of individuals to accept innovation: innovators, early adopters, early followers, after the late actor and laggards.

2. RELATED RESEARCHES ON O2O MODE

There are many domestic scholars who focus on O2O, while both on the model itself and O2O marketing

Yue Sun reveals that O2O is an ecosystem from information ecology visual O2O mode. You can always exchange information between consumers and business in systems. It is conducive to the formation of a healthy messaging ecosystem and it promotes maturation and development of O2O e-commerce.

Lei Zhang thinks that O2O is a model combined "offline store" and "online shop".

Na Wang (2012) proposed that O2O is to create a kind of "consumer experience" mode.

Guanbin He proposed that O2O uses new techniques and products identify ways to identify the target users and targeting incremental market, the concept has been gradually to the user experience of real products. O2O personalized consumer groups more obvious and its applications should move towards differentiation.

Fei Sun (2013) believes O2O enables network to be the foreground of traditional line trading services, and provides local service companies achieve precision marketing through tracking of consumer information.

Shuai Zhuang who is the CEO of Space Network thinks: O2O takes advantage of the characteristics, such as portable of mobile terminal, uniqueness of user identity, traceability of the user's location to seize a number of potential consumer users. And these consumers do not coincide with the regular consumption store-based traditional district. Acquisition costs of online users are far less than the store itself. And it will greatly develop the market.

Chunjia Shi said O2O is concerned about how to use network to map fragmentation of content and information with each other, in order to accurately locate the target population. O2O marketing cares the behavior of the transfer process more than other marketing. It displays the contents of the product in an appropriate channel, so that consumers are interested in and produces consumer behavior.

Zhangguang Wu (2012) think O2O commercial ecosystem fused, while well integrated social, mobile and local together to form three-dimensional marketing network. O2O takes one-way communication into a two-way interaction in marketing mode. It increases the fun of the consumer experience, and optimized the consumers buying experience.

3. O2O MODEL UNDER SOCIAL NETWORKS

3.1. *Social network marketing*

The 21st century is the information society. It is also a fragmented era of information society as a whole constitute a large network of community. There are a variety of new media in social networks, and the development of social media spawned a new marketing model. Social media as the leading new marketing model is gradually established. Social media, that is the online media, is the plat and tool people share ideas, insights, experiences and perspectives with each other. It includes social networking sites, stage, blog, microblogging, wechat, forums, podcasts, QQ, etc.

Any kind of media could become a marketing tool, and different marketing tools play different roles in their respective fields. So does social media. According to investigations by Nixon such, there are 22% of the total Internet population spend time on social media, and people who use social media are more than 24% of using e-mail on the Internet every day. As a new media forms of communication, social media is communicative, community-based, low-cost, fast, strong adhesion itself. Social media makes users to both their audience and also the maker of content. People could locate the media platform of target group through data analysis faster, because of the highly digital digitized and informatization of media.

There are deeply interactive and communication with consumers, emphasizing the relationship between users in the strategies of social media marketing. Especially the humane interact with consumers in social media marketing, and the social media drives marketing transformation. Huge commercial value of social media is to understand the needs of users through the user's social behavior in order to expand the finely marketing. It is very important to promote economic and social development. It is good for higher market value and to promote the upgrading of product marketing theory by using new media. The input-output ratio and the general public aware of the product can be improved through new marketing channels. Thereby, the market can be flourished by manner of cost-efficient, thus contributing to the development of the industry.

The core of social network marketing is "participation that is marketing". O2O E-commerce is a multi-level, multi-dimensional complex ecosystem, and it keeps to the multi-level, diverse and in-depth development. If the enterprises develop social marketing, then the contribution of social network online shopping site traffic growth of 77% a year. Users will make purchasing decisions based on social networks of friends or strangers recommendation, involving offline and on-line purchase. Social networks need to establish a dedicated marketing team, and creates a website space on the popular social networks, such as microblogging of Sina, WeChat, Tianya, Douban and other marketing activities. Based on the social network, marketers dig deeper potential customer needs from different perspectives, and establish relationship with the customer. During the delivery of product, we should establish the comprehensive marketing ideas. Marketing activities begin in market research, ending after consumer satisfaction. The goal of marketing activities is to maximize consumer value.

According to the demand of users, O2O mode could provide potentially relevant services for users. The demand can come from social network real-time location of users, also can be obtained through modern network positioning tool, completed payment through the online network, and then go to the offline store to achieve enjoying the merchant service.

3.2. *O2O marketing under social network*

In social networks, the new marketing reality is that it is an era of big data, while a variety of new media continues to be born. As Drucker pointed out that "the purpose of marketing is to understand customer needs deep, and constantly improve the products and services, and ultimately self-product sales."Under the social network, a new chain of social relationship is established on the internet by social media. The intersection of virtual and the real world become larger than before, and affect people's life, work, learn and play because of the existence and development of social media. O2O is concerned about how to use network to map fragmentation of content and information with each other, in order to accurately locate the target population. O2O marketing cares the behavior of the transfer process more than other marketing. It displays the contents of the product in an appropriate channel, so that consumers are interested in and produces consumer behavior. Demand of China's market for modern service industry is growing rapidly, and its potential is enormous. As a new carrier business model, spread which is serviced for products is growing more rapidly and widely because of social media. Through social network, consumers could interact with multiple and recommendation trust. We can enable the sharing of social relations chain of dissemination information, and businesses could locate marketing target more precise than before. O2O commercial ecosystem fused, while well integrated social, mobile and local services together to form three-dimensional marketing network. Sustainable stickiness of consumer can be promoted by aggregation of social relationships. One or more aggregation point at the center of the community can form a niche market. So precise marketing can be done. Under the social needs, O2O could improve customer loyalty, and generate greater business value.

Social integration, localization, mobile Internet is the trend of Internet development future. Localization is the geographic base of mobile business model. Socializing focuses user resources for new models of mobile business (Guoqiang, 2012).

Mobile is the technical support and vector of mobile commerce, which promotes innovation and upgrading user experience of mobile phone application model. Popularity of smart phones provide guarantee for commercial value of the localization, meanwhile, localization is a typical service model of mobile Internet. Moreover, smart phones provide a vector for consumption and sharing experiences anywhere of users.

In the environment of social network, O2O mode could carry out marketing, including relationship marketing, one-to-one marketing and so on, through a PC or a smart phone, and combined with advanced technical support, such as moving and positioning technology. Moreover, O2O could use wechat, forums and other public service platform. Under the third service platform, O2O could complete interactive between consumers and businesses, and complete service experience, thus achieving the purpose of supply chain integration, mining flow, service quality improvement and enhance the brand value. Meanwhile, a wealth of products and efficiency level will be enhanced, too. Based on the above analysis, a marketing diagram of O2O mode under social network is mapped out, it is shown in Figure 1.

4. O2O MODE APPLICATIONS UNDER SOCIAL NETWORS

There are so many O2O mode networks such as Meituan, aijia home, Uniqlo, Suning, dianping.com, eLong, Ganji, airbnb, LEHO, ju.taobao.com and koubei.comin and so on (Rong Zhang, 2013). Because of the huge social network, there are so many consumers of O2O online. So that consumers take advantage of the fragmentation time, and free to browse the content they are interested in any place, and complete the online payment, and then they use their right time, select convenient location to sale. After the selling, consumers can return to the online to share feelings of its own experience with others.

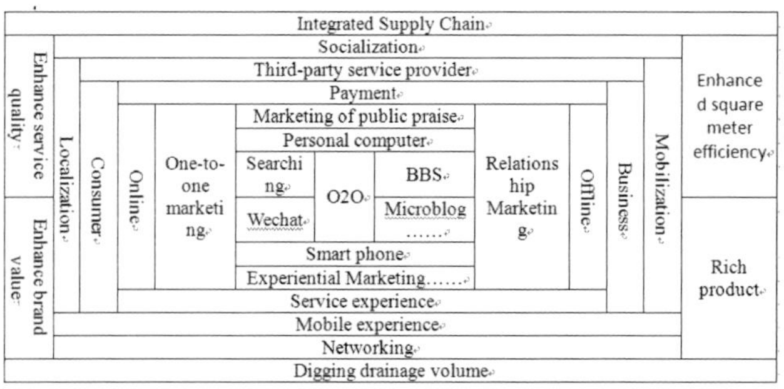

Figure 1. O2O mode under social network.

Currently, one problem of O2O mode generally faced is how to guide consumers to the line, and how to integrate suppliers well, and provide satisfactory service for consumers. Another problem is how to retain existing customers and attract new customers. At the same time, for different customers, how to recommend their interested products based on past purchases records. It will make more consumers glad to share their good consumer experience on social networking platforms, such as Wechat, Sina miroblog, Tianya BBS, Douban and so on. Table 1 shows the effect of social networking sites in several O2O mode of marketing and the effect they achieved.

Table 1. Several O2O models of web marketing and the results achieve.

No.	Name	Category	How to marketing	Effect
1	meituan.com	Food	Relationship marketing and experience marketing	Integrated supply chain and service quality
2	ajhome	Home	Experience marketing and one-to-one marketing	Enhanced brand value and service quality
3	uniqlo	Clothing	Experience marketing	Enhanced brand value
4	dianping	Complex	Marketing of public praise and relationship marketing	Enhanced service quality and square meter efficiency
5	e-long	Trip	Experience marketing and relationship marketing	Integrated supply chain, enhanced square meter efficiency
6	ganji	Complex	Relationship marketing and one-to-one marketing	Integrated supply chain, enriching the product
7	airbnb	Life	One-to-one marketing and community Marketing	Integrated supply chain and service quality
8	leho	Life	One-to-one marketing	Integrated supply chain and service quality
9	suning	Electronics	Experience marketing and relationship marketing	Enhanced brand value
10	ju	Complex	Relationship marketing and experience marketing	Integrated supply chain
11	koubei	Complex	Marketing of public praise	Enhanced brand value

5. CONCLUSIONS

The network is becoming the platform of traditional service business trading offline because of O2O mode. Every aspect of consumers' lives has become very convenient. Network marketing is the combination of online and offline, which has changed the traditional way of retail and extended the localization friends. They could both exchanges leisure experience, and interactive recommended businesses which have a good reputation. It is a good choice for traditional services to enhance performance and brand, to retain existing customers and develop new customers.

In the future, with the improvement of people's consumption level, the experience consumption will be much more than before, and not only simply selling and buying. It will also be shown in all of the world characteristics. O2O commerce market is likely to become the biggest piece of cake in the next e-commerce. There is no platform, so it is not cut yet. Movies, dining and entertainment, etc. are the biggest market, because they cannot be sold online. It is because seeing the huge potential of this market, Wanda, Baidu, and Tencent cooperates with each other to develop Wanda e-commerce. Wanda e-commerce do not sell goods, but sell services. Wanda is expected there will be 5 billion people use this Wanda e-commerce platform in 2020. The ultimate goal of Wanda electronic business platform is to become an open platform. With this platform, all of China companies which manage resort center, cinema, culture and food, can carry O2O marketing. If the idea of Wanda electricity supplier can be implemented, the value of this platform is very large, because of the exploration for the entire line of business. It is a development trend of mobile Internet to carry out O2O marketing through cooperation. And it is an innovation, too.

REFERENCES

- [1] Lei Zhang, Hua Xing, Ping Wu. Preliminary study on the O2O mode of pharmaceutical e-commerce. Shanghai Pharmaceutical [J]. 2013(11):47-49.
- [2] Na Wang. O2O mode in E-commerce. Journal of Shandong Academy of Governance [J]. 2012(10).76-78.
- [3] Fei Sun. The application of two-dimensional code in O2O e-commerce mode. Science & Technology Information [J]. 2013(19):87-88.
- [4] Zhangguang Wu. A study of business model based on SoLoMo & O2O. Journal of Changzhou Institute of Technology [J]. 2012(10):57-60.
- [5] Guoqiang Wei, Ying Liu. Research on mobile e-commerce business models based on LBS and O2O. Pioneering with Science & Technology Monthly [J]: 2012(6). 36-37.
- [6] Rong Zhang. The development of O2O model enterprises. Logistics Engineering and Management [J]. 2013(12):127-129.

Fluid-Structure Interaction Analysis of Bioprosthetic Heart Valve

B.S. Shen, Q. Yuan*, X. Zhang & X. Zhang
School of Mechanical Engineering Shandong University, Key Laboratory of High-efficiency and Clean Mechanical, Manufacture (Shandong University) Ministry of Education, Jinan 250061, P. R. China.
**E-mail: yuanquan66@sdu.edu.cn, Tel: +86-18769789399*

ABSTRACT: In order to improve long term durability of bioprosthetic heart valve, we analyze and compare stress distribution of bioprosthetic heart valve leaflets with different thickness under the same load. We will establish the elliptical leaflets models via computer aided design. Based on the parametric models of the heart valve, three kinds of thickness (0.3 mm, 0.4 mm, and 0.5 mm) of BHV is analyzed by us and finite element analysis is used to simulate the mechanical performance of HBV during the diastolic phase. We can conclude that the bioprosthetic heart valve leaflet with different thickness has a significant effect on the dynamic behavior of the bioprosthetic heart valve. According to the whole loading process, we can conclude that the thickness of the elliptical valve leaflet with 0.4 mm is better than others. The finite element analysis on the HBV could provide reliable and useful testimony for the HBV manufacturing and optimizing.

KEYWORDS: Bioprosthetic heart valve; Finite element analysis; Stress distribution; Fluid structure interaction.

1. INTRODUCTION

Bioprosthetic heart valve has been widely used since 1965. During the 1980s the scale of the bioprosthetic heart valve has been closed to the mechanical heart valve. The use of bioprosthetic heart valves in replacing diseased natural valves has become a routine procedure. These tissue-derived valves have the advantage of low rates of thromboembolic complications without chronic anticoagulation therapy. However, their long-term durability remains limited due to structural degradation of BHV tissue include mineralization and associated leaflet damage, and mechanical damage independent of calcification [1-3].

In order to improve long-term durability of bioprosthetic heart valve, stress distribution of bioprosthetic heart valve leaflets are analyzed and compared based on the study of fluid solid interaction performance of bioprosthetic heart valve. The computation of fluid structure interaction is among the most hot and difficult problems in many fields. In America, more than half of the famous university were engage in the application and researched on fluid structure interaction for a longtime [4-7]. Study of a fluid-structure interaction is fluid and solid mechanics of interaction that takes into account the fluid acting on the solid, solid deformation of reaction in the fluid, affecting the direction of the fluid velocity and other mechanical parameters. When bioprosthetic heart valve implanted in the human body, the blood flow field may be changed. The changes of the blood velocity field and shear stress field are closely associated with the destruction of the red cell, the formation of thrombosis and the reconstruction of vascular. Thus the fluid-structure interaction analysis was carried out on the bioprosthetic heart valve is very important.

The elliptical leaflets are created for FSI analysis and the FSI analysis results are compared by us. Geometrical design and the FSI analysis on the bioprosthetic heart valve could provide direct and more comprehensive information for the bioprosthetic heart valve designer, which is closely related to thrombosis and the damage of red cell. This work is very helpful to prolong the lifetime of the BHV and its clinical practice.

2. METHOD

2.1. *Mathematical modeling of BHV*

The flow field of bioprosthetic heart valve is similar to that of the human heart valve. The valve design must meet three basic requirements:

(1) Three leaflets intersect with the root of the aortic at the lines which divide the circle into three equal parts.

(2) There should be no leak when the valves close.

(3) Projecting the free edge of valve leaflets at the normal direction, the sum area should be larger than that of the suture ring [8-10]. Based on these three requirements, we construct a dimensional model using the Pro/ENGINEER software as shown in Fig. 1.

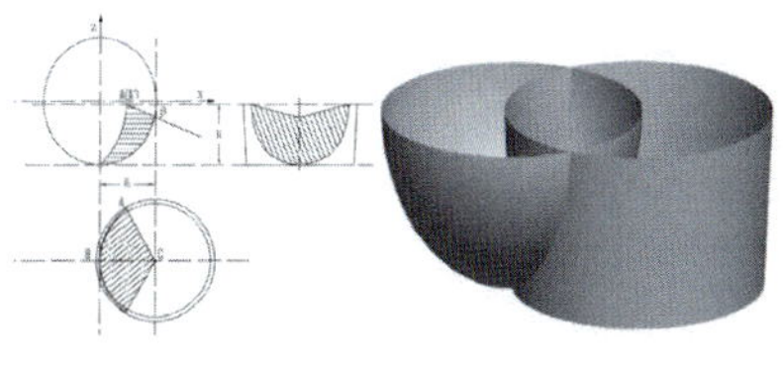

Figure 1. Effective view of the ellipsoidal leaflets.

Eq. (1) is the mathematical description of ellipsoidal surface leaflet (ELV):

$$\begin{cases} \dfrac{x^2}{13.4^2} + \dfrac{y^2}{13.4^2} + \dfrac{z^2}{14.8^2} = 1 \\ (x-13)^2 + y^2 = (z \tan 3^{\circ} - 13)^2 \end{cases} \quad (1)$$

2.2. *The establishment of a solid model*

For elliptical valve leaflet, in order to form a ellipsoid leaves ,seeing the axis that formed the inverted conical surface of the elliptical valve leaflet as the axis of rotation, and using geometry array command get three geometric model of the valve leaflet. Geometric model with a certain thickness of three-piece valve leaflets were imported into geometric unit of ANSYS FLUENT software modules. We can get the original model and the finite element models are shown in Fig.2. The valve material was served as linear elastic material, the density is $1.0\times10^{9}\, ton/mm^{3}$, and the modulus of elasticity is 5.4 Mpa and the poisson's ratio of 0.45.

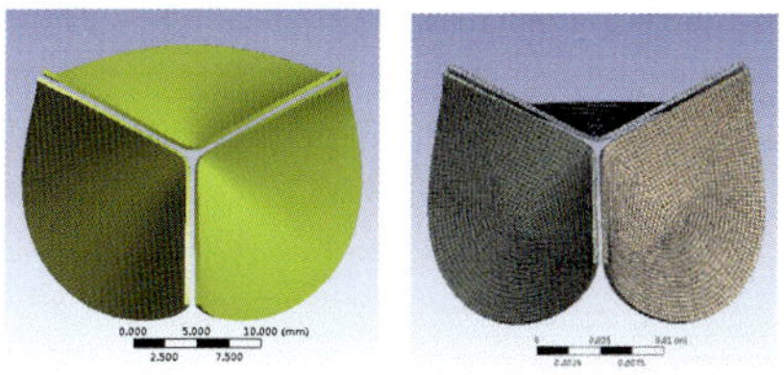

Figure 2. Disc solid model and finite element model.

2.3 *The establishment of a fluid model*

In the work of BHV, massive amounts of blood around the valve, the valve leaflets achieved closed and open by themselves by the transvalvular pressure between the valve leaflets. According to the actual situation, we believe that the arterial wall sinus and vessels are filled with blood in this fluid-structure interaction analysis. If the inlet and outlet of the arterial wall were closed and materialized, we can consider the whole arterial model as a fluid model. We imported the arterial wall model into in ANSYS software as shown in Fig. 3. In this analysis, we assume that the density of blood is $1.15\times10^{9}\, ton/mm^{3}$, the viscoelastic modulus is $5\times10^{5}\, pa$ and the Poisson's ratio is 0.3.

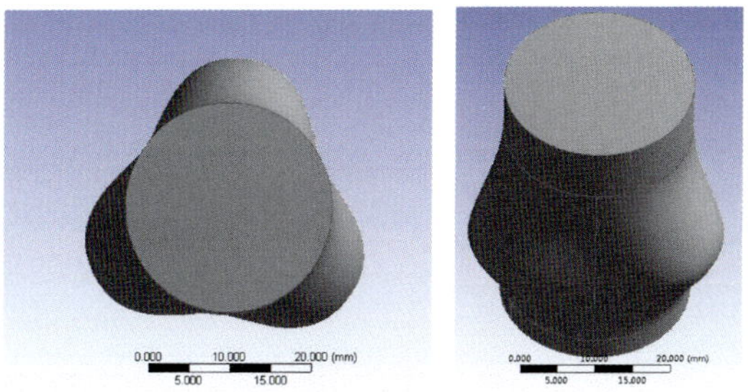

Figure 3. Fluid model.

We meshing fluid model by ANSYS. The finite element model for fluid model is showed in Fig. 4.

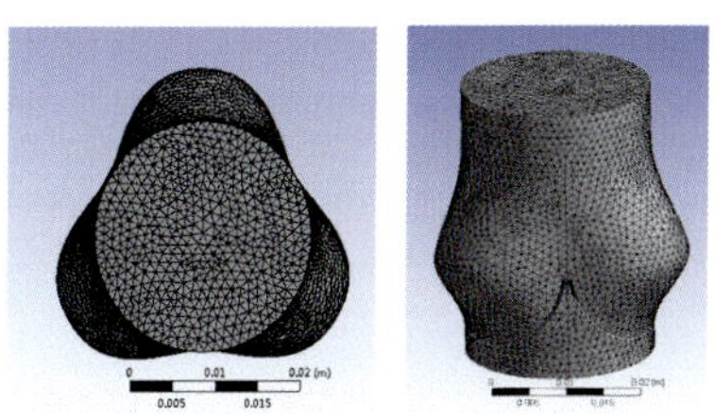

Figure 4. The finite element model for fluid.

After obtained the fluid model and the solid model, we can get the fluid-structure interaction analysis model through Boolean operations showed in Fig. 5.

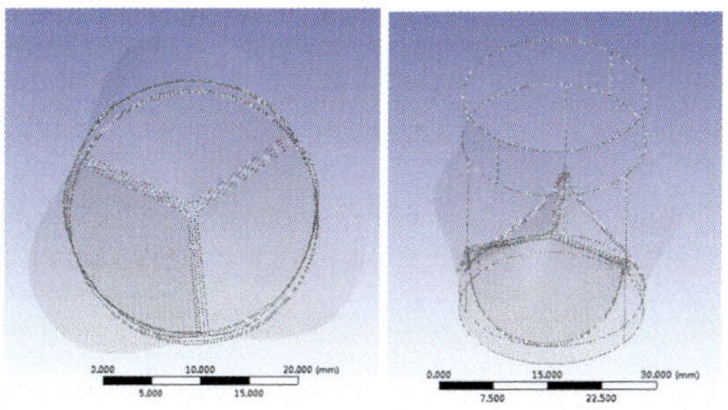

Figure 5. The fluid structure interaction model.

2.4 *On the surface of the fluid-structure interaction definition and boundary conditions are applied*

The fluid-structure interaction analysis needs to define the fluid-structure interaction surface and fluid inlet and outlet. According to the working principle of the valve, we definition of fluid and solid interaction surface for three valve leaflet thickness of upper and lower surfaces and valve free edge of the direction of the cross section. Fluid and solid interaction surface, the fluid inlet and outlet as shown in Fig. 6.

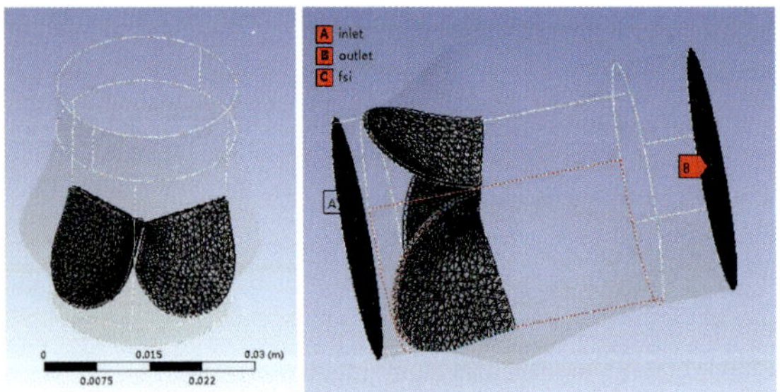

Figure 6. Fluid and solid coupling surface and the fluid inlet and outlet.

A surface is the fluid inlet, at the inlet boundary conditions we are set in velocity-inlet. According to the clinical data, we set the speed of the fluid is 1 m/s, the energy of turbulent kinetic is 1 m^2/s^2 and the rate of turbulent dissipation is 1 m^2/s^2. B surface as the fluid outlet, at the inlet boundary conditions we set in pressure outlet and set pressure value is 0. The turbulence value of the outlet is the same as the inlet. After the initial flow field, the iteration to around 100 step flow convergence. In setting load, the valve leaflets have borne the brunt of blood nine surface loading diagram in Fig. 7. Suture of the valve leaflet was fixed and its degrees of freedom is 0.

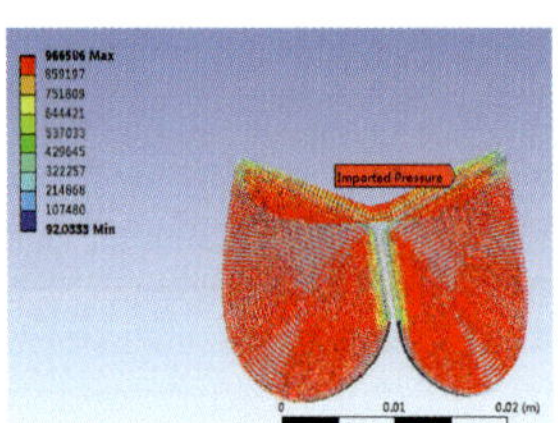

Figure 7. Stress distribution of valve leaflets.

3. RESULTS AND DISCUSSIONS

The finite element results of the thickness of the HBV with 0.3 mm, 0.4 mm and 0.5 mm are presented in Fig. 7, 8 and 9. We focus on our attention on the maximum equivalent stress and tangential stress.

3.1. *Stress distribution of the HBV with 0.3 mm thickness*

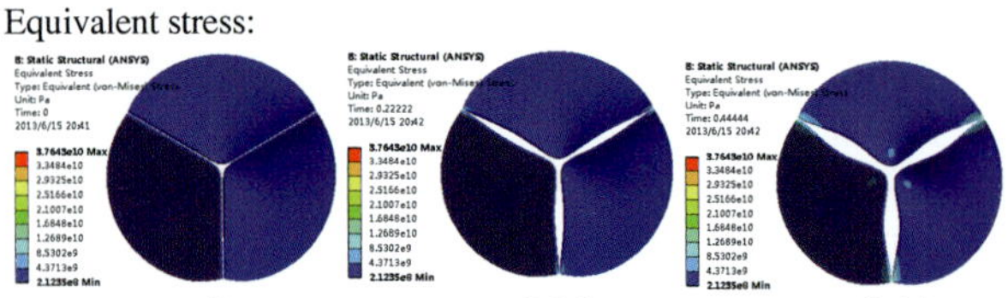

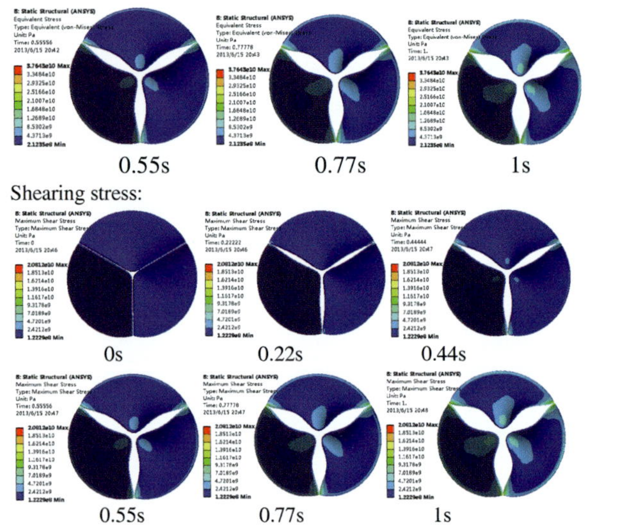

Figure 8. Stress distribution of the HBV with 0.3 mm thickness.

From the above analysis of stress, we can find that with the blood impacting, the valve leaflet gradually opened and at the same time the stress concentration mainly appears at the top of the attachment edge. The max Equivalent stress with 0.3 mm thickness is 37600Mpa and the max shearing stress is 20800Mpa.

3.2. *Stress distribution of the HBV with 0.4 mm thickness*

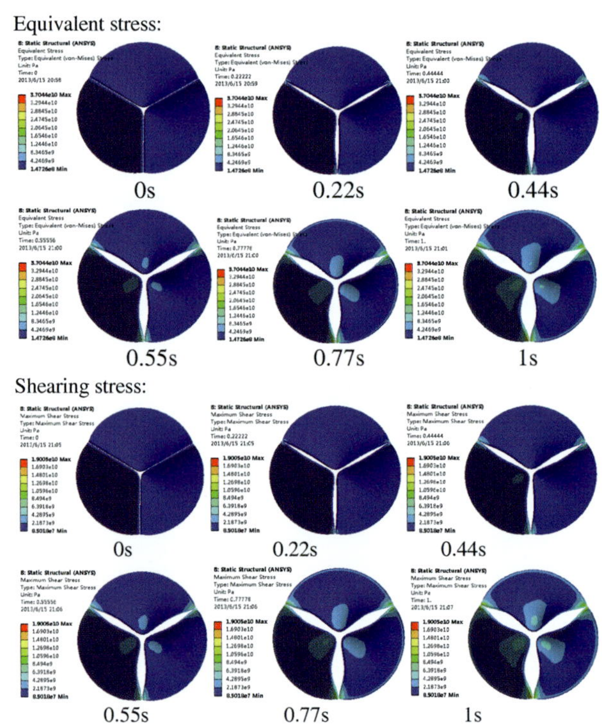

Figure 9. Stress distribution of the HBV with 0.4 mm thickness.

Depending on the analysis what we have done above, we can conclude that the stress concentration mainly appears at the top of the attachment edge and the abdomen of HBV with 0.4 mm thickness. The max Equivalent stress with 0.4 mm thickness is 37000Mpa and the max shearing stress is 19000Mpa.

3.3. *Stress distribution of the HBV with 0.5 mm thickness*

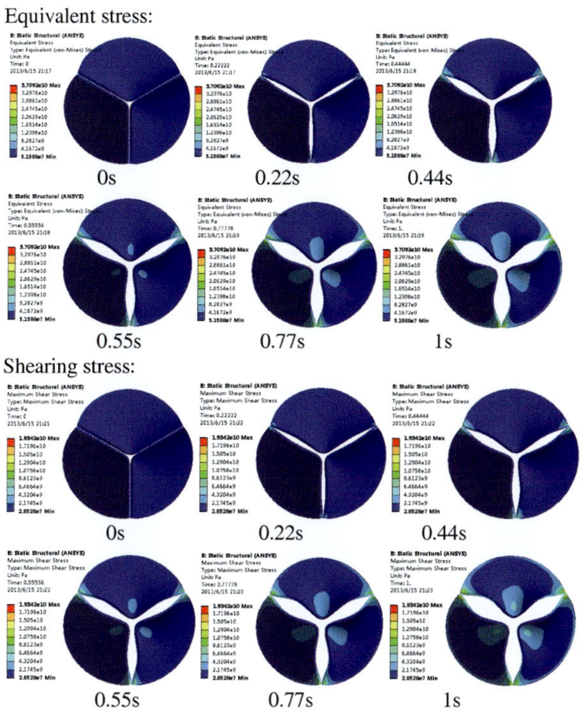

Figure 10. Stress distribution of the HBV with 0.5 mm thickness.

According to the analysis results, we can conclude that the max stress mainly appears at the top of the attachment edge and the min stress mainly distributes at the mid of the free edge. The max equivalent stress with 0.5 mm thickness is 37100Mpa and the max shearing stress is 19300Mpa.

3.4. *Comparison*

On the basis of the finite element analysis results, we can conclude that the stress concentration mainly appears at the top of the attachment edge and the abdomen no matter what thickness of the valve leaflet. The value of the peak von-Mises under different thickness as shown in Table 1.

Table 1. Value of von-mises of valve leaflet.

Stress Thickness	0.3mm		0.4mm		0.5mm	
	max	min	max	min	max	min
Equivalent stress/Mpa	37600	212.4	37000	147.3	37100	51.6
Shearing stress/Mpa	20800	122.3	19000	85	19300	28.5

From the finite element analysis of valve leaflets with different thickness, we can learn that the value of peak von-Mises not only the equivalent stress but also the shearing stress has declined from 0.3 mm to 0.4 mm and risen from 0.4 mm to 0.5 mm. The Table 1 shows that the value of peak von-Mises both the equivalent stress and the shearing stress with 0.4 mm thickness is lower than that of 0.3 mm and 0.5 mm and further more the min stress. In addition there occurs non-uniform stress distribution at the attachment edge under low thickness which indicates that the thickness has more effect on the attachment edge.

4. CONCLUSIONS

The paper constructs the parametric model of the elliptical HVB via computer aided design and the dynamic properties of the valve leaflet with different thickness are researched using the ANSYS software. The analysis results are compared and clearly confirmed that the fluid structure interaction has a significant effect on the mechanical properties of the valve leaflets. According to the whole loading process, we can conclude that the thickness of the elliptical valve leaflet with 0.4 mm is better than others Thus when manufacturing the bioprosthetic, we can use 0.4 mm thickness to make the leaflets.

ACKNOWLEDGMENT

This work was supported by grants from Natural Science Foundation of State (No: 31170906) and Clean Mechanical Manufacture (Shandong University) Ministry of Education.

REFERENCES

- [1] Vongpatanasin W, Hillis LD, Lange RA: Prosthetic Heart Valves. New Engl J Med, 1996, pp. 407-406.
- [2] Peter Zilla, Paul Human and D. Bezuidenhout, "Bioprosthetic heart valves: the need for a quantum leap," Biotechnol; Appl; Biochem, vol. 40, pp. 57–66, 2004.
- [3] Rivero G, Garcia-Paez JM, Alvarez L, Multigner M, Valdes J, Carabias I, Spottorno J, Hernando A: Magnetic sensor for early detection of heart valve bioprostheses failure. Sens Lett, 2007, pp.263-266.
- [4] Dong, S. and X. Yuan, Pretension process analysis of prestressed space grid structures. Journal of Constructional Steel Research, 2007. 63(3): p.406-411.
- [5] Bathe, K., Z. Hou and S. Ji, Finite element analysis of fluid flows fully coupled with structural interactions. Computers & Structures, 1999. 72(1–3): p.1-16.
- [6] Bathe K.J., Zhang H, S. Ji, A flow-condition-based interpolation finite element procedure for incompressible fluid flows [J], Computers & Structures, vol.80, pp.1267-1287, 2002.

- [7] Kohno H., Bathe K.J., A nine quadrilateral FCBI element for incompressible fluid flows [J], International Journal for Number Methods in Fluids, vol. 22, pp.673-699, 2006.
- [8] Eckert C, Zubiate B, Vergnat M, Gorman J, Gorman R, Sacks M, "In Dynamic Deformation of the Mitral Valve Annulus," Ann Biomed Eng, 2009, pp. 1757-1771.
- [9] Hou J, Yang Z, Zhou M, "Impact Action Between Concrete Blocks in Collapse Analysis of Reinforced Concrete Structures," Adv Sci Lett 2011, pp.986-995.
- [10] I. Vesely, "The evolution of bioprosthetic heart valve design and its impact on durability," Cardiovascular Pathology. vol. 12, pp.277– 286, 2003.

Improvement of Business Performance Based on ERP Technical Management

J.H. Liu[1] & J.H. Lin[2]
Education Technology Center, Experimental Teaching Center, Guangdong University of Foreign Studies, Guangzhou 510006, China
School of Economics & Trade, Guangdong University of Foreign Studies, Guangzhou, 510006, China
Email: [1]200511422@oamail.gdufs.edu.cn, [2]ljh@oamail.gdufs.edu.cn

Y.J. Hong
School of Economics & Trade, Guangdong University of Foreign Studies, Guangzhou, 510006, China

ABSTRACT: The paper aims to analyze the problems of implementing ERP management system, and the implementation progress of the maintenance of some contradictory information, system security and other aspects. Equipped with the management of ERP system in production and business operation activities, it can help enterprises to improve the management performance and the implementation of ERP. This paper provides the corresponding technical solutions for enterprises. In reality, through the use of Virtual Desktop technology for centralized management and the use of the ERP system, enterprises can improve management performance.

KEYWORDS: Enterprise resource planning; Virtual desktop; Enterprise performance.

1. INTRODUCTION

The globalization and informationization of economy has provided advantageous conditions for the improvement of the management level of corporation. The Enterprises Resource Planning system, also called ERP, adopts systematic management idea, achieves corporate strategic decision through information technology and provides a modern platform for management for the staff. It combines the ideas of modern information technology and corporate management through integrating resources like human resources, operation flow, information and data, hardware and software, and management idea. Through enhancing the operating ability and effectiveness as well as controlling the cost, it can help the company to maximize its economic benefits and thus make the most of the advantages in global market competition. ERP has been commonly used in developed countries. However, the usage rate of ERP in China is rather low. Consequently, it is the emphasis for both the academic and business circles to study the implementation of ERP.

2. THE TECHNOLOGICAL PROBLEMS WHEN USING ERP

In 1990s, an American IT company proposed the idea of ERP, enterprise resource planning, according to the information and computer technology at that time and the infomatization innovation of enterprise management which was supposed to have met the requirements toward the whole society's supply chain management of American enterprises, protesting the development tendency of enterprises in information era. ERP satisfies the development requirements of enterprises in market economy. It has become one of the most effective management tools of enterprise management [1], and it was the only way that enterprise management has to pass to mature. Manufacturing companies can use ERP to integrates almost all of the industry processes and improve enterprise's performance, helping management make decisions, making sure that enterprise to develop steadily. Moreover, ERP has greatly developed in health care system, transportation system, science and education system, import and export trade, service and so on [2]. ERP integrates enterprise's internal resources to make planning and management to the production, procurement, inventory, sales, cost, finance and human resource, in order to help enterprise get the most benefit result. But some enterprise management fails to consider the special management patterns and operation procedures of the companies when choosing which kind of ERP to use. They did not analyze the feasibility of the ERP software and carry out the targeted process reengineering, so they found all of the models of the software cannot adapted to the companies, resulting in the waste of enterprises' capital and the lower working efficiency before using ERP system.

Enterprises should fully understand ERP in a right way. ERP is not only a system software providing to enterprises, but also a modern resource management of a new management theory and integrated enterprise management thoughts. Conducting ERP is the tendency of enterprises' development. Nowadays, the successful rate of Chinese companies' using ERP is not high. The main reason is the enterprises fail to clearly understand the purposes of using ERP. On the other hand, some enterprise managers take ERP as software, lacking the overall implementation planning of ERP. They think ERP can be used as soon as it is installed. This kind of thought leads to many technological problems when enterprise conducting ERP.

2.1. *The security of the system and the implementation processes*

ERP system also has various hidden security problems as the software platform of enterprise management, including the information malfunction produces by the system itself, and the threats from the outside of the system: network hackers, the spy behaviors of competitors, the virus invasion problem and so on. In addition, the natural factors and the influence toward the enterprise of the accidental forces, which will all brings disastrous consequences of the enterprise production and daily operation.

Moreover, the information ERP system dealt with also has the problems of storage, reading speed, information security and so on, especially when coming down to the information security of the enterprise secretes, which will directly influence the future of the enterprise. ERP system can make sure of the data's quality through the unified access database, and is more convenient on sharing data. Through setting different operation access for the users of the system, employees of different departments can better understand the current production procedures of the enterprise. In this way, they can control better the operation progress of the enterprise and guarantee the normal operation. In addition, through setting permission, the system can improve the confidentiality of the enterprise data, making the enterprise use data more secure.

After ERP system operates in the internal system of the enterprise, managers may easily neglect the coordination, updating and maintenance of the system. In fact, the installation and usage of information system need a rather long period of time to test run and maintenance. ERP system needs the enterprise to make targeted adjustment according to the enterprises' concrete business and the change of organization, including test finding, repairing system errors, updating system models and so on. If the operation of ERP system is too complex, it will lead to the using difficulty of the employees, or the inadequate training, which will all result in the risk of the system's usage, even cannot guarantee the normal operation of the system. If you wait until the occurrence of these problems, and think solutions until having certain consequences, the enterprise will face a rather great loss.

2.2. *The contradiction and uncontrollable factors of ERP implementation*

There are lots of contradictions when implement ERP, including the problems of inter-coordination of different departments, influence the integration of ERP system, the deviation of the working focus of the system and needs of the enterprise, the inconsistent state between ERP's advanced thoughts and the enterprise's employees' quality weak, the accuracy of enterprise resource planning and the poor information system basic data, the fast updating of computer technology and ERP's rather long implementation period, all of which lead to the development of ERP system is very difficult to keep pace with the new technology. ERP training and consulting and maintenance, computer terminal, network equipment, storage and server hardware costs, the development of ERP system, the purchase and system upgrade software cost, for the ERP implementation of IT talent recruitment, deployment of ERP system in the process of Chinese and foreign hire staff training for employees, the contradiction of the high investment to carry on maintenance of the system and slow income; traditional manufacturing oriented enterprises mainly rely on intensive manpower to improve the productivity, which belongs to the intensive production. In the business process, the inevitable problems of human resources management difficulties, high cost etc. Therefore, ERP can help enterprises to save the human resource. The maximum possible work is completed with a minimum of human. Human resources cost is also an important cost of enterprise operation.

The deployment of ERP systems is rather complex, a successful deployment of ERP system is just the start of enterprises to use the ERP project, the actual process of the system need to integrate with the enterprise, through the oscillation period, the formation of enterprise ERP resources and improve enterprise performance. There are difference and the relation between the essence of implementation and technical management of enterprise ERP. Technological management needs to integrate with enterprise ERP, and carry out technological management of the implementation of ERP through ability, quality and benefits. By analyzing its performance, provide a clearer thought and scientific method for the construction of enterprise ERP implementation performance.

2.3. *System integration problems*

The implementation of ERP by enterprises needs rather more integration process. The installation of an ERP system is very complicated, the project is large, and the implementation of the performance of enterprise system influences directly the performance of the enterprise [3]. According to Melville and other scholars' IT resource computing models, the relation between IT technology resource, IT human resource and the organization performance are all positive [4]. At present, the researches of the application of ERP system in enterprise management is more about the problems encountered when purchasing and conducing ERP, among them, many of the situations are the unsatisfactory implementing process and performance [5]. Partial researcher starts to pay attention to the invisible or middle benefits brought by ERP system. Enterprise can be used as innovation leads to the reform of enterprise's management. Therefore, we need to study the problems of technical management of ERP system and the strategies to solve these problems of the traditional financial index and financial performance.

The implementation of ERP includes the network construction, software configuration, working mode and enterprise management system [6]. If the enterprise's procurement, production, sales departments and finance, department management have remote offices, buying the software without the implementation of remote access to the site, will lead to the installed system cannot use. In addition, configuration, implementation, maintenance and updating of the system, modify the work presents a challenge to the IT department [7]. There are certain hidden security problems when using ERP system. Information data of the ERP system processing relates to storage and confidentiality issues, especially the confidentiality of business information, and will directly affect the future survival of enterprises. In addition to the system itself and system fault, external factors, such as the network hacker attacks, competitors intrusion, virus threats, and the influences from natural uncontrollable factors, various unexpected will undoubtedly have great impacts on the production management of the enterprise. A clear understanding of these factors that influence the implementation of ERP will help the enterprise effectively use the ERP system, and help the enterprise find and solve management problems and bottlenecks, which will play a decisive role in the development of the enterprise.

3. THE ADVANTAGE OF ERP DESKTOP VIRTUALIZATION

3.1. *The introduction of virtual desktop technology*

In recent years, the virtual desktop technology has been widely used in many fields. Being a typical application of cloud computing, the core technology of virtual desktop virtualization is virtualizing the operating system of the personal computer's desktop, separating the operating system from the operation of the computer environment. In this way, users can not be restricted by space and time, and they can access to desktop operating system anytime and anywhere via laptop, portable mobile devices, desktops and other non-specified equipment. All in all, virtual desktop technology can support enterprises to conduct real-time remote access to desktop system and support enterprise to host data center uniformly.

The wide application of personal computer began to bring many new problems. The biggest problem is the increasing complexity of the system operation maintenance, forcing people to focus on deployment of computing resources delivery once more [8].Virtual desktop technology contributed to the user-centered calculation mode [9], hardware cost dropping substantially. With the promotion of data computing capacity, the size of the data center gets bigger, the operating costs of enterprises have been reduced, the rate of resource utilization has also been improved, and at last the business performance has eventually been improved. In a word, the deployment of virtual desktop leads to reductions of the enterprise operation cost and obvious improvements of its performance. Through virtual desktop technology, there is no direct connection between desktop, application system, operating systems and hardware. By encapsulating the desktop operating system, applications, and the corresponding user data, they are isolated to each other, and this solution enables IT staff to update, modify, and deployment of each component in a higher speed, the business process to get a higher flexibility, and the system response time to be shortened. In addition, the virtual machine can construct a complete operating system, desktop environment, application and configuration. The application of the virtual desktop technology will be able to make the enterprise get higher rates of manageability, security, and lower overall cost. Make use of virtualization service to realize the dynamic infrastructure environment in a system, further improve the system architecture and its enterprise management mode, and reach to a better data center based on service and security in the future.

3.2. *The advantages of ERP virtualization*

The aims to strengthen the management of enterprise ERP implementation technology are improving the utilization efficiency of enterprise ERP, reducing the enterprise operation and maintenance cost, improving security access mechanism and the safety of the enterprise data confidentiality, reducing risk, and improving enterprise performance.

On one hand, enterprise users freely access to and use the ERP system. In traditional ERP technology management mode, enterprise employees can only be limited to using a specific computer, and when the computer software and hardware failure, the user can only passively waiting for the enterprise system administrator to solve the problem of system, which seriously affects the work efficiency. Using virtual desktop technology, users of the ERP system are no longer limited to specific equipment, and they can use it anywhere at any time through a variety of free access to the virtual desktop terminal equipment and application of ERP system. Enterprise users operate in their own virtual desktop and all the data will be dealt with in the back-end servers. So even if the virtual machine system is infected by the virus or suffers a sudden power emergency, both the background data on the server and the operation will not be affected.

On the other hand, the install upgrade and maintenance of ERP system are conducted in the back-end servers. The ERP system of the company users' computers and installation procedure of enterprise client are very complicated, which leads to a higher requirement of computers' hardware, more difficulty of management and maintenance, and a bigger hidden security risk. All of these make it more likely to a slow computer running and even system crash. But the virtual desktop technology can exactly solve these problems. The virtual desktop provides services based on the user's identity. And its strong identify authentication design will protect the system from hacking or attacking, effectively strengthening the confidentiality of the enterprise information.

4. THE BUILDING OF ERP SYSTEM UNDER VIRTUAL DESKTOP

A lot of managers think that it is quite easy for corporates to use ERP system because it only needs setting up and using software instead of manually operating. And thus they tend to implement ERP as soon as they decide to use ERP. However, only after actual using, they come to realize that ERP cannot be fluently operated. For one reason, departments such as manufactory, purchase department, store, and financial department are located in different places but managers have not considered communication problems among different departments. And thus the system cannot be used after setting up. Besides, the system may be broken in the middle of the process if the corporate has not equipped with enough specialists of ERP. Consequently, the actual application and implementation of ERP requires the operators to be familiar with corporates' internal operational process and some specialists who have capabilities of ERP management and IT techniques. Also, managers should realize the difficultness of the implementation of ERP and pay attention not only to the building of the Internet, software and hardware, but also corporate's daily working modes and management system so as to cut the risk of ERP implementation. At present, there are quite a great number of problems in the application of ERP so it is necessary to take some successful corporate applications as examples, because ERP system has great using potential in China.

ERP system needs to be continually updated and the upgrading of ERP is an essential part of the application of ERP. Although the upgrading of ERP can enhance the effectiveness of the whole system, some working habits and processes should be changed and improved, which may lead to collision of the staff. It is important for the technology department of a corporate to control and supervise the implementation of ERP and allocation of hardware and software, the modification of data and the maintenance. And managers should know more about the whole system in order to better apply ERP. Otherwise, it will be a disaster for the company if problems arise in the system.

ERP can integrate the resource and system operation, span multiple departments or company deployed ERP system. The main purpose of resources integration is to set up the transfer channel for data flow, information flow among the various departments or companies between data flow, so as to shorten the circulation time, thereby reducing the waste of human, material and financial resources. The realization of data sharing, keeping the information consistency and improving the efficiency of the system, have become an effective management means for enterprises. The correct use of ERP among multi-departments and branches can be effective for system integration and operation. Build the systematic platform of information sharing and corporate decision-supportive data base for each department and branch of resource integration and management. The integrated system will help the enterprise managers to grasp the overall business process so as to improve the efficiency of enterprise management.

The virtual desktop technology will virtualize the traditional computer and manage it based on a virtualization platform. All the computer programs are installed and used in virtual machines, and employees can be managed through the virtual desktop access to thin client, computer, notebook and tablet computer and other equipment for the desktop. And those are all used in ERP system installed in the virtual desktop. Computer desktops and applications of staff's terminals can be controlled and centralized. Those data can be unified management by the administrator. The management processes include the real time monitoring data acquisition system, a variety of data analysis system, transmission of the collected data in the running to the administrator. The working model is as followed.

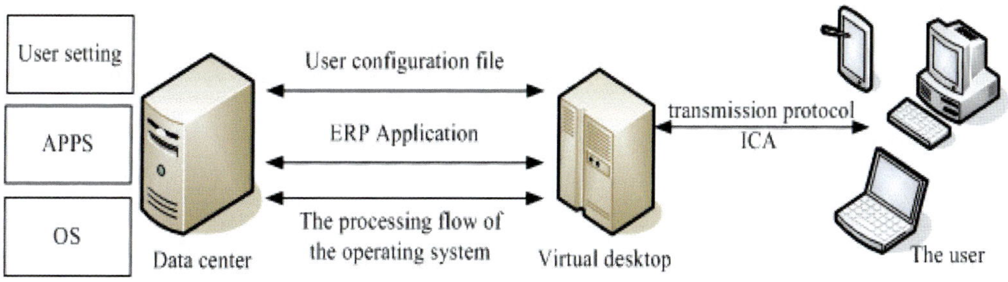

Figure 1. Working model based on virtual desktop.

Virtual desktop physically separates into 3 parts, which are user profile, system of stream processing and application. After the user logins, virtual desktop then dynamically combines the three parts into an independent operation of the desktop. The virtual desktop operating system uses ICA protocol in the terminal device. At the same time, it can also according to the needs of enterprises, create a set of independent personalized desktop operating system for each enterprise user, and with related applications deployed in the desktop system, users will have higher desktop management authority.

ERP uses a new management mode to change the traditional management mode of enterprise, integrating with management idea and advanced management method. It uses the concept of enterprise management, ERP technology and information management technology to reflect the comprehensive management of enterprises. The Effective implementation of ERP also needs to place large emphasis on staff skills training throughout the whole process of project. It needs to conduct training on fixed time hierarchically covering contents. Based on the knowledge integrity of the study, validity, scientific and practical, the staff awareness of ERP should be improved ERP. The key point is to prevent simply regarding ERP system as an unrealistic electronic tool in manual style, and come to the understanding that the essence of ERP is assisting the company to find better management solutions.

ERP system is related in nature with the management of enterprise. Merged the enterprise management theory into the process of implementing ERP, enterprises can improve the effect of implementation of ERP largely through the ERP implementation and operation process reengineering in enterprises. Also, the virtual desktop turns the implementation of ERP into the enterprise performance and value solidified in the enterprise products and services, and thus improving staff quality and enterprise ability and value. It then becomes the enterprise ERP management performance. ERP system's complexity is more than other system, relating to the enterprise operation in all aspects, especially in the aspect of enterprise management. To a certain extent, the actual operator of ERP system in the enterprise operation process system consider that the operation is more difficult, however, managers believe that the system can provide a large amount of data and the reasonable reference for decision makers. In addition, a substantial increase in financial sector financial settlement efficiency. The managers of the enterprise can achieve effective management with the data of ERP system. Various departments should learn the advanced management concepts, the use of new technology and business process reengineering and the development trend of enterprise management mode, and reestablish the management mode. This requires enterprises to study the performance of ERP system from the long-term macro view.

5. CONCLUSION

Through implementing virtual desktop technology and management as well as the implementation of construction technology and management, on one hand it raises the hard power of economic efficiency of enterprises. On the other hand, improve the soft power of the competitiveness of enterprises. Enterprises can achieve the fusion process between the enterprises, employees, ERP system, which is the enterprise ERP implementation process to improve enterprise performance management process of the virtual desktop technology. Through the above analysis, the ERP system can effectively help enterprises to reduce operating costs and improve enterprise management efficiency. At the same time, using the virtual desktop management for enterprise ERP implementation technology, it can enhance the enterprise information level, maintenance management, information and system security level, and it greatly enhances the enterprise operation ability and work efficiency, saving the cost of management and making the enterprise economic benefit maximization. Moreover, it can improve the overall business performance management, bringing greater potential for development, making enterprises remain invincible in the fierce market competition.

6. ACKNOWLEDGEMENT

This research was financially supported by the Innovation and Entrepreneurship Training Project of Guangdong University of Foreign Studies in 2014 (No. 201411846022).

REFERENCES

- [1] P. Ekman, P. Thilenius, T. Windahl, Extending the ERP system: considering the business relationship portfolio, Business Process Management Journal 20 (2014) 480-501.
- [2] P. Ruivo, B. Johansson, T. Oliveira et al, Commercial ERP Systems and User Productivity: A Study Across European SMEs, Procedia Technology 9(2013) 84-93.
- [3] R. Rajnoha, J. Kádárová, A. Sujová et al, Business Information Systems: Research Study and Methodological Proposals for ERP Implementation Process Improvement, Procedia - Social and Behavioral Sciences 109(2014) 165-170.
- [4] Kanellou, C. Spathis, Accounting benefits and satisfaction in an ERP environment, International Journal of Accounting Information Systems 14(2013) 209–234.
- [5] J. Ram, D. Corkindale, M.L. Wu. Implementation critical success factors (CSFs) for ERP: Do they contribute to implementation success and post-implementation performance? International Journal of Production Economics 144(2013) 157–174.
- [6] LING, The Integration Model and Key Technologies of E-commerce and ERP Systems, Journal of Computational Information Systems 5(2009) 665-671.
- [7] Y. WEI, C. LV, Mian ZHANG, Design and Implementation of a New Integrated E-commerce System based on AJAX, Journal of Computational Information Systems 5(2009) 755-762.
- [8] P. Calyam, R. Patali, A. Berryman et al, Utility-directed resource allocation in virtual desktop clouds [J]. Computer networks 55(2011) 4112-4130.
- [9] Z. Haiman, E. Fuentes, A virtual-desktop revolution has arrived, Caribbean Business 38 (2010) 32-33.

An Attribute-based Access Control Scheme in Cloud Storage Environment

M.H. Xing* & W.M. Li
buptxingminhong@163.com
State Key Laboratory of Networking and Switching Technology, Beijing University of Posts and Telecommunications, Beijing, 100876, China
**Email: buptxingminhong@163.com*

ABSTRACT: Access control plays an important role in cloud storage. Attribute-based encryption enables the data owner embedded the access policy in the data. Many solutions have been proposed to ensure data security on cloud. However, in the existing indirectly revocation schemes, the efficiency and computational costs need to be improved. In order to realize fine-grained access control and reduce the computing burden of the data owner and users, we propose a scheme which includes attribute-based access control with revocation. The scheme could ensure data security, achieve higher computing efficiency and realize expressive policy.

KEYWORDS: Cloud storage; Attribute-based encryption; Access control.

1. INTRODUCTION

The cloud storage service provider offers convenient services which is altering the traditional storage method [1]. More and more people store their data file on the cloud in order to synchronize and share with friends. When people enjoy this kind of services they also worry about their privacy and data security. Therefore access control is necessary for prevent the unauthorized user from illegally getting access to the secret information. In the context of cloud storage, data owner is independent of the cloud service provider [2], which means after uploading the files the data owner will not have direct interaction with the users. So the traditional control approaches [3], will not be suitable in cloud storage systems. To address this problem, researchers have worked to find some feasible solutions.

Sahai and Waters [4] firstly proposed a promising version for encryption, attribute-based encryption (ABE), so that the data owner could distribute encrypted data to the people who hold some certain attributes. The basic ABE could be divided into two categories, ciphertext policy ABE (CP-ABE) [5-7] and key policy ABE (KP-ABE) [8-10]. In CP-ABE the attributes are associated with the private key and the access policy is associated with the ciphertext, which enables the data owner to define the access policy. To be applicable in multiple scenarios, some variants of ABE have been proposed. The multi-authority schemes [11-13] aim to solve the problem of attributes in different domains. The proxy re-encryption schemes [14-16] could efficiently solve the problem of computational cost while protecting the security of the original data file. The ABE schemes with revocation [17-20] mainly solve the problem of access control. Since multiple users holds the same attributes, it is necessary to ensure that revoking one user or dropping one attribute of a user will not influence the other users. Among these ABE schemes with revocation, there are mainly two types, the indirect method [17, 18] and the direct method [19, 20].

(1) In the indirect schemes, the authority updates secret key periodically or updates the private key of the user who is not revoked. The cloud does not have to know the revocation list. However, there are also drawbacks. The update may not be immediate. Or in the key update phase, there may be large data communication costs between cloud and the user.

(2) In the direct schemes, the sender needs to specify a revocation list and directly revoke the user. The interaction between unrevoked user and trusted authority is direct and there is no need for key update. However, a revocation list should be maintained.

In this paper, we proposed an attribute-based access control scheme using in cloud storage environment. Inspired by the schemes proposed by Waters [7], Hur [18] and Green [21], we construct a user binary tree to generate CEK and use a proxy to do the partially decryption. The user binary tree is aimed at realizing access control by share parameters between the user and cloud. The proxy helps reduce the computating costs of the user. Our scheme is efficient and secure in the cloud storage environment.

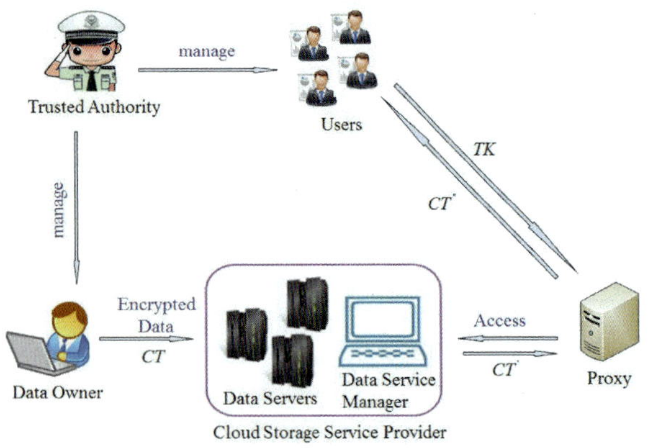

Figure 1. Cloud storage system.

2. PRELIMINARIES

2.1. *Access structure*

$\mathcal{U} = \{U_1, U_2, \cdots, U_n\}$ is a set of participants. For $\mathcal{A} \subset 2^U$, if $\forall B, C$: when $B \in \mathcal{A}$ and $B \subseteq C$, then $C \in \mathcal{A}$. We will call that $\mathcal{A}$ is monotone [7]. The monotone access structure $\mathcal{A}$ is the monotone set of nonempty subsets of participants. The set in $\mathcal{A}$ is called the authorized set, and the set out of $\mathcal{A}$ is called the unauthorized set. The member of the authorized set will successfully recover secret value $s \in S$ by using the secret shares $\{\omega_i \mid U_i \in \mathcal{A}\}$.

2.2. *Bilinear pairings*

Let G_1 and G_2 be two cyclic groups of prime order p. We call the map $e: G_1 \times G_1 \to G_2$ is a bilinear map [18] if it satisfies the following properties.

(1) Bilinearity. For $\forall P, Q \in G_1$ and $\forall a, b \in Z$, $e(P^a, Q^b) = e(P, Q)^{ab}$.

(2) Non-degeneracy. For $\exists P \in G_1$, $e(P, Q) \neq 1$.

(3) Computability. For certain $P, Q \in G_1$, there exists an efficient algorithm to calculate $e(P, Q)$.

2.3. *Decisional bilinear Diffie-Hellman exponent*

The Decisional q-Bilinear Diffie-Hellman Exponent (Decisional q-BDHE) problem [7] is defined as follows.

Choose a group $\mathbb{G}$ of prime order p. Let g be a generator of $\mathbb{G}$ and $a, s \in \mathbb{Z}_p$ are chosen randomly. Let g_i denotes g^{a_i}. When given $\vec{y} = (g, g_1, \cdots g_q, g_{q+2}, \cdots, g_{2q}, g^s)$, the adversary has to distinguish $e(g,g)^{a^{q+1}s} \in \mathbb{G}_T$ from a random element in $\mathbb{G}_T$.

We will say that algorithm $\mathcal{B}$ which outputs $z \in \{0,1\}$ has advantage ε when solving decisional q-BDHE problem on $\mathbb{G}$, if $|\Pr[\mathcal{B}(\vec{y}, T = e(g,g)^{a^{q+1}s}) = 0] - \Pr[\mathcal{B}(\vec{y}, T = R) = 0]| \geq \varepsilon$,.

Definition 1. The decisional q-BDHE assumption stands, if there is no poly-time algorithm that has a non-negligible advantage when solving the decisional q-BDHE problem [7].

3. SECURITY REQUIREMENTS AND SYSTEM MODEL

3.1. *System model and description*

Our cloud storage system model [18] involves five entities as shown in Figure 1. We will give specifications of these entities.

(1) Trusted authority (TA). It is the only entity that can be fully trusted by the users in the cloud storage system. TA generates system public key and private key, and also maintains a revocation list.

(2) Data Owner (DO). The data owner owns the original data file, and wants to share it on the cloud. He will define the access control policy and encrypt the data file under this policy before uploading it to the cloud.

(3) Users. The user hopes to receive the encrypted data. Each user holds a set of keys associated with attributes. Only if the attributes satisfy the access policy and the user is not revoked, will the user decrypt the ciphertext.

(4) Cloud storage service provider (CSSP). The cloud storage service provider offers data services on the cloud. It consists of a data management server and several data storage servers. The data storage server is responsible for storing data on the cloud. The data management server is responsible for access control. It will construct a user binary tree for re-encrypting the data and release some parameters to the users. Moreover, we consider the cloud is curious-but-honest, which means the cloud will execute the algorithm correctly but try hard to find as much sensitive information as possible.

(5) Proxy server (Proxy) [21]. We assume that the proxy has certain computational capacity and offers proxy computation service in order to reduce the computational cost of the user. Plus, the proxy does not need to be reliable. When the user holds some computation capacity limited devices, such as a mobile phone, the proxy can be used to do partial decryption. The user will use a secret value to construct a proxy key TK and send it to the proxy. The proxy cannot obtain the plaintext after receiving the TK and will decrypt the ciphertext honestly.

3.2. *Security requirements*

The data owner only wants to share the data file on the cloud with the authorized user. When there is revocation of user or attribute possession modification, the system is still secure. Moreover, the illegal users cannot collude to recover the secret information [18].

(1) Data Confidentiality. Firstly, the curious-but-honest cloud storage service provider cannot obtain

the secret information. Secondly, the illegal user who does not hold the attributes satisfy the access policy or is revoked cannot decrypt the ciphertext. Thirdly, the proxy server cannot get access to the secret information.

(2) Resistance to the collusion. If multiple users whose attributes do not satisfy the policy share their attributes, they still cannot obtain the secret information.

(3) Backward and forward secrecy. The new joining user, who gains new attribute so that the access policy can be satisfied, cannot obtain the data generated before this modification. This is the backward secrecy of the system. When a user is revoked or part of his attributes is dropped so that the access policy cannot be satisfied, the user cannot get access to the data generated after this modification. This is the forward secrecy of the system.

4. OUR CONSTRUCTION

4.1. *System setup*

In this phase, the trusted authority runs the Setup algorithm. The system inputs max and d, where max is the maximum number of the attributes, and d is the maximum number of $|\text{cover}(R)|$ for all the revocation lists. The master key MSK and public key PK are the outputs. TA first chooses a bilinear group $\mathbb{G}$ of prime order p with generator g and random elements $h_1, \ldots, h_{max}, u_1, \ldots, u_d$ in group $\mathbb{G}$. Then TA chooses two random $\alpha, a \in Z_p$. The master key is $MSK = < g^{\alpha} >$ and the public parameters are $PK = < g, e(g,g)^{\alpha}, g^{a}, h_1, h_2, \ldots, h_{\max}, u_1, u_2, \ldots, \quad u_d >$.

Plus, TA define a function $P(x)$ on $\mathbb{Z}_p \to \mathbb{G}$ as $P(x) = \prod_{j=0}^{d} u_j^{(x^j)}$.

4.2. *Data encryption*

When the data owner wants to share his file through the cloud storage services, he will run the Encrypt algorithm to enforce attribute-based access control over data $\mathcal{M}$. DO specifies the access policy (M, ρ) according to the universe of attributes S and encrypts $\mathcal{M}$ under (M, ρ). ρ is an injective function mapping attributes to rows of matrix $M_{l \times n}$. The algorithm randomly chooses a vector $\vec{v} = (s, y_2, \ldots y_n) \in \mathbb{Z}_p^n$, where $i = 1, \ldots, l$, and computes $\lambda_i = \vec{v} \cdot M_i$, where M_i denotes the i th row of the matrix M.

The ciphertext is then constructed as follows:

$$CT = (C = \mathcal{M}e(g,g)^{\alpha s}, C' = g^{s}, \forall i = 1, \ldots, l \;\; C_i = g^{a\lambda_i} h_{\rho(i)}^{-s}).$$

After generating the ciphertext, the data owner uploads it to the cloud.

4.3. *Key generation*

The key generation phase consists of the private key generation for each user and cloud encryption key generation, namely the CEK [21]. The private key is generated by TA while the CEK is generated by the data management service provider.

Phase 1: Attribute private key generation

After constructing the MSK and PK, TA runs the AttrKeyGen algorithm. Taking MSK and attribute set S as inputs, TA first randomly chooses $t \in Z_p$, and outputs the private key for each user as $SK = < K = g^{\alpha} g^{at} \;\; L = g^{t} \;\; \forall x \in S \;\; K_x = h_x^{t} >$.

TA sends the revocation list R to the data management server on the cloud.

Moreover, for each $\lambda_i \in \mathbb{A}$, TA also sends the attribute group information G_i to the data management server. For instance, user id_1, id_2, id_3 holds attributes $\{\lambda_1, \lambda_2\}$, $\{\lambda_1, \lambda_2, \lambda_3\}$, $\{\lambda_1, \lambda_3\}$ separately, therefore the corresponding attribute group will be $G_1 = \{\text{id}_1, \text{id}_2, \text{id}_3\}$, $G_2 = \{\text{id}_1, \text{id}_2\}$, $G_3 = \{\text{id}_2, \text{id}_3\}$. Then TA will sends the information to the data management server.

Phase 2: CEK generation

After obtaining the revocation list R and attribute group G_i, data management server runs the CoverGen algorithm.

Data management server firstly constructs the user binary tree. Set $\mathcal{X}$ denotes all the nodes in the tree. Each leaf node in the tree denotes a user $\text{id}_i \in \mathcal{U}$. $\text{Path}(\text{id}_i)$ denotes a series of nodes from the leaf to the root, such as $\text{Path}(id_7) = \{x_7, x_{12}, x_{14}, x_{15}\}$ in Figure 2.

Then the data management server calculates the minimal cover set $\text{cover}(R)$ according to the revocation list R. The nodes in minimal cover could cover all the leaf nodes $x \in \mathcal{U} \setminus R$ which are not in the revocation list. Take Figure 3 to illustrate. Assume $R = \{id_2, id_3\}$, since x_1, x_4 and x_{14} could cover id_1, id_2 and $\text{id}_5, \text{id}_6, \text{id}_7, \text{id}_8$ separately, so that we consider x_1, x_4 and x_{14} are nodes in the minimal cover set, namely $\text{cover}(R) = \{x_1, x_4, x_{14}\}$.

Data management server constructs CEK as follows:

a. Randomly selects the secret values $\hat{s}, \beta \in \mathbb{Z}_p$ to construct $CEK = e(g,g)^{\beta \hat{s}}$

For all the nodes $x \in \mathcal{X}$ in the binary tree, randomly chooses secret value $a_x \in \mathbb{Z}_p$ to construct a first degree polynomial $f_x(z) = a_x z + \beta$.

b. Computes and releases CEK parameters: $F =< F^{(1)} = g^{\hat{s}}, F_x^{(2)} = \{P(x)^{\hat{s}}\}_{x \in \text{cover}(R)} >$

c. For $r_x \in \mathbb{Z}_p$, randomly chooses the secret value and calculates the CEK sub-keys: $D =< D_x^{(1)} = g^{f_x(1)}, D_x^{(2)} = g^{f_x(x)} P(x)^{r_x}, D_x^{(3)} = g^{r_x} >$. Then it shares the CEK sub-keys with the user.

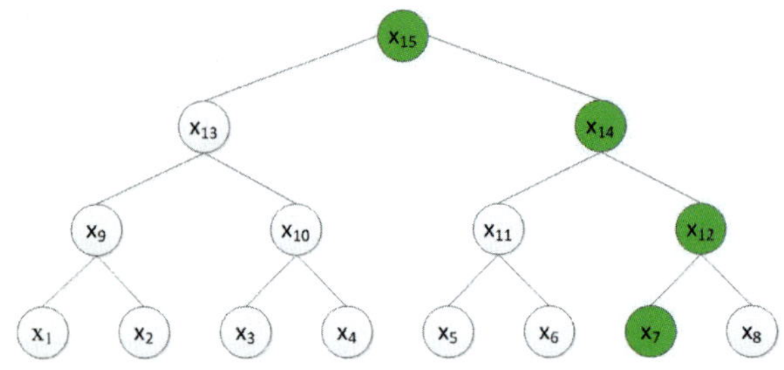

Figure 2. Path(id).

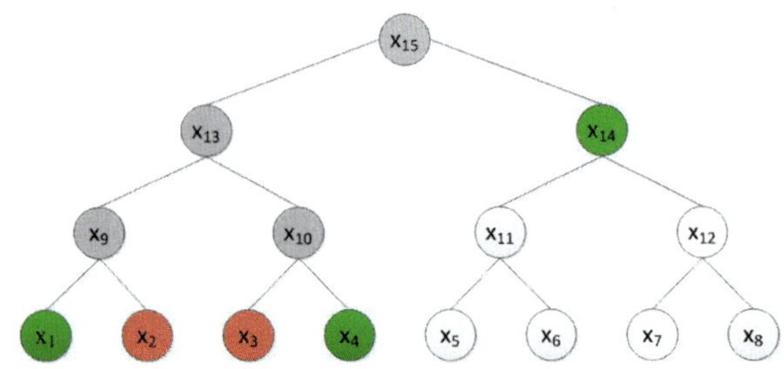

Figure 3. Minimal cover set.

4.4. *Data re-encryption*

After formally releasing the data, the data management server needs to execute the ReEncrypt algorithm and re-encrypts those attributes existing in the access structure. Therefore access control can be realized.

The data management server firstly chooses a random number as secret key, and construct the re-encrypted ciphertext CT':

$CT' = (C = \mathcal{M}e(g,g)^{\alpha s}, C' = g^s, \forall i = 1,\ldots,l$,
$C_i = (g^{a\lambda_i} h_{\rho(i)}^{-s})^{K_{\lambda_i}})$.

Afterwards, according to the attribute group information from TA, the data management server constructs the message header file. Using CEK to encrypt K_{λ_i}, the cloud sends the header file Hdr containing this information to the authorized users. $Hdr = (i = 1,\ldots l : \{E_k(K_{\lambda_i})\}_{K=CEK})$

Here a symmetric encryption method E_k is used, which $E_k : \{0,1\}^k \to \{0,1\}^k$.

When a user queries the server to access to the file, the data management server sends the file (Hdr, CT') to the user. As long as the user is authorized and is not revoked from the attribute group, he can achieve the content from the header file and decrypt the ciphertext. Moreover, this is a "stateless method" and the user does not have to update his key state constantly.

4.5. *Data decryption*

The user gets message (Hdr, CT') from the cloud, decrypts the CEK in the header file Hdr and decrypts the ciphertext using CEK and his own private key.

Phase 1: Attribute Key Decryption

Firstly the user needs to decrypts the attribute key corresponding to each attribute by using the CEK derived from Hdr.

If the user is not in the revocation list, namely $\mathrm{id} \notin R$, there must exist a node x so that $x \in Path(\mathrm{id}) \cap \mathrm{cover}(R)$. The user randomly chooses $z \in Z^*$ and makes $t' = 1/(1-x)z$. Then user constructs the proxy key TK for the proxy server as follows.

$$D_x^{(1)'} = \left(g^{f_x(1)}\right)^{\frac{x}{x-1}\frac{1}{z}} = (g^{f_x(1)})^{(-xt')}$$

$$D_x^{(2)} = \left(g^{f_x(x)} P(x)^{r_x}\right)^{\frac{1}{1-x}\frac{1}{z}} = \left(g^{f_x(x)} P(x)^{r_x}\right)^{t'}$$

$$D_x^{(3)} = (g^{r_x})^{\frac{1}{1-x}\frac{1}{z}} = (g^{r_x})^{t'}$$

The proxy constructs the blind CEK using the TK from user.

$$e(D_x^{(1)'}, F^{(1)}) \cdot \left(\frac{e(D_x^{(2)'}, F^{(1)})}{e(P(x)^{\hat{s}}, D_x^{(3)'})} \right)$$

$$= e((g^{f_x(1)})^{(-xt')}, g^{\hat{s}}) \cdot \left(\frac{e(\left(g^{f_x(x)} P(x)^{r_x}\right)^{t'}, g^{\hat{s}})}{e(P(x)^{\hat{s}}, (g^{r_x})^{t'})} \right)$$

$$= e(g,g)^{\beta \hat{s}/z}$$

The proxy returns the blind CEK to the user, and the user using his own secret value z which helps construct TK to recover CEK $= (e(g,g)^{\beta\hat{s}/z})^z = e(g,g)^{\beta\hat{s}}$. The user could obtain the attribute key K_{λ_i} .

Now the user could update his private key as follows.

$$SK' = < K = g^{\alpha} g^{at}; \forall x \in S, K_x = h_x^t, L_x = (g^t)^{\frac{1}{K_{\lambda_x}}} >$$

Phase 2: Ciphertext decryption

The user then decrypts the ciphertext with a proxy.

a. The user chooses a random $z \in Z^*$, and constructs the proxy key TK. Let $t' = t/z$, the proxy key TK was constructed as follows.

$$K' = (g^{\alpha} g^{at})^{1/z} = g^{\alpha/z} g^{at'}$$

$$K_x' = (h_x^t)^{1/z} = h_x^{t'}$$

$$L_x' = ((g^t)^{\frac{1}{K_{\lambda_x}}})^{1/z} = g^{\frac{t'}{K_{\lambda_x}}}$$

$$TK = < K' = g^{\alpha/z} g^{at'} \ \forall x \in S \ K_x' = h_x^{t'} \ L_x' = (g^{t'})^{\frac{1}{K_{\lambda_x}}} >$$

b. The proxy partially decrypts the ciphertext CT' with TK.

$$\frac{e(C', K')}{\left(\prod_{i\in I}(e(C_i, L_i') \cdot e(C', K_{\rho(i)}'))^{\omega_i}\right)} = \frac{e(g,g)^{\alpha s/z} e(g,g)^{ast'}}{\prod_{i\in I} e(g,g)^{t' a \lambda_i \omega_i}}$$

$$= e(g,g)^{\alpha s/z}$$

$$CT'' = (C, e(g,g)^{\alpha s/z})$$

Then the proxy sends the partially decrypted ciphertext CT'' to the user.

When receiving the partially decrypted ciphertext, the user decrypts it with the secret value z and obtains the plaintext $\mathcal{M}$.

$$\frac{C}{(e(g,g)^{\alpha s/z})^z} = \frac{Me(g,g)^{\alpha s}}{(e(g,g)^{\alpha s}} = \mathcal{M}$$

4.6. *Key update*

The user will notify the trusted authority when he wants to hold or drop the attributes. TA will then send the updated attribute group information to the data management server on the cloud and notify the cloud about the modification. When a user lost his data access privilege, TA sends the updated attribute revocation list to the data management server. The data management server will update those re-encrypt key parameters and CEK parameters which are influenced by the user privilege modification. Only the influenced parameters need to be updated. Through giving the computational work to the cloud in the update procedure, the user and data owner do not have to stay online constantly and the efficiency of the system can be improved.

The key will be updated as follows.

(1) Assume the attribute that has been influenced is j, and the data management server randomly chooses $s' \in \mathbb{Z}_p^*$, a new key K'_{λ_j} differing from the former key K_{λ_i}, and use the public parameter PK to re-encrypt ciphertext.

$$CT' = (C = \mathcal{M}e(g,g)^{\alpha(s+s')}, C' = g^{s+s'},\ C_j = (g^{a(\lambda_j+s')}h_{\rho(j)}^{-s})^{K'_{\lambda_j}},$$
$$\forall i \in S\backslash\{j\} : C_i = (g^{a(\lambda_i+s')}h_{\rho(i)}^{-s})^{K_{\lambda_i}})$$

(2) Based on the modification of the attribute ownership, data management server randomly chooses $\hat{s}' \in \mathbb{Z}_p$, updates and releases CEK parameters.

$$F' =< F^{(1)} = g^{\hat{s}'}, F_x^{(2)} = \{P(x)^{\hat{s}'}\}_{x \in \text{cover}(R)} >$$

Therefore those unauthorized user cannot calculate the new CEK. In this way forward and backward secrecy can be guaranteed.

The updated header file contains updated re-encryption key,

$$Hdr = (\{E_k(K'_{\lambda_j})\}_{CEK'} \forall i \in S\backslash\{j\} : \{E_k(K_{\lambda_i})\}_{CEK'}).$$

If a user sends a data request after the above update operations, the data management server will sends the new *Hdr* and ciphertext CT' which is encrypted by the updated key.

The key updated procedure realizes the fine-grained access control. When a user is revoked, the user-level access control can be guaranteed through key update as well as attribute-level access control. By selectively updating the attribute key and sending it in the *Hdr* to the user, the immediate revocation can be achieved and the user does not need to keep staying online.

5. COMPARISON

In this section, we will analyze the efficiency and expression policy, and compare with the previous scheme.

We introduce a proxy server instead of the user to execute the decryption algorithm which costs high computational capacity. By constructing proxy key and transferring the computational work to the proxy, the user only needs to do exponential operation once and will get the plaintext. Therefore the computational burden of the user can be reduced.

In Hur's scheme, when realizing access control, the data management server needs to set a binary tree for each attribute, and each leaf node of the tree denotes the user who holds this attribute. When the number of the system is large and half of the users hold one same attribute, there will be large key storage cost. For instance, when the total number of users in the system is n, and one certain user holds m attributes, namely he is the member of m attribute groups. Moreover, if each of the m attribute groups own $n/2$ users, then each user needs to store $m \cdot (\log_2^{\lfloor n/2 \rfloor} + 1)$ keys. However, in our scheme, we only need to maintain one user binary tree, therefore each user only needs to keep $\log_2^{\lfloor n \rfloor} + 1$ key parameters and one private key. Our construction largely reduces the storage cost of each user.

In our scheme, we use the LSSS access structure. It can express more formula. So our scheme have a more expressive policy than Hur's scheme.

In our scheme, using the injective function $\rho(i)$, the length of the ciphertext is reduced, and thus the computational burden is reduced. Assume that the number of attributes related to the access structure is l. In the encryption phase, the number of multiplications is $l+1$, and the number of exponentiations is $l+1$. Assume that the number of attributes that each user possesses is n. In the attribute key encryption phase, the number of multiplications is 1, and the number of exponentiations is $n+2$. In the phase of key update, taking the situation that there is only one attribute possession modification, the number of multiplications is $l+2$, and the number of exponentiations is $2l+2$.

6. CONCLUSION

In this paper, we use the attribute encryption algorithm and minimal cover set techniques to construct an efficient access control scheme. We transfer most of the user computational work to the proxy server, which is especially applicable for users who are using computational limited devices. Our scheme could ensure system security and reduce the key storage cost. Moreover, it is also expressive.

ACKNOWLEDGMENTS

This work is supported by NSFC (Grant Nos. 61300181, 61202434), the Fundamental Research Funds for the Central Universities (Grant No. 2015RC23).

REFERENCES

- [1] Wikipedia. Cloud Storage [EB/OL]. 2007. http://en.wikipedia.org/wiki/Cloud_storage.
- [2] Yu, S., Wang, C., Ren, K., & Lou, W. (2010, April). Attribute based data sharing with attribute revocation. In *Proceedings of the 5th ACM Symposium on Information, Computer and Communications Security* (pp. 261-270). ACM.
- [3] Anderson, J. P. (1972). *Computer Security Technology Planning Study. Volume 2*. Anderson (James P) and Co Fort Washington PA.
- [4] Sahai, A., & Waters, B. (2005). Fuzzy identity-based encryption. In *Advances in Cryptology–EUROCRYPT 2005* (pp. 457-473). Springer Berlin Heidelberg.
- [5] Bethencourt, J., Sahai, A., & Waters, B. (2007, May). Ciphertext-policy attribute-based encryption. In *Security and Privacy, 2007. SP'07. IEEE Symposium on* (pp. 321-334). IEEE.
- [6] Cheung, L., & Newport, C. (2007, October). Provably secure ciphertext policy ABE. In *Proceedings of the 14th ACM conference on Computer and communications security* (pp. 456-465). ACM.
- [7] Waters, B. (2011). Ciphertext-policy attribute-based encryption: An expressive, efficient, and provably secure realization. In *Public Key Cryptography–PKC 2011* (pp. 53-70). Springer Berlin Heidelberg.
- [8] Goyal, V., Pandey, O., Sahai, A., & Waters, B. (2006, October). Attribute-based encryption for fine-grained access control of encrypted data. In *Proceedings of the 13th ACM conference on computer and communications security* (pp. 89-98). ACM.
- [9] Ostrovsky, R., Sahai, A., & Waters, B. (2007, October). Attribute-based encryption with non-monotonic access structures. In *Proceedings of the 14th ACM conference on Computer and communications security* (pp. 195-203). ACM.
- [10] Attrapadung, N., Libert, B., & De Panafieu, E. (2011). Expressive key-policy attribute-based encryption with constant-size ciphertexts. In *Public Key Cryptography–PKC 2011* (pp. 90-108). Springer Berlin Heidelberg.
- [11] Chase, M. (2007). Multi-authority attribute based encryption. In *Theory of Cryptography* (pp. 515-534). Springer Berlin Heidelberg.
- [12] Liu, Z., Cao, Z., Huang, Q., Wong, D. S., & Yuen, T. H. (2011). Fully secure multi-authority ciphertext-policy attribute-based encryption without random oracles. In *Computer Security–ESORICS 2011* (pp. 278-297). Springer Berlin Heidelberg.
- [13] Chase, M., & Chow, S. S. (2009, November). Improving privacy and security in multi-authority attribute-based encryption. In *Proceedings of the 16th ACM conference on Computer and communications security* (pp. 121-130). ACM.
- [14] Liang, X., Cao, Z., Lin, H., & Shao, J. (2009, March). Attribute based proxy re-encryption with delegating capabilities. In *Proceedings of the 4th International Symposium on Information, Computer, and Communications Security* (pp. 276-286). ACM.
- [15] Emura, K., Miyaji, A., Nomura, A., Omote, K., & Soshi, M. (2009). A ciphertext-policy attribute-based encryption scheme with constant ciphertext length. In *Information Security Practice and Experience* (pp. 13-23). Springer Berlin Heidelberg.
- [16] Seo, H. J., & Kim, H. (2012). Attribute-based proxy re-encryption with a constant number of pairing operations. *Journal of information and communication convergence engineering*, *10*(1), 53-60.
- [17] Ibraimi, L., Petkovic, M., Nikova, S., Hartel, P., & Jonker, W. (2009). Mediated ciphertext-policy attribute-based encryption and its application. In *Information security applications* (pp. 309-323). Springer Berlin Heidelberg.
- [18] Hur, J., & Noh, D. K. (2011). Attribute-based access control with efficient revocation in data outsourcing systems. *Parallel and Distributed Systems, IEEE Transactions on*, *22*(7), 1214-1221.
- [19] Staddon, J., Golle, P., Gagné, M., & Rasmussen, P. (2008, March). A content-driven access control system. In *Proceedings of the 7th symposium on identity and trust on the Internet* (pp. 26-35). ACM.
- [20] Attrapadung, N., & Imai, H. (2009). Conjunc-tive broadcast and attribute-based encryption. In *Pairing-Based Cryptography-Pairing 2009* (pp. 248-265). Springer Berlin Heidelberg.
- [21] Green, M., Hohenberger, S., & Waters, B. (2011, August). Outsourcing the Decryption of ABE Ciphertexts. In *USENIX Security Symposium* (p. 3).

Crown Dimension of Plant with Trigeminal Tree Structure

X.Y. Nie*, K. Fang & D.P. Rao
College of Information Science and Technology
Hunan Agricultural University, Changsha, China
Email: Nxiaoyi@hunau.net

ABSTRACT: The plant crown can be considered as fractal, how to describe the dense degree of plant crown by fractional dimension, there is a little research. In this paper, the Crown dimension of plant with trigeminal tree structure is calculated by box dimension method, the box dimension is $\lg^3/\lg^{1/m(\frac{2}{\sqrt{3}}\sin\alpha)}$.

KEYWORDS: Plant crown; Trigeminal tree structure; Box counting dimension.

1. INTRODUCTION

In Euclidean geometry, the point is usually defined as zero-dimensional geometric shape, the line is defined as one-dimensional geometric shape, the plane is defined as two-dimensional geometric shape, the space is called as three-dimensional geometric shape. The concept of this dimension is the topological dimension of Euclidean geometry. Topological dimension of Euclidean geometry is represented by D_T. Since fractal is a graphic, then we can use dimension to quantitatively describe the fractal complexity, this is the fractal geometry [1].

There are many methods for calculating the fractal geometry fractal dimension, some of which are classical calculation methods, such as self-similar dimension and box dimension [2].

Suppose that A is a non empty bounded subset in R^n, for an arbitrary real number $r > 0$, $N_r(A)$ represents the minimum number of n-dimension cube (side length r) which covers subset A. If there exists a real number d, such that $N_r(A)$ and $1/r^d$ are the same order infinity, namely there exists is a positive number k, such that

$$\lim_{r\to 0}\frac{N_r(A)}{1/r^d} = k$$

or

$$\lim_{r\to 0}\log\frac{N_r(A)}{1/r^d} = \log k$$

We have

$$d = \lim_{r\to 0}\frac{\lg k - \lg N_r(A)}{\lg r} \approx -\lim_{r\to 0}\frac{\lg N_r(A)}{\lg r}$$

So called d box dimension calculation for A, referred to as box dimension for A.

The box dimension method can not only calculate the dimension of Cantor set and Kock curve, but also measure the irregular degree of signal [3]. In this paper, we tried to calculate the dimension of plant crown by box dimension method.

2. TRIGEMINAL TREE STRUCTURE OF 3D PLANT MODEL

In order to effectively and objectively simulate the growth of authentic plants and the genetic relationship among plant organs, much attention is paid to the selection of virtual plant growth models in the field of virtual agricultural research. Plant growth model is the simulation of the structure development and the growth process of plants in a virtual three-dimensional space [4].

The base model of virtual 3D plants is composed by trunks and branches [5], and we can produce a 3D model of trees by multiple iteration of basic model. Therefore, the 3D plant model there exist two basic fractal characteristics, it is very suitable for fractal description and simulation.

The plant with completely trigeminal tree structure is as shown in fig. 1, the simulation result is as shown in fig. 2.

Figure 1. Plant with trigeminal tree structure.

Figure 2. Simulation result.

In nature, the plants with completely binary tree structure or trigeminal tree structure does not exist, the true tree with missing or dead branches is shown in fig. 3.

This paper mainly researches the crown dimension of plant with completely trigeminal tree structure.

Figure 3. True tree.

3. CROWN DIMENSION OF PLANT WITH TRIGEMINAL TREE STRUCTURE

The plant crown is closely related to the growth rate and branching structure of plant. At present, how to describe the dense degree of plant crown by fractional dimension, there is a little research. Here we use the box dimension method to calculate the dimension of plant crown, trying to use the dimension of plant crown to explain the relationship between plant crown and the rate of growth.

Three dimensional plants with trigeminal tree structure are as shown in fig. 4.

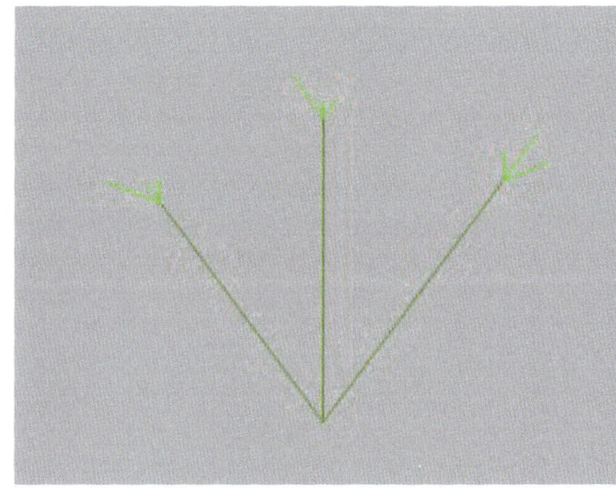

Figure 4. 3 D model of plant with trigeminal tree structure.

Every time plant branches, suppose that angles between the parent branch and each of child branches are all

$$\alpha(0 < \alpha < \pi / 2)$$

Let the first parent branch length is l , and its child branch length is

$$l_1 = ml(m < 1)$$

Then the side length of the least cube which covers two child branches is

$$L^{(1)} = l_1 \frac{2}{\sqrt{3}} \sin\alpha$$

And so on, when the n-th branch, its child branch length is

$$l_n = m^{n-1} l$$

The side length of the cube which covers two child branches is

$$L^{(n-1)} = l_n (\frac{2}{\sqrt{3}} \sin\alpha)^{n-1} = m^{n-1} l (\frac{2}{\sqrt{3}} \sin\alpha)^{n-1}$$

Now we know that 3^{n-1} cubes with the side length $L^{(n-1)}$ covers the plant crown. Therefore, the box counting dimension of plant crown with trigeminal tree structure is

$$d_3 = -\lim_{n\to\infty} \frac{\lg^{3^{n-1}}}{\lg^{L^{(n-1)}}}$$

$$= -\lim_{n\to\infty} \frac{(n-1)\lg^3}{(n-1)\lg^{m(\frac{2}{\sqrt{3}}\sin\alpha)} + \lg^l}$$

$$= -\frac{\lg^3}{\lg^{m(\frac{2}{\sqrt{3}}\sin\alpha)}}$$

$$= \frac{\lg^3}{\lg^{1/m(\frac{2}{\sqrt{3}}\sin\alpha)}}$$

When $m = \frac{\sqrt{3}}{2}$, the box counting dimension of plant crown is

$$d_3 = \frac{\lg^3}{\lg^{1/\sin\alpha}}$$

When $m = \frac{\sqrt{3}}{4}$, the box counting dimension of plant crown is

$$d_3 = \frac{\lg^3}{\lg^{2/\sin\alpha}}$$

When $m = \frac{\sqrt{3}}{2^k}$, the box counting dimension of plant crown is

$$d_3 = \frac{\lg^3}{\lg^{k/\sin\alpha}}$$

Explained above, the plant grows faster, the greater the crown dimension, so the denser the crown.

In nature, the plants with completely binary tree structure or trigeminal tree structure does not exist, when plant branches, there are missing or dead branches, so the crowns of plants with crown missing branches has to be studied further.

ACKNOWLEDGMENT

This paper is supported by the "Twelfth Five-Year" national science and technology support program (No. 2011BAD21B03) and the scientific key planning project of Hunan province (No. 2009NK4038).

REFERENCES

- [1] B.B. Mandelbrotr, Fractal, chance and dimension, W.H. Freeman and Company, Sanfraneiseo, 1977.
- [2] Zhu Hua, Ji Cui Cui, Fractal Theory and Its Applications, Science Press, 2011.
- [3] Zhao Chun-hui, Ma Shuang, Yang Wei-chao, "Spectrum Sensing in Cognitive Radios Based on Fractal Box Dimension" Journal of Electronics & Information Technology, Vol. 33, No. 22, pp: 475-478, 2011.
- [4] A. Lindenmayer, "Mathematical models for cellular interaction in development", Parts I and II, Journal of Theoretical Biology. Vol.18, pp.80-95, 1968.
- [5] M.T. Allen, P.P. Rusinkiewicz, "Using L-systems for modeling source-link interactions, architecture and physiology of growing trees: The L-PEACH model", New Phytologist, Vol. 166, pp. 869-880, 2005.

Frequent Pattern Mining for Massive XBRL Data in Internet Information Disclosure System

T. Feng* & Z.Y. Zeng
Yunnan University of Finance and Economics, Kunming, Yunnan, 650000, China
**Email: vonpower@gmail.com*

ABSTRACT: Information disclosure system is the law that listed companies must obey in order to insure the benefits of investors and hold up to public scrutiny. Information like financial statement changes and operation condition of listed companies must be to the public according to the system. XBRL is an XML-based extensible language for exchanging business information. The language is widely used in financial information disclosure system and becomes the standard data format of the system. The specification, taxonomy and instance documents of XBRL are researched in this paper and the method of parallel data mining for the frequent pattern of massive XBRL data is proposed based on MapReduce and HDFS. The XBRL instances of the listed companies in China are processed by using this method and proved it to be effective.

KEYWORDS: XBRL; Frequent pattern; Parallel computing; Information disclosure.

1. INTRODUCTION

Information disclosure system requires listed companies to have their information like financial statement changes and operation condition to be reported to the stock management and stock exchange, and published to the society. To set up effective information disclosure system is of vital importance for the development of the stock market and also has significant effects on judgment of stock price for investors.

XBRL (eXtensible Business Reporting Language) is an XML-based markup language that is used for definition and exchange of financial information. The XBRL Specification is developed and published by XBRL International, Inc. (XII). XBRL allows software vendors, programmers and end users to enhance the creation, exchange, and comparison of business reporting information [1]. Early users of XBRL included regulators such as the U.S. Federal Deposit Insurance Corporation [2] and the Committee of European Banking Supervisors [3]. Common functions in many countries that make use of XBRL include regulators of stock exchanges and securities, banking regulators, business registrars, revenue reporting and tax-filing agencies, and national statistical agencies. However, when the benefits of XBRL were commended, the cost of mass information processing for investors and financial analysts is increasing. It is worth studying on how to discover useful information from the massive disclosed data.

The X-SIR system based on relational database was developed in 2008 in order to solve the storage problem of XBRL [4]. A model was built to store and analyze XBRL data tested by experiments in 2011 [5]. A common warehouse meta-model was proposed to reveal the multidimensional structure of XBRL which cannot be implemented in plain relational database [6]. The XBRL data analysis system based on Hadoop was implemented in 2013 [7]. The XBRL data has been stored in distributed file system after extraction and transformation from Map /Reduce distributed computing model. Then investment feasibility of listed companies can be evaluated by the way of Interval Analytic Hierarchy Process.

Based on the above research results, a method of frequent pattern mining in massive XBRL data is proposed in this paper.

2. RELATED CONCEPT

2.1. *XBRL system*

XBRL system includes specification, schema, taxonomy, and XBRL instance.

According to the specification, XBRL file structure, taxonomy, syntax and semantics of XBRL instance are defined in detail. Information typing architecture from Electronic Industry Code of Conduct for the listed companies in China follows XBRL2.1

specification. Financial statement based on XBRL specification must follow the architecture. Taxonomy consists of schema definition file (*.xsd) and linkbase. It is used to provide schema validation for instance.

The abstracts of periodical reports (including annual reports, semi-annual reports, and quarterly reports) from listed companies completely follow the XBRL file format used by Shanghai Stock Exchange and Shenzhen Stock Exchange. "The Information Disclosure Electronic Specification for Listed Company" must be strictly formed according to ASBE (Accounting Standards for Business Enterprises) revised in 2006 and corresponding regulations about information disclosure of listed companies from CSRC (China Securities Regulatory Commission). And the specification must also be written based on XBRL 2.1 specification and FRTA (Financial Reporting Taxonomies Architecture). The newest taxonomy consists 12 Schema, 2679 Elements, and 36 Linkbase [8]. XBRL instances are processed according to the taxonomy in this paper.

2.2. *MapReduce and hadoop*

MapReduce is a distributed computing pattern proposed by Google that is used for parallel computation of large-scale dataset. Apache Hadoop is an implementation of MapReduce programming paradigm and also includes a distributed file system named HDFS. Hadoop releases as an open software based on Apache 2.0 license.

Data is processed by Map and Reduce functions of which key-value pair is mapped into a new key-value pair by Map function and the outputs from Map will be merged by Reduce function. Computation process of MapReduce is as follow: 1. Several MAP functions are executed where one or more DFS files as input for each MAP are ready to convert into key-value series. 2. Master controller collects several key-value pairs from each Map node and makes them sorted by key sequence. The sorted key-values are delivered to Reduce taks, which means all the key-values with same key is processed by one Reduce function. 3. Reduce would process one key each time and combines all the corresponding values in a certain way. Several Map and Reduce tasks on many compute nodes can be managed to parallel execution by Hadoop. And task failures caused by soft or hardware can also be handled in Hadoop platform.

3. METHODOLOGY

There are three steps of frequent pattern mining method for massive XBRL data proposed in this paper (Figure 1).

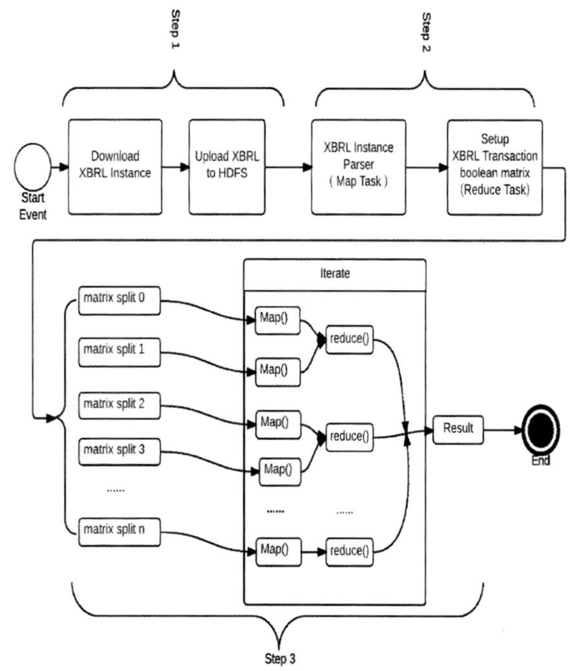

Figure 1. Massive XBRL data mining workflow.

Step 1: Upload XBRL instances from the internet to HDFS. All information in the massive XBRL instances can be completely saved in HDFS distributed database. Information in the database would be extracted and analyzed in the next step.

Step 2: XQuery language is used to analyze XBRL instance through Map function. The analyzed information will be merged by Reduce function and constructed boolean matrix of XBRL transaction data.

Step 3: Parition boolean matrix of XBRL transaction data into small pieces and find frequent pattern by using Map and Reduce functions.

The boolean matrix of XBRL transaction data formed in the second step and the parallel mining for XBRL frequent pattern in three step are the most important parts in this paper. They will be presented in detail in the following chapter.

3.1. *Boolean matrix of XBRL transaction data*

In the second step, small (only about 50-100kb each) but vast XBRL instances are merged into an integrated boolean matrix of XBRL transaction data according Map/Reduce task. Because of the huge data volume of XBRL instances, standalone processing is inefficient and even crashed. So they are operated on the Hadoop platform.

Map functions are used to extract XBRL information according to XBRL specification. The filename of XBRL instance is as the key with the format of "CN_SZ_000001_GB0110_20140313.xml" in which CN represents for China, SZ for Shenzhen

Stock Exchange, 00001 for stock serial number of listed companies, GB0110 for annual report, 20140313 for the time financial reports handed in. And the corresponding file input stream is as the value. The file path list where massive XBRL instance stored in is divided into n parts and put them into n Map functions in order to lead the functions to read the instances. According to the key of the filename, XBRL parser can process file stream of the value. After the Map functions have been executed, the new key composed of "C+T" is generated where C represents for listed companies code and T for information disclosure time. The value related to the key is the financial data from C Company published at T time.

To read the XML files of XBRL instances needs Taxonomy.xsd, References.xml, Presentations.xml, and other relevant files. The relationship between taxonomy and instance is shown in figure 2. Taxonomy provides schema validation for XBRL instance. The rules of the schema validation must be obeyed by the instance. For example every element in the instance must be declared in the present taxonomy definition file, or in other files called by the present one. The link-base library makes further description for the taxonomy definition file and instances should also obey the rules from the library. When data have been extracted from instance by Map function, the library provides relationship between these data.

Reduce functions are responsible for the index calculation, discretization, and generating boolean matrix of XBRL financial data.

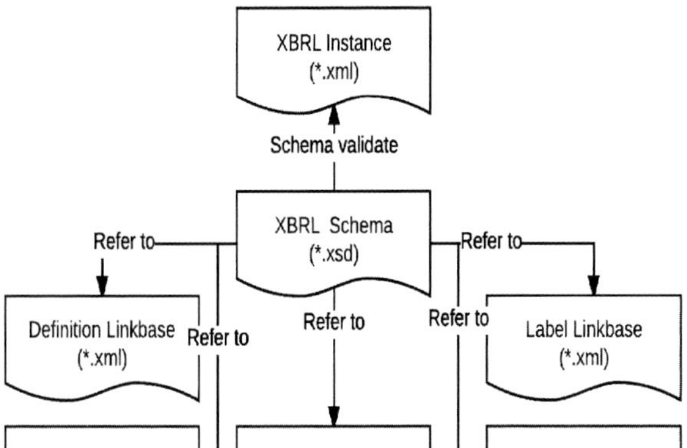

Figure 2. Relationship between taxonomy and xbrl instance.

The financial data and index, like NAVPS, asset-liability ratio, equity ratio and so on, are most of continuous data which cannot formed transaction database and need to be discretized. The important financial index in XBRL is listed in Table 1[9].

Table1: Important financial index in XBRL

net asset value per share(NAVPS)/yuan= stockholder's equity/ general capital
NAVPS after adjustment/yuan=NAVPS -adjustment
share capital fund/yuan=capital fund/ general capital
undistributed profit per share/yuan= undistributed profit/ general capital
asset-liability ratio/%= total liabilities/ total assets*100
equity-to-asset ratio/%=stockholders equity/ total assets
long-term liability rate/%= long-term liability/ total assets*100
cash ratio/%= cash and cash equivalents/ liquid liability*100
stock ratio/%=stock/liquid assets*100
liquid assets ratio/%= liquid assets/ total assets*100
fixed assets ratio/%=fixed assets/ total assets*100
liquid ratio= liquid assets/ liquid liability
quick ratio= (liquid assets- stock)/ liquid liability
turnover of account receivable= main business income/(initial collect net amount + final collect net amount)/2
inventory turnover ratio= main business cost/(initial stock net amount + final stock net amount)/2
turnover of total capital= main business income/(initial total amount of assets + final total amount of assets)/2
net capital increasing rate/%=(current net asset value per share-prior net asset value per share)/abs(prior net asset value per share)*100
total assets increasing rate/%=(current total assets-prior total assets)/abs(prior total assets)*100
rate of return on investment=current return on investment/prior return on investment-1= net capital increasing ratio/ total assets growth rate-1
increasing rate of fixed assets and current assets ratio=(current fixed assets/current liquid assets)/(prior fixed assets/prior liquid assets)-1

Definition for the XBRL financial index discretization: A is a continuous financial index and the range is [a,b]. A division of [a,b] is a set formed by K interval:

$$\pi_A = \{[a_0, a_1], [a_1, a_2], \ldots, [a_{k-1}, a_k]\}$$

where a0=a, ak=b. Discretization for A is the process of creating π_A. Supervised discretization algorithm based on minimum entropy is used to realize discretization for XBRL continuous financial data in this paper. Distributed information of class is used to count and confirm classified point. In order to make A discretized, minimum entropy from A is chosen as the classified point and the results are divided recursively.

Definition for entropy:

$$Entropy(D) = -\sum_{i=1}^{m} p_i \log_2(p_i)$$

Where m is the number of D class, p_i is the probability of i class. The purpose of discretization is to find a numerical point to divide range D into D_1 and

D_2. Thus harmonic information entropy of D after the division is minimized:

$$\text{Info}(D)=\frac{|D_1|}{|D|}\text{Enytopy}(D_1)+\frac{|D_2|}{|D|}\text{Enytopy}(D_2)$$

Fayyad & Irani recursive minimum entropy algorithm [10] provided in Weka [11] is used to make XBRL financial index discretization in our experiment.

3.2. *XBRLPA algorithm*

Frequent itemset mining should scan transaction data first. All of frequent itemset mining algorithms maintain many counting numbers in memory after the scanning. Any counting's change would need to load another page into memory from disk. So if there is not enough memory, it will cause memory thrashing and slow down running speed.

We can partition XBRL transactions on both horizontal and vertical way. Vertical partition is used in this paper.

Rule 1: Subset of frequent item set on the local node Si must be frequent one. Superset of infrequent item set must be infrequent one.

Rule 2: Global frequent item set X must be local frequent one on the node Si(1<=i<=n).

Based on the above rulers, XBRLPA algorithm proposed in this paper can calculate support count of candidate item set in each node. Figure 2 shows the XBRLPA work flow. Parallel execution of Map tasks makes candidate set as Key to output and the related Value as the local support count. Local support stored count is calculated by Reduce function in order to get global support count of candidate set. Then frequent item set and infrequent item set are calculated according to global support count which will be used for the next candidate item set calculation. The process iterates until the end of the algorithm.

XBRLPA pseudocode:

```
main()//entrance
{
   isEmpty=false;
   k=1;
   //task instance acquisition
   Job job = Job.getInstance();
   job.setJarByClass(XBRLJob.class);
   //specify Map functions
   job.setMapperClass(XBRLMapper.class);
   //specify Partitioner calss
   //results from map are allocated to Reduce function
  job.setPartitionerClass(XBRLPartitioner.class);
   //specify Reduce functions
   job.setReducerClass(XBRLReducer.class);
   //acquire XBRL transaction matrix from HDFS
   xbrlTransMatrix xtm=getHdfsXbrlMatrix();
   candiSet=getCandidate1(xtm);//procude 1-item candidate set
   while(candiSet!=null){
      // execute a loop when candidate itemset is not empty
      //set XBRL Job parameter:
      //matrixPath(input),candidateItemset(input),
      //min_support(input),frequentItemset(output)
(XBRLJob)job.setParams(matrixPath,candiSet,min_sup,frequentSet);
      //submit tasks to Hadoop cluster
      job.waitForCompletion(true);
      //frequnetSet is k-1 item set, candiSet is candidate k item set
      candiSet =CreateCandidate(frequentSet,k);
      k++;
   }
}
XBRLMapper
//candiSet is candidate item set, xtm_i is local matrix
input:candiSet,xtm_i
//count is local matrix support countding
output:<candiSet,count>
{
   for(Item item : candiSet){
      //pairs of row vectors in the matrix related to item are made AND operation
      vector=vector vector(item);
      //make AND operation with CS(transaction counting vector)
      vector=vector⊗vector[CS];
      //c is local support degree
      c=|vector|;
      emit(candiSet,c);
   }
}
XBRLReducer
//[c1,c2,...] is the list of local support counting of map node
input:<candiSet,[c1,c2,...]>
//frequentSet is frequent k item set, frequentSet is infrequent when k=0
output:<frequentSet,k>
{
   t=sum([c1,c2,....]);
   emit(candiSet,t>=min_sup?k:0);
}
```

4. EXPERIMENT AND ANALYSIS

Experiment condition: Hadoop Cluster composed by 8 PCs with Ubuntu 13.10, Oracle JDK1. 7, and Hadoop 2.4.0.

Experiment data: The best way to get XBRL data is by RSS technology. And XBRL service platform of listed companies is online (http://xbrl.cninfo.com.cn) when RSS is not provided by CSRC. Regular instances and history data of listed companies in the stock markets of Shanghai and Shenzhen in XBRL format are provided on the site. For example, from the URL: "http://xbrl.cninfo.com.cn/XBRL/Info.jsp?stkid=s1&getyear=s2&reportType=s3" Report from the listed company which stock number is s1 during the time s2 can be found, where s3 = {GB0110, GB0310, GB0510, GB0710} respectively represents annual report, semiannual report, the first quarter report, and the third quarter report.

We select 2% minimum support and 137 XBRL instances as experimental data. Frequent item set is acquired in the algorithm presented in chapter 3. It is obviously shows that some discrete financial index, such as UDPPS, asset-liability ratio, equity ratio, cash ratio, inventory turnover ratio, growth rate of net assets, and total assets turnover, appear repeatedly in the frequent item set which can built corresponding association rules with non-financial index like company financial condition rating and financial fraud.

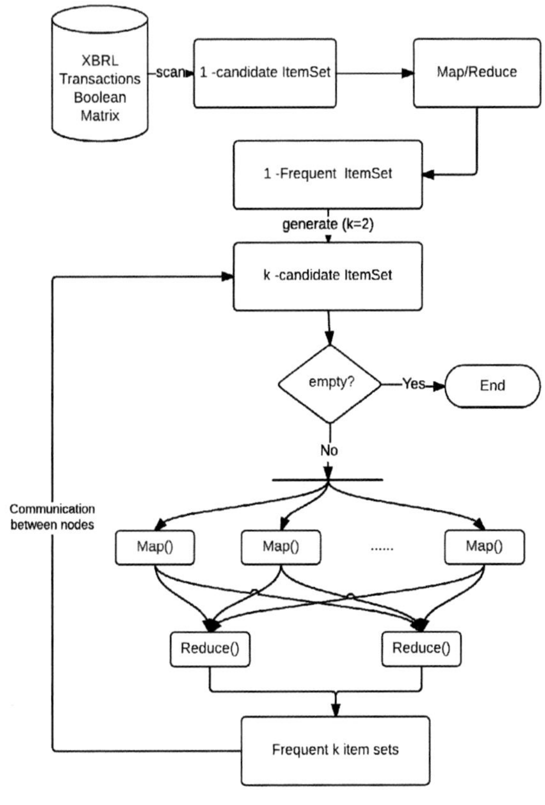

Figure 3. XBRLPA algorithm.

5. CONCLUSION

Financial information analysis and mining with computer technology always attract attention of many researchers. Theories and methods about them are constantly getting improved. Meanwhile, network information disclosure is becoming mature. Vast XBRL financial information will be accumulated in the next few years. Based on the above analysis, we are trying to find a method to efficiently acquire frequent itemsets from massive XBRL financial data under the network information disclosure mechanism. After research on the XBRL Specification, Taxonomy, and Instance, an algorithm of XBRL frequent parallel mining based on HDFS and MapReduce is proposed in this paper. It is proved to be practicable after the experiment. A good example on processing vast frequent XBRL data mining is set up in this paper.

ACKNOWLEDGEMENT

Supported by MOE (Ministry of Education in China) Project of Humanities and Social Sciences (Project No. 112YJCZH047, No. 10YJCZH004).

Supported by Natural Science Foundation of Yunnan Province, China (Project No. 2011FZ150)

Supported by the Research Foundation of Education Bureau of Yunnan Province, China (Project No. 2010Y121).

REFERENCES

- [1] XBRL International, Extensible Business Reporting Language (XBRL) 2.1[R].2013.
- [2] FFIEC, Improved Business Process Through XBRL: A Use Case for Business Reporting [R].2006.
- [3] Eurofilinginfo., Eurofiling Initiative [R].2013.
- [4] LI, R.B., LI, J., LIAO, H.M., XBRL Storage System Based on Relational Databases [J]. Computer Engineering, 2008, 5, 77-78.
- [5] ZHAO, J.Y., Storage and Analysis System of Financial Report based on XBRL [D], DaLian University of Technology. 2011.
- [6] WANG, X.L., Research of XBRL Data Storage Application Based on Common Warehouse Metamodel [D]. DaLian University of Technology. 2013.
- [7] JIA, S.P., Design and Implementation of XBRL Data Analyzing System Based on Hadoop [D]. DaLian University of Technology. 2013.
- [8] http://wwww.xbrl.org/Home/[EB/OL], 2014.
- [9] FENG, M., data mining research and application base on financial analysis [D]. East China Normal University. 2007.
- [10] WEKA, http://www.cs.waikato.ac.nz/ml/weka/[EB/OL]. 2014.
- [11] Fayyad, U.M., Irani, K.B., Multiinterval discretization of continuous valued attributes for classification learning [C]. In: Proceedings of the 13th International Joint Conference on Artificial Intelligence, France (Morgan Kaufmann), 1993, 1022~1027.

Parallel Scheduling Optimization Framework Based on Feedback Mechanism

B. Yin[1], P. Chi[2] & Y.Q. Yang[3]
Department of Computer Science and Technology, Ocean University of China, Qingdao, China
Email: [1]ybfirst@ouc.edu.cn, [2]ouc_cp@163.com, [3]i@yangyongquan.com

ABSTRACT: For large-scale data processing, complex scale, and the large amount of data, this paper proposes a new parallel scheduling optimization framework and corresponding algorithms, to improve the actual application effect of data processing. Parallel scheduling framework which is suitable for the large-scale data processing designed in this paper, this framework can further improve the parallel data processing. The main feature of the framework is the task of classification, dynamic scheduling and task feedback information, to provide further support for dynamic adjustment of the whole framework. Through the cooperation of each module in the framework, we can realize the parallel processing of data and ensure the accuracy, the stability and efficiency of data processing.

KEYWORDS: Data processing; Parallel scheduling; Scheduling framework; Information feedback.

1. INTRODUCTION

Data processing [1] is the core of the information system. Data processing refers to the data storage, processing, retrieval, statistics and maintenance operations, and its basic purpose is drawing and deriving valuable, meaningful data from the large data which may be difficult to understand. With the increasing number of data processing and the complexity of dealing with problem, data processing technology in general can't meet the requirement of efficiency, so that we put forward the idea of parallel scheduling [2] of data processing.

On the one hand, with the development of large-scale production of electronic process accelerate in modern enterprises, more and more data processing is needed. On the other hand, with the development of network technology, the Web can be regarded as an unlimited source of data, applications can access data from the data source. These data have the characteristics of classification, sub broad, deep, large scale; in view of this situation, in order to improve the efficiency of data processing, according to the existing parallel scheduling framework for data processing, we analysis its shortcomings, and then propose an optimization framework for parallel scheduling by using task classification, dynamic scheduling and information feedback, the three function modules, to realize the parallel processing of massive data of this type, so that we can make full use of the computing resources [3], improve data parallelism [4].

2. RELATED WORK

In order to improve the efficiency of data processing, it is very important to achieve data processing parallelism. In order to realize it, we can achieve that through the dynamic scheduling of the system environment. Firstly We must parallel processing on the data processing program, tasks will be divided into several sub modules, and determine the interdependence relationship of each sub module through the basic framework, then determine the sequence of concurrent working,we can parallel scheduling in various resources conveniently.

At present, there are some similar parallel scheduling framework, which can meet the requirements of the basic data parallel processing.

A method is proposed for real time dynamic scheduling of parallel tasks, through this framework to achieve a variety of real-time task scheduling parallel processing on heterogeneous environment. These studies bring some inspiration for the dynamic scheduling of this article, although they also have cut the size of the task reasonably, can't reduce the size and complexity of processing tasks, at the same time, the task completion also lack detection and feedback [5] control.

Another method is proposed for the parallel task scheduling framework, this framework proposes division of the multi queue scheduling task, it has great inspiration for this article. But the framework will put sub tasks which is cut in the same cohort, and scheduling according to the FIFO. So that, for a variety of the types of tasks, they are sequentially stored in the queue, which makes the treatment of multiple tasks in a certain extent is still in a serial mode; at the same time, the framework does not explicitly put forward the scheduling strategy and feedback strategies.

When the above data processing framework dealing with large scale and deep level data, can't make full use of resources, can't maximize the parallel processing of resources, so there are relatively large defects.

Therefore, in order to improve the efficiency of the data processing, through the practical application, we propose a parallel scheduling optimization framework based on feedback mechanism, the core is the decision-making of task classification, dynamic priority scheduling and feedback information. We can realize the optimization of the parallel scheduling through these three mechanisms.

3. THE PARALLEL SCHEDULING OPTIMIZATION FRAMEWORK BASED ON THE FEEDBACK MECHANISM

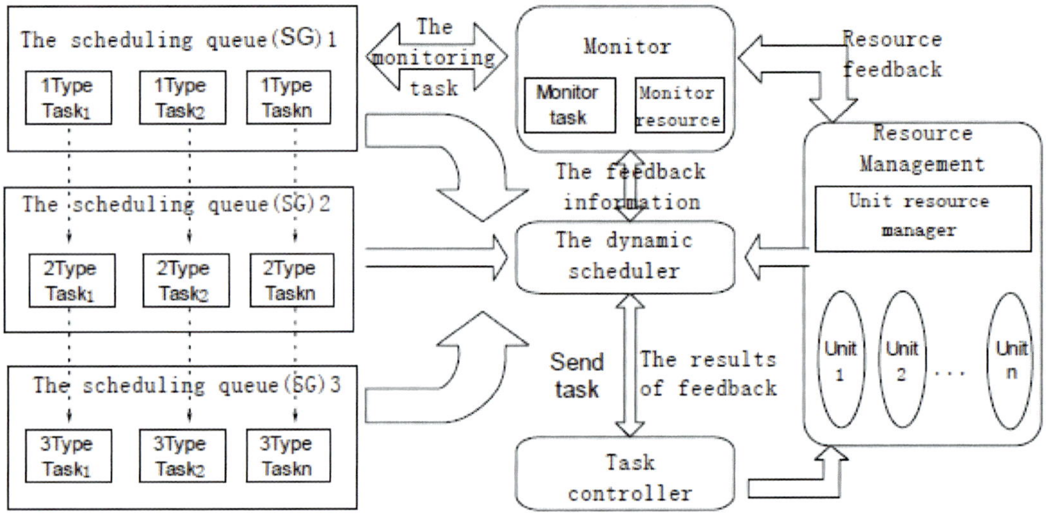

Figure 1. The parallel scheduling optimization framework based on the feedback mechanism.

Special frame can be seen from the above picture. Parallel scheduling optimization framework based on feedback mechanism is the framework which schedules according to the different tasks and response according to the framework of feedback. For different types of tasks, with different scheduling timeliness, tasks are classified by the framework. According to one type of tasks, we can dynamically generate a corresponding queue to achieve cooperation, and for different types of task queue, set different priority of queue scheduling, then we can dynamic scheduling according to priority. At the same time, when the task and processing unit are detected in this scheduling framework, the framework receives feedback information of task and then provides support for dynamic scheduling strategy.

4. THE KEY ALGORITHM OF PARALLEL SCHEDULING OPTIMIZATION FRAMEWORK

4.1. *The scheduling algorithm of parallel scheduling optimization framework*

The key scheduling algorithm under the framework is an algorithm which based on the multiple queens scheduling of dynamic table. The main idea of the algorithm can be concluded as the following three main steps.

Step 1. Identify the new priority of each scheduling queen. Identify the priority of all nodes which are not scheduled in the queen.

Step 2. Select the current highest priority queue and then put the task node that has the highest priority into the mission controllers [7].

Step 3. The mission controllers allocate the scheduling tasks to the processing unit resources which has the earliest startup time.

While the key parts of this scheduling algorithm is the child algorithm that drastically identify the queen and the priority of each task node. It is also the child algorithm who determines the scheduling according to the priority [6].

4.1.1. *The child algorithm with identified priority*

Firstly, the priority of the scheduling queen can be identified by HLF. Here is the main idea of the algorithm. Identify the sequence set of the key task queen according to the order and importance of processing flow of the various types of the task queen and give each task queen a corresponding level in the sequence from high to low. While give the lowest level to all those non-critical task queens. This is the way to identify the scheduling priority of each task queen.

In order to identify the priority of each task node [9] in the queen, we use the algorithm who has the highest response ratio after the queen is been selected. The HRN algorithm takes both the execution time and waiting time of the task into consideration and then selects out the task who has the highest response ratio. If more than one task nodes corresponding to the highest response ratio appear, identify the priority according to the FIFO manner.

4.1.2. *The child algorithm based on the scheduling of the priority*

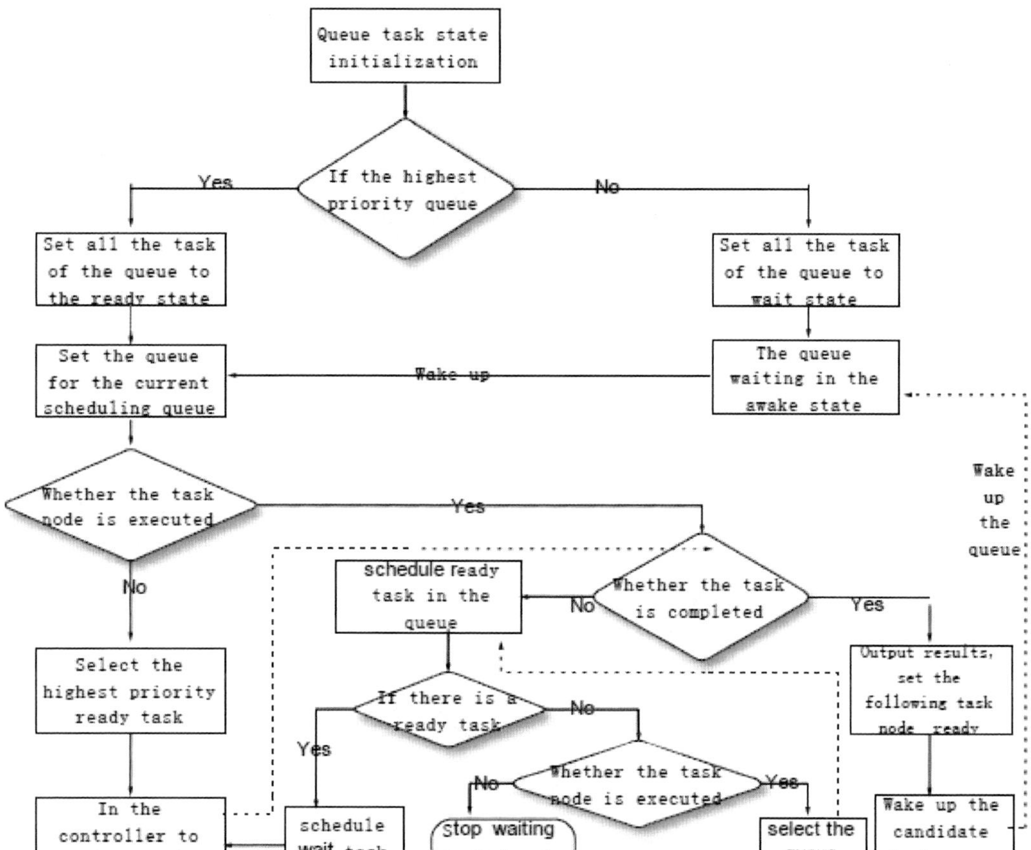

Figure 2. The algorithm based on the scheduling of the priority.

Step 1. Make sure that all the tasks in the queen that has the highest initialization level on the ready state of the process while others all on the waiting state. This is because that tasks with other levels must use the results of the front of the queen as their inputs and then they can enter into the ready-managed state.

Step 2. Determine whether the current tasks are in execution by the result feedback of the task detection. If there is no task, select the ready state of task node that has the highest priority level in the highest priority queen [8] and put it into the task controller. Obtain processing unit resource, generate task controlling thread and execute the task in the processing unit.

Step 3. Determine whether the task has been finished or not if a task is in execution. If there is no outcome returns, continue the scheduling of other tasks on the ready state in the queen. If there is no more ready-state task, check out if there has a task queen with higher levels. If the answer is yes, put the ready-state task in the task controller. On the contrary, stop and wait for the arrival of other ready-state tasks.

Step 4. If a certain kind of task has been finished, output the outcomes. Select the queen whose scheduling priority is one level lower than the current one. Use the result as the input of the corresponding subsequent task node in the queue. Set the subsequent task on the ready state and wake up the task queen that containing it.

Step 5. Repeat the approach b until all the task queens are empty.

4.2. *The feedback algorithm on the basis of parallel scheduling optimization framework*

The feedback scheduling algorithm optimized the scheduling strategy by analyzing the feedback information of the task. The information feedback model collects the feedback information of all kinds of tasks in the operational process of this framework. In order to further optimize scheduling policy, the model analyzes on the basis of the feedback information and modulates the scheduling and the allocation of the resources dynamically to obtain a more reasonable resource allocation fashion and a bigger concurrency. The main process is as follows:

Step 1. Initialize the feedback information. Classify the feedback information relatively according to the type of the task queen and then create a QRTable based on the number the resource. The table recorded the executive performance of each resource in each type of queen. Set the default maximum at the initialization time.

Step 2. Obtain the type of the task queen and resource of last mission by the feedback information. Obtain the performance record of which corresponds the named type and resource in the QRTable. Compare this performance record with the record in the feedback information of this type.

Step 3. Take the optimal performance as a standard. We know that the performance record is showed as the ratio of task size and execution time. Thus if the performance record of the new feedback information is bigger than that in the QRTable, update the record corresponding to the table. Otherwise, make sure that the record unchangeable.

Step 4. Firstly, obtain the current free processing unit resource in the QRTable when the scheduler is in execution. Then analyze its task types and find out the performance record of the execution of the free resource according to the number of free resource in the QRTable. Select out the task type who has the largest performance ratio by comparison. Finally, make a comparison between each free resource to find out the task scheduling who has the largest performance ratio and then make it into execution.

5. APPLICATION EXAMPLES AND PERFORMANCE TEST

5.1. *Examples of parallel scheduling optimization framework*

Parallel scheduling framework presented in this paper, which can handle the data with characteristics of a lot of classification, sub broad, deep and large scale. Now video data in the video surveillance system has the characteristics of large amount of data, a lot of classification and so on. In the process of handling, the stability of data, accuracy of data and data processing efficiency was relatively higher required. In this paper, the parallel scheduling optimization framework can be used as a parallel processing solution for data processing in video detection.

Now in a data processing system of the video surveillance platform, We have implemented the parallel scheduling optimization framework. For the data processing in the video detection of this school, the data is 3000 in a process of processing and need to be processed 30000 per hour. At the same time, the video data is divided into image detection, the preset position detection, PTZ detection, video detection, device detection. The use of the parallel scheduling optimization framework can realize parallel processing of the data.

Through the deployment of school equipment and data acquisition, according to the logic process of the corresponding data processing, tasks will be divided into four categories: Interactive acquisition of equipment, processing operation of cache data, data checking and cache data storage. So the scheduling framework will be established four scheduling queue (SG). For a building was incorporated into the school's monitoring [10], the data processing task is cut into four sub corresponding tasks which were taken into the four scheduling queue, and A unified scheduling by the parallel scheduling optimization framework, thus it can realize the parallel of data processing and improve the speed and efficiency of video monitoring data.

5.2. *Performance testing of parallel scheduling optimization framework*

Before proposing the framework, data processing of video surveillance detection is based on a common parallel framework , we call this way first scheme, Parallel scheduling optimization framework for data processing scheme is proposed in this paper is second scheme. In order to illustrate the feasibility of the scheduling framework, data processing of video surveillance detection in this school is compared according to the above two kinds of schemes.

5.2.1. *Test preparation*

Test on the actual effect of the parallel scheduling optimization framework is proposed in this paper, to study the framework in performance of large-scale complex data processing.

The test environment is two sets of PC machines, with the 100M Ethernet connection between machines. A PC is used for scheduling framework of the above two kinds of schemes, another PC as the processing unit for resource scheduling. In the test environment, we respectively study the comparison of two schemes' data processing. Each experiment repeated many times, the results are averaged.

5.2.2. *The test contents and results*

Experiment one: video surveillance detection of single number of concurrent for test of data processing results.

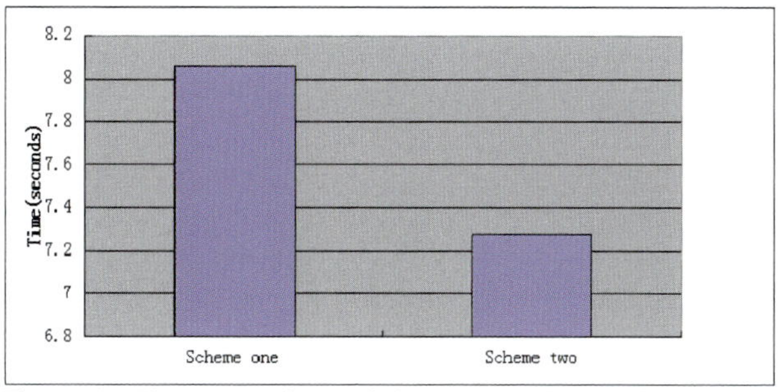

Figure 3. The comparison of data processing performance of single number of concurrent.

Experiment two: video surveillance detection of fifteen numbers of concurrent for test of data processing results.

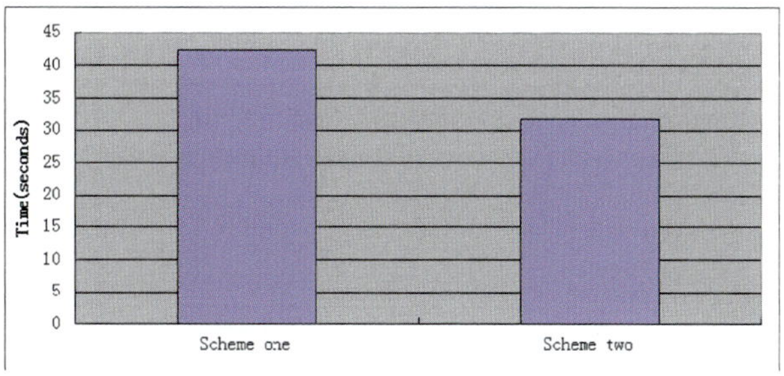

Figure 4. The comparison of data processing performance of fifteen numbers of concurrent.

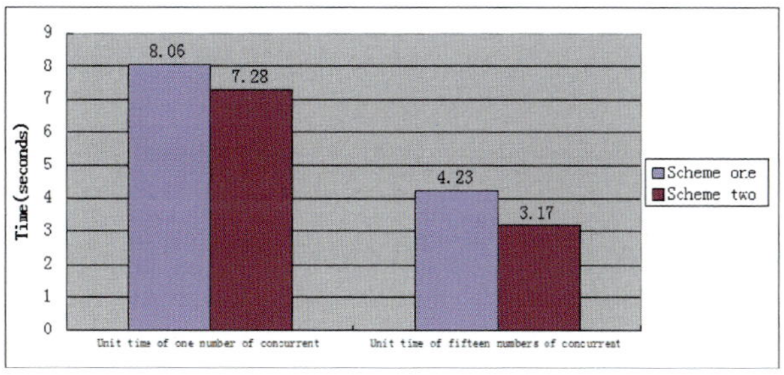

Figure 5. The comparison of the data processing time of unit of concurrent.

Experiment three: The test results on the data set with the increase of the number of concurrent.

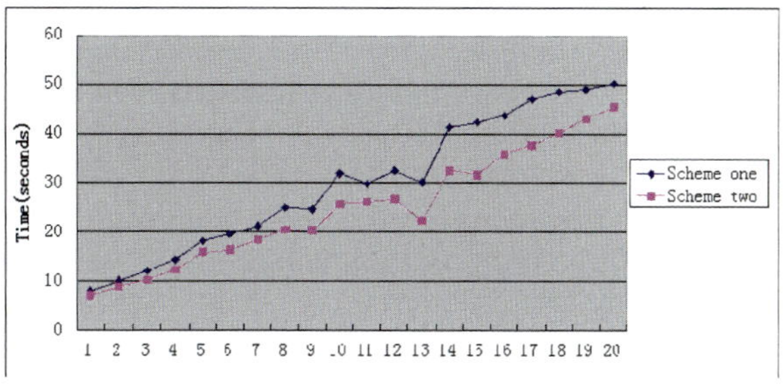

Figure 6. The comparison of the data processing time with the increase of the number of concurrent.

5.2.3. *Analysis of test results*

For the video monitoring system with single number of concurrent, in a process of processing the data quantity is 5 considering network delay and other reasons. After testing, the normal processing time of one concurrent is about 8 seconds. Testing results of the above two kinds of parallel program were compared and analyzed according to the standard.

Seen from experiment one, in the processing of single number of concurrent, two kinds of schemes and the normal processing time had no significant difference, this is because the Single number of concurrent testing still needs to rely on the logical steps, and task completed basically.

Seen from the experiment two, the concurrent quantity value increases to 15, the processing time of scheme two is obvious decrease than scheme one (Figure 4). It can be seen that the use of task classification, dynamic scheduling, information feedback, scheduling parallel scheduling framework can achieve better effect in the data processing of the parallel program two. From Figure 5 we can see, after using a parallel framework, data processing time of unit of fifteen numbers of concurrent than a normal processing time of the unit of concurrent is greatly reduced, so the parallel processing of data has played a role in this system. Further, we also can see the unit processing time of scheme two is less than scheme one, so that it proves that the optimization framework of parallel scheduling based on feedback has better application effect.

Seen from the experiment three, with the increase of number of concurrent, data processing time of scheme two is less than the scheme one, This also proves that with the increase of the number of concurrent, the optimization framework of parallel scheduling based on feedback can makes full use of the feedback information to help scheduling decision, then selects the appropriate tasks and assigns the suitable unit processing resources to deal, in order to achieve more parallelism and high efficiency of the data processing.

Seen from the above experiments, The use of parallel scheduling optimization framework based on feedback is proposed in this paper, through the task classification, dynamic scheduling and information feedback mechanism has a significant effect on the optimization of parallel scheduling, can further improve data parallelism of the parallel scheduling framework.

6. SUMMARY AND PROSPECT

Aiming at the regular feature of data processing, the thesis introduces a kind of parallel scheduling optimized framework design on the basis of feedback. The framework is mainly been made up by the multi-stage classification [11] scheduling queues, core scheduler and information detecting feedback. The framework not only processes the parallel data, but also enforces the real-time detection of resources and task status of the whole process flow. It also drastically modulates the scheduling strategy of the data processing to further improve the efficiency of the process.

The parallel scheduling optimized framework proposed in the thesis has been used in the real project currently. It plays a crucial role in the data processing unit. The result showed that the research achievement has high flexibility, stability and efficiency. It can further improve the parallelism of mass-data processing and meet its processing requirements.

There still has something to be perfected in the future. We need to further enforce and improve the scheduling and monitoring function of the framework to make it achieve the function of automation monitoring and self-adaption studying adjustment. We need to improve the intelligence [12] of the framework and perfect its integral function.

ACKNOWLEDGMENT

This paper is supported by strategic emerging industry development scheme of Qingdao City (13-4-1-45-hy), science and technology research of Shandong province (2014GGX101005), Inter -national scientific and technological cooperation projects (2013DFA10490).

REFERENCES

- [1] Dean J, Ghemawat S. MapReduce. 2008. simplified data processing on large clusters [J], *Communications of the ACM* 51(1): 107-113.
- [2] Cole R, Vishkin U. 1988. Approximate parallel scheduling. Part I: The basic technique with applications to optimal parallel list ranking in logarithmic time [J], *SIAM Journal on Computing* 17(1): 128-142.
- [3] Caron E, Desprez F, Loureiro D, et al. 2009. Cloud computing resource management through a grid middleware: A case study with DIET and eucalyptus [C], *Cloud Computing. CLOUD'09. IEEE International Conference on. IEEE*: 151-154.
- [4] Tarditi D, Puri S, Oglesby J. 2006. Accelerator: using data parallelism to program GPUs for general-purpose uses [C], *ACM SIGARCH Computer Architecture News. ACM* 34(5): 325-335.
- [5] Skogestad S, Postlethwaite I. 2007. Multivariable feedback control: analysis and design [M]. New York: Wiley.
- [6] Sha L, Rajkumar R, Lehoczky J P. 1990. Priority inheritance protocols: An approach to real-time synchronization [J]. *Computers, IEEE Transactions on*, 39(9): 1175-1185.
- [7] Martin S C, Whitcomb L L, Yoerger D, et al. 2006. A mission controller for high level control of autonomous and semi-autonomous underwater vehicles [C], *OCEANS. IEEE*: 1-6.
- [8] Monfroy E, Castro C, Crawford B. 2006. Adaptive enumeration strategies and metabacktracks for constraint solving [M], *Advances in Information Systems*. Springer Berlin Heidelberg: 354-363.
- [9] Lo V M. 1988. Heuristic algorithms for task assignment in distributed systems [J]. *Computers, IEEE Transactions on*, 37(11): 1384-1397.
- [10] Schena M, Shalon D, Davis R W, et al. 1995. Quantitative monitoring of gene expression patterns with a complementary DNA microarray [J]. *Science*, 270(5235): 467-470.
- [11] Abou EL-Magd I, Tanton T W. 2003. Improvements in land use mapping for irrigated agriculture from satellite sensor data using a multi-stage maximum likelihood classification [J]. *International Journal of Remote Sensing*, 24(21): 4197-4206.
- [12] Russell S, Norvig P. 1995. Artificial Intelligence: A Modern Approach [J]. Prentice-Hall, Egnlewood Cliffs, 25.

Research on the Construction of Yang Zhou Travel Ontology

J. Feng
School of Information Engineering, Yangzhou University, Yangzhou, China
Email: 18352764125@163.com

Y. Jiang
School of Information Engineering, Yangzhou University, Yangzhou, China

ABSTRACT: An Ontology is a shared formal specification of a conceptual model. This paper stated the necessity of constructing travel ontology from the perspective of ontology, inspected the design of class structure in the case of Yang Zhou Slender West Lake. By OWL DL, one ontology description language, this paper defined the ontology classes, relationship and constraints between attributes of ontology classes, and defined creation of class instances to complete the construction of domain ontology knowledge base. The visualization of ontology was performed through the ontology editing tools protégé 4.2 and graphviz 2.28.

KEYWORDS: Travel Ontology; OWL DL; Domain ontology knowledge base; Protégé 4.2.

1. INTRODUCTION

"Ontology" is a branch of philosophy, originally used to study the existence and the essence and law theory. In the ancient Chinese philosophy, it is the theory which is used to explore the root cause and basis for universe to produce, exist, develop, change [1].

Since the early 1990s, Ontology develops gradually into a hot topic and appeals to lots of team on artificial intelligence field, including the knowledge of engineering, natural language processing, and knowledge representation. There are a lot of ontology definition, one of the most famous is Gruber [2] "Ontology is the standardization of the conceptualization of specified". Ontology has become a common tool of knowledge engineering, which is used to solve the bottleneck problems knowledge acquisition in the knowledge engineering [3].

With the development of social economy, the national holiday system of regulation and perfect makes more and more people choose to travel during the holidays. In particular, since the industry scale developed quickly in the near decade, China's tourism becomes one of the important services that has promoted the growth of economy in our country and expanded employment channels. Compared to other cities, the tourism in Yang Zhou is more important why adds value of a share of GDP of 6.9%. While tourism is highly dependent on information industry. Traditional access mode is achieved by artificial narrative, but tourism has strong social disciplines, considering space, time and the restriction of many aspects, such as user preferences. Artificial knowledge acquisition mode cannot meet the timeliness and authenticity of the information. In order to make a better arrangement for the relevant service facilities and tourism resources, coordinate various services, and can give attention to different interests and hobbies in various visitors. One kind of intelligent and efficient travel information system needed to develop for this reason. To design such a system, we must learn from the knowledge theory which can be seen as the foundation, however this research at domestic or abroad has not been a knowledge base for the scenic spot. This paper introduced the concept of ontology to analyze tourism area information, establish a reusable, knowledge sharing and basis of tourism knowledge ontology library.

OWL (Web Ontology Language) is a W3C developed a web ontology language, which used to ontology for semantic description. OWL DL (Description Logic) is one of the OWL language of neutron make the reasoning skills and stronger expressivity as a priority. OWL DL includes all the ingredients of the OWL language, but must comply with certain constraints when use it. OWL DL provides the function of description logic reasoning, description logic is a formal foundation of OWL. This paper will use protégé 4.2 & graphviz2.28 ontology to build tourism as the OWL ontology editor environment.

1.1. *Construction of tourism ontology*

We denote Ontology by letter O: O={C, P, R, C, I}, these five elements respective:

1) $c: concept = \{c_1, c_2, \dots, c_n\}$ indicates the set of concept. “Concept” is a knowledge unit formed by the unique combination of features. The German Industrial Standard 2342 defines “Concept” as “A thinking unit with common features, which respond by something towards the use of abstract thinking way to extract”. It can refer to any objects, such as behavior, function, description and so on. As we build in the Tourism Ontology “stay”, “attractions”, “shopping”, “catering” are part of the concept.

2) p: $property = \{p_1, p_2, \dots, p_m\}$ shows the attributes set of concept. The properties of concept are divided into two partial: Object Property and Data Property. For instance: As for this class “attractions” has an object property “scenic spot name”; then like as “address” and “price” are data property.

3) $r: relation = \{r_1, r_2, \dots, r_l\}$ is a collection of all kinds of relationships between attributes of the concept. Such as: “parent child class relationship”, “equivalent class relationship”, “disjoint with relationship”. For example, there are two attributes "scenic spot name "and" nickname", all represent the same class and at the same level. SO they are belong to the equivalent class relationship;" Chinese food "," Japan and Korea food "are the subclass of" catering, they constitute “parent child class relationship”; there is no one accommodation has two object properties "economic" and "top grade" simultaneously. So the "economic" and "top grade" is a “disjoint with class relationship”.

4) C: $constrainsts = \{c_1, c_2, \dots, c_i\}$ represents some restrictions about two instances and the range and domain of properties. It is a restriction attribute, such as the concept is a part of the concept b. Denoting such constraints is order to reasoning.

5) I: $individuals = \{i_1, i_2, \dots, i_s\}$ shows the set of instance. It is the response to a specific class. Fox example: the class “Stay” has two instances “ru jia kuai jie hotel” and “Yangzhou hotel”.

1.2. *Inductions of Ontology editing tools*

Ontology is a editor tool to sharing and exchange information on the semantic Web. It is the premise which makes the semantic web apply widely, by achieve the ontology edited easily and quickly. There are many Web ontology editing tools, such as OTLED, Protege, Web Onto [4].

After analyzing their properties found that they have in common, they all design interface in GUI form to facilitate the users. In order to facilitate ontology generation, most of them integrates the functions of ontology reasoning. Table 1 shows the differences among three editing tools:

Table 1. Comparison of Ontology editor tools [5]

Features	OIL Ed	Protege	Web Onto
Construction	Independent	Independent	Client/Server
Input language	RDF(S);OIL; DAML+OIL	XML;RDF(S) OWL	OCML
Output language	OIL;RDF(S); DAML+OIL; SHIQ; Dotty; HTML	XML;RDF(S); XML Schema; Flogic; CLIPS Java; HTML	OCML; Ontolingua GXL;RDF(S); OIL
Storage form	File	File	File
Scalability	No	Yes	No
Ontology	Yes	Yes	Yes
Reasoning	Yes(FaCT)	Extended	Yes(OCML)

Ontology editor tool has outstanding advantages through analysis of three tools in a comprehensive perspective. Protege software is developed by Biological Information Research Center of Stanford University, based Java language. Used for ontology editing and knowledge acquisition. This software can be customized according to the user's needs. By customizing the user interface better adapt to the new language utility; You can set your own data entry mode and change the internal expression of protege to various forms of text-format. Protege as the core development tools in semantic web, used for building ontology mainly. It provides “concept” “property” “relation” “individuals”, and shield specific describe language. Users first build the domain ontology mode on the conceptual level, and ultimately with a plug graphviz2.28 for displaying a graphical interface.

2. DOMAIN ONTOLOGY DESIGN

2.1. *Knowledge acquisition*

The traditional approach of knowledge acquisition mainly by knowledge engineers, through take conversations with experts to acquire [6]. But as the introduction said, knowledge acquisition about tourism domain ontology was restricted by time, space and human subject and other factors. Obtained from the expert, it is difficult to ensure the accuracy of the knowledge sources and there is no compliance with personal preferences and circumstances moment. To solve this problem, the paper obtained knowledge source from the text has obvious advantages compared to traditional measure obtained from the expert. We know that text is always organized by natural language, and the randomness of natural language and context-sensitive feature make it is almost impossible to achieve knowledge automatically for the computer. A lot of people have done research on this, but under the current context of the knowledge still unable to achieve complete artificial intelligence. Therefore, this paper uses a semi-automatic formal to acquire knowledge.

This article is aim to semi-structured text for automatic knowledge acquisition. Semi-structured text is between structured and unstructured data. In the modern information society, information is divided into two categories: one category can be expressed in what we call structured data, which represented by unified structure or data, such as numbers, symbols; the other information cannot be expressed in numbers or unified structure, such as text, web pages, we define it unstructured data. Semi-structured text, as opposed to unstructured data has some structural. As like as "Baidu Encyclopedia entry" is a semi-structured. Our automated knowledge acquisition is for this type of text, therefore requires we do a lot of manual work before acquire knowledge that transfer semi-structured text to structured data.

2.2. *Define class of travel ontology and its inheritance*

There are three kinds of development methods to define the structure of class: top-down method bottom-up method and mixture of them. This paper uses top-down method, which firstly summarizes a category from the domain ontology, then analyses and classifies step by step and establish relevant subclass. Taking Slender West Lake for example, this method firstly takes "Slender West Lake" as a category, analyses subclass relevant to the entire scenic that is concentrated in the seven elements: "Stay", "Catering", "Attractions", "Traffic", "Travel route", "Shopping", "General", then refines this seven subclass gradually, builds their own subclass whose refinement should be detailed to each element. We establish the class of the Slender West Lake as follows: Table 2 indicates that the establishment of domain ontology of Slender West Lake, then establish class based on the broad framework for the entire Slender West Lake.

Table 2. Building Slender west lake Domain.

```
<Owl: Ontology rdf: about="">
<rdfs: comment>travel ontology</rdfs: comment>
</owl: Ontology>
```

For instance, establishing the subclass of slender west lake named "Stay", Table3 describes how to establish a class of stay in the Slender West Lake.

Table 3. Building Stay Class.

```
<owl: class rdf: ID="Stay">
<rdfs: subclass of rdf: resource="#slender west lake""/>
</owl: Class>
```

2.3. *Designs of class attributes and relationships*

According to the structure of the ontology, the relationship between concepts needs to be set after the definition of the class defining. In the modeling of this article, there are two attributes between concepts: object property and data property. Data property refers to a concept connected to a fixed value. According to the class inheritance, data property has inner generality, this means all the properties which the concept of the class possess are inherited by its subclass and its instances.

Object property, each class has its own specific properties. In addition to the unique value of fixed connections, there are some descriptive properties which are convenient to provide more information for class.

In this paper, date property and object property have more than 50 properties. For the above-mentioned establishment of "stay", this class has 9 association properties. As show in Table 4:

Table 4. Properties of Stay.

Object property	Data property
Hotel facility	address
comfort	tel
economic	price
top grade	grade
has wifi	
has a parking	
Disjoint with	
economic & top grade & comfort	

2.4. *Constraints of ontology*

OWL have some properties, a function, inverse function, symmetric, anti-symmetric, transfer, reflexive, anti-reflexive. It also supports cardinality constraint for property values, to facilitate inference reasoning. Owl complete a constraint for property by declaring the property belongs to a particular class. We assume that there is a relationship attribute $f(x,y)$, indicates that the relationship f between x and y.

1) Function: For any function attribute f, if there is $f(x,y)$ and $f(x,z)$ then y = z. The feature is one attribute only corresponds to a value; the same is the inverse function of a given individual, and only up to an individual by the property is connected to the individual

2) Symmetry: For any symmetric property f, if there is $f(x,y)$ then there must be $f(y,x)$. "Location" property belongs to symmetry property of "attractions".

3) Transitive: For any transitive property f, if there is $f(x,y)$ and $f(y,z)$ then $f(x,y)$ is also true. In this paper, the relationship established property "has a way "and "is a part of" are transitive properties.

4) Reflexivity: In this article has designed no reflexive.

It should be noted that the above properties all belong to in the object property, but does not allow any data property declared as Transitive or Symmetry property. According to the description logic theory, both of a function and symmetrical attribute will cause problems nondeterministic reasoning. Therefore, data attributes can only be declared as a function of the property.

①Suppose a attribute relation $p(x,y)$, p both of function and transitive property

Proof: $\because p$ has a transitive attribute,

$$\therefore p(x,y) \wedge p(y,z) \Rightarrow p(x,z)$$

$\because p$ has a function attribute,

$$\therefore p(x,y) = p(x,z) \Rightarrow y = z$$

$$\therefore z = y \wedge p(y,z) \Leftrightarrow p(y,y)$$

There is no reflexive has been denoted, it will cause reasoning conflict. Therefore it is false.

② Suppose a attribute relation $f(a,b)$, f has symmetric property

Proof: $\because f$ is symmetric,

$$\therefore f(a,b) \Leftrightarrow f(b,a)$$

While there is $tel(a,b)$, then $tel(b,a)$ will not be existed, so data property has no symmetry.

2.5. *Creating instances of ontology*

The concept is defined as a class or as an individual that is dependent on the needs of creating and the application of ontology. It's not incomplete for ontology that it only contains the description of the class. The ontology also requires some specific examples to supplement it, thus making information richer and making knowledge base more robust. In this paper, we define 400 instances. Table 3 indicates the instance creation of "Stay".

Table 5. Instance Sample.

```
<Stay rdf: ID="ru jia kuai jie hotel of wenchang">
<has Comfort rdf: resource="#economic"/>
<has Grade rdf: data type="&xsd; float">4.9
 </has Grade>
<has Address rdf: data type="&xsd; string">邗江区念
四桥路15号
  </has Address>
<has Tel rdf: data type="&xsd: long">051487317222
   </has Tel>
<has Price rdf: data type="&xsd: int">76
 </has Price>
</Stay>
```

3. VISUAL INTERFACE

After coding the ontology, showed under the owl viz view. Figure 1 shows all subclass of slender west lake. Figure 2 shows that included properties in travel ontology, Figure 3 shows how to represent structure type of travel ontology in the tree diagram. IT reflects the design approach of layer by layer and top-down. Among them inheritance relationship exists between parent and grandparent class.

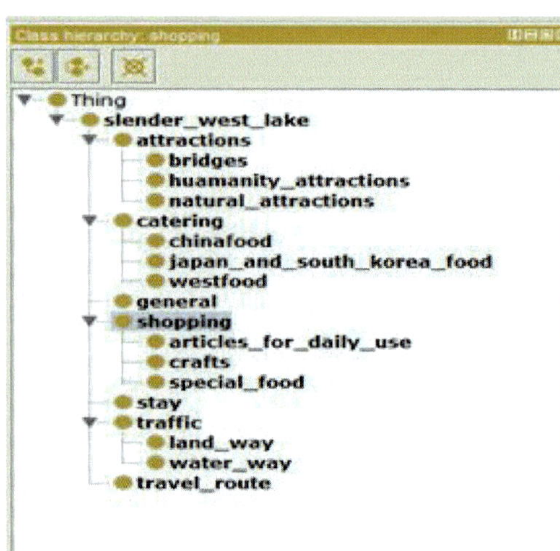

Figure 1. Classes graph.

Figure 2 shows some properties existed in travel ontology, such as "builder" "building background" are the special features in an old town.

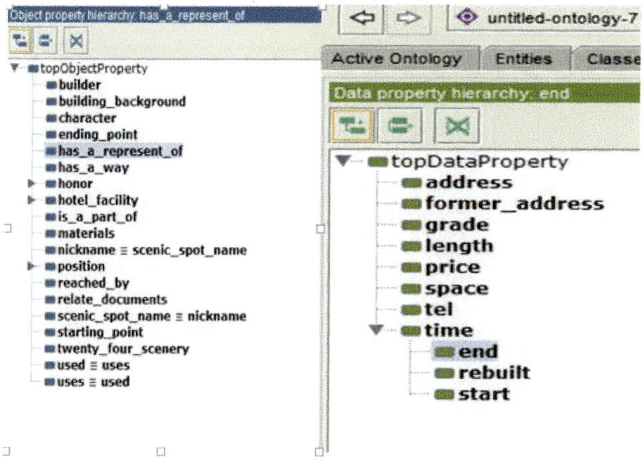

Figure 2. Object property and data property.

Completing the edit of protege and needing visual graphics. Because itself does not own visualization tools, you need to install plug-ins. The paper installed graphviz2.28. Figure 3 is to show the entire class of model, it can be seen from the figure, the subclass inherits the parent class is a relationship show.

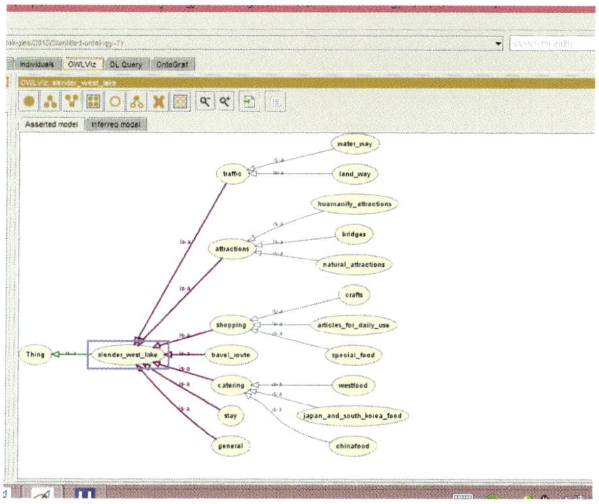

Figure 3. Visualization.

4. REASONING AND QUERY

Recently reasoning tools used mainly Jena, Racer, Jess, Pellet, FacT++. The paper used Fact ++ comes with its own inference engine. FacT ++ is the newest product of Fact which is a description logic tool developed by the University of Manchester. It can be achieved on the satisfiability testing of concept description logic.

According to the existing inference engine analysis and comparison [6] found that, compared to other inference engine, the advantages of FacT ++ is that have a good performance on checking the consistency on ontology and high efficiency and used comfortably. The feeble is that does not provide the interface of Owl and A Box query can not be done. In other word, inquiry the fact that the existing knowledge base. Such as query for the instance itself, including the the properties of the instance and relations between two instances. Choose reasoner tool what you need according to different user. The paper used original inference engine FacT++, and through reasoning ontology to test information consistency. Figure 4 shows that after the completion of the reasoning, ontology according to the rules will have some changes. It will no results while the information is inconsistent.

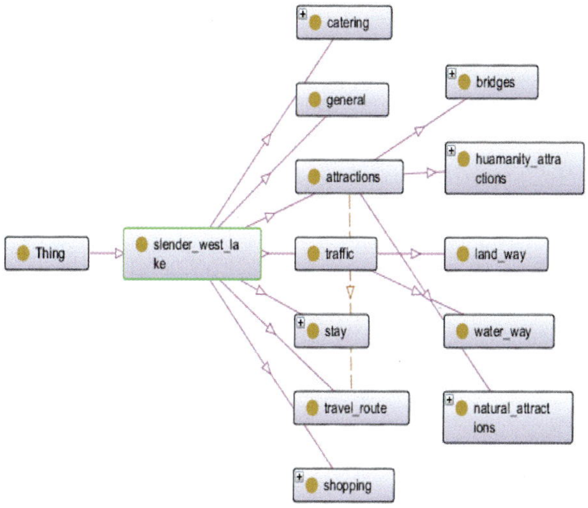

Figure 4. Onto graph.

5. CONCLUSION

With the development of the tourism industry, the traditional pattern of information search are no longer suitable for today's fast-paced development. Ontology research in knowledge engineering application has become more and more mature. If a set of shared travel knowledge established based on ontology, Ontology knowledge base can provide users with convenient services. Because the characteristics of FacT++ reasoning machine, it could not meet the demand of information query such as the properties of the relationship between attribute and the instance. In the future work, we will try to develop a new ontology reasoner to add query in individuals and in the details of the thing instance. This reasoner will make the information more complete.

ACKNOWLEDGEMENT

Project supported by the National Nature Science Foundation of China (Grant No. 61170201, No.

61070133, No. 61472344), Six talent peaks project in Jiang su Province (Grant No.2011-DZXX-032).

Innovation Foundation for graduate students of Jiangsu Province (Grant No. CXLX120916), National Undergraduate Innovative Training Program of China (Grant No. KYLX 1349), Natural Science Foundation of the Jiangsu Higher Education Institutions (Grant No. 14KJB520041).

REFERENCES

— [1] Xiao Kun Tao, Li De Shun. Ontology Theory. Encyclopedia of China Philosophy I. 1987.3

— [2] Gruber T. Ontoligua: a Translation Approach to Portable Ontology Specifications. Knowledge Acquisition, 1993, 5 (2): 199~200.

— [3] Gu Fang & Cao Cun Gen. Ontology Research and Existing Problems in Knowledge Engineering. Computer Science [J], 2004: 31(10).

— [4] Tao Wan & Liao Shu Mei. Analysis and research of current ontology editing tools. Computer Engineering and Design [J]. 2005: 26(3).

— [5] IST Project 2001-29243. A survey on ontology tools [M]. Onto web Deliverable 1.3, Final version, 2202-05.

— [6] Xu De Zhi & Wang Zhi Yong, Wang Bin. Analysis and research of current ontology editing tools. Computer Engineering and Design [J], 2006:12.

— [7] Zhou Xiao Bin. Medicine ontology and medical Acquisition. TP3.

— [8] Zeng Qing Tian, Cao Cun Gen, Gui Yue Fei, Si Jin Xin, Tian Guo Gang, Liu Han Wu. Research on Ontology-based Mathematical Knowledge Acquisition and Knowledge Heritance Mechanism. Microelectronics and Computer, 2003:(9).

— [9] Gong Hua Ming, Zhang Yuan Hong, Xue Zheng Shan, Zhang Yan Mei. Study on the Building of Ontology for Travel.

— [10] Xu Shao Fei. Garden style of Yangzhou Window Series, No. 1.

The Research of Data Mining Based on Improved Shuffled Frog Leaping Algorithm

Y.T. Wang
Department of Information Engineering, Hainan Institute of Science & Technology, Haikou, China

*J.H. Ku[1,2]
1. Department of Information Engineering, Hainan Institute of Science & Technology, Haikou, China
2. School of Computer Science, China University of Geosciences, Wuhan, China
Email: kujunhua@163.com

ABSTRACT: As the fuzzy C- means (FCM) clustering algorithm is easy to fall into local optimal value, this paper presents a new FCM clustering algorithm based on improved shuffled frog leaping algorithm (SFLA). The algorithm uses shuffled frog leaping algorithm for its fast global searching ability to generate initial clustering centers of FCM, and then use FCM to optimize the initial cluster centers. Finally we get the global optimal solution. In order to improve shuffled frog leaping algorithm ability to solve complex problems, Cauchy variation and chaos optimization mechanism is introduced in the frog update strategy, and improves the performance of shuffled frog leaping algorithm. In order to enhance the classification accuracy, a characteristic index weighting factor is introduced in the FCM, and the clustering accuracy and speed of FCM is improved. The results of experiment on real data show that searching ability and precision of the new algorithm (ISFLA-FCM) are improved obviously contrast with the traditional FCM clustering algorithms.

KEYWORDS: Data mining; Fuzzy C-means clustering; Shuffled frog leaping algorithm; Cluster analysis.

1. INTRODUCTION

Along with the rapid development of computer technology, communication technology, and network technology, the human has to face the explosive growth of data information. As it can obtain useful information from large and complex data, the data mining technology has aroused great concern in the database, the information decision-making areas and so on. As an important part of data mining technology, the cluster analysis has been widely used in image processing, computer vision, and text analysis field [1]. Clustering algorithm refers to make the unknown data having same attribute into one class as much as possible, according to the degree of similarity [2]. Clustering algorithms are often divided into the traditional clustering algorithm and fuzzy clustering algorithm. Based on fuzzy theory, fuzzy clustering algorithm has better clustering performance, and the fuzzy C- means (Fuzzy C-Means, FCM [3]) algorithm is the most widely used clustering algorithm. The FCM algorithm has simple concept, fast convergence, and strong local searching ability, but it is sensitive to initial value, easy to fall into local optimal solution, and can only identify clusters having cluster shape [4]. Therefore the domestic and foreign scholars have done many in-depth researches for the shortcomings of FCM algorithm, and propose some improved methods.

In paper [5], based on the FCM algorithm, an improved fuzzy partition clustering algorithm (IFP-FCM) is proposed. Through introducing the membership degree constraint function, this algorithm makes membership iterative formula more clear, and has better robustness to noise and outliers. In paper [6], a data mining algorithm for outlier data is proposed. Through given each attribute of data a certain weight, this algorithm improves the algorithm clustering effect. The fusion of intelligent algorithms and fuzzy clustering algorithm is one of the hot topics research, and has obtained many fruits, such as: C-Means clustering based on immune genetic algorithm [7], fuzzy clustering algorithm based on particle swarm, fuzzy clustering algorithm based on selection and mutation mechanism shuffled frog leaping algorithm [8]. These algorithms use different intelligent algorithm for FCM algorithm, and improved the performance of FCM algorithm to a certain extent.

Shuffled frog leaping algorithm (SFLA), is a kind of swarm intelligence based on heuristic computing technology, and has many characteristics such as easy to be realized, fast convergence speed, strong global optimization capability. At present, the basic theory of SFLA [9] and improvement methods for frog update strategy algorithm [10] have been carried out in-depth research, and successfully applied to the optimization problem in [11].

In this paper, Cauchy variation and chaos optimization mechanism are introduced into the basic SFLA frog update strategy, and a characteristic index weighting factor is introduced for FCM. This paper puts forward an improved Fuzzy C-means clustering algorithm (ISFLA-FCM) based on ISFLA. For SFLA fast convergence characteristics, this paper uses SFLA to generate the initial clustering center for FCM algorithm, and then use FCM to optimize the initial clustering center. Finally we get the global optimal solution.

2. FUZZY C-MEANS CLUSTERING ALGORITHM (FCM)

As the important method for unsupervised pattern recognition, the purpose of clustering analysis is to divide data into a number of categories, and the data in same category has higher similarity. Based on the fuzzy theory, fuzzy clustering method becomes mature, and the fuzzy clustering method based on objective function has been widely used. As the clustering problem is transformed into constrained nonlinear programming problem, it is easier to realize the classification problem. Among the objective function clustering algorithm, fuzzy C-means (FCM) algorithm is widely used. FCM algorithm is an iterative optimization algorithm, which can be described as a minimization of the exponential function.

For the data set $X=\{x_1,x_2,\cdots,x_k,\cdots x_n\}\in R^n$, x_k ($k=1,2,\cdots,n$) is a sample of individuals. We divide X into c ($C\in[2,n]$) classes, and cluster centers can be described as $V=\{v_1,v_2,\cdots,v_i,\cdots v_C\}$. We set the membership between x_k and v_i ($i=1,2,\cdots,C$) as μ_{ik}, and the classification results can be described as: $U_{n\times C}=(\mu_{ik})$. We give the objective function for the FCM clustering algorithm as follows:

$$\min J_{FCM}(U,V)=\sum_{k=1}^{n}\sum_{i=1}^{C}(\mu_{ik})^m \bullet \|x_k-v_i\|^2 \tag{1}$$

The constraint condition is:

$$\sum_{i=1}^{C}\mu_{ik}=1 \tag{2}$$

Where m is the fuzzy weighted factor. It controls the fuzziness of the FCM algorithm clustering results, and experimental results show that m value interval is [1.25, 2.5]. Update formula for v_i and μ_{ik} as follows:

$$v_i=\frac{\sum_{k=1}^{n}(\mu_{ik})^m \bullet x_k}{\sum_{k=1}^{n}(\mu_{il})^m},i=1,2,\cdots,C \tag{3}$$

$$\mu_{ik}=\left[\sum_{j=1}^{C}\left(\frac{\|x_k-v_i\|}{\|x_k-v_j\|}\right)^{\frac{2}{m-1}}\right]^{-1} \tag{4}$$

2.1. *Characteristic index weight factor*

Practice has proved that the FCM algorithm is one of the most effective methods in fuzzy clustering algorithm [12]. FCM assumes that each sample characteristics are the same, but in many areas, the contribution of each sample characteristic is different, and some attributes contribution is very small. In order to distinguish the affection of different attributes for the classification result, and improve the speed and accuracy of FCM, a characteristic index weighting factor w is introduced to the traditional FCM algorithm. We set that each x_k has l different characteristic attributes ($x_k=\{x_{k1},x_{k2},\cdots,x_{kq},\cdots,x_{kl}\}$), and the weight factor for each attribute x_{kq} is w_q, so W can be described as $W=\{w_1,w_2,\cdots,w_q,\cdots,w_l\}$. We give the improved objective function for the FCM clustering algorithm as follows:

$$\min J_{FCM}(U,V)=\sum_{k=1}^{n}\sum_{i=1}^{C}(\mu_{ik})^m \bullet \sum_{q=1}^{l}[w_q(x_{kq}-v_{iq})]^2 \tag{5}$$

Where $\sum_{q=1}^{l}w_q=1$, and the improved update formula for μ_{ik} is:

$$\mu_{ik}=\left[\sum_{j=1}^{C}\left(\frac{\sum_{q=1}^{l}[w_q(x_{kq}-v_{iq})]^2}{\sum_{q=1}^{l}[w_q(x_{kq}-v_{jq})]^2}\right)^{\frac{2}{m-1}}\right]^{-1} \tag{6}$$

There are many determining methods for attribute weight factor. According to [13], a determining method based on neural network supervised learning method is given, and the process is shown in Figure 1.

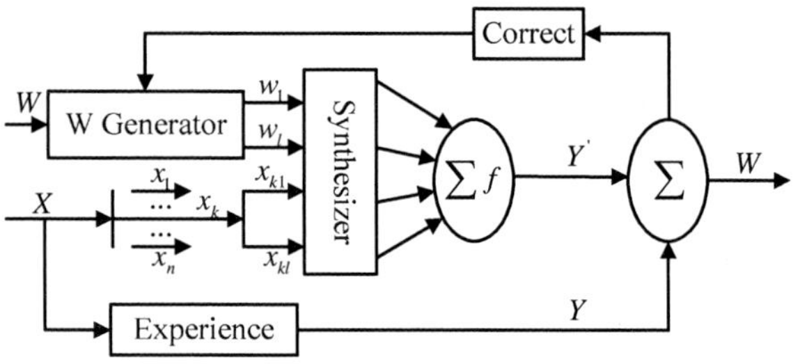

Figure 1. The determination of weight factor.

In Figure 1, the update theory for w_q as follows:

$$w_q^{t+1} = w_q^t + \alpha\left(y_k - y_k^{'m}\right)x_{kq} \tag{7}$$

Where w_q^t is the weight factor for x_{kq} after t times cycling.

2.2. *Improved FCM algorithm*

The improved FCM algorithm steps are as follows:

Step 1: Determine the number of clustering c, data set X and the weighting factor w.

Step 2: Randomly generates initial clustering centers $V^{(0)}$, set the terminate error ε, and initialize the iteration number t.

Step 3: Calculates the $U_{n \times C}^{(t)}$.

Step 4: Calculates the $V^{(t+1)}$, if $\left\|V^{(t+1)} - V^{(t)}\right\| \le \varepsilon$, then end iteration, and output the optimal cluster centers. Otherwise, $t = t+1$, and go back to Step 3.

3. SFLA

3.1. *Basic SFLA*

In 2003, based on Memetic algorithm and PSO algorithm, Eusuff and others present a shuffled frog leaping algorithm. Many researches show that SFLA can converge to the global optimal solution.

For s-dimensional objective optimization problem, the solution spaces can be described as: $S = \left\{P \middle| P = (P_1, P_2, \cdots, P_s)^T\right\} \subseteq R^s$. The frog initial population has F frogs and can be described as: $P = \{P_1, \cdots, P_k, \cdots, P_F\}$, $k = 1, 2, \cdots, F$. The position for frog k is: $P_k = \{p_{k1}, p_{k2}, \cdots, p_{ks}\}$. The frog population are sorted by the fitness values $f[P_k]$, and equally distributed into M groups. Each group frog number is N. The first frog put into the first ethnic group, second frog put into the second ethnic groups, until the M frog into the M ethnic group. Then, the $M+1$ frog is placed in the first ethnic group, the $M+2$ frog and put second ethnic group ... Until the finally frog M put into the M ethnic group.

In order to improve ethnic local search speed, according to the fitness value of frogs, frogs are chosen by triangular probability to form sub ethnic group in each ethnic group. Each sub population number is q, the probability for each frog is:

$$p_j = \frac{2(n+1-j)}{n(n+1)}, j = 1, 2, \cdots, N \tag{8}$$

For SFLA, only fogs with the worst value (P_w) are updated. The update strategy is (as shown in Figure 2 (a)):

$$D = r \bullet [P_b - P_w] \tag{9}$$

$$X' = X_w + D \tag{10}$$

where $r \in [0,1]$ and is a random number. P_g and P_b are the best solution in the entire frog population and each sub ethnic group. If the P' fitness is better than that of P_w, we use P' instead of P_w. Otherwise, we use P_g instead of P_b and re-run update strategy (9-10). If P' is still not better than P_w, then randomly generates a frog instead of P_w. The process is repeated in each sub ethnic group, until the local search time is met.

When all groups performed the local search, frogs are mixed again, and we get the new value of $f[P_k]$. The frogs are sorted by the fitness values $f[P_k]$, and equally distributed into M groups again. We make sub ethnic group division and do local search operation until meeting the algorithm terminates conditions.

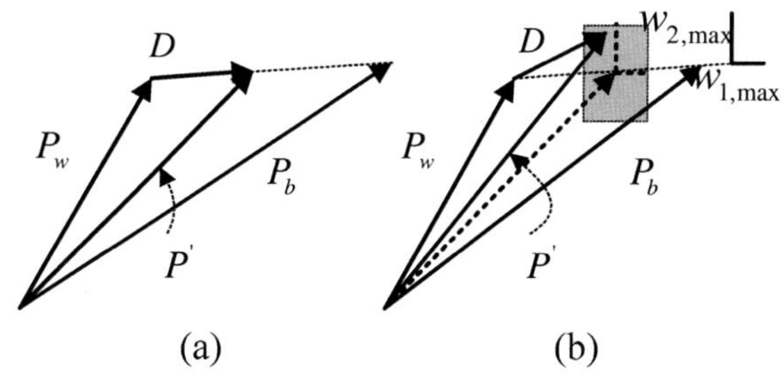

Figure 2. The frogs update strategy.

3.2. *Improved SFLA*

In the basic SFLA, simply by using sub groups or global optimum implementation for frog update strategy, it may restrict the local search range, and reduce the sub ethnic local search speed, resulting in local optimal solution. Therefore, in order to improve SFLA convergence speed, avoid falling into local optimum, the frog update strategy and global information exchange mechanism are improved, which improve the SFLA algorithm performance.

3.2.1. *Improvement for frog updating strategy*

According to literature [14], this paper gives the frog particle update strategy (as shown in Figure 2 (b) shown below) as follows

$$D(t) = r \bullet c \bullet (P_b - P_w) + W \tag{11}$$

$$W = \left[r_1 \cdot w_{1,\max}, r_2 \cdot w_{2,\max}, \cdots, r_n \cdot w_{n,\max}\right]^T \tag{12}$$

$$P' = \begin{cases} P_w + D & , if \|D\| \le D_{\max} \\ P_w + \dfrac{D}{\sqrt{D^T D}} D_{\max} & , if \|D\| > D_{\max} \end{cases} \tag{13}$$

where $c \in [1,2]$ and is a constant. $r_i \in [-1,1]$ and is a random number. $w_{i,\max}$ is the i dimension search space maximum uncertainty. The introduction of the search space uncertain factor increases the sub groups search space, improves the sub population sample diversity, and improves search speed to a certain degree.

3.2.2. *Cauchy mutation*

In the basic SFLA, if P' is still worse than P_w, then randomly generates a new frog instead of P_w. The randomly generated individuals approach increases the SFLA blindness, and reduces the convergence speed. In order to make full use of the disturbance information, this paper uses the Cauchy mutation to replace the randomly generated frog individual operation. The one-dimensional distribution density function for Cauchy is:

$$f(x) = \frac{\alpha}{\pi(\alpha + x^2)}, x \in (-\infty, +\infty) \tag{14}$$

When $\alpha = 1$, (13) is the standard Cauchy distribution, and we describe it as $C(0,1)$. Compared with the Gauss mutation, Cauchy mutation has better performance in jumping out of local optimal. The definition for Cauchy variance is:

$$P' = P_b + P_b \bullet C(0,1) \tag{15}$$

3.2.3. *Chaos optimization algorithm (COA)*

Chaos optimization algorithm means introducing chaos in variables, and expands chaos to the variables scope. COA uses chaos variables for global search and COA has good global search ability. Logistic mapping is the most used in the chaos optimization algorithm and logistic mapping has good randomness. The iterative equation for logistic mapping is:

$$x_{n+1} = \mu \times x_s \times (1 - x_s), 0 < x_n < 1 \tag{16}$$

Where μ is a chaotic variable. In paper [15], when μ value is among [3.85, 4], logistic mapping has the best performance. We give COA steps as follows:

Step1: Expands chaos to the variables scope.

$$p_{ks} = a_k + (b_k - a_k) \bullet p_s \tag{17}$$

Where a_k and b_k are the minimum and maximum values for frog P_k.

Step 2: Do chaos search strategy.

Step 3: Determine whether a termination condition is satisfied, if satisfied, end algorithm and output the results; otherwise, the iteration number plus 1, and moving to Step 1.

In the SFLA global information exchange process, by using chaos optimization strategy, the algorithm can avoid falling into local optimum.

3.2.4. *Fitness function*

In order to improve FCM algorithm by using improved SFLA, We chose the FCM objective function as the fitness function for ISFLA. When the clustering objective function gets the minimum value, the ISFLA has the smallest fitness value. We set each frog position is the clustering center, that means frog position can be describe as $P_V = \{p_{v_1}, p_{v_2}, \cdots, p_{v_i}, \cdots p_{vC}\}$. So the frog fitness function is:

$$f(P_V) = J_{FCM}(U,V) = \sum_{k=1}^{n}\sum_{i=1}^{C}(\mu_{ik})^m \bullet \sum_{q=1}^{l}[w_q(x_{kq} - p_{v_{il}})]^2 \tag{18}$$

4. ISFLA-FCM

Improved fuzzy C-means clustering algorithm (ISFLA-FCM) uses ISFLA produce the initial cluster centers at first, and then use the FCM algorithm adding weight factor to optimize the initial clustering center. Finally we get the global optimal solution. Figure 3 shows the ISFLA-FCM algorithm flow.

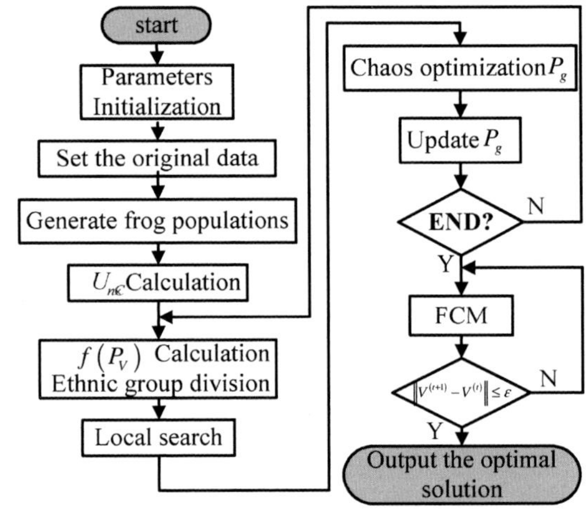

Figure 3. ISFLA-FCM algorithm flow.

5. SIMULATIONS

In order to verify the performance of ISFLA-FCM algorithm, this paper uses SFLA-FCM, FCM and ISFLA-FCM to test on the classic simulation data. We use Matlab as the simulation platform. ISFLA-FCM parameters setting: ε=10-3, m=2, $F = 200$, $M = 20$, $N = 10$, $q = 10$. The local iteration is 10, and the global iteration number is 500. The parameter setting is referred to [16], and this literature points out that using such parameters, SFLA has better performance.

5.1. *IRIS data experiment*

This paper adopts IRIS simulation data for test. The IRIS data has 150 samples, and each sample is 4 dimensional variable. The samples are divided into 3 categories, and each category includes 50 samples.

In the Matlab simulation platform, using SFLA-FCM, FCM and ISFLA-FCM and running 100 times, the simulation results is given. We set V as average accuracy rate, T as average running time, t as the average number of iterations, σ as variance. Table 1 gives the results of clustering on IRIS, and Figure 4 gives 3 kinds of algorithm convergence curve of average fitness.

Table 1. IRIS clustering results.

Index	***IRIS data***		
	ISFLA-FCM	***FCM***	***SFLA-FCM***
$\bar{V}$ /%	97.1	92.3	94.2
$\bar{T}$ /s	23.4	3.2	31.8
$\bar{t}$	15	17	23
σ	4.3	2.3	14.3

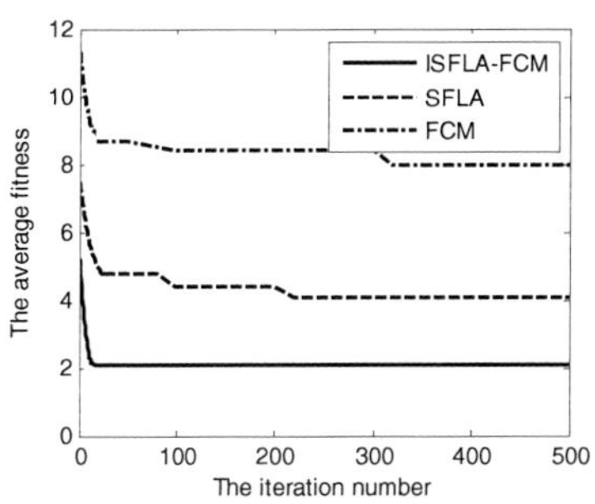

Figure 4. 3 algorithms convergence curves.

From Table 1 and Figure 4 we can see that ISFLA-FCM clustering has better accuracy and precision than the other two algorithms, and the running time is smaller than SFLA-FCM apparently.

5.2. *High dimensional data experiment*

In order to further validate the ISFLA-FCM performance in processing high dimension and multiple data problems, we chose the 3 algorithms to test on the multiple features data and diagnostic data. The simulation results are shown in Table 2 and Figure 5.

Table 2. High dimensional data clustering results.

Index	multiple features data			Diagnostic data		
	ISFLA	FCM	SFLA	ISFLA	FCM	ISFLA
$\bar{V}$ /%	95.3	88.7	90.2	93.1	81.4	89.5
$\bar{T}$ /s	52.1	34.7	67.2	43.2	20.4	69.1
$\bar{t}$	65	68	93	123	134	210
σ	16.1	33.6	27.9	13.8	65.1	31.9

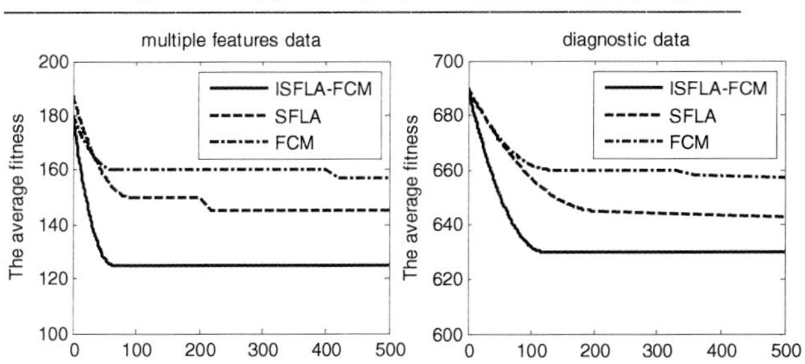

Figure 5. 3 algorithms convergence curves.

From Table 2 and Figure 5 we can see that, ISFLA-FCM has better performance in solving high dimension data, and its precision and accuracy are higher than the other two algorithms. This is because the ISFLA-FCM using improved SFLA to generate the initial cluster centers, and then use the FCM optimal cluster centers, which enhances the global searching ability of the algorithm.

6. CONCLUSIONS

This paper has researched the application of improved FCM based on improved SFLA in data mining. The frog update strategy is improved, and the Cauchy mutation is introduced to replace the randomly generated frog theory. Based on the chaos optimization strategy, the SFLA convergence rate is improved. This paper puts forward the characteristics index weight factor, which avoids FCM algorithm being trapped in local optimal solution. The simulation results show that the improved FCM has better performance and avoids the local optimum solution.

ACKNOWLEDGMENT

This work is supported by The Natural Science Foundation of Hainan Province (No. 610216, 614248), Scientific Research Fund of Hainan Provincial Education Department (No. Hjkj201591) and Scientific Research Fund of Hainan University (No. KYQD1118).

REFERENCES

— [1] Xiu Yu, Wang Shitong, Wu Xisheng, et al. The directional similarity based clustering method DSCM [J]. Journal of Computer Research and Development, 2006, 43(8): 1425-1431.

— [2] Zhu Lin, Wang Shitong, Deng Zhaohong. Research on Generalized Fuzzy C-Means Clustering Algorithm with Improved Fuzzy Partitions [J]. Journal of Computer Research and Development, 2009, 46(5):814-822.

— [3] Khotanzad A, Sadek N. Ulti-scale high-speed network traffic prediction using combination of neural networks [C] Proceedings of the International Joint Conference on Neural Networks. Portland, OR, USA: IEEE Press, 2003: 1071-1075.

— [4] Zhao Xiaoqiang, Liu Yueting. Fuzzy clustering algorithm based on selection and mutation mechanism shuffled frog leaping algorithm [J]. Application Research of Computers, 2012, 29(6): 2068-2071.

— [5] Hoppner F, Klawonn F. Improved fuzzy partitions for fuzzy regression models [J]. Journal of Approximate Reasoning, 2003, 32(2): 85-102.

— [6] Li Xingyi, Bao Congjian, Shi Huaji. Outlier data mining algorithms based on weighted fast clustering [J]. Computer Engineering and Applications, 2007, 43(35):153-155.

- [7] Sun Yang, Luo Ke. C-Means clustering based on immune genetic algorithm [J]. Computer Engineering and Applications, 2009, 45(23): 152-153, 169.
- [8] Chen Zhiya, Fang Xiaobin, Lei Ding-you. Fuzzy Clustering Algorithm Based on Particle Swarm [J]. Computer Engineering, 2007, 33(22): 198-199.
- [9] Alireza R V, Ali H M. Solving a bicriteria permutation flow shop problem using shuffled frog-leaping algorithm [J]. Soft Computing, 2008, 12(5): 435-452.
- [10] Huynh T H. A modified shuffled frog leaping algorithm for optimal tuning of multivariable PID controllers [C]. IEEE Int Conf on Industrial Technology. New York: IEEE Press, 2008: 1-6.
- [11] Rahimi-Vahed A, Mirzaei A H. A hybrid multi-objective shuffled frog-leaping algorithm for a mixed model assembly line sequencing problem [J]. Computers and Industrial Engineering, 2007, 53(4): 642-666.
- [12] Xiong Z, Orchard M, Ramchandran K. Inverse half toning using wavelets[J].IEEE Transactions on Image Processing, 1999, 8(10): 1479-1483.
- [13] Wang Xizhao, Wang Yadong, Wang Lijuan. Improving fuzzy C-means clustering based on feature weight learning [J]. Pattern Recognition Letters, 2004, 25: 1123- 1132.
- [14] Huynh T H. A modified shuffled frog leaping algorithm for optimal tuning of multivariable PID controllers [C]. IEEE Int Conf on Industrial Technology. New York: IEEE Press, 2008: 1-6.
- [15] Xu Hong-li, Qian Xu, Yue Xun. New ant colony optimization algorithm based on logistic chaotic image to resolve VRP problem [J]. Application Research of Computers, 2012, 29(6): 2058-2060.
- [16] E. Elbeltagi, T. Hegazy, D. Grierson. Comparison among five evolutionary-based optimization algorithms [J]. Advanced Engineering Informatics, 2005, 19(1): 43-53.

Five-Category Classification Prediction for "Three Rural" Loan Risk Based on Support Vector Machine

Y. Hu[1], K. Fang[1,*], X. Fang[2], C. Xu[2]
1 College of Information Science and Technology, Hunan Agricultural University, Changsha 410128, China
2 Information Center, Changsha University, Changsha 410001, China
**E-mail: fk@hunau.net*

ABSTRACT: Based on the data mining method, Support Vector Machine technology, Correlated Analytical Variable Selection method and Principal Component Analytical Variable Dimension Reduction method, setting five-category classification and prediction model for "Three rural" loan risk of commercial bank, then make classification prediction for an Agricultural Bank of China in Changsha and verify the outcome through this prediction model, and make comparative analysis with the classification prediction accuracy of neural network and the time consumed for processing, the advantage of this method is obvious. This five-category classification and prediction model for loan risk have great meanings for bank to establish more robust customer relationship management system and attract more high-quality customer resources.

KEYWORDS: Three rural loans; Support vector machine; Classification prediction.

1. INTRODUCTION

At present, domestic and foreign financial sector and academia generally agreed that the comprehensive five-category classification rating information is obtained by the bank credit inspectors, they divide borrowers into different levels based on the assessment of their repayment ability and the inherent risk degree of credit [1]. But this description is mainly focused on the classification process of credit risk, have no description on the ultimate goal of credit risk classification. The ultimate goal of classification management should be to facilitate the financial institutions to grasp client assets quality, and help them implement real-time control and processing on different levels of asset status by increasing the risk management and control level.

In 1998, the loan risk of People's Bank of China were divided into five categories: normal, secondary, concerns, doubtful and loss [2]. At present, since description on classification level is not clear, the understanding of goal is not detailed, subjective handling is too casual, the lack of actual operation of quantitative methods and a series of objective factors caused the accuracy and authenticity of credit risk classification, and the result of follow-up management on credit is not satisfactory. The following is a leader of "three rural" loan classification case in 2013 and 2014 of an Agricultural Bank of China in Changsha, as shown in Table 1.

Table 1 "Three rural" loan classification case in 2013 and 2014, of an Agricultural Bank of China in Changsha.

		2013		2014	
		Balance (million)	Proportion(%)	Balance (million)	Proportion(%)
Normal	nomal	88802	68.6	96256	65.9
	attention	15281	11.8	16463	11.3
	sum	104083	80.4	112729	77.15
Bad	secondary	3737	2.9	6843	4.7
	suspicious	14678	11.3	18896	12.9
	loss	6962	5.4	7653	5.2
	sum	25377	19.6	33392	22.9

As can be seen from the table, compared to 2013, the proportion of the “three rural” nonperforming loans increased by 3.3 percentage points in 2014, if this bank cannot take effective measures to reduce the proportion of bad loans For the long run, the cooperation between the Agricultural Bank of China and the “three rural” will be devastating. This case is just a tip of the iceberg of bad phenomenon of bad “three rural” loan which appears in commercial banks in China.

Currently, academia and the financial sector have proposed that financial institutions can improve the level of classification prediction and control on the risk of bank loans according to the principle of Fuzzy Mathematical Model, Matrix Method but because of the lack of empirical research, it didn’t receive the leadership’s attention in financial institutions sector.

Support Vector Machine is a rapidly developing method of learning machine, based on Statistical learning theory and follow Structural Risk Minimization principle, it nonlinearly map inseparable dataset into a high dimensional space by constructing a linear kernel function to make it linearly separable in this space, and get the optimum predicted outcome through balancing experienced risk and confidence interval confidence interval [3].

The main theory of Support Vector Machine how to classify “three rural” credit into different categories is that basing on the training of known data of loan, deducing the function model which is used for infer the risk level of this “three rural” credit data set, then judge and predict the risk type of unknown credit data [4]. Based on risk minimization principle, Support Vector Machine requires the maximum classification separation distance, the most concentrated classification subset, which coincide with the classification needs of the risk the “three rural” credit.

2. DATA SOURCES

Randomly extract and organize the data of 500 customers captured from the Customer Relationship Management Profile of an Agricultural Bank of China in Changsha. Then exclude the name, ID number and other properties that have nothing to do with mining, merely retain nine independent variables properties and one attributes properties, which are gender (x_1), age (x_2), domicile (x_3), the nature of work (x_4), education level (x_5), monthly income (x_6, Yuan), deposits (x_7,Yuan), credit (x_8, Yuan) and agro mode (x_9), as well as the type of loan risk (Y). There are five-category classification for the type of loan risk, which are normal (1), attention (2), secondary (3), suspicious (4), loss (5).

Four properties, the monthly income, deposits, loans and number of family members, have specific numerical, while other properties have no specific numerical, we have other attributes classified according to this bank’s statistics, as shown in the following table.

Table 2. Classification of properties with no specific numerical.

Gender		Age		Domicile		Nature of work		Education level		Customer type	
male	1	0-20	0	Changsha	1	Government agency	0	Postdoctor	0	VIP Customer	0
female	0	20-30	1	Other	0	Institutions	1	Dr.	1	Ordinary Customer	1
		30-40	2			SOE	2	Master	2		
		40-50	3			Private Enterprise	3	Undergraduate	3		
		50-60	4			Self-employed	4	College	4		
		>60	5			other	5	Secondary	5		
								Senior high school	6		
								Junior high school and below	7		

3. MODELING AND CLASSIFICATION PREDICTION

3.1. *Arguments standardization*

Data standardization contributes to SVM kernel function selecting parameters and the improvement of training rates. In this article, the entire data set of arguments is standardized by the following formula:

$$x_i' = -1 + 2(x_i - x_{\min}) / (x_{\max} - x_{\min}) x_i \subset [-1,1] \quad (1)$$

In this formula, $x_{\max}$ and $x_{\min}$ are respectively the maximum value and minimum value of x_i.

3.2. *Arguments screening*

Carrying out data normalization process before screening arguments is also needed. Then apply Correlation Analysis Method and Principal Component Analysis Method to execute linear and nonlinear filtering on arguments.

3.2.1. *Correlation analysis method*

Correlation Analysis is a statistical analysis method which analyzes and process dependencies between two peer vectors. Through mathematical calculations, it is able to calculate an abstract value that reflects the interaction degree and the associated direction of the two vectors, i.e., the correlation coefficient [5]. For vector X and vector Y, the sample values respectively are x_i and y_i ($i, j = 1, 2, \cdots n$), the mathematical description about correlation coefficients of X and Y is as follows:

$$\left.\begin{aligned} R &= \frac{\sum_{i=1}^{n}(x_i - \bar{x})(y_i - \bar{y})}{\sqrt{\sum_{i=1}^{n}(x_i - \bar{x})^2}\sqrt{\sum_{i=1}^{n}(y_i - \bar{y})^2}}, R \in [-1,1] \\ &\qquad (2) \\ \bar{x} &= \frac{1}{n}\sum_{i=1}^{n} x_i \\ \bar{y} &= \frac{1}{n}\sum_{i=1}^{n} y_i \end{aligned}\right\}$$

The correlation coefficients of variables and the dependent variables are as shown in Table 3.

It can be easily seen from the table that the correlation coefficient of variable x_1 (gender) and x_9 (family members) as well as Y (loan type) is small, that is say, these attributes, the gender and number of family members of customer, have weak influence on the type of loan, so that gender and the number of family members can be filter out, and leave seven attributes as independent variables for subsequent analysis.

Table 3. Correlation coefficients of variables and the dependent variables.

$\lvert R \rvert$	X_1	X_2	X_3	X_4	X_5	X_6	X_7	X_8	X_9
Y	0.23	0.91	0.86	0.92	0.92	0.91	0.95	0.92	0.34

3.2.2. *Principal component analysis*

Execute principal component analysis on the "three rural" borrowers (after Correlation analysis) by DPS6.55, the input sequence of arguments are age x_2, domicile x_3, nature of agro x_4, education level x_5, monthly income x_6, deposits x_7, loan x_8, the results are shown in table 4.

Table 4. The Principal Components Result of the Affecting Factors of "Three rural" loan customers.

Normalized feature vectors							
	Factor 1	Factor 2	Factor 3	Factor 4	Factor 5	Factor 6	Factor 7
x(1)	0.3894	0.1002	-0.0764	-0.3189	0.0415	-0.1342	-0.6993
x(2)	0.3678	-0.1104	-0.1453	0.5226	-0.3666	0.6012	-0.0251
x(3)	0.3546	0.0502	-0.2567	-0.5930	-0.0339	0.4229	0.1234
x(4)	0.3889	0.8109	0.4434	0.1340	-0.0230	0.0339	0.0549
x(5)	0.3298	-0.1471	-0.0878	0.2882	-0.3756	-0.5608	-0.1531
x(6)	0.3674	0.0311	-0.1468	-0.2163	-0.1776	-0.3515	0.6546
x(7)	0.3244	-0.5345	0.8324	-0.1675	0.1456	0.0673	0.0389

Feature values			
No	Feature values	Percentage %	Cumulative Percentage%
1	7.1253	89.0662	89.0662
2	0.5632	7.0400	96.1062
3	0.2635	3.2938	99.4000
4	0.0251	0.3138	99.7138
5	0.0121	0.1513	99.9651
6	0.0075	0.0938	99.9589
7	0.0033	0.0009	100

It can be seen from the table that the cumulative feature values have the first principal component approach to 90%, which indicates that the first principal component covers all information that affect the type of "three rural" loan customers. In addition, the normalized results of feature values also indicates that the first principal component contains all the information of the remaining seven independent variable, so the results of principal component analysis doesn't have to delete any independent variable factors, we leave all seven driving factors for subsequent analysis.

4. SVM PREDICTION

The steps of training and prediction of SVM are as follows:

1) Execute 10 cross-validation according to the

size of sample, apply Radial Basis Function to find optimal parameter c, g, according to the Mean Square Error minimum principle, c is an important parameter of loss function in SVM kernel function.

[c,g,mse]=mygridr_mex(train_y,train_x,10,'-s 3 -t 2'); // Select c,g combinations which enable mse obtain the minimum numerical

canshu=['-s ',num2str(3),' -t ',num2str(2), '-c ',num2str(c),' -g ',num2str(g)'];

2) Under the combination of optimal kernel parameter, establish prediction model for training samples by using svm_train.
model=svm_train(train_y,train_x,canshu);

3) Execute forecast verification on training model mode by utilizing svm_predict.
predict=svm_predict(test_y,test_x,model)

4) If it is verified to be reasonable and accurate through the verification model, then leave it for further prediction on forecast samples, If the opposite, back to the 1) step and restart to find optimal kernel function parameter, until find a reasonable MODEL.

5) Make actual prediction on forecast samples by using tools svmp_redict combined with reasonable MODEL, and obtain the predicted outcome.

Randomly select 100 customers from 500 compiled customer data as validation sample, and the other 400 customers are retained as training samples, measure the reasonableness of the training model according to the prediction accuracy of verification sample.

4.1. *Comparison method and results analysis*

4.1.1. *Comparison method*

BP neural network is also introduced as a comparison model. Put standardized independent variables and screened related analysis variables into BPNN and SVM to make classification prediction. BPNN prediction process is achieved by using MATLAB (R2011a) program calling Toolbox Neural Network, SVM forecasting process is implemented by using MATLAB (R2011a) program calling toolbox LIBSVM2.9.

4.1.2. *Results analysis*

Through compiling data, in 100 loan verification samples, we know that there are 21 normal (1) loans, 11 attention (2) loans, 31 secondary (3) loans, 28 suspicious (4) loans, 9 loss (5) loans. Among them, normal and attention loans are recognized as good loans, so there are 32 good loans and 68 poor loans. BPNN and SVM adopt multi-step prediction method to validate 100 verification samples, the prediction results of BPNN and SVM are shown in Table 5 and Table 6.

It can be seen from the table that BPNN's overall prediction accuracy of the type of "three rural" loans 57%, for normal (1) loan classification, the accuracy is 76.19%, for attention (2) loans classification, the accuracy is 63.64%, for secondly (3) loan classification, the accuracy is 51.61%, for suspicious (4) loan classification, the accuracy is 42.86%, for loss (5) loan classification, the accuracy is 55.6%. While for good loans, the prediction accuracy is 90.625%, the prediction accuracy of poor loans is 83.67%.

SVM's overall prediction accuracy of the type of "three rural" loans is 70%, for normal (1) loan classification, the accuracy is 85.71%, for attention (2) loans classification, the accuracy is 81.82%, for secondly (3) loan classification, the accuracy is 61.29%, for suspicious (4) loan classification, the accuracy is 60.71%, for loss (5) loan classification, the accuracy is 66.67%. while for good loans, the prediction accuracy is 100%, the prediction accuracy of poor loans is 91.18%.

Through analyzing, it's visible that SVM's individual prediction accuracy of Five-category Classification Prediction for "Three rural" Loan is much better than the prediction accuracy of BPNN, and the process for SVM to establish the whole model to predict is more efficient than BPNN, whether time consuming or prediction accuracy, SVM is significantly higher than BPNN, which indicates that SVM multi-classification model's identification process is fast, reasonable and effective. From the results, we can know that the prediction accuracy of Five-category classification prediction model for "three rural" loan that based on the SVM reaches to 100%. Which help the Agricultural Bank of China grasp high-quality the customer resources. Its prediction accuracy for non-performing loans reaches to 91.18%, which is conducive for the Agricultural Bank of China to avoid the risk of "three rural" credit, so as to reduce bank losses.

After establishing five-category classification prediction model for "three rural" bank loan, they can classify unknown type of new application for "three rural" loan into different categories through this model, then adopt different lending policies on loans based on the classification results, help bank intelligently select "three rural" loan customers, facilitate bank to review and monitoring lending process.

5. CONCLUSION

Based on the application data of "three rural" loan of an Agricultural Bank of China in Changsha and SVM, establish five-category classification model of "three rural" loan for this bank, both the time consuming of processing and the prediction accuracy of which is significantly better than BPNN five-category classification model established by BP neural network, which is a more efficient classification method of "three rural" bank loan. SVM-based five-category classification model of "three rural" bank loan make the implementation of banks' lending policies stronger, not only does this model reduce the "three rural" credit risk, it improve the efficiency of lending, it serves for "three rural" loan applicants, which have great significance for "three rural" and bank to establish smooth, harmonious and sustainable mutual-cooperated relationships.

REFERENCES

- [1] Liu Lizhong. The study of loan risk classification management of Agriculture Bank of China [D]. Changchun: Jilin University, 2005: 1-2.
- [2] Feng Xiantao. Bank credit decision and financial and risk identification of listed companies [D]. Shanghai: Shanghai Jiao Tong University, 2009:10-15.
- [3] Vapnik V N. The nature of statistical learning theory [M]. New York: Springer Verlag Press, 1995: 267-279.
- [4] Huyi, Fangkui, Zhuxinghui. Bank Customer Classification Model and Application Based on SVM [J]. ISSP2015, 667-674.
- [5] An Qianqian. Research on the development of agricultural loan based on the relation analysis between the agricultural loan and the agricultural economical growth [D]. Shanghai: Shanghai Ocean University, 2014: 4-5.

Table 5. Predicted Results of BPNN Verification Sample.

Actual Y	1	4	5	1	3	2	2	4	4	5	2	5	3	1	3	4	1	3	4	5
Predicted Y	1	4	4	1	3	1	2	5	1	3	1	5	2	1	3	3	1	5	5	5
Actual Y	1	4	3	3	4	5	4	1	3	1	3	4	2	1	3	4	4	1	4	3
Predicted Y	1	5	3	3	1	5	4	1	2	1	4	3	2	1	4	5	4	1	4	3
Actual Y	2	3	4	1	3	1	2	4	4	5	1	3	3	1	3	4	1	3	4	3
Predicted Y	1	3	3	3	3	2	2	4	2	5	1	3	2	1	3	4	2	3	5	1
Actual Y	1	4	4	3	3	5	3	1	3	1	4	4	1	2	3	4	5	1	5	3
Predicted Y	3	4	3	3	3	5	2	1	2	1	3	4	1	2	4	5	5	1	3	4
Actual Y	2	3	2	4	3	3	1	4	3	2	1	4	3	4	3	2	3	4	3	4
Predicted Y	2	2	1	4	3	1	1	4	3	2	2	4	4	5	3	2	3	3	4	4

Table 6. Predicted Results of SVM Verification Sample.

Actual Y	1	4	5	1	3	2	2	4	4	5	2	5	3	1	3	4	1	3	4	5
Predicted Y	1	4	5	1	3	1	2	4	3	4	2	5	3	1	3	4	1	4	4	5
Actual Y	1	4	3	3	4	5	4	1	3	1	3	4	2	1	3	4	4	1	4	3
Predicted Y	1	5	3	3	3	5	4	1	2	1	3	4	2	1	4	5	4	1	3	2
Actual Y	2	3	4	1	3	1	2	4	4	5	1	3	3	1	3	4	1	3	4	3
Predicted Y	1	3	3	2	3	1	2	4	3	5	1	3	2	1	3	4	2	3	4	1
Actual Y	1	4	4	3	3	5	3	1	3	1	4	4	1	2	3	4	5	1	5	3
Predicted Y	2	4	3	3	4	5	2	1	3	1	2	4	1	2	4	4	5	1	4	4
Actual Y	2	3	2	4	3	3	1	4	3	2	1	4	3	4	3	2	3	4	3	4
Predicted Y	2	3	2	4	3	2	1	3	3	2	1	4	4	4	3	2	3	3	3	4

Oscillation of Even Order Half-linear Neutral Differential Equation with Distributed Deviating Arguments

Y.H. Zeng
College of Mathematics and Statistics, Hengyang Normal University
Email:chj8121912@sina.com

ABSTRACT: In this paper, oscillation of even order half-liner neutral differential equation with distributed deviating arguments is studied. By means of yang inequality, the generalized Riccati transformation and the averaging technique, several sufficient conditions are obtained for oscillation of all solutions of the equation.

KEYWORDS: Even order; Distributed deviating arguments; Neutral; Half-linear; Oscillation.

1. INTRODUCTION

This paper is concerned with the problem of oscillation of even order neutral differential equation with distributed deviating arguments

$$\left(r(t)\left|z^{(n-1)}(t)\right|^{\alpha-1}z^{(n-1)}(t)\right)'+$$

$$\int_a^b q(t,\xi)\left|x(g(t,\xi))\right|^{\alpha-1}x(g(t,\xi))d\sigma(\xi)=0,$$

$$t\geq t_0\geq 0, \qquad (1)$$

where $z(t)=x(t)+m(t)x(t-\tau)$, $n\geq 2$ is an even integer and $\alpha>0$ is a constant.

Throughout this paper, we always assume that:

(H_1) $r(t)\in C([t_0,\infty),(0,\infty)), r'(t)\geq 0$, $R(t)=\int_{t_0}^t r^{-\frac{1}{\alpha}}(s)ds$, $\lim_{t\to\infty}R(t)=\infty$;

(H_2) $q(t,\xi)\in C([t_0,\infty)\times[a,b],[0,\infty))$, and $q(t,\xi)$ is not eventually zero;

(H_3) $g(t,\xi)\in([t_0,\infty)\times[a,b],R)$, $g'(t,a)>0$, $g(t,\xi)\leq t,\xi\in[a,b],g(t,\xi)$ is not `decreasing function for ξ, and such that $\lim_{t\to\infty}\min_{\xi\in[a,b]}\{g(t.\xi)\}=\infty$; and $\sigma(\xi)\in C([a,b],R)$ is not decreasing function for ξ, and the integral of (1) is in the sense of Riemann-Stieltjes.

2. MAIN RESULTS AND PROOF

Lemma 1[3] Let $x(t)\in C^n(I,R^+), x^{(n)}(t)$ is of one sign and not identically zero, then there exist $t_x\geq t_0$ and an integer l, $0\leq l\leq n$, with

$n+l$ even if $x^{(n)}(t)\geq 0$ or $n+l$ odd if $x^{(n)}(t)\leq 0$

such that $l>0$ implies

$$x^{(k)}(t)>0\ t\geq t_{x,}, k=0,1,\cdots,l-1$$

and $l\leq n-1$ implies

$$(-1)^{l+k}x^{(k)}(t)>0, t\geq t_{x,}, k=l,l+1,\cdots,n-1.$$

Lemma 2[3] Assume that $x(t)$ satisfies all the conditions in Lemma 1 and $x^{(n-1)}(t)x^{(n)}(t)\leq 0$, $t\geq t_x$, then there exist constants θ, $0<\theta<1$ and M>0 such that $x'(\theta t)\geq Mt^{n-2}x^{(n-1)}(t)$, for all sufficiently large t.

Lemma 3[3] Let X and Y be non-negative real numbers. Then

$$X^\lambda-\lambda XY^{\lambda-1}+(\lambda-1)Y^\lambda\geq 0,\ \lambda>1,$$

where the equality holds if and only X=Y.

stant $\lambda>\alpha$ such that

$$\limsup\frac{1}{t^\lambda}\int_T^t(t-s)^{\lambda-\alpha-1}\left[(t-s)^{\alpha+1}Q(s)-(q-1)\cdot\left(\frac{\lambda}{q}\right)^{\alpha+1}\left[\alpha\theta Mg^{n-2}(s)g'(s)\right]^{-\alpha}r(s)ds=\infty,\right.$$

where $\frac{1}{\alpha+1}+\frac{1}{q}=1$, $g(s)=g(s,a)$, $Q(s)=\int_a^b c(s,\xi)(1-m[g(s.\xi)])^\alpha d\sigma(\xi)$, then every solution of (1)is oscillatory.

Proof. Assume that Equation (1) has non-oscillatory solution $x(t)$. With loss of generality, we may assume that $x(t)>0$, $x(t-\tau)>0, x[g(t,\xi)]>0$, $t\ge t_1 \ge t_0\ge 0, \xi\in[a,b]$, we have $z(t)>0, t\ge t_1$ and

$$\left(r(t)\left|z^{(n-1)}(t)\right|^{\alpha-1}z^{(n-1)}(t)\right)'\le 0, t\ge t_1. \quad (2)$$

Then $r(t)\left|z^{(n-1)}(t)\right|^{\alpha-1}z^{(n-1)}(t)$ is decreasing function and $z^{(n-1)}(t)$ is of one sign and not identically zero.

Thus we assert that

$$z^{(n-1)}(t)>0, \quad (3)$$

otherwise if $z^{(n-1)}(t_2)<0$, $t_2\ge t_1$,from (2) we have

$$r(t)\left|z^{(n-1)}(t)\right|^{\alpha-1}z^{(n-1)}(t)\le r(t_2)\left|z^{(n-1)}(t_2)\right|z^{(n-1)}(t_2)\equiv -C,$$

$C>0, t\ge t_2$.

Hence

$$-r(t)\left(-z^{(n-1)}(t)\right)^{\alpha}\le -C, \quad t\ge t_2.$$

Integrating the above inequality from t_2 to t, we obtain

$$z^{(n-2)}(t)\le z^{(n-2)}(t_2)-C^{q-1}\left(R(t)-R(t_2)\right),$$

where $\dfrac{1}{\alpha+1}+\dfrac{1}{q}=1$ .Let $t\to\infty$ in the above, we obtain $\lim\limits_{t\to\infty}z^{(n-2)}(t)=-\infty.$

Thus $z(t)$ is an eventually negative function which contradicts $z(t)>0$. Hence inequality (3) holds.

By (2) and (3), we have

$$r'(t)\left(z^{(n-1)}(t)\right)^{\alpha}+\alpha r(t)\left(z^{(n-1)}(t)\right)^{\alpha-1}z^{(n)}(t)\le 0,$$

hence

$$z^{(n)}(t)\le 0, t\ge t_2. \quad (4)$$

Based on (4) and Lemma 1, since n is even, and then we have

$$z'(t)>0, t\ge t_3\ge t_2. \quad (5)$$

Hence, By (5) we can obtain

$$x(t)\ge\left(1-m(t)\right)z(t), t\ge t_3. \quad (6)$$

In view of (3) and (6), we have

$$\left[r(t)\left(z^{(n-1)}(t)\right)^{\alpha}\right]'+.$$

$$\int_a^b q(t,\xi)\left(1-m\left[g(t,\xi)\right]\right)^{\alpha}\left(z\left[g(t,\xi)\right]\right)^{\alpha}d\sigma(\xi)\le 0,$$

and then

$$\left[r(t)\left(z^{(n-1)}(t)\right)^{\alpha}\right]'+Q(t)\left(z\left(\left[g(t)\right]\right)\right)^{\alpha}\le 0, t\ge T\ge t_3, \quad (7)$$

where $Q(t)=\int_a^b q(t,\xi)(1-m[g(t,\xi)])^{\alpha}d\sigma(\xi)$.

Define

$$W(t)=r(t)\left(\frac{z^{(n-1)}(t)}{z(\theta g(t))}\right)^{\alpha}, t\ge T. \quad (8)$$

Differentiating (8) and making use of (7), it follows that

$$W'(t)\le -Q(t)\left(\frac{z(g(t))}{z(\theta g(t))}\right)^{\alpha}-\frac{\alpha\theta g'(t)r(t)\left(z^{(n-1)}(t)\right)^{\alpha}z'(\theta g(t))}{\left(z(\theta g(t))\right)^{\alpha+1}}, \quad (9)$$

In view of Lemma 2 and conditions (3)-(5), we have

$$z'(\theta g(t))\ge Mg^{n-2}(t)z^{(n-1)}(t). \quad (10)$$

Using (8) and (10) in (9), then we may obtain

$$W'(t)\le -Q(t)-\alpha\theta M g^{n-2}(t)g'(t)r^{1-q}(t)W^{q}(t), t\ge T,$$

where $\dfrac{1}{\alpha+1}+\dfrac{1}{q}=1$, integrating the above inequality from T to t, we obtain

$$-(t-T)^{\lambda}W(T)+\lambda\int_T^t(t-s)^{\lambda-1}W(s)ds+$$
$$\alpha\theta M\int_T^t(t-s)^{\lambda}g^{n-2}(s)g'(s)r^{1-q}(s)W^{q}(s)ds+$$
$$\int_T^t(t-s)^{\lambda}Q(s)ds\le 0, t\ge T. \quad (11)$$

Since $\alpha>0, q>1$, using Lemma 3, we have

$$X^{q}+(q-1)Y^{q}-qXY^{q-1}\ge 0, \qquad X\ge 0, Y\ge 0.$$

Let

$$X=[\alpha\theta M g^{n-2}(s)g`(s)]^{\frac{1}{q}}(t-s)^{\frac{1}{q}}r^{\frac{1-q}{q}}(s)\left|W(s)\right|$$

and

$$Y=\left(\frac{\lambda}{q}\right)^{\frac{\alpha+1}{q}}(t-s)^{\frac{\lambda-\alpha-1}{q}}\left[\alpha\theta M g^{n-2}(s)g'(s)\right]^{\frac{\alpha+1}{q^2}}r^{\frac{1}{q}}(s),$$

then for $T\le s<t$, we obtain

$$\alpha\theta M g^{n-2}(s)g'(s)r^{1-q}(s)(t-s)^{\lambda}\left|W(s)\right|^{q}\ge$$
$$\lambda(t-s)^{\lambda-1}\left|W(s)\right|-(q-1)\left(\frac{\lambda}{q}\right)^{\alpha+1}(t-s)^{\lambda-\alpha-1}.$$
$$\left[\alpha\theta M g^{n-2}(s)g'(s)\right]^{\frac{1}{1-q}}r(s). \quad (12)$$

Based on (11) and (12), we have

$$\int_T^t (t-s)^{\lambda-\alpha-1}\left[(t-s)^{\alpha+1}Q(s)-(q-1)\left(\frac{\lambda}{q}\right)^{\alpha+1}\cdot\right.$$

$$\left.\left[\alpha\theta M g^{n-2}(s)g'(s)\right]^{-\alpha}r(s)\right]ds \le (t-T)^{\lambda}W(T).$$

Hence

$$\limsup_{t\to\infty}\frac{1}{t^{\lambda}}\int_T^t (t-s)^{\lambda-\alpha-1}\left[(t-s)^{\alpha+1}Q(s)-\right.$$

$$\left.(q-1)\left(\frac{\lambda}{q}\right)^{\alpha+1}\left[\alpha\theta M g^{n-2}(s)g'(s)\right]^{-\alpha}r(s)\right]ds$$

$$\le W(T).$$

The last inequality contradicts (C1). The proof of theorem 1 is complete.

Theorem 2 Assume there exists a function $\rho(t)\in c'(I,R^+)$ such that

$$\limsup_{t\to\infty}\int_T^t\left[\rho(s)Q(s)-\frac{\rho'(s)r(s)}{(\alpha+1)^{\alpha+1}}\left(\frac{\rho'(s)}{\theta M\rho(s)g^{n-2}(s)g'(s)}\right)^{\alpha}\right]ds$$

$$=\infty \tag{C2}$$

for $T\ge t_0$, then every solution of equation (1) is oscillatory.

Proof. Let $x(t)$ be a nonoscillatory solution of equation (1), with loss of generality, we may assume that $x(t)>0$, $x(t-\tau)>0$, $x[g(t,\xi)]>0$, $t\ge t_1\ge t_0\ge 0$, $\xi\in[a,b]$. We proceed as in the proof of Theorem 1 until we find inequality (7).

Define

$$w(t)=\rho(t)r(t)\left(\frac{z^{(n-1)}(t)}{z(\theta g(t))}\right)^{\alpha},t\ge T, \tag{13}$$

from (10) and (13), we have

$$w'(t)\le-\rho(t)Q(t)+\frac{\rho'(t)}{\rho(t)}w(t)-$$

$$\alpha\theta M g^{n-2}(t)g'(t)\left(\rho(t)r(t)^{1-q}\left|w(t)^{q}\right|\right),t\ge T, \tag{14}$$

where $\frac{1}{\alpha+1}+\frac{1}{q}=1$. using Lemma 3, we have

$$qXY^{q-1}-X^{q}\le(q-1)Y^{q},q>1,\ X\ge0,Y\ge0. \tag{15}$$

Set

$$X=\left[\alpha\theta M g^{n-2}(t)g'(t)\right]^{\frac{1}{q}}\left[\rho(t)r(t)\right]^{\frac{1-q}{q}}\left|w(t)\right|$$

and

$$Y=\left(\frac{\alpha}{\alpha+1}\right)^{\alpha}\left(\frac{\rho'(t)}{\rho(t)}\right)^{\alpha}\left[\alpha\theta M g^{n-2}(t)g'(t)\right]^{\frac{-\alpha}{q}}\left[\rho(t)r(t)\right]^{\frac{\alpha}{\alpha+1}}$$

then (15) implies the following inequality

$$\frac{\rho'(t)}{\rho(t)}w(t)-\alpha\theta M g^{n-2}(t)g'(t)\left[\rho(t)r(t)\right]^{1-q}\left|w(t)\right|^{q}$$

$$\le\frac{\left[\rho'(t)\right]^{\alpha+1}r(t)}{(\alpha+1)^{\alpha+1}\left[\theta M\rho(t)g^{n-2}(t)g'(t)\right]^{\alpha}},t\ge T. \tag{16}$$

Combining (14) and (16), we obtain $w'(t)\le-\rho(t).,t\ge T.$

Integrating the above from T to t, we obtain $w(t)-w(T)\le$

$$\left[Q(t)-\frac{\rho'(t)}{(\alpha+1)^{\alpha+1}\rho(t)}\left(\frac{\rho'(t)}{\theta M\rho(t)g^{n-2}(t)g'(t)}\right)^{\alpha}\right]-$$

$$\int_T^t\left[\rho(s)Q(s)-\frac{\rho'(s)r(s)}{(\alpha+1)^{\alpha+1}}\left(\frac{\rho'(s)}{\theta M\rho(s)g^{n-2}(s)g'(s)}\right)^{\alpha-1}\right]ds.$$

Taking the lim sup of both sides of the above inequality as $t\to\infty$. So we have a contradiction to the condition (C2). This complete the proof of Theorem 2.

Now, let $\rho(t)\equiv1$ in Theorem 2, then we have the following results.

Corollary 1 Let $\limsup_{t\to\infty}\int_T^t Q(s)ds=\infty,T\ge t_0$, and then every solution of equation (1) is oscillatory.

Let

$$D_0\equiv\{(t,s)\in R^2:t>s\ge t_0\}$$

and

$$D\equiv\{(t,s)\in R^2:t\ge s\ge t_0\}.$$

The function $H\in C(D,R)$ is said to belong to class $\Re$ if

$H(t,t)=0,t\ge t_0,H(t,s)>0$ on D_0 and H has a continuous partial derivative about $\frac{\partial H(t,s)}{\partial s}$ on D_0 with respect to the second variable.

Theorem 3. Assume there exists a function $\rho(t)\in C^1(I,R^+)$, $H(t,s)\in C(D,R)$ and $h(t,s)\in C(D_0,R)$ belong to class $\Re$ such that

$$-\frac{\partial H}{\partial s}(t,s)-H(t,s)\frac{\rho'(s)}{\rho(s)}=h(t,s)H^{\frac{1}{q}}(t,s),$$

$(t,s)\in D_0$ and $\int_{t_0}^t\left|h(t,s)\right|^{\alpha+1}ds<\infty,\forall t\ge t_0$,

where $\frac{1}{\alpha+1}+\frac{1}{q}=1$.If

$$\limsup_{t\to\infty}\frac{1}{H(t,t_0)}\int_{t_0}^t\left[H(t,s)\rho(s)Q(s)-\right.$$

$$\left(\frac{1}{\alpha+1}|h(t,s)|\right)^{\alpha+1}\frac{\rho(s)r(s)}{\left[\theta Mg^{n-2}(s)g'(s)\right]^{\alpha}}\Bigg]ds=\infty.$$

and then every solution of equation (1) is oscillatory.

Proof. Let $x(t)$ be a nonoscillatory solution of equation (1) , with loss of generality we may assume that $x(t)>0$, $x(t-\tau)>0$, $x[g(t,\xi)]>0$, $t\ge t_1\ge t_0\ge 0$, $\xi\in[a,b]$. We proceed as in the proof of Theorem 2 until we find inequality (14),

$$w'(t)\le-\rho(t)Q(t)+\frac{\rho'(t)}{\rho(t)}w(t)-$$
$$\alpha\theta Mg^{n-2}(t)g'(t)(\rho(t)r(t))^{1-q}\left|w(t)^q\right|,t\ge T.$$

We use the following notations for simplicity: $G(t)=\theta Mg^{n-2}(t)g'(t)$.

Based on

$$\int_{t_0}^t|h(t,s)|^{\alpha+1}ds<\infty,\forall t\ge t_0,$$

for $t\ge T\ge T_0$,we have

$$\int_T^t H(t,s)\rho(s)Q(s)ds$$
$$\le H(t,T)W(T)-\int_T^t\left(-\frac{\partial H}{\partial s}(t,s)\right)W(s)ds+$$
$$\int_T^t H(t,s)\frac{\rho'(s)}{\rho(s)}W(s)ds-$$
$$\alpha\int_T^t H(t,s)G(s)\left[\rho(s)r(s)\right]^{1-q}|W(s)|^q ds$$
$$=H(t,T)W(T)-\int_T^t h(t,s)H^{\frac{1}{q}}(t,s)W(s)ds-$$
$$\alpha\int_T^t\frac{H(t,s)G(s)|W(s)|^q}{|\rho(s)r(s)|^{q-1}}ds$$
$$\le H(t,T)W(T)+\int_T^t H^{\frac{1}{q}}(t,s)|h(t,s)W(s)|ds-$$
$$\alpha\int_T^t\frac{H(t,s)G(s)|W(s)|^q}{\left[\rho(s)r(s)\right]^{q-1}}ds. \tag{17}$$

In view of (17), we set

$$X=\left[\alpha H(t,s)G(s)\right]^{\frac{1}{q}}\left[\rho(s)r(s)\right]^{\frac{1-q}{q}}|W(s)|$$

and

$$Y=\left(\frac{1}{q}\right)^{\alpha}|h(t,s)|^{\alpha}\left[(p-1)G(s)\right]^{\frac{-\alpha}{q}}\left[\rho(s)r(s)\right]^{\frac{1}{q}},$$

and then

$$H^{\frac{1}{q}}(t,s)|h(t,s)W(s)|-\alpha\frac{H(t,s)G(s)|W(s)|^q}{\left[\rho(s)r(s)\right]^{q-1}}$$
$$\le\left(\frac{1}{\alpha+1}|h(t,s)|\right)^{\alpha+1}\rho(s)r(s)\left[G(s)\right]^{-\alpha},t>s>T_0. \tag{18}$$

Combining (17) and (18) we have

$$\int_T^t\left[H(t,s)\rho(s)Q(s)-\left(\frac{1}{\alpha+1}|h(t,s)|\right)^{\alpha+1}\frac{\rho(s)r(s)}{G^{\alpha}(s)}\right]ds$$
$$\le H(t,T_0)W(T_0)\le H(t,T_0)|W(T_0)|\le H(t,t_0)|W(T_0)|.$$

Hence

$$\int_{t_0}^t\left[H(t,s)\rho(s)Q(s)-\left(\frac{1}{\alpha+1}|h(t,s)|\right)^{\alpha+1}\frac{\rho(s)r(s)}{G^{\alpha}(s)}\right]ds$$
$$=\left\{\int_{t_0}^{T_0}+\int_{T_0}^t\right\}\left[H(t,s)\rho(s)Q(s)-\left(\frac{1}{\alpha+1}|h(t,s)|\right)^{\alpha+1}\frac{\rho(s)r(s)}{G^{\alpha}(s)}\right]ds$$
$$\le H(t,t_0)\int_{t_0}^{T_0}\rho(s)|Q(s)|ds+H(t,t_0)|W(T_0)|$$
$$=H(t,t_0)\left\{\int_{t_0}^{T_0}\rho(s)|Q(s)|ds+|W(T_0)|\right\}\forall t\ge t_0.$$

Taking the lim sup of both sides of the above inequality as $t\to\infty$. So we have

$$\limsup_{t\to\infty}\frac{1}{H(t,t_0)}\int_{t_0}^t\left[H(t,s)\rho(s)Q(s)-\left(\frac{1}{\alpha+1}|h(t,s)|\right)^{\alpha+1}\cdot\right.$$
$$\left.\frac{\rho(s)r(s)}{G^{\alpha}(s)}\right]ds\le\int_{t_0}^{T_0}\rho(s)|Q(s)|ds+|W(T_0)|,$$

which is a contradiction to the condition (C3).

This complete the proof of Theorem 3.

ACKNOWLEDGMENT

This research was supported by science and technology projects foundation of Hengyang (2014KJ22), social science fund project of Hengyang (2014D060) and construct program of the key discipline in Hunan Province [2011(76)].

REFERENCES

- [1] Philos Ch G. A New criterion for the oscillatory and asymptotic behavior of delay differential Equations. Bull. Acad. Pol. Sci. Ser. Sci. Mat., 1981, 39:61-64.
- [2] Hardy G H, Littlewood J E, Polya G. Inequalities, 2nd ed. Cambridge: Cambrige Univ. Press, 1988.
- [3] Zhang Quanxin. Oscillation of even order half-linear neutral delay differential equation with distributed deviating arguments. Academic Mathematicae Applicatae Sinica, 2011, 34(5): 895-905.
- [4] Zeng Yun-hui, Luo Li-ping, Luo Zhen-guo. Oscillation criteria of second-order half-linear damped differential equations with distributed deviating arguments. Journal of Vibration and Shock, 2013, 32(8), 1-5.

— [5] Kamenev I V. I ntegral criterion of linear differential equations of second order. Math. Zametki, 1978, 23: 249-251.
— [6] Li H J, Yeh C C. An Integral Criterion for Oscillation of Nonlinear Differential Equation. Math. Japonica, 1995, 41:185-188.
— [7] Wang P G, Teo K L, Liu Y Q. Oscillation Properties for Even order Neutral Equations with Distributed Deviating Arguments. J. Comput. Appl. Math., 2005, 182: 290-303.

The Association Rule Mining of Armored Equipment Maintenance Material Consumption Data Based on MapReduce

Z. Lei*, Y. Sun, L.Y. Sun & Y. Zhang
Department of Scientific Research, Academy of Armored Force Engineering, Beijing, China
Email: williamjohnmail@126.com

ABSTRACT: To explore consumption law of armored equipment maintenance material, and to guide reserve and serve issues, this paper studied the association rule mining of the equipment maintenance material consumption data. Two typical association rule mining algorithms are expatiated and compared based on Hadoop MapReduce. Taking a typical equipment maintenance material consumption data as an example, this paper illuminated the executive processes of algorithms and analyzed the mining results. The study can provide reliance to the consumption standards perfection of current equipment.

KEYWORDS: Maintenance materials; Equipment support; Association mining; FP-Growth algorithm.

1. INTRODUCTION

Along with the development of the equipment support information technology, equipment support departments at all levels accumulated a large number of relevant data in the process of maintenance management. A lot of data is semi-structured or unstructured, to discover the valuable laws and service the security decisions is a very difficult task. In addition, the use of equipment maintenance material and storage time all have strict requirements, a lot of, long-term inventory backlog is bound to reduce the use of the equipment performance, causing immeasurable loss. Therefore, it is necessary to strengthen the research of equipment maintenance of material consumption law [Zhao P., Liu B.P., Huang D. 2014], formulate the corresponding standards and inventory consumption quota, guarantee the reasonable configuration and effective utilization of equipment, to provide a more accurate armored equipment.

In order to establish and improve the mechanism of armored equipment support information management, make the information serve equipment safeguard work better, provide information support, the research of data mining in the application of the equipment support decision support system is urgently needed. Data mining is to find the implicit knowledge or rules from the data. In the task of data mining, a kind of problems are called frequent itemset or association rules mining [Fan M., Meng X.F. 2001], the purpose of this kind of mining is to find the intimacy degree of two or more objects. If the number of occurrences at the same time reaches a certain threshold, you can think that the two or more objects are high relevant, or called the frequent itemsets. When the size of data set is small, a lot of machine learning and data mining algorithms can effectively work, but after the data scale reaches a certain degree, the existing algorithms will be difficult to complete the computing task, which requires designing parallel mining algorithm for big data. The building process of the association mining environment was introduced in this paper [Dean J. and Ghemawat S. 2008], and the two commonly used key mining algorithms are compared. MapReduce parallel processing technology is used to complete the k-frequent itemsets mining of equipment consumption data and equipment consume rule analysis. The construction of the experimental environment uses the popular Hadoop architecture, JDK, secure shell protocol (SSH), etc.

2. THE CONSTRUCTION OF CLUSTER ENVIRONMENT

2.1. *Hardware environment*

This experiment adopts three virtual machines into a cluster environment. The virtual machines run on the high performance blade servers, which support Intel ® TM 5600 series multi-core processors. One of the virtual machines serves as the primary server (Master), the remaining two servers serve as the slave servers. Set the IP address of each virtual machine.

2.2. *Software environment*

Mainly use the following software:

① Citrix XenCenter
② CentOS
③ Hadoop
④ SSH
⑤ Eclipse
⑥ JDK
⑦ MySQL

The whole distributed cluster environment of Hadoop system process is as follows:

(1) the installation of virtual machine and CentOS. First installing Citrix XenCenter software on the client Windows platform, to create virtual machine in the environment and install CentOS operating system on virtual machine.

(2) the installation of JDK. Hadoop is written in the Java language, and therefore need to install Java, here we have Sun JDK, version is jdk-6u33-linux-x64. The jdk-6u33-linux-x64 is copied to the required installation directory, then execute the installation file named jdk-6u33-linux-x64.bin, use vi to revise the /etc/profile file and configure JAVA_HOME and CLASS_PATH, save and makes configuration file effective.

(3) to create the Hadoop users, download and install Hadoop.

(4) to configure SSH. This configuration is mainly in order to realize free password to log in.

(5) to configure Hadoop environment. Mainly is to change the configuration file under the conf directory in the Hadoop installation directory.

(6) the installation of MySQL. Here the version is Navicat for MySQL 8.2.20.

(7) the Eclipse environment. Hadoop program can be developed in local LAN Hadoop, using Eclipse to program and debug, and then upload to the Hadoop cluster to run, can also download the Eclipse IDE for Java development kit of Linux version, which is installed in the Linux system, a method adopted here is the former, so that we can improve the development efficiency.

3. THE ALGORITHM USED IN THE EXPERIMENT

Two representative association rule mining algorithms are Apriori algorithm [Agrawal R., Srikant R., 1994] and FP-Growth algorithm [Han J., Pei J., Ming Y.Y. 2000]. FP-Growth algorithm abandoned the idea of Apriori algorithm, proposed a new computing way. The algorithm is not affected by basic data set number of data items, has better execution efficiency than Apriori algorithm. In addition, paper [Huang Y.H., Miao K.X. etc. 2014] introduces an association rule mining algorithm based on subset calculating, having more parallelization design characteristics than Apriori algorithm. Many researchers compared Apriori algorithm with the FP-Growth algorithm, the advantage of the latter is obvious on execution efficiency. Due to the subset-calculating based association rule mining algorithm is mentioned in 2014, the idea of the algorithm is relatively novel, therefore, FP-Growth algorithm and subset-calculating based algorithm are expatiated and compared on execution efficiency.

3.1. *Subset-calculating based algorithm*

The algorithm is based on an obvious fact: assume that the database is D, then a frequent item set is necessarily a subset of the transaction in D, that is to say, do not need to know the whole item set, the frequent item set can be computed just based on transaction data itself. The basic idea is to complete frequent item set mining quickly through calculating the subset. The idea of the algorithm is as follows:

(1) First assume that the database is D, transaction is T, the size of item set is k.

(2) Scanning the database, all subsets with size of k are calculated from the transaction in database.

(3) Output all the number of subsets, if the number of a subset is more than a certain threshold value S, then the subset is regard as frequent itemset.

3.2. *FP-growth algorithm*

FP-Growth algorithm needs not to generate candidate itemsets in the process of calculation of frequent itemsets, the algorithm adopts a novel frequent pattern Tree (FP-Tree). During read operations on database, FP-Growth algorithm stores all data items into the frequent pattern Tree, then mines frequent pattern tree, finally got all the frequent itemsets.

From the point of the implementation process of the algorithm, FP-Growth algorithm requires operating database for three times. Firstly, put the data into the FP-Tree. Secondly, order itemsets. Thirdly, judge the frequent itemsets in turn. Thus the number of database operations in FP-Growth algorithm is much less than the Apriori algorithm. It isn't hard to see that the promotion of the efficiency of FP-Growth is mainly attributed to the following four aspects:

(1) No candidate itemsets, save space and time;

(2) The adoption of high-integration data structure;

(3) Mining FP-Tree in recursive way, implementation is simple;

(4) The fewer database operations.

4. THE EXPERIMENTAL RESULTS

This experiment takes a certain armored equipment support maintenance material consumption data as analysis object, and compares the performance of two frequent itemsets mining algorithms, find out the law of material consumption. Before the data mining, usually some processing of the original data is needed, such as the continuous data discretization, dimension reduction, gap value filling processing, in order to make it more suitable for application of the mining algorithm, and makes the mining results more accurate.

(1) The comparison of two typical algorithm for mining frequent itemsets

The subset-calculating based algorithm and FP-Growth algorithm are compared in this study. First the subset-calculating based algorithm is adopted, the results are unexpected, system resources are inadequate and the algorithm cannot proceed. To see the analysis process of the algorithm, we settle for second best, a subset of containing the whole property was tested, then the algorithm is able to run normally. When the item set size is 3 and the support threshold is 50, some of its intermediate process is shown as follows:

Below is the status of file to read and write in the process of task execution of distributed file system HDFS, it can be seen that the pace of reading and writing is consistent.

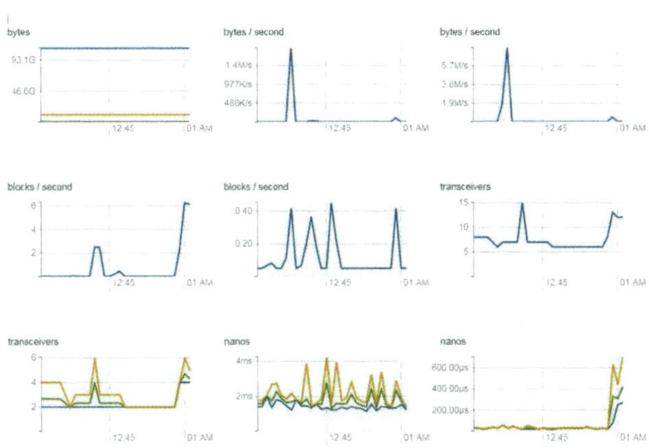

Figure 1. HDFS running status.

Below is the execution process of JobTracker in Hadoop. The JobTracker acts as the Master role, which is in charge of the jobs submitted by client and monitor their running status.

Kind	% Complete	Num Tasks	Pending	Running	Complete	Killed	Failed/Killed Task Attempts
map	0.74%	83943	83309	12	622	0	0 / 0
reduce	0.00%	3	3	0	0	0	0 / 0

	Counter	Map	Reduce	Total
File System Counters	FILE: Number of bytes read	0	0	0
	FILE: Number of bytes written	105,291,382	0	105,291,382
	FILE: Number of read operations	0	0	0
	FILE: Number of large read operations	0	0	0
	FILE: Number of write operations	0	0	0
	HDFS: Number of bytes read	40,684,902	0	40,684,902
	HDFS: Number of bytes written	0	0	0
	HDFS: Number of read operations	1,244	0	1,244
	HDFS: Number of large read operations	0	0	0
	HDFS: Number of write operations	0	0	0
Job Counters	Launched map tasks	0	0	634
	Total time spent by all maps in occupied slots (ms)	0	0	2,310,706
	Map input records	622	0	622
	Map output records	622	0	622
	Map output bytes	46,650	0	46,650
	Input split bytes	80,238	0	80,238

Figure 2. The implementation of JobTracker in Hadoop.

Then FP-Growth algorithm was tested on the same set of data collection, the result is very encouraging. Mining results show that for the same data set, the mining result is the same, but the time difference is very big, The subset-calculating based algorithm consumed 1 minutes and 27 seconds, while the FP-Growth algorithm consumed only 19.6 seconds, suggesting that while the design of subset-calculating based algorithm is novel and simple, but the execution efficiency is not high. As to the cause of the inefficient, it's because that the algorithm focuses on mining process on one MapReduce in order to overcome the poor performance of the iterative processing. In theory, it needs more cluster nodes, but only 2 virtual machine is adopted as the Slave server in the setting-up cluster test environment, which impacts on some of the proposed algorithm to a certain extent. While FP-Growth algorithm has higher integration of the data structure and less access of database. It still has a high efficiency even if in the case of only two slave nodes.

(2) Equipment material consumption pattern analysis

As mentioned earlier, FP-Growth algorithm has obvious advantages in association mining. In order to find out the equipment consumption pattern, an armored equipment support maintenance material consumption data are analyzed using the algorithm in this experiment. The analysis process and results are as follows:

The whole process lasts 58.6 seconds, part of the obtained numerical results are as follows:

① the Itemsets is 2, and the support threshold is 1430

([32kka012y, 9017000],467)
([32kka012y, 8072094],452)
([32kka012y, 8070080],436)

([0a66b90b4d9, dfsdfhghg0013],6170)
([0a66b90b4d9, dfsdfhghg0033],3255)
([odjfd20145b, dfsdfhghg0067],2761)
……

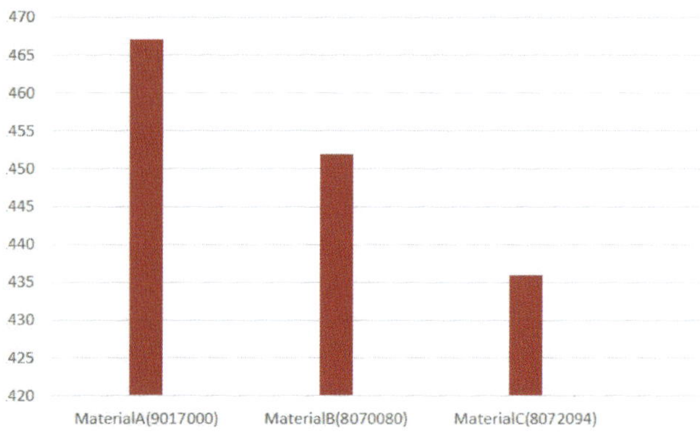

Figure 3. The association mining results when itemsets is 2 and the support threshold is 430.

It can be seen from the first three results, three kinds of materials whose identification code is 9017000, 8070080 and 8072094 respectively relevant to the equipment whose identification code is 32kka012y, have the highest support, they are 467, 452 and 436 respectively. It shows that this three kinds of materials are the most consumed ones. Remaining two itemset results suggest the correlation between some type repair activities and various types of equipment, which are discussed in part 2 below.

② the Itemsets is 2, and the support threshold is 6000

([32kka012y, b90b4d9],38998)
([32kka012y, d20145b],18109)
([32kka012y, e7a95e9],13543)
([32kka012y, 770e42d],7958)
([d20145b, fhghg0031],7478)
([b90b4d9, fhghg0013],6170)
([d20145b, fhghg0017],6028)

Above association rules analysis results can be more intuitively shown in the form of three dimensional histogram:

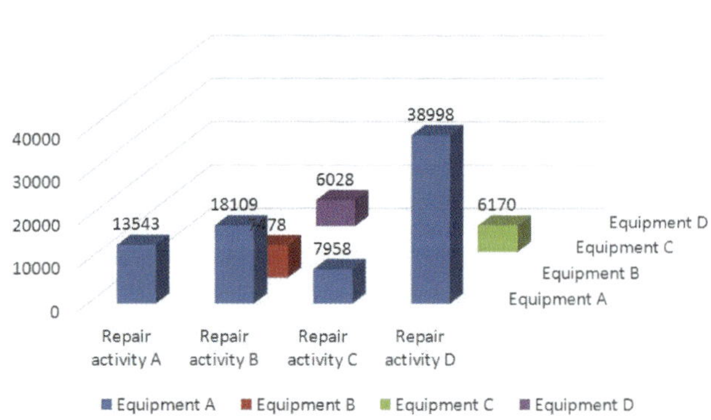

Figure 4. The association mining results when itemsets is 2 and the support threshold is 6000.

As can be seen from the above results, for the equipment whose identification code is 32kka012y, repair activities whose identification codes are 0a66b90b4d9, odjfd20145b, 23joe7a95e9 and 356q770e42d are carried out degressively. The decision supports for equipment support business, maintenance plan implementation, equipment financing and supply, resource allocation, equipment storage structure optimization can be provided based on the results analysis.

5. CONCLUSIONS

It's of great significance to study and master the consumption rule of armored equipment maintenance equipment. This paper compares two kinds of typical association mining algorithms, carries through association mining and analysis based on the armored equipment maintenance material consumption data, and gets some rules which cannot be found using conventional database retrieval methods.

It has certain reference value for the setting of equipment consumption standard, equipment financing and supply, and so on. Later many questions are still worth further studying, such as how to give a more reasonable way of data preprocessing, how to mine more effective, more valuable rules, etc.

REFERENCES

— [1] Agrawal R., Srikant R., 1994. Fast Algorithm for Mining Association Rules [C]. Proceedings of 20th Int. Conf. Very Large Data Bases (VLDB), Jorge B. Bocca, Matthias Jarke and Carlo Zaniolo, eds. Morgan Kaufmann Press: 487-499.
— [2] Dean J. and Ghemawat S. 2008. MapReduce: Simplified Data Processing on Large Clusters [J]. Communications of the ACM 51(1):107-113.
— [3] Fan M., Meng X.F. 2001. Data mining concepts and techniques [M]. Beijing: Mechanical Industry Press: 150-184.
— [4] Han J., Pei J., Ming Y.Y. 2000. Frequent Patterns without Candidate Generation [C]. Proceedings of 2000 ACM-SIGMOD Int. Conf. Management of Data (SIGMOD'00) [C] Washington DC: 1-12.
— [5] Huang Y.H., Miao K.X. etc. 2014. Deep understanding of big data: data processing and programming practice [M]. Beijing: Mechanical Industry Press: 335-340.
— [6] Zhao P., Liu B.P., Huang D. 2014. The prediction of ship service equipment consumption law based on data mining [J]. Journal of Equipment Manufacturing Technology 7:66-69.

Reductive Debronimation Pathway and Quantitative Structure Property Relationship Models for Polybrominated Diphenyl Ethers

X.D. Shi[1, a], L.Y. Li[1, b], J.L. Li [2, c], Y.M. Lin[1, d], M.Y. Fan[1, e], H. Yang[2, f] & J.W. Hu[1, g*]

1 Guizhou Provincial Key Laboratory for Information System of Mountainous Areas and Protection of Ecological Environment, Guizhou Normal University, Guiyang, 550001, P. R. China

2 Institute of South China Karst, Guizhou Normal University, Guiyang, 550001, P. R. China

*Email: [a]xuedanshi1991@163.com, [b]lingyunli1989@126.com, [c]lijieling1203@163.com, [d]yimiaolin2013@163.com, [e]fanmingyifmy@163.com, [f]yanghaosc1989@foxmail.com, *[g]jiweihu@yahoo.com, jwhu@gznu.edu.cn*

ABSTRACT: Polybrominated diphenyl ethers (PBDEs), used as an important class of additive flame retardants in polymers, post potential hazards to the environment, wildlife and humans, and it is thus essential to find an efficient way to eliminate the PBDEs contamination. The reductive debronimation pathway of BDE-47 and BDE-99 was investigated in this study. The stepwise debromination was shown as the dominant reaction process for PBDEs. The quantitative structure property relationship (QSPR) was also performed in this study to develop models for predicting the reactions of reductive debromination. And the predictive results from the QSPR studies show that the nonlinear model (back propagation artificial neural network (BP-ANN)) is better than the two linear models (principal component analysis-multiple linear regression (PCA-MLR) and partial least square regression (PLSR)). For the BP-ANN model, we also considered the overfitting problem with limited number of hidden neurons.

KEYWORDS: PBDEs; Reductive debromination; QSPR; BP-ANN.

1. INTRODUCTION

Polybrominated diphenyl ethers (PBDEs) are one typical class of persistent organic pollutants (POPs) [1]. They are anthropogenic chemicals and commonly used as additive brominated flame retardants, which have been used in a series of products including plastics, textiles and electronics [2]. During the use of these products, PBDEs can enter the environment through volatilization and leakage [3]. They are in general bioaccumulative and can undergo long-range atmospheric transport (LRAT) [2]. Since 2009, tetra-BDE, penta-BDE, hexa-BDE and hepta-BDE have been officially listed under the Stockholm Convention on Persistent Organic Pollutants by the United Nations Environment Programme.

PBDEs have aroused special environmental concerns due to the potential toxicities to humans and wildlife worldwide [2]. They can lead to endocrine disruption, neurotoxicological effects and carcinogenicity [4], posing a potential danger to ecosystems and human health [5]. Thus it is critical to find a way to eliminate PBDEs contamination. Recently, the reductive debromination of PBDEs has attracted a great attention [4]. And the stepwise debromination from n-bromo- to (n-1)-bromodiphenyl ether was observed as the dominant reaction process for PBDEs [1]. Quantum mechanics, which governs the electronic structures responsible for properties, such as conformational properties, reactivity and lipophilicity, offers an attractive alternative approach [6]. Numerous quantum chemical methods have recently been used for the geometry optimization of the PBDEs via the methods including semi-empirical, ab-initio and density functional theory (DFT) [4, 7, 8, 9]. These theoretical studies are needed to help understand the properties of the compounds and provide valuable insight into the related reaction mechanisms and kinetics [8].

Quantitative structure-property relationship (QSPR) methodology is based on the development of a mathematical relation between the macroscopic property and the molecular structure for a particular set of similar compounds [10]. However, overfitting occurs when a model has too many parameters relative to the number of observations. Generally, the models will have poor predictive performance when they have been overfit [11]. For the back propagation artificial neural network (BP-ANN), the number of the neurons in hidden layer should be minimal in case of overfitting. Some of previous studies on QSPR models established between the molecular descriptors and the logarithm of normalized reaction rate constants have ignored the overfitting problems [9, 12]. Li et al. used 10 neurons in hidden layer with only 10 observations in the training set, when they predicted the reaction rate constants for the reductive debrominated of PBDEs. In their studies, the number of connection was 50 that was totally over fitted [9, 12].

In the present work, water was chosen as the solvent in the calculations with the polarized continuum model (PCM) to study the debromination pathway for 2,2',4,4'-tetrabromodiphyenyl ether (BDE-47) and 2,2',4,4'5-pentabromodiphyenyl ether (BDE-99) [11]. And the linear and non-linear methods were employed for building QSPR models between the molecular descriptors and the logarithm of normalized reaction rate constants of fourteen selected BDE congeners obtained from the previous experiments [1, 7, 13]. The overfitting problems were also considered to improve the performance of the models.

2. COMPUTATIONAL METHODS

All calculations in this work were performed using Gaussian03 programs suite [14], and GaussView 4.1 was used as the molecular modeling system for constructing models and visualizing the results of the calculations. The geometries of the selected neutral BDE congeners were optimized by DFT calculations using the B3LYP (Becke, three-parameter, Lee–Yang–Parr correlation functional) [15, 16], with 6-31G(d) basis set in vacuum. We used the DFT calculations (PCM/B3LYP/6-31G(d)) to investigate the geometries of radical anions of BDE-47 and BDE-99 with solvent of water. All of the minimum geometries were confirmed by a frequency analysis. The partial least squares regression (PLSR) was carried out by SIMCA-P software (demo version 11.5.0.0, Umetrics AB). The principal component analysis-multiple linear regression (PCA-MLR) was undertaken with the use of PASW (Version 18.0.0, SPSS Inc.). The back propagation artificial neural network (BP-ANN) was built by using MATLAB software (2010a) with the Neural Network Toolbox (the MathWorks, Inc).

The IUPAC names and the congener numbers of the fourteen PBDEs selected in this study are listed in Table 1.

Table 1. IUPAC names and the congener numbers of the fourteen selected BDE congeners.

No.	IUPAC Name	No.	IUPAC Name
BDE-209	deca-bromodiphenyl ether	BDE-21	2,3,4-tri-bromodiphenyl ether
BDE-183	2,2',3,4,4',5',6-hepta-bromodiphenyl ether	BDE-12	3,4-di-bromodiphenyl ether
BDE-153	2,2',4,4',5,5'-hexa-bromodiphenyl ether	BDE-7	2,4-di-bromodiphenyl ether
BDE-100	2,2',4,4',6-penta-bromodiphenyl ether	BDE-5	2,3-di-bromodiphenyl ether
BDE-66	2,3',4,4'-tetra-octa-bromodiphenyl ether	BDE-3	4-mono-bromodiphenyl ether
BDE-47	2,2',4,4'-tetra-bromodiphenyl ether	BDE-2	3-mono-bromodiphenyl ether
BDE-28	2,4,4'-tri-bromodiphenyl ether	BDE-1	2-mono-bromodiphenyl ether

3. RESULTS AND DISCUSSION

3.1. *The debromination pathway of BDE-47 and BDE-99*

For BDE-47, the calculation results with the DFT method demonstrated that the cleavage of C-Br bond occurred first at the ortho-position of the one benzene ring, and then the other ortho-Br is replaced, as shown in Figure 1. For BDE-99, the para-Br in the aromatic ring with the higher-bromination was removed at first, as shown in Figure 2. For lower brominated diphenyl ethers, the cleavage of the C-Br bond preferentially occurred in the benzene ring with the higher-bromination. The degradation pathways obtained from the DFT calculations for these two low brominated diphenyl ethers are consistent with the experimental results [17]. This can be used for predicting the degradation pathway of other PBDE congeners.

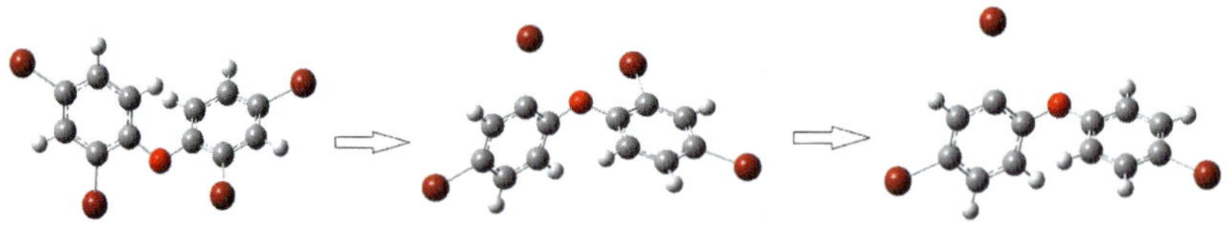

Figure 1. Debromination pathway of the BDE-47 congeners based on the structure of radical anions with solvent of water.

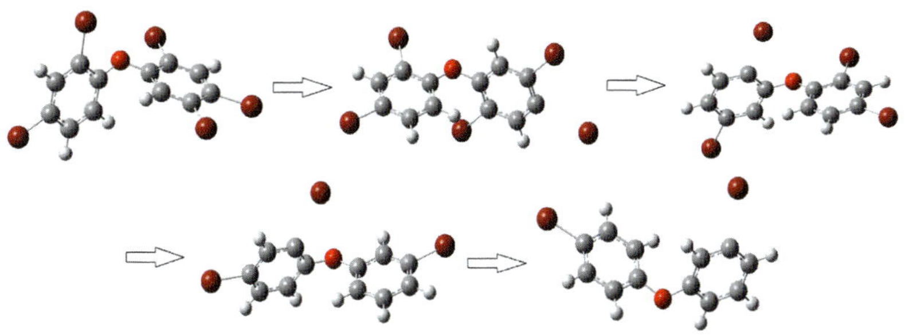

Figure 2. Debromination pathway of the BDE-99 congeners based on the structure of radical anions with solvent of water.

3.2. *Quantitative structure-property relationship (QSPR)*

The reaction rate constants of the fourteen BDE congeners used in this QSPR study were collected from the literatures [1, 7, 13], which were normalized using specific surface area (SSA) with respect to different-sized NZVI by Zhang et al. [1]. Four molecular descriptors obtained from the quantum chemical calculations were chosen as the independent variables, including the energy of highest occupied molecular orbital (E_{HOMO}), the energy of lowest unoccupied molecular orbital (E_{LUMO}), dipole moment (μ), and the number of Br (N_{Br}). The value of the molecular descriptors and the experimental debromination data are listed in Table 2.

Table 2. Experimental normalized reaction rate constant and molecular descriptors of selected BDE congeners by DFT method.

Congener	$logK_{SA}$[a] [L/d·m^2]	Reference[b]	μ [debye]	E_{LUMO} [hartree]	E_{HOMO} [hartree]	N_{Br}
BDE-1	-5.401	[1]	2.2298	-0.01952	-0.22711	1
BDE-2	-5.317		3.0974	-0.01929	-0.22882	1
BDE-3	-5.417		2.2504	-0.02072	-0.22428	1
BDE-5	-4.298		4.0020	-0.03195	-0.23301	2
BDE-12	-4.351		3.7720	-0.03286	-0.23168	2
BDE-21	-3.378		4.3427	-0.05254	-0.23576	3
BDE-153	-2.611	[7]	0.7353	-0.05615	-0.24732	6
BDE-183	-2.060		1.3846	-0.07716	-0.24809	7
BDE-209	-1.423		6.0294	-0.12648	-0.22833	10
BDE-7	-4.159	[13]	2.2089	-0.03193	-0.24163	2
BDE-28	-3.509		1.2939	-0.03685	-0.23487	3
BDE-47	-3.660		2.3067	-0.04159	-0.23989	4
BDE-66	-3.329		2.0124	-0.04220	-0.24034	4
BDE-100	-2.810		2.4408	-0.05845	-0.24275	5

As shown in Table 3, a significant intercorrelation was found between molecular descriptors via the Pearson correlation analysis, therefore we adopted the PCA-MLR model and the PLSR model to solve this problem. For the PCA-MLR approach, two principal components (PC1, PC2) were extracted from the original data (Table 4) for reducing the complexity. Then they were applied as the variable to establish the linear regression equations (Eq. 1, Eq. 2). The PLSR model can also eliminate the effects caused by multicollinearity among independent variables. The multiple linear regressions were carried out using PASW to better understand the relationship between the molecular descriptors and logarithm of the normalized reaction rate constants. The regression equations (3) and (4) were obtained.

Table 3. The Pearson correlation matrix between the normalized reaction rate constants and the molecular descriptors of the BDE congeners.

	μ	E_{LUMO}	E_{HOMO}	N_{Br}	$logK_{SA}$
μ	1				
E_{LUMO}	-0.423	1			
E_{HOMO}	0.532	0.243	1		
N_{Br}	0.199	-0.962**	-0.419	1	
$logK_{SA}$	0.121	-0.905**	-0.590*	0.950**	1

* Significant at 0.05 level (two-tailed), ** Significant at 0.01 level (two-tailed).

Table 4. PC1 and PC2 extracted from the 6 descriptor variables of the BDE congeners.

Congener	PC1	PC2	Congener	PC1	PC2
BDE-1	1.13493	0.42908	BDE-28	0.43888	-0.51153
BDE-2	1.0042	0.6555	BDE-47	-0.03453	-0.4762
BDE-3	1.18076	0.64804	BDE-66	-0.02294	-0.62669
BDE-5	0.43736	0.73188	BDE-100	-0.55268	-0.60243
BDE-7	0.42776	-0.62624	BDE-153	-0.61036	-1.65912
BDE-12	0.47939	0.73856	BDE-183	-1.20018	-1.4107
BDE-21	-0.1593	0.70899	BDE-209	-2.52331	2.00086

$$PC1 = 0.393E_{HOMO} + 0.985\ E_{LUMO} - 0.982\ N_{Br} - 0.335\ \mu \quad (1)$$

$$PC2 = 0.860\ E_{HOMO} - 0.136\ E_{LUMO} - 0.095\ N_{Br} + 0.889\ \mu \quad (2)$$

$$\log K_{SA} = -\ 0.001\ (\pm 0.118)\ \mu - 29.547\ (\pm 20.016)\ E_{LUMO} - 59.349\ (\pm 15.367)\ E_{HOMO} + 0.065\ (\pm 0.205)\ N_{Br} - 19.301\ (\pm 3.678)$$

(n = 11, R2 = 0.966, F = 63.997, p = 0.000) (3)

$$\log K_{SA} = -1.169\ (\pm 0.071)\ PC1 - 0.289(\pm 0.071)\ PC2 - 3.695\ (\pm 0.069)$$

(n = 11, R2 = 0.963, F = 143.250, p = 0.000) (4)

where n = the sample size; R^2 = the square of correlation coefficient; F = the F value for analysis of variance; p = the significance level.

When a BP-ANN model is overfitted, this can exaggerate minor fluctuations in the data [11]. Thus, the model will generally have a poor predictive performance. As shown in Figure 3, three hidden neurons were chosen to satisfy the theories that the number of connection in the network should be smaller than the number of observations to avoid the overfitting problem. The training goal was set by 0.01, and the learning rate was set by 0.02. All values of the inputted molecular descriptors were normalized between 0.1 and 0.9 using the following equation:

$$Vn = 0.1+(V-Vmin)/(Vmax-Vmin)\times(0.9-0.1) \quad (5)$$

where Vn = stands for the normalized value; V = original value; Vmax = maximum value of the descriptors; Vmin = the minimum value of the descriptors.

$$RMSE = \sqrt{\frac{\sum(\text{observed - predicted})^2}{n}} \quad (6)$$

Due to the random initialization of initial connection weight values, their final values are slightly different for different trainings [8]. In addition, the average values of the predictive results are shown in Table 4, which were simulated for 20 repetitions and expressed as mean value ± standard error. The performance was evaluated by root-mean-square error (RMSE) (Eq. 6, Table 4).

As shown in Table 4, for PLSR, MLR, PCA-MLR and BP-ANN models, the RMSE values of training set were 0.262, 0.235 0.246 and 0.174, while the RMSE values of the test set were 0.259, 0.218, 0.227 and 0.129, respectively. The results showed that predictive performance of the models was satisfactory. Thus, all of them can be applied to predict the reaction rate constants. The nonlinear BP-ANN method seems to have a better predictive ability and be more accurate than the other two methods due to the predictive results and the RMSE values. The main reason is that PCA-MLR and PLSR can only deal with the linear relationship between experimental data and the molecular descriptors [18, 19]. However, the BP-ANN model can deal with the nonlinear relationship to obtain more comprehensive predictive results.

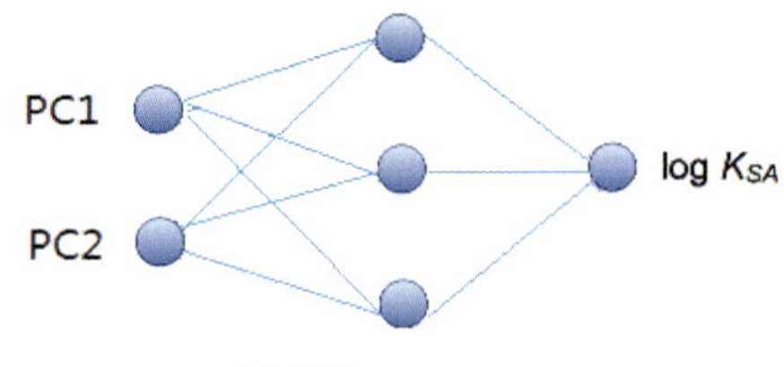

Figure 3. The architecture of the BP-ANN neural network.

Table 5. Predicted results of the QSPR models by PLSR, PCA-MLR and BP-ANN in training set and test set (values ± standard error) using the reported logarithm of the debromination rate constants ($logK_{SA}$) [1, 7, 13].

Congener	PLSR	MLR	PCA-MLR	BP-ANN	$logK_{SA}$
training set					
BDE-1	5.132±0.108	5.183±0.146	5.145±0.110	-5.490±0.092	-5.401
BDE-2	5.019±0.103	5.089±0.127	5.058±0.109	-5.252±0.056	-5.317
BDE-5	4.358±0.079	4.402±0.153	4.417±0.092	-4.320±0.047	-4.298
BDE-7	4.065±0.073	3.890±0.168	4.014±0.087	-3.803±0.135	-4.159
BDE-12	4.411±0.081	4.454±0.120	4.468±0.093	-4.390±0.045	-4.351
BDE-21	3.644±0.069	3.566±0.188	3.713±0.086	-3.364±0.117	-3.378
BDE-28	4.114±0.073	4.080±0.147	4.060±0.084	-3.908±0.113	-3.509
BDE-47	3.554±0.070	3.578±0.146	3.517±0.077	-3.485±0.148	-3.660
BDE-66	3.537±0.070	3.533±0.118	3.487±0.082	-3.410±0.107	-3.329
BDE-153	2.631±0.093	2.575±0.175	2.502±0.143	-2.665±0.139	-2.611
BDE-209	1.126±0.164	1.369±0.262	1.322±0.239	-1.445±0.069	-1.423
RMSE	0.262	0.235	0.246	0.174	
test set					
BDE-3	5.235±0.113	5.316±0.179	5.262±0.118	-5.461±0.109	-5.417
BDE-100	2.913±0.083	2.845±0.103	2.874±0.090	-3.012±0.231	-2.810
BDE-183	1.983±0.121	1.844±0.179	1.884±0.149	-2.451±0.407	-2.060
RMSE	0.259	0.218	0.227	0.129	

4. CONCLUSION

In this research, the calculational results for BDE-47 and BDE-99 using DFT method with solvent effect showed the cleavage of C-Br bond by the way of stepwise debromination. The results are also compatible with experimental results. For BDE-47, the Br atom at the ortho-position was first replaced, while the initial cleavage of C-Br bond occurred at the para-position of higher-brominated ring for BDE-99. The mechanism for the cleavage of C-Br bond is complex, thus this needs a further research to clarify the debromination pathway of PBDEs congeners. In addition, the QSPR models obtained in the present study, especially the BP-ANN model, can well describe and predict the dehaogenation rates.

ACKNOWLEDGMENT

This research was supported by the National Natural Science Foundation of China (Grant No. 21367009) and Government of Guizhou Province (Project No. LKS [2013]09).

REFERENCES

- [1] Zhuang, Y. Ahn, S. & Luthy, R.G. 2010. Debromination of Polybrominated Diphenyl Ethers by Nanoscale Zerovalent Iron: Pathways, Kinetics, and Reactivity. *Environmental Science Technology* 44(21): 8236-8242.
- [2] Pan, L. & Bian, W. 2013. Theoretical Study on the Photodegradation Mechanism of Nona-BDEs in Methanol. *ChemPhysChem* 14(6): 1264-1271.
- [3] Lin, Y.M. Li, L.Y. Hu, J.W. Fan, M.Y. Zhou, C. & Shi, X.D. 2014. A comparative study on the removal of 2,2',4,4' - tetrabrominated diphenyl ether (BDE-47) by four different methods. *Applied Mechanics and Materials* 700: 211-215.
- [4] Luo, J. Hu, J. Zhuang, Y. Wei, X. & Huang, X. 2013. Electron-induced reductive debromination of 2,3,4-tribromodiphenyl ether: a computational study. *Journal of Molecular Modeling* 19(8): 3333-3338.
- [5] Yuan, G.L. Han, P. Xie, W. Che, X.C. & Wang, G.H. 2012. Altitudinal distribution of polybrominated diphenyl ethers (PBDEs) in the soil along Central Tibetan Plateau, China. *Science of the Total Environment* 433: 44-49.
- [6] Hu, J. Eriksson, L. Bergman, A. Kolehmainen, E. Knuutinen, J. Suontamo, R. & Wei, X. 2005. Molecular orbital studies on brominated diphenyl ethers. Part I—conformational properties. Chemosphere 59(7): 1033-1041.
- [7] Li, A. Tai, C. Zhao, Z. Wang, Y. Zhang, Q. Jiang, G. & Hu, J. 2007. Debromination of decabrominated diphenyl ether by resin-bound iron nanoparticles. *Environmental Science Technology* 41(19): 6841-6846.
- [8] Hu, J. Zhuang, Y. Luo, J. & Wei, X. 2012. A Quantitative Structure-Property Relationship Study on Reaction Rate Constants for Reductive Debromination of Polybrominated Diphenyl Ethers by Zero-valent Iron. *Advanced Materials Research* 550-553: 2668-2675.
- [9] Li, L. Lin, Y. & Hu, J. 2014. A Study on Pathway and QSPR Models for Debromination of PBDEs with Pseudopotential Method. *Advanced Materials Research* 997: 25-32.
- [10] Hu, J. Zhang, X. & Wang, Z. 2010. A Review on Progress in QSPR Studies for Surfactants. *International Journal of Molecular Sciences* 11(3): 1020-1047.
- [11] Luo, J. Hu, J. Wei, X. Li, L. & Huang, X. 2015. Excited States and Photodebromination of Selected Polybrominated Diphenyl Ethers: Computational and Quantitative Structure—Property Relationship Studies. *International Journal of Molecular Sciences* 16(1): 1160-1178.

- [12] Li, L. Lin, Y. & Hu, J. 2014. A QSPR Study on Debromination of PBDEs with CPCM Solvation Model. *Advanced Materials Research* 1010-1012: 3-9.
- [13] Keum, Y.S. & Li, Q.X. 2005. Reductive Debromination of Polybrominated Diphenyl Ethers by Zerovalent Iron. Environmental Science Technology 39(7): 2280-2286.
- [14] Frisch, M.J. Trucks, G.W. Schlegel, H.B. Scuseria, G.E. Robb, M.A. Cheeseman, J.R. Montgomery, Jr. J.A. Vreven, T. Kudin, K.N. Burant, J.C. Millam, J.M. Iyengar, S.S. Tomasi, J. Barone, V. Mennucci, B. Cossi, M. Scalmani, G. Rega, N. Petersson, G.A. Nakatsuji, H. Hada, M. Ehara, M. Toyota, K. Fukuda, R. Hasegawa, J. Ishida, M. Nakajima, T. Honda, Y. Kitao, O. Nakai, H. Klene, M. Li, X. Knox, J.E. Hratchian, H.P. Cross, J.B. Adamo, C. Jaramillo, J. Gomperts, R. Stratmann, R.E. Yazyev, O. Austin, A.J. Cammi, R. Pomelli, C. Ochterski, J.W. Ayala, P.Y. Morokuma, K. Voth, G.A. Salvador, P. Dannenberg, J.J. Zakrzewski, V.G. Dapprich, S. Daniels, A.D. Strain, M.C. Farkas, O. Malick, D.K. Rabuck, A.D. Raghavachari, K. Foresman, J.B. Ortiz, J.V. Cui, Q. Baboul, A.G. Clifford, S. Cioslowski, J. Stefanov, B.B. Liu, G. Liashenko, A. Piskorz, P. Komaromi, I. Martin, R.L. Fox, D.J. Keith, T. Al-Laham, M.A. Peng, C.Y. Nanayakkara, A. Challacombe, M. Gill, P.M.W. Johnson, B. Chen, W. Wong, M.W. Gonzalez, C. & Pople, J.A. Gaussian 03. Gaussian, Inc., Wallingford CT, 2004.
- [15] Lee, C. Yang, W. & Parr, R.G. 1988. Development of the Colle-Salvetti correlation-energy formula into a functional of the electron density. *Physical Review B* 37(2): 785-789.
- [16] Becke, A.D. 1993. Density–functional thermochemistry. III. The role of exact exchange. *Journal Chemical Physics* 98(7): 5648-5652.
- [17] Fang, L. Huang, J. Yu, G. & Wang, L. 2008. Photochemical degradation of six polybrominated diphenyl ether congeners under ultraviolet irradiation in hexane. *Chemosphere* 71(2): 258-267.
- [18] Li, X. Xie, C. He, Y. Qiu, Z. & Zhang, Y. 2012. Characterizing the moisture content of tea with diffuse reflectance spectroscopy using wavelet transform and multivariate analysis. *Sensors* 12(7): 9847-9861.
- [19] Luo, J. Hu, J. Wei, X. Fu, L. & Li, L. 2015. Dehalogenation of persistent halogenated organic compounds: A review of computational studies and quantitative structure–property relationships. *Chemosphere* 131:17-33.

Applying Big Data to Food Safety Risk Monitoring

X.H. Kuang
Hunan Police Academy, Changsha, China
Key Laboratory of Network Crime Investigation, Colleges of Hunan Province, Changsha, China
Email: tacom@sohu.com, tacom@163.com

D. Tang
Hunan Police Academy, Changsha, China
Key Laboratory of Network Crime Investigation, Colleges of Hunan Province, Changsha, China

Z.X. Zhou
Central University of Finance and Economics, Beijing, China

ABSTRACT: Big Data has enabled businesses to monitor large amounts of data and extract pertinent patterns necessary for decision making. Food safety on the other hand, has necessitated the deployment of quality control (QC) systems like the hazard analysis and critical control points (HACCP) framework to reduce the amount of harmful pathogens that consumers are exposed to through food. However, the complexity of adapting Big Data to the food safety concern has exposed the lack of proper control of variables that dictate whether practitioners are in agreement on which aspects of food processing and supply chain management are most important to the control process. This research will propose a generic framework, which adapts Big Data to food safety risk monitoring systems more efficiently.

KEYWORDS: Big Data; Food safety; Risk monitoring; Generic framework.

1. INTRODUCTION

Information systems technologies combine the computational powers of specialized software and automated data capture devices to populate databases that, in turn, enable processing or inform business strategy. Big Data, as a variation of information technology, provides the capability necessary to process large amounts of data, in fields like data analytics and mining [1]. The technology befits the gravity associated with food safety [2]. Accordingly, several computational systems manage the task of assessing and monitoring food safety [2]. The hazard analysis and critical control points (HACCP) system, for example; incorporates technologies that support food safety management approaches. Big Data poses an efficient model for HACCP because using existing data capture setups like radio frequency identification (RFID) it is adaptable to the general framework that risk management processes (RMP) and supply chain risk management Process (SCRMP) outline [3, 4, 5]. Notwithstanding the existing food safety and risk monitoring systems, there exists a need to review the efficiency and application of these systems to generate a model capable of managing the increasing food safety-related incidences.

2. APPLYING BIG DATA

Although there does not exist an all-encompassing definition of big data; information system practitioners are all in agreement that conventional computing technologies cannot keep up with the high rates of data throughput occasioned by the highly internetworked nature and proliferation of data generating devices. The management of high-volume data, as pertains to Big Data, has served to improve the efficiency of data management for data mining and analytics purposes. Existing studies have established that Big Data can aptly manage the concerns associated with large volumes of data; namely data, (1) velocity; (2) complexity; (3) variability; and (4) variety (see Fig. 1) [6]. The capabilities inherent of Big Data systems have enabled business to increase their competitiveness. Issues pertaining to supply chain management (SCM) and the risk management process (RMP) have leveraged Big Data to capture the trends and patterns, otherwise untraceable using traditional computer systems [5].

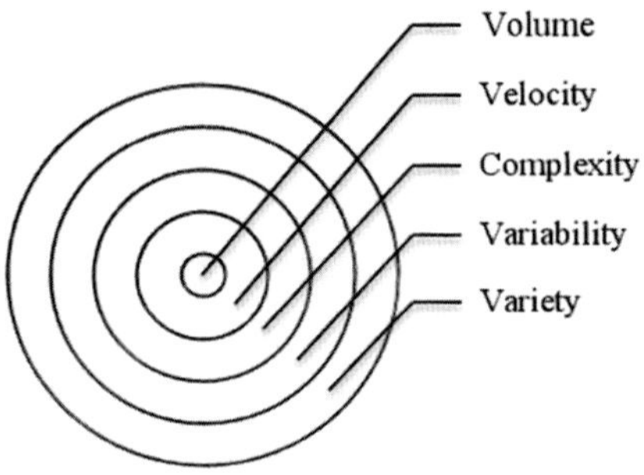

Figure 1. Factors of large data volumes addressed by big data.

3. FOOD SAFETY CONCERNS

Food, as a large constituent of consumer consumption, also acts as a carrier of microbes that cause disease; hence, acting as a transmitter of foodborne diseases. When quality control (QC) measures, SCM and RMP fail to identify dangerous levels of microorganisms, for instance, E.Coli, "Salmonella, Campylobacter and Listeria" [2], in food; consumers are at risk of foodborne diseases. As a result, public health initiatives have instituted policies requiring businesses to monitor and report their food safety practices. However, the requirements involve processing of large amounts of pertinent food safety-related data. HACCP has served to streamline food safety systems. The application nevertheless suffers from data collection and evaluation inefficiencies related to the specialized knowledge that transcends biological, medical and information systems fields [2]. Microbiological contamination presents the greatest risk to food safety (at 47.22%). The risk is nearly twice as that posed by both the contamination of processed foods' raw materials and poor sanitation (at a corresponding level of 22.22%) [4]—see Table 1.

Table 1. Prevalence of food safety risks.

Risk	***Prevalence***
Microbiological contamination	47.22%
Raw materials' contamination	22.22%
Poor sanitation	22.22%
Foreign objects contamination	8.34%

4. FOOD SAFETY RISK MONITORING

The risks associated with food safety have informed the formal methods of risk management, namely: "(1) risk identification; (2) risk measurement; (3) risk assessment; (4) risk evaluation; and (5) risk control and monitoring". [5] As pertains to Big Data, risk monitoring benefits from the argument that there is a "growing respect for correlations rather than continuous quest for elusive causality" [7]. Moreover, the complexities associated with risk monitoring of food safety keeps pace with the corresponding data generation that the processes of food production, SCM and QM experience. [9] Associations like the International Commission on Microbiological Specifications for Foods (ICMSF) have argued that practitioners should adapt their food safety risk management approaches to include data that is more efficiently exploitable by computing systems [8]. The ICMSF, for instance, proposes a control entity—the Food Safety Objective (FSO), which it assumes can enable the practitioners to monitor "the level of a hazard (in terms of concentration and/or frequency) that can be tolerated in" a food product at the time of consumption [8]; see Fig. 2.

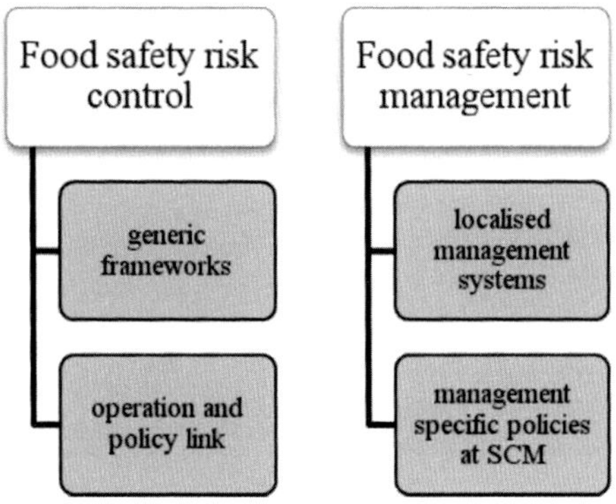

Figure 2. Risk monitoring in terms of food safety.

5. GENERIC FRAMEWORK

The generic framework notes two major categories of the variables pertinent to assessing food safety risks, namely; (1) risks; and (2) operational controls. The subsequent sections will present the variables' categories before formulating the framework and consequently examining the architecture capable of adapting Big Data.

5.1. *Big data model for food safety risk monitoring*

In 1983, the American Institute of CPAs (AICPA) presented an audit risk framework that can inform the design of a generic framework for managing risk. According to the AICPA, risk (P) is a function of three major components, namely;

- Inherent risk (I);
- Control risk (X); and
- Detection risks (Δ) [10]—see equation (1).

In turn, the three components inform the three data management components of:

- Validation
- Monitoring
- Verification

$$P = (I) * (X) * (\Delta) \quad (1)$$

The aspect of Big Data applies to the aforementioned framework, because compared to the time of AICPA's proposal; data management has increasingly faced the challenges illustrated in Fig. 1. More importantly, the high-level framework borrows from the principles employed in food safety management techniques, like the HACCP [8]. Furthermore, existing studies advises that the major challenge exists in the manner risk management practitioners manipulate the data, which indicates the "level of the pathogen that is achieved at the end of the chain" [8].

5.2. *Proposed architecture*

The use of a Big Data framework is crucial to food safety because the stages between the procurement and supply of food products to markets involve multiple players. When, for example, the 'raw food material' moves from the fields into the processing stage, it demands the use of a supply chain that fulfills economic requirements [4]. At this phase, the common practice is to verify that the producer; for instance, the farmer, has used the correct transport means. However, certain factors could go unnoticed at the produce reception stage—hence; farmers could participate in the risk monitoring process, from the farming phase. Using mobile devices is the most cost effective approach of transmitting the fertilizer levels and, in case of animal produce, the chemicals deployed in medication and treatment.

Since by the time the food processor receives the raw material the central database would contain farming details of the supplying farmer, the processor could verify whether the food stuffs contain the acceptable levels of chemicals. On reception, the processor populates the central database with the details of the food stuffs that have been accepted according to the set quality standards. [4], [5]. The QC phase, where the processor conducts further tests to determine whether the food stuff contains the levels of chemicals and pathogens that pose no risk to the consumer, the central database would already indicate which food stuffs demand keener inspection. By this point, therefore, the central database plays a key role in determining which food stuffs are deemed fit for human consumption or those that require disposal. Subsequently, the QC process generates RFID-compatible tags, which are readable by authorities and wholesalers. When external bodies, like food safety authorities get access to the central database, they can compare the food manufacturers QC benchmarks against the raw materials' indicators, which suggest the level of danger that consumers are potentially exposed [3].

While in the market, the RFID tag carries the data necessary to identify the particular food processor that contravenes the set food safety standards in case of a risk incident. For instance, when food stuff 'A' causes poisoning to infants, the food safety authorities could identify the manufacturer and the history of the raw materials through reference to the central database. Consequently, apart from the related legal procedures that the processor has to contend with, the authorities could isolate the raw material suppliers and examine the food growing or animal husbandry practices that could be potentially introducing harmful levels of pathogens or chemicals into the processed foods. On the other hand, the RFID tags could inform the authorities of the QC methods that had failed to mitigate the distribution of harmful food products. Additionally, including the QC details into the central database could offer more insight into the manufacturing processes that had failed to either reduce the dangerous levels of pathogens or dispose of unacceptable raw food materials.

In terms of risk management, the raw materials' procurement and processing phases are tasked with isolation and controlling the inherent risks (I). Likewise, the QC phase; that is monitoring phase; is tasked with the control risk (X), while the food packaging and distribution employ the RFID tags in order to provide for verification, which corresponds to detection risks (Δ) [10]. According to equation (1), the three categories of risk and their management approaches are in direct correlation, whenever any aspect of the risk management fails, therefore; the total risk to food safety increases comparably. As a result, Big Data, as a paradigm meant to minimize the risks passed on to consumers through dangerous levels of harmful contaminants, should feature in all the phases (see Fig. 3).

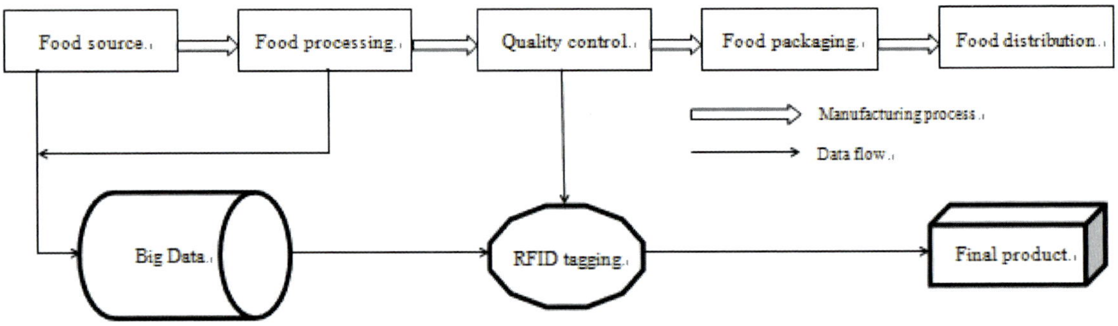

Figure 3. Generic Big Data framework.

6. CONCLUSION

The Big Data paradigm manages the aspects of data, which conventional underpowered computing systems cannot adequately handle. When combined with other enterprise computing models, for instance distributed or cloud computing, Big Data can serve the needs of the food industry in the aspect of monitoring food safety risks. This research has exposed the prevailing food concerns and the associated food safety risks; and argued that the Big Data paradigm can monitor risks efficiently. It has proposed a generic framework based on the AICPA's definition of risk management and adapted it to a computing model, where the multiple phases of food production interact with a central database to create an efficient model for validation, monitoring and verification. Consequently, the proposed model has indicated that the food safety authorities and the manufacturers could refer to the central database to determine aspects of food risks, which would otherwise continue to pose harm to the consumers.

REFERENCES

- [1] B. Weinberg, L. Davis and P. Berger, "Perspectives on big data", Journal of Marketing Analytics, Vol. 1, No. 4, pp. 187-201, 2012.
- [2] T. McMeekin, et al., "Information systems in food safety management", International Journal of Food Microbiology, Vol. 112, No. 3, pp. 181-194, 2006.
- [3] A. Regattieri, M. Gamberi and R. Manzini, "Traceability of food products: General framework and experimental evidence", Journal of Food Engineering, Vol. 81, No. 2, pp. 347-356, 2007.
- [4] S. Kumar and E. Budin, "Prevention and management of product recalls in the processed food industry: a case study based on an exporter's perspective", Technovation, Vol. 26, No. 5-6, pp. 739-750, 2006.
- [5] R. Tummala and T. Schoenherr, "Assessing and managing risks using the Supply Chain Risk Management Process (SCRMP)", Supply Chain Management: An International Journal, Vol. 16, No. 6, pp. 474-483, 2011.
- [6] D. Power, "Using 'Big Data' for analytics and decision support", Journal of Decision Systems, Vol. 23, No. 2, pp. 222-228, 2014.
- [7] V. Mayer-Schönberger and K. Cukier, Big Data: A Revolution that will transform how we Live, Work, and Think. New York: Houghton Mifflin Harcourt Publishing Company, 2013.
- [8] L. Gorris, "Food safety objective: An integral part of food chain management", Food Control, Vol. 16, No. 9, pp. 801-809, 2005.
- [9] L. Manning and J. Soon, "Mechanisms for assessing food safety risk", British Food Journal, Vol. 115, No. 3, pp. 460-484, 2013.
- [10] L. Manning, "Development of a food safety verification risk model", British Food Journal, Vol. 115, No. 4, pp. 575-589, 2013.

Research on the Employment Option of College Graduates Based on Bayesian Algorithm of Data Mining and Inclusion Degree

X.S. Zhang
Chongqing University of Science & Technology, 401331, Chongqing, China
Email: 276567574@qq.com

ABSTRACT: In recent years, the problem of the employment option of college graduates is paid more and more attention in the society. Every year the situation for the employment option of college graduates is faced with many uncertain factors. Therefore, the study on the employment of college graduates has very important practical significance. At present, we have accumulated a wealth of data about the employment options of college graduates in previous years. Data mining in handling high-volume data, excavate potential relationship has incomparable advantage. Therefore this paper proposes using bayesian data mining classification algorithm, through training the existing data of the employment option of college graduates, analyze the birth to the students graduated that were Satisfied with their jobs. And then we gain the classification feature set rules, and establish classification model about the employment option of college graduates. Using the model, we can divide the employment option of college graduates into three categories: the first that they were satisfied with their jobs, the second that they were General satisfied with their jobs, and the third that they were not satisfied with their jobs at all. Using the method of fuzzy mathematics and according the actual situations of the college graduates, we can calculate the inclusion degrees so as to determine which category they belong to. It is proved by the experiments that this model is selected user groups with high accuracy. The data of employment option of college graduates is of certain guidance.

KEYWORDS: High-risk claims; Bayes classification algorithm; Data mining.

1. INTRODUCTION

In recent years, many people have paid more and more attention to the problem of the employment option of college graduates in the society. It is difficult for the college graduates to find a job, which has become a fact. We analysis the reason and get the results above: the fresh graduates have poor stability, there is a big difference between the expected salary and actual salary, lack of practical experience, the students who graduate from popular major are often surplus, the orders of the employment markets should be further standard. And then it is more and more important to research the employment option of college graduates. Leading to these reasons the existing methods often use traditional statistical methods or simple professional analysis, with only experience decisions and neglected mass claims data implied in the valuable information. In dealing with mass data, data mining technology has the incomparable advantage. In recent years, many domestic and foreign articles specially discussed from several aspects of data mining in the application of the employment option of college graduates.

From a new perspective, data mining provides a method of handle the mass information for the employment option of college graduates. The method is that collected the mass dates which were not used actual many years, through the data mining technology, showed the type of customs and their features for the employment option of college graduate. The results of data mining also tell us more clearly about the employment option of college graduates.

The employment option of college graduates of China has accumulated the massive users' data. In view of this situation, this article introduces bayesian algorithm, analysis of large amounts of data of the employment option of college graduates, uses the bayesian classification algorithm, and establishes a college graduated crowd of bayesian filters. Thus putting the college graduated that were satisfied with their jobs personnel isolated, centralized analysis and find in guarantee slip so as to guide the employment option of college graduates.

2. RELATED THEORY

The bayesian theory originated from the British scholar Thomas Bayes (1763), his paper played an important role for modern probability and statistics. Thomas Bayes (1702-1761) proposed computation of conditional probability formula which used to solve uncertainty knowledge problem: suppose D[,1], D[,2]... mutexes and constitute a complete event, the probability of them: $P(D[,n])n=1,2,...$, now we observed "A" and $D[,1],D[,2]...$ accompanies appear, and known condition Probability $P(A/D[,n])$, how to get $P(D[,n]/A)$; Bayesian formula is:

$$P(D[,n]/A)=\frac{P(D[,n])P(A/D[,n])}{P(D[,1]P(A/D[,1])+P(D[,2]P(A/D[,2])+...}.$$

3. MODEL BUILT

The building of bayes classification algorithm model generally requires four steps:

The first step: data collection. Collect data, thus obtaining the users' data modeling required, including the choice of data items work directly determines the final whether the model with research objectives;

The second step: pretreatment data. On the initial users' data pretreatment, because the initial users' data must not meet our requirements, including modeling there will also be data noise and so on many kinds of problems, so for the pretreatment is to guarantee the inevitable requirement of modeling results are accurate;

The third step: training data. According to the collection of specific a group of data, through training these data, it is proved that the data is some characteristics of data collection, deposit features;

The last step: have characteristics set and classification algorithm, the tectonic classifier, as shown in figure 1.

Establish good bayes classification algorithm model, the user data for new join, we can detect through figure 2, first to be detected the user information to quantify, let them comply with a specific format, through the classifier are classified, through comparing, draw the conclusion.

4. CASE ANALYSIS

After decades of development, the employment option of college graduates of China has accumulated the massive users' data, and these enough we construct a bayesian classification algorithm model.

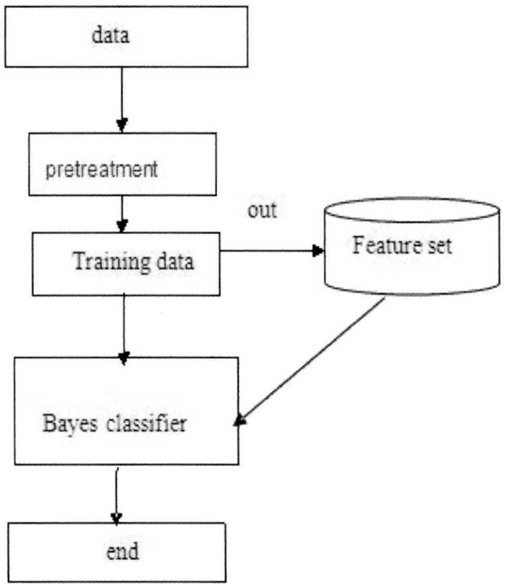

Figure 1. Model built.

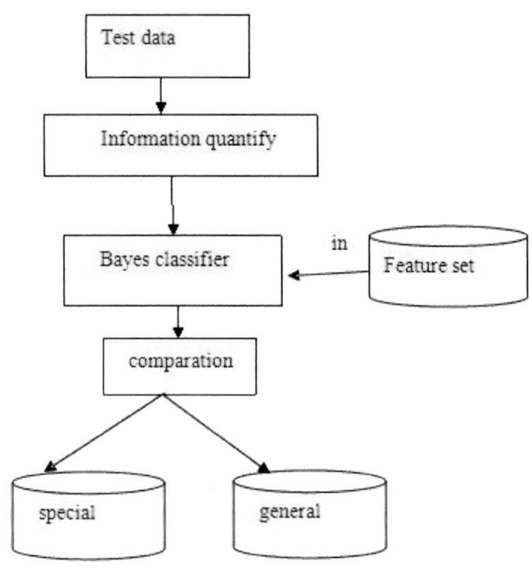

Figure 2. Test data.

Step 1: preprocessing the large number of claims data, and getting vector D (ID, age-related, it all, credibility), these are used as the training data;

Step 2: train data according to the classification algorithm and get classification rule, put the classification rules into feature set, fig. 3 shows,

Establish good classification algorithm model, when insurance companies find suspicious user, can use establish good classification algorithm model test. Extracting user information, according to the characteristics of the classification rules set get classification, judge this user genre.

5. CALCULATE INCLUSION DEGREE

We mark the system for B getting by f bayesian algorithm. So for a given new university xi, we can get its equivalent class.

$[x_i]_B = \{x \in U | f_a(x) - f_a(x_i), a \in A\}$

When the objects given are plentiful, $[x_i]_B \neq 0, \forall D_j (1 \le j \le k)$, we can calculate a Inclusion Degree. According to the maximum subjection principle, $D = \max\{d | d = D(D_j / [x_i]_B\}$, When D reaches maximum, xi belong to D_j class.

In the system, according to the age, study results, areal distribution and so on, We will divide them into three categories: D1 is category that they were satisfied with their jobs, D2 is category that they were General satisfied with their jobs, and D3 is category that they were not satisfied with their jobs at all. So to a new object x, $D(D_i / [x]_B), (i = 1,2,3)$, x belongs to a classification as follows:

$$x \in \begin{cases} D_1 & D = D(D_1 / [x]_n) \\ D_2 & D = D(D_2 / [x]_n) \\ D_3 & D = D(D_3 / [x]_n) \end{cases}$$

If $D = D([x]D_1 / B)$, then x belongs to D1, that is, namely you don't consider x;

If $D = D(D_2 / [x]B)$, then x belongs to D2, that is, you may consider x;

If $D = D(D_3 / [x]B)$, then x belongs to D3, that is, you can choose x.

Training data			
ID	age	study results	areal distribution
1	<=20	excellent	big city
2	21--23	good	medium-sized city
3	>23	general	better
.....	.....	.....	.....

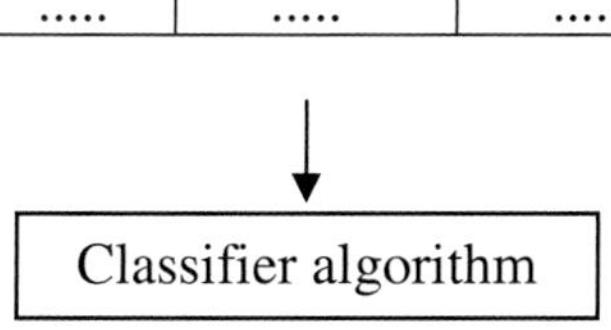

Figure 3. Training data.

6. CONCLUSIONS

Facing graduation, the college graduates all hope to find satisfied works. And every year the situation for the employment option of college graduates is faced with many uncertain factors. It has much important practical significance for them to establish a kind of effective method so as to lead to their employment. In this paper we use bayesian algorithm of data mining to establish a model of bayesian classification. The data mining technology is a broad prospect of data processing and analysis technology. It will have a large amount of information in all walks of industry and will play an inestimable role.

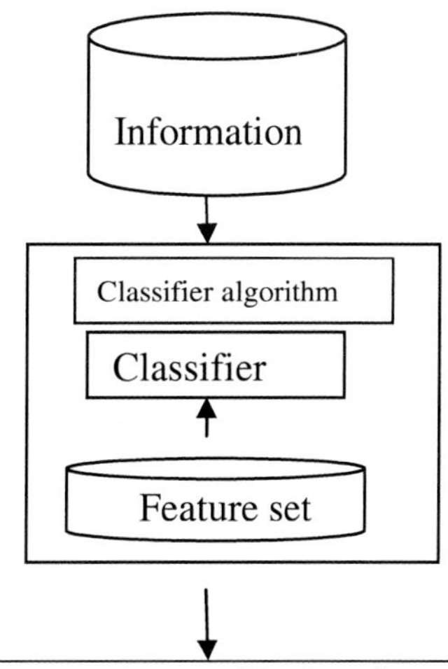

Testing data			
ID	age	study results	areal distribution
11	<=20	excellent	big city
12	21—23	good	medium-sized city
13	>23	general	village
.....	.....	.....	.....

Figure 4. Testing data.

REFERENCES

- [1] Davis, H. Putnam. A computing procedure for quantification theory. Journal of ACM, 7(3)(1960) 201-215.
- [2] Mitra S., Pal, S. K., Mitra P., Data mining in soft computing framework: a survey, IEEE Transactions on Neural Networks, 2002, 13(1):3-14.
- [3] Li Yuanjin, Yang Lianhe. The data mining technology in car insurance application [J], page 80-81.
- [4] Chen Yongqiang, Hu Leifang. The data mining technology in the life insurance CRM system application research [J]. Modern production and management technology, page 39-42.
- [5] Chen M-S, Han J., Yu P. S., Data mining: an overview from a database, Perspective, IEEE Transactions on Knowledge and Data Engineering, 1996, 8(6):866-883.
- [6] Hu De-min, Feng Ke-feng, One method of new attribute reduction based on discretization of continuous attributes [J]. Application Research of Computers, 2009, 1(5):64-65.
- [7] Yue Ha-i liang, Yan De-Qin, New Algorithm for Discretization Based on Information Entropy [J], Computer Science, 2010, 4(15):231-233.
- [8] Friedman N, Geiger D, Goldszmidt M, Bayesian network classify, Machine Learning, 1997.1, Vol 29,131-163.

Chapter 3
Algorithm and Simulation

An Automatically Learning Chinese Word Segmentation Algorithm Based on Particle Swarm Optimization

P. Nie
Computer Center of Practice Teaching, Jiangxi University of Finance and Economics, Nanchang, China
Email: zeanet@163.com

ABSTRACT: Nowadays, the automatically learning Chinese word segmentation algorithms based on particle swarm optimization (PSO) were presented and discussed. However, most of the papers employed PSO as the parameter optimizer for neural networks. We proposed a novel pure PSO-based CWS schema (PSO-CWS) and tested the practicability on the bakeoff 2005 dataset. Firstly, the content is split into a mass of clauses without any punctuation. Then clause-centered PSO-CWS generates the PSO swarm in the segment searching space. Led by the self-knowledge and the social knowledge, PSO-CWS covers the best segmentation schema with the highest fitness. Experiment results show that PSO-CWS proposed in this paper achieved the acceptable accuracy of Chinese word segmentation and the practical efficiency.

KEYWORDS: Chinese word segmentation; Particle swarm optimization; Heuristic algorithm.

1. INTRODUCTION

The statistical models in CWS are discussed wildly in a mass of lectures. There are three kinds of methods in general.

The first is to use unsupervised learning algorithm to segment texts, like branching entropy (BE) [1], normalized variation of branching entropy (nVBE) [2].

The second is to use unsupervised or domain-independent features in supervised learning for Chinese word segmentation, such as punctuation and mutual information (MI), word accessory variance [3-5].

The third is to use semi-supervised learning in sequence labeling to address the difference in source and target distributions [6].

Another branch of CWS schema is the automatically learning algorithms, such as neural networks. Collobert et al. [7] developed the SENNA system that approaches or surpasses the state-of-the-art systems on a variety of sequence labeling tasks for English. Zheng et al. [8] applied the architecture of Collobert et al. to Chinese word segmentation and POS tagging and proposed a perceptron style algorithm to speed up the training process with negligible loss in performance.

However, PSO is rarely introduced into the CWS works. PSO is an efficiently heuristic algorithm for the optimal solution in the searching space of the merits of the article to find the best results. In this paper, we proposed a novel pure PSO-based CWS schema (PSO-CWS) and tested the practicability on the bakeoff 2005 dataset.

The rest of this paper is organized as follows. Section 2 presents the idea of the particle swarm optimization. Section 3 introduces our PSO-based CWS algorithm in detail. The experiment and analysis are presented in Section 4. Finally, Section 5 concludes this paper.

2. PARTICLE SWARM OPTIMIZATION

PSO is a population based heuristic optimization technique developed by Kennedy and Eherhart [9]. As an algorithm, the main strength of PSO is its fast convergence, which compares favorably with many global optimization algorithms. Another advantage is that PSO can be implemented and applied easily.

The basic idea of PSO-CWS is to model the set of potential segments which can gain the best fitness as a swarm of particles moving around in a virtual search space. PSO-CWS generation starts with a random population initialization of a clause segmentation in the search space. Next, the CWS particles move around in the search space for the optimal result. During the movements, each particle's segment position is estimated by the fitness function. According to the estimations, the best particle of the entire swarm is selected as *gBest*. PSO-CWS generation converges to *gBest* by adjusting the trajectory of each individual particle towards its own best location (self-knowledge) and towards *gBest* location (social knowledge) on each iteration. PSO-CWS generation iterates one generation after another until the particle fitness or the number of the iterations reaches the termination condition.

The social knowledge sharing of information among PSO-CWS offers an evolutionary advantage: this hypothesis is fundamental to the development of PSO-CWS.

The rate equations which the PSO-CWS generation depends on are shown as Equation (1) and (2).

$$v_{id} = \begin{cases} wv_{id} + c_1 r_1 (p_{id} - x_{id}) + c_2 r_2 (p_{gd} - x_{id}), & v_{id} \le v_{maxd} \\ v_{maxd} & , v_{id} > v_{maxd} \end{cases} \quad (1)$$

$$x_{id} = x_{id} + v_{id} \quad (2)$$

Where,

w : the inertia weight

c_1, c_2 : the coefficients, the balance factors between the effect of self-knowledge and social knowledge in the CWS particle movement towards the target position

r_1, r_2 : the random numbers between 0 and 1, and different at each iteration

x_{id} : the position of the *i*-th CWS particle (p_i) in the *d*-th dimension of the search space

v_{id} : the velocity of p_i in the *d*-th dimension of the search space

p_{id} : the best position that p_i experienced in the *d*-th dimension of the search space

p_{gd} : the best position that *gBest* experienced in the *d*-th dimension of the search space

v_{maxd} : the maximum velocity for p_i

p_i updates its own velocity based on three aspects. wv_{id}, the first aspect, represents the segmentation position that p_i inherits from its previous movement. The second aspect is $c_1 r_1 (p_{id} - x_{id})$, called the *cognition* part, which represents the best segmentation position experience of p_i in the *d*-th dimension of the search space. p_i shares *gBest* experience to adjust its segmentation position by the third aspect $c_2 r_2 (p_{gd} - x_{id})$, which is called the *social* part. Finally, p_i renew its position by Equation (2).

3. PSO-BASED CWS ALGORITHM

3.1. *Framework*

In this section, we introduce our idea of PSO-based CWS algorithm in detail. Figure 1 gives the framework in general.

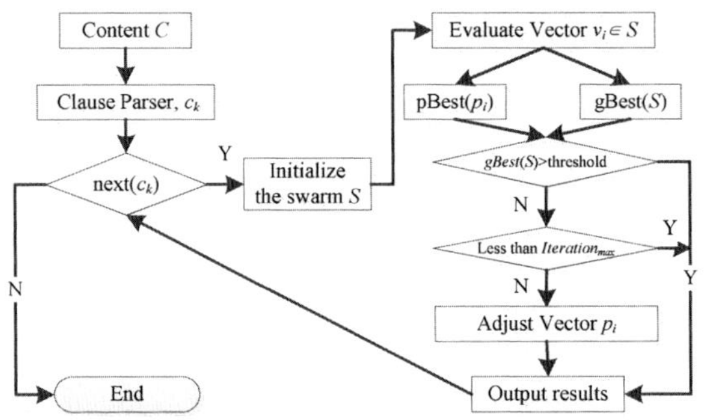

Figure 1. PSO-based CWS algorithm framework.

Step 1. The input content is split into a clause set $C = \{c_1, c_2 \cdots c_n\}, n \in N$; each c_k includes no more punctuation.

Step 2. Initialise the swarm by assigning a random segmentation to the copies of each c_i. The individual copy is called a CWS particle (p_i).

Step 3. According to the predefined objective function, evaluate the fitness for each p_i.

Step 4. For each individual p_i, compare the particle's fitness value with its *pbest*. If the current value is better than the *pbest*, then set the current segmentation value as the new *pbest*.

Step 5. Identify p_i that has the best fitness value. The value of its *pbest* is identified as *gbest*.

Step 6. Adjust p_i to vary the population. Update the velocities and positions of all the particles using Equations (1) and (2). If the velocity of one particle exceeds the upper limit v_{maxd}, $v_{id} = v_{maxd}$.

Step 7. Repeat Step 3 to Step 7 until a stopping criterion (e.g., a maximum number of iterations or a sufficiently good fitness value) is achieved and output the *gBest* as the segment result of c_i.

Step 8. Repeat Step 2 to Step 8 until each c_i has been run by Step 2 to Step 7.

3.2. *Swarm generation*

PSO-CWS firstly initialises the swarm with *N* particles by random from c_i. Each particle is a vector including different segment piece s_i as the following case.

In of case of c_i=南非与中国同是发展中国家 (South Africa and China are both developing countries), 5 particles in the initial swarm may be p_{m-2}: 南 非 与 中国 同是 发展 中国 家 with 8 s_i, p_{m-1}: 南非与 中国 同 是 发展中 国家 with 6 s_i, p_m: 南 非与 中 国同 是发展 中国家 with 6 s_i, p_{m+1}: 南非 与中 国同是发展 中国 家 with 5 s_i, p_{m+2}: 南非 与 中 国 同是 发展 中 国家 with 8 s_i.

The PSO-CWS creates each segment of p_i within *windowSize* 5, which means the max maximum segment length is less than six.

Before PSO-CWS generate the swarm, the input content has been split into causes, and each cause has finite Chinese characters in it. Usually, the length of a cause is less than 30. This makes the PSO-CWS run in a smaller search space to get the target.

3.3. *Fitness*

In this paper, the fitness function as Equation (3) is designed to be affected by two factors of the word frequency and the word length. We tend to encourage the longer word has the greater fitness against the noise from the short word with a high word frequency.

$$fitness(p_i) = \sum_{j=1}^{m} f(s_j) \times \alpha^{length(s_j)-1} \qquad (3)$$

where s_j denotes the *j-th* segment piece in p_i with m segment pieces in total, $f(\bullet)$ denotes the word frequency, $length(s_j)$ denotes the length of the *j-th* segment piece, and α is the coefficient to regulate the weight of the segment length.

3.4. *Swarm adjusting*

p_i after the evaluation process tries to adjusting itself in order to get a better fitness score. Each p_i in the swarm has a variable dimension segmentation space. The scale of the n-dimension space depends on the amount of s_j. Figure 2 shows the adjusting process for p_i from the n-th iteration to the next iteration.

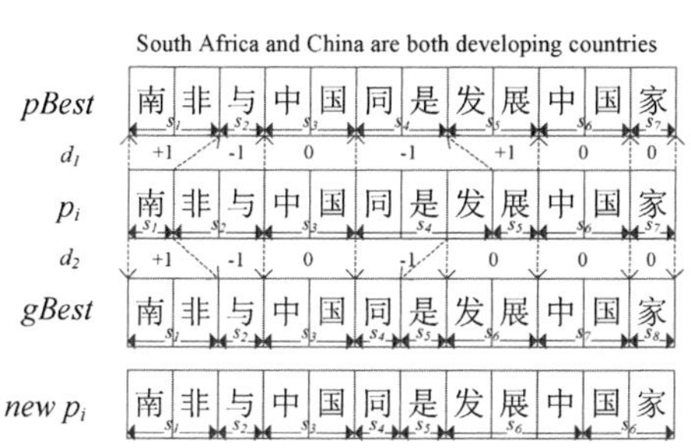

Figure 2. A case to illustrate the evolution of p_i.

In the n-th iteration, p_i measures both distances of $d_1 = distance(p_i, pBest)$ and $d_2 = distance(p_i, gBest)$. In the first case that the distance is greater than zero, p_i adds a random distance value v_{id} less than $\frac{windowSize}{2}$ to its current segment position to get close to *pBest* or *gBest*. In the second case that the distance is less than zero, p_i decreases a random distance value v_{id} less than $\frac{windowSize}{2}$ to its current segment position to get close to *pBest* or *gBest*. In the last case that the distance is equal to zero, p_i maintains itself.

We discussed how to perform the new distance to p_i. However, the new s_j may cover part of the old s_{j+1}. In this case, the next new s_{j+1} takes the residue of the old s_{j+1} as the segment start point. In another case, the new s_j may cover all of the old s_{j+1} and even part of s_{j+2}, so the segment start point of new s_{j+1} takes the residue position of the old s_{j+2}.

Finally, d_1 is used as $p_{id} - x_{id}$ and d_2 is used as $(p_{gd} - x_{id})$ in Equation (1). The new p_i in the next generation is created by Equation (1) and Equation (2) with some new random feature introduced by c_1 and c_2. In the case of Figure 2, new p_i has the best fitness and the most logical result.

We chose 5 for the hyper-parameters *windowSize* of the PSO-based CWS algorithm used in all our experiments, considering a larger corpus will be used in the following experiments, and the sparseness problem would be alleviated. Furthermore, we would like to "observe" a character within a slightly larger window to better discover its syntactic and semantic information in order to obtain character embeddings by using large unlabeled data.

4. EXPERIMENT AND ANALYSIS

In our experiment, the corpus with 1.7 million Chinese words released by Peking University consists of one month's (January 1998) newspaper material published by the People's Daily is taken as the dataset. The corpus grammar is used correctly and appropriately for the presentation. All of the Latin letters, the Arabic numerals and the punctuation are in the Chinese double byte format.

4.1. *Comparison*

We employed the wide used precision, recall, F-measure, IV recall, OOV recall as the features to test our CWS Algorithm.

Table 1 shows the results of PSO-based CWS on the word segmentation task for mandarin Chinese text in bakeoff-2005: c (Closed track), o (Open track).

Table 1: The results of PSO-based CWS.

		c_1	c_2	P	R	F	IV	OOV
A	c	0.1	0.1	0.706	0.812	0.755	0.754	0.138
	o	0.1	0.1	0.813	0.753	0.782	0.762	0.605
B	c	0.5	0.5	0.882	0.875	0.878	0.913	0.297
	o	0.5	0.5	0.909	0.903	0.906	0.924	0.709
C	c	1	1.5	0.921	0.902	0.911	0.912	0.731
	o	1	1.5	0.933	0.935	0.934	0.945	0.759
D	c	2	2.5	0.914	0.915	0.914	0.943	0.617
	o	2	2.5	0.937	0.939	0.938	0.947	0.806

Table 2 shows the comparision between our system results and results in bakeoff-2005.

Table 2: The comparision between PSO-based CWS results and results in bakeoff-2005.

	F (PSO-based CWS)	F (best bakeoff-2005)	F (average bakeoff-2005)
c	0.914	0.950	0.920
o	0.938	0.969	0.942

From those tables, we observe that PSO-based CWS with smaller c_1 and c_2 has lower score than the algorithm with greater c_1 and c_2. c_1 and c_2 represent the speeding figure, regulating the length when flying to the most segmentation schema of the whole swarm and to the most optimist individual segmentation. If the figure is too small, the segmentation schema is probably far away from the target field, if the figure is too big, the segmentation schema will maybe fly to the target field suddenly or fly beyond the target field. The proper figures for c1 and c2 can control the searching accuracy and the solution will not be the partial optimism.

Experimental results also show that PSO-based CWS has the biggest speed of convergence when w is between 0.8 and 1.2. While experimenting, w is confined from 0.9 to 0.4 according to the linear decrease, which makes PSO-based CWS search for the bigger space at the beginning and locate the position quickly where there is the most optimist solution. As w is decreasing, the speed of the particle will also slow down to search for the delicate partial.

In general, with the Bakeoff-2005 corpus, we compare the best F-score of ours to the second international Chinese word segmentation bakeoff algorithm and achieve the score close to the average level of Bakeoff-2005.

4.2. *Fitness convergence*

In this section, the fitness average increasing curves are shown in Figure 3.

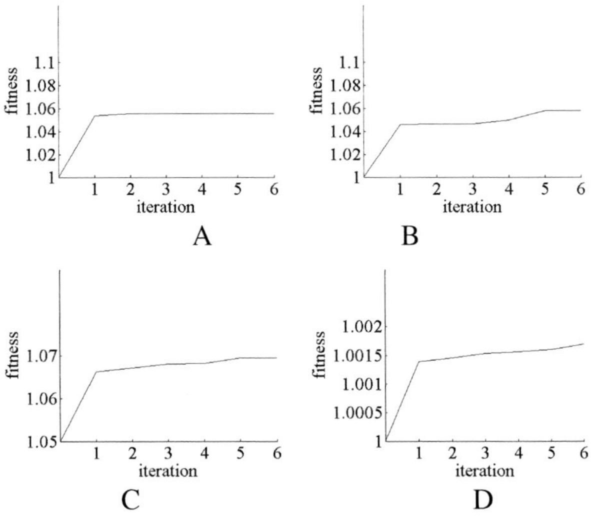

Figure 3. The fitness average increasing curves for different c_1 and c_2 in 4 cases.

First of all, all above cases show that the PSO-based CWS consumed less than 6 iterations to achieve the stable fitness. That means the time consumption is good. Secondly, as c_1 and c_2 were increased, the curves went more active, which resulted in better segments. Finally, in our experimental testing, the swarm with great size has no better result than the small size swarm. This reduced the CPU and the memory occupation greatly without reducing the performance of PSO-based CWS.

5. CONCLUSIONS

In this paper, we focused on PSO in the issue of Chinese word segmentation and proposed a novel pure PSO-based CWS schema (PSO-CWS). PSO-CWS is a heuristic algorithm and develop the segment schema to the best target automatically. Our algorithm was tested on the bakeoff 2005 dataset, and achieved good results in minuscule amount of iterations from a small size swarm.

REFERENCES

— [1] Jin, Z.H. & Kumiko, T.I. 2006. Unsupervised segmentation of Chinese text by use of branching entropy. *Proceedings of the COLING/ACL'06 on Main conference poster sessions*: 428-435, Sydney, Australia, 15-23 July 2006.

— [2] Magistry, P. & Sagot, B. 2012. Unsupervized word segmentation: the case for mandarin Chinese. *Proceedings of the 50th Annual Meeting of the Association for Computational Linguistics*: 383-387, Jeju, Republic of Korea, 8-14 July 2012.

— [3] Feng, H.D., Chen, K. & Deng, X.T. 2004. Accessor variety criteria for Chinese word extraction. *Computational Linguistics* 30(1): 75-93.

— [4] Zhao, H. & Kit, C. 2008. Unsupervised segmentation helps supervised learning of character tagging for word segmentation and named entity recognition. *In The Sixth SIGHAN Workshop on Chinese Language Processing*: 106-111, Hyderabad, India, 11-12 January 2008,.
— [5] Sun, W.W. & Xu, J. 2011. Enhancing Chinese word segmentation using unlabeled data. *In Proceedings of the Conference on Empirical Methods in Natural Language Processing*: 970-979, Edinburgh, UK, 27-29 July 2011.
— [6] Suzuki, J. & Isozaki, H. 2008. Semi-supervised sequential labeling and segmentation using gigaword scale unlabeled data. *In Proceeding of Association for Computational Linguistics*: 665-673, Columbus, Ohio, USA, June 2008.
— [7] Collobert, R. 2011. Deep learning for efficient discriminative parsing. *In Proceedings of the 14th International Conference on Artificial Intelligence and Statistics*, Fort Lauderdale, FL, USA, 2011.
— [8] Zheng, X. Q., Chen, H. Y. & Xu, T. Y. 2013. Deep Learning for Chinese Word Segmentation and POS Tagging. *In Proceedings of the 2013 Conference on Empirical Methods in Natural Language Processing*: 647–657, Seattle, USA, 18-21 October, 2013.
— [9] Kennedy, J. & Eberhart, R.C. 1995. Particle Swarm Optimization, *In Proceedings of IEEE Int'l. Conf. on Neural Networks*: 1942-1948, Piscataway, NJ, USA, 1995.

Design Implementation and Application of Swarm Intelligence Algorithm Optimization Function Simulation Platform

S.M. Duan*, J.L. Mao, J.L. Li & L.X. Fu
Department of Automation, Faculty of Information Engineering and Automation, Kunming University of Science and Technology, Yunnan, Kunming, China
**Email: dsm_2005@163.com, 529345484@qq.com*

ABSTRACT: This paper discusses the five kinds of swarm intelligence algorithm. On this basis, the interactive user interface simulation of swarm intelligent algorithm optimization function was designed with the function of GUI in MATLAB. This platform has the advantages of friendly interface, simple operation, strong interactivity, visualization, scalability etc. And any continuous function can be simulated, analysed and compared using the algorithm in the platform. At the same time, this paper proposed real coded chaotic quantum genetic algorithm based on catastrophe. The simulation results in the platform and improved algorithms are compared, which can get rid of the understanding of multiple swarm intelligent algorithm in the platform and save time. The simulation results are distinctive and highlight, and it shows that the improved algorithm has high precision, overcoming the premature and the advantages of fast convergence.

KEYWORDS: Swarm intelligence algorithm; Function optimization; Simulation design; Quantum genetic algorithm.

1. INTRODUCTION

Optimization technology is a mathematical basis for application of technology solutions for optimization problems in various engineering; used in function optimization, combination optimization, system engineering, production scheduling. Because of the complexity of the actual engineering problems, constraints and multi peak, non-linear and difficulties of modeling, using optimization algorithm suitable for large-scale and has intelligent feature optimization technology has become main research goal and direction. Swarm intelligence algorithm is applied to optimization technique, simulation on community phenomenon of biological populations in nature theory and thought source; have been widely used in the field of function optimization, combination optimization, transportation problem, scheduling optimization, engineering optimization design; domestic and foreign raised the research upsurge of swarm intelligence algorithm. But at present a lot of books by theoretical derivation and analysis of a single intelligent algorithm based, and this algorithm is used in a certain field, gives the optimization results; and no combination of swarm intelligence algorithm for the same optimization problems comparing results for the readers to observation and analysis, also does not have a suitable environment for simulation and analysis and compare the performance of these algorithms and features.

Based on the realization of each swarm intelligence algorithm programming, using the MATLAB GUI[1] user interface development function design "swarm intelligence algorithm optimization function simulation platform", has realized the simulation of swarm intelligence algorithm optimization function analysis and comparison of the integration and platform; and then an improved algorithm -- Based on the real coded chaotic quantum genetic algorithm (catastrophic real-coded chaotic quantum-inspired disaster genetic algorithm, CRCQGA), which were compared with the simulation platform of the five swarm intelligence algorithm, extends the application of the simulation platform; the simulation results show that the improved algorithm for high precision, fast convergence speed.

2. DESIGN OF THE SIMULATION PLATFORM OF SWARM INTELLIGENCE ALGORITHM OPTIMIZATION FUNCTION

2.1. *The design target of the platform*

The design of the target group function simulation platform of intelligent optimization algorithm are: simulation environment with interactive interface, open, good simple visualization; integrated a variety of swarm intelligence algorithm, and can modify the parameters of the algorithm; swarm intelligence algorithm for continuous function optimization with stochastic input to any platform; the simulation results are shown, the program running time, function the graphic description and eventually in the population distribution, optimization of trend diagram; to the same problem, will use a different algorithm platform optimized trend chart, random fitting comparison; optimization results can save the current problems of different swarm intelligence algorithms of data, compared the new algorithm and its expansion.

2.2. *The platform interface design*

Swarm intelligence algorithm optimization function simulation platform to simple and clear, only an interface, namely the simulation operation panel, as shown in figure 1. Mainly include:

(1) The information input part: parameter setting, the optimization objective function and interval of the input, optimization, swarm intelligence algorithm to select the direction of;

(2) The perform operation part: optimizing the start button, parameters and interface clear key, optimizing the end (platform off) select image fitting bond, swarm intelligence algorithm;

(3) The results showed part of the simulation results value display, the program running time display, graphic description and function groups in the final distribution shows, algorithm with evolutionary algebra optimization tendency chart display, a plurality of swarm algorithm fitting display graphics.

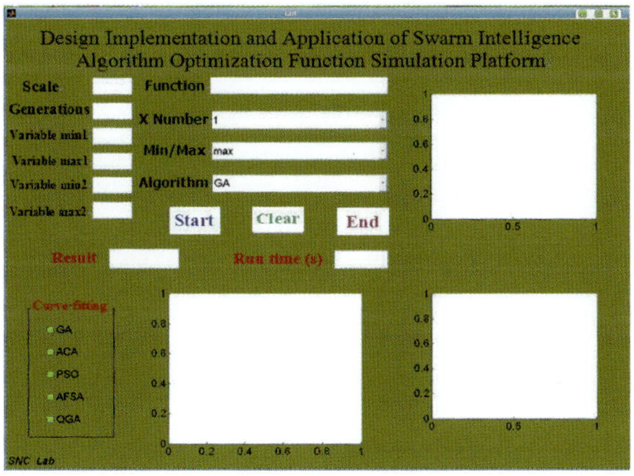

Figure 1. The simulation platform interface work.

2.3. *Swarm intelligence algorithm program implementation*

In the group of function simulation platform of intelligent optimization algorithm, the main five swarm intelligence algorithm design: genetic algorithm (genetic algorithm GA), ant colony algorithm (ant colony algorithm, ACA), particle swarm optimization (particle swarm optimization, PSO), artificial fish swarm algorithm (artificial fish swarm algorithm, and the quantum genetic algorithm (AFSA) quantum genetic algorithm, QGA).

2.3.1. *Genetic algorithm*

The specific implementation steps of genetic algorithm for [2]:

Step 1: group: the initial chromosomes randomly generated set of initialization of a certain scale;

Step 2: calculation of individual fitness;

Step 3: selection: select the copy operation;

Step 4: Cross: according to the crossover principle and crossover probability;

Step 5: variation: implementation according to the variation principle and the mutation probability, producing new individuals;

Step 6: termination conditions to judge whether or not, if not go to Step 2 else Step 7;

Step 7: output: the final will be the best individual best individual or the whole evolution process of population in genetic algorithm solution as output.

2.3.2. *Ant colony algorithm*

The specific steps [2] of ant colony algorithm:

Step 1: initialization searching for 0 times; the arc edge track initialization strength, edge arc length trajectory information left unit element quantity; initial ant population randomly generated a certain scale;

Step 2: the initial position point of each ant into the current solution set; for each ant with the probability of a given move on to the next point; and the point into the current section in the collection;

Step 3: for each ant objective function values were calculated and recorded on the current best solution;

Step 4: according to the update equations to modify the trajectory of strength;

Step 5: will track unit length information prime amount of each side on the legacy of the 0, and the iteration times accumulated 1;

Step 6: if the iteration times did not reach a set of terminating iteration times and no degradation appear, go to Step 2;

Step 7: output current optimal solution.

2.3.3. *Particle swarm algorithm*

The specific steps [3] of particle swarm optimization algorithm:

Step 1: initialization parameters of particle swarm optimization; random position and speed of the initial setting;

Step 2: To adapt to the value is calculated for each particle;

Step 3: for each particle, the adaptation values are compared, the best Pi value position and experienced if better, the best position of the current;

Step 4: for each particle, their fitness best position Pg experience and the global adaptation values are compared, if better, the current global best position;

Step 5: according to the formula (1), the formula (2) evolution of the velocity and position of particles;

$$v_{ij}(t+1) = v_{ij}(t) + c_1 r_{1j}(t)(p_{ij}(t) - x_{ij}(t)) + c_2 r_{2j}(t)(p_{gj}(t) - x_{ij}(t)) \quad (1)$$

$$x_{ij}(t+1) = x_{ij}(t) + v_{ij}(t+1) \quad (2)$$

Step 6: if not meet the end condition, Step 2 is returned.

2.3.4. *Fish swarm algorithm*

The specific steps [4] of fish swarm algorithm:

Step 1: fish initialization; within a given range of initial individuals randomly generated a certain scale set;

Step 2: for each individual fish test following behavior, to judge whether there is progress; if not, the Step 3 is executed; if so, executing Step 4;

Step 3: Test for each individual fish swarm behavior, to judge whether there is progress; if not, then the implementation of foraging behavior; if yes, then the implementation of the swarming behavior;

Step 4: if the iteration times did not reach a set of terminating iteration times or does not meet the other has a set of termination conditions, go to Step 2;

Step 5: output current optimal solution.

2.3.5. *Quantum genetic algorithm*

The specific steps [2] of quantum genetic algorithm:

Step 1: initialize the individual parameters and quantum chromosome;

Step 2: by the quantum chromosomes generated quantum collapse;

Step 3: fitness evaluation group;

Step 4: program stop condition judgment, when the stopping condition is met, the display output current best individual, otherwise continue;

Step 5: cross, to individual variation, produce new.

Step 6: using quantum rotation gate on the population is updated, the formula (3) (4), a new generation of quantum chromosome, i.e.

$$\begin{pmatrix} \alpha_{t+1} \\ \beta_{t+1} \end{pmatrix} = u(\theta) \cdot \begin{pmatrix} \alpha_t \\ \beta_t \end{pmatrix} \quad (3)$$

Quantum rotation gate:

$$\begin{pmatrix} \alpha_{t+1} \\ \beta_{t+1} \end{pmatrix} = u(\theta) \cdot \begin{pmatrix} \alpha_t \\ \beta_t \end{pmatrix} \quad (4)$$

The rotation angle is obtained from the look-up table; after the update, back to Step 2.

Step 7: meet the end condition, the output current optimal solution.

3. THE INSTANCE SIMULATION AND EXTENDED APPLICATION

According to the group function simulation platform of intelligent optimization algorithm, enumerates a binary function and function of two variables in the optimization of the steps in the platform.

3.1. *The simulation examples of function of one variable*

The simulation platform of operation steps are as follows:

The first step: open platform; fill algorithm population scale and algorithm evolving algebra; variable interval; input for optimizing the objective function. For example, the objective function for "input exp (-2*log (2) * ((x-0.1) /0.8).^2) * (sin (5*pi.*x)).^6", interval [0,1]; variable number in the objective function to be optimized selection; optimal choice of direction of the objective function, that is searching for the maximum or minimum max the value of min;

The second step: choose the use of optimization algorithms, there are five kinds of algorithm selection;

The third step: after the completion of the one or two step, click the 'start' button in the platform. Results such as the second step:

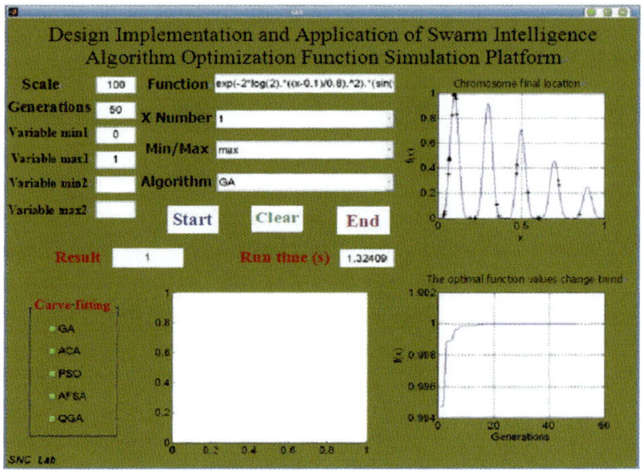

Figure 2. The interface of the simulation examples of function of one variable.

The middle of the platform displays maximum optimization after finding algorithm selection of objective function, that is, the global optimal solution; also shows the whole process of optimization program running time. The upper right corner of the platform shows the optimization objective function graph description, as well as in the graphic description indicating, the last generation after the end of operation optimization, the final position of individual. The optimal choice of swarm evolutionary algorithm in each generation to find the value saved, drawn into evolution curve is displayed in the lower right corner of the platform.

The fourth step: curve fitting in the lower left corner of the platform. The operation platform is in the lower left of curve fitting, select the required comparison algorithm, namely, click a certain algorithm, algorithm in front of the box will automatically call hook.

For the same optimization objective function in the same interval, choose the same population size and evolving algebra, optimization in the same direction, while the use of different optimization algorithms were optimized after the evolution curve of each algorithm can be obtained respectively choose fitting, and shown on the bottom left platform.

Only fit two algorithms, namely the two evolution curve results figure such as platform left below the fitness curves in figure 3.

The fifth step: the clear button. Click on the platform in the clear button, can clear the current result of the algorithm platform and preservation, and the MATLAB command window empty.

The sixth step: the end button. Click on the finish button, namely closure algorithm platform.

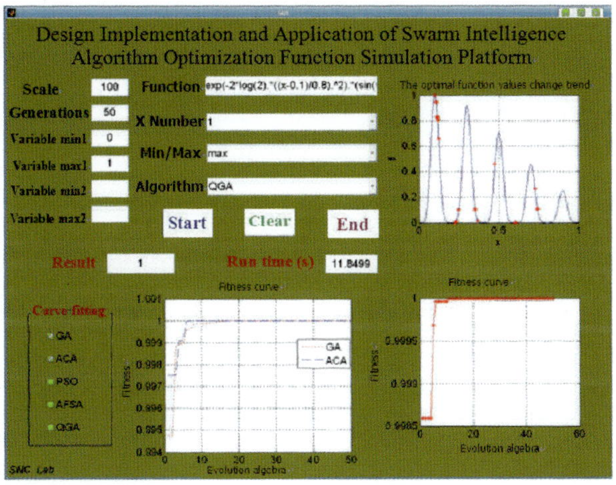

Figure 3. The two evolution curve fitting the graphical interface.

3.2. *The simulation examples of the binary function*

The simulation platform of operation steps are as follows:

The first step: open platform; fill algorithms that population size and evolution algebra algorithm, variable interval optimization function, input for optimizing the objective function. For example, the objective function input "0.5- (((sin (sqrt (x.^2+y.^2))) * (.^2-0.5) (1+0.001* (x.^2+y.^2)).^2).^-1)", interval [-5,5][-5,5]. The number of parameters is two, the optimal direction of Max, that is, find the maximum value.

The second step: choose different algorithms are optimized, click the 'start' button to search.

The genetic algorithm (GA), ant colony algorithm (ACA), particle swarm optimization (PSO), artificial fish swarm algorithm (AFSA), quantum genetic algorithm (QGA) optimization, the results were as below figure 4-8.

The third step: curve fitting in the platform;

In the same population size 100, algebra 50, evolution algorithm optimization function variable interval [-5,5][-5,5], the same to be optimized target function 0.5- (((sin (sqrt (x.^2+y.^2))) * (.^2-0.5) (1+0.001* (x.^2+y.^2)).^2).^-1). By fitting the choice to evolve curves of five kinds of algorithms, the results in figure 9.

The fourth step: click on the 'end' button, close the algorithm optimization platform.

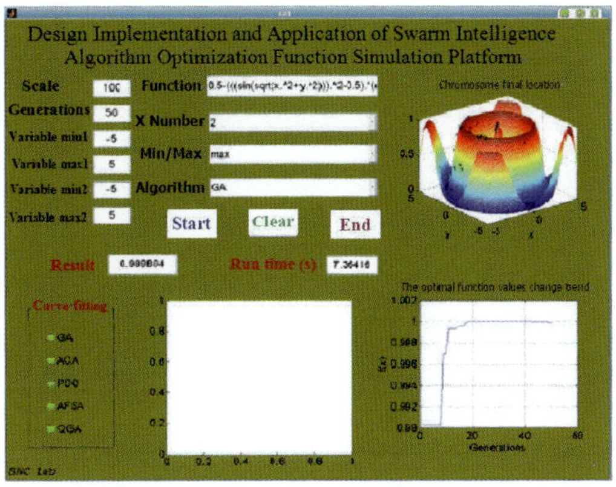

Figure 4. A two-dimensional function interface GA algorithm simulation examples.

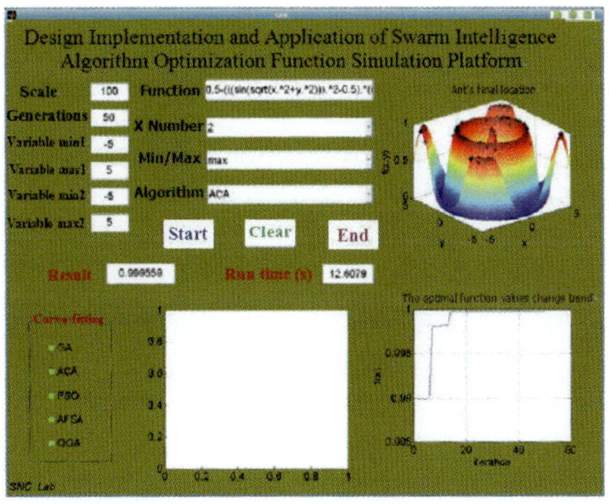

Figure 5. A two-dimensional function interface ACA algorithm simulation examples.

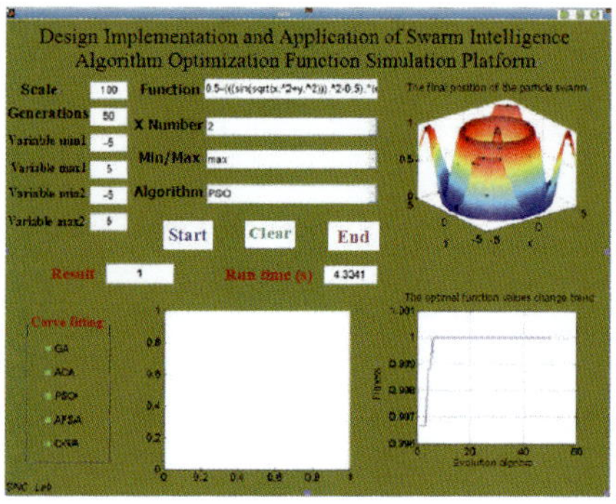

Figure 6. A two-dimensional function interface PSO algorithm simulation examples.

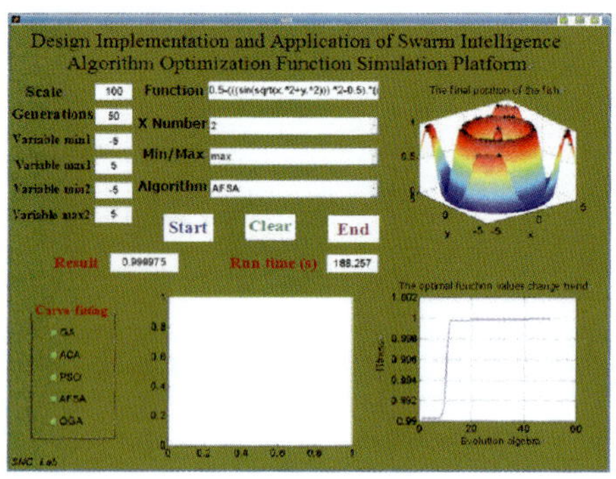

Figure 7. A two-dimensional function interface AFSA algorithm simulation examples.

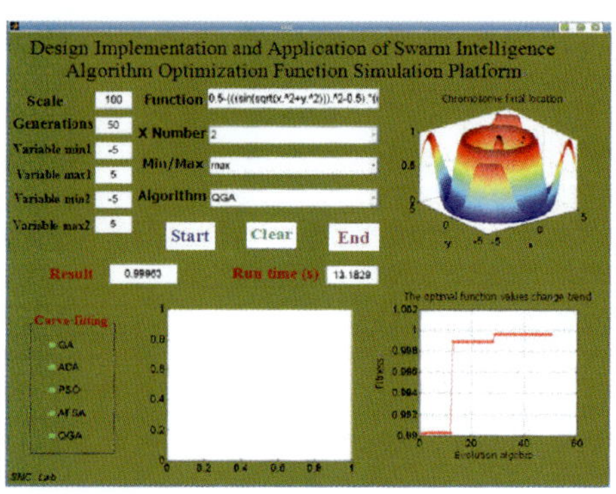

Figure 8. A two-dimensional function interface QGA algorithm simulation examples.

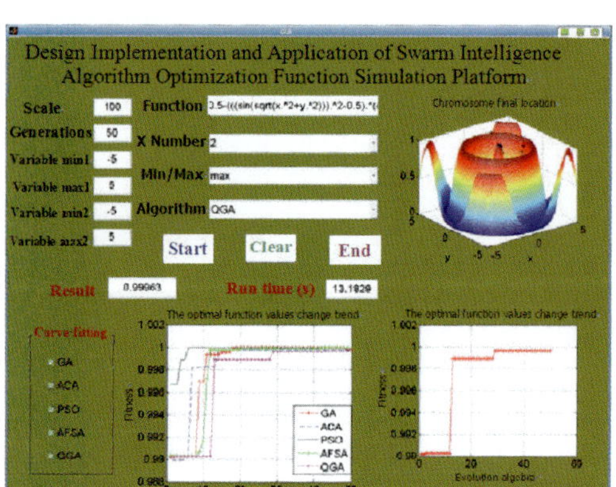

Figure 9. Function five evolution curve fitting two-dimensional graphical interface.

3.3. *Platform application development*

Swarm intelligence algorithm optimization function simulation platform can use the platform to arbitrary continuous function in the algorithm simulation, analysis and comparison; can also be the results of the simulation platform and improvement of the algorithms are compared. This paper presents a real coded chaotic quantum genetic algorithm based on catastrophe (CRCQGA), were compared with the simulation platform of the five swarm intelligence algorithm, extends the application of the simulation platform; at the same time, the simulation results also show that the improved algorithm for high precision, overcome premature convergence speed.

3.3.1. *The improved algorithm is proposed*

This paper presents real coded chaotic quantum genetic algorithm based on catastrophe (CRCQGA). The main improvement is to join disaster in the references [5] based real coded chaotic quantum genetic algorithm based on chaotic sequence [6], change the mapping model [7] [8], change the crossover and mutation ratio.

The specific process description is as follows:

Step 1: initialization individual parameters and population;

As with the RCQGA adopts real coding, a group size is N, the variable interval randomly generated N points x_i (i.e. a qubit representation of a chromosome), $i = 1, 2, ...N$. It composed of N points $P(0) = \{x_{10} \quad x_{20} \quad ... \quad x_{N0}\}$ of the initial population, and make use of type (5) to calculate the initial population of each individual corresponding phase Angle is expressed as type (6), (a, b) for variable interval.

$$\omega_i = \arcsin \frac{x_i - a}{b - a} \tag{5}$$

$$\omega(0) = \{\omega_{10} \quad \omega_{20} \quad ... \quad \omega_{N0}\} \tag{6}$$

In (0, 1) interval random chaotic sequence is generated in the initial values of Y (1).

Step 2: judge whether meet the catastrophic conditions, while satisfying the conditions will preserve the best individual, the rest of the individual to generate and continue with the next step; otherwise directly to take the next step;

Step 3: evaluation of population fitness, recording the best individual and fitness value;

Step 4: termination condition judgment, when meet terminates, otherwise continue;

Step 5: real probability of cross;

Set up a generation to keep the best individual and its phase angle respectively p_{best} and ω_{best}, population $P(t) = \{x_{1t} \quad x_{2t} \quad ... \quad x_{nt}\}$, corresponding phase angle for $\omega(t) = \{\omega_{1t} \quad \omega_{2t} \quad ... \quad \omega_{Nt}\}$.

The individuals in a population average are divided into two halves, the half use type (7) and (8) probability of crossover, get a new generation of individuals, replacing the old individual. Unlike RCQGA, real cross and evaluation function value has nothing to do.

$$\Delta\omega_{it} = \omega_{it} - \omega_{best} \quad (7)$$

$$x_{i(t+1)} = p_{best} \times \cos^2(\Delta\omega_{it}) + x_{it} \times \sin^2(\Delta\omega_{it}) \quad (8)$$

Step 6: chaos mutation;

Will the Step 5 population before real probability cross the other half of the individual, according to type (9) ~ (15) chaos mutation. Chaotic sequence generated by the three order Chebyshev mapping to generate chaos sequence.

The formula is as follows:

$$x_n = \cos(\omega \cdot \arccos x_n) \quad -1 \le x_n \le 1 \quad (9)$$

$$r_i = e^{\frac{F_b - f(x_i)}{F_b}} \quad (10)$$

F_b is the optimal individual fitness

$$\Delta\omega_i = y \cdot r_i \quad (11)$$

$$\begin{pmatrix} \alpha_i \\ \beta_i \end{pmatrix} = \begin{pmatrix} \dfrac{x_i - a}{b-a} \\ \sqrt{1-\left(\dfrac{x_i - a}{b-a}\right)^2} \end{pmatrix} \quad (12)$$

$$u = \begin{bmatrix} \cos(\Delta\omega_i) & -\sin(\Delta\omega_i) \\ \sin(\Delta\omega_i) & \cos(\Delta\omega_i) \end{bmatrix} \quad (13)$$

$$\begin{pmatrix} \alpha_{i(t+1)} \\ \beta_{i(t+1)} \end{pmatrix} = u \cdot \begin{pmatrix} \alpha_{it} \\ \beta_{it} \end{pmatrix} \quad (14)$$

$$x_{i(t+1)} = \alpha_{i(t+1)}(b-a) + a \quad (15)$$

To carry out the variation of individuals, using the type (9)-(11) calculates the rotational angle range, then the use of type (12), the real numbers are normalized, using type (13) quantum rotation gate and type (14), (15) to get a new generation of individual to replace the old individuals, thus forming a new generation of population, turning to Step 2.

Step 7: meet the end condition, save and output the current optimal solution.

3.3.2. *The comparison between improved algorithm and swarm intelligence algorithm in the simulation platform*

The objective function of 0.5- (((sin (sqrt (x.^2+y.^2))) * (.^2-0.5) (1+0.001* (x.^2+y.^2)).^2).^-1), interval [-5,5][-5,5], using -- improved CRCQGA algorithm to optimize them, find the maximum value; in the algorithm the evolution algebra is set to 50, the population number was 100, setting and parameters of platform of swarm intelligence algorithm are the same. The simulation of computer configuration for core 2CPU and SATA2 hard disk, frequency of 2.53GHz, memory 2.00GB. Function graphics description and final individual distribution in Figure 10; for the maximum value 1, the program running time is 8.38391425 s, get the fitness curves in figure 11. The platform adopts GA, and in ACA, PSO, AFSA, QGA is optimized to obtain fitness curve fitting, which is shown in Figure 12, the algorithm to find the optimal solution, the first to find the optimal solution of the algebraic and the running time are summarized in table 1.

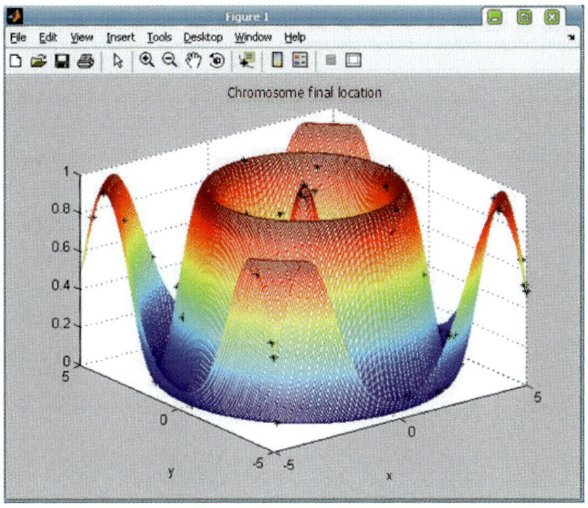

Figure 10. CRCQGA optimization function graph description.

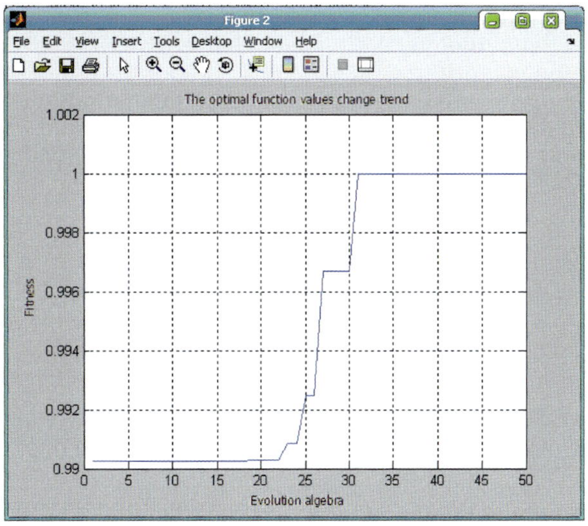

Figure 11. CRCQGA fitness optimization function curve.

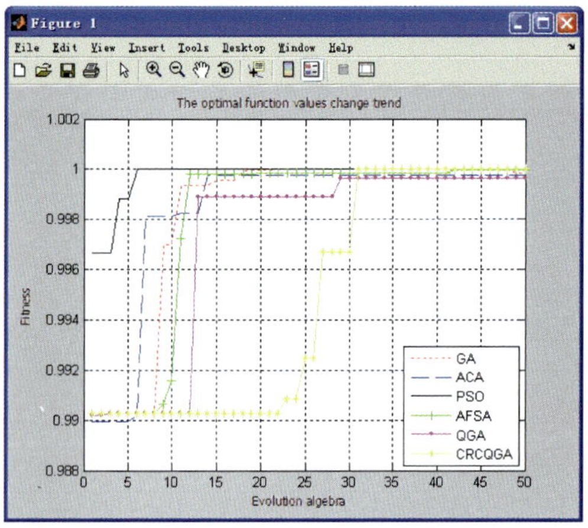

Figure 12. CRCQGA and swarm intelligence optimization algorithm to the degree of curve fitting.

Table 1. The results of using different algorithms of the same function.

The algorithm name	The optimal solution reference value	Algorithm to find the optimal solution	Find the optimal solution what generation (generation)	Program running time (s)
CRCQGA	1.00	1.00	31	8.38391
QGA	1.00	0.99963	29	13.1829
AFSA	1.00	0.999975	42	188.257
PSO	1.00	1.00	6	4.3341
ACA	1.00	0.999559	14	12.6079
GA	1.00	0.999864	18	7.36416

According to figure 12 and table 1 shows that only two algorithms find optimal solution in 1, PSO in the sixth generation to find the optimal solution; the CRCQGA to find the optimal solution of CRCQGA in the thirty-first generation; two yuan in this function optimization searching ability than PSO, but better than the other four swarm intelligence algorithm is strong, not easy to fall into premature convergence. Faster. CRCQGA compared with QGA, using quantum gates and quantum gate function update to complete the evolutionary search; rotation angle without looking up table, comparison, reduces the computational complexity; has the characteristics of small population size, the performance of the algorithm, the convergence speed; real number coding is used, suitable for multi parameter optimization and precision requirements; through the improvement of overcoming for multi parameter complex function optimization premature convergence phenomenon.

3.4. *The function and characteristics of the platform*

"Group" function simulation platform of intelligent optimization algorithms to continuous function as the optimization objective function, using GA, PSO, AFSA and QGA ACA, a total of five species of intelligent algorithm to respectively to optimize the objective function, and show the graph of a function described in the platform, mark out each individual finally group position in the graph; will some optimal algorithm of group evolution in each generation to find the value saved, drawn into evolution curve display in the platform. After the evolution, displays the global optimal algorithm to find the value in the platform, and running time. The platform also can be the evolutionary curve fitting algorithm for the same objective function together, and displayed. This platform has the advantages of simple operation, can be optimized for any continuous function, there are five kinds of algorithm on the algorithm, also optional, results and program running time comparison, clear description, contrast. The platform also can be the results compared with other algorithms, application development platform.

4. CONCLUSION

This simulation platform to realize the interface of the simulation of five swarm intelligence algorithm comparison functions and procedures of the user, for observation, analysis, comparison and research group to provide a convenient continuous function optimization intelligent algorithm; also can be extended compared with other algorithms, this paper proposed an improved algorithm and the algorithm is compared in the platform and analysis, the improved algorithm advantages and disadvantages clearly; and the platform has the advantages of simple operation, strong visualization, can expand. The next step of work but also can increase the types of platform of algorithm, expand the scope of the objective function optimization algorithm.

REFERENCES

- [1] Chen Yaoguang, Mao Taotao, 2011. Proficient in MATLAB GUI design (Version 2) [M]. Beijing: Electronic Industry Press, 2011.
- [2] Huang Yourui, Intelligent optimization algorithms and its application, Defense Industry Press, 2008.
- [3] Duan Haibin, Zhang Xiangyin, XU Chunfang. Bionic intelligent computing [M]. Beijing: Science Press, 2011.
- [4] Shi Feng, Wang Hui, Yu Lei. Intelligent algorithm 30 case analysis [M]. Beijing Aerospace University Press, Beijing (in Chinese), 2011.
- [5] Chen Hui, Zhang Jia-shu, Zhang Chao, Real-coded Chaotic Quantum-inspired Genetic Algorithm, Control and Decision, Vol. 20, No. 11, 1300-1303, 2005.

— [6] Jin Xidong, Li Ye, Genetic Catastrophic Algorithms and Its Application in Nonlinear Control System, Journal of System Simulation, Vol. 9, No. 2, 111-115, 1997.
— [7] Landford III O.E. Introduction to the mathematical theory of dynamical system [M]. Iooss G, Helleman R II G and Stora R Eds. Chaotic behavior of deterministic system. Amsterdam: North-Holland, 1983.
— [8] Mi Liang, Zhu Zhongliang, Optimization of Chaotic Direct Spreading Sequences and Comparison of Performances Between Chaotic and Conventional Sequences, Systems Engineering and Electronics, Vol. 24, No. 8, 110-117, 2002.

Design and Implementation on Marine Surveillance Intelligent Detection System Based on Ant Colony Optimization Algorithm

D.N. Jia[1], D.L. Shi[2] & Y.P. Cong[3,*]
Department of Computer Science and Technology, Ocean University of China, Qingdao, China
Email: [1]me@jiadn.com, [2]checkin001@seiouc.net, [3,]congyp@ouc.edu.cn*

ABSTRACT: Ant colony optimization algorithm is applied to loading balancing mechanism of marine surveillance intelligent detection system to increase its monitoring efficiency. Pheromone updating role and routing role is optimized to increase concurrency performance, and load balancing architecture is designed for the system to implement the algorithm. Practical test results demonstrate the efficiency and performance of the ant colony optimization algorithm.

KEYWORDS: Marine surveillance; Ant colony optimization; Load balancing.

1. INTRODUCTION

Marine surveillance technology is an important part of marine science, which has a great significance to maintain maritime rights and interests, develop marine resources, warn marine disaster and protect the marine environment, etc. Marine surveillance real-time fault detection is particularly important for real-time analysis, object tracking and monitoring in order to timely provide exception report to regulators. A marine surveillance intelligent detection system is implemented in this paper to deal with this difficulty of artificial maintenance. As the high concurrency performance is the key to detection efficiency, an improved ant colony optimization algorithm is used the system to implement load balancing mechanism.

2. RELATED WORK

Inspired by way of ant colony foraging, Colorni A. and Dorigo M. put forward Ant Colony algorithm [1] in 1992. On the performance of combinatorial optimization problem, ant colony algorithm has shown its excellent efficiency. Stutzle T., Hoos H.H. put forward Max-Min ant colony algorithm, which features its control mechanism of the pheromone updating mechanism [2]. Gambardella L.M. proposed Ant Colony System in the basis of ant colony algorithum, and its main characteristic is the combination of local pheromone update mechanism and the global update mechanism [3,4]. Ant colony algorithm has been applied to more complex applications due to its excellent solution finding ability. Dorigo M. and Birattari M. listed some typical application of ant colony algorithm, which includes vehicle routing problem, route choice problem, assignment problem, scheduling problem and subset problem such as set covering problem and multiple knapsack problem [5,6].

3. LOAD BALANCING MECHANISM

3.1. *Load balancing architecture*

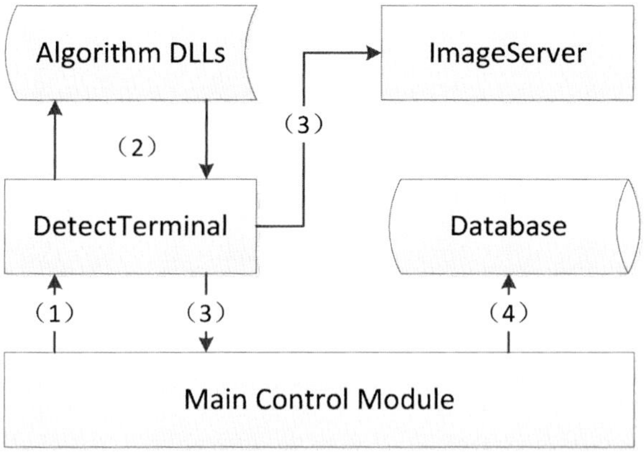

Figure 1. Load balancing scheduling architecture.

Parallel detection module is one of the main module implemented in the system, and its specific implementation process is shown in Figure 1: First, detection task queue is sent to terminal detection module from the main control module. When receiving the task queue, terminal detection module will first call the algorithm DLLs for detecting, and send the corresponding image to image server. Finally, detecting results is deposited in the database through the main control module. Load balancing mechanism is mainly implemented in this module.

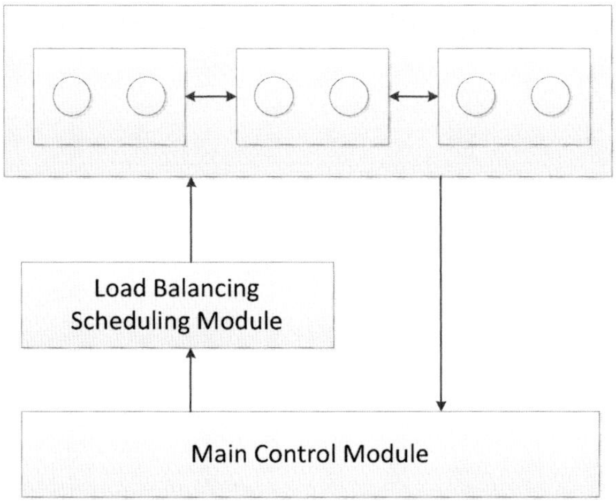

Figure 2. Load balancing scheduling architecture.

As is shown in Figure 2, load balancing scheduling module is implemented between the main control module and terminal detection module, which will schedule load balancing of the detection task queue using ant colony optimization algorithm. Task assigned to each server node can be transferred between the nodes by scheduling module.

3.2. *Problem definition*

In the load balancing problem, all problem parameters are assumed to be deterministic. K is the set of parallel machines, and |K| denotes the number ofmachines, i.e., the cardinality of set K. Similarly, J is the set of jobs that needs to be processed on these machines. K_j is the subset of machines on which job j can be processed, and J_k is the subset of jobs that can be processed onmachine k. Jobs are available at time zero. If job i precedes job j on machine k, then there is a sequence- dependent setup time of S_{ijk} between jobs i and j. Let p_{ik} be the processing time of job I on machine k.No preemption of jobs is allowed. Each job is processed on only one machine and only once.

Let C_k be the total completion time of all jobs assigned to machine k. The imbalance is defined as $\mathrm{C}_{\max} - C_k$, where the minimization objective will force $\mathrm{C}_{\max}$ to have the value of maximum completion time of jobs on all parallel machines.

$$\mathrm{C}_{\max} = max_{k\in K} C_k \tag{1}$$

The relative imbalance on machine k is the ratio of imbalance and the maximum completion time on all machines.

$$imbalance_k = \frac{\mathrm{C}_{\max} - C_k}{\mathrm{C}_{\max}} \tag{2}$$

Below is the evaluation criterion fo the problem. The goal of the problem is to schedule jobs to minimize the average relative percentage of imbalance (ARPI), which is described in Equation 3.

$$\mathrm{ARPI} = \min\left(\frac{1}{|K|}\sum_{k\in K}\frac{\mathrm{C}_{\max} - C_k}{\mathrm{C}_{\max}}\right)\times 100 \tag{3}$$

3.3. *Ant colony algorithm optimization*

With reference to the original framework of ant colony optimization algorithm, ant colony optimization algorithm implemented in this system applies local search algorithm [7] and tabu search algorithm [8], and optimizes pheromone updating and node choosing rule.

Let $\tau_{((i,k),(i',k'))}(t)$ be the artificial pheromone trail on an arc from (i,k) to (i',k') at iteration t. Similarly, $\Delta\tau_{((i,k),(i',k'))}(t)$ is the incremental pheromone amount, which is found as a function of the fitness of the solutions that are found by all ants at iteration t. Initially, the pheromone level on each edge is set to an arbitrary but small level of τ_0. After an iteration is completed, the level of pheromone level on each arc is updated.

Let $ARPI^{\gamma}(t)$ be the average relative percentage imbalance for the solution obtained by ant γ at iteration t. Then, after iteration t is completed, the pheromone level on ant γ's path is updated using Equation 4:

$$\Delta\tau^{\gamma}_{((i,k),(i',k'))}(\mathrm{t}) = \begin{cases} \dfrac{1}{\mathrm{ARPI}^{\gamma}(t)} & \text{if ant } \gamma \text{ travels on edge((i,k),(i',k'))} \\ 0 & \text{otherwise} \end{cases} \tag{4}$$

As the most optimal value of $ARPI^{\gamma}(t)$ is 0, when a solution with zero ARPI is obtained, then the ant colony algorithm stops. The overall change in the pheromone level is calculated using Equation 5:

$$\Delta\tau_{((i,k),(i',k'))}(\mathrm{t}) = \sum_{\gamma=1}^{\gamma}\Delta\tau^{\gamma}_{((i,k),(i',k'))}(t) \tag{5}$$

The total amount of pheromone level at any edge on the network is described using Equation 6:

$$\tau_{((i,k),(i',k'))}(t+1) = (1-\rho)\tau_{((i,k),(i',k'))}(\mathrm{t}) + \Delta\tau_{((i,k),(i',k'))}(\mathrm{t}) \tag{6}$$

where ρ is an evaporation rate that represents the evaporation of the trail between iteration t and t+1.

Selection of the next node, which has not been-visited yet, can be made in three ways:

(1) With probability q, select the node that has the maximum pheromone amount, as described in Equation 7:

$$(i',k') = \max_{(\bar{i},\bar{k}) \in tabu^{\gamma}} \left\{ \left[\tau_{((i,k)(i',k'))}(t) \right] \right\} \quad (7)$$

(2) With probability d, select the node with respect to a discrete probability function, which is a function of pheromone trails on all edges, as described in Equation 8:

$$Pr^{\gamma}_{((i,k),(i',k'))}(t) = \begin{cases} \dfrac{\left[\tau_{((i,k),(i',k'))}(t)\right]}{\sum_{(\bar{i},\bar{k}) \in tabu^{\gamma}} \left[\tau_{((i,k),(\bar{i},\bar{k}))}(t)\right]} & (i,k) \in tabu^{\gamma} \\ 0 & otherwise \end{cases} \quad (8)$$

where $Pr^{\gamma}_{((i,k),(i',k'))}(t)$ is the transition probability from node (i,k) to node (i',k') for ant γ.

(3) With probability r, select the next node randomly from the tabu list.

Note that $q+d+r=1$.

The pseudocode for the ACO algorithm is summarized in Figure 3.

Ant Colony Optimization Algorithm

STEP 0: Initialize:

- a) Set iteration counter t=0.
- b) Set pheromone level on all edges to τ_0.

STEP 1: Construct solutions for each ant γ (i.e., for γ=1 to n)

Generate a tour by adding an edge from $tabu^{\gamma}$ using the following:

- a) With probability q, the node with the maximum pheromone level.
- b) With probability d, a discrete probability distribution with edge probability $Pr^{\gamma}_{((i,k),(i',k'))}(t)$.
- c) With probability r, random selection.

STEP 2: Local search (Optional)

STEP 3: Evaluate the fitness of each solution.

STEP 4: Keep the best solutions in a list. If not optimal (i.e., ARPI is not zero) and t < MaxIterationCount, then update the pheromone levels on the network via evaporation and incremental pheromone update processes.

STEP 5: Set t=t+1. Go to Step 1.

Figure 3. Pseudocode for ACO algorithm.

4. OPTIMIZATION RESULT

After optimizing with load balancing mechanism, the concurrency performance of the system is tested with CPU as Intel Core i3-2120 and Memory as 4G DDR3. In two figures below, v4.11 represents system before optimazation, ACO represents system using original ant colony optimazation alogrithm, and ACO* represents system using improved ant colony optimazation alogrithm.

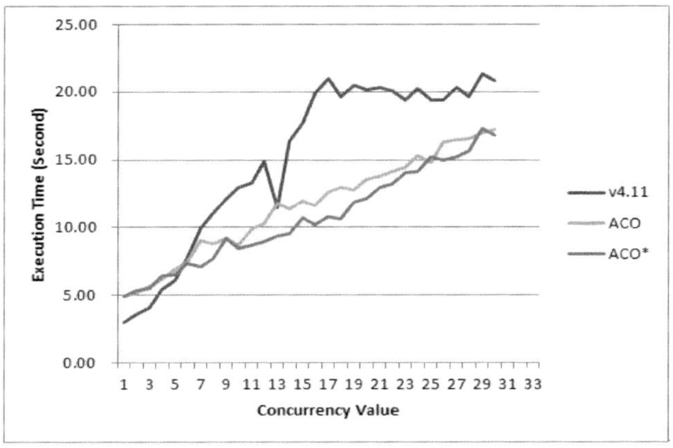

Figure 3. Image detection execution time.

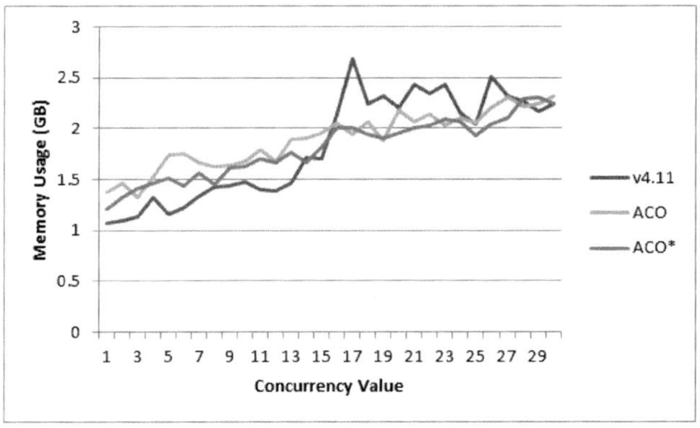

Figure 4. Memory usage.

In terms of concurrent execution time, when the concurrency value is less than 5, the execution time of two load balancing version is longer than the original version with the mean difference of 1.33 seconds. when the concurrency value is greater than 5, the execution time of two load balancing version is shorter than v4.11 with the mean difference of 5.035 seconds. As for the two load balancing version, when the concurrency value is less than 5, the improved ant colony optimization algorithm has little difference with ant colony optimization algorithm with the mean difference of 0.21 seconds. When the concurrency value is greater than 5, the gap of the execution time increases with the mean difference of 1.17 seconds.

In terms of memory usage, when the concurrency value is less than 15, the memory usage of two load balancing version is higher than v4.11 with the mean difference of 255 Mb. When the concurrency value is greater than 15, the memory usage of two load balancing version become less than v4.11 with the mean difference of 235 Mb. As for the two load balancing version, the memory usage between them only have a small gap with the mean difference of 65 Mb.

5. CONCLUSION

Marine surveillance intelligent detection system applied with load balancing mechanism improves on concurrent execution efficiency and stability than the original version. However, with the limit of load scheduling framework, the memory usage of the new version increased slightly than the original version, which will be studied and improved in further research. Meanwhile, the execution time of the optimized algorithm performs better than the original algorithm with little memory usage difference.

ACKNOWLEDGEMENT

This paper is supported by Qingdao innovation and entrepreneurship leading talent project (13-cx-2), Shandong province science and technology project (2013GHY11519) and Qingdao strategic industry development project (13-4-1-15-HY).

REFERENCES

- [1] Dorigo M, Gambardella L M. Ant colony system: a cooperative learning approach to the traveling salesman problem [J]. Evolutionary Computation, IEEE Transactions on, IEEE, 1997, 1(1): 53–66.
- [2] Stützle T, Hoos H H. MAX--MIN ant system [J]. Future generation computer systems, Elsevier, 2000, 16(8): 889–914.
- [3] Gambardella L M, Dorigo M. Solving Symmetric and Asymmetric TSPs by Ant Colonies.[A]. International conference on evolutionary computation[C]. 1996: 622–627.
- [4] Dorigo M, Gambardella L M. Ant colonies for the travelling salesman problem [J]. BioSystems, Elsevier, 1997, 43(2): 73–81.
- [5] Gaertner D, Clark K L. On Optimal Parameters for Ant Colony Optimization Algorithms. [A]. IC-AI[C]. 2005: 83–89.
- [6] Dorigo M, Birattari M. Ant colony optimization [A]. Encyclopedia of Machine Learning [M]. Springer, 2010: 36–39.
- [7] Stutzle T, Hoos H. MAX-MIN ant system and local search for the traveling salesman problem [A]. Evolutionary Computation, 1997, IEEE International Conference on [C]. 1997: 309–314.
- [8] Laguna M, Kelly J P, González-Velarde J. Tabu search for the multilevel generalized assignment problem [J]. European Journal of Operational Research, Elsevier, 1995, 82(1): 176–189.

Using Ant Colony Optimization and Cuckoo Search in AUV 3D Path Planning

X.L. Luan[1], F.X. Gong[2], Z.Q. Wei & B. Yin
College of Information Science and Engineering, Ocean University of China
Email: [1]578542663@qq.com, [2]gongfeixiang@gmail.com

Y.T. Sun
Institute of Oceanographic Instrumentation, Shandong Academy of Sciences.

ABSTRACT: People need a fast and efficient modeling method to describe the 3D of Marine environment. Three-dimensional modeling provides a precondition for the path planning. This paper introduces a way for modeling three-dimensional with ant colony optimization and cuckoo search which has strong robustness. The selection of the initial line is not high. Then the hybrid optimization does not need manual adjustment in the process, and its parameter is relatively small. Some simulations and experiments in this paper show that the ways with ant colony optimization and cuckoo search have a good performance in modeling three-dimensional path planning, the path is shorter than other algorithm. It prove that the method is effective both in establishing the corresponding data space, combining with the data for the path planning.

KEYWORDS: Three-dimensional modeling; Ant Colony Algorithm; Cuckoo Search; Path planning.

1. INTRODUCTION

With the improvement of science and technology, the human's exploration of Marine also is gradually strengthened. People need a fast and efficient modeling method to describe the 3D of Marine environment. The 3D spatial modeling is a means for computing, which put the real three-dimensional space into coordinate form in a certain way. Three-dimensional modeling is an important part of the three-dimensional path planning, because it provides a precondition for the path planning. A good 3D modeling of the space, can improve the efficiency of path planning.

Three dimensional path planning in underwater inspection, underwater exploration, development and salvage, sea life-saving, and other fields have a very important role. We need a kind of efficient path planning algorithm to realize the three-dimensional path addressing. The problem of three-dimensional path planning is mainly divided into two aspects: one is to extract the seabed environment, establish the corresponding data space; another is to use a reasonable algorithm, which is combined with the data for the path planning.

Ant colony algorithm (ACO) has strong robustness, compared with other algorithms, the require of selection of the initial line is not high. Ant colony algorithm does not need manual adjustment in the process, and its parameter is relatively small, so the ant colony algorithm can be applied to the underwater three-dimensional path planning problem.

Advantages of CS over other optimization algorithms are [1]:

- Simplicity, flexibility and robustness
- Use of fewer control parameters compared to many other search techniques.
- Ease of hybridization with other optimization algorithms.

This study proposes hybrid optimization technique with ACO and Cuckoo Search (CS) for optimization of path planning.

2. RELATED WORDS

People have adopted some algorithms to explore the problem of path planning in the three dimensional space:

In Hao Yanling's paper [2], she put the application of genetic algorithm to the path planning problem of AUV. According to the different characteristics of 3 d terrain in the path, the path is divided into three types. Using the penalty function and heuristic knowledge, they can realize the optimal path planning problem; Duan Junjie [3] compared the advantages and disadvantages of the global path planning, the real-time path planning and dynamic path planning; Kevin P Caroll [4] used A * search path planning method in three dimensional space; In addition, there are artificial potential field method and case-based reasoning method and so on. On the path planning problem in three-dimensional space, these algorithms have certain limitations exist compared with ant colony algorithm, so this paper uses ant colony algorithm to realize the three dimensional space.

Three-dimensional path planning based on ant colony algorithm, and also has carried on the related research. In many papers [5][6], the robot's initial position is set to S, the end position is set to D, and put the obstacle Oi as sphere, to establish 3D space rectangular Cartesian coordinate system. For the convenience of the study, he put the origin of coordinates on S, let the positive direction of axis Z via D, so that obstacles are between the plane that parallel to the OXY plane and pass through s and the OXY plane.

In the perpendicular direction of axis Z, put the space into N+1 equal pieces, then in each plane make sure the X axis and the Y axis is divided into 2M parts in the direction positive and negative positive and negative, so that each point in the coordinate system can be represented.

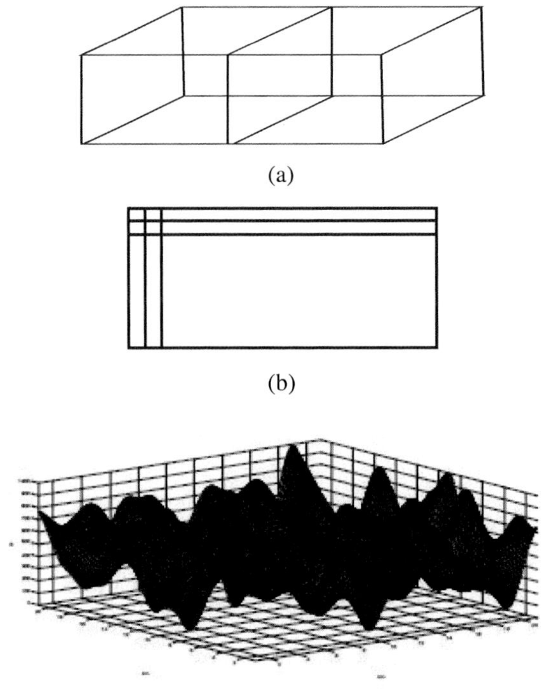
(a)

(b)

(c)

Figure 1. The process of 3D environment modeling.

3. ENVIRONMENTAL MODELING

The 3D spatial modeling is a means for computing, which put the real three-dimensional space into coordinate form in a certain way. Three-dimensional modeling is an important part of the three-dimensional path planning, because it provides a precondition for the path planning. A good 3D modeling of the space, can improve the efficiency of path planning.

In our paper, we used Liqiang Liu's [7] method to describe the 3D space. The abstract modeling of 3D environment space uses the equal grid point's method, which is based on the 3D seabed terrain data. As shown in the picture, taking the point which corresponded the point in the chart with the minimum longitude, the minimum latitude and the deepest point as the coordinate origin O (or A), the OX axis follows the latitude degree increment direction and passes the point O in the sea level. The OY axis follows the longitude degree increment direction and passes the point O in the sea level. The OZ axis is the perpendicular of the sea level, which pass the point O and upward to the sea level. According to the z axis direction that space can be divided into n plane, the distance between each plane is equal. (Fig. 1 (a)) The next step, in each plane make sure the X axis and the Y axis is divided into 2M parts in the positive direction, so that each point in the coordinate system can be represented. (Fig. 1 (b)) Finally, we use MATLAB to describe space as shown in figure 1.(c).

4. METHODOLOGY

4.1. *Ant Colony Optimization (ACO)*

Ant colony algorithm is a kind of intelligent optimization algorithm, biomimetic has found that ants transfer information between individuals through a material called pheromone, ants can sense this substance, and so as to guide the direction. Therefore, when a large number of ants take action collective, the more through a path of ants, the greater probability the newcomers choose the path, and finally ant colony can find the shortest path between food source and the nest [8].

Three-dimensional path planning problem of environment model is the manner in which the discrete point set S * said, these discrete points in corresponding solution of ant colony algorithm namely the nodes in the graph. If the connection between each discrete point set S * as pheromone storage carrier, the space complexity of the algorithm will be unable to bear. Therefore, we adopt the node representation, the pheromone is stored in the environment model of discrete point, arbitrary point corresponding to a pheromone values, the size of the pheromone amount on behalf of the discrete points on the degree of attract ants. This method greatly reduces the space complexity of the algorithm.

First of all, according to the initial position and the final location of plane, determine the path to the area, make the barrier between the two surfaces. In this way, the path of the main direction for the direction of x or y direction, the direction is the forward direction of underwater robots. Through this method, when choosing the path, it can be simplified as a choosing probability problem of point when the robot wants to go to the next plane. So, when the direction of x axis is the main direction, it can be expressed as the following formula:

$$P(x+1,y,z)=\begin{cases}\dfrac{\tau^{\alpha}_{x+1,y,z}\cdot H^{\beta}_{x+1,y,z}}{\sum \tau^{\alpha}_{x+1,y,z}\cdot H^{\beta}_{x+1,y,z}} & \textit{Feasible point}\\ 0 & \textit{else}\end{cases} \quad (1)$$

(1) α and β are the coefficients which representative of relative important grade of the factors above.

(2) $\tau_{x+1,y,z}$ is the pheromone amounts saved in the node $(x+1, y, z)$ in the next plane.

(3) H is the heuristic function.

Heuristic function is an important component of the path planning algorithm in 3D space. It plays an important role for fast, efficient and high quality planning a feasible path. The factors considered in the function represent the optimization criteria of the algorithm in the path construction. In this paper, we consider the shortest path and safety factors, to find the shortest path in a safe situation. The heuristic function $H(x, y, z)$ of the arbitrary point (x, y, z) in the environment abstract model designed according to this standard is shown as follows:

$$H(x,y,z)=[T(x,y,z)]^{\varphi}[S(x,y,z)]^{\lambda} \quad (2)$$

Where $S(x, y, z)$ is the safety factors for the consideration of environmental obstacles, $T(x, y, z)$ is the factors of quick navigation (the shortest path); φ and λ are the coefficients which representative of relative important grade of the factors above.

Pheromone update consists of two parts, which are local pheromone trail update and global pheromone trail update. Local pheromone trail is updated in the process of path construction; the update method is shown as follows:

$$\tau_{(x,y,z)}=(1-\xi)\cdot\tau_{(x,y,z)}+\xi\cdot\tau_0 \quad (3)$$

Where $\xi(0<\xi<1)$ is a parameter, τ_0 is the initial value of each feasible point.

Global pheromone trail is updated after all ant have constructed its path. In the algorithm, the evaluate value of each ant's path is computed by equation as follows:

$$f_{eval}(m)=\sum_{x=1}^{n+1}L_m(x) \quad (4)$$

Global pheromone update method is shown as follows:

$$\tau_{(x,y,z)}=(1-\rho)\cdot\tau_{(x,y,z)}+\rho\cdot\Delta\tau_{(x,y,z)} \quad (5)$$

$$\Delta\tau_{(x,y,z)}=\frac{1}{\min_m[f_{eval}(m)]} \quad (6)$$

Where $f_{eval}(m)$ is the evaluate value of the NO. m ant's path, and $L_m(x)$ is the length of the NO. x path section in the NO. mant's path, ρ (0< ρ <1) is evaporation factor.

4.2. *Cuckoo search*

4.2.1. *Cuckoo behavior*

Cuckoo is fascinating birds [9], not only because of the beautiful sounds they can make, but also because of their aggressive reproduction strategy. Some species such as the ani and Guira cuckoos lay their eggs in communal nests, though they may remove others' eggs to increase the hatching probability of their own eggs [10]. Quite a number of species engage the obligate brood parasitism by laying their eggs in the nests of other host birds (often other species). There are three basic types of brood parasitism: intraspecific brood parasitism, cooperative breeding, and nest takeover. Some host birds can engage direct conflict with the intruding cuckoos. If a host bird discovers the eggs are not it owns, it will either throw these alien eggs away or simply abandons its nest and builds a new nest elsewhere. Some cuckoo species such as the New World brood-parasitic Tapera have evolved in such a way that female parasitic cuckoos are often very specialized in the mimicry in color and pattern of the eggs of a few chosen host species [10]. This reduces the probability of their eggs being abandoned and thus increases their reproductivity.

4.2.2. *Efficiency of Lévy flights*

In nature, animals search for food in a random or quasi-random manner. In general, the foraging path of an animal is effectively a random walk because the next move is based on the current location / state and the transition probability to the next location. Which direction it chooses depends implicitly on a probability which can be modeled mathematically. For example, various studies have shown that the flight behavior of many animals and insects has demonstrated the typical characteristics of Levy flights [11, 12, 13].

A recent study by Reynolds and Frye shows that fruit flies or Drosophila melanogaster; explore their land scape using a series of straight flight paths punctuated by a sudden 90o turn, leading to a Lévy-flight-style intermittent scale-free search pattern [12]. Even light can be related to Lévy flights [14]. Subsequently, such behavior has been applied to optimization and optimal search, and preliminary results show its promising capability [13].

When generating new solutions $x^{(t+1)}$ for, say, a cuckoo i, a Lévy flight is performed

$$x_i^{(t+1)} = x_i^{(t)} + \alpha \oplus L(\lambda) \quad (7)$$

Where $\alpha > 0$ is the step size which should be related to the scales of the problem of interests. In most cases, we can use $\alpha = 1$. The above equation is essentially the stochastic equation for random walk. In general, a random walk is a Markov chain whose next status/location only depends on the current location (the first term in the above equation) and the transition probability (the second term). The product $\oplus$ means entry wise multiplications.

The Lévy flight essentially provides a random walk while the random step length is drawn from a Lévy distribution

$$L(s,\lambda) \sim u = t^{-\lambda},\ (1 < \lambda \le 3) \quad (8)$$

which has an infinite variance with an infinite mean. Here the steps essentially form a random walk process with a power law step-length distribution with a heavy tail. Some of the new solutions should be generated by Lévy walk around the best solution obtained so far, this will speed up the local search.

According to the above algorithm, we use the MATLAB simulation of three-dimensional path planning, simulation results are shown below:

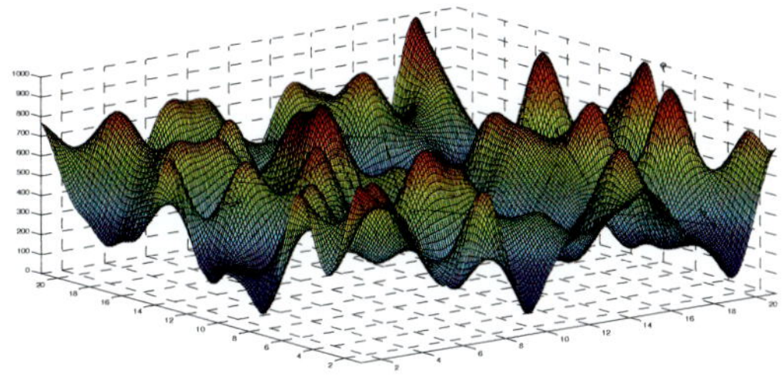

Figure 2. 3D view under certain visual angle.

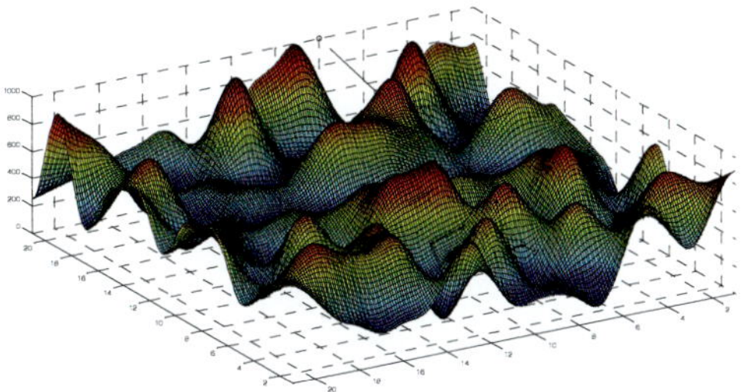

Figure 3. 3D view under certain visual angle.

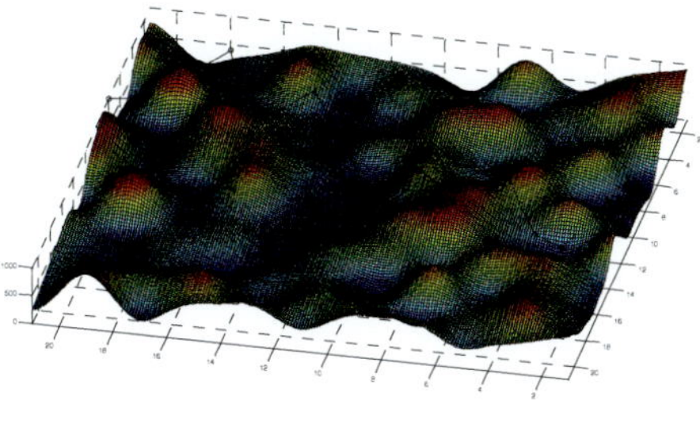

Figure 4. 3D view under certain visual angle.

5. CONCLUSION

Summary, this paper describes an effective method for modeling three-dimensional with Ant Colony Optimization and Cuckoo Search, it does not need manual adjustment in the process, and its parameters is relatively small, and have good performance both in establishing the corresponding data space, combining with the data for the path planning.

ACKNOWLEDGEMENT

*This research is supported by the Qingdao innovation and entrepreneurship leading talent project (13-cx-2), Qingdao strategic industry development project (13-4-1-15-HY) Shandong province science and technology project (2013GHY11519).

REFERENCES

-[1] Kaveh, A., & Bakhshpoori, T. (2012). Optimum design of space trusses using Cuckoo Search algorithm with Lévy flights. Iranian J Sci Technol, Vol. 37, pp.1-15.

-[2] Hao Yanling, Zhang Jingjuan. AUV Path Planning in 3D Seabed Environment Using Genetic Algorithm, Engineering Science, 2003.11.

-[3] Duan Qunjie. Research on Real Time Path Planning Method of Autonomous Underwater Vehicle, Harbin Engineering University, 2010.04.

-[4] Kevin P Caroll, Stephen R McClaran, Eric L Nelson, et al. AUV Path Planning: An A* Approach to Path Planning width Consideration of Variable Vehicle Speeds and Multiple, Overlapping, Time-Dependent Exclusion Zones [C] Proc. Symp. on AUV Technology, Washington DC: IEEE, 1992: 79-84.

-[5] Hu Hui, Cai Xiu-Shan. Path Planning of Robots in 3D Space Based on an Improved Ant Colony Algorithm College of Mathematics, Physics and Information Engineering, Zhejiang Normal University, Jinhua 321004, China.

-[6] Hu Xiaobing, Huang Xiyue. Path planning in 3-D space for robot based on ant colony algorithm, Journal of Chongqing University (Natural Science Edition), 2004.08

-[7] Liqiang Liu, Yuntao Dai. 3D Space Path Planning of Complex Environmental Underwater Vehicle, 2009 International Joint Conference on Computational Sciences and Optimization.

-[8] Peng Meng, Tengfei Ning. Path Planning Based on Hybrid Adaptive Ant Colony Algorithm for AUV 2012 11th International Symposium on Distributed Computing and Applications to Business, Engineering & Science.

-[9] Xin-She Yang, Suash Deb. Multiobjective cuckoo search for design optimization. Computers & Operations Research, 40 (2013) 1616–1624.

-[10] Payne RB, Sorenson MD, Klitz K. The cuckoos. Oxford University Press, 2005.

-[11] Brown C, Liebovitch LS, Glendon R. Lévy flights in Dobe Ju/'hoansi foraging patterns. Human Ecology 2007; 35: 129–38.

-[12] Reynolds AM, Frye MA. Free-flight odor tracking in Drosophila is consistent with an optimal intermittent scale-free search. PLoS One 2007; 2:e354.
-[13] Pavlyukevich I. Lévy flights, non-local search and simulated annealing. Journal of Computational Physics 2007; 226:1830–44.
-[14] Barthelemy P, Bertolotti J, Wiersma DS. A Lévy flight for light. Nature 2008; 453:495–8.

The Optimization of Sensing Delay in Cognitive Small Cell: A Fast Algorithm to Find Sequential Sensing Order

Q.F. Che
Hexi University, College of Information Technology and Communication, Zhang Ye, Gansu, China
Email: mmnown@163.com

Y. Fang
Hexi University, College of Information Technology and Communication, Zhang Ye, Gansu, China

ABSTRACT: This paper studies the problem of low delay oriented optimal sequential sensing order in cognitive small cell (CSC). CSC is a promising technology in the evolving 5G networks, which could opportunistically use the free channels unoccupied. The finding of idle channels could be carried out via spectrum sensing. We propose a sensing delay oriented fast sequential sensing order discovery algorithm. The capacities of channels, idle probabilities of channels, sensing delay and the target resource are jointly considered. The theoretic analysis gives out the sensing order decision condition. The computing complex of the proposed algorithm is also analyzed. Simulation results show that the proposed approach outperforms existing methods.

KEYWORDS: Cognitive small cell; Sequential sensing order; Sensing delay.

1. INTRODUCTION

The 5G network [1] has been drawn widely attention recently, which is expected to be composed of heterogeneous small cells, such as fem-to-cells, micro-cells and so on. The small cell would play an extreme important role in the spectrum discovery and access management. Specially, the cognitive small cell (CSC) [2] is expected to have certain degree of intelligence. The intelligence includes the capability of discovering the idle channels, which are not occupied by other users currently. The discovery of the idle channels could be realized by the technology of spectrum sensing, which is a widely used method in the cognitive radio. The spectrum sensing has been widely studied in cognitive radio related references [3-4]. In the widely used energy spectrum sensing, the CSC considers a channel free if the power received on that channel is smaller than the spectrum sensing threshold.

The 5G network is time delay sensitive. For the CSC, the fast discovery of idle channels among multi possible channels is very important. Sequential sensing is one important type of channel discovery, which could achieve high spectrum utility. One of the key problems is the sensing order of the multi channels. There are also some researches about the sensing order among the cognitive radio networks. Authors in [5] investigated the optimal sensing sequence in a multichannel cognitive MAC protocol. Sensing the channels in descending order of their achievable rates was proposed in [6]. Authors in [7] minimize the delay in discovering a single channel by descending order of the idle probabilities. The traffic based sequential sensing was proposed in [8]. Authors in [9] studied the optimal channel sequential sensing by finding the optimal sensing time. The strategy to determine the sensing channel and the time to transmit was proposed in [10]. However, rare works jointly considered the capacities of channels, idle probabilities of channels, sensing delay and the target resource.

In this paper, we focus on the low delay oriented optimal sequential sensing order in cognitive small cell (CSC). We propose a sensing delay oriented fast sequential sensing order discovery algorithm, considering the capacities of channels, idle probabilities of channels, sensing delay and the target resource. The computing complex of the proposed algorithm is also analyzed. Simulation results show that the proposed approach outperforms existing methods.

2. SYSTEM MODEL

We consider a network consisting of N channels, and the period of the slotted frame is T [2]. The CSC senses channels one by one through the energy spectrum sensing, until the target resource is obtained, i.e., the CSC needs find the target spectrum bandwidth before stopping the channel sensing. Denote the capacity of channel n as R_n, the idle probability of channel n as I_n, the on or off state of the channel n is denoted as S_n, the sensing time need for sensing channel n is denoted as τ_n. The target sensing resource is denoted by R_{need}.

Denoted a channel sensing order as $S=\{s_1,s_2,...,s_N\}$. The CSC carries out energy spectrum sensing on channel one by one to find the idle channels, until the target sensing resource R_{need} is achieved. The purpose of the sensing optimization is to minimize the sensing delay for obtaining the target sensing resource R_{need}, i.e.,

$$S^* = \arg\min \mathrm{E}\left[\sum_{i=1}^{N} \tau_{s_i}\right] \quad st. \ \sum_{j=1}^{i-1} R_{s_j}\left(1-S_{s_j}\right) < R_{need} \tag{1}$$

Considering all the possible state of the channels, the average sensing delay of the given sensing order $S=\{s_1,s_2,...,s_N\}$ is given by:

$$\tau^S = \sum_{S_{s_1}=0}^{1}\sum_{S_{s_2}=0}^{1}\cdots\sum_{S_{s_N}=0}^{1}\left\{\begin{array}{l}\left(1-I_{s_j}\right)^{S_{s_j}}\left(I_{s_j}\right)^{1-S_{s_j}} \\ \prod_{j=1}^{N} \times \left(\begin{array}{l} I_{s_1}^{S} + \\ \sum_{j=2}^{N} I_{s_j}^{S}\,\delta\left(\sum_{m=1}^{j-1} R_{s_m}\left(1-S_{o_m}\right) < B_{need}\right)\end{array}\right)\end{array}\right\} \tag{2}$$

Obviously, the exhausive searching approach could achieve the optimal sensing order. However, the computing complexy would be extremely high when the number of channels is large. The purpose is to find a low computing complexy algorithm.

3. THE FAST ORDER SEARCHING ALGORITHM

Denote the optimal sensing order as $S^*=\left(s_1,s_2,...,s_{k-1},s_k,s_{k+1},s_{k+2},...,s_N\right)$, and the counter sensing order is $S'=\left(s_1,s_2,...,s_{k-1},s_{k+1},s_k,s_{k+2},...,s_N\right)$ by exchange the k-th sensing channel in the order. For the optimal sensing order S^*, we have:

$$\begin{aligned}\tau_{B_{need}}^{S} &= \tau_{S_{k-1},B_{need}}^{S} \\ &+ \Pr\left(\sum\nolimits_{s_i\in O_{k-1}} R_{s_i}\delta\left(S_{s_i}=0\right)<B_{need}\right)\tau_{s_k}^{S} \\ &+ \Pr\left(\sum R_{s_i}\delta\left(S_{s_i}=0\right)<B\right)\tau_{s_{k+1}}^{S} \\ &+ \Pr\left(\sum R_{s_i}\delta\left(S_{s_i}=0\right)<B\right)\tau_{S_{k+1}^{-},B_{need}}^{S}\end{aligned} \tag{3}$$

Similarly, for sensing order S', we have:

$$\begin{aligned}\tau_{B_{need}}^{S'} &= \tau_{S_{k-1},B_{need}}^{S'} \\ &+ \Pr\left(\sum\nolimits_{s_i\in O_{k-1}} R_{s_i}\delta\left(S_{s_i}=0\right)<B_{need}\right)\tau_{s_k}^{S'} \\ &+ \Pr\left(\sum R_{s_i}\delta\left(S_{s_i}=0\right)<B\right)\tau_{s_{k+1}}^{S'} \\ &+ \Pr\left(\sum R_{s_i}\delta\left(S_{s_i}=0\right)<B\right)\tau_{S_{k+1}'^{\sim},B_{need}}^{S'}\end{aligned} \tag{4}$$

Because the S^* is the optimal sensing order, then

$$\tau_{B_{need}}^{S} \le \tau_{B_{need}}^{S'} \tag{5}$$

Combining equation (3), (4) and (5), we have

$$\begin{aligned}&\frac{\tau_{s_k}^{S}}{I_{s_k}\left(\Pr\left(\sum_{s_i\in S_{k-1}} R_{s_i}\delta\left(S_{s_i}=0\right)<B_{need}\right)-\Pr\left(\sum_{s_i\in S_{k-1}} R_{s_i}\delta\left(S_{s_i}=0\right)<B_{need}-R_{s_k}\right)\right)} \\ &\le \frac{\tau_{s_{k+1}}^{S}}{I_{s_{k+1}}\left(\Pr\left(\sum_{s_i\in S_{k-1}} R_{s_i}\delta\left(S_{s_i}=0\right)<B_{need}\right)-\Pr\left(\sum_{s_i\in S_{k-1}} R_{s_i}\delta\left(S_{s_i}=0\right)<B_{need}-R_{s_{k+1}}\right)\right)}\end{aligned} \tag{6}$$

Focusing on the first channel of the remained channels, we have:

$$\tau_{B_{need}}^{S^*} \le \tau_{B_{need}}^{S'} \Leftrightarrow \tau_{S_k}^{S} I_{S_{k+1}} - \tau_{S_{k+1}}^{S} I_{S_k} \le 0 \tag{7}$$

The analysis result tells us that the optimal sensing channel in the next slot would be determined by equation (7). The exhaustive searching would not be needed. Finding the next channel to sensing according to equation (7) would be a much fast algorithm.

4. THE COMPLEXITY ANALYSIS

With the exhaustive searching algorithm, the computing complexity would be $O(N!)$. However, with the proposed fast algorithm, there are $N-k+1$ strategies to compare at the k-th step, then the computing complexity would be:

$$N+(N-1)+...+1 = N(N+1)/2 \sim O\left(N^2\right) \tag{8}$$

which is much lower than the exhaustive searching algorithm.

5. NUMERICAL RESULTS AND DISCUSSIONS

We verify the proposed approach by the MATLAB simulation. Without the generality, the system is set up as follows: the number of channels is 12. The channel capacity is $R=[1,1.5,2,2.5,3,3.5,4,4.5,5,5.5,6,6.5]$ M bit/s, the sensing delay for channels is $\tau=[25,22,20,18,16,14,11,9,7,5,3,1]$ ms. We simulate the average delays for different target resources to verify the algorithm's performance. The result is the average value of 1000 independent experiments.

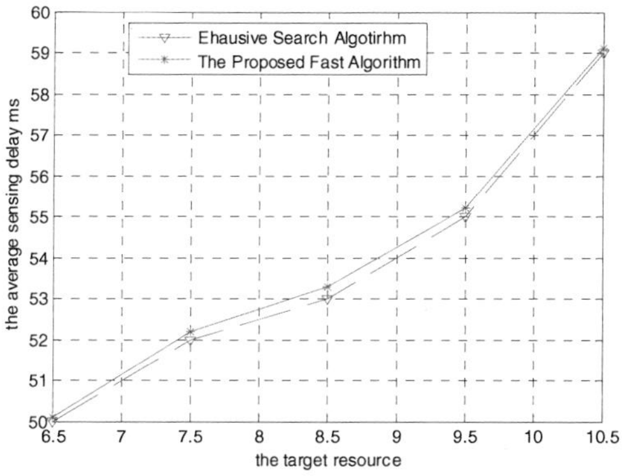

Figure 1. The average sensing delay.

Fig. 1 shows that the proposed algorithm achieves almost the same performance with the exhausive searching algorithm. In other words, the proposde fast algorithm is almost the optimal method. The average sensing delay would increase when the target resource increases, because the number of the idle channels need to be found would increase.

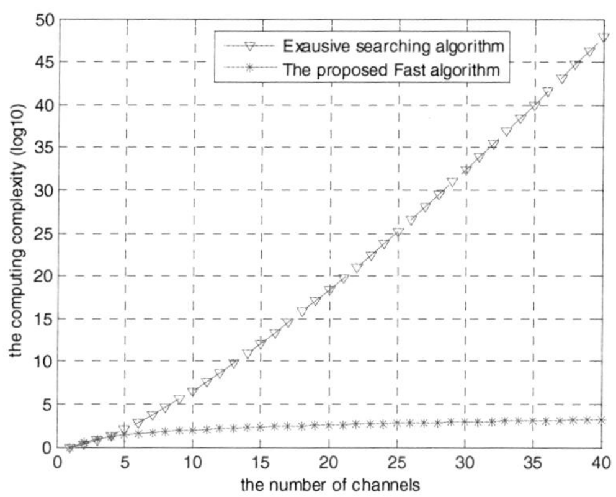

Figure 2. The computing complexity comparison.

Fig. 2 shows that the proposed fast algorithm is much lower computing complexity compared with the exhausive searching algorithm, especially when the number of channels is large. The traditional exhausive searching algorithm would not be carried in practical scenarios because the computing complexity is too high when there are much channels to be sensed.

In all, the proposed fast algorithm could achieve almost the same performance with the exhausive searching algorithm, but with much lower computing complexity, which provides a practical solution to the sequential channel sensing problem.

6. CONCLUSIONS

This paper proposed a sensing delay oriented fast sequential sensing order discovery algorithm for the CSC, by jointly considering the capacities of channels, idle probabilities of channels, sensing delay and the target resource. The finding of idle channels could be carried out via spectrum sensing. The theoretic analysis gives out the sensing order decision condition. The computing complex of the proposed algorithm is also analyzed. Simulation results show that the proposed approach outperforms existing methods.

REFERENCES

— [1] P. Demestichas and A. Georgakopoulos, "5G on the horizon: Key challenges for the radio-access network," IEEE Vehicular Technology Magazine, pp. 47-53, Sep. 2013.
— [2] Hesham ElSawy and Ekram Hossain, Dong In Kim, "HetNets with Cognitive Small Cells: User Offloading and Distributed Channel Access Techniques," IEEE Communications Magazine, Jun. 2013.
— [3] Changhua Yao and QihuiWu, "A Hybrid Combination Scheme for Cooperative Spectrum Sensing in Cognitive Radio Networks," DOI: 10.1155/2014/106106, Mathematical Problems in Engineering, 2014.
— [4] Changhua Yao and Qihui Wu, "Traffic Based Optimization of Spectrum Sensing in Cognitive Radio Networks," DOI: 10.1155/2014/349350, Mathematical Problems in Engineering, 2014.
— [5] H. Jiang, L. Lai, R. Fan, and V. Poor, "Optimal selection of channel sensing order in cognitive radio," IEEE Trans. Wireless Commun., vol. 8, no. 1, pp. 297-307, Jan. 2009.
— [6] H. T. Cheng, W. Zhuang, "Simple channel sensing order in cognitive radio networks," IEEE J. Sel. Areas Commun., vol. 29, no. 4, pp. 676-688, Apr. 2011.
— [7] H. Kim, K.G. Shin, "Efficient Discovery Spectrum Opportunities with MAC-Layer Sensing in Cognitive Radio Networks," IEEE Trans. Mobile Computing, vol. 7, no. 5, pp. 533-545, May. 2008.
— [8] Changhua Yao, Qihui Wu and Yuhua Xu, "Sequential Channel Sensing in Cognitive Small Cell Based on User Traffic", vol. 19, no. 4, pp. 637-640 IEEE Communications Letters, April. 2015.
— [9] T. Shu and M. Krunz, "Throughput-Efficient Sequential Channel Sensing and Probing in Cognitive Radio Networks Under Sensing Errors," Proc. ACM MobiCom, Sept. 2009.
— [10] N.B. Chang and M. Liu, "Optimal Channel Probing and Transmission Scheduling for Opportunistic Spectrum Access," Proc. ACM MobiCom, Sept. 2007.

An Algorithm for Generating EMD Mixed Mean Line Used to Extract Roughness Profile from Engineering Surfaces

H. Zhang & S.B. Liu*
Harbin Institute of Technology Shenzhen Graduate School, Shenzhen, China
**Email: mesbliu@hitsz.edu.cn*

ABSTRACT: Surface roughness of an engineering surface is composed of short-wavelength components, and it is formed by subtracting long-wavelength components from the raw profile of an engineering surface. A mean line is commonly used to express long-wavelength components during surface evaluation. In our previous research, we proposed an EMD mean line to separate surface roughness profile from raw profile, but it suffers from some deviations at two ends of an evaluation length. This article tries to overcome the problem by using an EMD mixed mean line. Firstly, Empirical Mode Decomposition (EMD) is utilized to decompose the raw surface profile into a series of Intrinsic Mode Functions (IMFs) and a residue. Secondly, IMFs with frequency less than 10 within an evaluation length and the residue, are selected for reconstructing an EMD reference line. An Amplitude Weighting Factor (AWF) is further applied to the selected IMF with maximum frequency to form an EMD mean line. Finally, an EMD mixed mean line is created by mixing the middle segment of EMD mean line with the two boundary segments of EMD reference line. Varied Amplitude Weighting Factor (VAWF) is designed to complete and smooth the EMD mixed mean line. Experimental results show that the deviations at two ends are suppressed and the EMD mixed mean line is more accurate for roughness profile extraction.

KEYWORDS: Surface roughness profile; EMD; IMFs; Mean line.

1. INTRODUCTION

A typical engineering surface consists of roughness, waviness and form, which influences the performance of mechanical system (Whitehouse 2011, Boryczko 2010). To evaluate various roughness parameters, it is necessary to extract surface roughness profile. Surface roughness is composed of short-wavelength components. The extraction of roughness profile is realized by subtracting long-wavelength components from the raw profile of an engineering surface. Long-wavelength components are commonly expressed with a mean line during surface evaluation. The variations of engineering surface to the mean line are surface roughness.

Filtering methods are commonly adopted to determine the mean line of an engineering surface (Raja 2002). Gaussian filter determines a point of a mean line by averaging a local area of raw surface profile with Gaussian weighting factors. It is the most common filter in the assessment of surface morphology, but it suffers from edge distortion effects (ISO 1996, Yuan 2000). The Spline filter and Wavelet filter are recent advances in the filtering of engineering surface. Spline filter gets the mean line by solving a spline filtering equation which contains an unknown n-dimensional vector representing a mean line (ISO 2003, Krystek 1996). Wavelet filter decomposes raw surface profile into different frequency components based on a wavelet base, and uses low-frequency components to reconstruct the mean line. However, the mean line reconstructed from a same engineering surface is varied with different wavelet bases (Fu 2003).

Empirical Mode Decomposition (EMD) can be used to analyze nonlinear and time-varying signal (Huang 1998). The empirical mode decomposition is self-adaptive and doesn't need any base function. A complex signal can be decomposed into a series of Intrinsic Mode Functions (IMFs) and a residue. In theory, the EMD method can be used for decomposition of any type of time-signal, especially for non-stationary and nonlinear signals. In our previous research, we proposed an EMD mean line based on empirical mode decomposition. The EMD mean line can be used to separate surface roughness profile from raw profile (Liu & Zhang 2015), but it exhibits weak edge effects at two ends of an evaluation length.

In this paper, an EMD mixed mean line is further proposed to overcome the problem. For a raw profile of an engineering surface, EMD decomposes it into a series of IMFs with different frequency and a residue. An EMD reference line is first constructed with the IMFs of low frequency. By applying an Amplitude Weighting Factor (AWF) to the selected IMF with maximum frequency, an EMD mean line is then formed. The EMD mixed mean line is further created by mixing the middle segment of EMD mean line with the two boundary segments of EMD reference line. The roughness profile is thus separated based on the new mean line, and roughness parameters are calculated.

2. IMFS OF RAW PROFILE AND DEFINITION OF IMF FREQUENCY

2.1. *Generation of IMFs*

The EMD decomposes a signal into many components called IMFs. The implementation of EMD is a sifting process generating IMFs. For a raw surface profile $x(t)$ as shown in Figure 1(a), the EMD algorithm is described as follows:

Algorithm EMD

1) Pick out all maxima and minima of $x(t)$.

2) Fit the maximum envelope $e_{max}(t)$ of $x(t)$ by passing a natural cubic spline through the maxima. Similarly, fit the minimum envelope $e_{min}(t)$ with the minima.

3) Compute the mean, $r(t) = (e_{max}(t) + e_{min}(t)) / 2$.

4) Check whether $r(t)$ is a monotonic function. If yes, let $r_n = r(t)$, and terminate the sifting procedure; If no, continue the next step.

5) Compute the new sequence $m_i(t) = x(t) - r(t)$.

6) Check whether $m_i(t)$ is an IMF. If $m_i(t)$ is not an IMF, let $x(t)= m_i(t)$, and turn to the step 1); If $m_i(t)$ is an IMF, then let set $c_i(t) = m_i(t)$, and $x(t) = x(t) - c_i(t)$, and turn to the step 1).

Once the sifting procedure is completed, n-empirical modes of the surface profile are extracted. Then the $x(t)$ is expressed as

$$x(t) = \sum_{i=1}^{n} c_i(t) + r_n(t) \qquad (1)$$

where $r_n(t)$ is the residue (not an IMF), $c_i(t)$ is an IMF, a special wave with varied amplitude. Figure 1 illustrates a raw surface profile, the last four IMFs, and a residue.

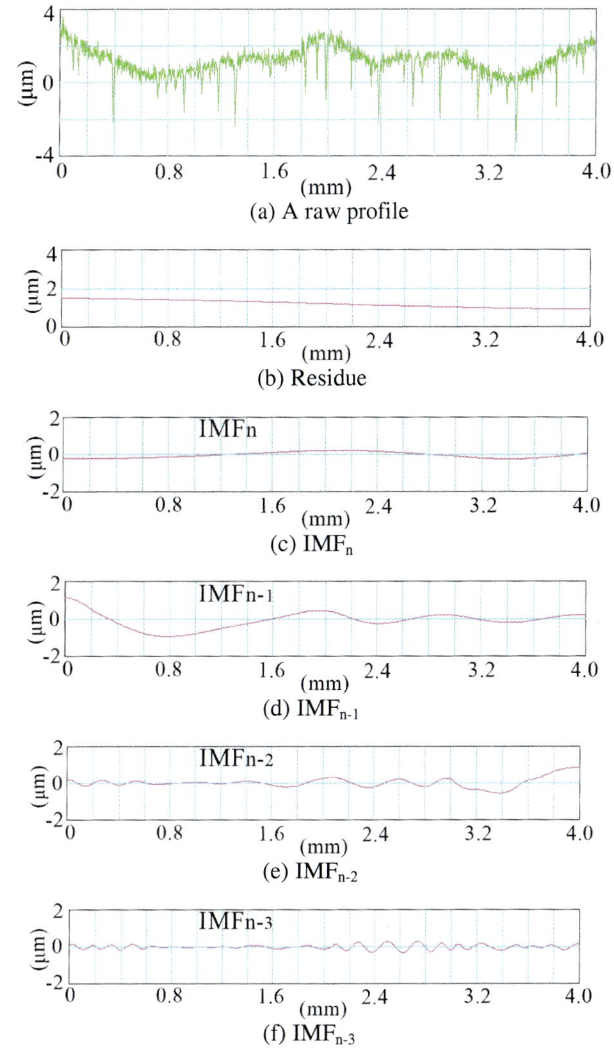

Figure 1. The measured raw profile (a) is decomposed into a residue (b), and a series of IMFs where the last four IMFs are presented in (c)-(f).

2.2. *Calculation of IMF frequency*

The frequency of an IMF within a unit length (1 mm) is defined as the average value of the individual quarter-wave's frequency covered by the evaluation length. It can be expressed as

$$f = \frac{1}{m} \sum_{i=1}^{m} \omega_i \qquad (2)$$

where f is the frequency of an IMF within a unit length, ω_i is the frequency of the i-th quarter-wave within a unit length, m is the total number of the quarter-waves covered by the evaluation length, while a quarter-wave is defined as an interval from a cross-zero point to its consecutive extreme point, or from an extreme point to its consecutive cross-zero point.

To calculate the frequency of the i-th quarter-wave within a unit length, ω_i, seven period values are involved where four period values, $T_{1,i}^1$, $T_{1,i}^2$, $T_{1,i}^3$ and $T_{1,i}^4$ are from four full-waves, two period values, $T_{2,i}^1$ and $T_{2,i}^2$ are from two half-waves, and one period value, $T_{4,i}$ is from a quarter-wave, as shown in Figure 2. It can be expressed as (Huang 2009)

$$\omega_i = \frac{1}{12}\left\{\frac{1}{T_{4,i}} + \left(\frac{1}{T_{2,i}^1} + \frac{1}{T_{2,i}^2}\right) + \left(\frac{1}{T_{1,i}^1} + \frac{1}{T_{1,i}^2} + \frac{1}{T_{1,i}^3} + \frac{1}{T_{1,i}^4}\right)\right\} \quad (3)$$

The frequency values of IMFs within an evaluation length can be calculated by the frequency values of IMFs within a unit length (1 mm) times the value of evaluation length in millimeter. The frequency values of IMFs corresponding to Figure 1(c)-(f) are shown in Table 1.

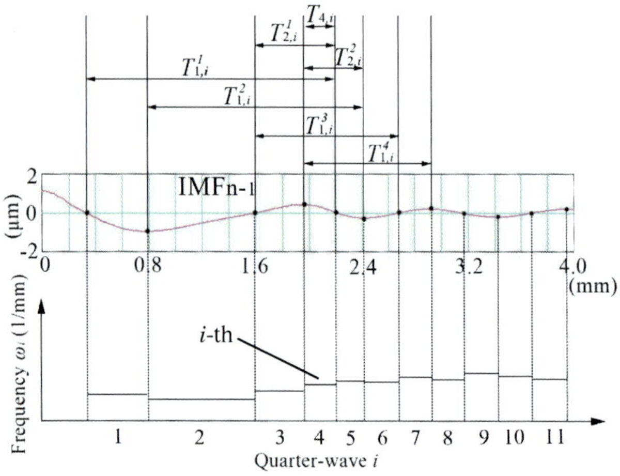

Figure 2. The full-wave periods, half-wave periods, and a quarter-wave period used to calculate the i-th quarter-wave's frequency ω_i within 1 mm.

Table 1. The frequency and wavelength of IMFs.

	IMF_{n-3}	IMF_{n-2}	IMF_{n-1}	IMF_n
Wavelength (mm)	0.1844	0.4188	1.0064	—
Frequency(1/mm)	5.4224	2.3877	0.9936	0
Frequency(1/4mm)	21.690	9.5508	3.9744	0

3. GENERATING EMD MIXED MEAN LINE

3.1. *Generation of EMD reference line*

In the field of surface evaluation, the frequency of trend profile of surface roughness is usually less than 2 within a cut-off length. Then we deduce that the frequency of an IMF should be less than 10 within an evaluation length, supposing that it is composed of five cut-off lengths. As a result, the IMFs of frequency less than 10 within an evaluation length are selected to reconstruct the EMD reference line. The EMD reference line is defined as

$$Reference = r_n(t) + c_n(t) + \cdots + c_{n-i}(t) \quad (4)$$

where *Reference* is the EMD reference line, $r_n(t)$ is the residue, $c_n(t)$ is the last IMF, $c_{n-i}(t)$ is the IMF with maximum frequency among the selected IMFs. According to Table 1, the frequency of IMF_n, IMF_{n-1}, IMF_{n-2}, satisfy the criterion. The EMD reference line is reconstructed by

$$Reference = r_n(t) + c_n(t) + c_{n-1}(t) + c_{n-2}(t)\,. \quad (5)$$

The comparison between an EMD reference line and a Gaussian mean line is shown in Figure 4. More details for Gaussian mean line via Gaussian filtering are presented in ISO 11562 (ISO 1996). According to Figure 4, it is obviously to see that the EMD reference line has some fluctuations in the middle relative to the Gaussian mean line but it follows well at two ends of the raw surface profile.

3.2. *Generation of EMD mean line*

To get a mean line which correlates well with Gaussian mean line in most locations, an Amplitude Weighting Factor (AWF), μ, is used to multiply the IMF whose frequency is the maximum among the selected IMFs. The EMD mean line is defined as

$$Mean = r_n(t) + c_n(t) + \cdots + \mu \bullet c_{n-i}(t) \quad (6)$$

where *Mean* is the EMD mean line, μ is an AWF ranged from 0.3 to 0.5 with a fixed value in the program. According to Table 1, μ should be applied to IMF_{n-2}. The EMD mean line is expressed by

$$Mean = r_n(t) + c_n(t) + c_{n-1}(t) + \mu \bullet c_{n-2}(t)\,. \quad (7)$$

Figure 3 shows an EMD mean line with μ=0.4. It can be found that the EMD mean line correlates well with Gaussian mean line in the middle locations but it suffers from weak edge effects at two ends.

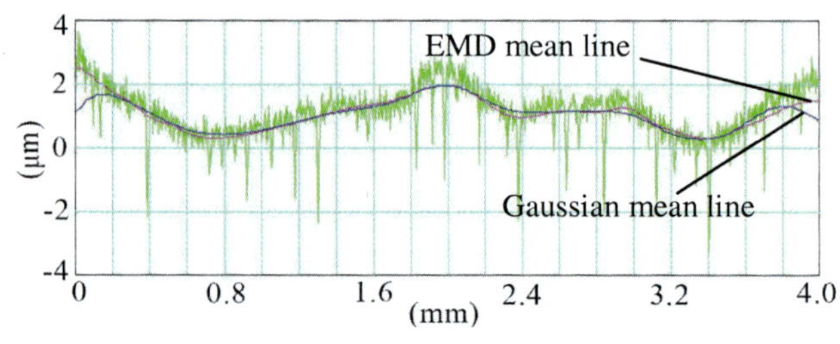

Figure 3. A comparison of Gaussian mean line and EMD mean line with μ=0.4.

3.3. *Generation of EMD mixed mean line with VAWF*

Figure 4 illustrates a comparison between EMD reference line, and EMD mean line, and Gaussian mean line. EMD reference line exhibits a good following capacity at two ends of the surface profile, but it has some fluctuations in the middle location relative to Gaussian mean line. EMD mean line correlates well with Gaussian mean line in the middle location, but it also has edge effects as those of Gaussian mean line.

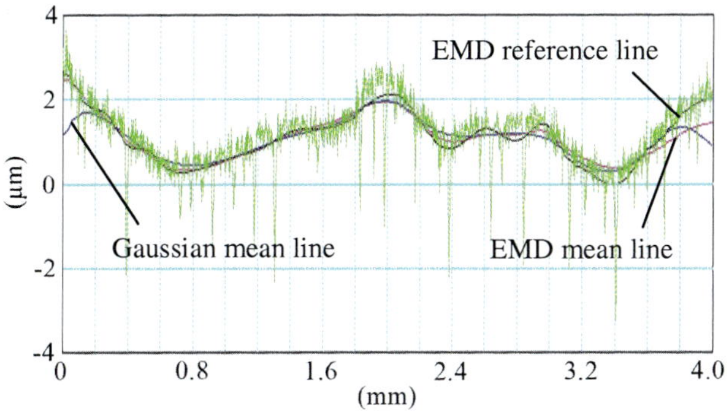

Figure 4. A comparison of EMD reference line, EMD mean line, and Gaussian mean line.

To suppress edge effects of EMD mean line, we propose a method to combine EMD mean line with EMD reference line, and to form a new mean line, named as EMD Mixed Mean Line. It will correlate well with Gaussian mean line and avoid edge effects.

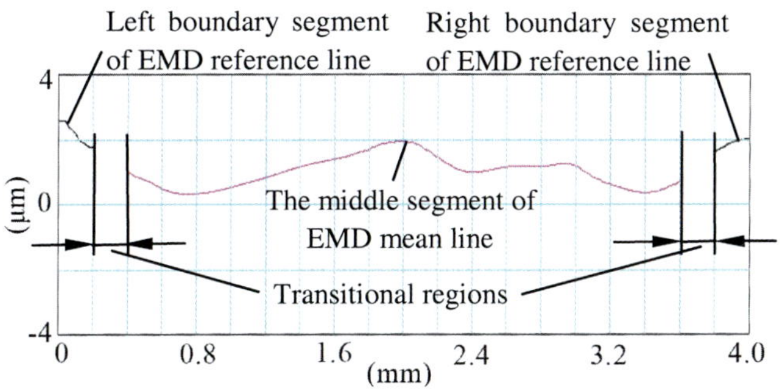

Figure 5. The middle segment and the two boundary segments used for constructing the EMD mixed mean line.

We define the middle segment of EMD mean line as the interval between the first half cut-off and the last half cut-off. It is used to constitute the middle segment of the new EMD mean line. We define the left boundary segment as the interval of the first quarter cut-off of EMD reference line, and define the right boundary segment as that of the last quarter cut-off. They are used to constitute the two boundary segments of the new EMD mean line. Two transitional segments are to be determined at the transitional regions, as shown in Figure 5.

To determine the transitional segments, the reconstructing process of the EMD reference line and the EMD mean line need to be analyzed. In the reconstructing of EMD reference line, the AWF applied to IMF_{n-2} is 1. In the reconstructing of EMD mean line, the AWF, μ applied to IMF_{n-2} are 0.4. As shown in Figure 6, we use a sine function in the transitional regions to connect the AWF curves smoothly. This results in varied AWF within an evaluation length, and it is named as Varied Amplitude Weighting Factor (VAWF).

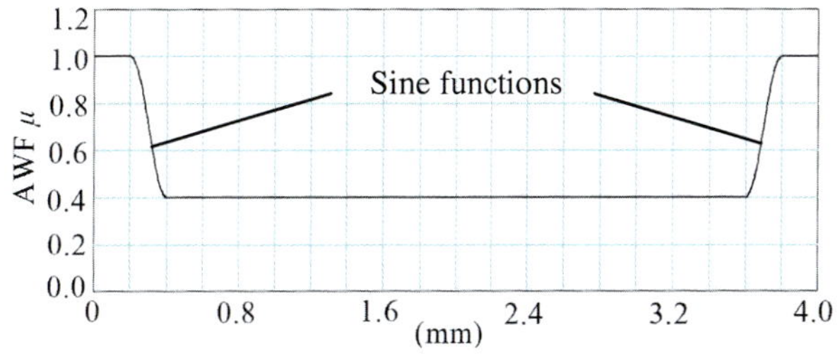

Figure 6. Varied Amplitude Weighting Factor constructing with sine functions.

To achieve an intelligent algorithm, the VAWF can be expressed with a diagonal matrix, A. Then, two transitional segments are given by

$$Mixed\ Line = r_n(t) + c_n(t) + c_{n-1}(t) + A \bullet c_{n-2}(t) \quad (8)$$

where A is a diagonal matrix, and it is given by

$$A = \begin{bmatrix} 1 & & & & & & & & & & & & 0 \\ & \ddots & & & & & & & & & & & \\ & & 1 & & & & & & & & & & \\ & & & \ddots & & & & & & & & & \\ & & & & t & & & & & & & & \\ & & & & & \ddots & & & & & & & \\ & & & & & & \mu & & & & & & \\ & & & & & & & \ddots & & & & & \\ & & & & & & & & \mu & & & & \\ & & & & & & & & & \ddots & & & \\ & & & & & & & & & & t & & \\ & & & & & & & & & & & \ddots & \\ & & & & & & & & & & & & 1 \\ & & & & & & & & & & & & & \ddots \\ 0 & & & & & & & & & & & & & & 1 \end{bmatrix} \quad (9)$$

where t is a value of a sine function ranged from 1 to μ (or from μ to 1). It can be calculated by

$$t = \mu + \frac{1-\mu}{2}(\sin x + 1) \quad (10)$$

where x is a local horizontal coordinate in the transitional regions.

Moreover, the Formula (8) can also express a completed EMD mixed mean line, and it can be generalized as

$$Mixed\ Line = r_n(t) + c_n(t) + \cdots + A \bullet c_{n-i}(t) \quad (11)$$

where *Mixed Line* is the EMD mixed mean line.

The resulting EMD mixed mean line with Formula (8) is shown in Figure 7(a). It can be found that the EMD mixed mean line correlates well with Gaussian mean line in the middle location and follows surface profile well at the marginal areas. Based on the EMD mixed mean line, the roughness profile is extracted and its roughness parameter *Ra* is 0.3466μm, as shown in Figure 7(b). Based on the Gaussian mean line, roughness parameter *Ra* is 0.3467μm. The relative error E_r is 0.03%.

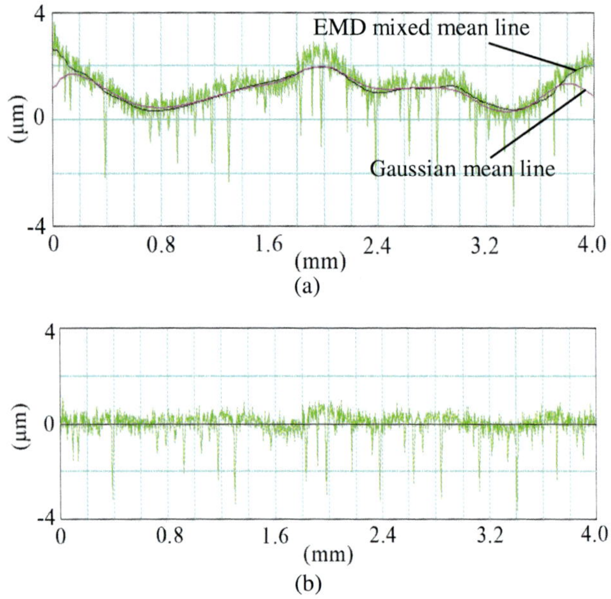

Figure 7. A comparison of EMD mixed mean line and Gaussian mean line (a), and the extracted surface roughness profile based on EMD mixed mean line (b).

3.4. *The algorithm of EMD mixed mean line*

Based on the above analysis, the algorithm for generating EMD mixed mean line can be briefly described as follows:

Algorithm EMD Mixed Mean Line

1) Read surface profile data *x(t)*.

2) Do empirical mode decomposition with ***Algorithm EMD*** and obtain residue $r_n(t)$ and IMF_n, IMF_{n-1}, IMF_{n-2}, ..., IMF_2, IMF_1.

3) Calculate individual IMF frequency within 1 mm with Formula (2) and (3), and convert it into frequency within an evaluation length.

4) Select IMFs with frequency less than 10 within an evaluation length, and record the IMF of maximum frequency as IMF_{n-i}.

5) Determine the diagonal matrix *A* using Formula (9), (10), and the selected value of μ.

6) Calculate the EMD mixed mean line using Formula (11).

4. EXPERIMENT

Another measured surface profile is shown in Figure 8(a). The evaluation length l_n is 4mm and the cut-off length λ_c is 0.8mm.

According to ***Algorithm EMD Mixed Mean Line***, we first do the empirical mode decomposition of the raw surface profile, and obtain the IMFs and the residue of the raw profile. Then the individual IMF frequency within 1 mm is calculated by Formula (2) and (3), and the frequency within an evaluation length can be calculated. The residue and several IMFs with low frequency within an evaluation length are shown in Figure 8(b)-(e). The frequency values of IMFs are shown in Table 2. From Table 2, the frequency values of IMF_n and IMF_{n-1} are less than 10 within an evaluation length, and the IMF_{n-1} is the one whose frequency is the maximum between IMF_n and IMF_{n-1}. The next step is to construct the diagonal matrix *A* by the selected value of μ=0.3, Formula (9), and (10). Finally, based on Formula (11), the EMD mixed mean line is calculated by

$$Mixed\ Line = r_n(t) + c_n(t) + A \bullet c_{n-1}(t) \qquad (12)$$

The EMD mixed mean line is shown in Figure 9(a).

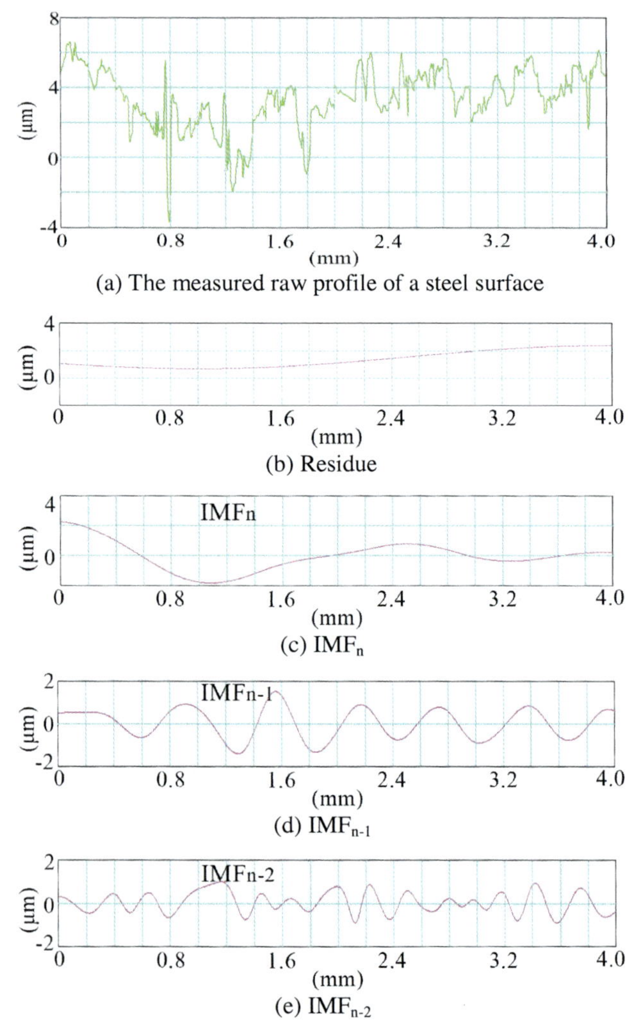

(a) The measured raw profile of a steel surface

(b) Residue

(c) IMF_n

(d) IMF_{n-1}

(e) IMF_{n-2}

Figure 8. The measured raw profile of a steel surface (a), its residue (b), and the last three IMFs (c)-(e).

Table 2. The frequency and wavelength of IMFs.

	IMF_{n-3}	IMF_{n-2}	IMF_{n-1}	IMF_n
Wavelength (mm)	0.1221	0.2591	0.6119	2.4295
frequency (1/mm)	8.1883	3.8599	1.6342	0.4116
frequency (1/4mm)	32.753	15.440	6.5868	1.6464

A comparison between the EMD mixed mean line and the Gaussian mean line is shown in Figure 9(a), where Gaussian mean line is generated by Gaussian filtering with a cut-off length of λ_c=0.8mm. As can be seen in Figure 9(a), the EMD mixed mean line not only correlates well with Gaussian mean line in the middle location, but also follows surface profile well at margin areas. Based on the EMD mixed mean line, the surface roughness profile is separated, as shown in Figure 9(b), and its roughness parameter Ra is 0.8335μm. Based on the Gaussian mean line, roughness parameter Ra is 0.8285μm. The relative error E_r is 0.60%.

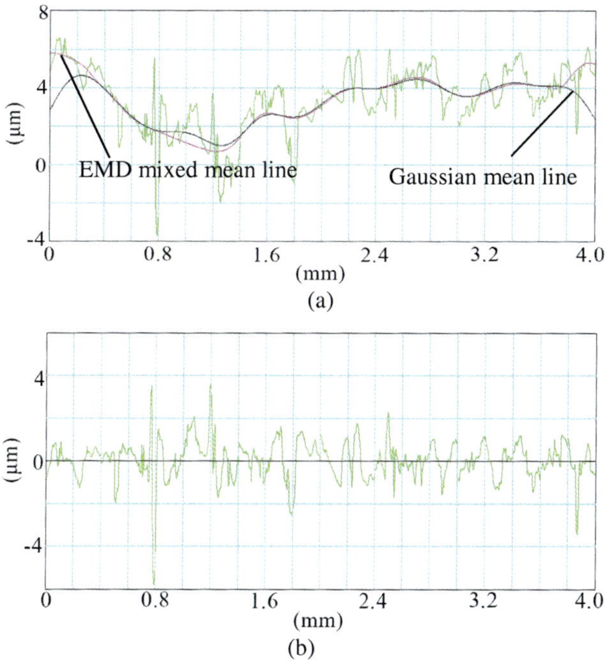

Figure 9. A comparison of EMD mixed mean line and Gaussian mean line (a), and the extracted surface roughness profile based on EMD mixed mean line (b).

5. CONCLUSION

An algorithm for generating EMD mixed mean line is proposed to separate surface roughness profile from an engineering surface. The residue, IMFs with frequency less than 10, the VAWF is used to reconstruct the EMD mixed mean line. The EMD mixed mean line can correlate well with Gaussian mean line in the middle location of surface profile and suppress edge effects in the marginal areas. In our experiments, EMD mixed mean line will be more accurate than EMD mean line for the reason that the VAWF is applied. Therefore, it can act as a candidate of mean lines without edge effects for the assessment of surface topological characteristics.

ACKNOWLEDGMENT

This research was sponsored by the National Natural Science Foundation of China under grant No. 60873141 and the Shenzhen Basic Research Project grant No. JCYJ20140417172417154.

REFERENCES

— [1] Boryczko, A. 2010. Distribution of roughness and waviness components of turned surface profiles. *Metrology & Measurement Systems* 17(4): 611-620.
— [2] Fu, S. et al. 2003. Engineering surface analysis with different wavelet bases. *Journal of Manufacturing Science and Engineering* 125(4): 844-852.
— [3] Huang, N.E. et al. 1998. The empirical mode decomposition and the Hilbert spectrum for nonlinear and non-stationary time series analysis. *Proceedings of the Royal Society of London A* 454: 903-995.
— [4] Huang, N.E. et al. 2009. On instantaneous frequency. *Advances in Adaptive Data Analysis* 1(2): 177-229.
— [5] ISO 11562. 1996. *Geometrical product specification (GPS)-surface texture: profile method-metrological characteristics of phase correct filters.* Geneva: International Organization for Standardization.
— [6] ISO/DTS 16610-22. 2003. *Geometrical Product Specifications (GPS)-Filtration-Part 22: Linear profile filters: Spline filters.* Geneva: International Organization for Standardization.
— [7] Krystek, M. 1996. Form filtering by splines. *Measurement* 18(1): 9-15.
— [8] Liu, S.B. & Zhang, H. 2015. Separation of surface roughness profile from raw contour based on Empirical Mode Decomposition. *Advances in Engineering Research* 15: 406-411.
— [9] Raja, J. et al. 2002. Recent advances in separation of roughness, waviness and form. *Precision Engineering* 26(2): 222-235.
— [10] Whitehouse, D. 2011. *Handbook of surface and nanometrology.* Boca Raton: CRC Press.
— [11] Yuan, Y.B. et al. 2000. A fast algorithm for determining the Gaussian filtered mean line in surface metrology. *Precision Engineering* 24(1): 62-69.

A Study of Multi-layer Swarm Path Planning

X. Xu*, K. Zou & R.S. Liang
Department of Computer Engineering, University of Electronic Science and Technology of China Zhongshan Institute, Zhongshan 528402, China
**Email: xuxiang8@mail2.sysu.edu.cn, 467796538@qq.com*

ABSTRACT: Swarm animation is an important research direction in the field of computer animation, which aims at computer simulation of swarm behavior, real-time rendering of swarm animation and other relevant aspects. In these aspects, swarm path planning is a key issue and has received widespread attention. Some global path planning methods, such as **A*** and **Dijkstra**, due to need predefined environment information and high computation burden, is not suitable for swarm path planning; But some optimization algorithms based on swarm intelligence theory, such as particle swarm optimization (**PSO**), ant colony optimization (**ACO**) and artificial bee colony (**ABC**), etc. Because of its simplicity and fast convergence, has become the best choice of swarm path planning. This paper presents a multi-layer swarm path planning method. Firstly we divide the virtual environment into three layers, including geometry layer, topology layer and navigation layer. On the basis of this environmental model, the swarm path planning model is divided into inner layer and outer layer model, outer layer adopts an improved **A*** algorithm for topological path planning, inner layer adopts a hybrid algorithm based on **ABC** and **PSO** for dynamic path planning, then path data derived from two layers are joined together to form a final path result. Experimental results show this multi-layer swarm path planning method effectively reflected intelligence and authenticity of individuals, improved execution efficiency of the algorithm, and prevented premature convergence.

KEYWORDS: Swarm path planning; Artificial bee colony (**ABC**); Particle swarm optimization (**PSO**); **A***; Multi-layer.

1. INTRODUCTION

Swarm refers to a collection of individuals which gather together and interact with neighbors and outer environment, these individuals have similar thinking logic and behavior rules. When they gather together, often emerge some swarm behaviors different from simple individual behaviors. In order to better simulate these swarm behaviors, scholars put forward the concept of Swarm Animation. Swarm Animation aims to simulate intelligent swarm behaviors and reveal its base rules by using computer technique and swarm intelligence theory. Swarm Animation can be applied to movies, games, virtual reality, military training, disaster prevention, transportation planning, and other fields. In these fields, Swarm Animation need to provide consistent motion of the whole swarm as well as personalization behavior of each individual, these two aspects of demand should also be satisfied when planning swarm path.

As early as 1987, Reynolds proposed *leader follow* and *path following* group motion patterns [1]. The *leader follow* pattern divided group members into the leader and the follower, the follower's motion is completely controlled by the leader, so only just need to plan the leader's path. The *path following* pattern by means of a predefined trajectory to restrict all individual's motion. These two group motion patterns can be used for small team, but for the large-scale swarm, still has a big gap in authenticity and efficiency. In 2002, Bayazit et al. used global *roadmaps* to improve the quality of group path planning in a complex environment [2], through embedding behavior rules in individual flock members and in the *roadmaps*, obtained better group behaviors, such as homing, goal searching, traversing narrow areas and shepherding. In 2003, Kallmann et al. proposed a fast path planning algorithm based on a fully dynamic constrained Delaunay triangulation [3]. Tang et al. used an improved **A*** algorithm for path planning and used terrain meshes generated by the height map as interaction environment [4]. In 2004, Lamarche and Donikian proposed a new topology structure of the geometric environment in order to implement the rapid multi-layer path planning, as well as a new navigation algorithm for virtual swarm motion [5]. In 2005, Pettre et al. presented how to automatically decompose multilayered surfaces or uneven terrains into navigation map, their research showed that the path planning can reuse the calculated results for all individuals in the group [6]. All these methods are superior to the traditional global path planning methods in computation efficiency when applied to swarm path planning, but they still have some shortcomings, such as neglecting the simulation of authentic individual behaviors, especially for quickly obstacle avoidance and interaction with each other in the complex dynamic environment, still remains to be improved.

Combining with evolutionary computation and swarm intelligence theory, this paper carried on the thorough analysis for the key issues of Swarm Animation, including virtual environment modeling and swarm path planning, and proposed a multi-layer swarm path planning method. On the one hand, for the modeling of virtual environment, we divided the whole environment model into three layers, including geometry layer, topology layer and navigation layer. Geometry layer used to geometric environment modeling; Topology layer used to partition of environment node and manage entity attributes within this node; Navigation layer used to complete path planning by means of geometry layer and topology layer. This kind of multi-layer environment model ensures more realistic rendering and real-time interaction, and provides strong guarantee for swarm path planning and collision detection. On the other hand, when planning swarm path, we combined static global path planning method with dynamic intelligent path planning method, and divided the path planning procedure into two parts, one part is internode path planning based on topology layer environment information, we adopted an improved **A*** algorithm, which will generate a node sequence as outer layer path planning result; the other part is intra-node path planning based on dynamic environment information in the node, we adopted a hybrid algorithm based on **ABC** and **PSO**, **ABC** is used to search the optimal path, and **PSO** is used to provide an adaptive interaction behavior for individuals, which let individuals dynamic update their trajectory according to the change of environment. Finally we adopted a random splicing function to composite these two parts of path data and form a final path result.

2. ALGORITHM DESCRIPTION

Swarm path planning involves every individual's path planning in a complex dynamic environment, whether path planning algorithm is efficiently adapted for the environment is the most critical problem. Path planning method based on swarm intelligence theory is able to quickly generate optimal path, but these algorithms exist parameter setting, premature convergence and local optimum, etc. With the increasing of population, these problems will be more apparent. For this purpose, this paper proposed a multi-layer swarm path planning method. On the basis of the environment model, the path planning model is divided into two layers: inner layer and outer layer. Outer layer adopted topological path planning based on an improved **A*** algorithm and implemented on inter-node; Inner layer adopted dynamic path planning based on a hybrid swarm intelligence algorithm and implemented on intra-node. The algorithm architecture diagram is shown in Figure 1.

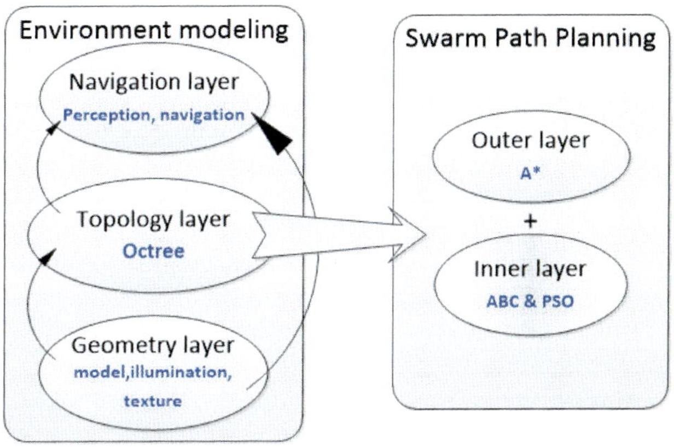

Figure 1. Architecture diagram of the proposed multi-layer swarm path planning method.

2.1. *Environment modeling*

Traditional virtual environment modeling refers to space modeling based on geometrical information, such as how to construct a 3D game scene vividly as much as possible. The visually realistic degree is the only evaluation criteria for the environment model. However, as people's rising requirement for more realistic swarm animation, merely geometrical information can not satisfy. Because in the virtual environment, in addition to geometrical information, also includes motion individuals and all kinds of virtual events, so the virtual environment model should be able to help individuals to plan their behaviors and interact with environment [7].

In view of the virtual environment modeling, different researchers have proposed different methods. *Grid map* is a technique derived from robot domain [8], which divided the virtual environment into uniform grid, each grid represents a region in the environment. Leonard et al. proposed *Featuremap* technology [9], which uses regular geometric elements to represent environment space, and give these geometric elements corresponding characteristics, these characteristics facilitate swarm to percept the environment. Lamarche et al. proposed a compound environment model [10], which compound environment description, path planning and interactive traversal together, can support hundreds of swarm motion simulation. Sung et al. proposed a method which combine the individual behavior model with the environment model, can dynamically adjust individual's behavior rules according to the current virtual environment [11]. In addition, a large number of mature virtual environment modeling software were emerged, Wei Shao et al. developed a hierarchical environment modeling system [12]. Bernard Moulin et al. developed a pedestrian shopping behavior simulation system called **MallMAGS** by using geographical environment information [13]. Julien Pettre et al. developed a multi-level uneven terrain environment modeling system [14], and so on. However, these methods and tools are mostly supposed that swarm have known in advance the complete virtual environment information, means planning path in a static environment. But in fact, the virtual environment is always changing, path planning on static environment may cause unharmonious between swarm with the environment, and in real world swarm is impossible to obtain complete environment information beforehand. Moreover, even if the virtual environment is static, with the increasing of environment complexity and swarm scale, using previous path planning methods still encounter large computation burden. Therefore, the more effective virtual environment model is needed.

This paper proposed a multi-layer virtual environment model, which divided environment into geometry layer, topology layer and navigation layer. Geometry layer mainly solve how to build a realistic virtual geometrical environment, including geometrical model of 3D objects, scene illumination setting, texture map and environment data storage, etc. some map editor tools like ***Unreal*** and ***Unity3D*** game engine and ***3DS Max*** modeling tools, etc. can help to build geometry layer information. Topology layer is used to manage topological structure and various entity attributes, usually adopts some spatial data structure for topology partition, such as Bounding Volume Hierarchy (**BVH**) [15], Binary Space Partitioning Tree (**BSP**) [16,17], **Octree** [18,19], etc. Relative to **BSP** which is usually applied for indoor environment, **Octree** is usually used in outdoor environment. **Octree** regards the whole environment model as a root node, the root node is divided into eight octants, corresponding to eight child nodes, each child node can also recursive partition if needed , eventually the decomposition process can be expressed as a tree. By using **Octree** partition, the virtual environment is converted into a node set. For each node, we need to define and store it's data structure, commonly a node data structure including information such as *node depth*, *parent node*, *children nodes*, as well as *entity set* within the node (static and dynamic obstacles entity), often we also need to define *weight value* of each node(marked as ω), which represents passable capacity of the node, ω can be calculated from the *entity set* within the node, if the node completely impassable, ω is set to *MAX*, otherwise ω is set to a value between 0~*MAX*, representing different passable capacity, which means the node needs to do further recursive partition. When path planning, we only need to focus on the nodes that we care for, without considering the other nodes. Navigation layer is used to support swarm path planning, this layer read geometrical information from geometry layer, and topological information from topology layer, then provide these information for path planning, collision detection and other applications.

2.2. *Path planning method*

In environment modeling, we adopted a multi-layer model, which converted a single large environment path planning problem into a hierarchical path planning problem [20], means the whole environment is divided into some small sub regional blocks, which often called *path node*. In path planning, we firstly implement inter-node searching at outer layer, the result is a node sequence with minimum path length. Then we implement inner layer dynamic path searching under this node sequence. Finally we adopt a random splicing function to combine these two layers data and generate the final path result. The proposed multi-layer swarm path planning method has both intelligence and authenticity, avoid premature convergence, and provide a significant promotion in execution efficiency.

2.2.1. *Outer layer topological path planning*

Outer layer topological path planning is based on **Octree** data structure, its goal is to find the shortest path from starting point to end point on the topology graph, each node uses weight value ω as fitness value. The global search algorithms such as **A*** and ***Dijkstra*** can be used to solve this problem. **A*** is a heuristic search algorithm which firstly proposed in [21]. **A*** has many advantages. Firstly, if exists an effective path from starting point to end point, **A*** must be able to find this path. Secondly, as long as the evaluation function *h(n)* is adopted, it must be able to find a shortest path. Thirdly, **A*** has least search states in all heuristic search algorithms. But for requirements of more intelligent an efficient path planning, **A*** still need to improve in some aspects: First of all, because **A*** algorithm does not know the final path in each search step, thus need to detect all possible nodes in the state space, each possible nodes need to calculate weight value and compare together, which not only slow down calculation speed, but also consume plenty of space resources. Second, **A*** algorithm carried out path planning in accordance with grid nodes, nevertheless the resulting grid path is the shortest, but often twists, too mechanization, so we often need to smooth the path before using it. This paper used an improved **A*** search strategy, which create a *global solution path table* beforehand for optimizing path planning procedure, the solution path table adopts reverse search manner, means when the target node is given, the search direction can be from the target node reverse extended to all passable nodes. The generated *global solution path table* can be saved as a look-up table. After finished the *global solution path table*, the path generation becomes quite simple, since each node contains the minimum cost of the parent node pointer, given an arbitrary starting point, only need to traverse its parent, until the target node, can obtain a global optimal path. Detailed flow chart is shown in Figure 2.

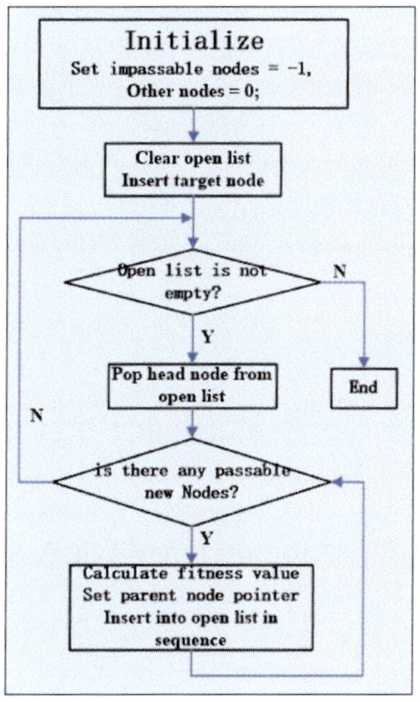

Figure 2. Flow chart of generating *global solution path table*.

2.2.2. *Inner layer dynamic path planning*

After finished outer layer path planning, we obtained a regional node sequence, this node sequence represents stage target for the swarm, but how to make the swarm migrate from one node to adjacent node, still need to use inner layer path planning. Inner layer path planning refers to path planning within one node and between adjacent nodes, it not only restricts range of swarm motion, but also let individuals demonstrate more intelligent and realistic behaviors, such as collision avoidance, aggregation and separation, etc. By means of swarm intelligence theory, this paper adopted a hybrid swarm path planning algorithm based on **ABC** and **PSO** for inner layer path planning.

The **ABC** algorithm is a kind of numerical optimization algorithm based on bee's self-organization model. In 1995, Seeley first proposed bee colony self-organization model [22]. Then, Duan Teodoroviá et al. proposed bee colony optimization algorithm in 2005 [23], Dervis Karaboga applied **ABC** algorithm on the function of numerical optimization problem in 2005 [24], and further in 2007, they applied **ABC** theory on the restrictive numerical optimization problem, and achieved good test results [25]. Based on the **ABC** algorithm, the swarm is considered as a bee colony, looking for an optimal path is considered as finding the optimal food source. Bee colony is divided into employed bees, onlookers and scouts, employed bees randomly obtain a food source and then return to the hive, share the information about nectar amount of the food source with the onlookers, onlookers use roulette method to choose a food source, then use greedy selection mechanism to update the target food source and return to the hive, which complete a cycle. Iteration within the maximum cycle times and finally finds the optimal solution. Scouts randomly search new food sources around the hive when the previous food source is abandoned.

The **PSO** algorithm was firstly proposed by Eberhart and Kennedy in 1995, it is also a kind of swarm intelligence optimization method [26], which comes from the study of birds foraging behavior. The **PSO** algorithm has fast convergence speed, less setting parameters and easy implementation. Considering the individual's interaction and change of environment, we introduced **PSO** into algorithm for controlling individual self-adaptive behavior and path update.

The main steps of the hybrid algorithm can be described as follows:

Step 1: Initialization. A random population is initialized, define initial position and velocity of each individual, input node sequence derived from outer layer path planning algorithm.

Step 2: Dynamic path planning. Searching regional optimal path based on the **ABC** algorithm. After initialization, for employed bees, onlookers, and scouts, respectively. A loop search procedure will conduct.

Step 3: Individual behavior control. Based on the **PSO** algorithm and information sharing mechanism, individuals can adaptively control their behaviors. Depending on the outer path node information, individuals can interact with the environment dynamically.

Step 4: Iterative loop. After limited loops, if the solution cannot be improved further, it will be abandoned and replaced by a new solution found by scouts, or else return to ***Step 2*** and continue.

Step 5: Obtain global optimal solution. After that again ***Steps 2, 3*** and ***4*** will be repeated until the stopping criteria is met.

In ***Step 1***, suppose population size is ***N***, the algorithm randomly generate ***m=N/2*** size of initial path. Each initial path can be regarded as a composition of ***d*** size of small segments, so each possible solution is a ***d***-dimensional vector, defined as $y_i = (y_{i1}, y_{i2}, ..., y_{id})$ $(i = 1,2,...,m)$. A passable initial path must ensure not collision with static obstacles. In order to simplify the calculation of fitness value, we choose ***path length***, ***obstacle avoidance force*** and ***target weight value*** as path quality factors, and weighted sum as fitness value of the path, detailed describe is shown in formula (1).

$$\text{fitness}(y_i) = \alpha \times L_i + \beta \times F_i + \gamma \times \omega_{id} \tag{1}$$

Where fitness (y_i) is the fitness value of path ***i***. L_i is the sum of segments which represents ***path length***. F_i represents ***obstacle avoidance force***, we calculate on each segment of the path and then summation. For each segment, the ***obstacle avoidance force*** is obtained by calculating the vertical distance between this segment with the nearest obstacle, the smaller the distance, the greater the ***force***, said the more likely collision, specific description is shown in formula (2). Where d_{ij} represents distance from segment ***j*** to the nearest obstacle, ***c*** is adjustment factor used to scaling d_{ij}, be attention if $d_{ij} = 0$, it means collision with obstacles happened, we need to choose again. ω_{id} is the weight value of target node, if $\omega_{id} = MAX$, the target is not feasible and need to choose again. α, β and γ are impact factors, and meet $(\alpha + \beta + \gamma) = 1$.

$$L_i = \sqrt{\Sigma(y_{ij}^2)},\ j = 1,2,..,d$$

$$F_i = \Sigma c / d_{ij} \tag{2}$$

Step 2 is one iteration for the optimal path searching by using **ABC** algorithm. When employed bees choosing target, they use formula (3) to find a new target around current target. Where ***k*** is randomly selected from *{1,2,...,m}* and $k \neq i, j \in (1,2,...,d)$, ***W*** is the **Octree** node size, $\phi_{ij}, \varphi_{ij} \in [-1,1]$ is a uniformly random variable. Thus employed bees can dynamic adjust target based on **Octree** node unit. Employed bee will judge $newx_{ij}$ and x_{ij}, if fitness of new source is less than old source, employed bee will accept the new one instead of the old one.

$$\text{newx}_{ij} = x_{ij} + \phi_{ij}(x_{ij} - x_{kj}) + \varphi_{ij} W \tag{3}$$

After employed bees finished searching, they will share information of food sources for onlookers, onlookers choose target according to nectar amount (fitness value of each path) and probability formula (4).

$$p_i = \frac{\exp(\frac{fitness_i}{T})}{\sum_{i=1}^{N} \exp(\frac{fitness_i}{T})} \tag{4}$$

Where p_i is the probability of selected food source ***i***, $fitness_i$ is the fitness value of food source ***i***, and $T = T_0(0.99^{c-1})$.

In ABC algorithm, iteration number is an important control parameter, it controlled algorithm convergence and decided the ability to jump out of local optimal solution. After limited iterations, if the fitness value of a food source is still in low level, it will be abandoned, and scouts will use formula (5) to generate a new solution to replace the old. Thus, onlookers and employed bees perform local search, scouts perform global search, which provide a balance between the global exploration search and local exploitation search.

$$x_i^j = x_{\min}^j + rand()(x_{\max}^j - x_{\min}^j) \tag{5}$$

Swarm path planning need to find the optimal path, at the same time keep intelligent and realistic of individual behaviors. So in ***Step 3***, we also introduced **PSO** algorithm to dynamic control individual's behavior, in order to realize the interaction with other individuals and outer environment. After onlookers have found the food source, Individuals for choosing the same food sources can form a small colony, through information sharing mechanism, individuals implement path planning and collision avoidance. Firstly, we initialized each individual's position x_i and velocity υ_i, Individual extreme ***pbest*** and global extreme ***gbest*** are also generated. The fitness of individual can be defined as formula (6).

$$fitness(x_i) = \alpha \times D_i + \beta \times fitness(y_{ij}) \tag{6}$$

Where D_i denotes the distance between individual ***i*** and the food source y_{ij}, $fitness(y_{ij})$ denotes the fitness value of the food source. Formula (6) comprehensive considered the distance between the individual and the food source, and the quality of food source factors, etc. Then according to the formula (7) and (8), update each individual's velocity and position, loop iteration to complete choice of the optimal path. In formula (7), ***ρ*** is inertia weight, c_1 is the individual weight coefficient and c_2 is the global weight coefficient, often $c_1 = c_2 = 2$.

$$\upsilon_{id} = \rho\upsilon_{id} + c_1 rand()(p_{id} - x_{id}) + c_2 rand()(p_{gd} - x_{id}) \tag{7}$$

$$x_{id} = x_{id} + \upsilon_{id} \tag{8}$$

2.2.3. *Path joining*

After finished Outer and Inner layer path planning, we need to join together two layers path data. We can use a simple sequence splicing method, but it will result in stretch, separation and other adverse phenomena. Here we use a random splicing function for path joining. Random splicing functions by selecting two random paths between adjacent topological nodes, and add some restriction on the velocity, which can achieve the balance of each individual's velocity.

3. EXPERIMENTAL RESULTS

In this section, we evaluated the performance obtained by the proposed multi-layer swarm path planning method. We choose two different swarm behaviors for testing, one is *dynamic target follow* behavior, and the other is *aggregation and diffusion* behavior. Two different experiments performed on the same simulation environment and the population size is set to ***100***. Firstly, we use **Octree** to segment the environment, and obtain **Octree** node set, each node represents a sub scene, the entities information within this node are stored in the node's data structure.

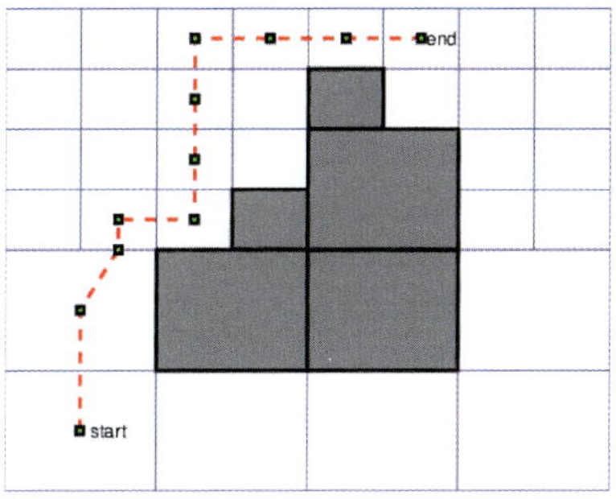

Figure 3. The optimal node sequence obtained from pre-build global solution path table.

For experiment 1, we first give target position and all individuals' initial position. All individuals are in the same node, this experiment simulated the swarm moving from initial position to the target. The simulation also demonstrated path following and collision avoidance behaviors, etc. Firstly, we used pre-build global solution path table to obtain the optimal node sequence, then inside each node of sequence, we finished individual's dynamic path planning by using the proposed hybrid swarm path planning algorithm. Detailed simulation results as shown in Figure 3 and Figure 4. Figure 3 shows the node sequence from start point to the target, as we can see, this node sequence has the shortest length and automatically avoids impassable regions. Figure 4 shows the dynamic path planning simulation result inside one node. As can be seen, individuals can find stage target position, two optimal paths are obtained by the proposed algorithm, when individuals are moving, and they can avoid collision with each other and follow one path.

For experiment 2, we simulated *aggregation* behavior. Firstly, we give an aggregation position, all individuals are dispersed to different path nodes at the initial time. Based on the outer layer path planning result from experiment 1, the algorithm grouped individuals according to their node location, each group implement corresponding dynamic path planning respectively. Simulation results as shown in Figure 5. As we can see, four groups of individuals are gathering together, each group can follow their optimal trajectory respectively.

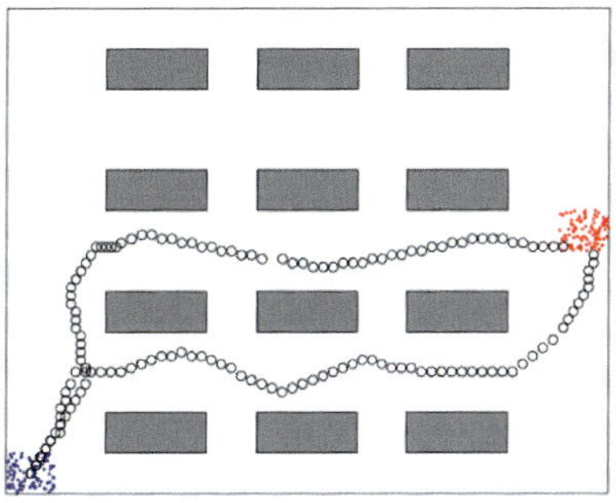

Figure 4. *Dynamic target follow* behavior simulation. Left bottom is the initial position, and right middle is the stage target position. The trajectory points for the optimal path are marked as circle point.

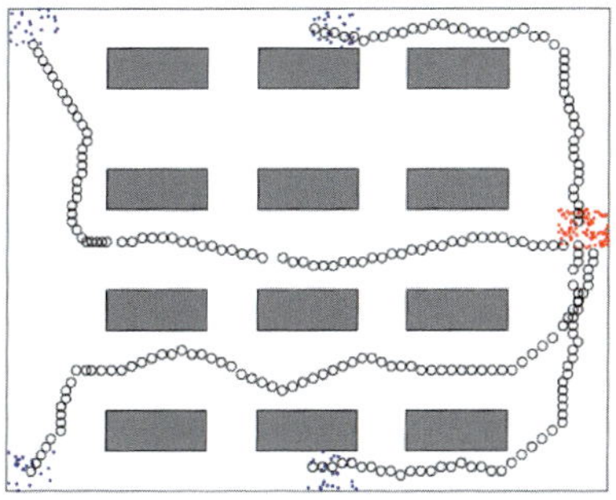

Figure 5. Aggregation behavior simulation. Four groups of individuals are dispersed to different position at the initial time, and right middle is the target position. The trajectory points for the optimal path are marked as circle point.

In order to test and verify the convergence of the proposed hybrid algorithm, in the process of iterative optimization, the number of iterations and convergence time are compared with the standard **ABC** algorithm, as shown in Figure 6. From Figure 6, we can clearly see that the proposed algorithm can accomplish the optimal solution in a minimum number of iterations, relative to the standard **ABC** algorithm, the performance of the hybrid algorithm has obvious improvement.

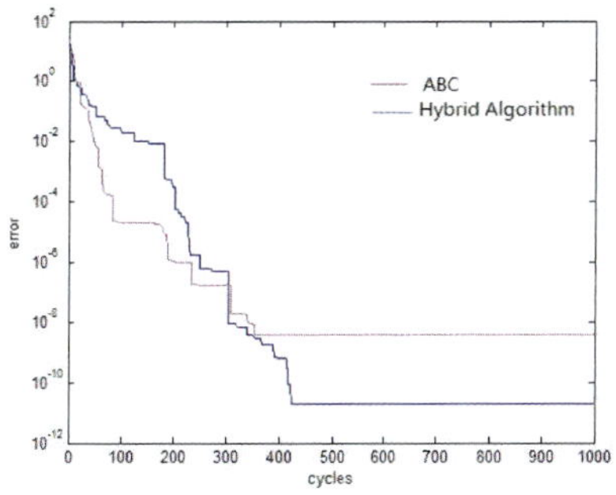

Figure 6. Performance compare between the proposed hybrid algorithm and the standard ABC.

4. CONCLUSIONS

A multi-layer method for swarm path planning is proposed in this paper, aiming to obtain advantages in individual intelligence and computation efficiency. The proposed two layers model work collaboratively, outer layer model drives the swarm to move from one path node to another, and inner layer provides behavior guidelines for each individual in order to avoid collision with each other or environmental obstacles. The Experimental results show that the multi-layer swarm path planning method not only improved the convergence of algorithm, and presented more intelligence and authenticity of the individual.

5. ACKNOWLEDGEMENTS

This research has been jointly supported by the Science and Technology Program of Guangdong Province under Grant No. 2013B090500035, and the Science and Technology Program of Zhongshan City under Grant No. 2013A3FC0284.

REFERENCES

- [1] Reynolds, C.W. 1987. Flocks, herds, and schools: A distributed behavioral model. Computer Graphics (ACM SIGGRAPH'87 Conference Proceedings), 21(4): 25–34.
- [2] Bayazit, O. B. & Lien, J.M. & Amato, N.M. 2002. Better group behaviors in complex environments using global roadmaps. Artificial Life, 362–370.
- [3] Kallmann, M. & Bieri, H. & Thalmann, D. 2003. Fully Dynamic Constrained Delaunay Triangulations. In Geometric Modelling for Scientific Visualization, Springer-Verlag, 241–257.
- [4] Tang, W. & Wan, T.R. & Patel, S. 2003. Real-time crowd movement on large scale terrains. 2003. Proceedings in Theory and Practice of Computer Graphics, 146–153.
- [5] Lamarche, F. & Donikian, S. 2004. Crowds of virtual humans:a new approach for real time navigation in complex and structured environments. Eurographics 04: Computer Graphics Forum, 23(3): 509–518.
- [6] Pettre, J. & Laumond, J.P. & Thalmann, D. 2005. A navigation graph for real-time crowd animation on multilayered and uneven terrain. In First International Workshop on Crowd Simulation, 81–89.
- [7] Farenc, N. & Musse, S. & Schweiss, E. & Kallmann, M. & Aune, O. & Boulic, R. & Thalmann, D. 2000. A paradigm for controlling virtual humans in urban environment simulations. Applied Artificial Intelligence, 14(1): 69–91.
- [8] Elfes, A. 1987. Sonar based real world mapping and navigation. IEEE Journal of Robotics and Automation, 3(3): 249 – 265.
- [9] Leonard, J.J. & Durrant-Whyte, H.F. 1991. Mobile robot localization by tracking geometric beacons. IEEE Transactions on Robotics and Automation, 7(3): 376–382.
- [10] Lamarche, F. & Donikian, S. 2004. Crowd of virtual humans: a new approach for real time navigation in complex and structured environments. Computer Graphics Forum, 23(3): 509–518.
- [11] Sung, M. & Gleicher, M. & Chenney, S. 2004. Scalable behaviors for crowd simulation. Computer Graphics Forum, 23(3): 519–528.
- [12] Shao, W. & Terzopoulos, D. 2005. Environmental modeling for autonomous virtual pedestrians. In SAE Symposium on Digital Human Modeling for Design and Engineering, 1–8.
- [13] Moulin, B. & Chaker, W. & Perron, J. & Pelletier, P. & Hogan, J. & Gbei, E. 2003. Mags project: Multi-agent geosimulation and crowd simulation. in Spatial Information Theory. Foundations of Geographic Information Science, 2825: 151–168.
- [14] Pettre, J. & Laumond, J. & Thalmann, D. 2005. A navigation graph for real-time crowd animation on multilayered and uneven terrain. In First International Workshop on Crowd Simulation.
- [15] Ratcliff, J. 2001. Sphere trees for fast visibility culling, ray tracing, and range searching. Game Programming Gems 2, 384–387.
- [16] Gordon, D. & Chen, S. 1991. Front-to-back display of bsp trees. Computer Graphics and Applications, IEEE, 11(5): 79–85.
- [17] Adam, J. 1999. Binary space partitioning for accelerated hidden surface removal and rendering of static environments. University of East Anglia.
- [18] Fan, O.Y & Zhang, T. 2012. Octree-based spherical hierarchical model for collision detection. 2012 10th World Congress on Intelligent Control and Automation (WCICA), 3870–3875.
- [19] He, H.Q. & Zhang, Y & Liu, H.H. 2007. A method used to dynamic scene management based on octree. Computer Graphics, Imaging and Visualisation, 2007. CGIV'07, 16–21.
- [20] Botea, A. & Muller, M. & Schaeffer, J. 2004. Near optimal hierarchical path-finding. Journal of Game Development, 1(1): 7–28.
- [21] Roth, U. & Walker, M. & Hilmann, A. & Klar, H. 1997. Dynamic path planning with spiking neural networks. Biological and Artificial Computation: From Neuroscience to Technology, Springer Berlin Heidelberg, 1355–1363.
- [22] Seeley, T.D. 1995. The wisdom of the hive: The social physiology of honey bee colonies, Harvard University Press.
- [23] Teodorovic, D. & Dellorco, M. 2005. Bee colony optimazation-a cooperative learning approach to complex transportation problems. Proceedings of The 10th EWGT Meeting, 13– 16.
- [24] Karaboga, D. 2005. An Idea Based On Honey Bee Swarm for Numerical Optimization, Erciyes University, Engineering Faculty. Computers Engineering Department.
- [25] Karaboga, D. & Basturk, B. 2007. Artificial bee colony (abc) optimization algorithm for solving constrained optimization problems. Foundations of Fuzzy Logic and Soft Computing, 4529: 789–798.
- [26] Kennedy, J. & Eberhart, R. 1995. Particle swarm optimization. IEEE International Conference on Neural Networks, 4: 1942–1948.

Study of Permanent Magnet Synchronous Motor Vector Control Based on Three-Level NPC Inverter-Fed

R. Hua*, W.Z. Liu, S. Lin & Z.T. Xia
School of Railway Transportation, Shanghai Institute of Technology, Shanghai 201418, China
Email: huarong@sit.edu.cn, huarong326@sina.com

ABSTRACT: The neutral point clamped (NPC) pulse width modulation (PWM) inverter has been put into practical use for large capacity AC motor drives because of its less distorted output, lower costs and better control performance. This paper suggests a way to improve the performance of permanent magnet synchronous motor (PMSM) by using the three-level NPC inverter. Firstly, the three-level NPC inverter space voltage vector pulse width modulation (SVPWM) technique is analyzed in detail. Then, the NPC inverter is applied in PMSM vector control. Finally, a simulation experiment of the proposed control algorithm is carried out. The simulation results show that the proposed method can effectively suppress the torque ripple and improve driving performance for the PMSM drive.

KEYWORDS: Three-level inverter-fed; Neutral point clamped; Vector control; Permanent magnet synchronous motor.

1. INTRODUCTION

The permanent magnet synchronous motor (PMSM) has been widely applied in various types of AC drives, due to its advantages in simpler structure, higher power density and higher productivity. Additionally, the development of power electronic technology, permanent magnetic materials and high-performance digital signal processor (DSP) bring new opportunities for a wider range of application of PMSM [1]. At present, two-level inverter commonly used in AC speed regulation system can play a good role for the cases with relatively low voltage and current change rates. But the traditional two-level inverter is difficult to meet the requirement of high speed drivers [2].

The multi-level inverter, as a new type of inverter, can reduce high voltage and current change rates caused by the peak voltage and other shortcomings in traditional inverter. It, mainly through the improvement of its main circuit topology, makes all the power components work at the fundamental frequency or lower to realize the purposes of reducing peak voltage and improving output waveform performance [3]. Topological structure of three-level inverter has common characteristics of multi-level inverter, so it is applicable to the high-voltage, large-capacity frequency conversion occasions. Three-level neutral-point-clamped (NPC) inverter gives a further solution on the low withstand voltage of power components and reduces voltage change rate, which was put forward by Nabale in 1980 [4]. It not only improves the output waveform of inverter, but also has advantages of lower switching losses, higher efficiency and smaller influence of electromagnetic interference. Therefore, it has been widely used in the many fields of the industry, and has become one of the hot spots of power electronics and electric drive technology for the time-being [5].

This paper suggests a vector control method of PMSM, in which three-level NPC inverter is combined with PMSM. At first, the vector control principle of PMSM is analyzed, and then space voltage vector pulse width modulation (SVPWM) technology of three-level NPC inverter is introduced. A simulation experiment of the proposed control algorithm by Matlab/Simulink software is carried out to verify excellent driving performances of the vector control system of PMSM based on three-level NPC inverter.

2. MODEL OF PMSM VECTOR CONTROL

For simplicity, magnetic saturation, magnetic hysteresis and eddy current are taken out of consideration, and a sinusoidal back electromotive force of the motor is assumed further. Therefore, the mathematical model of PMSM in rotating d-q coordinate system can be stated as follows [5],

$$u_d = Ri_d - \omega_e L_q i_q + L_d \frac{di_d}{dt} \tag{1}$$

$$u_q = Ri_q + \omega_e \psi_f + \omega_e L_d i_d + L_q \frac{di_q}{dt} \tag{2}$$

$$T_e - T_L - B_\omega \omega = J\frac{d\omega}{dt} \tag{3}$$

$$T_e = \frac{3\pi}{2\tau} P\left[\psi_\tau i_q + (L_d - L_q) i_d i_q\right] \tag{4}$$

where id and iq (A), ud and uq (V), Ld and Lq (H) are the currents, the voltages and the inductances in phase d and q respectively, R (Ω) is resistance, ωe and ω (rad/s) are the rotor electricity angular velocity and mechanical angular velocity respectively, Te and TL (N·m) are the electromagnetic torque and the load torque respectively, J (kg·m2) is the moment of inertia, Bω (N·s/rad) is the motor viscous friction constant, p is the rotor number of pole-pairs, ψf (Wb) is the amplitude of the flux linkage of permanent-magnet. In this paper, vector control under the condition id=0 is employed. Hence, the d-q axis current is naturally decoupled. The corresponding vector control for the PMSM scheme is shown in Fig. 1.

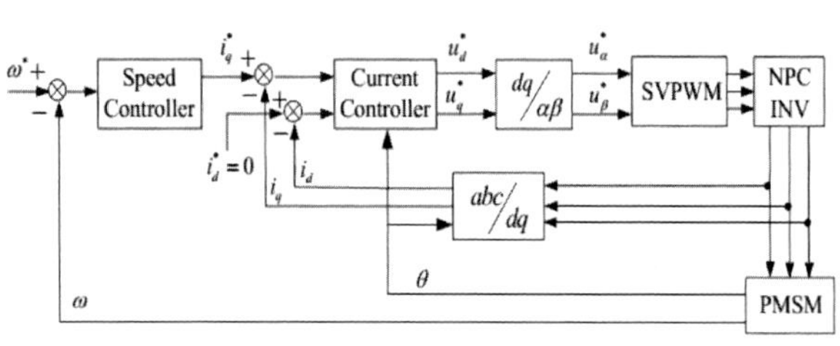

Figure 1. Overall control structure of PMSM vector control system.

3. THREE-LEVEL NPC INVERTER SVPWM CONTROL ALGORITHM

3.1. *Three-Level NPC inverter*

Fig. 2 shows the main circuit topology structure of three-level NPC inverter, including the capacitances C1, C2 used to provide two identical DC voltages to transform circuit, the diodes used to clamp levels. The bridge arms of the inverter's each phase can output three levels: Udc/2, 0, -Udc/2, where Udc/2 is DC voltage. P, O, N signifies these three kinds of potentials of the DC side respectively. Traditional two-level inverter only has 23=8 switching states, while three-level inverter has 33=27 switching states whose output states decide 19 different voltage vectors, as shown in Fig. 3. According to their amplitude lengths, these voltage vectors can be divided into four groups: three zero vectors, twelve short vectors, six medium vectors and six long vectors. As shown in Fig. 3, the long vectors respond to vertices of the outer hexagon, whose amplitudes are Udc; the medium vectors locate the angle bisector in each 60° sector, whose amplitudes are 2 3Udc; the short vectors locate in vertices of the inner hexagon and come in pairs, whose amplitudes are Udc 2.

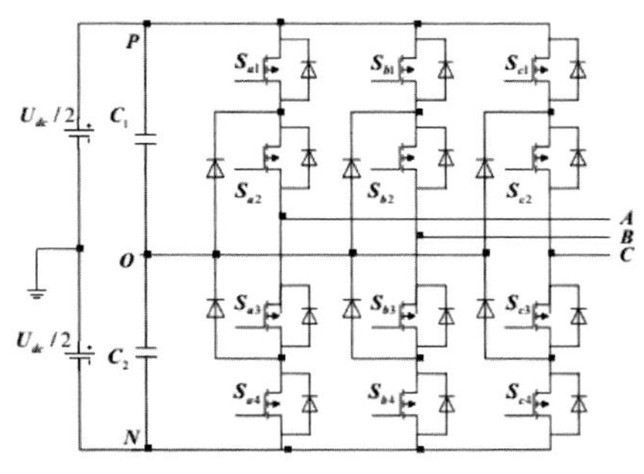

Figure 2. Three-level NPC inverter diagram.

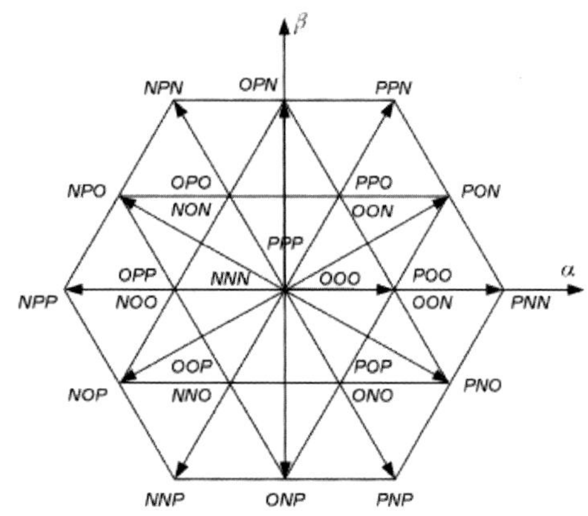

Figure 3.Voltage plane of three-level NPC inverter.

Accordingly, the zero and long vectors do not affect the neutral-point current at all. The midpoint voltage imbalance produced by the medium vectors can be compensated by the symmetry of the space voltage vectors. The short vectors can be used to control the midpoint potentials, because they always appear in pairs. In order to meet the vector control of PMSM requirements, the space vector control for three-level NPC inverter should be able to output adjustable SVPWM wave in frequency and amplitude.

3.2. *SVPWM control algorithm*

The primary task of SVPWM is to determine which one of those big sectors and then which one of those small triangles in the determined big sector the reference voltage vector Uref lies in, so that the corresponding reference output voltage could be determined. For the first step, according to the amplitude of the reference vector, we can identify which one of six triangle regions the vector is located in, as shown in Fig. 2. For the second step, we can further determine that it is located in which small triangle using the following three rules:

Rule 1: $U_{ref\alpha}+U_{ref\beta}/3\leq U_{\alpha}$; Rule 2: $U_{ref\alpha}-U_{ref\beta}/3\geq U_{\alpha}$;Rule 3: $U_{ref\alpha}<U_{\beta}$.

Where $U_{ref\alpha},U_{ref\beta}$ are the components which were decomposed into α, β axis respectively. Whether it meets the three rules or not can be immediately determined through the simple arithmetic operations. For example, vector diagram of the sector I is showed in Fig. 4, and then the relationship of rules and the small triangles can be obtained as shown in Table 1. Finally, according to the Table 1, the location of reference voltage vector can be determined, and then the output voltage vector of the synthesis of the reference vector can be obtained.

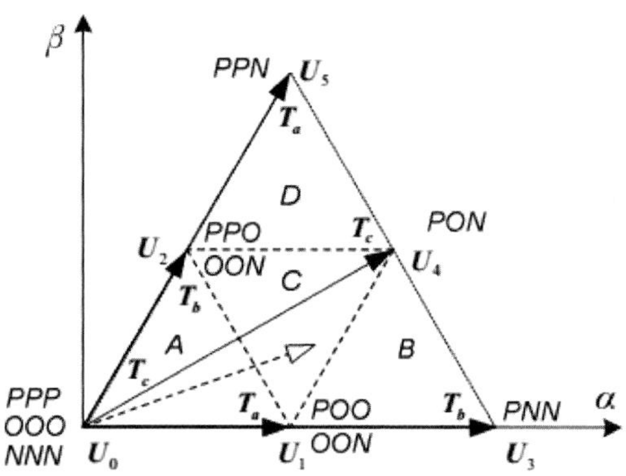

Figure 4. Vector diagram of the sector I.

Table 1. the relationship of rules and the small triangles.

	Rule1	Rule2	Rule3
A	*Yes(Y)*	----	-----
B	*No(N)*	*Y*	-----
C	*N*	*N*	*Y*
D	*N*	*N*	*N*

3.3. *Vector's functioning time*

Given the sector, small triangle and switching order of the reference vector, the functioning time of each output voltage vector should be further calculated, which is the total time of conduction and turn-off for switching devices within a cycle. Consider a simple example of calculating a vector's functioning time. The synthesis of a space voltage vector can be analyzed in sector ⊃ which has ten vectors, as shown in Fig. 4. Suppose that expected voltage vector falls in the Triangle C and it is the synthesis of U1, U2 and U4 under the principle of neighboring three-vector synthesis principle. According to the volt-second balance principle, the equation could be obtained as follows:

$$\begin{cases} U_1T_a+U_2T_b+U_4T_c=U_{ref}T_s \\ T_a+T_b+T_c=T_s \end{cases} \tag{5}$$

where Ta, Tb, Tc denote the functioning time of the vectors U1, U2 and U4 respectively, Ts is the control cycle of space vector modulation. When the Eq. 5 is decomposed in the α-β axis, the functioning time of each vector can be calculated as:

$$\begin{cases} T_a=T_s[1-2k\sin\theta] \\ T_b=T_s[1-2k\sin(\frac{\pi}{3}-\theta)] \\ T_c=2kT_s\sin(\theta) \end{cases} \tag{6}$$

where $k=2U_{ref}/\sqrt{3}$ represents modulation depth, θ stands for the expected reference space voltage vector angle. Similarly, the functioning time of the reference vectors located in triangle A, B and D can be obtained easily. Then it is not difficult to get the functioning time of the rest five sectors by symmetry. To ensure smoothness of the output voltage waveform, vector mutation should be avoided effectively in the process of switching vector. Therefore, in the proposed SVPWM modulation algorithm, short positive vector is selected as starting vector for the synthesis of four output vectors.

4. SIMULATION

A PMSM is used to test the proposed method. The main parameters are R = 2.875Ω, Ld = Lq = 8.5mH, Ψf = 0.175Wb, τ = 16mm, p = 4, J = 16kg·m^2, Bω = 4N·s/rad, Udc = 550V. To study the operation of the NPC with classical modulation, the SVPWM inverter-fed PMSM with the whole control scheme has been simulated using Matlab/Simulink software. Fig. 5 gives the simulation model. In the simulation process, the machine starts without load. In order to verify static and dynamic performance of the designed permanent magnet synchronous motor control system, the load torque TL is set as 10N·m at 0.05s after the system is stable and at the rated speed. The simulation results are shown in Fig. 6 through Fig. 9. From the simulation results, it can be seen that transient responses of the stator current and the motor speed are relatively fast and waveforms are relatively smooth; the stator current is nearly sinusoidal at steady-state; transition rate of the output voltage is relatively low; and waveform of the output voltage is standard three-level waveform and closer to sine wave than the two-level, that means it is a good waveform; harmonics of the output voltage is small. Then when into the steady state, the motor torque ripple is relatively small and stable.

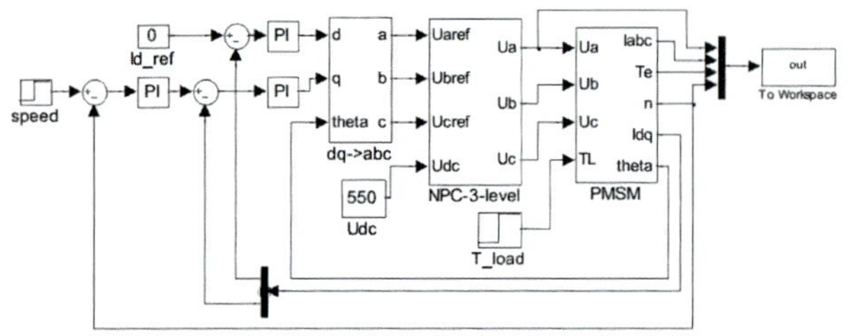

Figure 5. Simulation schematic of the three-level NPC inverter-fed PMSM vector control system.

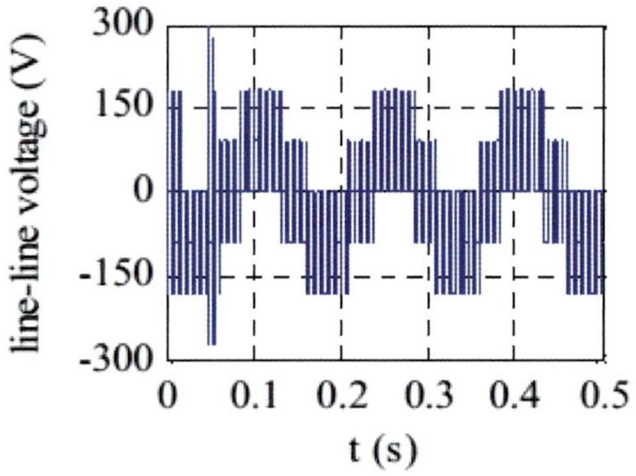

Figure 6. Line-to-line volt.

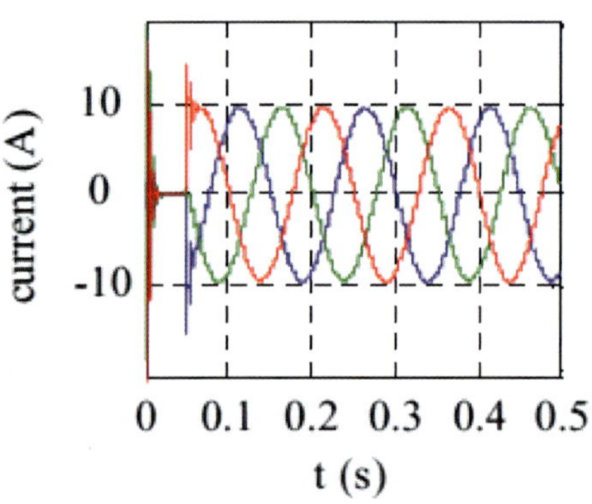

Figure 7. Stator current.

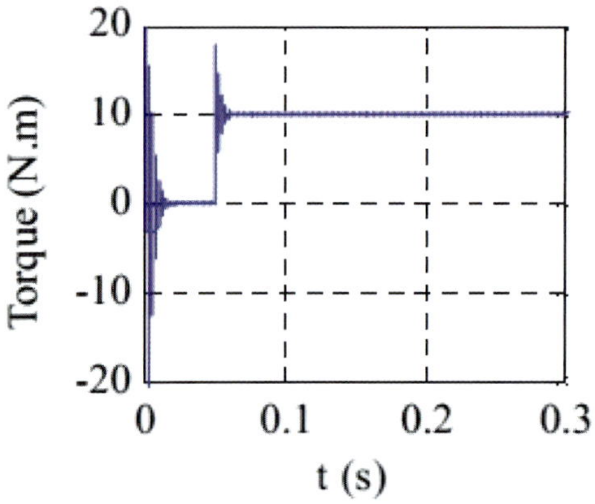

Figure 8. Torque response.

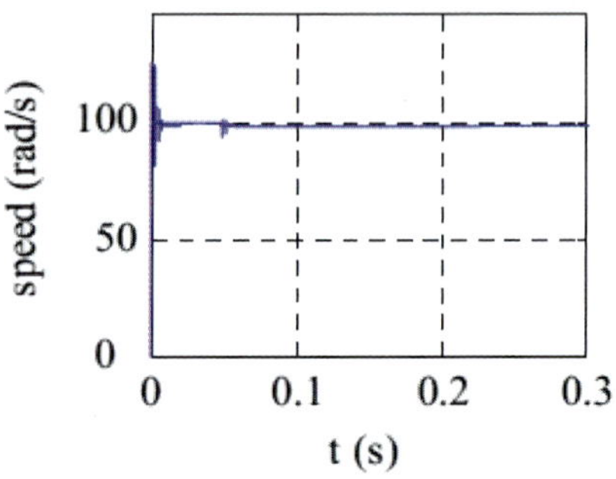

Figure 9. Rotor speed.

5. CONCLUSION

This paper has suggested a mathematical model and control design methodology for the vector control of SVPWM PMSM drives using three-level NPC inverter. The paper provided a detailed description of both three-level NPC inverter and SVPWM control algorithm. The simulation results show that the dynamic response of the speed drives is fast, the motor speed fluctuation and the torque ripple are reduced. Moreover, the steady state could be reached in a much shorter time, and the output voltage and current harmonic are small, when applied load. From this analysis, high dynamic performance, good stability and precision are achieved. As a conclusion, the proposed method could be used in high voltage and great power applications as electrical traction.

ACKNOWLEDGEMENTS

This work was financially supported by the Innovation Program of Shanghai Municipal Education Commission (12zz191).

REFERENCES

— [1] R. Souad, H. Zeroug. Comparison between direct torque control and vector control of a permanent magnet synchronous motor drive. *Power Electronics and Motion Control Conference*. Vol. 1 (2008), p. 1209.
— [2] W. D. Jiang, S. W. Du, L. C. Chang. Hybrid PWM strategy of SVPWM and VSVPWM for NPC three-level voltage-source inverter. *IEEE Transactions on Power Electronics*. Vol. 25 (2010): p 2607.
— [3] K. Yamanaka. A novel neutral point potential stabilization technique using the information of output current polarities and voltage vector. *IEEE Trans. on Industry Applications*, Vol. 38 (2002): p. 1572.
— [4] X. H. Lin, S. Gao, J. Li. A new control strategy to balance neutral-point voltage in three-level NPC inverter. *IEEE 8th International Conference on Power Electronics and ECCE Asia (ICPE & ECCE)*, Vol. 1 (2011), p. 2593.
— [5] N. Celanovic, D. Boroyevich. A comprehensive study of neutral-point voltage balancing problem in three-level neutral-point-clamped voltage source PWM inverters. *IEEE Trans. On Power Electronics*, Vol. 15(2000), p. 242.

Research on Travelers' Route Choice Behavior of Travelers Based on Fuzzy Reasoning and Prospect Theory

G.J. Zhang

Sichuan College of Architectural Technology, Department of Information Engineering, Deyang, Sichuan, China

H.X. Zhao*

Shenzhen Graduate School, Harbin Institute of Technology, Shenzhen, Guangdong, China

**Email: zhaohaixiahit@126.com*

ABSTRACT: Travelers' route choice behavior is usually based on analysis of objective information and is explained by expected utility theory. However, less researcher consider information effect on travelers' psychological feelings. In this paper, objective information affecting route choice is firstly analyzed and prospect theory is applied to do psychological mapping of the objective information of route choice contributing factors so as to forming subjective information. Then, the relationship model between the subjective information and evaluation levels is proposed. A BP fuzzy neural network method is designed to simulate relationship model and solve it. Route choice possibility evaluation value is obtained by fuzzy aggregation and defuzzification processing of evaluation levels, which reflects probability of traveler's route choice. Finally, a real network is used to test the validation of this model.

KEYWORDS: Route choice; Fuzzy reasoning; Prospect theory; Neutral network.

1. INTRODUCTION

With the continuous expansion of city scale, economic and social activities have become increasingly frequent, the number of cars increases rapidly, and city travel demand arises dramatically. As a result, the traffic problems have become increasingly prominent. Improving the utilization of facilities, strengthening traffic control and management is an effective way to enhance the operation efficiency of the traffic system and to ease the traffic congestion. Meanwhile, the further study of travelers' route choice behavior to provide reasonable method for traffic managers, is an idea to achieve this.

Improving the operational efficiency of road traffic system is one of the important issues of city traffic. Advanced traveler information system can help travelers to avoid the congested roads, choose the best path to shorten the travel time, and improve the efficiency of transportation network. But the ATIS's efficiency depends on travelers' reaction to this system as well as its confidence degree [1].

Improving the utilization of facilities, strengthening traffic control and management is an effective way to enhance the operation efficiency of the traffic system and to ease the traffic congestion. The study of travelers' route choice behavior and the establishment of the route choice behavior model would provide reasonable method for traffic managers, which would be an idea to achieve the effective way mentioned above. For the research about traveler route choice behavior, seen from the methods, foreign scholars Hoogerdoorn [2] found that Zadeh's fuzzy logic can explain and analyze travelers' route choice behavior and achieve better accuracy. But with further research, in some aspects, it is inadequate to study the routine choice behavior just based on the fuzzy theory. From the starting point of the study, the traditional research often use the expected utility theory to describe travelers, route choice behavior and think that man is "rational man." In fact, man's rationality is limited. The "prospect theory", which was proposed by Kahneman and Tversky in 1979, was based on a lot of the actual investigation and experimental analysis [3]. This theory studies people's actual decision making behavior and describes people's actual behavior under uncertainty situation. Almost all aspects involved people's wealth preference can expect the help of the prospect theory [4]. It is a good analysis of the relationship between objective information and subjective information and study decision markers' risk attitudes from the perspective of gains and losses [5]. However, applying the prospect theory to study travelers' routine choice behavior is rare.

2. ANALYSIS ON INFLUENTIAL FACTORS OF THE ROUTE CHOICE BEHAVIOR AND ITS PSYCHOLOGICAL INFLUENCE

2.1. *Influential factors of factors that affect travelers' route choice behavior*

In the process of personal growth, everyone has formed the relatively stable psychological characteristics influenced by the environment, education and social status and identity formed in the personal development, in route choice behavior study, it is reflected in travelers' gender, age, economic status, level of knowledge, personality and preferences, purpose and nature of trip and their familiarity with the road network, etc. In the process of travel, these conditions will affect the travelers' mental activities and the outcome of their behaviors.

When travelers choose one routine, the routine's road, environment and traffic information determines whether it will be selected by travelers or not in a large degree. Roads, environmental and traffic information mainly include the routine's length, travel time, travel costs, road congestion, the number of intersections and the way of controlling intersections, traffic environment and weather conditions and etc.

There are two ways of gaining the influence information involved in the routine's choice. They are obtained by experience and provided by ATIS respectively.

2.2. *Travelers' route choice behavior based on prospect theory*

(1) The application of value function.

The relationship between the value function and the reference point is very close. Kahneman and Tversky once pointed out that-people's decision can be controlled by the method of changing the reference point. From this the importance of reference point in the value function can be seen [6].

The travelers' psychological perception of information can be described by value function of prospect theory as shown in figure 1. The value function has two remarkable characteristics: one is that the function is an convex function in obtaining interval, but is an concave function in the loss interval, namely it performs for risk avoidance in the obtained interval, but performs for the risk seeking in the loss interval; the other feather is that near the reference point, loss is more steeply than gain, which phenomenon is called loss avoiding.

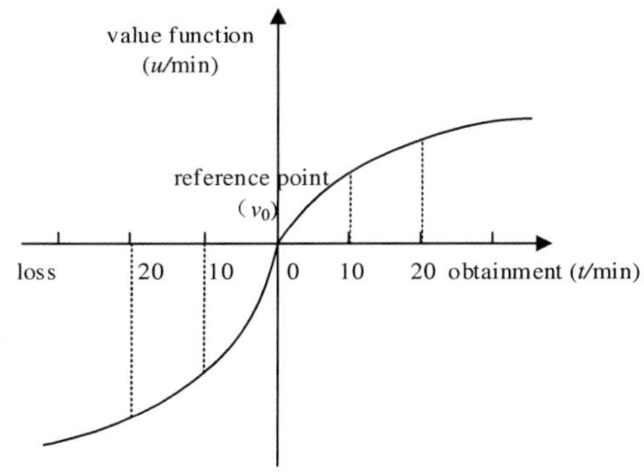

Figure 1. Value function.

According to the prospect theory, the paper defines the value function as follows.

When the value is larger, it is more beneficial to the traveler:

$$v(x) = \begin{cases} (x - v_0)^a & x \ge v_0 \\ \lambda(v_0 - x)^a & x < v_0 \end{cases} \quad (1)$$

When the value is smaller, it is more beneficial to for the traveler:

$$v(x) = \begin{cases} \lambda(x - v_0)^a & x \ge v_0 \\ (v_0 - x)^a & x < v_0 \end{cases} \quad (2)$$

Where, $v(x)$ is value function; x is the objective value of route choice value; a is risk attitude coefficient, $0 < a < 1$, and larger a indicates the traveler is more inclined to risk. When $a = 1$, it is the risk medium. λ is loss avoiding coefficient, and if $\lambda > 1$, it shows that traveler is more sensitive to loss.

(2) The application of weighting function

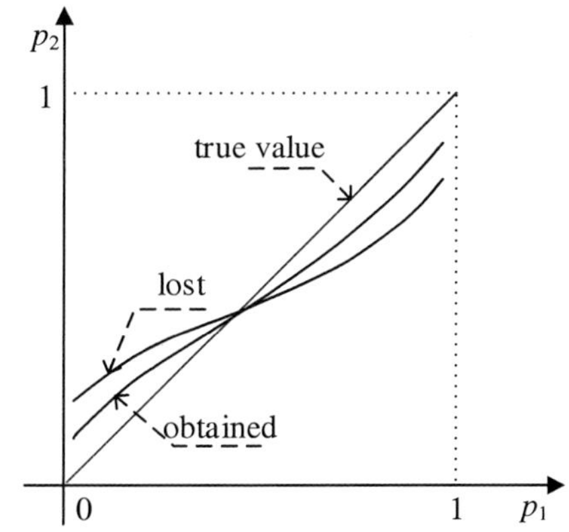

Figure 2. Weight function.

In the figure, p_1 represents the actual likelihood of the event occurring, and p_2 represents the psychological mappingm appingm apping of the actual likelihood of the event occurrence.

The weight function in prospect theory can describe risk decision making. On the basis of the weight function proposed by Kahneman in 1992, the weighting formula in this paper is as follows.

When obtained: $$w^{+}(p)=\frac{p^{\gamma}}{(p^{\gamma}+(1-p)^{\gamma})^{\frac{1}{\gamma}}} \quad (3)$$

When lost: $$w^{-}(p)=\frac{p^{\delta}}{(p^{\delta}+(1-p)^{\delta})^{\frac{1}{\delta}}} \quad (4)$$

Where, p is the possibility of the event. In addition, Kahneman calibrate $\gamma = 0.61$, $\delta = 0.69$ [3] after experiments.

The value function of prospect theory mainly carries on the psychological refection of the impact of the information on the route choice, and the weight function mainly to the route evaluation level.

2.3. *Travel routing choice behaviors based on fuzzy reasoning*

Since the factors affecting the choice of one routine and route evaluation are expressed in the fuzzy form, it needs to establish the relational model between factors affecting route choice and route evaluation grade to get the fuzzy comprehensive evaluation and route choice possibility evaluation value, and then carry on fuzzification, fuzzy rule base, fuzzy inference, and defuzzification operations. Combining with fuzzy system structure, the arithmetic logical structure of factors affecting travelers' route selection based on fuzzy reasoning is as shown as following:

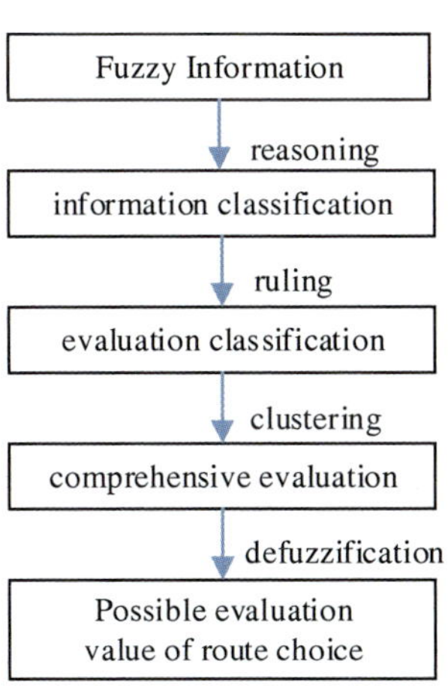

Figure 3. Three logical structure of fuzzy systems.

To achieve the above-described logical structure, it requires the use of selection of the basic operations of fuzzy sets and membership function of fuzzy theory, which acts as a basement of fuzzy reasoning and fuzzy model establishment.

3. THE MODEL FOR RELATIONSHIP BETWEEN INFLUENCING INFORMATION OF ROUTE CHOICE AND EVALUATION LEVEL

3.1. *Model establishment*

This paper extends the calculation method of the fuzzy rules apply degree of T-S fuzzy model. Originally, t-s fuzzy model has single approach to one consequence. For example, if A_1, A_2... A_n happen, then B occurs. While new model has multiple approaches to one consequence. For example, if A_1 happens, then B occurs in some extent, which weaken relationship between premises. The single approach to one consequence in the T-S model apply multiple equation, so does this paper. But when to merge approaches, the add equation is applied. Based on analysis, the equation for rules adaptability corresponding with evaluation level V is:

$$r_{iv}=\sum_{j=1}^{5} w_{\overline{T}} * u_{\overline{T}ij} * w_{\overline{T}jv}+\sum_{j=1}^{5} w_{\overline{D}} * u_{\overline{D}ij} * w_{\overline{D}jv}+\sum_{j=1}^{5} w_{\overline{S}} * u_{\overline{S}ij} * w_{\overline{S}jv} \quad (5)$$

Table 1. The parameter list.

Relevant parameters	Parameters description and explanation
$\overline{T}, \overline{D}, \overline{S}$	Value optimized by the value function of prospect theory of T, D, S
P	The possibility value of route choice corresponding to the evaluation level of
$\overline{P}$	The value of P optimized by the weight function of prospect theory namely the
$w_{\overline{T}}, w_{\overline{D}}, w_{\overline{S}}$	The weight of $\overline{T}, \overline{D}, \overline{S}$
i	The traveler sequence number
j	Various grades of $\overline{T}, \overline{D}, \overline{S}$
$\overline{T}j, \overline{D}j, \overline{S}j$	The membership function of j grade of $\overline{T}, \overline{D}, \overline{S}$
$u_{\overline{T}ij}, u_{\overline{D}ij}, u_{\overline{S}ij}$	The match degree of traveler i for all kinds of information and catalogue level
v	The various levels of route evaluation
$w_{\overline{T}jv}, w_{\overline{D}jv}\ w_{\overline{S}jv}$	The weight of the j grade on the v rating of a travelers information of $\overline{T}, \overline{D}, \overline{S}$, namely rule weights
r_{iv}	Application degree of the evaluation value of the i traveler to the route
Pv	Membership function of evaluation grade v
e_i	The total error value generated when the BP network training
cs	Layers of the BP neural network

The partial parameter boundary in the above table is: $i \in \{1,2\cdots,n\}$, $j \in \{1,2,\cdots,5\}$, $v \in \{1,2,\cdots,5\}$.

Rules adaptation involves two aspects: one is degree of fitting u between input and grade, and the other is inspiring intensity of input to each rule, that is weight of information multiplied by weight of rule, and the result is rule adaptation. The relationship model of information grade and evaluation grade has the same basic thought with t-s fuzzy model, while the difference is expressed as below.

Table 2. Comparison between t-s fuzzy model and model proposed in this paper.

Fuzzy rules	T-S fuzzy model	The relationship model in this paper
Conditional sentence (if)	Single point of fuzzy number	Fuzzy value
The results sentence (then)	The exact expression	Fixed value
Rule application degree calculation	Quadrature method	Quadrature method and Addition method

3.2. *Model solving structure based on BP algorithm*

In order to realize the output of the relationship model between, it is necessary to first determine the weight of factor information, the parameters of membership function and the weights of rules. Based on learning algorithm and the structure of relation model of BP neural network, the design of BP fuzzy neural network method for solving is made. The BP fuzzy neural network structure of the route choice influence information and evaluation degree is shown in figure 4.

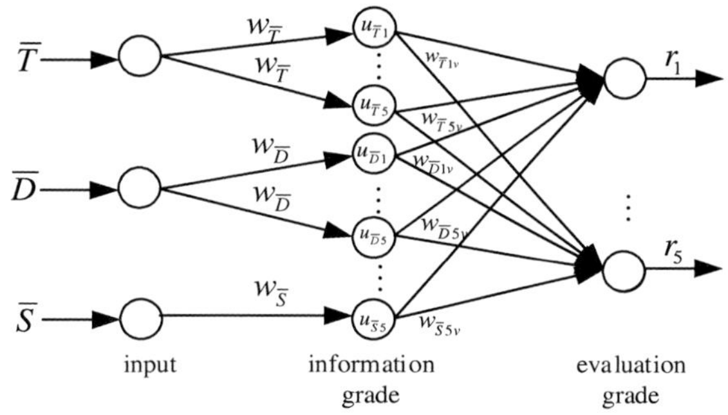

Figure 4. BP fuzzy neural network structure.

Based on the rule adaptation equation (5), and applying BP algorithm to solve the model's weight and parameters, total error of BP fuzzy neural network is obtained as follows:

$$e_i = \frac{1}{2}\sum_{v=1}^{5}(r'_{iv} - r_{iv})^2 \tag{6}$$

Where, r' is ideal output of network.

To minimize the total error, an adjustment of weight and parameters of the model is necessary, which contains adjustment for information weight, rule weight and membership function parameters.

3.3. *Possible evaluation value of route choice*

After establishing the relationship model for influencing information and evaluation grade of route choice, the output are the adaption of the adaptation degree between information and evaluation grade. For achieving route integrated fuzzy evaluation value, two steps are needed. Firstly, to build psychological mapping of route choice probability for each evaluation grade. Then, adaption and psychological mapping are dealt with fuzzy aggregation and defuzzification processing to obtain route choice probability evaluation value.

Evaluation grade reflects the route choice probability. For reflecting the map of route probability on traveler's psychology, optimizing weight for each grade evaluation membership function is necessary, to match each grade with psychological behavior.

Table 3. Membership function of psychological map for each evaluation grade.

Evaluation grade	The parameters of the weight function	Parameters of each grade of p_v ,namely μ_{p_v}	Mental mapping parameter, namely $\mu_{\bar{p}_v}$
Very poor	$\gamma = 0.69$	0.10	0.17
Poor	$\gamma = 0.69$	0.30	0.32
Modest	$\gamma = 0.69$ $\gamma = 0.61$	0.50	0.43
Good	$\gamma = 0.61$	0.70	0.53
Excellent	$\gamma = 0.61$	0.90	0.71

Integrated fuzzy evaluation value is simulated by maximum outcome method. The following figure shows membership function for each evaluation grade by applying maximum outcome method.

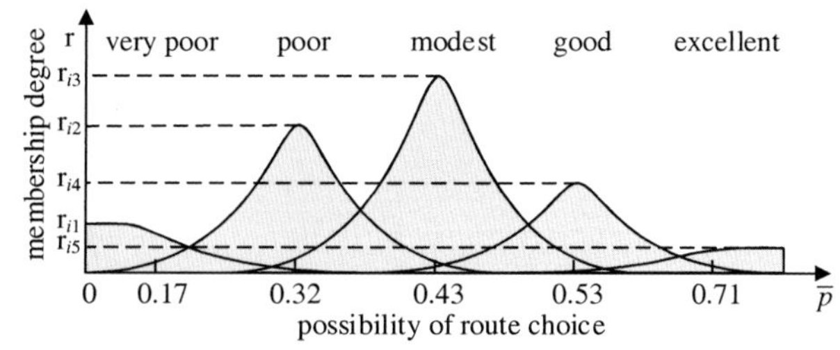

Figure 5. Fuzzy aggregation based on maximum outcome method.

Maximum membership degree for each evaluation degree is corresponded with outputting adaption, respectively.

Making a defuzzification for the fuzzy aggregation result based on maximum outcome method in figure 5, exact value is achieved, which represents the probability evaluation value for choosing one route. The defuzzification process uses the gravity method, and the result p_0 is the center of membership degree function covering area. p_0 is shown as:

$$p_0 = \frac{\int r(p)pdp}{\int r(p)dp} \tag{7}$$

Where, p_0 is the evaluation value of the route choice probability, corresponding with probability for traveler choosing certain route.

When the road and environment information is stable, traffic condition has close correction with travelers' behavior. Thus, this article only updates integrated travel time. For traveler i, assuming the experimental travel time for travel y is $T_{Ei}^{y} = (a_{Ei}^{y}, b_{Ei}^{y}, c_{Ei}^{y})$, and the travel time provided by ATIS is $T_{ATISi}^{y} = (a_{ATISi}^{y}, b_{ATISi}^{y}, c_{ATIS}^{y})$, and predicted travel time is $T_{ei}^{y} = (a_{ei}^{y}, b_{ei}^{y}, c_{ei}^{y})$, while the experimental travel time for travel $y+1$ is $T_{Ei}^{y+1} = (a_{Ei}^{y+1}, b_{Ei}^{y+1}, c_{Ei}^{y+1})$. The membership function of the experimental travel time for travel y is $\exp(-(T-\mu_{Ei})^2/2\sigma_{Ei}^2)$. For convenience, the membership function of experimental travel time is turned into $E_y(\mu_{Ei}, \sigma_{Ei})$. And so on, the membership function of travel time provided by ATIS, predicted travel time is changed into $E_y(\mu_{ATISi}, \sigma_{ATISi})$, the predicted travel time into $E_y(\mu_{ei}, \sigma_{ei})$. Besides, the membership function of experimental travel time for travel $y+1$ is simplified into $E_{y+1}(\mu_{Ei}, \sigma_{Ei})$.

Bayesian theory is adapted in the updating process of travel time parameters.

The predicted travel time for travel is obtained by both experimental travel time and travel time provided by ATIS. Based on Posterior Density formula adjusted by Bayesian theory, the simulation method of parameters in $E_y(\mu_{ei}, \sigma_{ei})$ is as follows:

$$\mu_{ei} = \frac{\sigma_{Ei} \cdot \mu_{ATISi} + \sigma_{ATISi} \cdot \mu_{Ei}}{\sigma_{Ei} + \sigma_{ATISi}} \tag{8}$$

$$\sigma_{ei} = \frac{\sigma_{Ei} \cdot \sigma_{ATISi}}{\sigma_{Ei} + \sigma_{ATISi}} \tag{9}$$

The experimental travel time for travel $y+1$ is obtained by both experimental and predicted travel time for travel y. The simulation method of parameters in $E_{y+1}(\mu_{Ei}, \sigma_{Ei})$ is as follows:

$$\mu_{Ei(y+1)} = \frac{\sigma_{Ei} \cdot \mu_{ei} + \sigma_{ei} \cdot \mu_{Ei}}{\sigma_{Ei} + \sigma_{ei}} \tag{10}$$

$$\sigma_{Ei(y+1)} = \frac{\sigma_{Ei} \cdot \sigma_{ei}}{\sigma_{Ei} + \sigma_{ei}} \tag{11}$$

The integrated travel time for travel $y+1$ is obtained by both experimental travel time and travel time provided by ATIS. The parameter updating method is the same in this article.

4. CASE ANALYSIS AND EVALUATION

This paper is a study of travelers' route choice behavior between the two points. To combine with the reality, the comprehensive analysis is made on the road network in Shenzhen, selecting Shahe East overpass as the starting point, Luohu Railway Station as the terminal point. The distance between two points is about 20 kilometers, and the main road that connects them are expressways and trunk roads. It can be seen from the map: their three main connecting road are North Central Avenue, Shennan Road and Marina Boulevard, and the map is as follows.

Figure 6. The route distribution of the background network.

Settling all survey index data of reflecting road, environment and traffic information, carrying psychological mappingm appingm appings respectively based on the corresponding reference point and value function to obtain subjective information, as the input of BP fuzzy neural network, the possibility of route choice for fuzzy reasoning is deducted and five actual rating levels in line with the extent of each traveler are solved out, namely the degree of application of the relationship model output, as the actual output of BP fuzzy neural network and then initializing the network's information weights, rule weights and membership function parameter values, to calculate all types of traveler information weights under the condition of different route, as shown in table 4.

The choosing probability for each path of travelers is calculated by the BP fuzzy neural network. The gap between the probable maximum or minimum excepted value for each choice is 0.075. The probability that the first class travelers' possibility of error less than 0.075 is 0.971 and the second class travelers' possibility of error less than 7.5 is 0.951, indicating the calculated route choice possibility evaluation value in the range of the average fuzzy values of travelers stated.

Table 4. Information weights value of various types of travelers in case of different routes.

Traveler category	route	$w_{\overline{T}}$	$w_{\overline{D}}$	$w_{\overline{S}}$
The first class travelers	L_1	0.7476	0.0527	0.0523
	L_2	0.7606	0.0513	0.1131
	L_3	1.0114	0.0512	0.0507
The second class travelers	L_1	0.7297	0.0505	0.0504
	L_2	0.7897	0.0512	0.0523
	L_3	0.8143	0.0528	0.1084

According to information feedback and update, using iterative computation on route choice behavior model, that the change of travelers route choice probability increased with travel times when the increase in travel times is predicted.

The choice probability for each route of travelers for each route choice probability with increasing travel times gradually change with increasing travel times, due to the continuous accumulation of information, travelers gradually has a fixed understanding on each route and their route choice possibility becomes stable.

Figure 7 describes an object which is one from the first class traveler and the corresponding possibility for path choosing changes more slowly with the increase of travel times. As can be seen from the graph, for the first class traveler, they prefer to choose the route 2, and then route 3, and the possibility to choose route 1 is minimum.

Figure 8 describes an object which is one from the second class traveler and the corresponding possibility for path choosing also changes more slowly with the increase of travel times. As can be seen from the graph, for the second class traveler, they prefer to choose the route 3,and the probability of choose route 3 is far greater than route 1 and route 2, and the probability of choose route 2 is slightly larger than route 1.

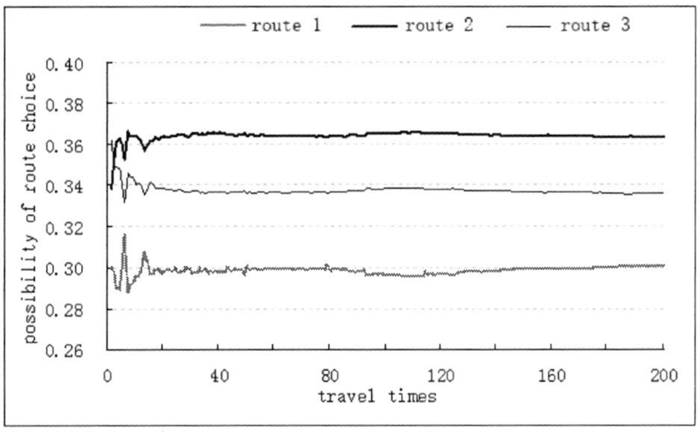

Figure 7. The first type of travelers' route choice probability curve.

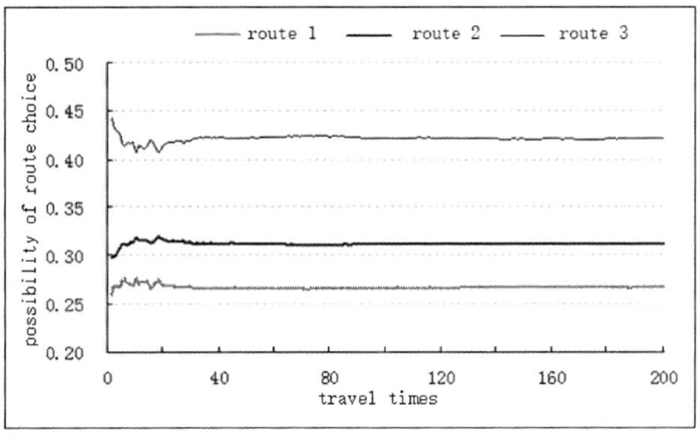

Figure 8. The second type of travelers' route choice probability curve.

5. CONCLUSION

This paper adopts fuzzy reasoning and prospect theory to research route choice problem, according to which, the travelers' route choice behavior is studied based on the subjective information, and then the method and expression form of influencing, route choice factor index are obtained. Secondly, the relation model between the subjective information and grade of evaluation is established, and the BP fuzzy neural network is constructed and calculated based on the route choosing behavior, which effectively reveals the feasibility of BP algorithm in route choice behavior, as well as its potential in improving aspects of traditional algorithms. Finally, the effectiveness and superiority of the proposed model and method based on fuzzy reasoning and prospect theory are verified with the help of the actual survey data.

REFERENCES

- [1] Cascetta E, Russo F. A Model of Route Perception in Urban Road Networks. Transportation Research Part B. 2002, 36(7):577~592.
- [2] Hoogendoorn S.P, Copinga G. Perspectives of Fuzzy Logic in Traffic Engineering. TRB 78th Annual Meeting. 1999, 247~253.
- [3] Zhao Lin, Zhang Xing-chen. A Prospect Theory-Based Route Choice Model of Traveler with Prior Information. Journal of Transportation System Engineering and Information Technology. 2006, 6(2):42~46.
- [4] Zou Yan, Guo Ju-e. Two Important Improvements of Prospect Theory-Study of the Loss Aversion Coefficient and the Reference Point. Operations Research and Management Science. 2007, 16(5):87~89.
- [5] Liu Rui-xia, Wu Dong-hua, Ling He-liang. New Research into Judgment and Decision-making under Uncertainty—Prospect Theory. Operations Research and Management Science. 2005, 14(2):14~18.
- [6] Song Hui. Analysis of Expected Utility Theory and Prospect Theory. Journal of Xi an University of Finance and Economics. 2008, 21(2):59~64.

Chapter 4

Signal and Image Processing

Cloud Model Based SaDE for Feature Selection in Hyper-spectral Image Data

J.H. Ku[1,2*]
1. Department of Information Engineering, Hainan Institute of Science & Technology, Haikou, China
2. School of Computer Science, China University of Geosciences, Wuhan, China

Z.H. Cai
School of Computer Science, China University of Geosciences, Wuhan, China

X.Y. Yang
Department of Information Engineering, Hainan Institute of Science & Technology, Haikou, China
Email: kujunhua@163.com

ABSTRACT: Hyperspectral images are captured from hundreds of narrow and contiguous bands from the visible to infrared regions of electromagnetic spectrum. Due to the presence of large number of bands, classification of hyperspectral images becomes computation intensive. In this paper, attempt has been made to develop a supervised feature selection technique guided by evolutionary algorithms. Cloud model based self-adaptive differential evolution (CMSaDE) is used for feature subset generation. Generated subsets are evaluated using a wrapper model where fuzzy k-nearest neighbor classifier is taken into consideration. Our proposed method also uses a feature ranking technique, *ReliefF* algorithm, for removing duplicate features. To demonstrate the effectiveness of the proposed method, investigation is carried out on KSC data set and the results are compared with four other evolutionary based state-of-the-art feature selection techniques. The proposed method shows promising results compared to others in terms of overall classification accuracy and Kappa coefficient.

KEYWORDS: Feature selection; Hyperspectral images; Evolution computation; Cloud model; Self-adaptive differential evolution.

1. INTRODUCTION

Hyperspectral imaging sensors [1] acquire a set of images from hundreds of narrow and contiguous bands of electromagnetic spectrum ranging from visible to infrared regions. Images captured by hyperspectral sensors have ample spectral information to identify and distinguish spectrally unique materials. Classification of hyperspectral images is a challenging task due to the presence of a huge number of bands in each pixel position. Performance of a classifier depends on the interrelationship between sample size and number of features and also on classifier complexity. Since the number of features in a hyperspectral image is quite large, to classify the patterns properly, the sample size should also be high, which is infeasible in real life situation. Another fact regarding the hyperspectral images is that the neighboring bands are usually strongly correlated. Therefore, feature selection [2] is one of the important tasks for reducing the dimensionality. Feature selection methods can be categorized as supervised and unsupervised ones according to availability of labeled patterns. Supervised feature selection methods [3–5] which are mainly feature selection techniques have been applied in hyperspectral images.

In recent years, the issue of the supervised classification of hyperspectral images has attracted much research from the remote sensing community. Compared with previous developments [9,10], the current objective that is set by researchers is to further boost the classification accuracy [11-14]. From these new works, one can discern that an important direction of the research is related to the choice of classification approach.

Various stochastic optimization based feature selection techniques for hyperspectral images are found in litera-ture exploiting the merits of genetic algorithm (GA) [5,18], ant colony optimization (ACO) [4], etc. In [3], Liu et al. used differential evolution for subset generation and used information entropy as objective function. A combi-nation of ACO and DE based methods is used for feature selection in [6], where the population upon which DE operators work are actually drawn from the solutions that the ACO finds.

DE is a powerful evolutionary algorithm for global numeric optimization [7]. Compared with most of the avail-able evolutionary algorithms, it is much simpler and straightforward to implement. The drawback of DE, is that the key parameters to be adopted for a problem needs to be determined by trial and error methods. This drawback is conquered in cloud model Based self-adaptive differential evolution (CMSaDE) [8] algorithm. In this algorithm, self-adaptive control mechanism is exploited to set the optimal parameter values automatically. In the present article, a supervised feature selection method for hyperspectral images is proposed by exploring the applicability of CMSaDE for finding out the suboptimal subset of features and uses wrapper model for evaluating them. Except objective function information, no other information like correlation of features is required to execute the process. In this procedure, classification accuracy of subset of features is treated as an objective function. For removing duplicate features from a subset of generated features, a feature list is formed considering the feature estimating technique ReliefF [16]. The advantage of ReliefF is its efficiency, awareness of the contextual information, and correct estimation of quality attributes for the problems having strong dependencies among them. Since the data usually have overlapping information, fuzzy kNN classifier [17] is used for calculating the classification accuracy.

The organization of this article is as follows: Section 2 contains the relevant techniques involved in the pro-posed work. The proposed method is described in Section 3. Section 4 contains description of the data set, experimental details and result analysis. Finally conclusive remarks are made in Section 5.

2. RELEVANT TECHNIQUES FOR THE PROPOSED METHOD

In this section a brief introduction to differential evolution and self-adaptive differential evolution are given.

2.1. *Differential evolution*

Differential evolution (DE) [7] can be viewed as a search and optimization technique. In DE, a population at generation G (denoted as $X_{i,G}$ where i varies from 1 to the size of the population, NP) consists of a set of d-dimensional parameter vectors where each population vector refers to a possible solution of the problem (target vector). Initially, population vectors are chosen randomly from the entire parameter space. Trial vector of each target vector is obtained by mutation and crossover operation. Depending on the cost values, the selection process selects the vectors for the next generation from the set of trial and target vectors. The steps of DE are as follows:

•Mutation: During mutation stage, the DE algorithm generates new vectors by adding the weighted difference of two vectors to a third vector. For each target vector $X_{i,G}$, a mutant vector for generation G+1 (denoted as, $V_{i,G+1}$) is generated as follows

$$V_{i,G+1} = X_{r1,G} + F(X_{r2,G} - X_{r3,G}) \quad (1)$$

where r1, r2, r3 are random indices and r1, r2, r3∈[1, NP]; $r1 \neq r2 \neq r3 \neq i$ and F∈[0, 2] is a scale factor which amplifies the difference between the two vectors $X_{r2,G}$ and $X_{r3,G}$ and thereby controls the evolution rate of the population vectors.

•Crossover: Uniform crossover technique is used in DE. To increase diversity, the trial vector $U_{i,G+1}$ is obtained from the elements of the mutant vector $V_{i,G+1}$ and the target vector $X_{i,G}$; $U_{i,G+1}$ is written as

$$U_{i,G+1} = (U_{1,i,G+1}, U_{2,i,G+1}, \cdots, U_{d,i,G+1}) \quad (2)$$

Where

$$U_{j,i,G+1} = \begin{cases} V_{j,i,G+1} & \text{if } r(j) \leq \text{CR or } j = rn(i) \\ X_{j,i,G+1} & \text{otherwise} \end{cases}$$

with j = 1,2,...,d, and $r(j)$ denotes the jth random number whose value lies between 0 to 1; CR, the crossover probability, controls the fraction of parameter values that are copied from the mutant vector. A randomly chosen index $rn(i)$ where $rn(i)\in 1,2,\ldots,d$ ensures that $U_{i,G+1}$ receives at least one parameter from $X_{i,G+1}$.

•Selection: In selection operation, if the trial vector at generation G+1 ($U_{i,G+1}$) yields more cost value than the target vector at generation G ($X_{i,G}$), then the trial vector replaces the target vector in the next generation. Hence, $X_{i,G+1}$ is determined as follows:

$$X_{i,G+1} = \begin{cases} U_{i,G+1} & \text{if } f(U_{i,G+1}) \leq f(X_{i,G}) \\ X_{i,G} & \text{otherwise} \end{cases} \quad (3)$$

Where $f(\cdot)$ denotes the cost function of the given vector.

2.2. *Self-adaptive differential evolution algorithm based on cloud model (CMSaDE)*

In DE, suitable values of the three control parameters namely, amplification factor of the difference vector (denoted by, F), crossover control parameter (denoted by, CR), and population size (denoted by, NP) are generally set using trial-and-error method. On the other hand, in CMSaDE [8], self-adaptive control mechanism is used for each population vector to determine the parameters F and CR during the execution of the program. The third parameter, NP is kept constant throughout the run. Let $F_{i,G}$ and $CR_{i,G}$ be the amplification parameter and crossover control parameter for ith population vector at Gth generation, respectively. In each generation, values of the parameters are adapted before mutation operation, so that the new values of the parameters can be used for the following mutation, crossover and selection operations. This is done using the following equations:

2.2.1. *Self-adaptive F*

F mainly controls search foot, we can dynamically adjust F according to the present circumstance. F is adjusted on the basis of continuous normal generations and continuous abnormal generations, the main operations is as follows.

In each generation, F_i is generated by forward normal cloud generator for each individual xi,

$$F_i = CG(Ex, En, He) \in [0,2] \quad (4)$$

where Ex is the mean of successful scale factors, that can produce offspring that can go into the next generation. Ex is initialized as 0.5, and adjusted following

$$Ex = (1-c)Ex + c \cdot mean_L(S_F) \quad (5)$$

where c is a constant in the range of [0,1], $mean_L$ is Lehrer mean [7].

$$mean_L(S_F) = \frac{\sum_{F \in S_F} F^2}{\sum_{F \in S_F} F} \quad (6)$$

En and He respectively controls breadth and stability. When there appears cross-age elite, we can shrink breadth (decrease En) and strengthen the stability (decrease He), making the drops of cloud look like normal distribution, which can increase accuracy and convergence; A simple way is to narrow K-fold to En, He adjusted according to [19]; When there no appears cross-age elite, that is continuous normal generations more than λ_{local}, this demonstrates that the algorithm is stagnated, when it should skip the present neighborhood; A simple way is to expand L times to En, He adjusted according to [19]. When there is still no cross-age elite after local adjustment, that is Continuous normal generations more than $\lambda_{gloal} \succ \lambda_{local}$, a reset of Ex, En, He is necessary.

2.2.2. *Self-adaptive CR*

In each generation, CR_i is randomly generated through normal distributions for each individual x_i

$$CR_i = N_i(CR_m, 0.1) \in [0,2] \quad (7)$$

where CR_m is the mean of successful crossover rates S_{CR} ,which can produce offspring that can go into the next generation. CR_m is initialized as 0.5, and adjusted following

$$CR_m = mean_A(S_{CR}) \quad (8)$$

Where $mean_A$ is arithmetic mean.

3. PROPOSED METHODOLOGY

Like any supervised feature selection method, the proposed algorithm also consists of two stages: subset generation and subset evaluation. In subset generations, a candidate subset is generated by using some search techniques and subset evaluation process evaluates the goodness of the corresponding candidate subset by some criterion. Here the self-adaptive differential evolution algorithm based on cloud model (CMSaDE) technique is used as search criterion and wrapper model is used for evaluating the subset of features.

Algorithm 1. Proposed algorithm

1. Initialization
   - Set the population size, NP.
   - Set the size of each vector (candidate subset) d.
   - Initialize the population (a set of population vectors).
   - Initialize the values of the parameters, F and CR for each vector.
   - For all the features, create a feature list using ReliefF algorithm.
   - Calculate fitness value (classification accuracy) of each vector using fuzzy kNN classifier.
2. Obtain the trial vectors using mutation and crossover operations by Eqs. 1 and 2.
3. If any element of the trial vector is a real number then round it to the nearest integer.
4. If any element of the trial vector is below/above the minimum/maximum feature index value, then it is replaced by the minimum/maximum feature index.
5. If there is any duplication of feature indices in a trial vector, replace one of the repeated index by another feature index (not present in the corresponding vector) which is on the top (or near to it).
6. Calculate fitness value (classification accuracy) of each trial vector using fuzzy kNN classifier.
7. Perform selection operation using Eq. 3.
8. Perform self-adaptation of the values of F and CR for the next generation using Eqs. 4 and 7.
9. Continue Steps 2–8 until termination condition is satisfied.

In any feature selection method, a number of d features is selected from a set of $D(>d)$ features, i.e., a possible solution (candidate subset) is of length d. Each subset is associated with an objective functional value. Differential evolution (DE) process tries to find out the optimum of this function. Classification accuracy is used as an objective criterion. In the proposed methodology, if any solution (candidate subset) contains correlated features, classification accuracy of it will be less and therefore, will be discarded in subsequent generations. This conveys that the present methodology implicitly takes care of correlation among the features while using wrapper models for evaluating the subsets. If any solution contains duplicate features, substitute one of these by a feature which has good discriminating ability for classification. To do so, a feature list is made according to their discriminating ability using ReliefF algorithm. Since, in our investigation, DE has been used in a discrete space, if any real number appears in mutation stage, it is rounded off to the nearest integer.

The step-by-step process of our proposed methodology is described in Algorithm 1. At the beginning, NP number of subsets each with d number of features are randomly selected from the range of feature indices $(1,2,\ldots,D)$. As mentioned earlier, each subset of features is treated as a population vector in DE. While initializing the population, it is ensured that for any subset no redundant feature index is present. After calculating the fitness value of each of these population vectors, using the objective function, mutation and crossover operations are performed on them using Eqs. 1 and 2. The new vector, produced after crossover operation, is called the trial vector. Fitness value of each of these trial vectors is again calculated. Higher classification accuracy corresponds to higher fitness value. Selection operation selects the trial vectors based on their fitness values using Eq. 3. Highly fitted vectors are more suitable than the lower fitted ones. If the fitness value of the trial vector is greater than that of the corresponding target vector, then the trial vector is selected as a member of the population for the next generation, otherwise the target vector remains as it is. This process continues until stopping criterion is reached.

As mentioned earlier, *ReliefF* algorithm is used to construct a feature list of all the features according to their rank and the said list estimates the quality of the attributes according to how well their values are used to identify the instances that are close to each other. The key idea of the algorithm is to estimate the quality of the attributes depending on how well their values help to classify the patterns.

The whole process is continued until stopping criterion is reached. Depending on user's need, one stopping criterion could be to execute the algorithm for some pre-specified number of generations. It could also be set to some specified number of generations for which the change of fitness value of the best subset of features is not significant.

4. EXPERIMENT AND EVALUATION

To evaluate the effectiveness of the proposed self-adaptive differential evolution based feature selection method, experiments are carried out on KSC images, corresponding to the geographical areas of Kennedy Space Center of Florida. The dataset is described in the following.

4.1. *KSC data set*

The KSC [20] images, acquired over Kennedy Space Center (KSC), Florida on March 23, 1996 by NASA AVIRIS, is of size 512×614.AVIRIS acquires data in 224 bands of 10 nm width with wavelengths ranging from 400 nm to 2500 nm. The data is acquired from an altitude of approximately 20 km and have a spatial resolution of 18 m. After removing the bands disturbed due to water absorption or with low SNR value, 176 bands are used for analysis. Training data were selected using land cover maps derived from color infrared photography provided by the Kennedy Space Center and Landsat Thematic Mapper (TM) imagery. The vegetation classification scheme was developed by KSC personnel in an effort to define functional types that are discernable at the spatial resolution of Landsat and the AVIRIS data. Discrimination of land cover for this environment is difficult due to the similarity of spectral signatures for certain vegetation type (Fig.1). Details of the 13 land cover classes considered in the KSC data area are listed in Table 1.

4.2. *Parameter details*

The value of the parameter NP is set before starting any operation. It is set to a value in between 5×d to 10×d. As mentioned earlier, self-adaptive technique is used for adjusting the values of the parameters F and CR. There are separate F and CR parameters for each target vector. The value of F and CR lie in [0.1,1] and [0,1], respectively. These two parameters adapt their values by themselves using Eqs. 4 and 5 from generation to generation before mutation.

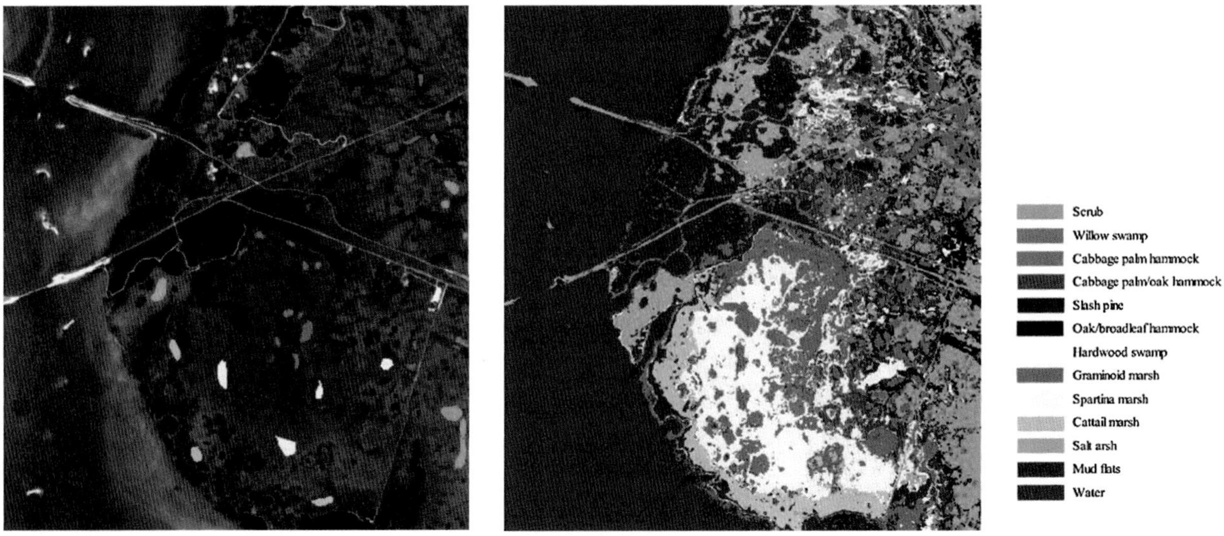

Figure 1. Band 11 image of KSC data.

Table 1. KSC data: class names and number of samples.

Class name	No. of samples
Scrub	761
Willow swamp	243
Cabbage palm hammock	256
Cabbage palm/oak hammock	252
Slash pine	161
Oak/broadleaf hammock	229
Hardwood swamp	105
Graminoid marsh	431
Spartina marsh	520
Cattail marsh	404
Salt marsh	419
Mud flats	503
Water	927

4.3. *Analysis of results*

Performance of the proposed CMSaDE based technique has been compared with that of a GA based [18] method, an ant colony based [4] one, a DE based [3] method and a combination of ACO & DE (ANTDE) [6] based one. As mentioned, experiments are performed on KSC data set described earlier. Before conducting the experiment, normalization of data has been done. The desired number of features to be selected is not known and it varies from image to image. In the present investigation, experiments are carried out for different desired number of features ranging from 9 to 25 with a step size 2. The algorithm is terminated when the difference between the fitness values of two consecutive generations for the best subset of features is negligible (e.g., <0.002) and the same scenario prevails for a certain number of generations for all the stochastic techniques.

For the proposed method, initial solutions are chosen randomly within the range of feature indices i.e., from 1 to 176 for KSC data. At termination of each of the algorithms, fuzzy kNN classifier is used on the selected subset of features using 10-fold cross validation. Performance of the proposed methodology is compared with those of other four existing techniques with respect to overall classification accuracy (OA) and Kappa coefficient (Kappa) [15]. For stochastic feature selection methods, twenty simulations are done with different random initializations and the average values of OA and Kappa measures are reported.

For KSC Data set, the results obtained using the proposed method as well as those using four other techniques with different desired number of features are provided in Table 2 and graphically depicted in Fig. 2. From the table, it is observed that in most of the cases (except the cases of selected number of features as 13 and 25), the proposed method is producing better results than all the four methods used. ANTDE based method is found to be better than both DE, ACO and the GA based methods in terms of both OA and Kappa measures. Between DE and ACO based techniques, the latter one is seen to produce slightly better results compared to the former one. For this data set, the best performance is obtained when the number of selected features is 19 for all the four stochastic methods.

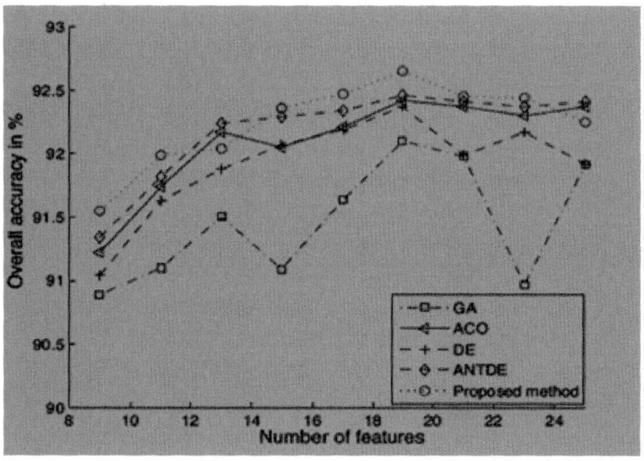

Fig. 2. Comparison of GA, ACO, DE, ANTDE and the proposed method in terms of overall accuracy with respect to the number of features used for KSC data set.

5. CONCLUSIONS

In this article, a new feature selection technique is proposed using cloud model based self-adaptive differential evolution for subset generation in hyperspectral images. A feature ranking method, named *ReliefF*, is used for removal of duplicity of features in a subset. Fuzzy kNN classifier is used for subset evaluation. Performance of the proposed method is compared with that of GA, ACO, DE and ANTDE based ones. Results of the proposed method show significant improvement over the existing algorithms with respect to overall accuracy and Kappa coefficient for KSC data sets used in our investigation. Future work will focus on the initialization of the population vectors and fast convergence of the DE algorithm from the perspective of hyperspectral feature selection.

ACKNOWLEDGEMENTS

This work was supported by Hainan Provincial Natural Science Foundation of China (No. 614248), the projects foundation of Hainan Institute of Science and Technology under grant No. HKYZQJ2014-05.

REFERENCES

— [1] P.K. Varshney, M.K. Arora, Advanced Image Processing Techniques for Remotely Sensed Hyperspectral Data, 2nd ed., Springer Verlag, Berlin, 2004.
— [2] A.K. Jain, R.P.W. Duin, J. Mao, Statistical pattern recognition: a review, IEEE Transactions on Pattern Analysis and Machine Intelligence 22 (1) (2000) 4–37.
— [3] X. Liu, C. Yu, Z. Cai, Differential evolution based band selection in hyperspectral data classification, in: Proceedings of the International Symposium on Intelligence Computation and Applications (ISICA'10), 2010, pp. 86–94.
— [4] F. Samadzadegan, T. Partovi, Feature selection based on ant colony algorithm for hyperspectral remote sensing images, in: 2010 2nd Workshop on Hyperspectral Image and Signal Processing: Evolution in Remote Sensing (WHISPERS), 2010, pp. 1–4.
— [5] L. Zhuo, J. Zheng, F. Wang, X. Li, B. Ai, J. Qian. A genetic algorithm based wrapper feature selection methods for classification of hyperspectral images using support vector machine, in: Proceedings of the International Archives of the Photogrammetry, Remote Sensing and Spatial Information Sciences, Vol. XXXVII, 2008, pp. 397-402.
— [6] R.N. Khushaba, A. Al-Ani, A. AlSukker, A. Al-Jumaily, A combined ant colony and differential evolution feature selection algorithm, in: Proceedings of the International Conference on Ant Colony Optimization and Swarm Intelligence, 2008, pp.1–12.
— [7] R. Storn, K. Price. Differential evolution: a simple and efficient heuristic for global optimization over continuous spaces, Journal of Global Optimization 11 (4) (1997) 341–359.
— [8] Jingjing Sun, Hongbin Dong, Yue Pan. A self-adaptive differential evolution algorithm based on cloud, in: Proceedings of the international conference on network and computational intelligence model, 2012, pp. 59-64.
— [9] J. Ham, Y. Chen, M. M Crawford, and J. Ghosh, "Investigation of the random forest framework for classification of hyperspectral data," IEEE Trans. Geosci. Remote Sens., vol. 43, no. 3, pp.492–501, Mar. 2005.
— [10] Y. Bazi and F. Melgani, "Toward an optimal SVM Classification system for hyperspectral remote sensing images," IEEE Trans. Geosci. Remote Sens., vol. 44, no. 11, pp. 3374–3385, Nov. 2006.
— [11] N. Alajlan, Y. Bazi, F. Melgani, and R.R.Yager, "Fusion of supervised and unsupervised learning paradigms for improved classification of hyperspectral images," Inf. Sci., vol. 217, pp. 39–55, Dec. 2012.
— [12] J. Li, P.R. Marpu, A. Plaza, J. M. Bioucas-Dias, and J.A. Benediktsson, "Generalized composite framework for hyperspectral image classification," IEEE Trans. Geosci. Remote Sens., vol. 51, no.9, pp.4816–4829, Sep. 2013.
— [13] M. Fauvel, Y. Tarabalka, J.A. Benediktsson, J. Chanussot, and J. C. Tilton, "Advances in spectral spatial classification of hyperspectral images," Proc. IEEE, vol. 101, no. 3, pp. 652–675, Mar. 2013.
— [14] J. Li, J. M. Bioucas-Dias, and A. Plaza, "Spectral-spatial classification of hyperspectral data using loopy belief propagation and active learning," IEEE Trans. Geosci. Remote Sens., vol. 51, no. 2, pp. 844–856, Feb. 2013.
— [15] R.G. Congalton, K. Green, Assessing the Accuracy of Remotely Sensed Data, 2nd ed., CRC Press, Boca Raton, London, 2009.
— [16] M. Robnik-ˇSikonja, I. Kononenko, Theoretical and empirical analysis of ReliefF and RReliefF, Machine Learning Journal 53 (2003) 23–69.
— [17] J.M. Keller, M.R. Gray, J.J.A. Givens, A fuzzy k-nearest neighbor algorithm, IEEE Transactions on Systems, Man, and Cybernetics SMC 15 (4) (1985) 580–585.
— [18] S. Yu, S.D. Backer, P. Scheunders, Genetic feature selection combined with composite fuzzy nearest neighbour classifiers for hyperspectral satellite imagery, Pattern Recognition Letters 23 (2002) 183–190.
— [19] Liyu, Li De-yi, Zhang Guang-wei et al., Atomize Feature in Cloud Based Evolutionary Algorithm [J]. Chinese Journal of Electronic, 2009, 37(8):1651-1658.
— [20] J. Ham, Y. Chen, M.M. Crawford, J. Ghosh, Investigation of the random forest framework for classification of hyperspectral data, IEEE Transactions on Geoscience and Remote Sensing 43 (3) (2005) 492–501.

Table 2 OA and Kappa value of GA, ACO, DE, and ANTDE based and the proposed methods for different number of selected features for KSC data set.

Selected no. of features	Method based									
	GA		ACO		DE		ANTDE		Proposed(CMsaDE)	
	OA	Kappa	OA	Kappa	OA	Kappa	OA	Kappa	OA	Kappa
9	90.89	0.8986	91.22	0.9022	91.04	0.9005	91.34	0.9032	**91.55**	**0.9057**
11	91.10	0.9009	91.74	0.9078	91.63	0.9068	91.82	0.9086	**91.99**	**0.9107**
13	91.50	0.9050	92.17	0.9126	91.88	0.9095	92.24	0.9133	**92.26**	**0.9134**
15	91.09	0.9008	92.05	0.9113	92.07	0.9116	92.29	0.9139	**92.36**	**0.9148**
17	91.64	0.9065	92.21	0.9131	92.19	0.9128	92.34	0.9144	**92.47**	**0.9159**
19	92.10	0.9121	92.42	0.9154	92.37	0.9147	92.46	0.9158	**92.65**	**0.9180**
21	91.98	0.9101	92.37	0.9149	91.99	0.9107	92.41	0.9152	**92.45**	**0.9158**
23	90.97	0.8994	92.30	0.9142	92.17	0.9126	92.37	0.9147	**92.44**	**0.9156**
25	91.92	0.9095	92.37	0.9149	91.92	0.9099	92.41	0.9153	**92.42**	**0.9154**

A Robust System for Online Handwritten Chinese/Japanese Character Recognition

B.L. Zhu* & Masaki Nakagawa
Department of Computer and Information Science, Tokyo University of Agriculture and Technology, Tokyo, 184-0012 Japan
**Email: zhubilan@cc.tuat.ac.jp*

ABSTRACT: This paper presents a robust system for online handwritten Chinese/Japanese character recognition. Online handwritten character recognition, recognizing characters from their trajectories, will be used more widely, with the development and proliferation of pen-based or touch-based input devices such as tablet terminals, smart phones, electronic whiteboards and digital pens (e.g., Anoto pen). This paper focuses on the online handwritten Chinese/Japanese character recognition, and describes its recent technology trends, problems and methods to solve them.

KEYWORDS: Online handwriting recognition; Character recognition.

1. INTRODUCTION

Due to the development and proliferation of pen-based or touch-based input devices such as tablet terminals, smart phones, electronic whiteboards, and digital pens (e.g., the Anoto pen), on-line handwritten character recognition is receiving even more attention than before. Realizing online handwritten character recognition with high performance is vital, especially for applications such as the natural input of text on smart phones, to provide a satisfactory user experience.

Although character classifiers with high recognition accuracy have been reported [1], the demand for speeding up recognition is very high for portable devices as well as for desktop applications for which handwriting recognition is incorporated as one of the modules. The performance of these relatively small devices requires having a fast as possible recognition speed while maintaining high accuracy. Even for a desktop PC with relatively high device performance, recognition speed within 0.5 seconds per page and memory consumption within 10 MB are required in actual applications since those applications need more memory consumption on top of the memory consumption for a character recognizer.

Chinese, Japanese, or Korean has thousands of different categories, and their large character set is problematic not only for the recognition rate but also for the recognition speed.

Handwritten character pattern recognition methods are generally divided into two types: online recognition and offline recognition [2]. Online recognition recognizes character patterns captured from a pen-based or touch-based input device where trajectories of pen-tip or finger-tip movements are recorded, while offline recognition recognizes character patterns captured from a scanner or a camera device as two dimensional images.

Both online and offline recognition methods can be roughly divided into two categories: structural and un-structural. Structural methods are based on stroke analysis and use structural features such as sampling points, line segments and/or strokes for offline recognition [3] and for online recognition [4]. Un-structural methods use un-structural features such as directional features, gradient histogram features and projection features such as those for offline [5] and online recognition [6], which eventually achieves stroke-order independence.

Structural methods are weak at collecting global character pattern information, while they are robust against character shape variations. In contrast, un-structural methods are robust against noises but very weak against character shape variations. By combining a structural method (structural recognizer) with an un-structural method (un-structural recognizer), the recognition accuracy improves since they compensate for their respective disadvantages [7].

For online recognition, structural features are often employed with hidden Markov models (HMMs) [8] or Markov random field (MRF) [9]. However, since the un-structural features are easily extracted from an online handwritten pattern by discarding temporal and structural information, we can apply the un-structural method as well. Therefore, we can combine the structural and un-structural methods.

In freely written string recognition, we need to consider whether we should select segmentation-free or over-segmentation-based methods. Character segmentation of cursive handwriting is difficult due to the fact that spaces between characters are not obvious. Without character recognition cues and linguistic context, characters cannot be segmented unambiguously. A feasible way to overcome the ambiguity of segmentation is called integrated segmentation and recognition, which is classified into segmentation-free and over-segmentation-based methods [10] as shown in Figure 1. Segmentation-free methods, mostly combined with hidden Markov model (HMM)-based recognition [11], simply slice the word pattern into frames (primitive segments) and label the sliced frames, which are concatenated into characters during recognition. Such methods do not sufficiently incorporate character shape information. On the other hand, over-segmentation-based methods attempt to split character patterns at their true boundaries and label the split character patterns [12]. Character patterns may also be split within them, but they are merged later. This is called over-segmentation. It is usually accomplished in two steps: over-segmentation and path search. The string pattern is over-segmented into primitive segments such that each segment composes a single character or part of a character. The segments are combined to generate candidate character patterns (forming a segmentation candidate lattice), which are evaluated using character recognitions incorporating geometric and linguistic contexts. However, character segmentation is a hard problem to solve. When handwritten words are not easily segmented, such as with cursive writing, over-segmentation may result in misrecognition. In this case, a segmentation-free method is appropriate. For Chinese/Japanese recognition, however, segmentation is easier than in English or other western languages.

Segmentation-free offline word recognition methods using un-structural features in sliding windows combined with hidden Markov models (HMMs) [13] and those using over-segmentation-based methods [14] can also be considered as un-structural methods since they use un-structural features.

Since over-segmentation-based methods can better utilize character shapes, they are considered to outperform segmentation-free methods [15]. Moreover, over-segmentation-based methods produce less primitive segments since they attempt to find the true boundaries of character patterns as segmentation point candidates; therefore, we consider that over-segmentation-based methods are effective and more efficient compared with segmentation-free methods for Chinese/Japanese string recognition. We show our online handwritten Chinese/Japanese string recognition system in Figure 2, where an over-segmentation-based method is used.

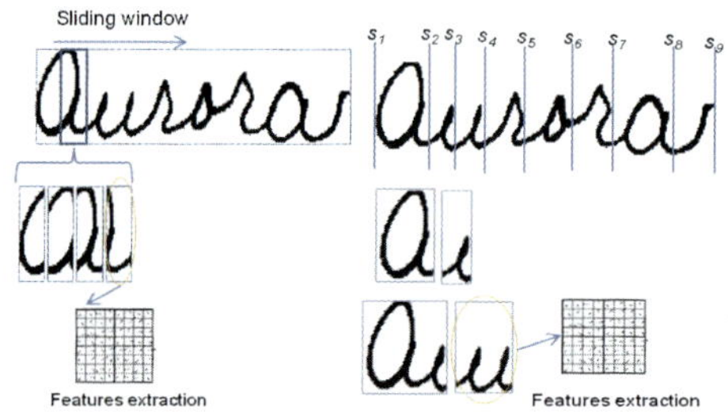

(a) Segmentation-free method (b) Over-segmentation-based method

Figure 1. Freely written string recognition.

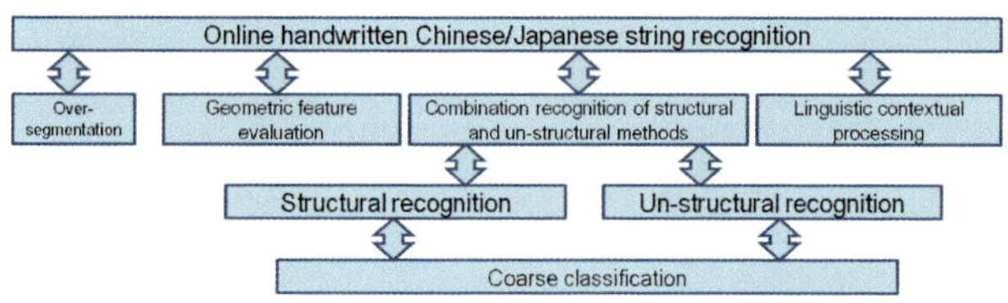

Figure 2. Online handwritten Chinese/Japanese string recognition.

In this chapter, we describe a robust system for online handwritten Chinese/Japanese character recognition, and the recent technology trends, problems and methods to solve them for the online handwritten Chinese/Japanese character recognition. The rest of this chapter is organized as follows. Section 2 presents an overview of our online handwritten string recognition system. Section 3 presents structural and un-structural recognitions. Section 4 describes coarse classification. Section 5 describes combination of structural and un-structural recognitions. Section 6 presents string recognition, and Section 7 draws conclusions.

2. RECOGNITION SYSTEM OVERVIEW

We process each online handwritten string pattern as follows:

(1) Segmentation candidate lattice construction.

Strokes in a string are grouped into blocks (primitive segments) in accordance with the features such as off-stroke (pen lift between two adjacent strokes) distance and overlap of bounding boxes of adjacent strokes. Each primitive segment is assumed to be a character or a part of a character. An off-stroke between adjacent blocks is called a candidate segmentation point, which can be a true segmentation point (SP) or a non-segmentation point (NSP). One or more consecutive primitive segments form a candidate character pattern. The combination of all candidate patterns is represented by a segmentation candidate lattice.

(2) Character pattern recognition.

There are thousands of categories for the Chinese/Japanese language. First, to improve the recognition speed, we reduce recognition candidates by using a coarse classifier for each online candidate character pattern. After coarse classification, we apply a structural recognizer and an un-structural recognizer to recognize the input pattern, and obtain two sets of character candidate classes from the two recognizers. Each candidate class of each set has a corresponding structural or un-structural recognition score. We combine the two sets of candidate classes considering their recognition scores to output a set of candidate classes to nominate them into the candidate lattice.

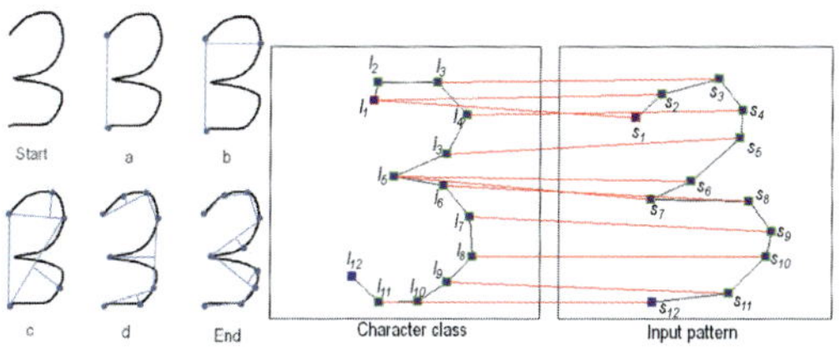

(a) (b)

Figure 3. Feature points extraction and labeling.

(3) Search and recognition.

We apply the beam search strategy to search for the candidate lattice. During the search, the paths are evaluated in accordance with the path evaluation criterion proposed Zhu et al. [1], which combines the scores of character recognition, linguistic context, and geometric features (character pattern sizes, inner gaps, single-character positions, pair-character positions, candidate segmentation points) with the weighting parameters estimated by a genetic algorithm (GA). This method selects an optimal path as the recognition result.

3. STRUCTURAL AND UN-STRUCTURAL RECOGNITIONS

3.1. *Structural recognition*

First, we include a brief description here on our structural character pattern recognition system [16]. Our system first normalizes an input online character pattern by a linear or nonlinear normalization method. An online character pattern is a sequence of strokes and a stroke is a time sequence of coordinates of pen-tip or finger-tip movements. Then, it extracts feature points by such a method as Ramner [17]. First, the start and end points of every stroke are picked up as feature points. Then, the most distant point from the straight line between adjacent feature points is selected as a feature point if the distance to the straight line is greater than a threshold value. This selection is done recursively until no more feature points are selected. The feature point extracting process is shown in Figure 3(a).

Then it uses a MRF model to match the feature points with the states of each character class as shown in Figure 3(b) and obtain a similarity for each character class. It then selects the character class with the largest similarity as the recognition result.

Site: Feature points from an input pattern $S=\{s_1, s_2, s_3,\ldots,s_{12}\}$

Label: States of a character class $L=\{l_1, l_2, l_3,\ldots, l_{12}\}$

Labeling problem: Assign labels to the sites such as $\{s_1= l_1, s_2 = l_1, s_3 = l_3,\ldots,s_{11} = l_9, s_{12} = l_{11}\}$

The system recognizes the input pattern by assigning labels to the sites to make the matching between the input pattern and each character class. MRF model is used to solve the labeling problem.

HMMs have been often used with online statistical structural recognition methods and offline English word recognition methods. HMMs probabilistically treat a sequence of feature vectors in writing or position order, so that they can only use the neighborhood relationships between the successively adjacent feature vectors in writing or position order (the so-called one-dimensional neighborhood relationships) and the two-dimensional neighborhood relationships, such as those among the neighboring feature vectors, on distances are not explicitly expressed. For one-dimensional neighborhood relationships, HMMs only use the state transition probabilities and unary features, but binary features are not used well. Moreover, the neighborhood relationships among more than two neighboring feature vectors, such as ternary features, cannot be used. Although some HMMs apply binary features, they only merge the binary features into the unary features and use a vector of larger dimension because HMMs do not take a new view of the binary features, which limits recognition accuracy.

The MRF model is described using an undirected graph in which a set of random variables have a Markov property, and MRFs can be used to effectively integrate information among neighboring feature vectors, such as binary and ternary features, and two-dimensional neighborhood relationships [9]. Therefore, MRFs have been widely and successfully applied to image processing [9]. However, MRFs had not been applied to online character recognition until our reports [16]. Current online handwritten character recognition tends to use HMMs (note that HMMs can be viewed as specific cases of MRFs). MRFs have more degrees of freedom than HMMs for explicitly expressing relations among multiple feature vectors.

We have proposed an MRF model for online recognition of handwritten Japanese characters [16]. We focused on an online structural method introducing temporal information into one-dimensional neighborhood relationships and compared their effects on HMMs and MRFs. Experimental results demonstrated the superiority of the method and that MRFs exhibited higher recognition accuracy than HMMs.

3.2. *Un-structural recognition*

For the un-structural recognizer, we do not need to transform each online character pattern to an offline character pattern (two dimensional images), and extract directional features directly from the online character pattern. From an online character pattern, we extract directional features: histograms of normalized stroke direction [6]. For coordinate normalization, we apply pseudo 2D bi-moment normalization (P2DBMN) [6]. The local stroke direction is decomposed into eight directions, and from the feature map of each direction, 8x8 values are extracted by Gaussian blurring so that the dimensionality of feature vectors is 512. To improve the Gaussianity of feature distribution, each value of the 512 features is transformed by the Box-Cox transformation (also called variable transformation). The input feature vector is reduced from 512D to *n*D by the Fisher linear discriminant analysis (FLDA) [10]. Then we use the *n*D feature vectors to create a modified quadratic discriminant function (MQDF) recognizer [18] as follows:

$$g_2(\mathbf{x},\boldsymbol{\omega}_i) = \sum_{j=1}^{k} \frac{1}{\lambda_{ij}} [\boldsymbol{\varphi}_{ij}^T(\mathbf{x}-\boldsymbol{\mu}_i)]^2 + \frac{1}{\delta}\{\|\mathbf{x}-\boldsymbol{\mu}_i\|^2 - \sum_{j=1}^{k}[\boldsymbol{\varphi}_{ij}^T(\mathbf{x}-\boldsymbol{\mu}_i)]^2\} + \sum_{j=1}^{k}\log\lambda_{ij} + (n-k)\log\delta \quad (1)$$

where μ_i is the mean vector of class ω_i, λ_{ij} ($j = 1, \ldots, k$) are the largest eigenvalues of the covariance matrix and φ_{ij} are the corresponding eigenvectors, k denotes the number of principal axes, and δ is a modified eigenvector that is set as a constant. The value of δ can be optimized on the training data set. However, for a convenience, we simply set it as $\gamma\lambda_{average}$ where $\lambda_{average}$ is the average of λ_{ij} ($i,j = 1, \ldots, n$) for all features of all classes and γ is a constant that is larger than 0 and smaller than 1.

According to previous works [6], the best unstructural recognition performance is obtained when n is about 160 and k is about 50 for the MQDF recognizer. When combining structural and unstructural recognizers and then combining them with linguistic context and geometric features for the string recognition, we have found the best combination performance is obtained when n is about 90 and k is about 10 for the MQDF recognizer. Therefore, we take n as 90 and k as 10, respectively.

4. COARSE CLASSIFICATION

A general approach to improving the recognition speed is to perform coarse classification, preclassification, or candidate selection before the fine classification [19].

The coarse classification typically uses simpler classification algorithms or fewer features in order to achieve a better speed than does the fine classification. It is used to select a relatively small subset of candidates out of a very large set quickly. The fine classification would then be used on these candidates to match an input pattern so that the whole recognition time is reduced. Current approaches for coarse classification typically use distance measures that are simpler than those for fine classification [20]. The confidence evaluation provides even more precise candidate selection [21]. Others use simple features different from those for fine classification [22]. Sequential (multi-stage) classifications using a partial set of features at each stage have also been used [23]. A common characteristic of these methods is that the entire candidate selection process is performed during the recognition process. We call these "dynamic approaches."

In contrast to dynamic approaches, prototypes may be organized prior to the search itself so that the search is performed on a subset of prototypes. We could mention a number of methodologies that vary slightly in how the data is organized. The simplest ones are proposals for ordered spaces and tree structures. The search on pre-structured spaces aims particularly at alleviating problems with search costs. As a result, recognition is accelerated. We refer to these methods as static approaches. In previous research within our group, we applied a static approach named "structuring search space" (SSS) as an off-line recognizer of handwritten Japanese characters [24]. In SSS, prototypes are organized by unsupervised clusters, and their centroids, for example, are used to represent the group. During recognition, an input pattern is first compared with all of the clusters' centroids, and second, only the clusters with centroids similar to the input are used as search space. This method was extended to a two-layered search space [25] and named the "layered search spaces (LSS) method". Being different from the approach by Tseng et al. [26] and that by Fujimoto et al. [27], the LSS method works in the original feature space for fine classification and, therefore, only has to assume one distance space. Waizumi et al. also presented a multilayer search space construction method for character class prototypes that uses LVQ [28].

In general, the previous methods for both the dynamic and static approaches have applied rather intuitive ideas for selecting simple recognition functions such as Euclidean distance or fewer features to speed up recognition. Therefore, they have to take a larger number of output candidates to maintain recognition rates, which causes recognition time to increase and limits the effects on speedup.

We have presented a systematic method for constructing an efficient and robust coarse classifier that uses a genetic algorithm (GA) for the online recognition of handwritten Japanese characters [29]. The method creates 243 basic recognizers with different classification costs and different classification accuracies by controlling the parameters of feature extraction and discriminant functions as well as the LSS method. It then uses these basic recognizers to construct a robust coarse classifier. It constructs a sequential cascade of basic recognizers and reduces the candidates after each basic recognizer. The parameters are estimated by using a GA so as to optimize the holistic character recognition performance. The coarse classifier thus developed follows the dynamic approach although it integrates the statistically tuned LSS. Experimental results demonstrated the superiority of our method.

5. COMBINED RECOGNITION

We have applied a discriminative method for MCE to optimize the parameters for combinations of structural and un-structural recognizers with a linear or nonlinear function for online handwritten Japanese string recognition [7]. To introduce an effective set of parameters, we applied a k-means method to cluster the parameters of all character categories into groups, and for categories belonging to the same group, we introduced the same weight parameters. We investigated how to construct the function and how to introduce effective parameters for discriminative methods under the condition of a limited amount of samples for classifier training. We designed the objective functions of parameter optimization so as to optimize the string performance. Moreover, we used GA to estimate super parameters such as the number of clusters, initial learning rate, and maximum learning times as well as the sigmoid function parameter for the MCE optimization. Experimental results demonstrated the superiority of our method.

6. STRING RECOGNITION

6.1. *Linguistic contextual processing*

String recognition applies not only character recognition, but also linguistic contextual processing. As shown in Figure 4 (a), by character recognition, each candidate character pattern is associated with a number of candidate classes with confidence scores. The combination of all character classes is represented by a character recognition candidate lattice. The linguistic contextual processing evaluates the combinations from character classes to character classes. By searching the candidate lattice by the Viterbi algorithm, the optimal path with maximum score gives the final result of string recognition.

Linguistic contextual processing methods can be roughly divided into two classes: methods using the character combinations and methods using the word combinations. As shown in Figure 4 (b), the linguistic contextual processing evaluates the probability P(C) of the string C that comprises a sequence of characters $\{c_1, c_2, \ldots\}$ or a sequence of words $\{w_1, w_2, \ldots\}$.

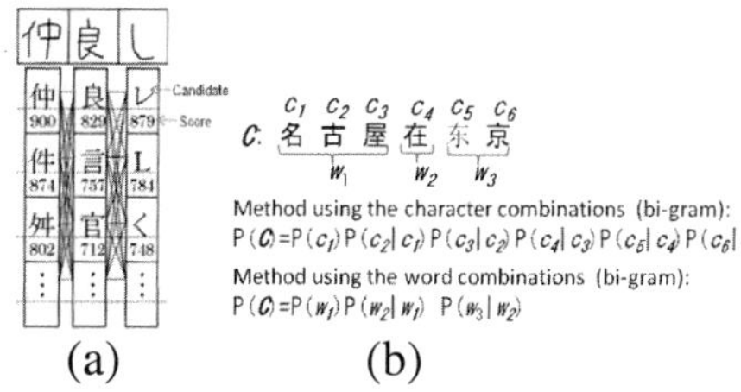

Figure 4. Character recogniton candidate lattice and linguistic contextual processing methods.

The methods using the character combinations evaluate the probability of the character combinations for each string candidate. We can use the appearance probability of only one character (unigram), bi-gram of two characters, tri-gram of three characters and generally called n-gram of n characters. The tri-gram is smoothed to overcome the imprecision of training with insufficient text by combining unigram, bi-gram and tri-gram using a linear function with weighting parameters.

In our experiment, under the condition with character writing boxes, using bi-gram improved the character recognition rate by 5 points from 92.9%, and using tri-gram improved the character recognition rate by one point. Moreover, under the condition without character writing boxes, using bi-gram improved the character recognition rate by 10 points from 81.3%, and using tri-gram improved the character recognition rate by 3 points.

The methods using the word combinations first divide string into words by morphological analysis, and then evaluate the probability of the word combinations for each string candidate. We can also use the appearance probability of only one word (unigram), bi-gram of two words, tri-gram of three words and generally called n-gram of n words. Although the methods have some problems such as unknown words and word dictionary memory, Nagata et al. have presented it could save more than 2/3 misrecognitions in a handwriting OCR simulation by dealing with unknown words [30].

We apply the methods using the character combinations for our system.

6.2. *Freely written string recognition*

With pen-based or touch-based input devices of large writing areas such as tablet PCs, Pad PCs, electronic whiteboards and digital pens, people tend to write text continuously with little constraints. This urges the need of handwritten string recognition. Compared to isolated character recognition, handwritten string recognition faces the difficulty of character segmentation because characters cannot be reliably segmented before they are recognized. Moreover, in continuous handwriting, characters tend to be written more cursively.

The integrated segmentation and recognition to overcome the ambiguity of segmentation, is dichotomized into segmentation-free method and over-segmentation-based method as shown in Fig. 1 [10]. Based on the advantages of over-segmentation-based method, we apply it for our recognition system.

By character recognition, each candidate character pattern is associated with a number of candidate classes with confidence scores. The combination of all candidate patterns and character classes is represented by a character segmentation-recognition candidate lattice, where each arc denotes a segmentation point and each node denotes a character class assigned to a candidate pattern as shown in Figure 5. The segmentation paths and corresponding string classes in the candidate lattice are evaluated by combining the scores of candidate characters and between-character compatibilities (geometric and linguistic contexts).

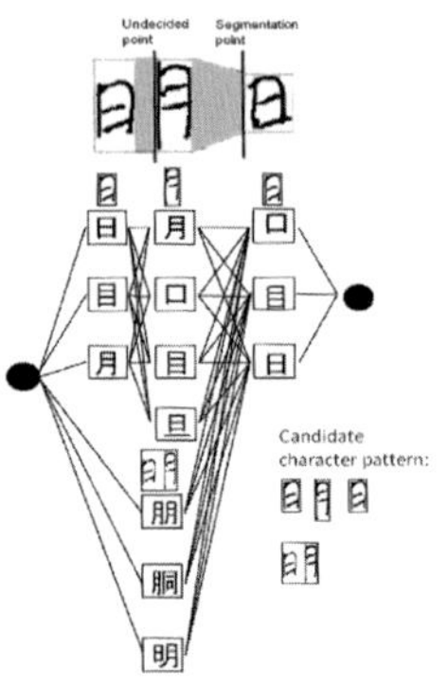

Figure 5. Character segmentation-recognition candidate lattice.

In over-segmentation based string recognition, how to evaluate the candidate characters (lying on paths in the candidate lattice) is a key issue. A desirable criterion should make the path of correct segmentation have the largest score. Unlike HMM-based recognition that classifies a unique sequence of feature vectors (each for a frame) on a string, the candidate lattice of over-segmentation has paths of different lengths, each corresponding to a different sequence of feature vectors, thus the comparison of different paths cannot be based on the Bayesian decision theory as for HMM-based recognition. Instead, candidate character recognition and context scores are heuristically combined to evaluate the paths. Such heuristic evaluation criteria can be divided into summation-based ones [31] and normalization-based ones [32]. A summation criterion is the summation of character-wise log-likelihood or the product of probabilistic likelihood. Since the likelihood measure is usually smaller than one, the summation (product) criterion is often biased to paths with fewer characters, and so, tends to over-merge characters. On the other hand, the normalized criterion, obtained by dividing the summation criterion by the number of segmented characters (segmentation length), tends to over-split characters.

To solve the problems, we have proposed a robust context integration model for online handwritten Japanese string recognition [1]. By labeling primitive segments, the proposed method can not only integrate the character shape information into recognition by introducing some adjustable parameters, but also is insensitive to the number of segmented character patterns because the summation is over the primitive segments. Experimental results demonstrated the superiority of our proposed string recognition model.

We include a brief description here on our recognition model [1]. Denote $\boldsymbol{X} = x_1 \ldots x_m$ as successive candidate character patterns of one path, and every candidate character pattern x_i is assigned a candidate class C_i. Then $f(\boldsymbol{X},\boldsymbol{C})$ is the score of the path $(\boldsymbol{X},\boldsymbol{C})$ where $\boldsymbol{C} = C_1 \ldots C_m$. The path evaluation criterion is expressed as follows:

$$f(\mathbf{X},\mathbf{C}) = \sum_{i=1}^{m} \left\{ \begin{array}{l} \sum_{h=1}^{6} [\lambda_{h1} + \lambda_{h2}(k_i - 1)] \log P_h + \lambda_{71} \log P(g_{j_i} \mid SP) \\ + \lambda_{72} \sum_{j=j_i+1}^{j_i+k_i-1} \log P(g_j \mid NSP) \end{array} \right\} + m\lambda \quad (2)$$

where P_{h}, h=1,…,6, stand for the probabilities of $P(C_i|C_{i-2}C_{i-1})$, $P(b_i|C_i)$, $P(q_i|C_i)$, $P(p^u{}_i|C_i)$, $P(x_i|C_i)$, and $P(p^b{}_i|C_{i-1}C_i)$, respectively. b_i, q_i, $p^u{}_i$, and $p^b{}_i$ are the feature vectors for character pattern sizes, inner gaps, single-character positions, and pair-character positions, respectively. g_i is the between-segment gap feature vector. $P(C_i|C_{i-2},C_{i-1})$ is the tri-gram probability. k_i is the number of primitive segments contained in the candidate character pattern x_i. λ_{h1}, λ_{h2} (h=1~7) and λ are the weighting parameters estimated by GA. $P(x_i|C_i)$ is estimated by the combination score of the structural and un-structural recognizers. We can also divide it into two parts $P(x^{str}{}_i|C_i)$, $P(x^{un\text{-}str}{}_i|C_i)$ where $x^{str}{}_i$ denotes the structural features of x_i, $x^{un\text{-}str}{}_i$ denotes the un-structural features of x_i, $P(x^{str}{}_i|C_i)$ is estimated by the score of the structural recognizer and $P(x^{un\text{-}str}{}_i|C_i)$ is estimated by the score of the un-structural recognizer. The path evaluation criterion is changed as follows:

$$f^1(\mathbf{X},\mathbf{C}) = \sum_{i=1}^{m} \left\{ \begin{array}{l} \sum_{h=1}^{7} [\lambda_{h1} + \lambda_{h2}(k_i - 1)] \log P_h + \lambda_{81} \log P(g_{j_i} \mid SP) \\ + \lambda_{82} \sum_{j=j_i+1}^{j_i+k_i-1} \log P(g_j \mid NSP) \end{array} \right\} + m\lambda \quad (3)$$

where P_{h}, h=1,…,7, stand for the probabilities of $P(C_i|C_{i-2}C_{i-1})$, $P(b_i|C_i)$, $P(q_i|C_i)$, $P(p^u{}_i|C_i)$, $P(x^{str}{}_i|C_i)$, $P(x^{un\text{-}str}{}_i|C_i)$, and $P(p^b{}_i|C_{i-1}C_i)$, respectively. λ_{h1}, λ_{h2} (h=1~8), and λ are the weighting parameters estimated by GA. By the path evaluation criterion, we re-estimate the combination of the structural and un-structural recognizers.

7. EXPERIMENTS

We investigated the results for our recognition systems using on-line Chinese handwriting databases (CASIA-OLHWDB1.0-1.2, 2.0) [33] and on-line Japanese handwriting databases (TUAT Nakayosi/Kuchibue, Kondate) [1, 34].

We trained the structural and un-structural character recognizers, the weighting parameters for combination, and geometric scoring functions using CASIA-HWDB1.0-1.2 for the Chinese recognition (7,356 classes, including 7,184 Chinese characters and 172 symbols), and using Nakayosi/Kuchibue for the Japanese recognition (4,443 classes, including 4,060 Chinese characters, 169 Kana and 211 symbols). For scoring linguistic context, we prepared a tri-gram table for Chinese recognition from a corpus of People's Daily, and that for Japanese from the 1993 and 2002 volumes of the *Asahi* and *Nikkei* newspapers, respectively. For training the weight parameters and evaluating the performances of character string recognitions, we use the database CASIA-OLHWDB2.0 (420 writters, 20,573 text lines) for Chinese recognition and the database Kondate (100 writters, 13,685 text lines) for Japanese recognition.

We used 336 people's Chinese text lines and 75 people's Japanese text lines for training the classifiers for the candidate segmentation point probability and the weighting parameters of the path evaluations. The performance test for the string recognizer used the text lines of the remaining 84 persons of CASIA-OLHWDB2.0 and 25 persons of Kondate. Table 1 shows the results, where the numbers without any parentheses or brackets are the recognition rates, those shown in parentheses are the average character recognition time and those shown in brackets are the memory costs. The experiments were implemented on an Intel(R) Xeon(R) CPU W5590 @ 3.36 GHz 3.36 GHz (2 processers) with 12 GB memory.

Table 1. Recognition results.

System	Chinese	Japanese
Performance	90.00%(25ms)[246MB]	92.99(20ms)[20MB]

For the Japanese recognition system, we build two compact structural/un-structural recognizers by compressing them using vector quantization (VQ) techniques [35, 36] and we did not built compact recognizers for the Chinese recognition system because of the time limitation. Therefore, the memory cost for the Japanese recognition system is lower than that for the Chinese recognition system. From the results we can see that we have realized the online handwritten Chinese/Japanese character recognitions with high performances that can be applied to actual applications. The Japanese recognition system exhibited higher recognition accuracies than the Chinese recognition system. We consider that it is because Chinese characters have simpler shapes than Japanese characters and Chinese people writes characters more fluently and more cursively than Japanese people resulting in low recognition accuracies.

8. CONCLUSION

This paper described the recent trends in online handwritten Chinese/Japanese character recognition and our recognition systems. We apply an over-segmentation-based method for our recognition system where the paths are evaluated in accordance with our path evaluation criterion, which combines the scores of character recognition, linguistic context, and geometric features (character pattern sizes, inner gaps, single-character positions, pair-character positions, candidate segmentation points) with the weighting parameters estimated by GA. We combine structural and un-structural methods to recognize each character pattern so that the recognition accuracy improves.

Improving recognition performance is the aim of our future work. This can be achieved by incorporating more effective geometric features, exploiting better geometric context likelihood functions and weighting parameter learning methods, and improving the accuracy of character recognizer. To speed up recognition and reduce memory size is another dimension of our future work. We should consider effective methods to remove invalid patterns from the lattice.

ACKNOWLEDGMENT

This work is being supported by the Basic Research Program (C) of Scientific Research Fund funded by Japan Society for the Promotion of Science (JSPS) / Ministory of Education, Culture, Sports, Science & Technology (MEXT) for "Research on Unified Model and Method for Recognizing Multilingual Handwriting from Touch Based Input Device".

REFERENCES

– [1] B. Zhu, X.-D. Zhou, C.-L. Liu and M. Nakagawa: A robust model for on-line handwritten Japanese text recognition, Int'l J. Document Analysis and Recognition (IJDAR), 13(2), 121-131, 2010.
– [2] R. Plamondon and S.N. Srihari: On-line and off-line handwriting recognition: a comprehensive survey, IEEE Trans. PAMI, 22(1), 63-82, 2000.
– [3] C.-L. Liu, I.-J. Kim and J. H. Kim: Model-based stroke extraction and matching for handwritten Chinese character recognition, Pattern Recognition, 34(12), 2339-2352, 2001.
– [4] M. Nakagawa and K. Akiyama: A linear-time elastic matching for stroke number free recognition of on-line handwritten characters, Proc. 4th IWFHR, 48-56, 1994.

— [5] C.-L. Liu and K. Marukawa: Pseudo two-dimensional shape normalization methods for handwritten Chinese character recognition, Pattern Recognition, 38(12), 2242-2255, 2005.
— [6] C.-L. Liu and X.-D. Zhou: Online Japanese character recognition using trajectory-based normalization and direction feature extraction, Proc. 10th IWFHR, 217-222, 2006.
— [7] B. Zhu, J. Gao and M. Nakagawa: Objective function design for MCE-based combination of on-line and off-line character recognizers for on-line handwritten Japanese text recognition, Proc. 11th ICDAR, 594-599, 2011.
— [8] M. Liwicki and H. Bunke: HMM-based on-line recognition of handwritten whiteboard notes, Proc. 10th IWFHR, 595-599, 2006.
— [9] S. Z. Li: Markov random field modeling in image analysis, Tokyo, Springer, 2001.
— [10] M. Cheriet, N. Kharma, C.-L Liu and C. Y. Suen: Character recognition systems - A guide for students and practioners, Hoboken, New Jersey, John Wiley & Sons, Inc, 2007.
— [11] S. Jaeger, S. Manke, J. Reichert and A. Waibel: Online handwriting recognition: the Npen++ recognizer, IJDAR, 3(1), 69-180, 2001.
— [12] C.-L. Liu, M. Koga and H. Fujisawa: Lexicon-driven segmentation and recognition of handwritten character strings for Japanese address reading, IEEE Trans. PAMI, 24(11), 1425-1437, 2002.
— [13] M. Mohamed and P. Gader: Handwritten word recognition using segmentation-free Hidden Markov Model and segmentation-based dynamic programming techniques, IEEE Trans. PAMI, 18(5), 548-544, 1996.
— [14] G. Kim and V. Govindaraju: A lexicon driven approach to handwritten word recognition for real-time applications, IEEE Trans. PAMI, 19(4), 366-379, 1997.
— [15] C.-L. Liu, S. Jaeger and M. Nakagawa: On-line recognition of Chinese characters: the state of the art. IEEE Trans. PAMI, 26(2), 198-213, 2004.
— [16] B. Zhu and M. Nakagawa: On-line handwritten Japanese characters recognition using a MRF model with parameter optimization by CRF, Proc. 11th ICADR, 603-607, 2011.
— [17] U. Ramer: An iterative procedure for the polygonal approximation of plan closed curves, Computer Graphics and Image Processing, 1, 244-256, 1972.
— [18] F. Kimura: Modified quadratic discriminant function and the application to Chinese characters, IEEE Trans. PAMI, 9 (1), 149-153, 1987.
— [19] S. Mori, K. Yamamoto and M. Yasuda, Research on machine recognition of handprinted characters, IEEE Trans. PAMI, 6, 386-405, 1984.
— [20] N. Sun, M. Abe, Y. Nemoto: A handwritten character recognition system by using improved directional element feature and subspace method, Trans. IEICE Japan, J78-D-2 (6), 922-930, 1995.
— [21] C.-L. Liu and M. Nakagawa: Precise candidate selection for large character set recognition by confidence evaluation, IEEE Trans. PAMI, 22 (6), 636-642, 2000.
— [22] T. Kumamoto, K. Toraichi, T. Horiuchi, K. Yamamoto, H. Yamada: On speeding candidate selection in handprinted chinese character recognition, Pattern Recognition, 24 (8), 793-799, 1991.
— [23] C.-H. Tung, H.-J. Lee, J.-Y. Tsai: Multi-stage precandidate selection in handwritten Chinese character recognition systems, Pattern Recognition, 27 (8), 1093-1102, 1994.
— [24] Y. Yang, B. Zhu and M. Nakagawa: Structuring search space for accelerating large set character recognition, IEICE Trans. Information and Systems, 88(8), 1799-1806, 2005.
— [25] Y. Yang and M. Nakagawa: Improving the structuring search space method for accelerating large set character recognition, Proc. 9th International Workshop on Frontiers in Handwriting Recognition, Tokyo, 251-256, 2004.
— [26] Tseng, Y. H., Kuo, C. C., Lee, H. J., Nov.: Speeding up Chinese character recognition in an automatic document reading system, Pattern Recognition, 31 (11), 1601–1612, 1998.
— [27] K. Fujimoto, H. Kamada, K. Kurokawa: Fast, precise pre-classification method using projections of feature regions, Technical report of IEICE, PRMU 97 (558), 25–32, 1998.
— [28] Y. Waizumi, N. Kato, K. Saruta and Y. Nemoto: High speed and high accuracy rough classification for handwritten characters using hierarchical learning vector quantization (in Japanese), Technical Report of IEICE, Vol.97, No.40, PRMU, 1-8, 1997.
— [29] B. Zhu and M. Nakagawa: A coarse classifier construction method from a large number of basic recognizers for on-line recognition of handwritten Japanese characters, Proc. 11th ICDAR, 1090-1094, Beijing, China, 2011.
— [30] M. Nagata: A Japanese OCR error correction method using character shape similarity and statistical language Model, Trans. IEICE Japan, J81-D-2 (11), 2624-2634, 1998.
— [31] M. Nakagawa, B. Zhu and M. Onuma: A model of online handwritten Japanese text recognition free from line direction and writing format constraints, Trans. IEICE Japan, E88-D (8), 1815-1822, 2005.
— [32] C.-L. Liu, H. Sako, H. Fujisawa: Effects of classifier structures and training regimes on integrated segmentation and recognition of handwritten numeral strings, IEEE Trans. PAMI, 26(11), 1395-1407, 2004.
— [33] C.-L. Liu, F. Yin, D.-H. Wang, Q.-F. Wang: Online and offline handwritten Chinese character recognition: Benchmarking on new databases, Pattern Recognition, 46(1): 155-162, 2013.
— [34] M. Nakagawa, K. Matsumoto: Collection of On-line Handwritten Japanese Character Pattern Databases and Their Analysis, IJDAR, 7(1), 69-81, 2004.
— [35] B. Zhu and M. Nakagawa: Building compact on-line MRF recognizer for large character set using structured dictionary representation and vector quantization technique, Proc. 13th ICFHR, 155-160, 2012.
— [36] J. Gao, B. Zhu and M. Nakagawa: Development of a Robust and Compact On-line Handwritten Japanese Text Recognizer, EICE Trans. Inf & Syst., Vol. E96-D, No.4, pp. 927-938, 2013.

Pixel-based Multi-focus Image Fusion by Color Appearance Model

C.C. Hsieh[1] & W.H. Wu[2]
Dept. of Computer Science and Engineering, Tatung University, Taipei, Taiwan
Email: [1]cchsieh@ttu.edu.tw, [2]hugown@gmail.com

ABSTRACT: The technology of multi-focus imaging is to fuse multiple images, which have the same scene but with difference focal distance, into one picture with several focusing simultaneously. General multi-focus image fusion technology can only process gray image mostly. In this paper, we process color images and use color saturation based on chrominance divided by luminance to do multi-focusing. The focus is calculated by deploying a star-light shaped mask. To deal with object displacement or deformation phenomena, image registration is necessary before fusion. The obtained mean correction rate and PSNR are 80% and 42dB for tested color images, respectively. For test gray images, the obtained mean correction rate and PSNR are 83% and 40dB, respectively. The experimental results proved that the proposed color saturation based star-light focusing detection can be applied to image fusion reliably.

KEYWORDS: Multi-focus images; Image fusion; Color saturation; Fusion mask.

1. INTRODUCTION

When taking photos, the photographer will set the focus of lens on the target object. Hence, the focus of lens will make the target object clearly display on the taken photo, while non-target objects of the scenery will be displayed indistinctly. Thus, it will create a depth of field photos, including clear target object and indistinct background.

Actual photographing scene may appear a kind of situation, i.e. several different target objects may exist under the same scene. Distances between these target objects and photographic equipment are also different. At the moment, the photographer may adjust the focus of lens to appropriate focal distance, so that different target objects can have clear outline. However, inspecting the image carefully, it can be discovered that except the target object on appropriate focus is clear, the rest target objects on inappropriate focus are indistinct. Therefore, to make each target object have quite clear outline, the photographer shall adjust each target object to appropriate focus before photographing. Hence, the result is multiple photos of the same scene with individual clear target object are taken respectively. At the moment, multi-focus image fusion technology can be used to fuse these photos into a photo with multi focusing target object, i.e. to select the sharpest and clearest parts of two or more images and fuse them into an image with more sharp and clear parts as shown in Fig. 1. The application scenes of multi-focus image fusion are plenty, such as fixed-focus photography and macro photography.

Figure 1. Multi-focused images fusion.

To do Multi-focus image fusion, whether each pixel on different images are in focusing status can be considered, and pixels that are viewed as focused are extracted and fused into one multi-focus image.

Additionally, considering the condition of using human eyes to check the image, human vision may feel clearer for more saturated region, i.e. colour saturation has certain degree of correlation with image clarity. Therefore, this paper will discuss these ideas. Hence, we propose using color appearance model for finding the optimal fusion mask for multi-focus images.

In the following section, we briefly review the several main approaches for multi-focused image fusion. In Section 3, the system architecture of the pixel-based fusion approach using color appearance model is presented. To address the movement or distortion problems, image registration has to be done before deciding the fusion mask. The focus metric is calculated by the proposed color saturation feature and star-light mask. For completeness, several color saturation models are evaluated and analyzed. In Section 4, experiments on popular test data sets including color and grey images are tested. Both visual and numerical verification of the results are given. Finally, discussions and conclusions are made in the last section.

2. RELATED WORKS

According to the classification made by Nikolov et al. [1], image fusion techniques can be categorized into two approaches: spatial domain and transform domain. Approaches based on spatial domain deal directly with intensity values of pixels from input images. The fused image is composed by selecting the sharper pixels at each pixel location over all the input images. Huang & Jing [2] evaluate several focus measures for pixel-based methods, such as variance, energy of image gradient, Tenenbaum's algorithm, energy of image Laplacian, sum-modified-Laplacian, and spatial frequency, to determine the degree how a pixel is focused. These pixel-based fusion methods are sensitive to registration accuracy, so that co-registration of input images is required. To remedy the presence of noise, block [3] or region-based [4] methods have been proposed by segmenting the input images into sharp blocks/regions and blurred blocks/regions. Then, the fused image is composed by selecting the sharper blocks/regions from the input images. Due to the inconsistencies between blocks/regions from different sources, artifacts may appear at the boundary of blocks/regions.

On the other hand, multi-focus image fusion [5] can also be performed in the transform domain. This approach is also called multi-scale methods which utilize Laplacian Pyramid transform [6], Discrete Wavelet transform (DWT) [7], curvelet transform [8], or contourlet transform [9, 10] to fuse images at different scale. The input images are decomposed by multi-scale transform into a hierarchy of levels, with each upper level corresponding to a coarser resolution. In addition to the spatial image for each level, there are high frequency/detail components produced and represented by transform coefficients to indicate sharpness. During the fusion of the high frequency sub-bands, the coefficients with the largest activity level at each pixel location are selected, and the coefficients are averaged while considering the low frequency sub-bands. Inverse multi-scale transform is then computed based on the composite of high and low frequency sub-bands to construct the fused image. Compare with spatial domain approach, wavelet-based fusion algorithms need greater computational complexity. Still, multi-scale methods are sensitive to shift-variant images and noises.

No matter spatial domain or transform domain approaches, several mathematical models were proposed to combine information from different sources. Image fusion methods based on probability theory were proposed to reduce uncertainty such as Bayesian theory [11] and Dempster-Shafer theory of evidence [12]. The priori probability needs to be given or estimated before solving the uncertainty. Hua et al. [13] formulate image fusion to the problem of assigning high weights to focused pixels and low weights to unfocused pixels. Several popular focus measures variance, energy of image gradient (EIG), energy of Laplacian (EOL), frequency selective weighted median filter (FSWM), and intensity value are initially evaluated to estimate the weights. These weights are represented as a fully connected graph and optimized globally by using Random Walker algorithm. Singh et al. [14] deployed computationally simple texture features and color saturation measure to generate weight map for multi-exposure images fusion. Color saturation is computed as the standard deviation within the RGB channel at each pixel. Weighted Least Squares (WLS) framework is utilized to refine the weight map. The advantage is that it is well suited for multi-focus images fusion.

Each fusion method has its own set of advantages and limitations. Combinatorial approach [15] integrating the advantages of spatial domain and transform domain based methods is proposed. Combination of different fusion schemes has also been approved to be useful [15, 16]. However, selection and arrangement of those candidate fusion schemes are quite arbitrary [5]. Table 1 makes comparison for above various kinds of methods. Most methods are to find out the feature or edge of each object in two groups (or more) of fused image and distinguish whether the object is in focusing status. Then, cut off the regions of objects, which are judged as focused, from the image. Finally, fuse these focusing objects with different sources into an image with multi focusing. Additionally, most image fusion methods process only grey images and the colour information of pixels are lost.

3. SYSTEM ARCHITECTURE

3.1. *Scope of color saturation*

Before doing colour image analysis, human eyes are used to examine two images with same composition. Scenery of one image is more indistinct while the scenery on the other image is clearer. When checking the two images by human eyes, the image with more saturated color makes people feel clearer, and the image with less saturated color makes people feel more indistinct, e.g. deep red color makes people feel clearer than the light red and black makes people feel clearer than grey. Therefore, the saturation of color may affect the clearness feeling of people, as shown in Fig. 2.

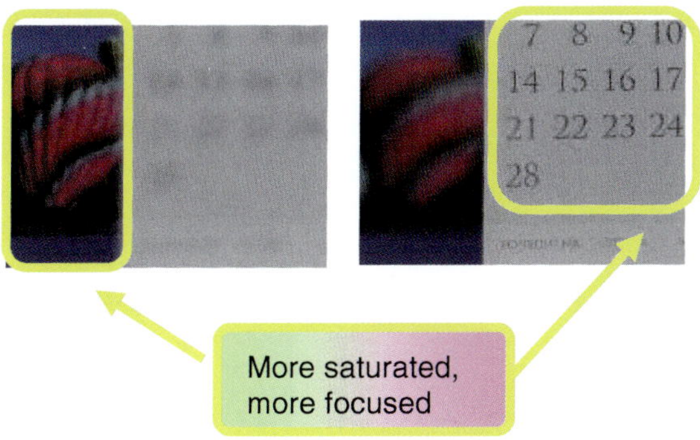

Figure 2. The relation between color saturation and focus in human visual system.

Color appearance models [17, 18] transform the color tri-stimulus values to perceptual attributes such as brightness, lightness, chroma, colorfulness and saturation for variety of applications. In this paper, color saturation is utilized to measure the focus between different source images. There are several color appearance models like CIELUV, CIELAB, and CIECAM02.

Generally, pixel color of image is presented by the color space of red, green and blue (RGB). To analyze the color saturation and luminance, it shall do color conversion as mentioned above. To simplify the calculation, we adopt YCbCr, in which the Y is Luminance and CbCr is Chrominance. To analyze color saturation of pixels further, it shall use square root to represent color saturation according. Considering the Luminance factor, Y is used to normalize color saturation, as in the following equation.

Figure 3 shows the S_{CY} distribution diagram of under B=0. The smaller R and G are, the larger C/Y is. It means that the darker the pixel is, the larger C/Y is; but the C/Y value changing is concentrated in the range of R and G values those are less than or around 64. Similarly, the influences of R values are more distinct to the values of C/Y if G<64.

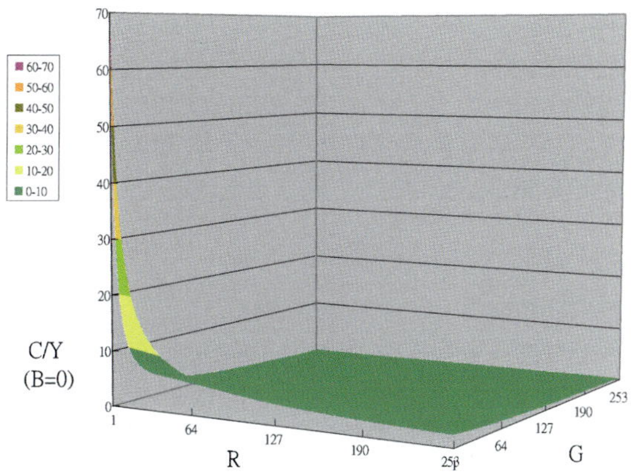

Figure 3. The C/Y scope when B equals to 0.

When the image luminance is in dark condition overall, C/Y is used to adjust the saturation status of color; however, when the image luminance is in bright condition overall, using C/Y value will be unfavourable to pixels those have larger Y. Hence, the calculation formula of saturation changing is C/(255-Y) and the obtained values from the formula are used to draw distribution diagram similar to Fig. 3.

From Fig. 3, it can be understood when the Luminance of image is darker overall, the influence of R, G and B to C/Y is larger as the saturation rises. Using C, Y and C/Y to draw distribution diagram, it can be viewed that the influence of C is larger than that of Y. Hence, when the larger C is and the smaller Y is, it is easier to process identification operation. Viewing from other aspect, when the Luminance of image is brighter overall, the saturation is changed along with C/(255-Y), and C, Y and C/(255-Y) values are used to draw distribution diagram. It can be viewed that the influence of C is larger than that of Y. Hence, when the larger C is and the larger Y is, it is easier to process identification operation.

Based on the above analysis, if pixel is adopted as the unit to do focusing identification, pixels of relative position on two images can be compared with extracted Chrominance (C_b and C_r) and Luminance (Y). The pixel with higher focusing degree can be selected as a focusing pixel. Furthermore, pixels are taken as the unit to analyze the condition of focusing. For image with more complex structure, such as images with more details, identification will be easier. It cannot be achieved when taking region as a focusing unit, because the focusing objects on certain images are composed of fewer pixels. If pixels are taken as the unit, this method can be used to extract details and fuse them into final results.

3.2. *Proposed system architecture*

Multi-focus image fusion system flow chart is proposed as in Fig. 4. Step 1 is to process registration for the two images to be fused. Step 2 is to process color space conversion for the two registered images to obtain chrominance and luminance of images. Step 3 is to use C/Y and C/(255-Y) to calculate possible fusion mask for fusing pixels. Step 4 is to analyze these possible masks to prepare final mask. The last step is to do image fusion using the registered pixels of image produced on Step 1 based on the final mask image.

Since the proposed fusion method takes pixel as the unit, focusing verification can only be performed on objects of the same relative positions on the images. Hence, different images shall take image registration processing first to avoid causing problems that pixels of different objects are taken to compare, as in Figure 6. For registration processing, we use cvCalcOpticalFlowPyrLK and calcOpticalFlow-Farneback functions both are Opencv functions. cvCalcOpticalFlowPyrLK function is using Pyramid Lucas-Kanade [19] method to calculate Optical flow vector of all same objects in different images. Before processing cvCalcOpticalFlowPyrLK function, we need to check the object feature points.

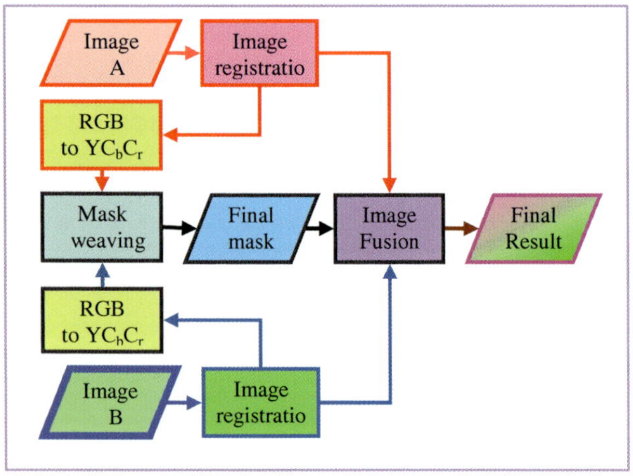

Figure 4. System flowchart.

3.2.1. *Star-Light focusing detection*

Before proceeding to mask image weaving, we will introduce the innovated focusing detection method called star-light focusing detection mentioned in this paper first. The principle of star-light focusing detection is to take the detected pixel as the center and extended in 8 different radial directions, i.e. up, down, left, right, upper left, lower left, upper right and lower right. Furthermore, accumulate the different (color saturation difference) values between each pixel on 8 directions and the central pixel as shown in Fig. 5.

This phenomenon can be seen in many images that the bright light is presented in radial light form. Therefore, the light energy strength of pixels on these directions has direct relation with the central pixel. The energy intensity difference values of each pixel and central pixel are accumulated to confirm the focusing degree of central pixel. This concept is used to calculate the difference between color saturation of each pixel and color saturation of central pixel on these directions. Then, sum up the absolute value of each difference value and take this value as the focusing degree value of central pixel, as in the Equations (1) and (2). The *C/Y* means saturation; *m* and *n* are the height and width of the star-light window mask.

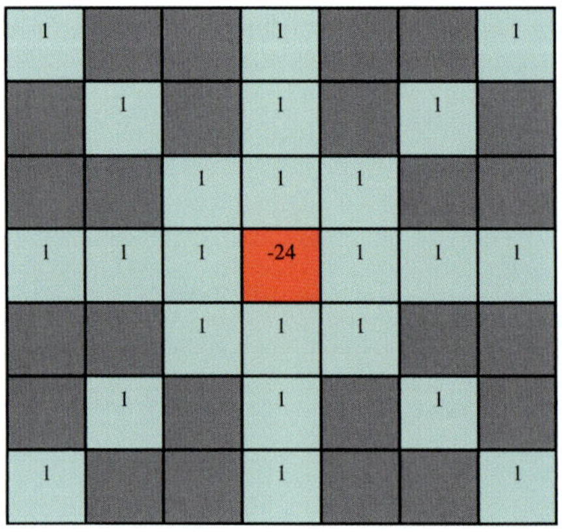

Figure 5. Star-light window mask for focus measurement.

$$F(x,y)=\sum_{i=1}^{n}\sum_{j=1}^{m}\left|CY(x+i,\, y+j)-CY(x,y)\right| \qquad (1)$$

$$S=\begin{cases} C/Y=\dfrac{\sqrt{C_b^2+C_r^2}}{Y} & \textit{darker mask} \\ C/(255-Y)=\dfrac{\sqrt{C_b^2+C_r^2}}{255-Y} & \textit{lighter mask} \end{cases} \qquad (2)$$

3.2.2. *Proposed focus metric*

After Registration processing is finished, focusing measurement can be processed. The measurement dimension used is the color saturation mentioned. It shall consider the Luminance of overall image. Redefinition is as in the following equation. To distinguish whether it is focusing further, we will take Laplacian of Gaussian (LoG) for color saturation image. Generally, the effect of LoG is to emphasize the edge part. It is to input image after filtering noise by Gaussian filter. Then, Laplacian is calculated from the results, so as to reduce the impact of random noise.

As the color saturation calculation may be different according to the Luminance of original image, using LoG to process individually for C/Y and C/(255-Y) of image A will obtain two images, A' and A''. Similarly, using LoG to process individually for C/Y and C/(255-Y) of image B will obtain two images, $\mathbf{B}'$ and $\mathbf{B}''$. Hence, 4 images are created, i.e. image $\mathbf{A}'$ and image $\mathbf{B}'$ are C/Y calculation based and image **A″** and image B" are C/(255-Y) calculation based.

3.2.3. *Image fusion*

After final mask image is prepared, resultant fused image can be processed. In this procedure, each pixel value on final mask image is used to determine whether pixel values of resultant fused image on relative position are to be extracted from image A or B for fusion. Hence, each pixel value on resultant fused image is from the original image. Figure 6 is an example to illustrate the evaluation method of pixels. On final mask image, when the pixel value is 255, R, G and B values of the corresponding pixel on image A is used as R, G and B values of the pixel on resultant fused image. If the pixel value of final mask image is 0, R, G and B values of the corresponding pixel on image B is used as R, G and B values of the pixel on resultant fused image. However, if the pixel value of final mask image is 128, it means that the R, G and B values of the pixels on the same position of two original images are very close. Hence, the average value of R, G and B values of pixels on the same position of image A and B is used, and the image fused by this method is the final resultant fused image.

4. EXPERIMENTAL RESULTS

The pixel-to-pixel position distortion takes place frequently when multi-focusing image fusion is carried out, so registration processing is necessary. In order to verify the effect of star-light focusing detection, we set up an experiment to compare the results of star-light focusing detection and Sobel edge detection by using color image. We analyze the correction rate and error rate of the synthetic mask image and the generated final mask image. Because we observe that the grey pixels of all mask images are almost the same as the RGB value of two original image pixels, we think that grey pixels of final mask image do not represent error; thus, the correction rate and error rate are calculated by the principle.

The experiment is carried out by the minimum 3×3 detection region; firstly, image A and B are calculated by RGB to YC_bC_r for the original C/Y and C/(255-Y) matrixes; and then the blur processing is carried out to obtain the blur C/Y and C/(255-Y) matrixes; finally, the original C/Y and C/(255-Y) matrixes minus the blur C/Y and C/(255-Y) matrixes to reinforce the focusing region and then to process LoG to get the analysed C/Y and C/(255-Y) matrixes. And then, star-light focusing detection analysis is carried out. Fig. 6(a) and 6(b) show images A and B; Fig. 6(c) and 6(d) are the images presented by C/Y matrixes; 6(e) and 6(f) are the images presented by C/(255-Y) matrixes; Fig. 6(g) and 6(h) are the initial mask image formed after calculating (c, d) and (e, f) by Star-light focusing detection; Fig. 6(i) and 6(j) are the initial mask image formed after calculating (c, d) and (e, f) by Sobel edge detection; figures (k) and (l) are the final mask image and resultant fused image formed by (g, h); Fig. 6(m) and 6(n) are the final mask image and resultant fused image fused by (i, j). After all mask images (g, h, i, j, k, m) are compared with figures (a, b), we can see that the grey regions of all mask images are almost the same as the same region of figures (a), (b); comparing mask image (k) with (m), we can see that (k) has greater black and white region and less different pixels within the regions. From the PSNR analysis of the above experiment, we can see that star-light has better effects than other methods as shown in Table 1.

In order to compare with the existing multi-focusing image fusion technologies, we use the test images from [7]. At present, we think Weighted Least Squares (WLS) [14] is the most related work. The results are almost the same if observed by human eyes. Object displacement is considered here so the overlapping problem of object is minimized; hereby, the central text is apparently overlapped and the central text has relatively fewer overlapping problems.

Table 1. PSNR error rate correction rate.

	PSNR(db)	False Pos. (%)	True Pos. (%)	False Neg. (%)	True Neg. (%)
book	43.1029	26.8012	73.1988	16.1456	83.8544
balloon	38.7309	16.1706	83.8295	6.2678	93.7322
disk	41.2487	10.8368	89.1632	6.2397	93.7603
leaf	39.6141	22.4715	77.5285	17.9061	82.0939

5. CONCLUSIONS AND FUTURE WORKS

This paper uses the ratio of chrominance to luminance as the basis of focusing status and proposes a new star-light mask to measure the focus. The results by using this method are very close to the one using traditional square (matrix) method to obtain the focusing degree values. However, Star-light is faster on analysis processing because it requires less pixels to be calculated. Additionally, when fusing mask image and resultant fused image, the units used are all pixels rather than blocks, which are composed of several pixels. Each pixel shall be identified so it will have better effect for small objects. Moreover, it obtains the pixels of original image as the pixels of fused image as many as possible rather than the pixel values of processed non-original image, so as to achieve detail resemblance of original image. However, the displacement vector of each pixel will affect the fusion results and registration is an important part for images fusion.

REFERENCES

— [1] Nikolov, S., Hill, P., Bull, D., & Canagarajah, N., 2001. Wavelets for image fusion, Wavelets in Signal and Image Analysis, *Computational Imaging and Vision Series*, 213–244, Kluwer Academic Publishers, Dordrecht, The Netherlands.

— [2] Huang, W. & Jing, Z. 2007. Evaluation of focus measures in multi-focus image fusion, *Pattern Recognition Letters*, 28(4), 493-500, ISSN 0167-8655.

— [3] Siddiqui, A.B., Jaffar, M.A., Hussain, A., & Mirza, A.M. 2010. Block-based feature-level multi-focus image fusion, In *the 5th International Conference on Future Information Technology*, 1-7, 21-23 May.

— [4] Li, S. & Yang, B. 2008. Multifocus image fusion using region segmentation and spatial frequency, *Image and Vision Computing*, 26(7), 971-979, DOI=10.1016/j.imavis.2007.10.012

— [5] Dong, J., Zhuang, D., Huang, Y., & Fu, J. 2011. Survey of multispectral image fusion techniques in remote sensing applications, *Image Fusion and Its Applications*, Intech., 1–22.

— [6] Wang W. & Chang, F. 2011. A multi-focus image fusion method based on Laplacian pyramid, *Journal of Computers*, 6(12), Dec., 2559-2566.

— [7] Yang, Y. 2011. A novel DWT based multi-focus image fusion method, *Procedia Engineering*, vol. 24, 177-181, ISSN 1877-7058.

— [8] Li, S. & Yang, B. 2008. Multifocus image fusion by combining curvelet and wavelet transform, *Pattern Recognition Letters*, 29(9), 1 July, 1295-1301.

— [9] Zhang Q. & Guo, B. Multifocus image fusion using the non-subsampled contourlet transform. *Signal Processing*, 89(7), July, 1334-1346.

— [10] Cunha, A.L., Zhou, J. & Do, M.N. 2006. The Non-subsampled contourlet transform: theory, design, and applications, *IEEE Transactions on Image Processing*, 15(10), 3089-3101, Oct., doi: 10.1109/TIP.2006.877507

— [11] Zhang, Y., De Backer, S., & Scheunders, P. 2008. Bayesian fusion of multispectral and hyperspectral image in Wavelet domain. *IEEE International on Geoscience and Remote Sensing Symposium*, 7-11 July, V-69-V-72.

— [12] Le Hégarat-Mascle, S., Richard, D., & Ottlé, C. 2003. Multi-scale data fusion using Dempster-Shafer evidence theory, *Integrated Computer-Aided Engineering*, 10(1), 9-22.

— [13] Hua, K. L., Wang, H.C., Rusdi, A.H., Jiang, S.Y. 2014. A novel multi-focus image fusion algorithm based on random walks, *Journal of Visual Communication and Image Representation*, 25(5), July, 951-962, http://dx.doi.org/10.1016/j.jvcir.2014.02.009.

— [14] Singh, H., Kumar, V., & Bhooshan, S. 2014. Weighted least squares based detail enhanced exposure fusion, ISRN Signal Processing, Article ID 498762, 2014. doi:10.1155/2014/498762

— [15] Song, M. & Guo P. 2012. A combinatorial optimization method for remote sensing image fusion with contourlet and HSI transform, *Journal of Computer-Aided Design & Computer Graphics*, Jan.

— [16] Krista, A., Yun, Z., & Peter, D. 2007. Wavelet based image fusion techniques — An introduction, review and comparison, *ISPRS Journal Photogram and Remote Sensing*, vol. 62, 249-263.

— [17] Fairchild, M.D. 2013. Color Appearance Models, In the *3rd Ed. Wiley-IS&T*, Chichester, UK, 2013, ISBN 978-1-119-96703-3.

— [18] Li, C. & Alastair, R.A. 2008. An image quality metric based on a colour appearance model, Advanced Concepts for Intelligent Vision Systems, *Lecture Notes in Computer Science*, vol. 5259, 696-707.

— [19] Bouguet, J.Y. Pyramidal Implementation of the Lucas Kanade Feature Tracker Description of the algorithm, Intel Corporation Microprocessor Research Labs, http://jean-yves.bouguet@intel.com

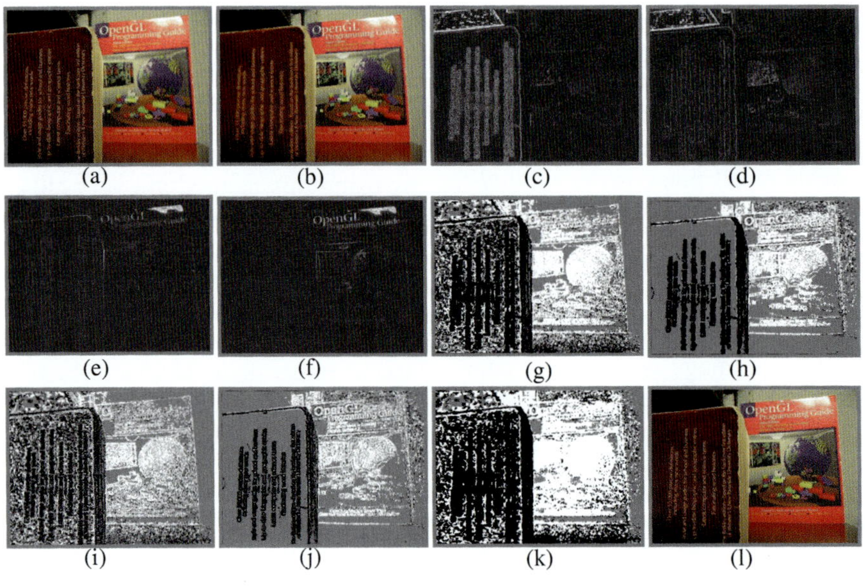

Figure 6. (a) and (b) are the original images. (c) and (d) are the produced matrixes by C/Y. (e) and (f) are the produced matrixes by C/(255-Y). (g) and (h) are the produced masks by Star Light. (i) and (j) are the produced masks by Sobel. (k) is the produced mask by (g) and (h) , and (l) is the produced result by (k).

Study on Fingerprint Classification Algorithm Based on Genetic Neural Network

F. Zhao
Hubei Institute of Fine Arts, Wuhan, Hubei, China
Email: 10035154@qq.com

ABSTRACT: Fingerprint classification is very important for improving the efficiency of fingerprint identification. In some sense, the process of fingerprint classification is also a rough process of fingerprint matching. This article discusses neural network and pattern identification technique in a combined manner, and proposes a kind of fingerprint classification algorithm based on genetic neural network. Judging from the simulation result, the algorithm could make basically accurate classification on fingerprint, and could reduce the time of fingerprint matching and search as well as calculation complexity. It increased the robustness of the identification system, and was conducive to enhancing the speed and anti-interference ability of fingerprint identification.

KEYWORD: Fingerprint identification; Fingerprint classification; Genetic algorithm; Neural network.

1. INTRODUCTION

Along with social development and continuous progress of computer technology, the application of computer-based biological characteristics identification is becoming more and more extensive. Due to their uniqueness and stability, fingerprint characteristics are often used as main bases for personal identity authentication and attract wide attention from the society. Fingerprint-related application has covered various fields of social life in an in-depth manner, such as the fingerprint identification used by the police and the public prosecution organs, etc. On the other hand, neural network has been widely applied in such fields as pattern identification, image processing and signal processing, and significant results have been seen in such applications. The idea to combine the neural network optimized by genetic algorithm and the traditional fingerprint classification and identification technology is a way which is worthy of attempt for improving the efficiency of fingerprint classification and the accuracy rate of fingerprint identification.

2. FINGERPRINT CLASSIFICATION AND IDENTIFICATION SYSTEM PROCESS AND THE PROBLEMS FACED

Generally, the fingerprint identification system uses fingerprint acquisition instrument to acquire fingerprint. After pre-processing, the only characteristic parameters that can represent a certain piece of fingerprint are extracted and stored into the sample database in the computer, serving as the benchmarks for comparison and search. Then, fingerprint acquisition instrument is used to acquire the to-be-identified fingerprint. After pre-processing, characteristics are extracted, and these characteristic points are compared with the template characteristic points stored in the sample database to judge if the to-be-identified fingerprint image and a certain fingerprint image in the sample database come from the same finger of the same person, so as to meet the requirement of identification.

At present, remarkable achievements have been made in fingerprint classification, identification and matching, the commercialized equipment for fingerprint acquisition and its market application are also becoming increasingly mature, and the scope of application is also becoming more and more extensive, yet a lot of problems are exposed during the actual using of such technology. For example, the environmental adaptability of the acquisition equipment is too poor; the finger print image extracted from the three-dimensional curved surface of the finger may easily be deformed when transformed into two-dimensional fingerprint image; although the fingerprint identification system adopts classification algorithm and indexing technology, during the identification process with the database that has less obvious classification or enormous classification contents, the speed of sample identification and matching is yet to be improved.

3. GENETIC NEURAL NETWORK STRUCTURE AND ITS ALGORITHM

BP neural network is a multilayer feed-forward neural network, a multilayer forwarding network of one-way communication. In the network, in addition to the input nodes and output nodes, there are also several hidden layer nodes, and the nodes on the same layer have no any coupling between each other. The transformation function of the nodes generally selects the Sigmoid-type function, which is one of the most extensively used activation functions in BP neural network and can normalize the input values into the range of 0~1 [1]. The selection of initial weights of BP neural network is highly random. Since the BP algorithm is based on gradient descent method, different initial weights may lead to totally different results, hence the BP neural network has the defects of low learning efficiency and low convergence speed.

The genetic algorithm is a calculation model that simulates the biological evolution process of Darwinian genetic selection and natural selection, and is a global probability search algorithm based on such biological mechanisms as natural selection and genetic mutation [2]. Its feature of global search can be used to find the most appropriate network connection weight and network structure. The three-layer neural network consists of input layer, output layer and hidden layer, while the number of input layer and output layer nodes is determined by the modeling sample. Therefore, the optimization of BP neural network structure is mainly about optimizing the number of its hidden layer nodes. The basic idea of genetic algorithm-based optimization is as follows:

1) Set the training times and training error of the network, input the training sample. After training, input the testing sample, and initially establish the value range of the network connection weights. Define the fitness function as:

$$F(w,v,\theta,r)=\frac{1}{\sqrt{\sum_{k=1}^{N_1}\sum_{t=1}^{n}[y_k(t)-\hat{y}_k(t)]^2}} \tag{1}$$

2) Work out codes according to the value range of the network connection weights to generate the code string which is composed of two parts — control code and weight coefficient code.

3) Determine the individual composition of initial population. Conclude the number of hidden nodes of the network from the control code string, and conclude the connection weight of the network from the weight coefficient code string, input the training sample, and calculate the adaptability of each individual in the population.

4) Duplicate the individual with the strongest adaptability directly into the next generation without letting them be involved in the crossover and mutation computing. Other individuals are selected by using the roulette method.

5) The crossover and mutation of the control code adopts the basic genetic algorithm method.

6) Mutate the number i individual to generate a new generation of population.

7) After repeated iteration, decode the finally-concluded individual with the strongest adaptability to conclude the corresponding numbers of the network connection weights and hidden nodes.

In this way, the combined use of genetic algorithm and neural network not only utilizes the global random search capability and robustness of the genetic algorithm, but also gives full consideration to the self-learning capability of the neural network. The simulation experiment result shows that the genetic neural network can effectively inhibit the early convergence of genetic algorithm and improve the learning efficiency and convergence accuracy of the multilayer forwarding neural network weight coefficient, and can also overcome the defects of the traditional BP learning algorithm and genetic algorithm of the multilayer forwarding neural network, indicating the feasibility and effectiveness of the method.

4. FINGERPRINT CLASSIFICATION BASED ON GENETIC NEURAL NETWORK

During the fingerprint identification process, the to-be-identified fingerprint samples need to be compared one by one with enormous fingerprint information in the sample database. When the volume of the sample database is too big, such identification process is quite time-consuming. In order to reduce the search time and calculation complexity, we may classify the fingerprints in the sample database into several categories, and store different types of fingerprints into different sub-databases. The pre-set categories as per this article include five types -- spiral type, left-ring type, right-ring type, arch type and unidentifiable type [3]. In this way, the to-be-identified fingerprint only needs to be compared with the sample fingerprints of the same category in the corresponding sub-database, which will significantly improve the speed of identification and matching.

Generally, the fingerprint classification algorithm can be categorized according to the theoretical method adopted, such as statistical method, structure method, artificial neural network method, etc.; it can also be categorized according to the fingerprint characteristic point information by using modeling or be categorized according to image ridge line characteristics and direction information by using global method, proceeding from the realistic problem [4]. Many experts have conducted a number of studies on fingerprint classification algorithm, such as the classification method proposed by Karu and Jain which features the identification of the center point and the triangular area [5]. Because human finger is a three-dimensional curve surface structure, during the acquisition of fingerprint image, if the force used is improper, the spacing and location of the fingerprint characteristic point will distort. In addition, there is certain extent of directional angle error between the to-be-identified fingerprint and the sample fingerprints during acquisition, which also adds to the difficulty in calibration. Therefore, how to use the extracted characteristics of the fingerprint samples to establish models for convenient and accurate identification of the to-be-identified image is a hot-spot issue in algorithm study.

Although the relative spacing and location of the fingerprint characteristic point has changed more or less during the acquisition of fingerprint image, the fingerprint structure characteristics need by the system for identification have not changed substantially. That is to say, no matter how the to-be-identified fingerprint rotates and mutates, the fingerprint structure characteristics model can be established. In reality, human fingerprint experts compare the similar characteristics between the acquired fingerprint image and the sample fingerprint to determine whether they come from the fingerprint of the same person. We can simulate such way of thinking to take any one fingerprint characteristic point as a center, and establish a six-dimensional characteristics vector based on the frequency of appearance of various local detail pattern characteristic points within the range of unit radius. Such vector can be expressed as (V, f(a1), f(a2), f(a3), f(a4), f(a5)), while as V represents the type of the central characteristic point, and f(a1)~ f(a5) respectively represents the number of end point, crossover point, isolated point, short-vein point and annular point. In this way, we can use the characteristics vector to represent the fingerprint samples image. During the process of fingerprint classification, we select the characteristics vector of the fingerprint samples center point as the input node for the genetic neural network. Hence, there are 6 input nodes for the genetic neural network. We take the identified fingerprint pattern binary code as the output node for the genetic neural network, whereas fingerprint pattern can be any one of the above-mentioned five types -- spiral type, left-ring type, right-ring type, arch type and unidentifiable type . So, we can set 3 output nodes, which is in line with the classification requirement for the number of classification types to be less than 8. The system will first generate code and initial population. After individual adaptability assessment, selective duplication, crossover and mutation will be carried out according to genetic algorithm, until meeting the conditions for termination. Finally, we use the well-trained network to classify the fingerprint samples. The process of the fingerprint classification algorithm based on genetic neural network is shown in Fig. 1.

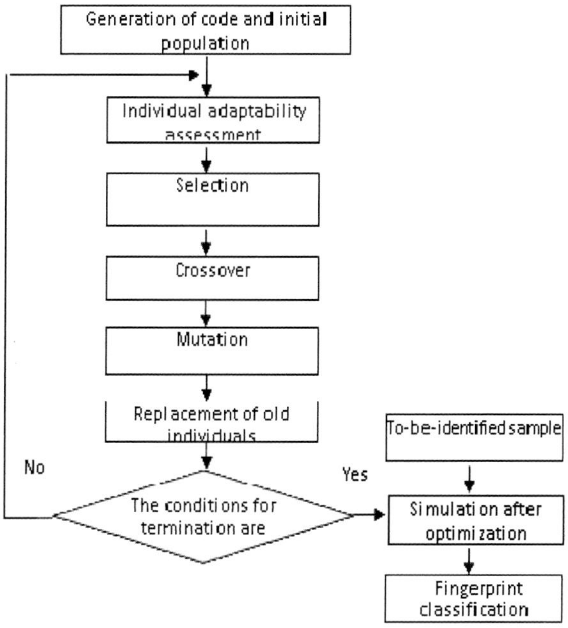

Figure 1. Process of the fingerprint classification algorithm based on genetic neural network.

In algorithm testing, we select 120 fingerprint images in the fingerprint database, including 12 spiral type images (10%), 42 left-ring type images (35%), 24 right-ring type images (20%), 30 arch type images (25%) and 12 unidentifiable type images (10%). The classification result shows that there are 117 times of accurate classification and 3 times of false classification, meaning that the classification error rate is 2.5%. Judging from the experiment of result, the algorithm can basically make accurate classification on fingerprints and reach certain degree of accuracy, yet there are also certain number faults. This indicates that there is still large room for the optimization of the algorithm. The proportion of unidentifiable fingerprint samples is high. Through analysis, we find that this is mostly caused by the low quality of the acquired images, indicating that the equipment acquisition process of fingerprint samples and image pre-processing process are yet to be improved, and the algorithm robustness is still to be enhanced.

5. CONCLUSION

Fingerprint classification is to classify fingerprints into several pre-set categories according to the structure characteristic point of fingerprints. The result provides an indexing mechanism for the later identification of fingerprints, which greatly improves the efficiency of comparing the to-be-identified fingerprint with the fingerprints in the sample database. This article elaborates on the practice of adopting the appearance frequencies of the central characteristic point and local detail pattern characteristic points as the vector of fingerprint samples characteristics, and utilizing the genetic neural network to optimize the classification. The classification result is basically accurate, yet the algorithm robustness is yet to be improved.

REFERENCES

- [1] B.Q. Chen, M. Sun. 2008. Practical Guidance for Digital Image Processing and Analysis. Beijing: Tinghua University Press, 292-298.
- [2] P.F. Yan, Ch.SH. Zhang. 2000. Artificial Neural Network and Simulated Evolution Computation. Beijing: Tinghua University Press, 396-421.
- [3] Y.L. Yin, X.B. Ning, X.M. Zhang. 2002. Improved Fingerprint Detail Characteristics Extraction Algorithm. *Chinese Journal of Image and Graphics,* 7(A):1302-1306.
- [4] A.M. Bazen, GT.B.Verwaaijen, S.H. Gerez, Veelenturf L.P.J. and van der Zwaag B.J. 2000. A Correlation-Based Fingerprint Verification System in *Proc. Workshop on Circuits Systems and Signal Processing (ProRISC2000):* 205-213.
- [5] K. Karu and A.K. Jain, Fingerprint Classification. 1996. *Pattern Recognition,* 29(3): 389-404.

Computing Intelligence Approach for an Eye State Classification with EEG Signal in BCI

Y.M. Kim, C.Y. Lee & C.G. Lim*
Chonnam National University, Yeosu, Jeonnam, South Korea
Email: cglim@jnu.ac.kr

ABSTRACT: Finding human cognitive state is very important and useful for medical cares in our daily life. Eye state classification is a kind of common time-series problem for detecting human cognitive state. One of approaches of EEG eye state classification is based on time series data. We propose a new neural fuzzy structure that is possible to use an eye state classification. The classification accuracy can be achieved by using the proposed approach in terms of the number of neurons in the hidden layer, which also leads types of membership function in fuzzy rules. The data of EEG signals for monitoring eye state saved by Machine Learning Repository, University of California, Irvine (UCI) is used for eye state benchmarking. We did experiments with 3 different networks for the architecture by changing the number of neurons in the hidden layer and random seed for weights. We found that tuning parameters asymmetrically gave us the best results through test cases. According to the test results, we have the best result with 4 neurons by managing parameters of standard deviations asymmetrically, with which showed a 4.0% average error rate with the test data.

KEYWORDS: Computing intelligence; Eye state classification; EEG; BCI; Machine learning.

1. INTRODUCTION

Humans have been imagined the ability to interact and communication with machines through thought, Brain Computer Interface (BCI). It mainly deals with the interfacing of our brain with computers or devices by adapting to given tasks. The system consists of the several factors such as brain signal measuring, feature extraction, and translating it to commands for output devices. Machine learning methods for specific tasks are reviewed in terms of robust feature selection [1].

Electroencephalography (EEG) is one of most popular ways to record brain signals, which is portable and inexpensive for BCI. The electrical activity of the brain is measured in non-invasive way recordings the sum of many postsynaptic potentials in the cortex. EEG (electroencephalography) signals in a feedback setup is the first published work for learning to control their alpha waves [2]. EEG activity patterns are classified by mapping between the EEG data and classes corresponding to mental tasks like movement of the left hand [3]. Interesting review of classification algorithms has been published to design Brain Computer Interface (BCI) systems based on EEG [4, 5].

Finding human cognitive state is very important and useful for medical cares in our daily life such as infant sleep-waking state identification [6] and driving drowsiness detection [7]. Eye state classification is a kind of common time-series problem for detecting human cognitive state. Machine learning and statistical methodologies are widely used for identifying the states.

Computing intelligence is an emerging problem solving technology for uncertain and nonlinear problems. It can be considered as collaboration between the Fuzzy Logic, Genetic Algorithms, and Neural Networks. They contribute their advantages to compensate for their weaknesses to find out optimal solution in the given problem. For example, fuzzy logic is useful for approximate reasoning but doesn't have any learning capability and vice versa in neural networks. It exploits a tolerance for imprecision, uncertainty, partial truth to achieve tractability, and robustness by merging these technologies [8].

Machine learning is a program, which automatically learns from data to construct the system for various applications such as Web search, spam filters, recommender systems, and pattern classification etc. It can be done by minimizing error obtained by training in general lead to fitting and robust behavior for the given system. Vidaurre et al. successfully used machine learning technique in which Brain-computer interfaces (BCIs) allow users to control a computer application by brain activity as acquired (e.g., by EEG). In this work, the participants undertake a calibration measurement without feedback to acquire data to train the BCI system [9].

The purpose of this paper is:

1) to prepare a new neural fuzzy structure that is possible to use an eye state classification;

2) to increase the classification accuracy that can be achieved by using the proposed approach in terms of the number of neurons in the hidden layer and types of membership function in fuzzy rules.

This paper is divided into five sections. The second one describes EEG eye state classification regarding existing works and data set for the work in this paper. The third section explains the new method used in the research by applying computing intelligence. The fourth section presents the results of the work proposed and the discussion of these results. Conclusion and future work are illustrated in the last section.

2. EEG EYE STATE CLASSIFICATION

2.1. *Previous works*

Recently several eye state studies have been proposed. One of approaches of EEG eye state classification is based on time series data. A log-linearized Gaussian mixture neural network is employed for EEG eye state classification [10]. Yeo et al. successfully used Support Vector Machines (SVMs) to detect drowsiness during car driving by eye blink [7].Furthermore, a hybrid system based on decision tree classifier and fast Fourier transform was applied on the detection of epileptic seizure by Polat et al. [11]. Sulaiman et al. also employed K-Nearest Neighbor (K-NN) for stress features identification [12].

Mind Switch Control System (MSCS) is developed to help disabled people control electrical devices, which are based upon changes in EEG signals between the two states [13]. Frequency analysis based on the Hilbert-Huang transform (HHT) is examined as an alternative to Fourier spectral analysis in the study of EEG signals. It is not necessary the need for the EEG signal to be linear and stationary [14]. Neural networks are used for EEG eye state identification using incremental attribute learning (IAL), which is a new machine learning strategy by gradually importing and training features one by one [15].

2.2. *Eye state dataset*

The data of EEG signals for monitoring eye state can be obtained eye state corpus for a benchmark problem saved by Machine Learning Repository, University of California, Irvine (UCI) [16]. It is from one continuous EEG measurement of the Emotive EEG Neuroheadset, which is shown in Figure 1. Röslerand Suendermann prepared the EEG eye state dataset and donate them for the research purpose [17]. All data were derived from one continuous EEG measurement with the Emotiv EEG neuroheadset.

The data set consists of 14 EEG values, with which each indicates the eye state. The total numbers of data instances are 14,980 patterns. The 14 instances of the features are the data obtained by 14 sensors from the headset. The duration of the measurement was 117 seconds. The eye state was detected via a camera during the EEG measurement and added later manually to the file after analyzing the video frames. All these works showed that machine learning and statistical methods are feasible in solving time series classification for EEG eye state identification.

3. COMPUTING INTELLIGENCE APPROACH FOR EYE STATE CLASSIFICATION

3.1. *Fuzzy logic system modeling*

The aim of constructing Fuzzy Inference System (FIS) is to obtain a set of fuzzy rules to describe the given tasks to be solved accurately. Figure 1 presents the essence of the FIS [18]. The FIS consists of a knowledge base and a processing stage part. The knowledge base provides MFs and fuzzy rules that are integrated to the process of the system. In the processing stage, the input values of the system are numerical as crisp variables. These variables are passed through a fuzzification stage where they are transformed to linguistic variables, which become the fuzzy input for the inference engine. This fuzzy input is transformed by the rules of the inference engine to fuzzy output. The linguistic results are then changed by a defuzzification stage into numerical values that become the output of the system.

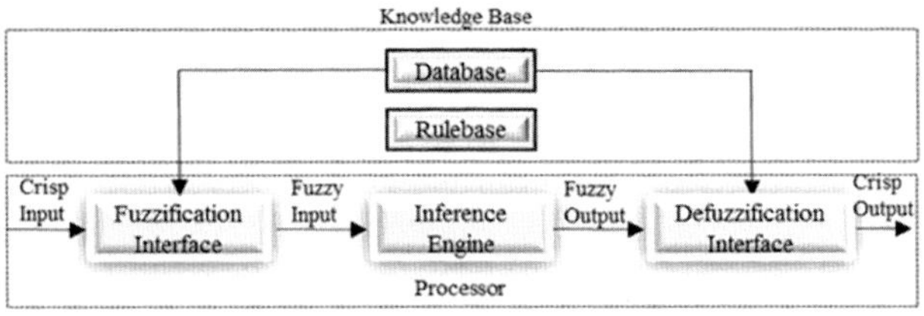

Figure 1. The essence of the Fuzzy Inference System (FIS) [18].

In this paper, Genetic Algorithms (GAs) tune fuzzy systems by adjusting the parameters of fuzzy MFs and its weights of neural network structure (see

Figure2). We use of the advantage of the GAs by adapting simple operations for tuning fuzzy system parameters automatically.

3.2. *Computing intelligence system as a classifier*

3.2.1. *The structure of the proposed system*

We discuss the formulation of the proposed system, which implements a fuzzy logic algorithm based on neural network structure in Figure 2. The general structure of the system is the multi-input and multi-output. The input layer accepts the input vector (x_1, x_2, x_3,....,x_n) and the neurons (s^1, s^2, s^3,....., s^m) of the hidden layer conduct fuzzy inference. The action of classification for each of fuzzy rule depends on the interconnected weighs between the hidden layer and output layer. The output layer gives the classification state.

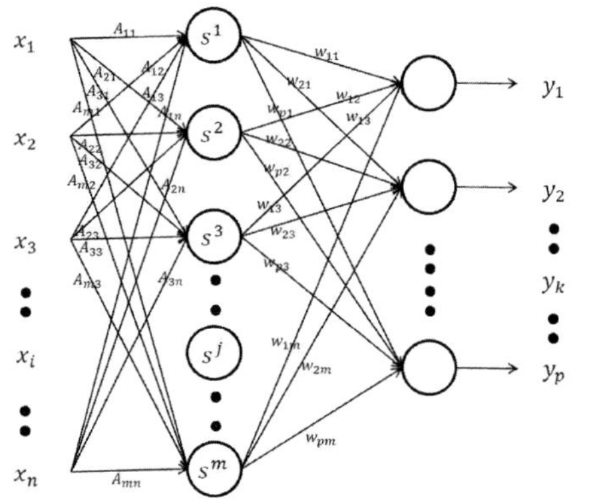

Figure 2. The structure of the proposed system for an eye state classification.

The fuzzy logic for the inference can be implemented the following rules which are written as

R^j: IF x_1 is A_{j1} and x_2 is $A_{j2}$and... x_i is A_{ji}...and x_n is A_{jn}

Then y_1 is w_1 and y_2 is w_2 and ... y_j is w_j...andy_p is w_p

Where A_j (j=1,2,3,...,m) is fuzzy set in the rules and m is the number of fuzzy rules.

Fuzzy logic basically involves three steps: fuzzification, inference process, and defuzzification. The fuzzification takes care of the IF part of the fuzzy rule. Inference process is mainly related to the membership function by applying all rules. The results of the rules are combined to generate the final results in the defuzzification stage.

3.2.2. *Gaussian membership function*

Membership functions provide the means to translate linguistic expressions by identifying the fuzziness in a given fuzzy set. The proposed system uses asymmetrical Gaussian function as the membership function, which can be represented as a mathematical formula as in Equation 1. **v** represents the mean (center) of each cluster in the rule base. **s** is the standard deviation (width) in the given membership function. Index *l* stands for left of the deviation and *r* is right of the deviation to maintain membership function asymmetrically. The main advantage of using a Gaussian function is its applicability to fuzzy systems.

$$A_{ji}(x_i) = \begin{cases} exp\left(\frac{-(x_i-v_{ji})^2}{2\left(s_{il}^j\right)^2}\right) & if x_i \leq v_{ji} \\ exp\left(\frac{-(x_i-v_{ji})^2}{2\left(s_{ir}^j\right)^2}\right) & if x_i > v_{ji} \end{cases} \tag{1}$$

i=1,2,3...,n

j=1,2,3...m

3.2.3. *Defuzzification for classification*

It is necessary to define fuzzy inference to apply knowledge base. To calculate membership function value of the given input vector, we use the Equation 2.

$$s^j = A_{j1}(x_1) \cdot A_{j2}(x_2) \cdot \ldots \cdot A_{jn}(x_n) \tag{2}$$

Membership function and weight values are still non-crisp values. The results are combined and distilled to classify given input vector by carrying out Equation 3. It can be viewed like a center of gravity defuzzification method. The output is a crisp value that will be one of the eye states, open or close for the system. Genetic algorithm will be used to find out the optimal parameters of the membership function in the fuzzy rules and weights. It uses simple operations to derive the optimal system by designing and automatic tuning, which is discussed in the next section.

$$y_k = \frac{\sum_{j=1}^{m} s^j w_{kj}}{\sum_{j=1}^{m} s^j}, \quad s^j = \prod_{i=1}^{n} A_{ji}(x_i) \tag{3}$$

3.2.4. *Design of gene type*

Gene is each of standard deviation of the membership function and weight to be tuned for the fuzzy rule base. Figure 3 represents the connection matrix format for the membership functions in terms of standard deviation. We fix the parameters for the mean in the membership function without tuning. The mean is to be represented for each cluster in the rules. The weight gene can be represented with matrix form as illustrated in Figure 4. The number of gene of the chromosomes in a population depends on dimension of input and output and the number of rules for the system.

$s^1_{1l}\, s^1_{1r}$	$s^1_{2l}\, s^1_{2r}$	$s^1_{3l}\, s^1_{3r}$	......	$s^1_{nl}\, s^1_{nr}$
$s^2_{1l}\, s^2_{1r}$	$s^2_{2l}\, s^2_{2r}$	$s^2_{3l}\, s^2_{3r}$	......	$s^2_{nl}\, s^2_{nr}$
$s^3_{1l}\, s^3_{1r}$	$s^3_{2l}\, s^3_{2r}$	$s^3_{3l}\, s^3_{3r}$	......	$s^3_{nl}\, s^3_{nr}$
......	......	......	......	......
$s^m_{1l}\, s^m_{1r}$	$s^m_{2l}\, s^m_{2r}$	$s^m_{3l}\, s^m_{3r}$	......	$s^m_{nl}\, s^m_{nr}$

Figure 3. Matrix representation of the standard deviation (gene) for membership function of the fuzzy rule base.

w_{11}	w_{21}	w_{31}	......	w_{p1}
w_{13}	w_{22}	w_{32}	......	w_{p2}
w_{13}	w_{23}	w_{33}	......	w_{p3}
......	......	......	......	......
w_{1m}	w_{2m}	w_{3m}	......	w_{pm}

Figure 4. Matrix representation for weight (gene) of the system structure.

3.2.5. *Learning algorithm of the system*

The main idea of a genetic algorithm is "survival of the fittest" by evolving a solution to a search problem. The goal of a genetic algorithm is to produce a chromosome with the highest possible fitness by applying GA operations. A proportion of the existing population is selected to generate new members of population through a fitness-based process. The chromosomes with higher fitness have more chances to be the next generation. The selected chromosomes can be reproduced as offspring according to the relative fitness of the individuals. They also exchange partially of the genes. Main operations of GA, which perform 'pseudo-random' walk through search space. The basic procedures of GA to be utilized in this paper are described as follows.

1) Prepare a population of chromosomes, each of length *n* genes, which consists of widths and weights in the structure for an eye state classification.
2) Test each chromosome from the population within the problem space and only the fitness survives to reproduce for the next generation.
3) Select parents based on their fitness using a roulette wheel.
4) Exchange portions of pair chromosomes at a randomly selected point with some crossover probability.
5) Mutate the values of genes of a selected chromosome at one or more positions randomly.
6) Create a new population by replacing a portion of the original population with the new chromosomes.
7) Test if the end condition is satisfied, stop, else go to step 2.

4. EXPERIMENT RESULTS AND DISCUSSIONS

4.1. *Experiment setup*

We consider the proposed model of an eye state classification using a computing intelligence approach. The data consists of two groups, eye close and open. Among 14,976 data, 8,254 are assigned to the eye open and rest of them is eye open. The prepared data were randomly divided into training and testing sets for experiments. 70 percent of data were used for training and the rest of them for testing.

For the eye state classification problem, the number of the input layer is 14 neurons. The output layer should be one neuron for two classes that represents the eye state, open or close that we want to classify. The number of neurons in the hidden layer isvaried according to the structure of the system, which depends on the number of cluster in the given data for the optimal configuration, with which we will explain the experiment results. For example, using 4 neurons in the hidden layer, we now have 32 genes (14x2 + 4x1) in the population of individuals to be tuned using GA. The 28 parameters of standard deviations in the hidden layer were determined in the clustering process and weight parameters between and output layer were set at the randomly.

The aim of the learning process is to minimize an average squared error function. The network parameters, $\{\mathbf{s}\}$ and $\{\mathbf{w}\}$, can be optimized by employing RMSE (Root Mean Square Error) for a given data set to minimize an objective error function:

$$RMSE = \sqrt{\frac{1}{N}\sum_{i=1}^{N} e_i^2} \quad (4)$$

where e is the model errors with N samples.

4.2. *Evaluation of the proposed system*

This section illustrates the experiment results obtained using the system explained in the previous section. To evaluate our approach's robustness for finding parameters in the system, we trained 3 different networks for the architecture by changing the number of neurons in the hidden layer and random seed for weights. We used networks with 3, 4, and 5 hidden neurons. Although we used 2 hidden neurons, there is no acceptable result. On the other hand, more than 6 neurons in the hidden layer leaded to time consuming with computation time for training without better results compared to 3, 4, and 5 ones.

The networks were trained for 100 generations for each network with termination condition less than 1 % of error rate. Roulette-wheel and best selection operations were used for selection. Single and multi-point points were selected for mutation. We created a new population by replacing a portion of the original population randomly with rate less than 1%.We prepared 3 different experiment studies by tuning parameters during training. The study design is useful for testing whether our theories and models actually work in the proposed problem. The experiments include: tuning weights only, weights and standard deviation symmetrically, and weights and standard deviation asymmetrically.

Figure 5 shows the learning curves in terms of the number of neurons in the hidden layer. It can be shown that 4 neurons in the hidden layer gives the best training result.

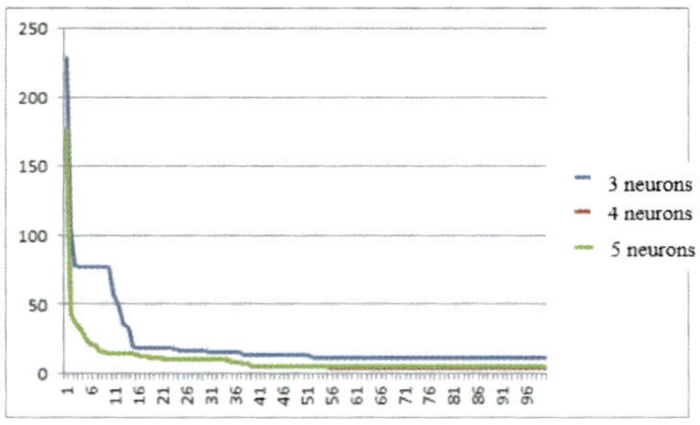

Figure 5. Learning curves depending on the nodes in the hidden layer.

The performance evaluation of the system measures the accuracy by testing the designed system. Once a network is converged, the input vector is presented as features to be classified in terms of close or open. In our experiments, we trained the system 10 times with different number of neurons in the hidden layer and by changing styles as we mentioned. Case 1 only tunes the weight in the structure without adjusting standard deviations as parameters. Standard deviations can be adjusted asymmetrically and asymmetrically based on the strategies for training for the best results in Case 2 and 3 respectively.

Table 1 gives experiment results obtained using all parameters of the proposed system in this paper. We tried 10 times for each test case with the different network structures based on fuzzy rules. Each row shows the number of neuron in in accordance with test cases. The average of test results is illustrated in the bottom of row to be compared easily.

Table 1. Experiment results according to test cases (perform 10 times each test case with different neuron numbers in the hidden layer).

Case	Case 1			Case 2			Case 3		
N	3	4	5	3	4	5	3	4	5
1	50.9	38.9	25.2	18.2	15.8	17.1	10.3	3.5	4.9
2	49.9	37.9	25.6	19.8	15.7	15.8	9.9	3.9	4.3
3	51.2	38.9	25.4	20.6	16.9	14.9	10.2	3.6	5.1
4	49.9	38.8	25.8	18.8	17.9	14.6	10.2	3.5	5.0
5	50.1	38.7	23.6	20.6	16.9	16.2	10.5	4.2	4.1
6	49.1	38.6	24.8	21.5	14.6	15.9	9.1	4.1	4.9
7	49.7	37.5	25.6	25.4	18.3	17.5	9.8	3.5	4.7
8	49.3	36.8	23.8	19.5	19.1	18.1	9.7	3.5	5.5
9	50.1	38.2	25.0	19.0	14.1	17.3	10.5	4.5	5.3
10	49.1	38.3	26.8	20.0	13.6	16.9	11.6	3.6	5.0
Avg.	50.0	38.2	25.2	20.3	16.3	16.4	10.2	4.0	4.9

4.3. *Discussion*

In this section, we prepared three cases of test results for eye state classification. Figure 6 shows a summary of 3 cases for validations of our approach. The results show that 3 neurons in the hidden layer of the structure gave more error rate compare to 4 and 5 neurons. On the other hand, when more neurons are used for training and testing, an improvement is not found in error rates. It has shown that the system requires optimal hidden neurons for better performance to the given problem. Although we can fix the structure in the neural network approach, we decided the number of neurons in the hidden layer. The number of iterations to converge is also less than that of neural networks, since our approach prepared the structure to converge fast with the optimal number of neurons for the recall phase. This is due to the rule and defuzzification process, which require more computation than neural networks do in the recall phase.

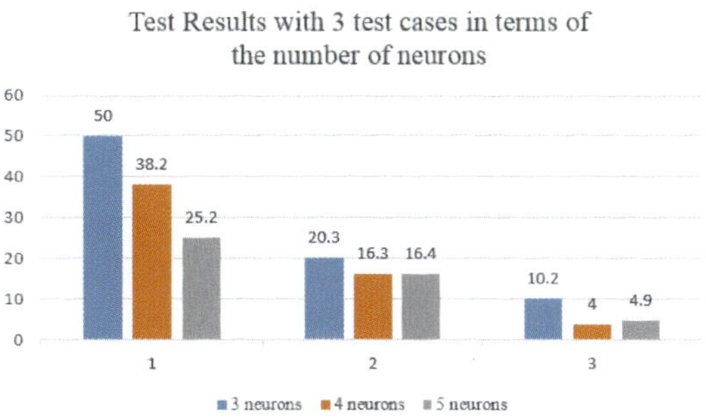

Figure 6. Test results with 3 cases in terms of the number of neurons in the hidden layer. Learning curves depending on the nodes in the hidden layer.

One thing we have to know in these experiments is parameters we have to tune in training phase. As we can see, test case 1 gave us the worst performances, in which we only tune the weights between hidden and output layer by fixing the standard deviations. The errors are decreased in the case 2 by updating parameters for standard deviations symmetrically compared to the case 1. We found that tuning parameters asymmetrically gave us the best results in case 3.

We knew how to update the parameters through the experiments. Now we need to know how to decide the number of neurons for the hidden layer. According to the test results in Figure 6, we have the best result in the test case 3 with 4 neurons, which is better than 5 neurons even though with more rules. 3 neurons for the hidden layer are not enough to get the acceptable result. We reached the conclusion that managing parameters of standard deviations asymmetrically is the right way to get the best performance to the given problem.

5. CONCLUSIONS AND FUTURE WORK

This paper presented a new computing intelligence system for classifying eye state using EEG data set. Our experimental results show that the proposed approach gives us a promising method with small number of fuzzy rules. It is a simple fuzzy system with neural network structure by tuning GA providing statistically superior solutions. In our research, we used the real dataset, which is a popular in eye state classification area provided by UCI.

An eye state was classified into two classes, open or close. To differentiate two eye states, we proposed the new neural fuzzy system tuning by GA. To evaluate the results according to the proposed approach the number of neurons in the hidden layer, various experiments were conducted. In the experiments, we maintained the Gaussian membership asymmetrically for an appropriate convergence into a desired result. The best result with 4 neurons in the hidden layer showed a 4.0% average error rate with the test data.

One thing we need to do in the future is comparing the performance of different ensemble methods for EEG signal classification for BCI system. We also will be in trying to classify more actions using other techniques for feature extraction to different areas such as robotic arm and imagined mental tasks. Finally, we need to automatically find out the optimal number of neurons in the hidden layer in the given task. It is one of possible ways to determine optimal number of fuzzy rules based on cluster validity values.

ACKNOWLEDGEMENT

This work (Grants No. C0214152) was supported by Business for Cooperative R&D between Industry, Academy, and Research Institute funded Korea Small and Medium Business Administration in 2014.

REFERENCES

- [1] Müller, K.-R., Krauledat M., Dornhege, G., Curio, G., & Blankertz1, B. Machine learning techniques for brain-compute interfaces. *Biomedical engineering*, 2004, Vol. 49, Num. 1, pp. 11-22.
- [2] Kamiya, J. Operant Control of the EEG Alpha Rhythm and Some of its Reported Effects on Consciousness. Biofeedback and Self-Control: An Aldine Reader on the Regulation of Bodily Processes and Consciousness, 1971.
- [3] Lotte, F., Congedo, M., Lecuyer, A., Lamarche, F. & Arnalsi. B. A review of classification algorithms for EEG-based brain-computer interfaces. Journal of Neural Engineering 2007, 4: R1-R13.
- [4] Wolpaw, J. R., Birbaumer, N., McFarland, D. J., Pfurtscheller, G. & Vaughan, T. M., Brain computer interfaces for communication and control. Clinical Neurophysiology, 2002, 113(6):767-791.
- [5] Vallabhaneni, A., Wang, T., & He, B. Brain computer interface. In He B (Ed): Neural Engineering, 2005, pp 85-121.
- [6] Estevez, P. A., Held, C. M., Holzmann, C. A., Perez, C. A., Perez, J. P. , Heiss, J., Garrido, M., & Peirano, P., Polysomnographic pattern ecognition for automated classification of sleep-waking states in infants. Medical and Biological Engineering and Computing, 2002, vol. 40, pp. 105-113.
- [7] Yeo, M. V. M., Li, X., Shen, K., & Wilder-Smith, E. P. V. Can SVM be used for automatic EEG detection of drowsiness during car driving? Safety Science, 2009, vol. 47, pp. 115-124.
- [8] Shukla, K.K. Soft computing paradigms for artificial vision. In: Sinha, N.K., Gupta, M.M. (Eds.), Soft Computing and Intelligent Systems: Theory and Applications. Academic Press, San Diego, 2000, pp. 405–417.
- [9] Vidaurre, C., Sannelli, C., Müller, K-R., & Blankertz, B. Machine-Learning-Based Coadaptive Calibration for Brain-Computer Interfaces. Neural Computation 23, 2011, 791–816.
- [10] Fukuda, O., Tsuji, T., & Kaneko, M. Pattern classification of EEG signals using a log-linearized Gaussian mixture neural network, in Proceedings of the 1995 IEEE International Conference on Neural Networks, 1995, Part 1, pp. 2479-2484.
- [11] Polat, K. & Gunes, S. Classification of epileptiform EEG using a hybrid system based on decision tree classifier and fast Fourier transform. Applied Mathematics and Computation, 2007, vol. 187, pp. 1017-1026.
- [12] Sulaiman, N., Taib, M. N., Lias, S., Murat, Z. H., Aris, S. A. M., & Hamid, N. H. A. Novel methods for stress features identification using EEG signals. International Journal of Simulation: Systems, Science and Technology, 2011, vol. 12, pp. 27-33.
- [13] Craig, A., Moses, Tran, P. P, Y., McIsaac, P., & Kirkup, L. The effectiveness of a hands-free environmental control system for the profoundly disabled. Arch. Phys. Med. Rehabil, vol 83 pp. 1455-1457.
- [14] Thuraisingham, R. A., Tran, Y., Craig, A. & Nguyen, H. Frequency analysis of eyes open and eyes closed EEG signals using the Hilbert-Huang Transform. 34th Annual International Conference of the IEEE EMBS San Diego, California USA, 2012, 28 August - 1 September.
- [15] Wang, T., Guan, S-U., LokMan, K., & Ting, T. O. EEG Eye State Identification Using Incremental Attribute Learning with Time-Series Classification. Mathematical Problems in Engineering, 2014, Volume 2014, Article ID 365101.
- [16] Frank, A. & Asuncion, A. UCI machine learning repository. 2010, http://archive.ics.uci.edu/ml.
- [17] Rösler, O. & Suendermann, D. First step towards eye state prediction using EEG, in Proceedings of the International Conference on Applied Informatics for Health and Life Sciences (AIHLS '13), 2013, Istanbul, Turkey.
- [18] Jang, J.-S.R., Sun, C.-T., Mizutani, E. Neuro-fuzzy and Soft Computing: A Computational Approach to Learning and Machine Intelligence. 1997, Prentice-Hall, Upper Saddle River, NJ.

Research on Automatic Registration and Fusion Technology for Multi-group images

Q. Wei[*], L. Zhao
Academy of Equipment, Beijing, China,
[*]*Email: weiqun@sina.com*

ABSTRACT: With the development of computer graphics technology, machine vision and virtual reality technology in recent years, 3D reconstruction method through the sequence of images of outdoor scenes has become a key research direction in computer vision and graphics. During the acquisition process of image, due to the measurement equipment and environment, single shot sequence of photos may not be able to extract enough surface information and lead to unable to complete the reconstruction of 3D objects. To solve this problem, fusion method of point clouds from multi-group images is adopted in the thesis. Firstly the color histogram matching is used to complete the supplement image sequence. Next the point cloud from the supplement image sequence is solely calculated. Then the transform parameters in overlap area of different point clouds are computed by using the improved iterative closest point algorithm. Finally the registration and fusion among the point cloud data of different photos is conducted. The experiments show that this method can effectively supplement point cloud data for reconstruction.

KEYWORDS: 3D reconstruction; Iterative Closest Point (ICP) algorithm; Color histogram matching; Point cloud registration and fusion.

1. INTRODUCTION

For a long time, computer workers hope for the reconstruction of spatial entities or scenes in a computer. With rapid development of computer technology and measurement technique, the 3D reconstruction of outdoor objects and environment has attracted much attention in recent years and has become the focus in computer vision and graphics related fields. At present, 3D reconstruction method is mainly classified 2 kinds: the 3D reconstruction depending on the depth detect equipment to acquire point cloud data and the 3D reconstruction based on sequence images [1]. The latter is convenient and low cost which has broad application prospects. Based on this, the paper aims at the registration and fusion of point cloud which are acquired from multi-group images.

At present, 3D reconstruction method with monocular stereo vision are often based on multi-view stereo technology and the technology of 3D reconstruction based on motion. Usually, firstly the camera calibration is used to obtain parameters of camera, and next a group of images of objects are imported. Text, correspond image points for the relevant regions are acquired by feature extraction and matching, and then the relative orientation method is adopted to calculate the relative orientation parameters of image. The 3D coordinate of corresponding image points are obtained by space intersection formula. Finally the reconstruction is completed by triangulation and texture mapping. The method is relatively mature. But when the engineering practice encountered more quantity of images, one-time input will take a very long time and accumulative stitching error of the model become larger. At the same time, if surface has complex structure it is not conducive to the further enhancement of the geometric details. Based on these problems, this paper presents a fusion method for point cloud of multiple groups of image sequences. The method can effectively complement the surface point cloud information and reduce the accumulated error to ensure the reconstruction accuracy.

2. RELATED WORK

At present, most methods adopt the combination of initial registration and accurate registration. That is, the initial matching should keep error down as much as possible. The initial matching accuracy will directly affect speed and convergence of the subsequent accurate registration. The commonly used method includes the turntable method, labeling and the surface characteristics. The accurate registration of point clouds makes the error minimum. The ICP algorithm (i.e., the iterative closest point algorithm) and its improved algorithm are the key algorithm for accurate registration. Now most of the registration algorithm is improved on this basis to solve the practice problem.

The main goal of improvement on ICP algorithm is to solve two problems: well initial values and a precise correspondence in iterative process.

Zhou Chunyan [2] takes into account the effect of initial registration parameters for accurate registration in iteration. In the algorithm, the principal component analysis is adopted to choose the initial registration parameters, which provides a good accurate condition for subsequent ICP algorithm. At the same time, the kd-tree is used to accelerate the finding of corresponding points, the preprocessing of point set is increased and the restrictions that assure no false matching points in searching points are added.

Based on the traditional ICP, Liu — fully considers the geometrical properties of point cloud and give a variety of constraints. The literature — integrates 3 kinds of constraints and effectively eliminate a large number of outliers, which greatly improves the ratio of the correct point. The improvement provides a good foundation for accurate solution to the subsequent acceleration of the iterative convergence process and the parameters of rotation and translation.

3. THE REGISTRATION AND FUSION METHOD OF MULTI GROUP OF POINT CLOUD

This paper presents a registration and fusion method of multi group of point cloud. This method of reconstruction of 3D objects can not only be used to complete the local geometric information, also can be used to surface stitching in different regions of the object. It can quickly supplement local point cloud information which is lacked by the environment and thereby reduce the time consumption of point cloud acquisition and the fusion error in 3D reconstruction process, also can be used to quantitative evaluation of fusion result.

According to the characteristics of multi group image sequences, this paper improves the ICP algorithm and is applied to stitching and fusion of point cloud. The algorithm mainly includes the self constructing overlap area, unifying the scale coefficient of being fused point clouds, calculating rotation and translation parameters by the ICP iteration, and then fusing overlap point cloud. Furtherly, experiment demonstrates that this method can quickly provide enough point cloud data for reconstruction, and the point cloud has been well stitched and fused.

Figure 1 shows point cloud registration and fusion method based on the multi group image sequence.

The method is mainly divided into two parts: (1) The acquisition of point cloud P1 from the original image sequence; (2) Complement of the supplemental image sequence, the acquisition of point cloud P2 from the supplemental image sequence and point cloud fusion of P1 and P2.

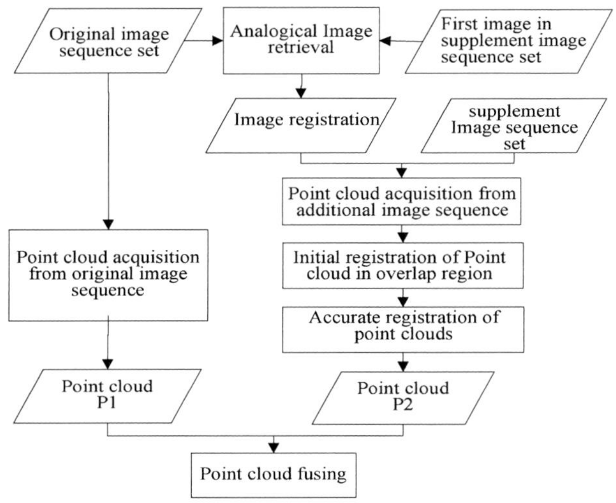

Figure 1. Process of the algorithm.

3.1. *Acquisition of point cloud from original image sequence and improved scale unifying method*

In the process of reconstruction, the extraction of corresponding points of two images is a key step. The distribution and quantity of extracted corresponding points determines the final effect of 3D reconstruction. In this paper image sequence to be reconstructed is obtained by the camera which has been calibrated. The object contour in the image is extracted and the image within the contour is transformed with SIFT and the corresponding points are used as seeds. Then extension of corresponding points are achieved with quasi dense matching algorithm. The relative orientation principle — is adopted to calculate matrix of external orientation elements. Next, the 3D coordinates of point clouds in each of their left view of the coordinate system are solved by spatial forward intersection method.

After the above processing, the coordinate axis of each corresponding point pair are parallel to each other, but the origins of the coordinate are inconsistency and the baseline components of each model are independent, so that the scales of models are not consistent. Therefore models need to be connected in order to unify 3D coordinates of the points to the coordinate system of the first image in the image sequence. The usual model connecting method — is that N corresponding points are chosen from the adjacent model 1 and 2 to calculate scale coefficient K and the mean value is as a result of the scale coefficient. But in this method the repeatability of the result is not strong and large cumulative error will be caused for a large number of images.

In this paper, the iterative method is utilized to calculate the K value. The three viewpoints are chosen to calculating scale coefficient. For the different coordinate systems of correspond points in different groups, what should to do is to make coordinates of these three viewpoint as consistent as possible by coordinate transformation, that is, minimizing the least square error of corresponding point pairs. Specific steps are as follows:

1) The mean of scale coefficient is calculated from n corresponding points which are taken arbitrarily from the model 1 and 2.

$$\frac{(Zw)_{\text{模型}1} - b_{Z1}}{(Zw)_{\text{模型}2}} = k_Z, \quad \frac{(Yw)_{\text{模型}1} - b_{Y1}}{(Yw)_{\text{模型}2}} = k_Y, \quad \frac{(Xw)_{\text{模型}1} - b_{X1}}{(Xw)_{\text{模型}2}} = k_X$$

$$K_1 = \frac{1}{3}(K_X + K_Y + K_Z), \quad K = \frac{1}{n}(K_1 + K_2 + \cdots + K_n) \tag{1}$$

Where, X_w, Y_w, Z_w is coordinate values of the point in the world coordinate system. b_{x1}, b_{x2}, b_{x3} is the baseline coefficient of three coordinate axes in model 1. K is the scale coefficient.

The coordinates of each point and the baseline component in the next model are multiplied by the coefficient, and then the translation transformation is made so that point clouds of models can be unified to model 1.

2) The calculation of the standard deviation of the distance of point pairs. The point whose distance of point pair is 3 times standard deviation is as a defective point and will be eliminated.

3) Calculation the least square error of corresponding points in model 1and 2.

$$d_k = \frac{1}{n}\sum_{i=1}^{n} ||P_1(i) - (KP_2(i) + \boldsymbol{B})||^2 \tag{2}$$

Where, $P_1(i)$, $P_2(i)$ are coordinates of corresponding points respectively. K is the scale coefficient. B is baseline vector.

4) After eliminating defective points in model 1 and 2, the same corresponding points are used to recalculated the scale coefficient. The coordinates of point cloud in next model are obtained and the least square error d_{k+1} of the corresponding points are calculated.

5) if $||d_k - d_{k+1}|| < \tau$ (τ is a given threshold), then stopping the calculating and the final scale coefficient K is got. Otherwise it returns step 1.

With the scale coefficient K, the 3D coordinates and shift coefficients of points in latter model are multiplied by K. Then the rotation and translation are made and eventually all points are unified to the coordinate system of the first image in image sequence so as to obtain the original point cloud P1.

3.2. *The acquisition, transformation and fusion of point cloud in supplemental image sequence*

3.2.1. *The expansion of supplemental image sequences*

Usually, the point clouds are unified in coordinate system of the first image of each image set and the scale coefficients are different. The scale coefficient impacts on the translation factor calculation in ICP iteration. So the point clouds of supplemental image sequence are need to unifying the scale before the registration. In this paper, two successive images from original image set C1 are chosen to the first location of supplemental image set C2. With the scale factor of the point cloud of these 2 images, the point cloud in image set C2 is converted so that coordinate scale of point cloud in C2 image set is identical as C1 set.

For the convenience to blend the point cloud information of C2 set into coordinate system of points cloud in C1 set, the expanding of the supplemental image set C2 is required. The method is as follows. The first image in C2 set is taken and searched in the original image set C1 with color histogram method to find the image which has the highest similarity. The 2 consecutive image Pic1, Pic2 which are most close to the image in C1 set is taken out and are placed in the first position of supplemental image set C2.

In this paper, h and s in the HSV color space is used to construct the histogram for comparing since the target object is easy to pick up in this color space and the ambient light has little effect on the matching. The chi square value of the histogram distance $d_{\text{chi-square}}(H_1, H_2)$ is calculated as following:

$$d_{chi-square}(H_1, H_2) = \sum_i \frac{(H_1(i) - H_2(i))^2}{H_1(i) + H_2(i)} \tag{3}$$

Where: $H_1(i)$ and $H_2(i)$ are respectively gray value of the histogram 1 and 2 in the same section. The lower the value, the higher the degree of matching.

As an experiment of car pictures shown in figure 2, the outsourcing polygon of object is calculated by tracking foreground of the image. According to the triangular decomposition of polygon, histogram of internal triangular is calculated and histogram matching data is as shown in table 1. The color histogram of image 4 has the minimum value so it has the highest degree of matching. The image 2 and 3 are chosen to added to C2 set as the first image.

Table 1. The result of histogram matching.

No. in image set	0	1	2	3	4	5
Matching result	0.14500	0.15110	0.30354	0.07102	0.04550	0.08654

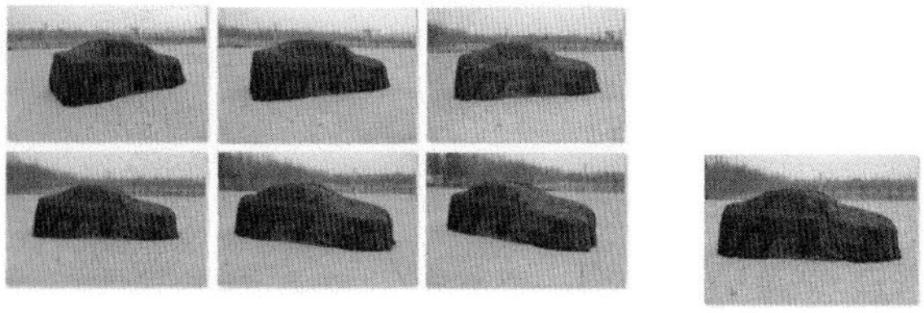

(a) (b)

(a) Partial original images (b) The first image of added pictures

Figure 2. Partial original images and the first image of the supplemental images.

3.2.2. *Point cloud acquisition and initial registration of the supplemental image set*

1) Point cloud acquisition. The scale coefficient K in C1 set of pic1 and pic2 is used as the initial scale coefficient to compute space coordinates in C1set. With the method in 3.1, point cloud P2 in C2 set is calculated.

2) The initial registration. The purpose of initial registration is to make the overlap area of point cloud P1 and P2 closer and to provide a well initial iterative environment for accurate registration.

The exterior orientation elements (the rotation matrix R and the translation vector T) of Pic1 and Pic2 in C1set are taken out to transform the 3D point cloud P2, that is, initial registration is achieved.

3.2.3. *The improved ICP algorithm for point cloud registration*

The initial registration reduces the dislocation of point cloud as much as possible. In order to make the stitching error of point cloud converge and minimize in the iteration, the accurate registration is required. At present, ICP algorithm and improved algorithm [7] is key algorithms in accurate registration. The most commonly used method is based on SVD decomposition and based on Quaternion.

ICP algorithm is an optimal transformation algorithm based on the least square algorithm. The algorithm repeats the process "determining the corresponding point set and calculating the optimal rigid body transformation", until that convergence conditions of the correct registration are met.

The first point set of the space is denoted as $\{P_i, i = 1,2,\ldots,N\}$. ICP algorithm requires transformation R and T of the second point set to minimize the objective function [8].

$$f(\boldsymbol{R},\boldsymbol{T}) = \sum_{i=1}^{N} ||Q_i - (RP_i + \boldsymbol{T})||^2 = min \quad (4)$$

In the formula, P_i as the target point set, Q_i as reference point set, R as rotation matrix and T as the translation matrix. Since the point cloud data is obtained from the images in this paper, the registration of point cloud should consider the scale coefficient K. So using the formula:

$$f(\boldsymbol{R},\boldsymbol{T},k) = \sum_{i=1}^{N} ||Q_i - (kP_i\boldsymbol{R} + \boldsymbol{T})||^2 = min \quad (5)$$

Here, k is a scale coefficient, other parameters is the same as formulae (4).

In this paper, the improved ICP algorithm is used to the step of accurate registration of point cloud. The flow is shown in figure 3. The algorithm mainly consists of 7 steps:

Step 1: Choosing control points. 3D coordinates of corresponding points of image Pic1 and Pic2 in C1 set and C2 set respectively constitute the points set P1 and P2.

Step 2: Searching for the corresponding point pairs. The corresponding points are matched from image Pic1 and Pic2 should be consistent in image set C1 and C2 and hereby establish corresponding point set P1 and P2, denoted as $P_i, i = 1,2,\ldots,N_p$ and $Q_i, i = 1,2,\ldots,N_q$.The object function $f(R,T,k)$ is constructed by the distance of corresponding points (formula 5).

Step 3: calculating the weight of point pair. According to Rusinkiewicz [9] method, weight ratio can be considered as the ratio of the distance of corresponding point and the maximum distance of point pair:

$$\text{weight} = 1\text{-}\text{Dist}(p1,p2)/\text{Dist}_{max} \quad (6)$$

Here, $\text{Dist}(p1,p2)$ denotes the distance of corresponding point, Dist_{max} denotes the maximum distance in all corresponding points.

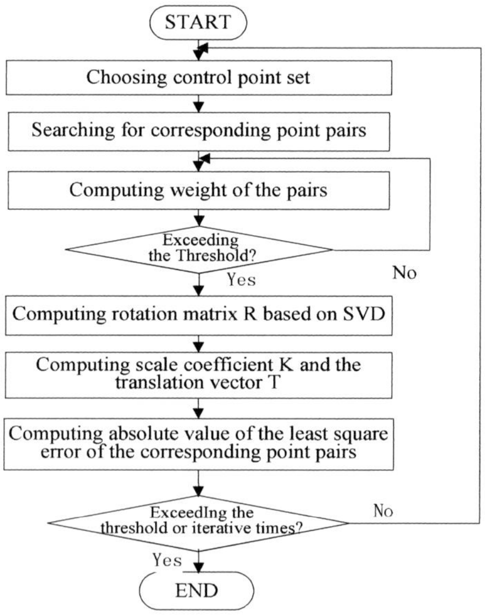

Figure 3. The flow of the accurate registration of point cloud.

When $Dist(p1,p2) = Dist_{max}$, the weight of the point pair is equivalently 0. Such kind of point can be seen as outliers and removed. Usually a weight threshold should be set and only points whose value is above the threshold are retained so that the robustness of the ICP algorithm is improved. In this paper, integrated with paper —, the point is regarded as a defective point and is eliminated when the distance of corresponding point pair is more than 2.5 times the standard deviation of point pair set.

Step 4: Calculating the transformation matrix and the scale coefficient. Calculating the barycentric coordinates of set P and Q and the difference between each point and the barycentre.

$$p = \frac{1}{N}\sum_{i=1}^{N} P_i \ , \ p' = \frac{1}{N}\sum_{i=1}^{N} Q_i$$

$$q_i = p_i - p \ , \ q_i' = p_i' - p'$$

Establishing the covariance matrix:

$$H = \sum_{i=1}^{N} q_i q_i'^t$$

Decomposing H matrix with SVD (7):

$$H = U\Delta V^t \tag{7}$$

Here: U and V are orthogonal matrix, Δ denotes nonnegative diagonal matrix.

Let $\mathrm{Pk1} = \sum_{i=1}^{N} q_i$, $\mathrm{Pk2} = \sum_{i=1}^{N} q_i'$, calculating the rotation matrix R and scale coefficient K and the translation vector T:

$$\boldsymbol{R} = \boldsymbol{V}\boldsymbol{U}^{\boldsymbol{t}} \tag{8}$$

$$k = trace(Pk2 * Pk2^T)/trace(Pk1 * Pk2^T * \boldsymbol{R})$$

(trace is the trace of a matrix) (9)

$$\boldsymbol{T} = p' - k * p * \boldsymbol{R} \tag{10}$$

Step 5: According to the scale coefficient K and the transformation matrix R and T, the point set P2 is transformed and a new point set P2_new is gained. The least square error of the distance of new corresponding point pair DK2 is calculated.

Step 6: Comparing the initial least square error DK with the least square error DK2. The threshold $\hat{o}$ is set to judge whether the iteration is terminated or the iteration number is set as the termination condition for iteration.

Step7: If the conditions to terminate iteration are not being met, the point set P2_new will be as the new point set P2 and the processing returns to Step2. Otherwise the process terminates.

In this paper, the improved ICP algorithm is used to accurate registration of point cloud. The image set is reorganized and divided into models. Each model is composed with two consecutive images. Theoretically, 3D coordinates of corresponding points in adjacent model should be the same. So the least square error of the distance of three point of view in 2 adjacent models is known as a parameter to measure the matching effect of point cloud. The error dk is as follow:

$$\mathrm{d_{kn}} = \frac{1}{\mathrm{N}}\sum_{\mathrm{i=1}}^{\mathrm{N}} ||\mathrm{PL_i}\text{-}\mathrm{PR_i}||^2 = \min \tag{11}$$

Of which: $\boldsymbol{PL_i}$ is the 3D coordinates of corresponding points in model 1, $\boldsymbol{PR_i}$ is the 3D coordinates of the corresponding points in adjacent model.

4. THE EXPERIMENTS AND DATA ANALYSIS

The two experiments were designed to verify the effect of stitching and supplement of surface geometry details.

Experiment 1: Verifying stitching effect.

In this paper, 4 groups of image sequence are acquired. The image numbers are respectively 10, 6, 8, 8. There are overlapping region between image groups.

According to this method, firstly the image set C2 is supplemented by the consecutive image Pic1 and Pic2 in image set C1 with the color histogram matching. Then 3D coordinates of corresponding points from C1 and C2 are respectively computed and point set P1 and P2 are gained. In accordance with the method mentioned above, the two group of point cloud are stitched and fused and formed the new point cloud P12. Next, the first and second image sets are regard as a new first image set and the third image set is regarded as the new second image set. The approach above is repeated until the last image set is processed. Finally the complete car point cloud is obtained and shown as figure 4.

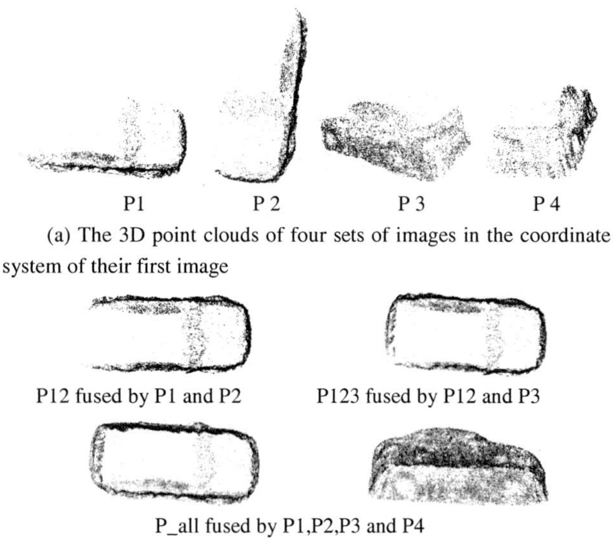

(b) The registration and fusion of points cloud

Figure 4. The point cloud of the car based on multiple sets of images.

The following is the quantitative analysis of the overlap region. Theoretically 3D coordinates of corresponding point pair in the overlapping area should be consistent. So the least square error of distance of the corresponding point can be considered as a measure parameter of the stitching result, as shown in table 2.

The experimental results show that, this method can effectively achieve stitching of the point cloud in different group. The error of the least square error of corresponding points in overlap area is reduced greatly than that of the standard ICP algorithm in accurate registration. The stitching result can support the subsequent reconstruction.

Table 2. The least square errors of corresponding points in overlapping region of the car.

Error / Combination	Initial registration	Standard ICP	This paper
P1 and P2	0.0204194	0.0030920	0.0003620
P12 and P3	0.0734500	0.0035880	0.0002500
P123 and P4	0.1506800	0.0036910	0.0007030

Experiment 2: Supplementing surface geometry detail.

In the experiment, a set of 24 images firstly are shot. Because of the dark backlight and less image numbers, there are not enough point cloud data for reconstruction. So an image sequence of 10 images is taken by strengthening brightness in dark face. The method is applied to compute the point cloud respectively and is fused to complete object information, as shown in figure 5.

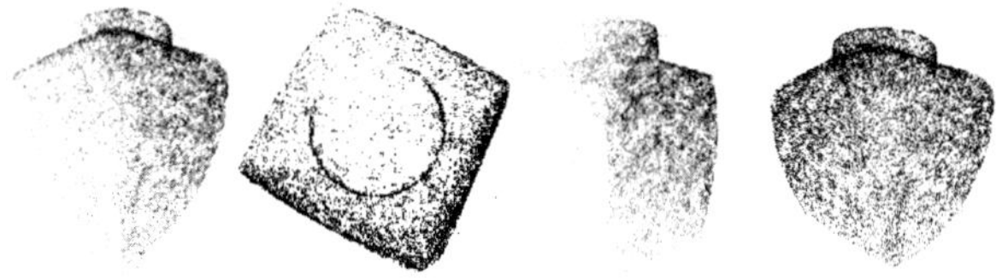

(a) (b) (c)

(a) P1 from original sets of images (b) P2 from supplement images (c)The whole points after registration

Figure 5. The supplement of the point cloud on shady face of the pot.

The least square error of distance of corresponding points in overlap region is calculated, shown as table 3. The experimental results show that the method of this paper can be used to strengthen the local geometric details of the 3D model. The error of the least square error of corresponding points in overlap area is reduced greatly than that of the standard ICP algorithm in accurate registration. The stitching and fusing result can support the subsequent reconstruction.

Table 3. The least square error of corresponding points in overlapping region of the pot.

Error / Combination	Initial registration	Standard ICP	This paper
P1 and P2	0.0204194	0.0030920	0.0003620

The method of stitching and fusing based on image sequence adopts the "matching + registration and fusion" technique. Via the above two experiments, it can be found that the method can be used not only to strengthen the local geometric details but also to stitch point clouds which are taken from multiple image sets. Because of separate calculating the coordinates of corresponding point from the supplement images, it is unnecessary to integrate the image set C1 and C2 together and save a lot of dealing time. The experimental results show that the stitching and fusion of the point cloud has good effect. The error in overlap area is small and the experiment verifies the convergence of iterative.

5. CONCLUSIONS

In the process of 3D object reconstruction based on image, the point clouds are sometimes lacked in place where the light is dark or due to the shooting angle. In order to obtain enough point cloud, some supplement images in these places are taken additionally to reinforce point cloud data. This paper adopts 2 connect images from the original image set and uses point cloud registration and fusion method to fuse point cloud data from supplement image set to the original one. Under the condition to ensure a certain error tolerance, the method improves the efficiency of point cloud data acquisition and verifies the convergence of the stitching parameters on iteration.

This method can well solve the problem of insufficient point numbers due to the light or camera angles. The further research should be devoted to 3D point cloud acquisition for weak texture object. The following work can be considered that a synthesis method of various feature extraction is applied in feature extraction of images to further increase the amount of corresponding point, so as to provide sufficient data support in reconstruction.

REFERENCES

- [1] Musialski, Wonka P, Aliaga D G, et al. A survey of urban reconstruction. Computer Graphics Forum, 2012, 31(2): 1 18.
- [2] Tu Z Q, Zhu X P. The modified ICP algorithm in 3-D model points registration. [J] Welding Journal, 2013, 34 (1).
- [3] Wang J, Zhu L. 3D building ade reconstruction based on image FA C matching point cloud fusion [J]. Computer Journal, 2012, 10.35 (10).
- [4] Nishino K, Ikeuehi K. Robust simultaneous registration of multiple range images comprising a large number of points [J]. Electronics and Communications in Japan (Part II: Electronics), 2004, 87 (8): 61-74.
- [5] Xu Zhaohe. The research and implementation of 3d reconstruction technology based on images. [D] Academy of Equipment, 2012, 11.
- [6] Wang Jun, Zhu Li. The image matching - point cloud fusion facade and 3D reconstruction based on [J]. Chinese Journal of Computers, 2012, 35(10).
- [7] Wang Jianqi. Mass point clouds registration and fusion of [D]. Technology research of Zhejiang University of Technology. 2012, 10.
- [8] Jiang C C, Hu T S, Zhou W. An improved algorithm of ICP [J]. Computer Systems and Applications, 2009 (08): 84-85.
- [9] Rusinkiewicz S, Levoy M. Efficient variants of the ICP algorithm [C]. 2001.

Face Recognition Based on Self-training for Large Margin Neighbor

K.L. Li[1], Y.R. Zhao[2], Y.B. Li, Y.X. Zhang & X.F. Geng
College of Electronics and Information Engineering, Hebei University
Email: [1]likunlun@hbu.edu.cn, [2]name_zhaoyiru@163.com

ABSTRACT: Compared to the dimension of face image samples, the number and face image is relatively small. The face recognition problem is essentially a small sample learning problem. Aiming at the small sample problem, in this paper, we propose the method of self-training for margin neighbor. Using the margin to represent decision confidence, and using the spatial adjacent to represent gradual change of face manifold, through self-training iteration, the sample distance of the same classifications is as compact as possible, the sample distance of the different classifications maintain a certain large distance. In the neighborhood, constantly mark the unlabeled samples of high credibility. Experiments show that, compared to other methods, self-training for large margin neighbor has relatively better recognition in small face samples.

KEYWORDS: Semi-supervised; Self-training; Margin; Face recognition.

1. INTRODUCTION

An object can form different face images. The set of all face images of an object is a high-dimensional data space formed by the distance, position, direction, intensity of illumination and other parameters. Generally, the data structure or limiting structure of high-dimensional space of face is difficult to determine, whether the Gauss distribution or the other distributions is uncertain. However, according to the center limit theorem for random variables, as samples increase, the high-dimensional space tends to be a Gauss distribution or a combination of projection in a low dimensional space. With the dimension increases, data space volume increases sharply, so a relatively small number of samples in high-dimensional space appear sparse. Commonly, the information will not fill the high-dimensional data space, there is a correlation between the variables, most of the data variables can be represented as a combination of a few variables, namely the redundancy of high dimensional data. The intrinsic dimension is low-dimensional and face is a potential low-dimensional manifold in high-dimensional space. The nature of manifold is essentially characterized by the continuity of slow change and space adjacent property [1].

In this paper, we propose a method of a self-training for large margin neighbor. Compared to Large Margin Nearest Neighbors, we strengthen the use of unlabeled data, Through self-training iteration and data editing, the unlabeled samples are constantly marked, meanwhile removing the wrong standard sample, to improve the quality of classification in the case of small face sample.

2. DISTANCE AND MARGIN

Maximizing the distance of the different classifications and minimizing the distance of the same classifications is the pursuit of the target of machine learning. Fisher discriminant analysis is one of the representatives, to find the most suitable projective direction, and to make the same classification sample distance as com-pact as possible while the different classification sample distance as far as possible. Compared to the principal component analysis (PCA) to find the principal axis direction of effective representation, Fisher is looking for effective classification direction. In face recognition, the performance of Fisherface is better than the Eigen-face in most cases.

The concept of margin from optimal linear classifier is proposed by V. N. Vapnik. Using kernel methods, the low-dimensional linear inseparable data could be map into high-dimensional space, constructing a separable hyperplane, so that the data points belonging to two different categories have a maximum margin, namely a theory of support vector machine, which has considerable advantages In the small sample size problem and generalization ability. Shawe Taylor derived the Generalization Inequality based on margin, proved that margin and generalization ability are closely related and proposed the subject: design margin of closed convex sets [2]. To explain the generalization error of Adaboost, Schapire derived an upper bound on the generalization error. The upper bound is concerned with margin distribution, the number of training samples, and the complexity of the space where the weak classifier works. And he concluded that the generalization ability of Adaboost does not depend on the training error, but final convergence margin distribution. The larger of the margin of trained samples, the better generalization performance of the classifier has [3].

Margin is a geometric measure for decision confidence. The further samples get away from decision boundary, the higher decision confidence will be, so does the robustness. According to the K.Crammer. R's paper, margin can be divided into the sample margin and hypothesis margin [4]: Hypothesis margin refers to the maximum distance of decision surface, keeping the sample label unchanged. The typical algorithms are Boost, Adaboost and Relief etc; The sample margin is the distance between samples and decision boundary, the typical algorithm is support vector machine. Margin theory gradually applied to clustering, ensemble learning, feature extraction algorithms or models, such as LPBoost [5], SoftBoost [6], EBBoost [7], Maximum Margin Bayesian Network [8], Novel Maximum-Margin Training Algorithms for Supervised Neural Networks [9]. Kilian.Q.Weinberger proposed large margin nearest neighbor algorithm is one of the typical [10]: The main idea of the large margin nearest neighbor algorithm is to learn a distance metric, in a new Mapping space, for a input xi, K neighbors belong to the same category, while the samples with different category maintain a certain large distance with xi. Although enough samples to ensure large margin nearest neighbor classifier accuracy in a certain extent, but in practical application, the initial labeled data training set number is small, it is difficult to train high quality classifier. Therefore, we propose a large margin neighbor based on self-training.

3. SELF-TRAINING FOR LARGE MARGIN NEIGHBOR

In practical applications, labeled samples are always relative small and the work of manual marking samples label are relative slow and expensive. The information provided by the small amount of labeled samples may be limited and unilateral. The massive unlabeled data is more easy to obtain and closer to the overall distribution of all the data. According to the study method of unlabeled samples, namely unsupervised learning, its accuracy effect is always poor than supervised learning for labeled samples. Therefore the commonly effective use of labeled data and unlabeled data is the reasonable methods to improve learning performance, semi-supervised learning is such a method. The relationship between the semi-supervised algorithm and data is based on the following assumed conditions. Manifold hypothesis: samples of the local neighborhood have similar properties and change slowly. Cluster hypothesis: a cluster sample is likely to belong to the same category in the generative model. Smooth hypothesis: if the samples are very close in high density area, then the corresponding output is possible related or the close, conversely, if the samples are separated in the low density regions, then the corresponding output is not possible related or close.

Self-training method is a typical semi-supervised algorithm: First in the labeled sample sets, train a basic classifier. Then use the basic classifier, to mark the unlabeled samples of high credibility. Add the new labeled samples to the original training sets. And use this new training set to retrain a new classifier to relay mark the unlabeled samples of high credibility. Repeat the above process until the iteration conditions.

The key point of self-training is the processing of labeled samples error. Because the expanded training set may be impacted by the wrong labeled samples, classify wrong categories and by the iterative, constantly mark wrong labeled samples, make the performance of classifier greatly reduced. On the contrary, if find these errors in early iteration, correct the mistakes, then the expanded training set quality will be better, classification performance is not decreasing with the iteration, the classifier will have good performance.

The Self-training algorithm for large margin neighbor is given:

I. Sets $\{(x_i, y_i)\}_{i=1}^{m}$ are m labeled samples, sets $\{(x_i)\}_{i=n-m}^{n}$ are n-m unlabeled samples, $x_i \in Rd$ is d dimension samples, y_i is the label. In the initial training sets, use large margin nearest neighbor algorithm, to obtain the Semi-definite matrix M and mapping matrix L, $M = L^T L$.

Minimize

$$\Sigma_{ij}\eta_{ij}(X_i - X_j)^T M (X_i - X_j) + c\Sigma_{ijk}\eta_{ij}(1 - Y_{ijk})e_{ijk} \quad (1)$$

Subject to $$M \geq 0 \quad e_{ijk} \geq 0 \quad (2)$$

$$(X_i - X_k)^T M(X_i - X_k) - (X_i - X_j)^T M(X_i - X_j) \geq 1 - e_{ijk} \quad (3)$$

II. Add labeled samples to unlabeled sample set $\{(x_i)\}_{i=1}^{n}$,

$$D(i,j) = (X_i - X_j)^T M(X_i - X_j) \quad (4)$$

Arbitrarily select unlabeled samples x_i and calculate from the nearest three samples. If three nearest samples are the same label, this sample x_i should be the category (The obtained new labeled samples in the steps of other unlabeled samples decision, still in accordance with the unlabeled data processing). If three nearest samples, one is an unlabeled sample and the other two are the same label, his sample x_i should be the category. Other circumstances do not to take any action.

III. Add new labeled samples from above step to the initial labeled sets, so obtain the new extended labeled sets. Repeat steps I and II, until all the unlabeled samples is marked. End.

In the actual process, the sample distance of the different classifications is greater than the sample distance of the same classifications. e_{ijk} leads to take the negative, the constraint conditions of D(i,k) - $D(i,j) \geq 1 - e_{ijk}$ rarely play a role. So it is solved by sub-gradient method.

On the ORL database, IMM face database and PolyU-NIRFD face database, We took the lmnn (large margin nearest neighbor), slmnn (Self-training for large margin neighbor) and fisher (Fisher discriminant analysis) comparison experiment in this case-different proportion of training sets and testing sets. For example, in ORL database, every individual has ten imagines, five images of each person for training and five other images for testing and proportion of training sets and testing sets is: 50%:50%.

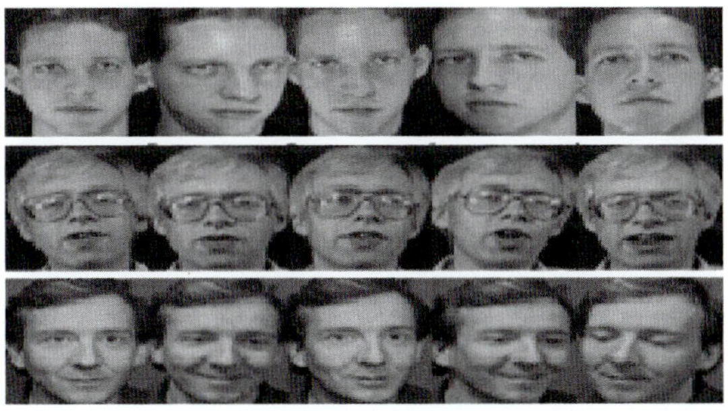

Figure 1. ORL database.

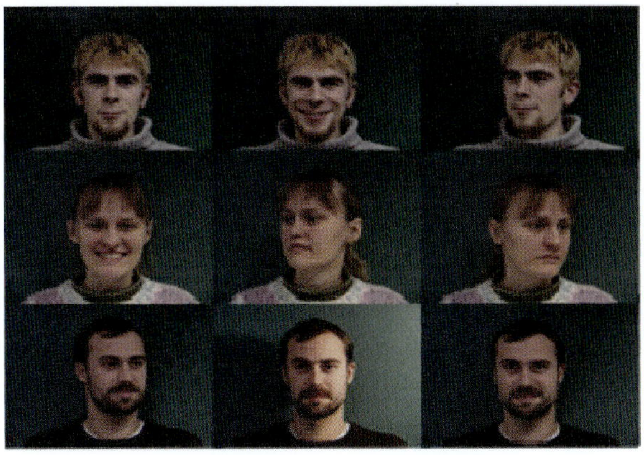

Figure 2. IMM database.

Table 1. Recognition rate on the ORL database.

Algorithm / *Proportion*	*LMNN*	*SLMNN*	*Fisher*
30%:70%	42.85%	76.72%	54.34%
40%:60%	64.84%	79.86%	62.34%
50%:50%	72.34%	80.72%	75.34%
60%:40%	82,73%	83.64%	80,73%
70%:30%	97.02%	85.91%	92.18%
80%:20%	96.36%	89.21%	95.55%
90%:10%	96.18%	92.87%	93.18%

Table 2. Recognition rate on the IMM database.

Algorithm / *Proportion*	*LMNN*	*SLMNN*	*Fisher*
30%:70%	49.77%	72.87%	51.34%
40%:60%	52.62%	74.98%	60.85%
50%:50%	67.84%	79.96%	72.10%
60%:40%	79,19%	81.81%	80.91%
70%:30%	90.45%	83.84%	89.18%
80%:20%	96.02%	88.91%	92.13%
90%:10%	95.17%	90.89%	95.03%

Table 3. Recognition rate on the PolyU-NIRFD database.

Algorithm / *Proportion*	*LMNN*	*SLMNN*	*Fisher*
30%:70%	36.71%	69.89%	50.34%
40%:60%	46.95%	72.67%	57.85%
50%:50%	54.34%	74.94%	67.10%
60%:40%	74.81%	75.82%	77.98%
70%:30%	88.49%	83.81%	85.46%
80%:20%	87.94%	85.91%	91.22%
90%:10%	90.17%	89.14%	96.01%

The experiment shows that good classifier requires a certain amount of labeled samples as the training set. When labeled samples are lack, the classification accuracy rate dropped significantly.

Since self-training for large margin neighbor not only uses the information of labeled samples, but also use the distribution information of unlabeled samples. Use the margin to represent decision confidence, use the spatial adjacent to represent gradual change, in the case of small face sample, the method has relatively better recognition.

4. CONCLUSION

Face is a potential low-dimensional manifold in high-dimensional space. Compared to the dimension of face image samples, the number and face image is relatively small. The face recognition problem is the high dimensional data problem and the small training sample size problem. In this paper, we proposed a self-training algorithm for large margin neighbor based on semi-supervised learning theory and Large

Margin Nearest Neighbors. Using the margin to represent decision confidence, use the spatial adjacent to represent gradual change of face manifold, through self-training iteration, the sample distance of the same classifications is as compact as possible, the sample distance of the different classifications maintain a certain large distance. In the neighborhood, constantly mark the unlabeled samples of high credibility. The method we proposed shows that unlabeled data can be used to augment the training set and can improve the accuracy of the final classifier. The experiment results show that it is appropriate for the case of small face samples and this method of utilizing large number of unlabeled data has a potential for significant benefits in practice.

But, many research questions remain. The effect of wrong labeled samples in the iterative process is still big. In the further, we will continue our research.

ACKNOWLEDGMENTS

We would like to express our gratitude to all those who gave us help to complete this paper, especially for Mr Yanbo Li, Jun Wang and Jian Song whose constructive suggestions and encouragements help us in all the time of research and writing of this paper. This research is supported by: the National Science and Technology Support Program under Grant No. 2013BAK07B04; the Natural Science Foundation of Heibei Province of China under Grant No. F2013201170; the Educational Commission of Hebei Province of China under Grant ZD2014008.

REFERENCES

- [1] Seung HS, Lee DD. The manifold ways of perception [J]. Science, 2000, 290(5500): 2268-2269.
- [2] Bartlett P, Shawe-Taylor J. Generalization performance of support vector machines and other pattern classifiers [J]. Advances in Kernel Methods—Support Vector Learning, 1999: 43–54.
- [3] R.E. Schapire, Y. Freund, P. Bartlett, et al. Boosting the margin: A new explanation for the effectiveness of voting methods. Annals of Statistics, 1998, 26(5): 1651-1686.
- [4] Crammer K, Gilad-Bachrach R, Navot A, et al. Margin analysis of the LVQ algorithm [C]. Advances in neural information processing systems. 2002: 462-469.
- [5] A. Demiriz, K.P. Bennett, and J. Shawe-Taylor. Linear Programming boosting via column generation. Mach. Learn. 2002, 46(1-3): 225-254.
- [6] M. Warmuth, K. Glocer and G. Rätsch. Boosting algorithms for maximizing the soft margin. In Proc. Advances in Neural Information Processing Systems, 2008, 1585-1592.
- [7] P. Shivaswamy and T. Jebara. Empirical Bernstein Boosting. In AISTATS, 2010L. Mason, J. Baxter, P. Bartlett and M. Frean. Boosting algorithms as gradient descent. In Proc. Adv. Neural Inf. Process. Syst., 2000, 512-518.
- [8] Franz Pernkopf, Michael Wohlmayr and Sebastian Tschiatschek. Maximum Margin Bayesian Network Classifiers [J]. IEEE Transactions on Pattern Analysis and Machine Intelligence, 2012, 34(3): 521-532.
- [9] O. Ludwig and U. Nunes. Novel Maximum-Margin Training Algorithms for Supervised Neural Networks [J]. IEEE Transactions on Neural Networks, 2010, 21(6): 972-984.
- [10] K.Q. Weinberger, J. Blitzer, and L.K. Saul. Distance metric learning for large margin nearest neighbor classification. Advances in neural information processing systems (NIPS), 2006.

A Digital Watering of 3D Image Scheme Based on Visual Cryptography

Y.Y. Han
Beijing Electronic Science & Technology Institute, Beijing 100070, China
X.N. Ge*
Xidian University, Xi'an 710071, China
W.C. He
Beijing Electronic Science & Technology Institute, Beijing 100070, China
Z.L. Xu
Xidian University, Xi'an 710071, China
Email: nannan19901228@sina.com

ABSTRACT: With the rapid popularity of the 3D-TV, it is becoming more and more significant to protect the copyright in 3D image. To cater this need, we proposed a novel digital watermarking of 3D image scheme based on visual cryptography. Anaglyph 3D image is separated into left eye view image, right eye view image and the depth view image, while the watermark is pretreated based on the visual cryptography. Watermarking content protection is done with the help of Discrete Wavelet Transform (DWT) on anaglyph 3D images.

KEYWORDS: Visual Cryptography; 3D image; DWT.

1. INTRODUCTION

With the development of 3D image, people pay more attention on its technology. Nowadays, the prosperous of 3D technology is dazzling. Hence, people all around the world show the prodigious interests on 3D technology, because it provides an immersive experience to the viewers. In this case, it becomes more and more momentous to enhance the data hiding techniques for 3D image when people enjoy the pleasant it brings to them. Watermarking, for example, it's an effective protection which is done with the help of Discrete Wavelet Transform (DWT) based on visual cryptography in this paper, while disposing the watermark is the hinge step as well.

In paper [1], Sanjay R. Zadokar proposed a watermarking system, which can be used to protect the copyright. The proposed watermarking scheme is effective to reduce the noise because watermark is embedded in all three layers of anaglyph 3D image. But as we know, that paper embedded an unprocessed watermark, it makes easier for attackers to take them out eventually. In order to improve that drawback, the watermark was processed by visual cryptography scheme (VCS) in this paper.

Tracing back to 1994, Shamir and Naor proposed a novel n-threshold sharing mechanism on black and white binary image. To put it simply, the visual cryptography scheme (VCS) separates an image to n shares and none of them obtains the meaningful information [2]. When recovery the image, one just need to print any k shares on transparencies, then stack them on a projector without the complicated computation. While stacking less than k shares is useless and no information will be got, in which way it can improve the quantity of information and increase the robustness of the scheme. Obviously, people need not to be equipped with cryptography knowledge and the implementation cost is also not so high [3]. Therefore, even the adversary obtained the watermark, it is pretty intricate to recover the original watermark in a short time.

2. THE ANALYSIS AND PROCESSING OF THE 3D IMAGE

Anaglyph 3D uses a rotating filter wheel to separate spectral information, while it uses a different color to filter the image, making it generate two images at the same time, which should be done in the same environment and condition. Hence, each eye of human being will see different images [4]. We got the left and right eye views of 3D anaglyph image by filtering the red and cyan separately, while warping is used to marge both of them to get the depth image.

In order to simulate how the human eyes work, we processed the pixels in the center color image to the virtual left and right views according to a corresponding depth image as follows

$$\mathrm{xl} = xc + \frac{tx}{2} \cdot \frac{f}{Z}, \quad \mathrm{xr} = \mathrm{xc} - \frac{tx}{2} \cdot \frac{f}{Z}, \qquad (3)$$

Where xc, xl and xr are x-coordinate of the pixels in the center view, the virtual left view, and the virtual right view respectively. While *tx* is a baseline distance, and *f* is a focal length. Z is a depth value corresponding to the coordinate of the center view pixel. Based on the equation, there's no doubts that the embedded watermarks should be embedded to guarantee the robustness when tx changes [5].

3. PROCESS THE WATERMARK

The process of watermark is shown in Fig. 1.

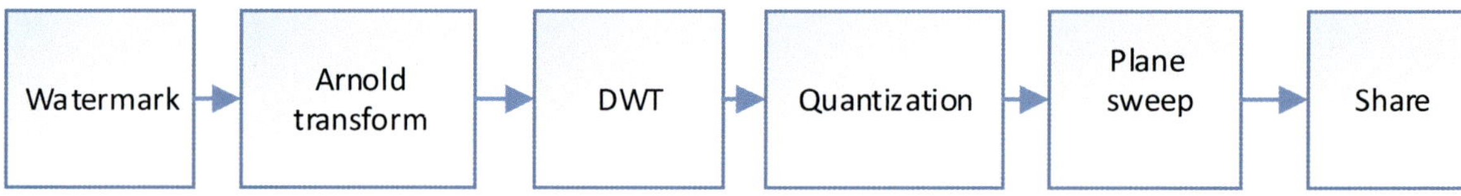

Figure 1. Process of watermark.

First of all, we need to encrypt the watermark by Arnold transform. After scrambled the image, we used the Discrete Wavelet Transform to get a relatively higher PSNR. We used the followed equation to quantize the DWT coefficient in 256 grey level.

$$B_j(x,\ y)' = B_j(x,\ y) + |Min_j| \qquad (2)$$

$$B_j(x, y)'' = B_j(x, y)' + Max_j \times 255 (x, y = 1, 2, 3, 4) \qquad (3)$$

Next, the quantized coefficient was arranged to be a string of pixel, then we employed the plane sweep to construct the new string of pixel, which has the characteristic that the front pixel has more information of the image. The process of the plane sweep is shown in Fig. 2, in which MSB denotes the highest bit, while the lowest is remarked as LSB.

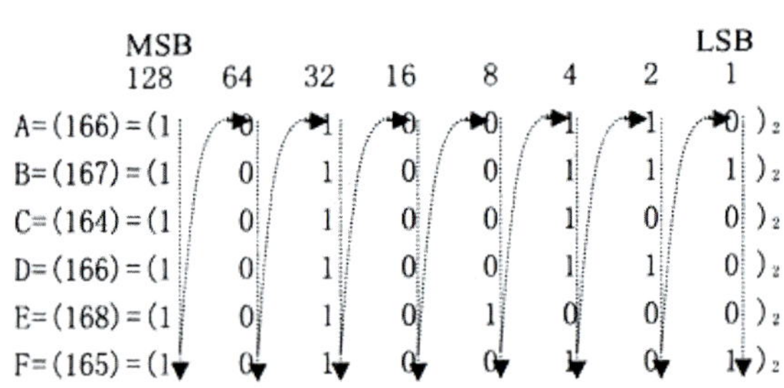

Figure 2. Plane sweep.

At the last of the process, the Lagrange interpolation polynomial is employed to realize the purpose of sharing the secret. The pixel of each block is regarded as the coefficient of polynomial, i.e. $a_1, a_2, \ldots a_{r-1}$, it follows

$$F_j^1(x) = (a_0 + a_1 x + \ldots + a_{r_1-1} x^{r_1-1}) \bmod p$$

$$F_j^2(x) = (a_{r_1} + a_{r_1+1} x + \ldots + a_{r_1+r_2-1} x^{r_1+r_2-1}) \bmod p$$

$$\ldots$$

$$F_j^i(x) = (a_{r_1+r_2} + a_{r_1+r_2+1} x + \ldots + a_{r_1+r_2+\ldots+r_k-1} x^{r1+r2+\ldots r_k-1}) \bmod p$$

Where $F_j^i(x)$ means the ith pixel in the jth block of the xth share.

4. WATERMARK IMPLANTING AND EXREACTING

4.1. *Watermark implanting*

The red component, green component and the blue component are extracted from each view image firstly, and the three components are decomposed into 3-level DWT, in which way can we get the decomposition coefficient $d_{cl}\theta(i,j)$, where *c* denotes the color component, *l*=1,2,3...denotes the level of the DWT, while $\theta = 0,1,2,3$ denotes the high-frequency part, horizontal part, vertical part and the diagonal part separately. Next we get the detail coefficient of 3rd level DWT and the average absolute value by

$$z_{cl}\theta = \frac{\sum_{i=1}^{M}\sum_{j=1}^{M}|d_{cl}\theta(i,j)|}{M \times M} \qquad (4)$$

Where M is the size of the 3rd DWT decomposition coefficient matrix. After revise the detail coefficient by formula (5), the watermark image is embedded into the R,G,B component repeatedly.

$$d'_{cl}\theta(i,j) = \left[round\left(\frac{d_{cl}\theta(i,j)}{z_{cl}\theta}\right) + (1/4)W'(i,\ j)\right] \qquad (5)$$

Where $d_{cl}'\theta(i,j)$ denotes the DWT coefficient after embedded the watermark. Finally we combined left eye view image, right eye view image and depth image to get the original 3D image with the watermark in it.

4.2. *Watermark extracting*

It's obviously the inverse process of implanting the watermark. First of all, the R,G,B component are extracted from the embedded image, then we got the watermark from that three component. The DWT decomposition coefficients are obtained by the process of 3-level DWT, and formula (2) is employed again to get $z_{cl}\theta$. Finally, we extracted the watermark from the 3rd DWT decomposition coefficients by formula (6)

$$W_{cl}\theta(i,j) = sgn\left\{z'_{cl}\theta \times B(i)\left[\frac{d'_{cl}\theta(i,j)}{z'_{cl}\theta} - round\left(\frac{d'_{cl}\theta(i,j)}{z'_{cl}\theta}\right)\right]\right\} \quad (6)$$

5. THE SIMULATION

Firstly, we chose an Anaglyph 3D image named *Bear*. In the next step, it was separated into the left eye view image, right eye view image and the depth view image as we conceived, the original image and the results are shown in Fig. 3 below. By this step, we finished the procedure of processing the anaglyph 3D image, they were prepared to be the carriers of the watermark we would get in the next step.

Figure 3. Original image and view images.

In the next step, the classical image of the Matlab *Lena* is shown in Fig. 4 (a), which is used to be the watermark in our stimulation. Just as we mentioned before, the Anorld transform was employed to get Fig. 4(b). Then after series of transforms based on visual cryptography, we got the three shares of the watermark, shown in Fig. 5, which would be employed to be embedded into the carriers.

Figure 4(a) Lena.

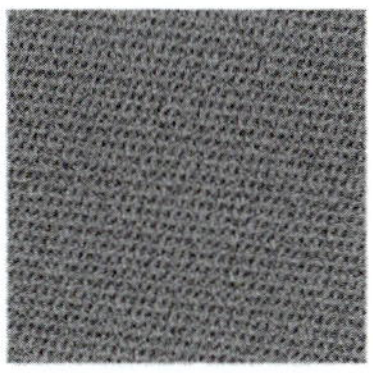

Figure 4(b) Anord transform.

Figure 5. Share 1 Share 2 Share 3.

Finally, using the Inverse Discrete Wavelet Transform, we inserted the shares into the Fig. 3. In order to recover the 3D image, we merged the processed left eye view image, right eye view image and the depth image together. In this way, we got the 3D image with watermark in it, the embedded image and the watermark image are shown respectively in Fig. 6 and Fig. 7.

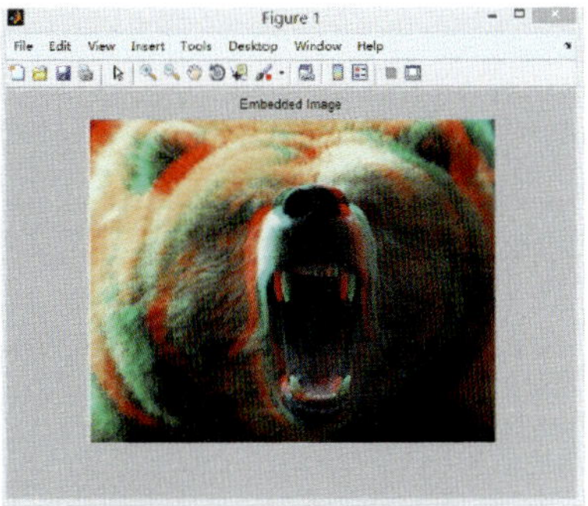

Figure 6. Embeded image.

Figure 7. Watermark extracted.

6. SECURITY ANALYSIS

In order to evaluate the security of our results, JPEG compression, cropping, adding Gaussian noise, rotation and median filtering are used to observe the transparence and robustness. We separately implemented each attack to get the relative parameters, in which the Peak Signal to Noise Ratio (PSNR) is used to show the transparence of watermarks, while Noise Correlativity (NC) is employed to present the robustness of the watermark.

6.1. *JPEG compression*

In the simulation, the quality factors (QF) of the JPEG compression are 90, 70, 50, 30, 10 to watermarked image. The watermark are extracted to gain PSNR (dB) and NC when QF changes.

Table 1. Attacked by jpeg compression.

QF	90%	70%	50%	30%	10%
PSNR	30.2341	27.6734	26.8394	25.3453	23.3647
NC	0.9814	0.9756	0.9612	0.9599	0.9470

Table 1 above presents that the watermark we embedded has a better transparence and robustness with JPEG compression attack.

6.2. *Cropping*

It is no doubt that cropping is a traditional way of evaluating the security of our result in this experiment, in which way we can get the result as shown in Fig. 8(a) and (b).

Figure 8(a) Cropping.

Figure 8(b) Watermark.

It's not difficult for us to explain that the watermark we embedded has a high security after attacked by cropping a quarter.

6.3. *Adding gaussian noise*

Considering adding Gaussian noise to the watermarked images, we got the further result of the robustness of our scheme. Given the variances of Gaussian noise of 0.01, 0.008, 0.005, the results are shown in Table II.

Table 2. Attacked by adding gaussian noise.

V	0.005	0.008	0.01
NC	0.9763	0.9624	0.9342

Table II adequately illustrates the good robustness after adding Gaussian noise.

6.4. *Rotation*

Rotation is also a normal method of watermarking attacks. The watermarked image is rotated 45 degrees anticlockwise. The extracted watermark are shown in Fig. 9(a) and (b).

It's no wonder that Fig. 9 shows the watermark has good robustness after attacked by rotation of 45 degree.

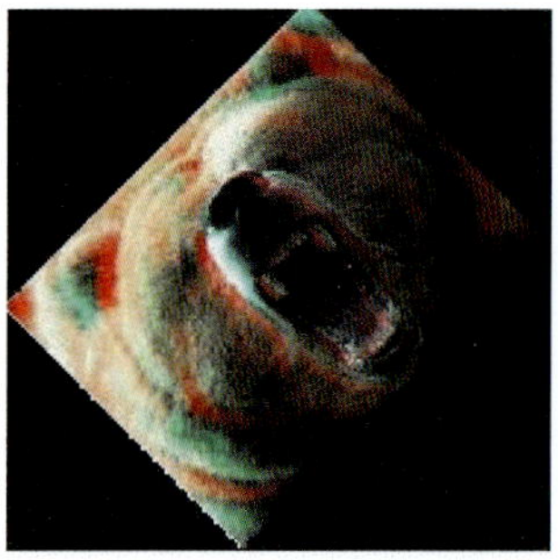

Figure 9 (a) Rotation.

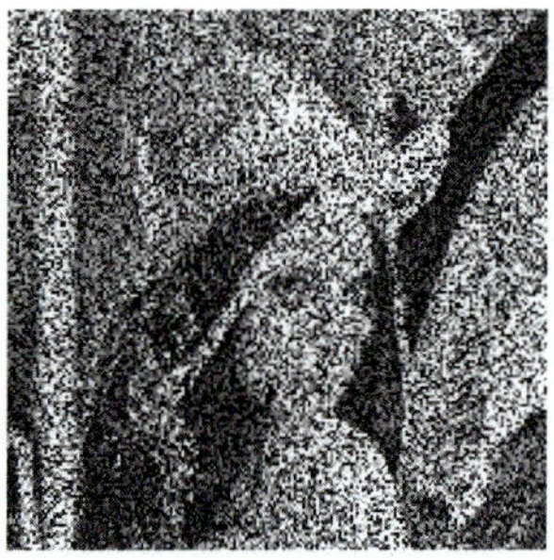

Figure 9(b) Watermark.

6.5. *Median filtering*

Finally, the median filtering is employed in texting the watermark we embedded, we chose the 3×3 median filtering as always did, the result is shown in Fig. 10(a) and (b) as followed.

Figure 10(a) Filtering.

Figure10 (b)Watermark.

As shown above, the watermark we embedded in 3D image has good robustness when attacked with median filtering by 3×3.

Above five, it's obvious that the scheme we proposed has a good character to resist the common attacks.

Besides that, the security of our scheme is in a relative high level. Compared with [1], the watermark we embedded is disposed by a series of transformation in our scheme, it's confused for adversarys to get the meaningless share of the watermark. Even if they find that we pretreat the watermark based on the visual cryptography eventually, which means that we embedded the shares of the watermark instead of itself, it will cost them lots of time to take the watermark out.

7. CONCLUSION

The scheme we proposed in this paper can be used to protect the copyright contents present in the 3D images. The original image is processed by its imaging principle, while the watermark is disposed based on the visual cryptography.

Also, the Anord transform and the DWT were employed in embedding the watermark. This paper just presents an effective scheme for 3D images, and it is just the start step toward exploiting this interesting and important topic and of course, there are lots of different issues worthy of further investigations.

REFERENCES

— [1] Sanjay R. Zadokar, Vishal B. Raskar. A Digital Watermarking for Anaglyph 3D images: 2013 International Conference on Advances in Computing, Communications and Informatics (ICACCI).

— [2] M. Naor, A. Shamir. Visual cryptography. Advances in Cryptography: EUROCRYPT, LNCS, Vol. 950, pages 1-12, 1995.

— [3] Yanyan Han, Study of visual cryptography technology, Xidian University, Xi'an, China, Apr 2009.

— [4] "3D Generation and Watermarking From 2D Images and Videos" by Badillo I. Elias, New Mexico Tech, EE Department Digital Image Processing.

— [5] Ruanaidh Q J, Bowling W J, Boland F M. Watermarking Digital Images for Copyright Protection. IEEE proceeding on Vision, Signal and Image Processing, 1996, 143(4): pp. 250-256.

A Novel Manifold Learning Algorithm for Image Classification

H.M. Tian
School of Information Technology, Jinling Institute of Technology, Nanjing, China 211169
Email: thm_jit@163.com

ABSTRACT: Manifold Learning algorithms are significant and have been popularly applied in artificial intelligent, image processing and computer vision applications. In this paper, we propose a novel manifold learning algorithm for image classification. It improves the locally linear embedding (LLE) algorithm, namely imp-LLE. The algorithm integrates the identification to preferably improve the optimation aiming at keeps the intrinsic topology composition of the initiate data. We apply the proposed imp-LLE algorithm into image classification visualization, which attains a better classification visualization result compared with existing manifold learning algorithms.

KEYWORDS: Manifold learning; Locally Linear Embedding (LLE); Image classification.

1. INTRODUCTION

It is well known that many artificial intelligent and data mining problems deal with the high-dimensional data representation and analysis. In the past few decades, numerous dimension reduction and feature extraction algorithms play an significant role in pattern recognition, computer vision, and image classification [1,2], and they have been devoted to find the resultful feature representation of the initiate data. The aim of dimensionality reduction is to reveal the intrinsic composition of the distribution of samples in the initiate high-dimensional space. In the literature, traditional linear dimensionality reduction algorithms like principal component analysis (PCA) [3], linear discriminant analysis (LDA) [4], multi-dimensional scaling (MDS) [5] and representative manifold learning-based dimensionality reduction algorithms like kernel PCA [6], locally linear embedding (LLE) [7], ISOMAP [8], Laplacian eigenmaps (LE) [9], locality preserving projections (LPP) [10] and local tangent space alignment (LTSA) [11] have been the most popular techniques.

Through the research and analysis of the above algorithms, they can present a good dimension reduction while samples are uniformity in the high-dimensional space. But, They can destroy the local intrinsic composition of the initiate data and lead to a bad low-dimensional embedding result when data points present the non-uniformity in high-dimensional space. To solve the solutions, we propose a novel manifold learning algorithm for image classification. It improves the locally linear embedding (LLE) algorithm, namely imp-LLE. The algorithm integrates the identification to preferably improve the optimation aiming at keeps the intrinsic topology composition of the initiate data. We apply the proposed imp-LLE algorithm into image classification visualization, which attains a better classification visualization result compared with existing manifold learning algorithms.

2. PROPOSED ALGORITHM

In this section, we propose a novel manifold learning algorithm for image classification, which can preferably improve the optimation aiming at keeps the intrinsic topology composition of the initiate data. Our proposed IMP-LLE algorithm integrates the identification information of the data to keep the correlation composition of initiate data while mapping samples from high-dimension to low-dimension. In summary, the IMP-LLE algorithm explores the intrinsic topology to mine hidden relationships of the data and find the representative dimensions. The technique enables us to keep intrinsic properties of the initiate samples and to derive a lower intrinsic dimensional space.

Next, we describe the IMP-LLE algorithm. IMP-LLE improves the locally linear embedding (LLE) algorithm. Now, let $X = \{x_1, x_2, \cdots, x_N\}$ be a given dataset of N samples in $\Re^D$, where $x_i \in \Re^D$ $(i = 1,2,\cdots,N)$, here D is the dimension of the dataset. LLE constructs locally linear compositions at each data point x_i by representing x_i using its selected k neighbors. The optimal weights are decided by dealing with the following optimation:

$$\begin{cases} \arg\min\limits_{w_{ij}} \sum\limits_{i=1}^{N} \left\| x_i - \sum\limits_{j=1}^{k} w_{ij} x_j \right\|_2^2 \\ s.t. \quad \sum\limits_{j=1}^{k} w_{ij} = 1 \end{cases} \tag{1}$$

Once the reconstruction weight matrix $W = \{w_i = (w_{i1}, w_{i2}, \cdots, w_{iN})\}^T$ is computed, LLE maps the set X to $Y = \{y_1, y_2, \cdots, y_N\}$ in a lower dimensional space that preserves the local combination properties according to (2):

$$\begin{cases} \arg\min\limits_{y_i} \sum\limits_{i=1}^{N} \left\| y_i - \sum\limits_{j=1}^{k} w_{ij} y_j \right\|_2^2, \\ s.t. \quad YY^T = I \end{cases} \tag{2}$$

where I is an unit matrix with $N \times N$. LLE deals with the optimization to attain d eigenvectors that construct the set Y in the low-dimensional space. LLE present a good dimension reduction while samples are uniformity in the high-dimensional space. But, They can destroy the local intrinsic composition of the initiate data and lead to a bad low-dimensional embedding result while samples present the non-uniformity in high-dimensional space. An intuitive example can be depicted as shown in Fig. 1 that presents the local embedding result from 3-dimension to 2-dimension by LLE. We can see clearly from Fig. 1 that LLE greatly changes the intrinsic topology composition of the initiate local data.

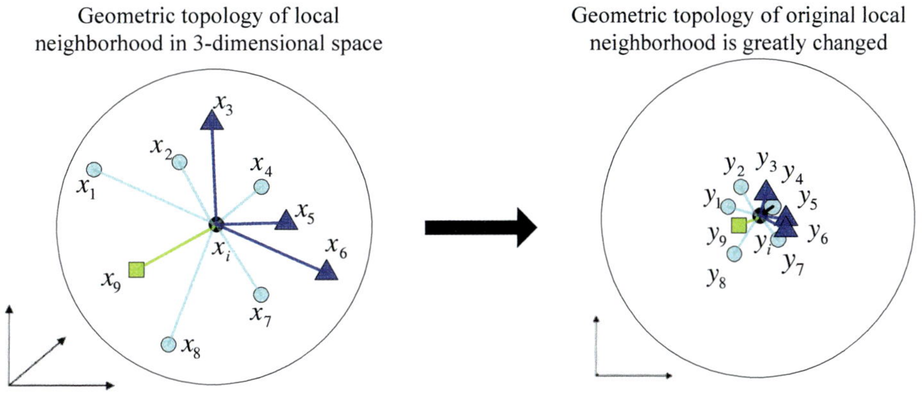

Figure 1. Schematic diagram of local embedding result from 3D to 2D by LLE.

To overcome this deficiency, we propose a novel local linear embedding algorithm integrating identification in this section, which can effectively keep the intrinsic topology composition of the initiate data. Specifically, LLE uses the reconstruction weights $\{w_{ij}\}$ to guarantee the intrinsic composition of the initiate data, but it cannot reflect the density information of nearest k neighbors for x_i. So, we use the identification information to attain better separability inter-class distance of the data. This aims to avoid bringing together the sample points of different classes when mapping an uneven distributed data. Fig. 2 illustrates this idea.

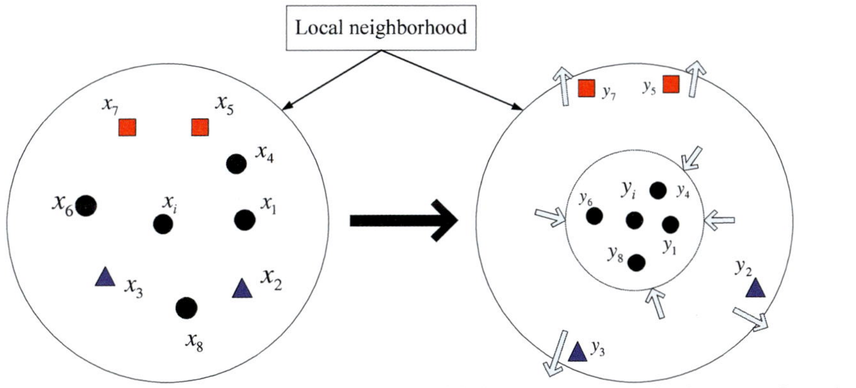

Figure 2. Local neighborhood optimization: the sample points with the same shape and color come from the same class.

The objective function can be used as follows:

$$\begin{cases} \underset{y_i}{\arg\min} \sum_{i=1}^{N} \left(\alpha \left\| y_i - \sum_{j=1}^{k_I} w_{ij}^{I} y_j \right\|_2^2 - \beta \left\| y_i - \sum_{j=k_I+1}^{k} w_{ij}^{2} y_j \right\|_2^2 \right) \\ s.t. \quad YY^T = I \end{cases} \tag{3}$$

where α and β are two scaling factors to unify different measures, $\alpha + \beta = 1$.

IMP-LLE Algorithm can be described as follows:

IMP-LLE Algorithm
Input: Dataset X of N samples with dimension D
Output: Embedded result Y;
1. Find k nearest neighbors of each x_i;
2. Calculate local reconstruction weights $\{w_{ij}\}$ according to (1);
3. Map the dataset $X \to Y$ in a lower dimensional space $\Re^d$;
4. Determine global Y by solving the optimization problem (3);

3. EXPERIMENTAL RESULTS

We first evaluate the effectiveness of the proposed IMP-LLE dimension reduction algorithm. The tested dataset is an artificial *S*-curve in $\Re^3$ as shown in Fig. 3(a). Fig. 3(b) shows the scatter plot of the *S*-curve dataset. As we can see, the *S*-curve data points are lying on a highly nonlinear manifold with randomly generated 2000 points. We compare IMP-LLE with LLE [8] for a 2D manifold with *S*-curve embedded in 3D space and run them with k=16. Note that k is the selected nearest neighbor number of each sample point x_i as mentioned in Section 2. We can see clearly from Fig. 4 that IMP-LLE keeps the intrinsic topology composition of the initiate *S*-curve data and generates better embedding results for different number of nearest neighbors. On the contrary, LLE greatly changes the intrinsic topology composition of the initiate data.

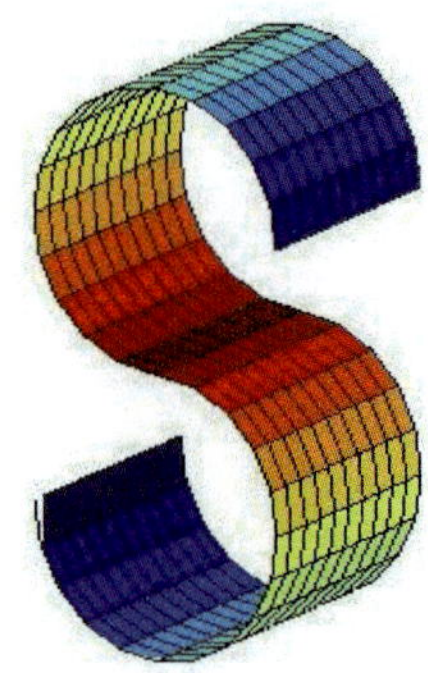

(a)

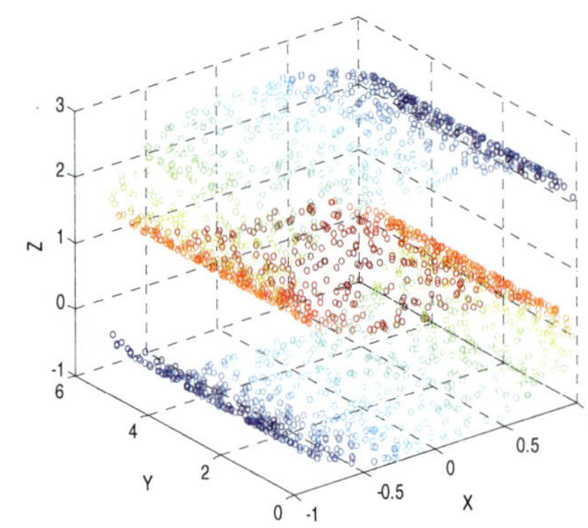

(b)

Figure 3. (a) *S*-curve dataset. (b) *S*-curve sampled points with $N = 2000$.

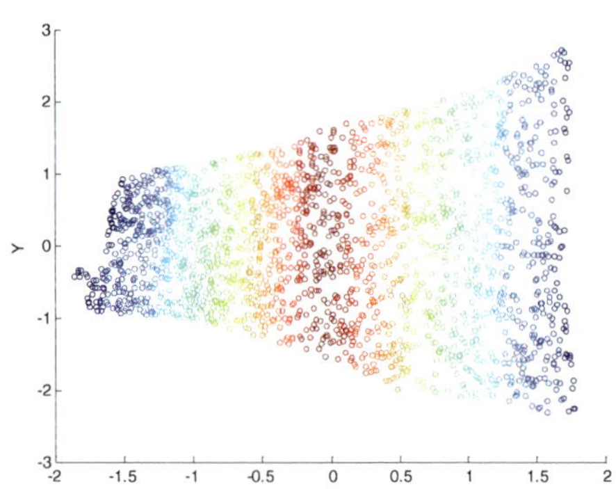

(a) LLE

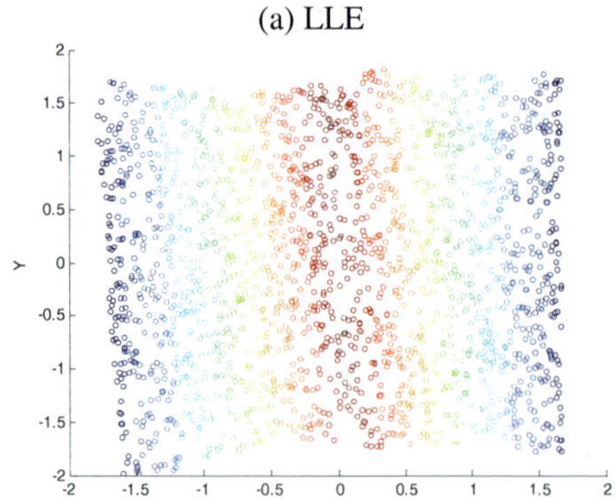

(b) IMP-LLE

Figure 4. 2-dimensional embedding results of *S*-curve data by LLE and IMP-LLE.

In order to evaluate our proposed algorithm in a real-world situation, we conduct the experiment: face classification on the FFace dataset [8]. To evaluate the uneven distribution situation, we randomly select 300 face samples in a 560-dimensional space. We classify the dataset into five classes according to facial expression: neutral faces, happy faces, unhappy faces, tongue faces and pouting faces. Fig. 5(a) and Fig. 5(b) present the visualization of 2D classification on the FFace dataset by LLE and IMP-LLE with k =6. We can see clearly that IMP-LLE can separates happy, unhappy and natural expression faces well in 2D space.

(a) LLE

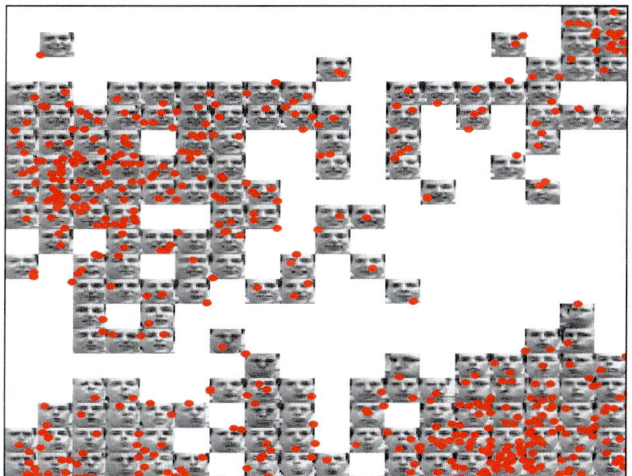

(b) IMP-LLE

Figure 5. 2D Visualization of FFace expression database.

4. CONCLUSIONS

In this paper, we propose a local neighborhood optimization strategy integrating identification information for dimension reduction. The proposed imp-LLE can attain better separability inter-class distance of the data in the low-dimensional space, which effectively keeps the intrinsic topology composition of the initiate data. The experimental results show that the proposed imp-LLE algorithm attains a better classification visualization result compared with existing manifold learning algorithms.

ACKNOWLEDGMENT

This work is supported by Project of Natural Science Foundation of Jinling Institute of Technology, Nanjing, China (No. 208.40410826).

REFERENCES

— [1] A. Shyr, R. Urtasun and M. I. Jordan, "Sufficient dimensionality reduction for visual sequence classification," *In Proceedings of Twenty-third IEEE Conference on Computer Vision and Pattern Recognition*, pp. 3610-3617, 2010.

— [2] Y. Koren and L. Carmel, "Robust linear dimensionality reduction," *IEEE Transactions on Visualization and Computer Graphics*, vol. 10, no. 4, pp. 459-470, 2012.

— [3] I. T. Jolliffe, "Principal component analysis," Springer-Verlag, New York, 1986.

— [4] P. Belhumeour, J. Hespanha and D. Kriegman, "Eigenfaces versus fisherfaces: recognition using class specific linear projection," IEEE Transactions on Pattern Analysis and Machine Intelligence, vol. 19, no. 7, pp. 711-720, 2007.

— [5] B. Scholkopf, A. J. Smola and K. R. Muller, "Nonlinear component analysis as a kernel eigenvalue problem," *Neural Computation*, vol. 10, no. 5, pp. 1299-1319, 1998.

— [6] S. T. Roweis and L. K. Saul, "Nonlinear dimensionality reduction by locally linear embedding," *Science*, vol. 290, no. 5500, pp. 2323-2326, 2000.

— [7] S. T. Roweis and L. K. Saul, "Nonlinear dimensionality reduction by locally linear embedding," Science, vol. 290, no. 5500, pp. 2323-2326, 2000.

— [8] J. B. Tenenbaum, V. de Silva and J. C. Langford, "A global intrinsic framework for nonlinear dimensionality reduction," *Science*, vol. 290, no. 5500, pp. 2319-2323, 2000.

— [9] M. Belkin and P. Niyogi, "Laplacian eigenmaps for dimensionality reduction and representation," *Neural Computation*, vol. 15, pp. 1373-1396, 2003.

— [10] X. He and P. Niyogi, "Locality preserving projections," *Advances in Neural Information Processing System*, vol. 16, pp. 153-160, 2004.

— [11] Z. Zhang and H. Zha, "Principal manifolds and nonlinear dimension reduction via local tangent space alignment," *SIAM Journal of Scientific Computing*, vol. 26, no. 1, pp. 313-338, 2005.

Chapter 5

Electrical Engineering

The Conversion between Left-linear Grammar and Right-linear Grammar in Finite Automata

R.H. Wang

Key Laboratory of Machine Learning and Intelligent Information System, Chongqing University of Arts and Sciences, Chongqing, China

Email: ruihuwang@126.com

ABSTRACT: Left-linear grammar and right-linear grammar are known collectively as regular grammar, which defines a description mechanism for lexical analyzing. Meanwhile Finite Automata (FA) provides a recognition mechanism for tokens, which can be constructed from regular grammar. This paper proposed a conversion method between left-linear grammar and right-linear grammar via finite automata. Firstly, one of them is converted to finite automata, and then rewrites the grammar based on the constructed finite automata.

KEYWORDS: Left-linear grammar; Right-linear grammar; Finite automata; Conversion.

1. INTRODUCTION

1.1. *Grammar and language*

The syntax for a variety of programming languages can be described with one of linguist Noam Chomsky's grammatical models named as context-free grammars [1]. Regular grammar is a special case of context-free grammar. It is mostly used for lexical analyzing phrase as it can be transformed into finite automata easily. As we well known, automata theory is the research of abstract computation machines [2], which provides a recognition mechanism for lexical analyzing. The simplest and most widely used automata model is finite automata, which can be applied to analyze finite-state systems [3]. In this paper, we will explore the intrinsic relationship between regular grammar, including left-linear grammar and right-linear grammar, and finite automata.

Definition 1 (***Grammar***) A ***grammar*** is a quadruple denoted by $G=(A,V_N,P,S)$ [4], where

-- A is an alphabet on which language is defined;

-- V_N is a finite set of non-terminal which is used to derive the strings of the grammar. Here the non-terminal means that it needs to be further defined;

-- P is a finite set of productions or rules;

-- S is a start or recognition symbol from which a derivation begins. It is also represent the ultimate syntax phrase which we want to describe.

Statement 1 *Recursive definition is an essential tool to represent an infinite set by finite elements.*

Example 1 An infinite string set {01, 0011, 000111, ...} can be formulated by

$$L(G)=\{0^n1^n \mid n\geq 1\}$$

which can be represented by some finite elements within a grammar G,

$G[S]$: $S\to 0S1$

$S\to 01$

where, $A=\{0,1\}$, $V_N=\{S\}$, and

$P=\{S\to 0S1, S\to 01\}$.

The string 0^n1^n is generated by derivation as follows:

$S\Rightarrow 01\Leftrightarrow 0^11^1$,

$S\Rightarrow 0S1\Rightarrow 0011\Leftrightarrow 0^21^2$

$S\Rightarrow 0S1\Rightarrow 00S11\Rightarrow 000111\Leftrightarrow 0^31^3$,

......

Apparently, the set of $L(G)$ is infinite while $G[S]$ is finite, in which $|A|=2$, $|V_N|=1$ and $|P|=2$.

1.2. *Finite automata*

Definition 2 (***Finite Automata***) A finite automata M is defined as a quintuple $(K,A,\to,\uparrow,\downarrow)$, where

- K is a finite set of states;
- A is an input alphabet which constructs the strings accepted by automata;
- $\to\subseteq K\times A\times K$ is a state transition map which defines which next state k_j reached when the current state k_i reads an input symbol a, where $k_i,k_j\in K$ and $a\in A$;
- $\uparrow$ is an initial state;
- $\downarrow\subseteq K$ is a set of terminal states [3].

One example of finite automata for recognizing unsigned digital is given in Figure 1 [5], where

$K = \{S, A, B, C, D, E, F\}$,

$A = \{e, d, \bullet, +, -\}$

$\rightarrow = \{<S, e, B>, <S, d, A>, <S, \bullet, C>, \cdots\}$

$\uparrow = S$

$\downarrow = \{A, E, F\} \subseteq K$.

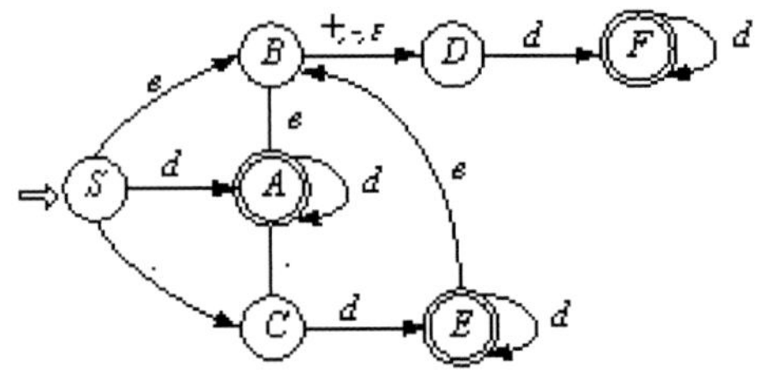

Figure 1. Example of finite automata.

In Figure 1, the input symbol *d* denotes digits varied from 0 to 9. The input string $45.76e+10$ can be accepted by this automaton. The transition procedure of states for accepting $45.76e+10$ is shown in Figure 2.

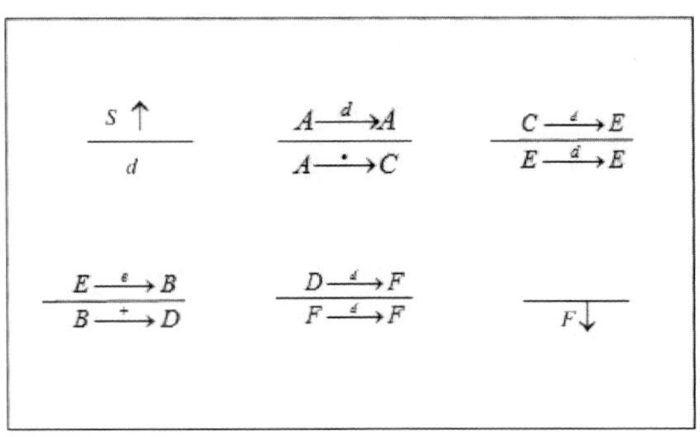

Figure 2. The transition states for accepting *dd.dde+dd*.

Statement 2 Finite automaton is a powerful tool for lexical analyzing. It is only constructed upon regular grammar, rather than any context-free grammar.

1.3. *Regular expression*

Definition 3 (***Regular Expression***) For a given alphabet set Σ, we define an auxiliary alphabet set $\Sigma' = \Sigma \cup \{\varepsilon, \Phi, \bullet, (,), |\}$. Here we make a recursive definition for regular expression and regular set as follows.

- For each a, $a \in \Sigma$, a is a regular expression, and the corresponding regular set is $\{a\}$.

- Both of ε and Φ are regular expressions, and the regular sets are $\{\varepsilon\}$ and Φ, respectively.

- If r_1 and r_2 are two regular expressions, and the corresponding regular set are $L(r_1)$ and $L(r_2)$ respectively, then (r_1), $r_1 | r_2$, $r_1 \bullet r_2$ and r_1^*, r_2^* are all regular expressions and their regular set are $L(r_1)$, $L(r_1) \cup L(r_2)$, $L(r_1)L(r_2)$, $L(r_1)^*$, $L(r_2)^*$.

Definition 4 (***Equivalence)*** If a set $L(G)$ consisted with all sentences derived from a given grammar G is equal to a regular set $L(r)$ described by a regular expression r, or equal to the strings set $L(M)$ running through the start state towards one of the end states of a finite automata M, we call the grammar G is equivalent with the regular expression r and with the finite automata M, denoted by $G \equiv M \equiv r$.

Example 2 Regular grammar *G*[*S*] is defined as,

$$S \rightarrow aA \mid a$$

$$A \rightarrow aA \mid dA \mid a \mid d$$

which can be used for defining **Identifier** of a program language[4]. It is equivalent with regular expression $r = a(a \mid d)^*$, which means each of identifier is start with a letter followed by any string constructed from *a* and *d*.

Theorem 1 For each right-linear grammar G_R there exists a finite automaton M such that $G_R \equiv M$.

Proof.

Let $G_R = (A, V_N, P, S)$ and $M = (K, A', \rightarrow, \uparrow, \downarrow)$.

- We associate the ith non-terminal $N^{(i)} \in V_N$ in G_R with a state $k_N^{(i)}$. $K_N = \{k_N^{(1)}, k_N^{(2)}, \cdots, k_N^{(n)}\}$. $n = |V_N|$.

$K = K_N \cup \{Z\}$, where Z is a newly imported terminal state. And $|K| = |K_N| + 1 = |V_N| + 1$ holds true.

- $A' = A$.

- The start symbol S of G_R is designated as the initial state of M, namely $\uparrow = S$.

- $\downarrow = \{Z\} \subseteq K$.

- The last tuple of M which has not been determined yet is $\rightarrow$.

For each production or rule like $A \rightarrow tB$ in P of G_R, $A, B \in V_N$, $t \in A$, we construct a transition map $<<A, t>, B> \in \rightarrow$; whereas each rule like $A \rightarrow t$ we make a transition map $<<A, t>, Z>$.

Example 3 The finite automaton of Example 2 is given in Figure 3.

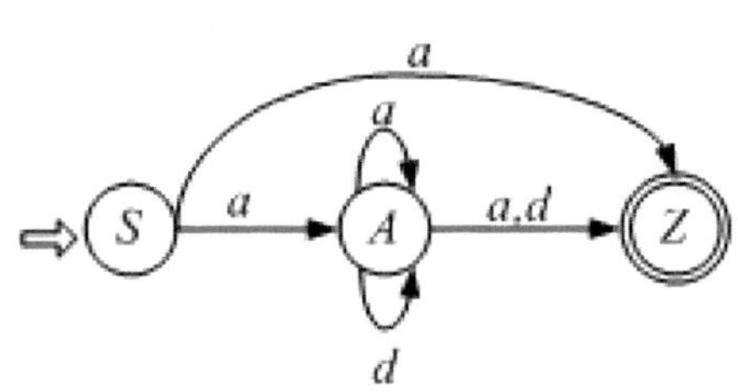

Figure 3. The finite automaton of identifier grammar.

2. CONVERSION BETWEEN LEFT-LINEAR AND RIGHT-LINEAR GRAMMAR

2.1. *Right-linear grammar to Left-linear grammar*

Theorem 2. For each right-linear grammar $G_R = \{A, V_N, P, S\}$, there exists a left-linear grammar $G_L = \{A', V_N', P', S'\}$ which is equivalent with G_R.

Proof. Firstly, we construct a finite automaton M_R with the given right-linear grammar G_R with Theorem 1.

For each transition function like,

$<< A, t >, B > \in \rightarrow$

In M_R, we write a production like $B \rightarrow At$, $B \rightarrow At \in P'$. As to the unique initial state S of M_R, adds a rule like $S \rightarrow \varepsilon, S \rightarrow \varepsilon \in P'$. The terminal state of M_R is regarded as the start symbol of the left-linear grammar G_L. So the quadruple of G_L has been determined.

Note: *There is a unique terminal state in* M_R *constructed from right linear grammar, which is viewed as the only start symbol of left-linear grammar.*

Example 4 Given a right-linear grammar G_R [6],

$P = \{S \rightarrow 0A \mid 1B, A \rightarrow 1S \mid 1, \ B \rightarrow 0S \mid 0\}$

The equivalent finite automaton M_R of G_R is shown in Figure 4. Obviously it is a nondeterministic finite automaton (NFA).

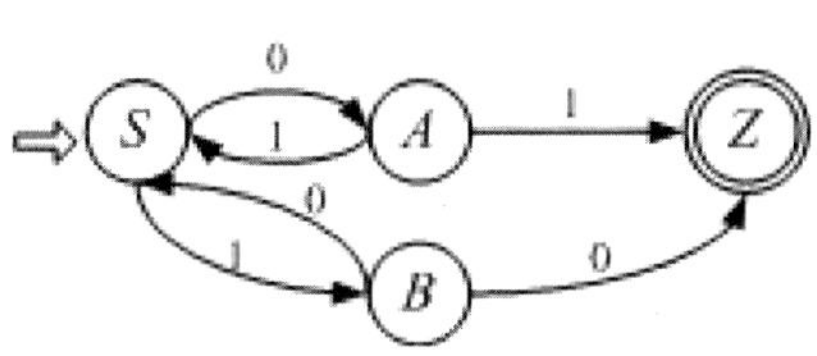

Figure 4. The NFA M_R of grammar G_R.

We construct a Deterministic finite automaton (DFA) M_D as shown in Figure 5.

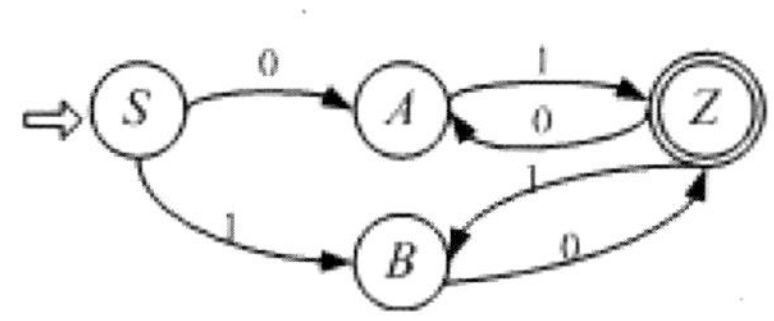

Figure 5. The Deterministic Finite Automata M_D of G_R.

where, $K = \{S, A, B, Z\}$,

$A' = \{0,1\}$

$\rightarrow = \{< S, 0, A >, < S, 1, B >, \cdots, < Z, 1, B >\}$,

$\uparrow = S$,

$\downarrow = \{Z\}$.

We can write a regular expression for DFA M_D given by Figure 5 as,

$$r_{M_D} = 01(01)^* \mid 10(10)^*.$$

The left-linear grammar G_L of M_D is $G_L = \{A', V_N', P', S'\}$, where $A' = A = \{0,1\}$, and $V_N' = \{S, A, B, Z\}, S' = Z$. And,

and

$$P' = \{Z \rightarrow A1, Z \rightarrow B0, A \rightarrow S0, A \rightarrow Z0, B \rightarrow S1, B \rightarrow Z1, S \rightarrow \varepsilon\}.$$

Now what we want to do is to proof that the grammar G_L is equivalent with G_R.

Proof. For rule $A \rightarrow S0$ and $S \rightarrow \varepsilon$, we can derive that $A \succ 0$;

For rule $Z \rightarrow A1$ and $A \rightarrow Z0$, we can deduce that $A \succ A10$;

Thus, $A \succ A10 \mid 0$ holds true.

Through eliminating the left recursion in $A \succ A10 \mid 0$ we get,

$$A \succ 0A', A' \succ 10A' \mid \varepsilon$$

The equivalent regular expression can be written as

$$r_A = 0(10)^*,$$

Furthermore, with $Z \rightarrow A1$ the regular expression for Z is $r_Z^A = 0(10)^*1$.

Similarly, for $B \rightarrow S1$ and $S \rightarrow \varepsilon$, we can derive $B \succ 1$.

For $Z \rightarrow B0$ and $B \rightarrow Z1$, we can deduce that $B \succ B01$,

Thus, $B \succ B01 \mid 1$ holds true.

Eliminating left recursion again,

$$B \succ 1B', B' \succ 01B' \mid \varepsilon$$

Now we can write an equivalent regular expression as

$$r_B = 1(01)^*$$

Meanwhile $Z \rightarrow B0$, so the regular expression for Z is $r_Z^B = 1(01)^*0$.

In the end, the regular expression for Z is,

$$r_Z = r_Z^A \mid r_Z^B = 0(10)^*1 \mid 1(01)^*0.$$

Obviously,

$$L(r_Z) = L(M_D) = L(G_L) = L(G_R).$$

2.2. *Left-linear grammar to right-linear grammar*

Theorem 3. For each left-linear grammar G_L there exists a finite automata M such that $G_L \equiv M$.

Proof. Let $G_L = (A, V_N, P, S)$ and

$$M = (K, A', \rightarrow, \uparrow, \downarrow).$$

We set $A' = A$ and $\downarrow = \{S\}$. The newly added state F is the start state of M, namely $\uparrow = F$. And $K = V_N \cup \{F\}$. For each rule like $A \rightarrow Bt$, we construct a transition function as $B \xrightarrow{t} A$; For each rule like $A \rightarrow t$, we construct a transition function as $F \xrightarrow{t} A$.

After that a map from a quadruple G_L to a 5-tuple M has been constructed and they are equivalent with each other.

Statement 3. For each left-linear grammar $G_L = (A, V_N, P, S)$, there always exists a right-linear grammar $G_R = (A, V_N', P', S')$ which is equivalent with G_L.

Example 5 Turn a left-linear grammar $G_L[S]$ into a right-linear grammar $G_R[F]$.

$$G_L[S]:\ S \to A0,\ \ A \to A0\,|\,S1\,|\,0$$

Firstly, we construct a corresponding finite automata of $G_L[S]$ with Theorem 3 as follows,

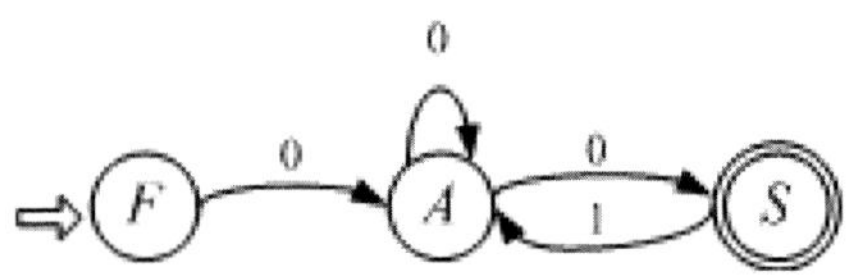

Figure 6. The Non-deterministic Finite Automata constructed from a left-linear grammar in Example 5.

Secondly, a determination matrix for NFA is formed as shown in Table 1,

Table 1. Determination matrix.

	0	1
[*F*]	[*A*]	
[*A*]	[*AS*]	
[*AS*]	[*AS*]	[*A*]

Let [*AS*]=[*S*], we can rewrite the NFA in Figure 6 to a DFA M_D in Figure 7,

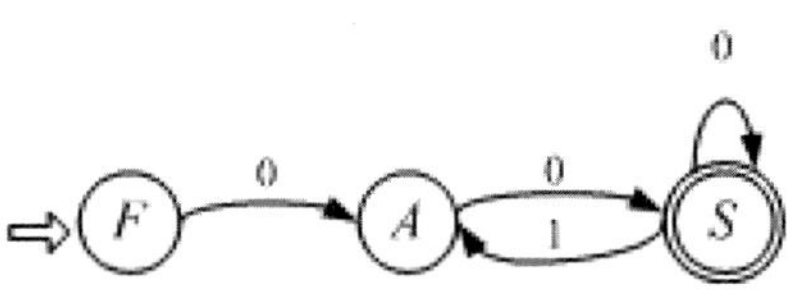

Figure 7. The Deterministic Finite Automata M_D of NFA.

Then a right-linear grammar $G_R[F]$ which is equivalent to $G_L[S]$ can be written as

$$G_R[F] = (A, V_N', P', S'),$$

where $A = \{0,1\}$, $V_N' = \{F, A, S\}$, $S' = F$, and

$$P' = \{F \to 0A, A \to 0S, S \to 1A,$$
$$S \to 0S, S \to \varepsilon\}$$

Furthermore, the regular expression of the DFA M_D in Figure 7 can be easily written as,

r_1=00(10)*0*,

Meanwhile, the regular expression of the right linear grammar $G_R[F]$ is

r_2=00(10|0)*,

And the regular expression of the left-linear grammar $G_L[S]$ is

r_3=0 (0|01)*.

Here $r_1 \equiv r_2 \equiv r_3$ holds true.

3. CONCLUSION

In this paper a conversion method is proposed between left-linear grammar and right-linear grammar via finite automata construction. It enriches the foundation framework of regular grammar and provides a new approach to study the Type-3 grammar.

ACKNOWLEDGEMENT

This research was supported by scientific and technological project of Yongchuan District under Ycstc 2013ad5001 and science and technology research project of Chongqing Municipal Education Commission under KJ31225, and Research Foundation of Nature and Science of Chongqing Municipal under cstc2012jjA1292.

REFERENCES

— [1] Tao Jiang, Ming Li, Bala Ravikumar, Kenneth W. Regan. Formal Grammars and Languages. Algorithms and Theory of Computation Handbook. 1998.

— [2] J.E. Hopcroft, R. Motwani, J.D. Ullman. Introduction to Automata Theory, Languages, and Computation. Pearson, 2006.

— [3] J.C.M. Baeten, P.J. L. Cuijpers, B. Luttik, P.J.A. van Tilburg. A Process-Theoretic Look at Automata.

— [4] Mikhail Barash, Alexander Okhotin. Linear grammars with one-sided contexts and their automaton representation.

— [5] Zhang Jing, Huang Weitong, Baikunth Nath. Compiler Principle and Implementation. Beijing: Tsinghua University Press, 2007.06.

— [6] Lv Yingzhi, Zhang Suqin, Jiang Weidu, Dai Guilan. Compiler Principle. Beijing: Tsinghua University Press, 2011.07.

Effect of Vacuum Level on the Performance of Vacuum Packaged Micromachined Quartz Tuning Fork Gyroscopes

M.Y. Fan[1] & L.F. Zhang[2]
1- School of Information Technology and Engineering, Yuxi Normal University
2- Office of Academic Affairs, Yuxi Normal University
Email: [1]fmy@yxnu.net

ABSTRACT: Through the study of MEMS packaging technology, the quartz tuning fork crystal oscillator is directly capsulated in MEMS vacuum packaged shell and the phase and amplitude comparison circuits are used to measure and monitor the degree of vacuum in the internal cavity of the MEMS package. The resistance welding method for vacuum packaging and the vacuum measurement technologies have been developed to improve the performance of the micromachined quartz tuning fork gyroscopes. The threshold is enhanced about 10 times.

KEYWORDS: Micromachined; Quartz tuning fork gyroscope; Threshold; Vacuum packaging; Vacuum level.

1. INTRODUCTION

Microelectromechanical systems (MEMS) is a rapidly developing new field. Typical MEMS devices or systems can not only sense the external environment, but also respond to changes in the external environment and perform their intended functions. Vacuum packaging can improve the performance of micromachined gyroscopes, but the gyroscope performance is not directly proportional to the degree of vacuum of the device package. If with insufficient vacuum, the gas in the device cavity will damp the devices and lead to low sensitivity and bad performance. If the degree of vacuum is too high, the oscillation phenomenon will occur. This requires to measure and control the vacuum level of the package [1]. The quality factor (Q-factor) is an important measure of the micromachined gyroscope vacuum packaging. The vacuum level of atmospheres in the cavity is the main factor affecting the Q-value. For measuring the vacuum level in a sealed device cavity, the degree of vacuum measured upon encapsulation should not be used as the gas pressure in the cavity after packaging. The packaged device must be actually measured. The quartz tuning fork crystal sensor is considered as a kind of vacuum sensor. The digital frequency synthesizer is adopted as the signal source to excitate the quartz crystal sensor and the phase and amplitude comparison circuit is employed to compare the phase and amplitude of signals at both ends of the quartz crystal sensor signal and output the corresponding voltage signals for measuring and monitoring the degree of vacuum inside the MEMS package [2].

2. MEMS VACUUM PACKAGING TECHNOLOGY

Packaging is the last step in the process from the chip testing to the product. Only after a chip is packaged, users can easily access to the signal interface of the chip, which achieves interaction and isolation with the environment through packaging. It can effectively improve the reliability of the chip. The package enables users to conveniently use various functions of the chip in a minimum size, the lowest cost and the simple structure, while effectively expanding the performance or functions of the chip according to users' needs. The main functional components of the vacuum packaged MEMS devices or systems include sensors and actuators. It is a typical characteristic that most MEMS devices have "moving" parts. Moving parts will be damped by air in the atmosphere and affect the Q-value of devices. After vacuum packaging, the device performance can be greatly improved [3]. The MEMS gyroscope measuring the angular rate has the two-dimensional vibrating damped system architecture and the tuning fork vibration system architecture; the gyroscope measuring the absolute angle adopts the system architecture of isotropic vibration in the plane, and due to energy conversion between the two spin axes, procession seems being observed in the vibrating direction of the non-inertial system and the precession angle is associated with the angle of rotation. The typical structure of the MEMS gyroscope measuring the angular rate employs the converse electric drive for vibration in the direction of drive and causes vibration in the detecting direction acted upon the Coriolis force. The vibration characteristics are closely related to the Q-value. The ultimate sensitivity of gyros is mainly determined by the measuring circuit noise and the Brownian heat engine noise:

$$\Omega_{\min} = \sqrt{\Omega_e^2 + \Omega_B^2} \tag{1}$$

Here: $\Omega_e \propto \frac{\omega_0}{Q} \cdot \frac{1}{q_{drv}} V_n \sqrt{BW}$, $\Omega_B \propto \frac{1}{q_{drv}} V_n \sqrt{\frac{4k_B T}{\omega_0 M Q}} \cdot \sqrt{BW}$, Ω_e is the ultimate sensitivity related to the measuring circuit; Ω_B is the ultimate sensitivity related to the Brownian motion; the Q value is the quality factor of the mechanical oscillator; q_{drv} is the drive amplitude; M is the effective mass of the oscillator; and BW is the effective bandwidth.

The Q-value of the oscillator in the gyro is one of the major factors that determine the sensitivity. In addition to the materials and structures, the air damping is the determinant of the Q-value. Gyroscopes are indispensable components in the areas of aerospace, military, automotive and other consumer products. When the acceleration sensitivity reaches the level less than $1\mu g\sqrt{Hz}$, the main factors influencing the sensitivity comprise the heat engine noise and the noise of the measuring circuit. The heat engine mainly contributes the noise caused by the air damping. Under the atmospheric pressure the sensitivity is at the order of magnitude of $1.8\mu g\sqrt{Hz}$ because of the heat engine noise. Under the pressure less than 1Pa, the sensitivity may reach $0.05\mu g\sqrt{Hz}$ by the heat engine noise. Therefore, the vacuum packaging can greatly improve the sensitivity of the devices. Currently due to the high cost and not very good reliability of vacuum packaging, the application of the vacuum package in the gyroscope is restricted. The vacuum packaging using the resistance welding free of fluxes and solders can be achieve the vacuum level of $10^{-2} Pa$ [4-6].

3. COMMON PROBLEMS EXISTING IN VACUUM PACKAGING

The technical difficulties confronted by the vacuum packaging are summarized at the physical mechanism level and some of the common problems faced by the MEMS vacuum packaging are as follows [7, 8]. (1) Evaluation of the leak rate for the vacuum packaging process. MEMS devices are small and require a leak rate lower than the traditional vacuum packaging process to maintain vacuum in the small or micro vacuum cavity. For such low leak rate, how to measure and evaluate by the conventional *He* helium mass spectrometer is a technical problem. (2) Online vacuum measurement. The vacuum packaging is commonly conducted in a vacuum environment, but the vacuum pressure in the vacuum environment is not equal to the pressure in the vacuum cavity of the MEMS devices. The most direct approach to check the effectiveness of the vacuum packaging process is measuring the vacuum pressure inside the vacuum cavity. (3) Method for maintaining vacuum and the assessment of reliability. For the vacuum packaged devices, the vacuum in the cavity should maintain more than 8 years of life, or else the packaging process cannot fulfill the requirements for practical use. Currently the common solution is using getters, but the traditional getters are restricted in MEMS packaging applications. The getters suitable for the vacuum packaging of MEMS devices need to be developed or the vacuum packing method without getters are researched. (4) Standardization of vacuum packaging process and equipment. The study on the MEMS vacuum packaging is to formulate a workable vacuum packaging process and put it into practice. An effective vacuum packaging process and the specific development are needed to attain the process.

4. PRINCIPLES OF VACUUM MEASUREMENT

When the X, Y types of quartz crystal oscillators in the flexural oscillation mode, the impedance varies greatly with the pressure. Oscillation of quartz crystal oscillators in the air can be understood as the damped oscillation caused by the air friction. The resonance impedance of tuning fork crystal oscillators is $Z = Z_0 + \Delta Z$ upon resonance. ΔZ denotes the impedance caused by the gas damping and can be calculated by the following formula:

$$\Delta Z = \frac{2\eta_0 V^2 \cos\theta}{A^2} \cdot f \tag{2}$$

Here: η_0 is the conversion factor for converting electrical energy to mechanical energy, V is the driving voltage, θ is the phase difference between voltage and current, A is the amplitude of the crystal oscillator, and f is the friction resistance coefficient. For a specific crystal oscillator, the coefficient $2\eta_0 V^2 \cos\theta / A^2$ is definite. ΔZ only changes with f, which has different calculation formulas under different gas flow patterns.

In the molecular flow mode: $f = R^2 \sqrt{\frac{8\pi M}{R_0 T}} \cdot P$; in the viscous flow mode: $f = 6\pi\eta R + 3\pi R^2 \sqrt{2\eta\rho\omega}$, where: P is the gas pressure; R is the radius of the sphere, approximately equal to the thickness of the tuning fork crystal oscillator; M is the molecular mass; R_0 is the gas constant; T is temperature; η is a coefficient of viscosity; ρ is the gas density, directly proportional to M and P; and ω is the resonance frequency. In the two different gas flow modes, ΔZ may change with the temperature change, so the degree of vacuum should be measured at a constant temperature as much as possible.

The schematic diagram of π network method to measure the resonance frequency of quartz wafer is shown in Figure 1. The box with dotted lines in the figure shows the equivalent circuit of the measured quartz wafer, L_1 denotes the dynamic inductance, C_1 indicates the dynamic capacitance, C_0 represents the static capacitance and R_1 means the resonance resistance. R_f and quartz wafers constitute a simple π network. By analyzing the equivalent circuit, it shows that there is an inherent series resonant frequency of the quartz wafer and when the applied excitation frequency is equal to the resonance frequency, the quartz wafer impedance is minimum and purely resistive. When the quartz wafer is in a resonant state, the π network is a purely resistive network with the smallest voltage drop at both ends of the network, so the test of quartz wafer parameters can be simplified as the test of impedance of the π network [9].

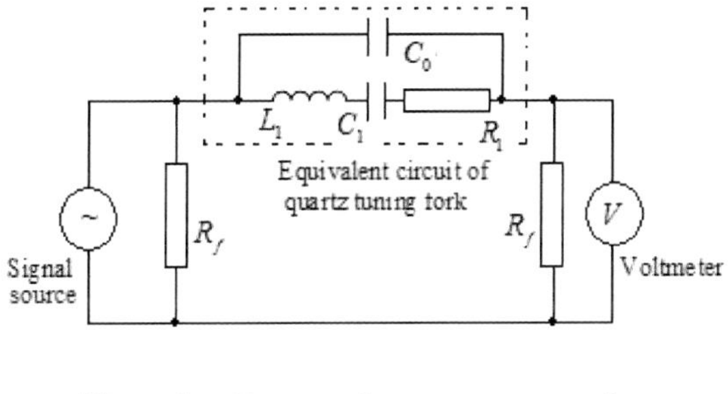

Figure 1. π network to test quartz wafer.

5. GYRO VACUUM PACKAGING PROCESS AND THRESHOLD MEASUREMENT

The technical roadmap for the MEMS device-level vacuum packaging is based either on the reflow soldering process with solders or on the resistance welding process of metal shells. Comparing the two processes, the MEMS device-level vacuum packing based on the resistance welding is obviously more advantageous. Resistance welding is a process in which heat is generated at the interface of the parts to be joined by passing an electrical current through the parts so that the metal parts attain the plastic state or the melted state under a controlled pressure and are firmly welded together. It is a welding process widely used in the hermetic package. The upper and lower portions of the welded parts contact with the upper and lower electrodes respectively. The resistances between the upper and lower electrodes comprise the following: the contact resistance between the upper electrode and the welded parts R_{c1}, the body resistance of the upper portion R_{n1}, the contact resistance between the upper and lower portions of the welded parts R_z, the body resistance of the lower portion R_{n2} and the contact resistance between the lower portion of the welded parts and the lower electrode R_{c2}. The joule heat generated from the flow of current from the upper electrode through the lower electrode is calculated as follows:

$$Q = I^2 \cdot \left(R_{c1} + R_{n1} + R_z + R_{c2} + R_{n2}\right) \cdot t \qquad (3)$$

Since the contact surface is not absolutely flat, only a number of microscopic points come in contact on the contact surface. When the current passes through the contact surface, the power line contracts at these contact points, and hence the formed additional resistance is the major part of the contact resistance, as shown in Fig. 2. For the contact resistance, the larger the area, the smaller the resistance. Since the contact area at the welding place is much smaller than the contact area of the electrodes and the welded parts, the contact resistance is the maximum at the welding place. Therefore, it is first heated to the desired temperature by the passage of current and forms the welding spots under pressure. The welding points are formed in three stages:

(1) Squeeze stage: Due to different levels of the shell production processes, the contact resistance at the interface of the parts to be joined may be too large and when the current passes through, excessive Joule heat will burn the contact surface, so the squeeze is needed before passage of current.

(2) Electric heating stage: After the squeeze stage, the passage of current through a resistance generates heat, plastic deformation occurs with broken grains at the interface under pressure and heat. The broken grains are recrystallized at a high temperature so that the grains are formed between the parts through mutual crystallization to complete the welding when the surface becomes plastic. As the temperature rises, the plastic area extends around and there is melting area in the center. Since the melting area is surrounded by the plastic area, the molten metal will not splash, but if the temperature is too high, the melting area expands to the edges of the parts and causes outflow of the molten metal.

(3) Hold stage: After cutting off the welding current, the electrode continues to extrude the welding points. Because of good cooling conditions around the weld, the peripheral are set first, the rigidity is enhanced surrounding the melting area, and the center setting and contracting are hampered. If it is not

pressurized to overcome this problem, welding defects such as cracks will form.

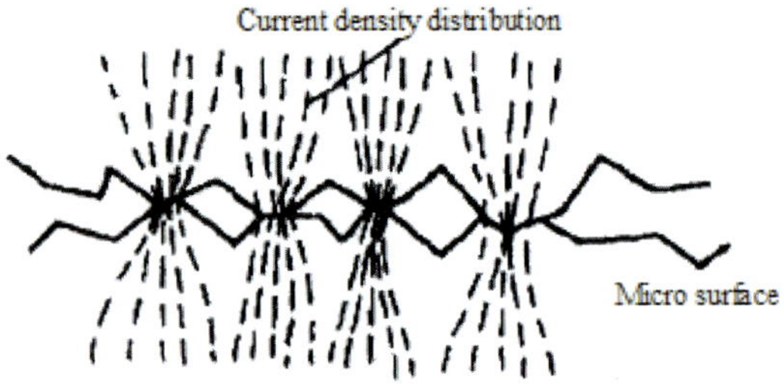

Figure 2. Schematic diagram of the contact resistance.

Resistance welding rapidly discharges the stored power from the energy storage capacitor bank through *RLC* discharge circuit to generate a large welding pulse current. The capacitance, inductance and resistance in the discharge circuit are the important design parameters of the vacuum welding machine and affect the amplitude and width of the current pulse. In order to adapt to the diversity of MEMS devices, the welding pulse energy for the resistance welding is designed as $30000J$ with the weld length greater than $30cm$ and the ultimate vacuum of the cavity of $2\times10^{-4}Pa$. The welding equipment integrates the advantages of the current domestic resistance welding equipment, and the advantages of resistance welding and vacuum packaging process. It comprises glove box, vacuum oven, vacuum system and welding mechanism, effectively improves the welding environment of components and increases the welding speed, so that it is more convenient and more practical for operation. The specific process is as follows: the parts are heated in a vacuum oven, placed directly into the glove box and then put into a die in the vacuum cavity, create vacuum and finally complete the welding. The working vacuum cavity is installed in the glove box for vacuum outgassing, protective transfer of shell and resistance welding integration process in a vacuum environment, so as to ensure the stability of the process. The entire process is completed in the sealed glove box. The photo of the vacuum resistance welding equipment is shown in Figure 3.

Figure 3. Vacuum resistance welding equipment.

In order to verify the sealing characteristics and the vacuum retaining of the metal package, the metal shell is vacuum packaged in the experiment according to the determined vacuum packaging process by the resistance welding method in a vacuum environment $10^{-3}Pa$ and set with crystal oscillators to monitor the vacuum pressure. In the experiment, the voltage change of the crystal oscillator resonance resistance is utilized for measure the vacuum pressure change and the voltage value corresponds to the appropriate vacuum pressure. A monitoring crystal oscillator is installed each shell. Due to the individual difference of the calibration curve of crystal oscillators, each crystal oscillator has been separately calibrated before packaging. The vacuum packaging equipment and technology developed by Huazhong University of Science and Technology are applied to vacuum packaging of the silicon MEMS gyroscopes. As shown in Figure 4, the size of the vacuum packaging is about $20mm\times10mm$, and the Q value is increased 6-12 times after vacuum packaging of gyroscopes [10]. Through the 60-day monitoring of the output characteristics of vacuum packaged gyros, the results are shown in Figure 5. The drive output detection voltage maintains a relatively stable output value and this means little leak of the vacuum packaged devices within this period of time.

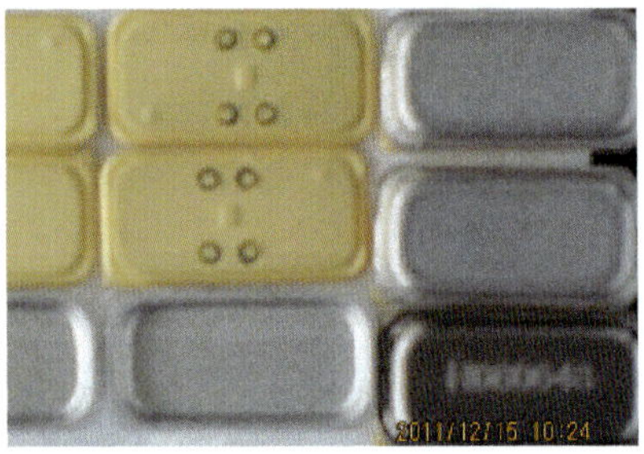

Figure 4. Vacuum packaged metal shell of micromachined quartz tuning fork gyroscope.

It is found in the experiment that the quality of the sealing process alone cannot satisfy the requirement for keeping more than 8 years of vacuum in the vacuum packaged devices and other methods are needed to further reduce the leakage rate. Study on the outgassing process of metal shell shows that heating in the high-temperature vacuum oven at above 250° C for over 48 hours can achieve a good outgassing effect; for a 10Pa vacuum package, the impact of the fixture may be neglected, but the fixture for a vacuum package with pressure of 0.1Pa or less must be strictly designed so that the degree of vacuum in the vacuum packaged shell is consistent with that in the vacuum cavity of the packaged devices.

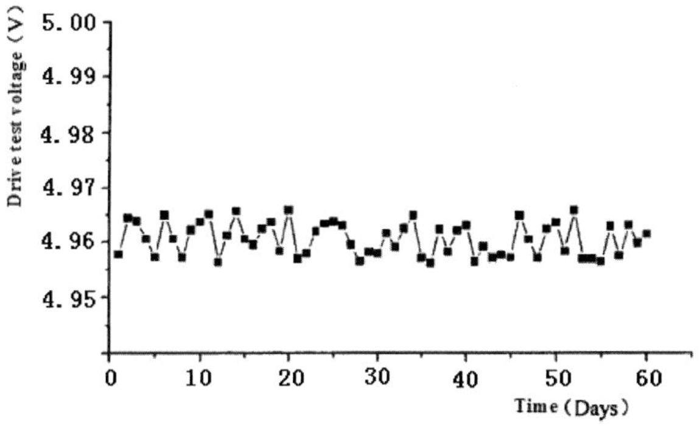

Figure 5. Micromachined gyroscope drive output signal.

Based on the optimization of packaging equipment parameters, the vacuum packaging process using the resistance welding optimizes the welding quality, the outgassing device and the experiment for measuring the impact of fixture on the vacuum package and shapes a reliable resistance welding-based vacuum packaging process.

(1) Outgassing of metal shell. Put the gold-plated Kovar alloy shell in the vacuum oven, bake at the high temperature 250°C for over 48 hours, and transfer the packaged shell in a nitrogen atmosphere to the vacuum cavity of the vacuum packaging equipment;

(2) Use the molecular pump to create vacuum to 10^{-3}Pa, observe the degree of vacuum, and conduct the electric resistance welding by the optimized resistance welding parameters;

(3) Release nitrogen to the vacuum cavity and transfer the encapsulated shell out;

(4) Measure the vacuum degree by the quartz crystal oscillator placed in the metal shell in advance.

The metal shell is vacuum packaged in accordance with this method. The experiments demonstrate that the success rate of over 95% can reliably achieve instantaneous vacuum packaging under 10Pa or less pressure. The main process parameters of the resistance welding-based vacuum packaging equipment include primary pressure, secondary pressure, welding voltage and number of turns in the secondary coil and so on. The shell used in the experiment is made of Kovar alloy. The welding experiment results show that the welding quality is good when the primary pressure takes 0.4MPa and the secondary pressure adopts 0.6MPa.

The experimental procedures are detailed as follows. (1) The crystal oscillator is used to directly measure the vacuum level in the cavity of the vacuum packaging equipment and the measured values are compared with those measured by the vacuum gauge. This is actually the calibration of the crystal oscillator. (2) The crystal oscillator is welded on the tube socket, put the tube cap on the tube socket, produce vacuum and measure the degree of vacuum in the shell by the crystal oscillator. (3) Lift up the tube cap (8mm higher than the tube socket) and then measure the vacuum level again. Because after the tube cap is lifted up, the measurement results of the crystal oscillator show a same trend of change with the calibration results and significantly different from the measurement results when the tube cap is covered. The relative impedance values are obviously different. Therefore, the degree of vacuum in the encapsulated shell cannot be simply equivalent to the degree of vacuum in the vacuum cavity. If the pressure is over 0.1Pa for the targets in the vacuum packaging, the impact of fixture on the vacuum packaging may not be considered, but it must be taken in account for a vacuum package under 0.1Pa.

The threshold of the micromachined quartz tuning fork gyroscope is generally smaller than $t0.01^{\circ}/s$. It can be determined by measuring the relationship between the zero voltage output and the angular rate input of the micromachined quartz tuning fork gyroscope. The measurement method is measuring noise after the gyro starts and stably outputs, from the input rate $0.001^{\circ}/s$ and increasing by $0.001^{\circ}/s$ each time. Record the output curve and calculate the mean value. When the noise to signal ratio of the output value reaches 63%, this input angular rate is sensitivity limit that is able to be identified, called the threshold. Figure 6 shows the output curve of the micromechanical quartz tuning fork gyro at the input rate $0.005^{\circ}/s$ for one minute and it can be determined that the threshold of the gyroscope is $0.005^{\circ}/s$. Tuning fork gyroscopes have no dead zone (insensitive zone) as a result of friction or other causes, so that the relationship between the threshold and the output noise is particularly obvious. The main source of the overall stochastic noises is the electrical noise, which is caused by a high-gain operational amplifier. Another source is coupling of the driving movement, which produces noise in the output and this effect can be minimized if the gyro works at the mechanical zero point.

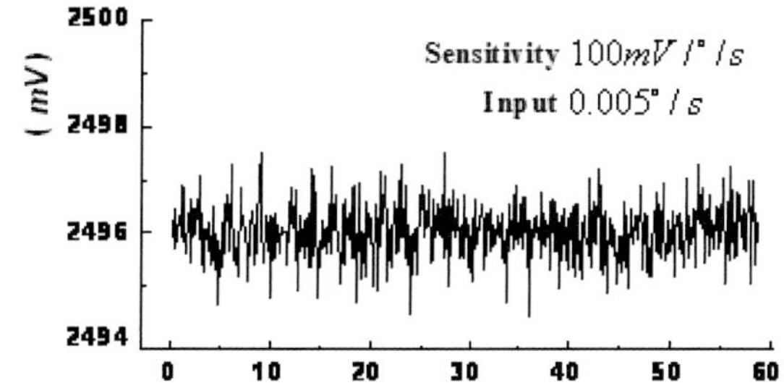

Figure 6. Threshold measurement of micromachined uartz tuning fork gyroscopes.

6. CONCLUSIONS

Through the long-term tracking and measuring of vacuum in the encapsulated cavity, the factors affecting the instability of the vacuum degree mainly are:

(1) leak in fine pores at weld seams; (2) leak at tube legs. Air damping and noise are the key factors impacting on the mechanical properties of micromachined quartz tuning fork gyroscopes. The greater the air damping, the lower the Q-value, and the lower the sensitivity. The quartz tuning fork of the micromachined gyroscope is used as the sensitive element for vacuum measurement. An online vacuum measurement system is designed for the real-time online vacuum measurement and determining the procedures and parameters of the resistance welding-based vacuum packaging process. The vacuum package can improve the comprehensive performance of the micromachined quartz tuning fork gyroscopes, reduce the degree of oxidation of the electrode film and extend their service life.

REFERENCES

— [1] Chen Deyong, Cao Mingwei, Wang Junbo, et al. Fabrication and wafer-level vacuum packaging of MEMS resonant pressure sensor [J]. Optics and Precision Engineering, 2014, 22(5):1235-1242.

— [2] Cao Mingwei, Chen Deyong, and Wang Junbo, et al. Research of a Micromachined Resonant Pressure Sensor Based on SOI Wafer [J]. Chinese Journal of Sensors and Actuators, 2013, 26(6):801-805.

— [3] Wang Chenggang. Investigation of Device Level MEMS Packaging based on Vacuum Resistance Welding Candidate [D]. Huazhong University of Science and Technology, 2013.

— [4] Huang Tianshu, and Chen Ranjing. Design and Research of Quartz Oscillator Frequency Measurement System [J]. China Instrumentation, 2005 (10): 83-115.

— [5] Cheng Yingjun, Zhu Rui, and Xu Wei, et al. Modelling and simulation of vacuum packaging of MEMS devices [J]. Journal of Transducer Technology, 2004, 23(12):86-88.

— [6] Tao Yi. Development of processes for vacuum packaging of microelectromechanical system [J]. University of Arkansas, 2003, 65(2):13-18.

— [7] Bustillo James M, Howe Roger T, Muller Richard S. Surface Micromachining for Micro- electro mechanical Systems [J]. Proceedings of the IEEE, 1998, 86(8): 1552-1573.

— [8] Zhiyin Gan. Study of vacuum packaging of MEMS devices [D]. Huazhong University of Science and Technology, 2008.

— [9] Shi Xiong, Zhu Gungxi, and Gan Zhiyin, et al. Vacuum degree measurement of MEMS vacuum package [J]. Chinese Journal of Scientific Instrument, 2007(28)10: 1906-1910.

— [10] Shen Qiang, Li Xiaoying, and Chang Honglong, et al. An Effective Method for Improving Mechanical Stability of Vacuum Silicon Micro-Gyroscope [J]. Nanotechnology and Precision Engineering, 2012(10)1:14-19.

Experiment and Simulation of Magnetizing Inrush Current Identification in Single-phase Traction Transformer

X.W. Li

Department of Electrical Engineering, Zhengzhou Railway Vocational and Technical College, Zhengzhou, Henan Province, China, 450052, xuewu6981@163.com

P.X. Ji

Network Information & Technical Center, Zhengzhou Railway Vocational and Technical College, Zhengzhou, Henan Province, China, 450052, pxji@sohu.com

ABSTRACT: The microprocessor differential protection is the main protection of single-phase traction transformer in the traction power supply system. The conventional algorithm based on differential protection is often unable to identify the magnetizing inrush current correctly, and causes the malfunction. The artificial neural network with the adaptive ability, based on the experimental data and the field data, can identify the magnetizing inrush current and the short-circuit current. This method is accurate, and has no misjudgment phenomenon.

KEYWORDS: Single-phase traction transformer; Magnetizing inrush current; Artificial neural network.

1. INTRODUCTION

The main protection of single-phase traction transformer adopts the longitudinal current differential protection. The magnetizing inrush current is the main reason of the malfunction [1]. Especially in the treatment on the internal fault of traction transformer, its technical requirements on reliability and fastness cannot be met [2].

The artificial neural network allows to describe the state of power system with multiple inputs completely, but the accuracy of input data is not too high [3]. Using the neural network to form the criterion, its input can fully reflect the characteristics of inrush current. After sufficient training, the neural network can take advantage of its excellent pattern recognition ability to distinguish the magnetizing inrush current and the internal faulty current, and to diagnose the traction transformer fault.

2. SAMPLE DATA ACQUISITION OF ARTIFICIAL NEURAL NETWORK

2.1. *Ideas of sample data acquisition*

The training sample data of neural network include the inrush current sample data and the faulty current sample data. The recording data in industrial field is the most real and convictive. But, when training, the neural network needs hundreds of sample data, it is almost impossible to find a sufficient quantity of inrush current and faulty current sample. There are a lot of digital simulation software for the transformer. The parameters can be adjusted by the digital simulation, its simulation process is controllable and its sample data format specification is normative. But there is a deviation for the data characteristic of the current sample between the digital simulation software and the actual traction transformer. The laboratory simulation test has a certain reality, and can change the model parameters to meet the test needs at the same time. So, giving priority to the sample of laboratory recording wave, and with the sufficient precision digital simulation model as a guiding sample, the neural network training and testing can be carried out in this paper

2.2. *Sample data acquisition of experiment*

In this paper, the single phase traction transformer is used as the research object, and a small test model has been set up in the laboratory. The connection of testing model is shown in Figure 1. A single-phase autotransformer is used as the testing traction transformer. Its nominal capacity is, and the rated voltage is. A AC contactor QK1 is used to simulate the switching circuit breaker, and a fuse FU is also used in the graph. The breaker QK2 is opened when no-load closing. The inter-turn fault can be completed through the breaker QK2 closing. After the short circuit occurring, the fuse melts in 140 ms,

Footnotes: X.W. Li (the abbreviated name of Li Xuewu); P.X. Ji (the abbreviated name of Ji Pengxiao).

and can record the fault waveform extended 6~7 periods.

The test is divided into three parts: the closing test with no-load, the internal fault test, and the test from the no-load closing to the internal fault. After processed, the waveform data recorded take part of the current fundamental value, which exceed than differential setting value, for valid data. The data window length of each sample is fixed for a cycle length (20 ms). The recording wave data on experiment include the three parts: the inrush current data of the traction transformer, the short circuit fault current data, and the current data from the no-load closing to the failure. Through the following measures such as changing the switching time of QK1, the regulating handle position of autotransformer, and the closing time of QK2 etc., the different switching time, short circuit time, and short circuit parameters of on-site transformer are simulated. The sample number of the inrush current data is 2456, the sample number of the fault current data is 1124, and the sample number of the current data from the no-load closing to the failure is 326 altogether. Among them, 2000 of the inrush current data and 1000 of the short circuit fault current data are used as the training samples of neural network, and the rest are used as the testing samples of neural network. All the current data from the no-load closing to the failure is used as the testing samples of neural network. Figure 2 shows the excitation inrush current waveform of the testing transformer when no-load closing and the short circuit current waveform of the testing transformer when the internal short circuit occurring.

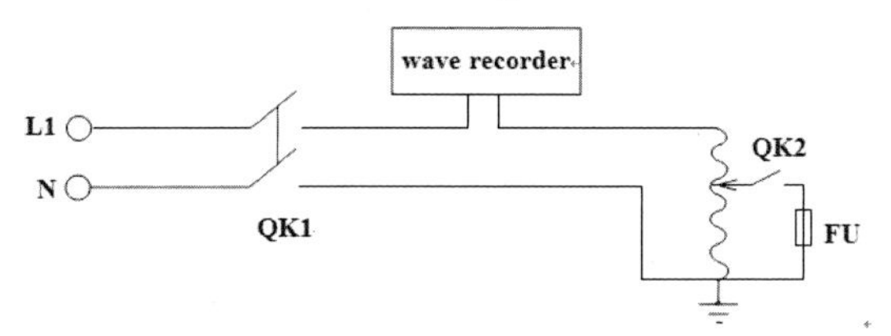

Figure 1. The connection of test model.

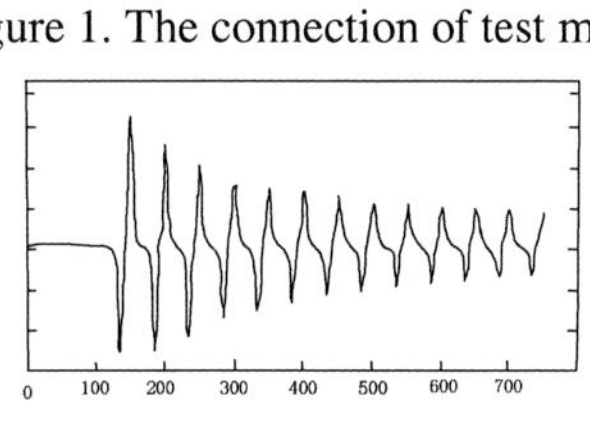

(a) the internal short circuit current waveform of the testing transformer

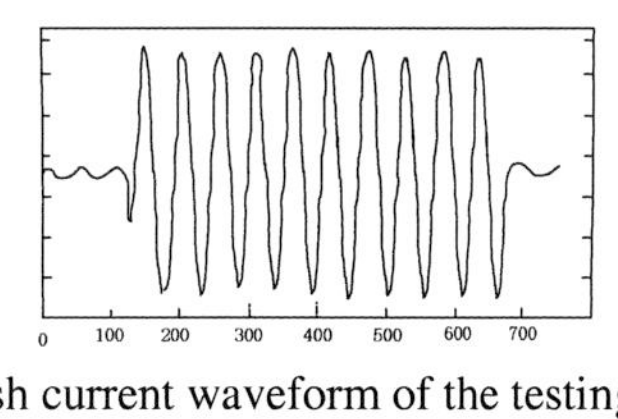

(b) the inrush current waveform of the testing transformer

Figure 2. The current waveform of testing transformer.

2.3. *Sample data acquisition of simulation*

A single-phase traction transformer is simulated by Matlab/Simulink tool kit in this paper [4]. The concrete parameters for the single-phase traction transformer are shown in the following: the capacity is 31.5MVA, the frequency is 50Hz, the voltage of the transformer primary windings is 220KV, the resistance of the transformer primary windings is 0.002p.u., the inductance of the transformer primary windings is 0.08p.u., the voltage of the transformer secondary windings is 27.5KV, the resistance of the transformer secondary windings is 0.002p.u., the inductance of the transformer secondary windings is 0.08p.u.,the excitation resistance is 500p.u. The simulation model is shown in Figure 3.

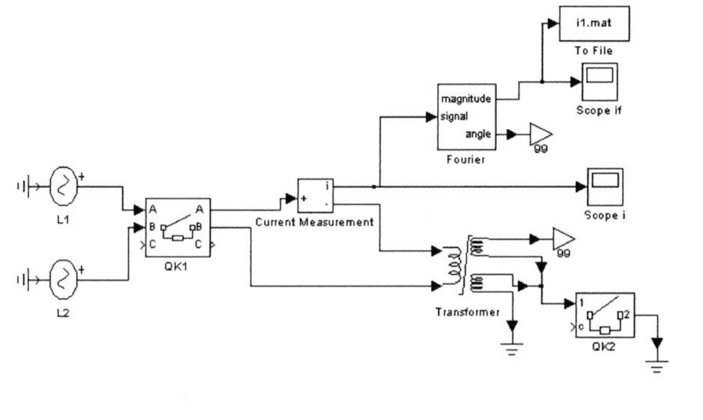

Figure 3.The Matlab simulation model of single-phase traction transformer.

The simulation is also divided into three parts: the no-load closing, the internal fault, from the no-load closing to the internal fault. The excitation inrush current waveform and the short circuit current waveform under different condition can be obtained by changing the different initial angle of alpha (°) of power supply switching and by changing the iron core remanence phi0 (p.u.) of traction transformer. The current waveform can be qualitatively observed through the oscilloscope of simulation model, and the related data can be kept into the corresponding file. The sample number of the inrush current data is 512, the sample number of the fault current data is 324, and the sample number of the current data from the no-load closing to the failure is 120 altogether. Among them, 400 of the inrush current data and 300 of the short circuit fault current data are used as the training samples of neural network, and the rest are used as the testing samples of neural network. All the current data from the no-load closing to the failure is used as the testing samples of neural network.

Figure 4 shows the excitation current waveform and the short-circuit current waveform of digital simulation transformer respectively. It can be seen that the short circuit fault current and the excitation current is an obviously different. The short circuit current is continuous, there is no dead angle, and its waveform is a symmetrical sine wave.

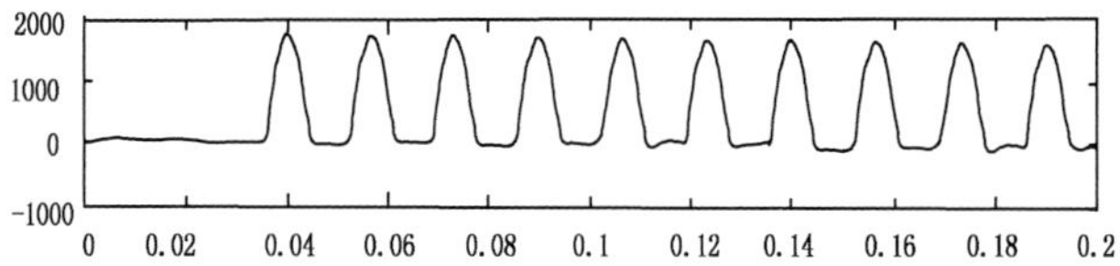

(a) The excitation current waveform of digital simulation

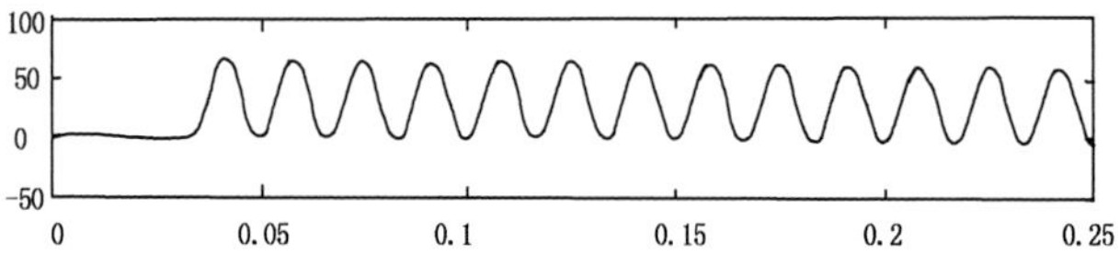

(b) The short-circuit current waveform of digital simulation

Figure 4. The current waveform of digital simulation.

3. ARTIFICIAL NEURAL NETWORK STRUCTURE BASED ON FULL-CYCLE FOURIER ALGORITHM

The fault current and excitation inrush current of traction transformer are identified by applying the three layer BP neural network in this paper. When no-load closing, the traction transformer locks in the differential output, and ensures the differential protection not malfunctioning. When the internal short circuit occurring or when from the no-load closing to the internal fault, the traction transformer opens the differential output, ensures the differential protection not resisting operation, and shortens the action time of differential protection. The neural network contains five input nodes totally. An output node is determined. When the inrush current sample were as the input, the output should be 1. When the fault current sample were as the input, the output should be 0. Generally, the number of hidden layer nodes is determined for over 2 times of the input layer. So, the number of hidden layer nodes is determined for 12 [5].

4. TRAINING TEST AND RESULT ANALYSIS OF ARTIFICIAL NEURAL NETWORK

Testing on the neural network is programmed in MATLAB environment. The excitation inrush current waveform and the internal fault waveform through experiment and simulation are expanded into Fourier series. Among them, the DC component and the harmonic component (from 1 to 5 times) are called the characteristic value, and can be used as the inputs of neural network after the normalization processing. Through training, the network converges quickly. The testing results are shown in Table 1. Testing results show that the excitation inrush current and the short-circuit current can be identified by the artificial neural network accurately.

Table 1. Testing results of the artificial neural network.

		The sample data of experiment	The sample data of simulation
The inrush current test	The sample number	456	112
	The sample output range	0.9997~1	0.9994~1.0024
	The gross error sample number	0	0
The fault test	The sample number	450	144
	The sample output range	-0.0014~0.0012	-0.0011~0.0014
	The gross error sample number	0	0

5. CONCLUSION

The neural network trained sophisticatedly, in the case of no-load closing or internal fault of the traction transformer, can show more superior performance. It is proved that the traction transformer fault is identified by the artificial neural network feasibly. This article adopts the method of digital simulation combined with experiment, giving consideration to both the advantages and the disadvantages of the three methods to obtain the sample data, and is worth promoting. But the testing traction transformer is used as a source of training sample, the capacity of selected traction transformer, the core material, and the winding structure etc. must be fully investigated. The training samples obtained by the testing traction transformer should be in accordance with the traction transformer in most cases. The traction transformer used as a source of training samples by digital simulation, its digital simulation model must have a sufficient accuracy.

REFERENCES

- [1] Ke zhimin, Suo Nan. Relay Protection Foundation [M]. Beijing: Beijing Jiaotong University Press. 2010.
- [2] Yang Xinmin, Yang Junlin. Power System Microcomputer Protection Training Materials (Version 2) [M]. Beijing: China Electric Power Press. 2008.
- [3] Jiang Zongli. Introduction to Artificial Neural Network [M]. Beijing: Higher Education Press. 2008.
- [4] Wu Tianming. MATLAB7 Power System Design and Analysis (Version 3) [M]. Beijing: National Defence Industry Press. 2010.
- [5] Feisi Science and Technology Product Research and Development Center. Neural Network Theory and MATLAB7 Implementation [M]. Beijing: Electronic Industry Press. 2005.

Exploitation of DC Servo Motor Controller

W. Wang* & H. Yu
Nanjing Forestry University, Nanjing, Jiangsu, China
**Email: cynlinwang@163.com*

ABSTRACT: Through the chip YT5188 and Trident 2SA695 setting up a circuit, this article mainly use a DC motor as a control object. A mechanical position sensor is driven by a bridge type circuit (potentiometer), composed of a digital feedback control system, forming the position closed-loop, so as to form a position controller, adjusting the potentiometer resistance to the effect of servo control. Through the method of PWM pulse width modulation, the Angle of the DC motor output can be controlled with a more convenient location.

KEYWORDS: DC motor; Servo; position control.

1. CURRENT RESEARCH AND SIGNIFICANCE

With the emergence of microcomputers, VLSI, new sensors, and the in-depth development of automatic control theory, power electronics technology, computer control, the DC motor control also continues to move forward.[1] DC servo system is a DC motor control system, with a wide range of speed, high output torque, strong overload capacity and large Motor moments of inertia.[2] It is widely used in steel rolling, paper-making machine, metal cutting machine tools and many other areas of automatic control system, it can achieve accuracy, speed and position control in a wide range. So it is widely used in demanding systems.

In recent years, position servo system developed on digital signal processing has become a hot research. Meanwhile, many chip manufacturers have also developed a number of special motor control chips and int the chips, simplifying the connection with power electronics power conversion device. It also has a powerful processing function which can complete some complex algorithm in modern control theory and intelligent control theory. The development period will be shorter and the hardware structure will be more simplified if using these control chips to complete the system. So in this paper the position servo control will be mainly controlled through a DC motor and a digital chip.

2. SERVO POSITION CONTROL

Position servo has been widely used in many high technology fields with the great progress of science and technology. Figure 1 introduces the function of servo position control briefly.

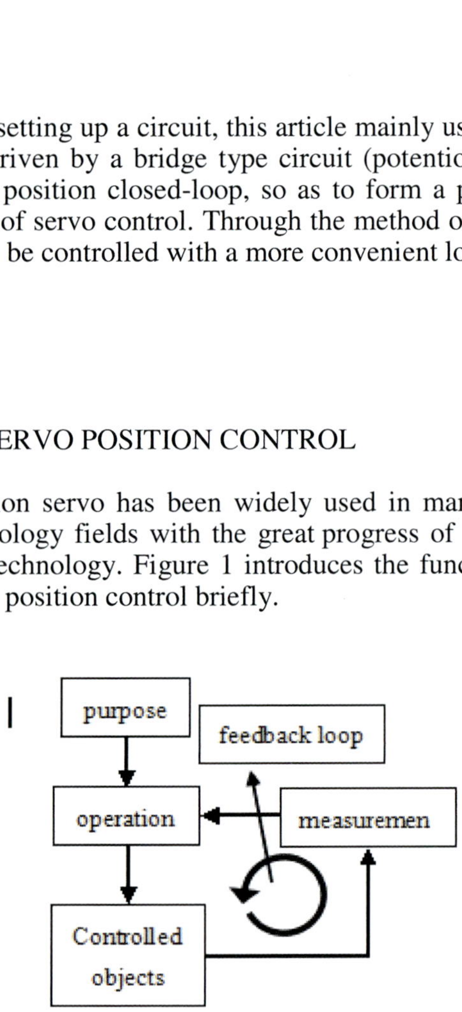

Figure 1. The function of servo position control briefly.

According to the structural characteristics of the system, it can be roughly divided into four basic structure forms. They are divided into open loop servo system (no position feedback), semi closed loop servo system (with position detection and anti control), full closed-loop position servo control (theoretically ideal) and mixed loop control system (with semi closed loop and the closed-loop at the same time).

3. HARDWARE DESIGN

The chip controlled by semiconductor integrated circuit can be applied to adjust the speed of the DC motor, as well as the additional use of transistors, bridge circuit and so on, which form the position control.

According to the function and characteristic of the integrated circuit chip YT5188 and a trident 2SA695, the preliminary design of the circuit shown in Figure 1.

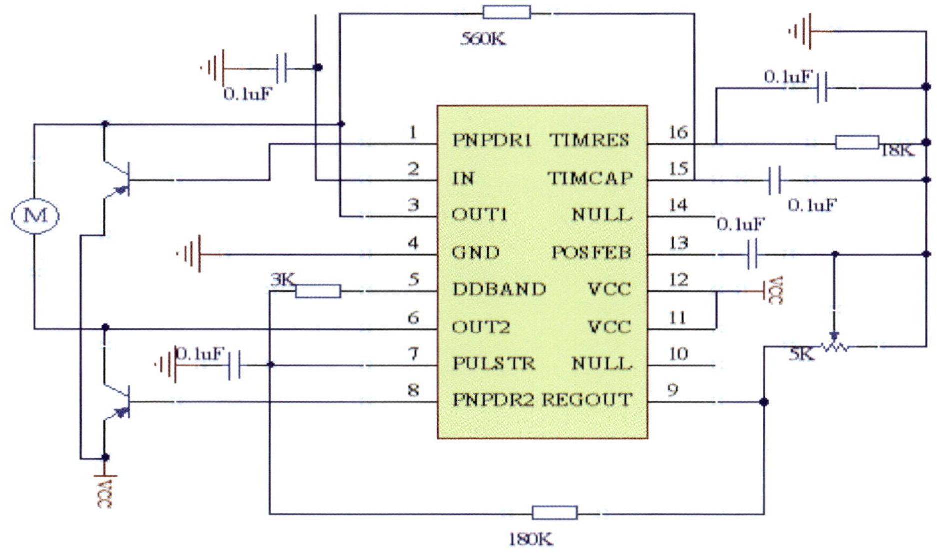

Figure 2. Hardware design.

Circuit Function Description:

YT5188 and peripheral PNP transistor can be composed of a DC pulse width modulation circuit. When inputting a signal at PIN2 (IN), the corresponding bridge circuit can output a positive-negative reversible voltage. When the input pulse width increases (decreases), one side of the bridge circuit (or the other side) starts conducting, the conduction time is proportional to the difference between input pulse width and zero. PIN11 can be adjusted to restore zero if the output is not zero. With this feature, the position closed-loop is formed by using the bridge circuit to drive a mechanical position sensor (potentiometer), so as to form a position controller.

4. THE PWM SIGNAL

PWM is the abbreviation of pulse width modulation, pulse width modulation PWM is a term in type switch regulated power supply. It is classified by the control of regulator, include PWM, PFM and PWM, PFM hybrid. PWM switching regulator circuit is adjusting the duty cycle through the voltage feedback in the case of controlling the circuit output frequency constant, so as to achieve the purpose of stabilizing the output voltage.

Programming the PWM signal of motor rotation into the microcontroller, and checking whether it meets the requirements with oscilloscope. The waveform is shown in figure 3.

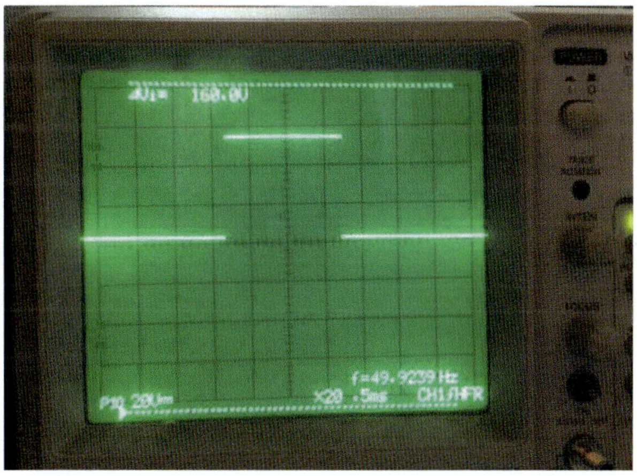

Figure 3. Waveform.

5. DEBUG

After the given PWM signal is input, the rotation of the motor varies along with the change of potentiometer resistance. Table 1 to make a brief description.

Table 1. Motor rotation situation.

Motor situation	Potentiometer resistance (KΩ)	Motor resistance at both ends (KΩ)
Forward	3.29	3.38
Stop	2.65	1.67
Reversion	1.39	-1.89

In the debugging process, the PPM protocol is used to observed the changes of the potentiometer resistance and the voltage across the motor when it is stopped, by changing the duty cycle of the waveform (signal shown as figure 4 and 5).

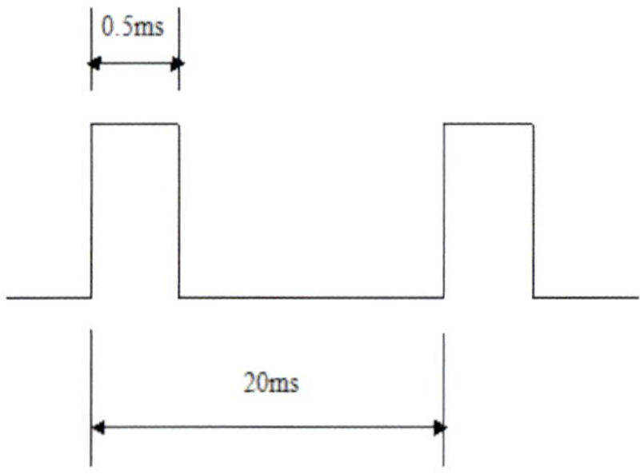

Figure 4. Min DC 2.5%.

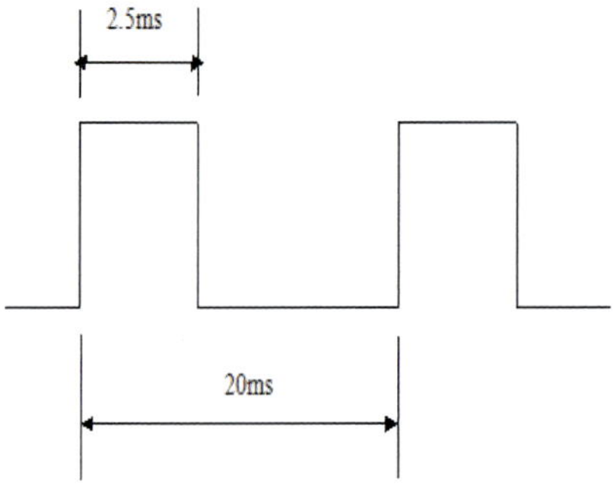

Figure 5. Max DC 12.5%.

By a given program, the PWM signal is adjusted to change the duty cycle between 2.5% and 12.5%. Meanwhile, changing the potentiometer resistance until the motor is stopped, and comparing the variations.

Table 2. Experimental data.

Motor situation	PPM duty cycle (%)	Potentiometer resistance (KΩ))	Voltage across the motor (V)
Stop	0	2.23	1.26
Stop	10	2.49	1.39
Stop	20	2.65	1.67
Stop	40	2.82	1.81
Stop	80	3.29	1.96
Stop	100	3.43	2.01

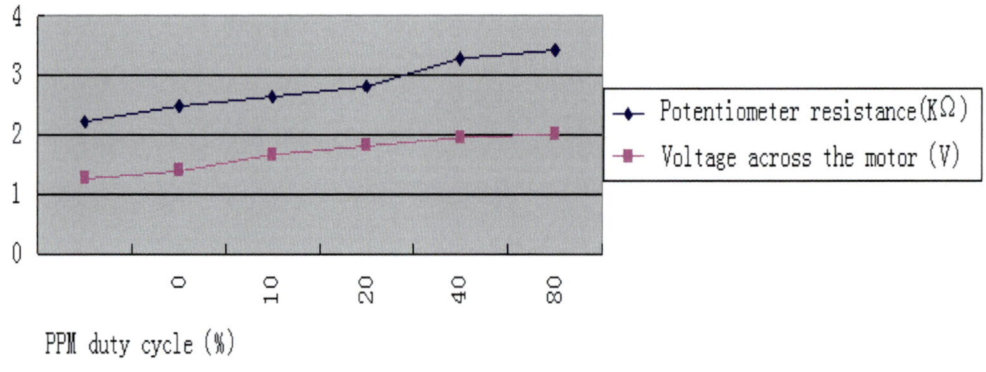

Figure 6. Line graph.

It can be seen from the line graph clearly that the fluctuation of the polyline is not great. Due to the sensitivity of the motor and some other objective reasons, there are some errors in the data, but the conclusion is still within a reasonable range. So the scheme designed in this paper has certain feasibility.

6. CONCLUSION

Through continuous improvement and debugging, the general structure of DC motor position servo controller has mainly completed. The DC motor can be expected to turn up in accordance with the idea of this article. Along with the changes of the potentiometer resistance the motor can be forward, reverse, or stop, reaching the position servo control effect and drive the PWM signal, the DC motor can be expected to turn up in accordance with the idea of this article, along with changes in the resistance of the potentiometer the motor can Story, reverse, stop, reaching the target of position servo control.

REFERENCES

- [1] Y.X. Jiang, The design of the remote PWM DC motor speed control using STC12C5404AD (in Chinese), Journal of Jjiangsu Teachers University of Technology (Natural Science Edition), 3(2009), 36-40.
- [2] S. Xie, Design DC motor servo control system (in Chinese), Science & technology information, 3(2010), 2.
- [3] J.G. Li and P.Y. Xu, The design of low-cost DC servo motor speed control system (in Chinese), Micro motor, 7(2008), 60-61.
- [4] X.M. Wang and W. Gao, SCM research on DC servo motor control (in Chinese), Science Technology and Engineering, 14(2007), 3588-3590.
- [5] X.Z. Xu and Digital Control System of High Precision DC servo motor (in Chinese), Engineering Journal of Wuhan University, 2(2006), 59-62.
- [6] J. Zheng and S.F. Qu, Design of small servo brushless DC motor driver (in Chinese), Electronic measurement technology, 3(2006), 130-132.
- [7] C.Y. Tuo, Design and development of DC motor PWM speed regulation system based on SCM (in Chinese), Coal technology, 6(2011), 62-63.
- [8] R. Xiao and S.G. Hao, Design of a DC motor position servo system using a digital controller MC9S12 (in Chinese), Embedded technology, 9(2007), 25-27.
- [9] J.W. Cheng and X.X. Yao, Control of Electric Actuator Using Brushless DC Motors and Its Performance Evaluation, Intelligent Computation Technology and Automation, 2009. ICICTA '09. Second International Conference on, 3(2009), 38-41.
- [10] J. Y. Hung, R. M. Nelms, and P. B. Stevenson, “An output feedback sliding mode speed regulator for dc drives,” IEEE Tran, 30(1994), 691-698.

PSO-BP Neural Network for State-of-charge Estimation in a New Lithium Battery

H.Z. Chen, X.D. Wang, *Y.P. Cong & B. Yin
Department of Computer Science and Technology, Ocean University of China, Qingdao, China
**Email: congyp@ouc.edu.cn*

ABSTRACT: In order to overcome the weakness of BP algorithm, a new type of lithium battery SOC estimation method which is based on particle swarm optimization and the BP neural network is proposed. This method uses network training error as particle swarm optimization's fitness value and then iteration to find the optimal individual as the network initialization thresholds and weights. The average error of the SOC estimation is 1% when compared with the real SOC obtained from a discharge test. This show higher accuracy compared with BP neural network.

KEYWORDS: State of charge; Particle swarm optimization; BP neural networks.

1. INTRODUCTION

Battery's state of charge (SOC) is one of the important parameters of characterization of the status of the battery; its measurement easily affected by many factors such as temperature and aging, and has strong nonlinear [1].

Traditional SOC estimation methods mainly include open circuit voltage method, ampere-hour method, impedance method, but in recent years, there appeared some new methods such as neural network, Kalman filtering method, and so on. Among them, the open circuit voltage method can more accurately reflect the battery SOC, but must stand of the battery after long enough [2, 3]. Ampere-hour method use the integral current to estimation battery SOC, it had many advantages, such as simple algorithm, high precision, but due to open loop estimation, it also lead to a measurement error accumulation for a long time or when the current volatile estimation precision is not high [4,5]. Internal resistance method is rarely used in the actual SOC estimation with the measuring unit price is high and the large size factors. Kalman filtering method uses a linear mean square criterion, it take the SOC as an internal state variables of battery management system, then combine the estimates of the moment with the real-time measurement of value, and estimate SOC by using the method of recursive in real-time [6,7]. Neural network has nonlinear characteristics, and at the same time have a strong ability of learn, adapt, as long as can quickly make the corresponding output responses when it has a little some external stimulation, this method is adapted to all kinds of battery SOC prediction [8].

Previously, we have studied the use of BP neural network and GA-BP neural network to predict the battery SOC, have achieved good results [9]. Considering that PSO optimization algorithm has significant effect in improving the BP neural network, we have studied the PSO-BP to predict SOC.

2. RELATED WORKS ABOUT PSO-BP

Neural network BP is the most widely used, it is a three-layer feedforward network, each layer node use the output of the previous layer as input, the input layer is provided by external signal, the signal input of each node corresponds to the value of a right, structure as shown in figure 1.

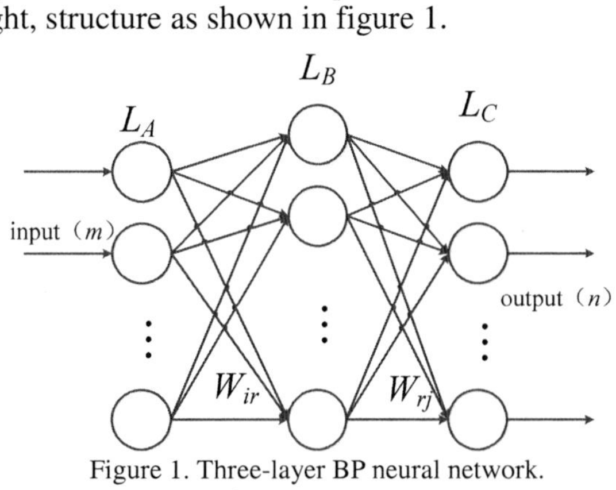

Figure 1. Three-layer BP neural network.

However, the BP neural network itself has some defects [10]: the selection of the structure of the network connection parameters lack of rigorous theoretical basis of design program, optimization process could fall into local minima, difficult to control the speed of convergence.

Particle swarm optimization is a new evolutionary algorithm developed in recent years, which invented by Dir. Eberhart and Dir. Kennedy [11]. PSO algorithm provides efficient solutions to specific problems as a global optimization algorithm, and shows great superiority in solving practical problems. Using PSO algorithm to optimize the structure of neural network has the advantage that it can automatically design neural network weights and thresholds, and the process does not require human interference, which has a lot of research work. Carvalho and Ludermir used PSO algorithm and two improved particle swarm optimization algorithm for BP neural network training, the conclusions show that the PSO algorithm enhance the generalization ability of neural network [12]. Hippert used particle swarm algorithm with inertia weight to train the neural network, the experiment showed that the particle swarm optimization algorithm is the fastest and easiest way to train the neural network [13].

In this paper, the PSO algorithm is applied to the optimization of the weights of BP neural network, through the establishment of the mathematical model of PSO and BP to forecast lithium battery SOC. The experiments show that PSO-BP has a more ideal result compare to the optimized BP neural network model and GA-BP model we did.

3. SOC PREDICTION METHOD BASED ON PSO-BP NRURAL NETWORK

3.1. *Design of neural network structure model*

According to Kolmogorov theorem, three-layer neural networks can approximation a continuous function with arbitrary precision [14], so use the three, so use the three layers BP neural network to predict the battery SOC, as shown in Figure 2.

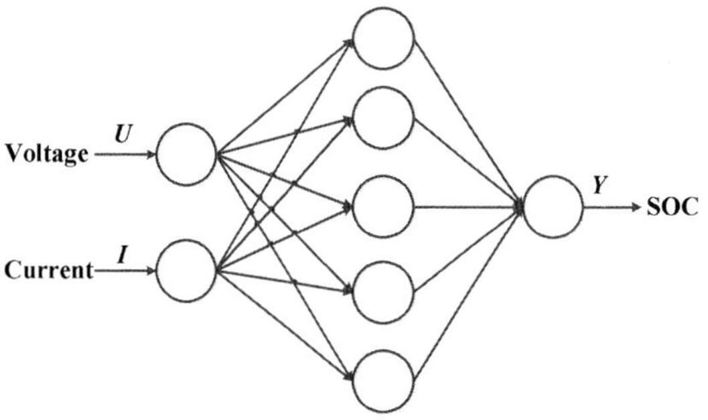

Figure 2. BP neural network SOC prediction model.

Using the network structure model, a total of 15 weights, 6 threshold settings, setting vector dimension of the particle swarm algorithm to 21, each vector corresponding to show a neural network whose weight value and threshold value have been determined.

The individual fitness function is as follows:

$$F = k(\sum_{i=1}^{n} abs(y_i - o_i)) \tag{1}$$

In the formula, n is the number of nodes from network output; y_i is the desired output from the node i of the BP neural network; o_i is the predicted output from the node I; k k is the coefficient.

3.2. *Design of network algorithm based on PSO optimization*

3.2.1. *Algorithmic process*

The process of optimizing BP neural network based on particle swarm optimization algorithm is divided into 3 parts, determining the structure of BP neural network, optimizing particle swarm optimization and forecasting BP neural network.

Assured parts of BP neural network's structure determined the structure of BP neural network according to the number of fitting function's input and output parameters, and then determine the dimension of particles from particle swarm optimization. Particle swarm optimization algorithm is used to the optimize weight value and threshold value of BP neural network, each dimension of vector represents the values of the weights or thresholds, to calculate the fitness value through the individual fitness function, Particle swarm optimization algorithm to find the optimal solution is obtained by iteration. BP neural network prediction obtains the optimal individual using particle swarm optimization algorithm to give the initial weights and thresholds of neural network assignment. The network after training can predict the output of function. As shown in figure 3:

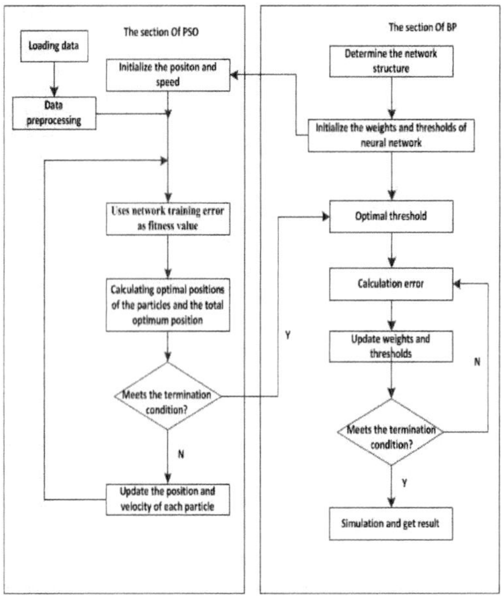

Figure 3. Flow chart of PSO-BP neural network.

3.2.2. *Algorithm description*

Implementation of particle swarm algorithm in part as follows:

Step 1. Matrix and initialize the particle velocity and optimal position of each particle and other variables and parameters:

$$V = [v_1 \cdots v_N]$$

$$P = [p_1 \cdots p_N]$$

Step 2. Update the velocity of particles according to the inertia weight method

$$V(t+1) = (0.9 - \frac{t}{2T_{max}}) V(t) + c_1 r_1 (P(t) - X(t)) + c_2 r_2 (p_g(t) - x_{id}(t)) \quad (2)$$

Step 3. Update the speed according to the particle velocity limit. Order

$$r(x) = \begin{cases} v_{max} & x > v_{max} \\ -v_{max} & x < -v_{max} \\ x & |x| \le v_{max} \end{cases} \quad (3)$$

Then

$$V(t+1) = r(V(t+1)) \quad (4)$$

Step 4. Update the position of each particle

$$X(t+1) = X(t) + V(t+1) \quad (5)$$

Step 5. Update the optimal position of each particle and the total optimal position according to the fitness function F

$$p_i(t+1) = \begin{cases} p_i(t) & f(p_i(t)) \le f(x_i(t+1)) \\ x_i(t+1) & f(p_i(t)) > f(x_i(t+1)) \end{cases} \quad (6)$$

$$p_g(t+1) = p_i(t+1) \quad f(p_i(t+1)) = \min f(P(t+1)) \quad (7)$$

Among them $f(x_1) = F$, $f(p_1) = F$;

Step 6. Check whether it reached the maximum number of iterations. If have reached the maximum number of iterations, then output the total optimal position and the best fitness, otherwise go to Step 2.

4. SIMULATIONS

4.1. *Select the test data*

This article selects the lithium ion battery data from a new soft carbon cathode material of lithium ion battery, which characteristics on the charging and discharging present a relatively strong nonlinear and is similar to the conventional. All experimental data are from the measured data provided by the battery manufacturer. The charge-discharge curves of samples are as follows:

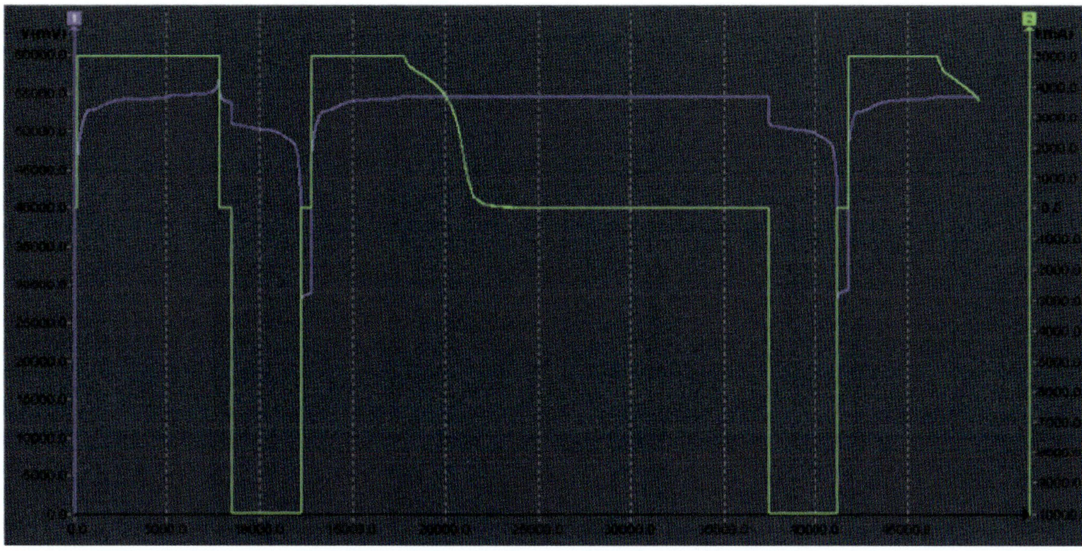

Figure 4. Battery charging and discharging curve.

Then we use the difference method for data processing to meet the shortage of samples. After the charging and discharging process data as shown below:

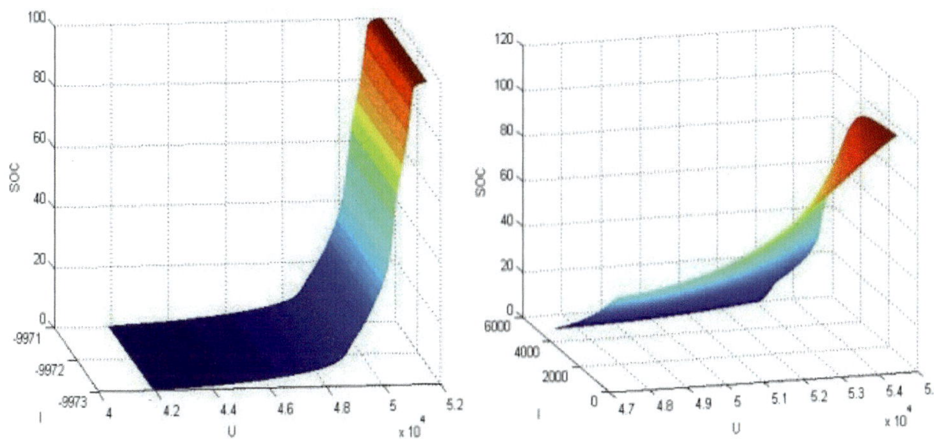

Figure 5. Experimental data.

During the experiment, we randomly selected 1038 groups as experimental data, 100 groups as test data. Then build a BP neural network model for training. And use the trained BP neural network to predict the function output.

4.2. *Optimization of simulation results with PSO-BP*

Load and carried on normalized processing to the experiment data, randomly selected 1038 groups as experimental data, 100 groups as test data. Then build a network model for training based on the set of network structure. Set for PSO algorithm dimension 21 based on the network structure 2-5-1. Initialize related value of the particle swarm algorithm, set maxgen=20, sizepop=20, c1=2, c2=2. Particle swarm optimization process, the best individual fitness value changes as shown below.

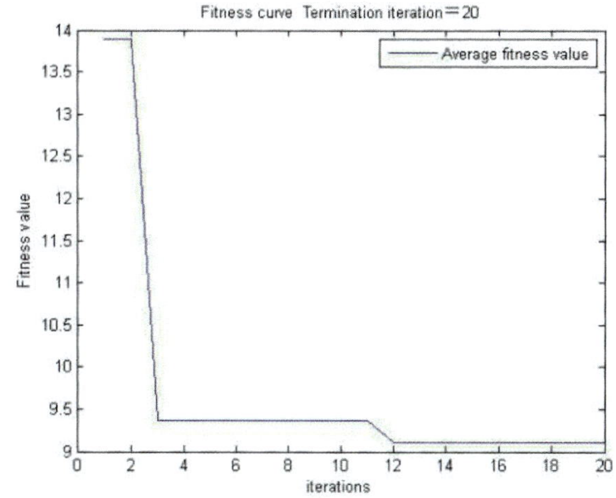

Figure 6. PSO fitness curve.

Particle swarm optimization of BP neural network to obtain the optimal initial weights and thresholds listed in the following table.

Table 1. The optimal initial weights and thresholds of BP neural network.

The weights between input layer and hidden layer	The threshold of hidden layer node	The threshold between hidden layer and output layer	The threshold of output layer node
-1.1711	2.9826	2.5699	-0.2623
-1.8513	3.3897	0.4768	—
-1.9190	3.3041	3.1258	—
2.2083	0.2471	0.6388	—
-2.7817	-3.8059	0.3571	—
3.8427	—	—	—
-0.8758	—	—	—
-0.8023	—	—	—
2.8911	—	—	—
2.4612	—	—	—

Assign the optimal initial weight and the threshold value to the neural network. The trained network optimized by particle swarm optimization is denoted as PSO-BP neural network. The prediction result is shown in Fig. 7. And errors of prediction are like Fig. 8.

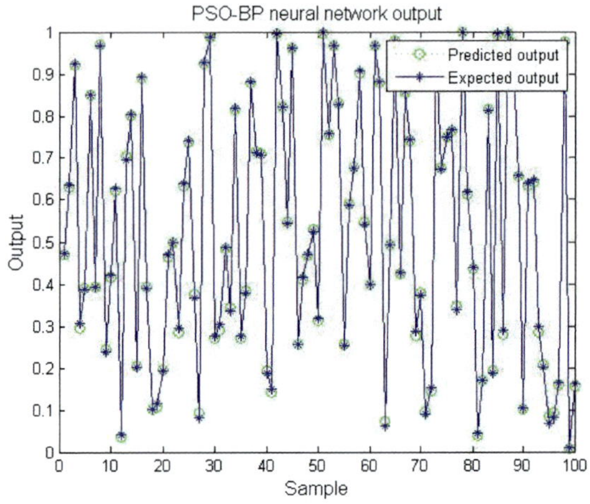

Figure 7. PSO-BP network predicting output.

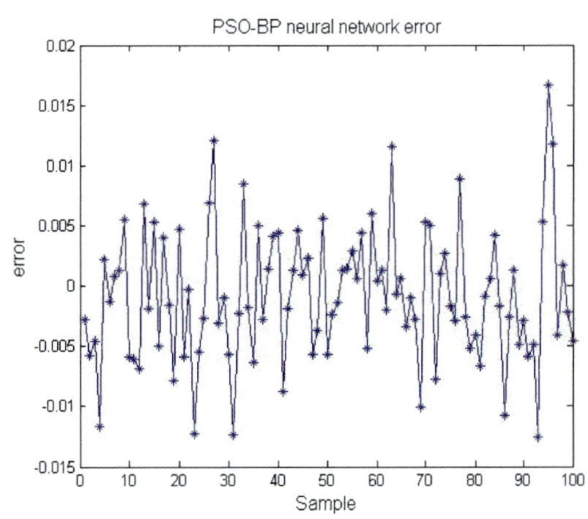

Figure 8. PSO-BP network predicting error.

The prediction result of the output with the trained BP neural network using the test data is shown in Fig. 9. And errors of prediction output and expected output are like Fig. 10 [9].

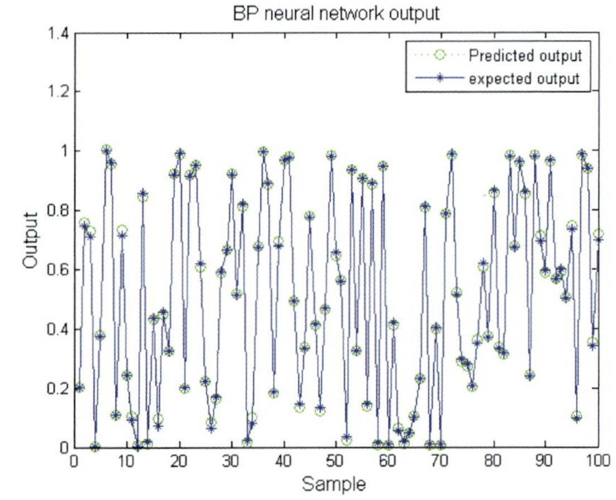

Figure 9. BP neural network predicting output.

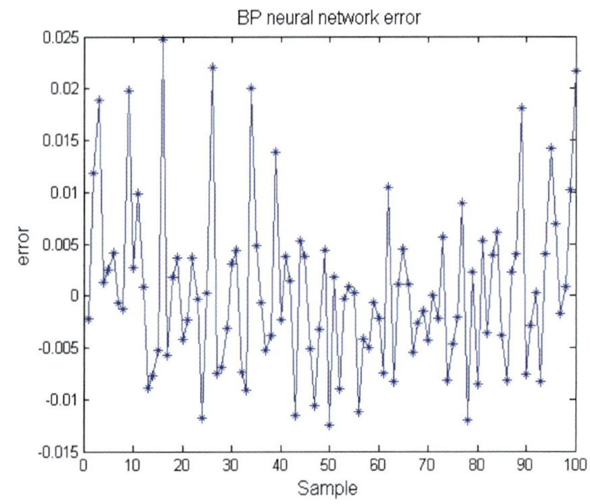

Figure 10. BP neural network predicting error.

The trained network optimized by genetic algorithm is denoted as GA-BP neural network [9]. The prediction result is shown in Fig. 11. And errors of prediction are like Fig. 12.

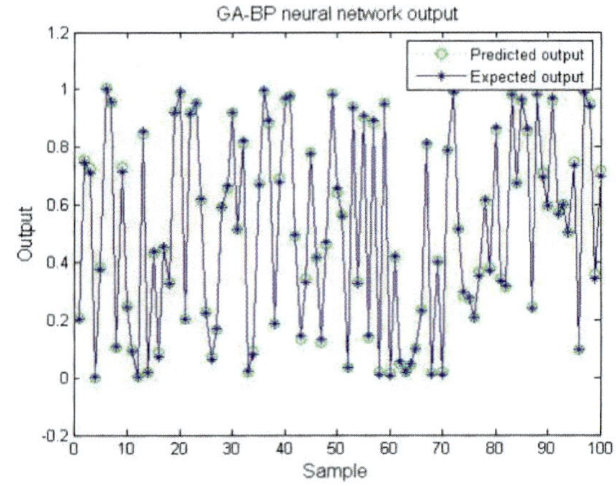

Figure 11. GA-BP network predicting output.

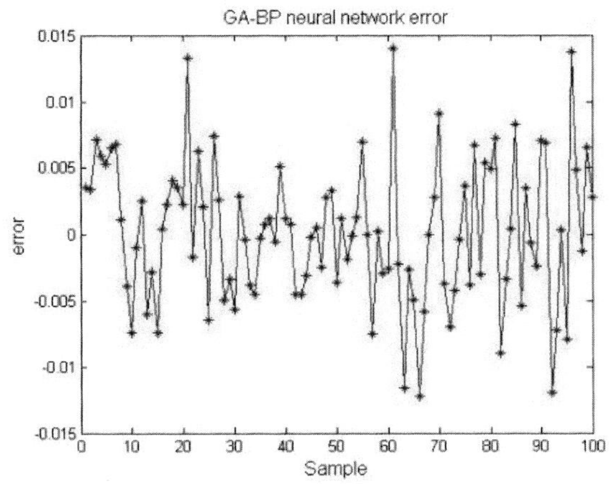

Figure 12. GA-BP network predicting error.

It is easy to see from Figs. 7 and 8 that all of the SOC estimation errors are not more than 1.7%. The average error is 1%.

4.3. *Analysis and comparison*

In addition to using BP network prediction SOC, we also studied the integration of GA-BP network prediction. The estimation results are shown in Table 2.

Table 2.The predicted value of PSO-BP network compare with the BP network and GA-BP network.

	maximum error	average error
BP	6%	2%
GA-BP	2.5%	1.2%
PSO-BP	1.7%	<1%

Comparison of three methods can be seen that in either the maximum or the mean error of PSO-BP network is dominant. Moreover, the time required for PSO network also faster than the BP network. It can be seen that the PSO-BP neural network has higher precision and faster convergence.

5. CONCLUSIONS

This paper establishes a SOC prediction model which is based on hybrid particle swarm optimization and BP neural network to predict lithium battery SOC. Experimental results show that SOC prediction method based on PSO-BP neural network is feasible. For selected samples, the maximum error of the improved algorithms decreases from 6% to 1.7% compared with the BP neural network prediction method. And the average error is reduced from 2% to 1%. The GSO-BP neural network prediction method has higher accuracy and stability. The prediction precision can meet the practical requirement and is of important practical value.

ACKNOWLEDGEMENT

This work was financially supported by national 863 plan project (2014AA052303-5), Qingdao strategic industry development project (13-4-1-15-HY) and Shandong province science and technology project (2013GHY11519).

REFERENCES

- [1] Manoj Kumar P. 2010. Kolar A K. Effect of cathode design on the performance of an air-breathing PEM fuel cell. *International Journal of Hydrogen Energy* 35(2): 671-681.
- [2] F Huet. 1998. A review of impedance measurements for determination of the state-of-charge or state of health of secondary batteries. *Journal of Power Sources* 70:59-69.
- [3] S Rodrigues, N Munichandraiah. A K Shukla. 2000. A review of state-of-charge indication of batteries by means of AC impedance measurements. *Journal of Power Sources* 87:12-20.
- [4] S Piller, M Perrin. A Jossen. 2001. Methods for state-of-charge determination and their applications. *Journal of Power Sources* 96:113-120.
- [5] J H Aylor, A Thieme, B W Johnson. 1992. A battery state-of-charge indicator for electric wheelchairs. *IEEE Transaction on Industrial Electron* 39(5):398-409.
- [6] G Plett. 2004. Extended Kalman filtering for battery management systems of LiPB-based HEV battery packs: Part 1. Background. *Journal of Power Sources* 134: 252-261.
- [7] G Plett. 2004. Extended Kalman filtering for battery management systems of LiPB-based HEV battery packs: Part 2. Modeling and identification. *Journal of Power Sources* 134:262-276.
- [8] Y. Shen 2010. Adaptive online state-of-charge determination based on neuro-controller and neural network. *Energy Conversion and Management* 51:1093-1098.
- [9] Guan K, Wei Z, Yin B. 2015. SOC Prediction Method of a New Lithium Battery Based on GA-BP Neural Network. *Proceedings of the 4th International Conference on Computer Engineering and Networks*: 141-153. Springer International Publishing.
- [10] Youkun Li. 2012. Analysis and improvement applications of BP neural network Huainan. *Anhui University of Science and Technology.*
- [11] Pu Shi, Chunguang Bu, Yiwen Zhao. 2005. The ANN models for SOC/BRC estimation of Li-ion battery. *Information Acquisition, 2005 IEEE International Conference on. IEEE*: 560-564.
- [12] Carvalho M. Ludermir T B. 2006. An Analysis of PSO Hybrid Alrorithm for Feed-Forward Nerual Nerworks Training. *Sixth International conference on hybrid intelligent systems*: 2-5.

— [13] Hippert H S, Pedreira C E, Souza R C. 2001. Neural networks for short-term load forecasting: a review and evaluation. *IEEE Transactions on Power Systems, November* 1(16): 44-45.
— [14] Kennedy J, Eberhart R C. 1995. Particle swarm optimization. *Proc IEEE int conf on neural networks Vol. IEEE service center, Piscataway, NJ*: 1942-1948.

Chapter 6
Software Engineering

A Method of Modelling Software Evolution Confirmation Based on LDA

J.M. Han
College of Software, Yunnan University, Kunming 650091, China, ynwshjm@126.com

W. Wang
Key Laboratory for Software Engineering of Yunnan Province, Kunming 650091, China, wangwei@ynu.edu.cn

Y. He
College of Software, Yunnan University, Kunming 650091, China, Arthus_he@hotmail.com

ABSTRACT: This paper research a method that can confirm the software evolution based on Latent Dirichlet Allocation (LDA). LDA is a method that can analyze the interdependency among words, topics and documents, and the interdependency can be expressed as probability. In this paper, adoption of LDA to modeling software evolution, take the package in source code as a document, regard names of function (method), variable names and comments as words, and figure out the probability between the three. Take results compare with update reports, can confirm the software of new version consistent with update reports.

KEYWORDS: LDA; Software evolution; Confirm; Probability.

1. INTRODUCTION

Nowadays, software became an indispensable part in our human society. However, in order to satisfy human changing requirements, software has to evolve. The evolved software satisfies the user's requirements or not, it needs a model to confirmation. LDA is a topic model that can confirm the software evolution. LDA was first presented as a graphical model for topic discovery by David Blei, Andrew Ng, and Michael Jordan in 2003.

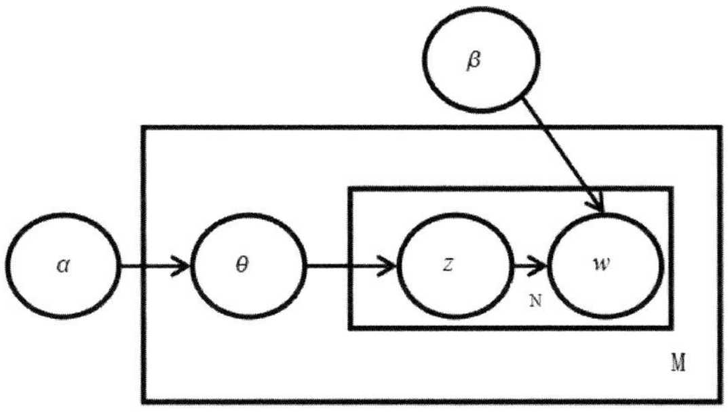

Figure 1. LDA Graphical model.

This graphical model represents a model of probability, and can be expressed as Eq. 1.

$$P(\theta, z, w|\alpha, \beta) = P(\theta|\alpha)\prod_{n=1}^{N} P(z_n|\theta)P(w_n|z_n, \beta) \qquad (1)$$

Latent Dirichlet Allocation (LDA) [1] is a document topic generation model, it has three layers structure including document, topic and word. Meanwhile, LDA is a kind of unsupervised machine learning techniques, it can recognizes the topics in the documents or corpus. In LDA, each document may be viewed as a mixture of various topics, and use bag of words that regards each document as a word frequency vector and regardless the sequence of words, so change the text information to the easily model numerical information.

LDA use Gibbs sampling [2] can get words from document collection or corpus. When direct sampling is difficult(Joint probability distribution is not available or difficult to obtain sampling directly, but the each variable's conditional known or easily), Gibbs sampling is a Markov chain Monte Carlo [3] method that can receive some observed number which are approximated from a specified multivariate probability distribution. Markov chain is a set of events, in this set, each event take place one by one, the next event occurrences only decided by contemporary events.

The structure of this paper organized as follows. Section 2, introduces the details of the LDA and Gibbs sampling. Section 3, describes the experimental data and how to obtaining the data. Section 4, shows the experiment and results. Finally, section 5, gives a conclusion.

2. THE LDA AND GIBBS SAMPLING

2.1. *The processing of LDA*

In LDA, have three layers structure including document, topic and word, or can redefines three layers Bayes Model.

LDA defines a generative process for each document [4]:

(1) For each document, from the distribution of topics extract a topic;

(2) Extract a word from the word distribution of the extracted topic;

(3) Repeat step (1) and (2), until traversing all words in the document.

There are some symbols' arrangements when LDA applies to topic modeling in document collection:

(1) Word is elementary cell is text information, using {***1, 2, …, V***} presents subitem of the index words. Using a N-dimensional vector $\boldsymbol{w}$ presents article n a word in vocabulary, and for any $u \neq v, w_v = 1$, $w_u = 0$;

(2) Document is a sequence of N words, present as $\boldsymbol{d} = \{w_1, w_2, \ldots, w_n\}$, w_n is the article n a word in the sequence.

(3) Document collection includes M documents, present as $\boldsymbol{D} = \{d_1, d_2, \ldots, d_n\}$.

Assume have $\boldsymbol{k}$ topics, the probability of $\boldsymbol{i}$ a word w_i in document $\boldsymbol{d}$ can present as follow formula:

$$P(w_i) = \sum_{j=1}^{T} P(w_i | z_i = j) P(z_i = j) \tag{2}$$

In the Eq. 2, z_i presents the word $\boldsymbol{i}$ named w_i come from this topic, and it is a latent variable. $P(w_i|z_i=j)$ presents the probability that word w_i belongs to topic $\boldsymbol{j}$. $P(z_i=j)$ presents the probability that probability belongs to document $\boldsymbol{d}$.

The topic j can present as $\boldsymbol{V}$ words' multinomial distribution $\phi_{w_i}^{j} = P(w_i | z_i = j)$, text representation into $\boldsymbol{K}$ implicit stochastic mixed on the theme $\theta_j^d = P(z_i = j)$, so the probability of word w "exists in" document $\boldsymbol{d}$ is:

$$P(w|d) = \sum_{j}^{T} \varphi_w^j \bullet \theta_j^d \tag{3}$$

By using EM (Expectation Maximization Algorithm) will get the maximum likelihood function:

$$l(\alpha, \beta) = \sum_{i=1}^{T} \log p(d_i | \alpha, \beta) \tag{4}$$

The number of topics will have an affect on adoption of LDA model the whole document. Meanwhile the LDA model has two critical parameters $\boldsymbol{\alpha}$ and $\boldsymbol{\beta}$. In the Eq. 4, can estimate the maximum likelihood estimators $\boldsymbol{\alpha}$ and $\boldsymbol{\beta}$, so the LDA model can be confirmed. The conditional probability distribution of document $\boldsymbol{d}$ "exists in" is:

$$P(d|\alpha, \beta) = \frac{\Gamma\left(\sum_i \alpha_i\right)}{\prod_i \Gamma(\alpha_i)} \int \left(\prod_{i=1}^{k} \theta_i^{\alpha_i - 1}\right) \left(\sum_{n=1}^{N} \sum_{i=1}^{k} \prod_{j=1}^{V} (\theta_i \beta_{ij})^{w_n^j}\right) d\theta \tag{5}$$

2.2. *MCMC method and Gibbs sampling*

The basic idea of Markov chain Monte Carlo (MCMC) [5] method is create a Markov chain, make the stationary distribution be the posterior distribution of parameters. Through the Markov chain will create samples of posterior distribution, then take Monte Carlo integration based on the samples which in the stable Markov chain. Assume in a sample space, $\boldsymbol{n}$ represents the total of whole sample space, $\boldsymbol{m}$ represents the number of samples which in the stable Markov chain, the MCMC method can summarized as follow steps:

(1) Create a Markov chain, make it converges to a stable distribution $\boldsymbol{\pi(x)}$;

(2) Create samples: from a point in the chain starts, take simulated sampling from the chain in step(1), createa series of points, like: $\boldsymbol{x}^{(1)}, \boldsymbol{x}^{(2)}, \ldots, \boldsymbol{x}^{(n)}$.

(3) Monte Carlo integration: the estimation of expectation of a functions $\boldsymbol{f(x)}$ is:

$$E[f(x)] = \frac{1}{n - m} \sum_{t=m+1}^{n} f(x)^t$$

Gibbs sampling is a procedure of algorithm that iterativemultivariate distribution then generate the samples of approximately obey one distribution. Gibbs sampling is a simple and practical MCMC method, the basic ideas as follow steps [6]:

Give an initial vector $\boldsymbol{x_{(0)} = (x_1^{(0)}, x_2^{(0)}, \ldots, x_n^{(0)})}$;

Extract a sample $\boldsymbol{x_1^{(1)}}$ ***from*** $\boldsymbol{\pi(x_1/x_2^{(0)}, \ldots, x_k^{(0)})}$;

Extract a sample $\boldsymbol{x_2^{(1)}}$ ***from*** $\boldsymbol{\pi(x_2/x_1^{(1)}, \ldots, x_k^{(0)})}$;

……

Extract a sample $\boldsymbol{x_j^{(1)}}$ ***from*** $\boldsymbol{\pi(x_j/x_1^{(1)}, \ldots, x_{j-1}^{(1)}, x_{j-1}^{(0)}, \ldots, x_k^{(0)})}$;

……

Extract a sample $\boldsymbol{x_k^{(1)}}$ ***from*** $\boldsymbol{\pi(x_k/x_1^{(1)}, \ldots, x_{k-1}^{(1)})}$;

Through n time iterations, can get the posterior samples, like $\boldsymbol{x_{(1)}, x_{(2)}, \ldots, x_{(n)}}$, and compute the matrix based on posterior samples.

This method choses different initial values, and create many Markov chains, finally if the chains are convergence, the algorithm is convergence.

3. GETTING DATA

Data is the most important part in the experiment. In order to get available and effective experimental data, some principles should be obeyed, like we can get the source code of the legitimate software easily, then the software should be evolved a long time and released many different versions, meanwhile have some reports about the update. Finally, we choose an open source software called jEdit(written by JAVA), because the source code of jEdit can download from its official website (http://jedit.en.softonic.com/).

Based on this paper's method believes that in the source code, the names of function (method), variable names and comments can represent what does the source code perform [7]. Like a method name called "toString", it may means that the method will changes other format information to format String. So the source code includs rich information that can help us confirm the software evolution.

The source codeof jEdit's, have 531 classes and 38 packages (use the Version 4.3, and only consider the file name extension is ".java"). In consideration some classes including a few words, take a package as a document will be better. Now, obtain the available experimental data is a key processing, the follow steps [8] are method to obtaining the experimental data in this paper:

(1) Download the jEdit's source code from its official website, the format of source code showed as Fig. 2:

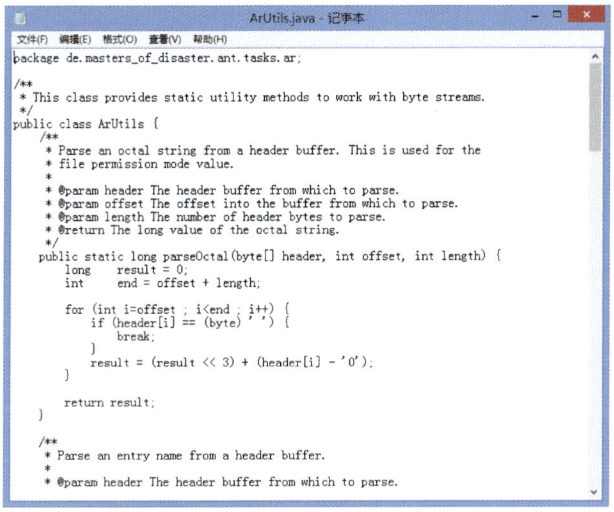

Figure 2. Example of source code.

(2) Extract the names of function (method), variable names and comments from each source code file.

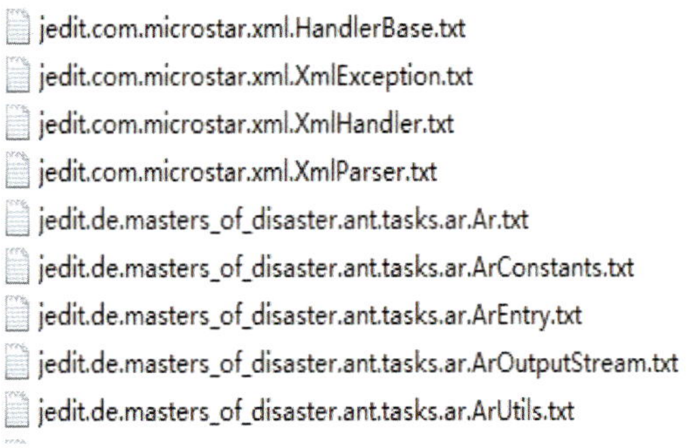

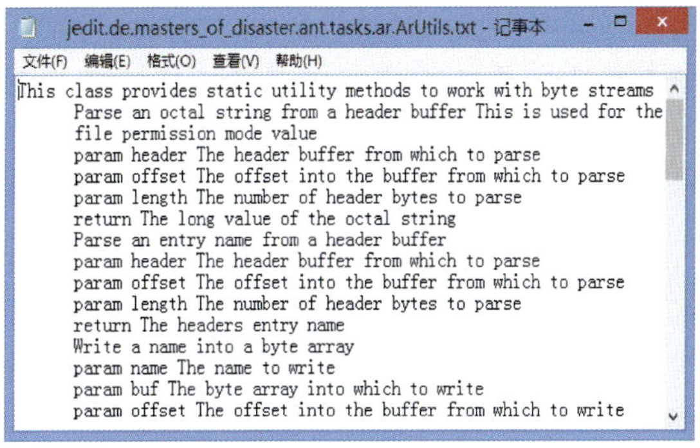

Figure 3. Example of file after extracted.

A program has been written to extract the useful information from source code file. As Fig. 3 shows, on the left is list of files after extracted, and the file named as its package name add its name. On the right, is content of the file that including names of function(method), variable names and comments.

(3) Put the whole contents of file after extracted into a file, then adjust the format meet the requirements of the LDA program.

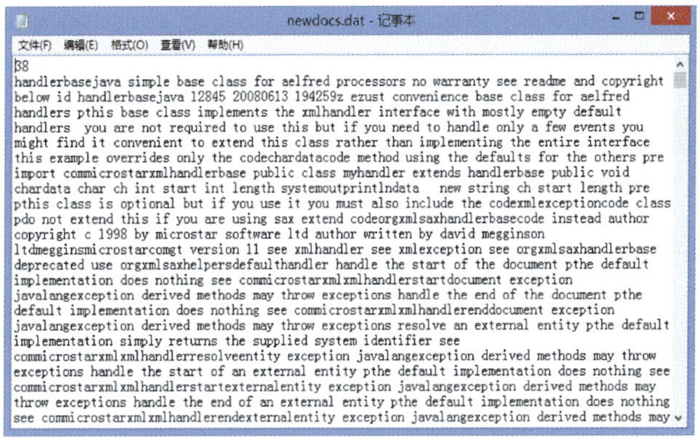

Figure 4. Data of after adjustment.

From Fig. 4, the source code becomes the available information and right format. The file information in the Fig. 4, the information of first line "38" means have 38 documents, because source code has been classified by package. The rest are names of function (method), variable names and comments, the whole information in a package occupied a line.

4. EXPERIMENTS AND RESULTS

4.1. *LDA experiment*

In this experiment, have some parameters should be initialized in LDA program before perform experiment.

Table 1. Parameters in experiment.

Variable name	Role in program
alpha(α)	an array, a parameter in Dirichlet distribution
beta(β)	a two-dimensional array, column represents topic, matrix unit represents the probability of a topic generates a word
ntopics(K)	specify the number of topics
niters	specify the number of iterations
savestep	specify the number of steps to save the model since the last save
twords	specify the number of most likely words to be printed for each topic

4.2. *Experimental results*

The parameters should be initialized before perform experiment. Give an example of set parameters as Table 2 shows:

Table 2. Parameters setting.

Variable name	Value
alpha(α)	0.2
beta(β)	0.1
ntopics(K)	10
niters	1000
savestep	100
twords	10

The output data will be formatted Table 3 shows:

Table 3. Output information.

File name	Details
model-XXXXX.others	Information file, save the value of parameters, like alpha, beta, ntopics and so on
model-XXXXX.phi	probability distribution file of word-topic, is a big matrix M, assume have 1000 topics, each topic will list 100 words, M have 100 rows and 1000 columns, each row is a set of words, each column is a topic, an element value in M means conditional probability P (word|topic), also represents the probability of each word belong to each topic
model-XXXXX.theta	is a big matrix, row is a document of training data, column is a topic, an element value means conditional probability P(topic|document), also represents the probability of the document belongs to different topics
model-XXXXX.tassign	the format data in this file is "wordID: category", means that the highest probability of a word belongs to a topic
model-XXXXX.twords	is result of the model, this file list the first ten of probability words belong to every topic(the "ten" assigned by variable "twords")

In table 3, the "XXXXX" is the iteration times, for example, if iterations is 900 times, the file will be saved and named "model-900.others", "model-900.phi", "model-900.theta", "model-900.tassign" and "model-900.twords". When last iteration is over, the "XXXXX" will be replaced by "final" rather than specific figures. As the Fig. 5 shows:

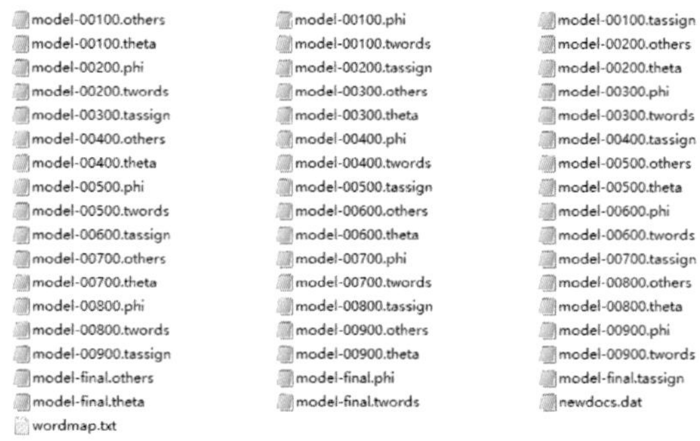

Figure 5. Result files.

As Table 4 shows, the data extracted from file "model-final.twords", and list the most likely words for one topic.

Table 4. Partial content in file "model-final.twords".

Word	Probability
search	0.014580406400986875
class	0.013209745399719013
actionperformed	0.008069766644964534
actionhandler	0.006699105643696673
match	0.006185107768221225
constructor	0.006013775143062742
bufferset	0.006013775143062742
file	0.005328444642428811
replace	0.005328444642428811

The information in the Table 4, a row means word "the" belongs to a topic with the probability of 0.1095188892216953.

5. CONCLUSIONS

In this paper, firstly extract the names of function (method), variable names and comments from source code file, then model them by LDA, finally analyze the results that the probability among words, topics and document. Download two versions of the source code, processing them by this paper's method, find differences from results, and identify distinctions between the differences and update reports. According to the distinctions that can confirm whether the software evolution satisfy the users requirements.

Hyperparameters ***α***, ***β***, and the topic number in this paper, assign their value by experience, so loss of generality. Another side, the names of function (method), variable names and comments extract from source code file, do not manipulate them by stemming reduction, synonym replacement or stop word removal. Find a reliable and reasonable way to solving these problems is a target in further research.

ACKNOWLEDGMENTS

This work were supported by the National Natural Science Foundation of China under Grant Nos. 61462092, 61262024, 61379032, the key project of Natural Science Foundation of Yunnan Province under Grant No. 2015FA014; the Natural Science Foundation of Yunnan Province of China under Grant No. 2013FB008.

REFERENCES

- [1] David M Blei, Andrew Y Ng, Michael I Jordan. Latent Dirichlet Allocation [J]. Journal of Machine Learning Research, 2003, 3(Jan): 993-1022.
- [2] Griffiths T L, Steyvers M. Finding scientific topics [J]. PNAS, 2004, 101(1): 5228-5235.
- [3] Stephen P Brooks. Markov chain Monte Carlo method and its application. The Statistician, 1998, 47(1), 69-100.
- [4] QuanzhuYao, Zhili Song, Cheng Peng. Research on text categorization based on LDA. Computer Engineering and Applications, 2011, 47(13): 150-153.
- [5] Haiyun Ma. Research on test case generation technology based on Gibbs sampling [J]. Automation & Instrumentation, 2011, (152): 11-1.
- [6] Zhong, Liu, Shisong, Mao. Bayes analysis for grouped data-Gibbs sampling method [J]. Chinese Journal of Applied Probability and Statistics, 1997, 13(2): 211-216.
- [7] Yun He, Wei Wang, Tong Li, et al. Behavior and topic oriented software feature location method. Journal of Frontiers of Computer Science and Technology, 2014, 8(12): 1452-1462.
- [8] Marcus A, Sergeyev A, Rajlich V, et al. An information retrieval approach to concept location in source code [C]. Proceedings of the 11th Working Conference on Reverse Engineering (WCRE '04), Delft, Netherlands, Nov 8-12, 2004. Washington, DC, USA: IEEE Computer Society, 2004: 214-223.

Using Dynamic Self-adaptation Threshold Algorithm to Optimize the Performance of SSD

Y.H. Lu[1, 2], W.L. Ruan[1,2] & B.X. Wang[1]

1. School of Computer Science, Northwestern Polytechnical University, Xi'an 710072, China

2. Y.H. Lu, email: yanhonglu@nwpu.edu.cn; Corresponding author, W.L. Ruan, junziyzgssd@163.com

ABSTRACT: In the field of application of parallel storage, the increased demand and system function expansion have put forward a higher requirement on the storage performance of reading and writing. On the basis of VxWorks, this paper makes a deep research of dos File System (dosFs) and raw File System (rawFs). And we found that the reading and writing speed of Solid State Disk (SSD) under rawFs is faster than it under dosFs. What's more, we proposed an algorithm named Dynamic self-Adaptation Threshold Algorithm (DATA) which takes advantage of the free time to write back some data into data buffer. The algorithm can reduce the waiting time so that it can increase the performance of SSD. In order to further increase the reading and writing speed, we applied this algorithm to rawFs. Through the experiment result we reach the conclusion that the performance of SSD under rawFs is better than it under dosFs. And the performance of SSD under rawFs which has been used DATA is better than it under rawFs which hasn't been used.

KEYWORDS: DATA; SSD; dosFs; rawFs; parallel storage.

1. INTRODUCTION

With the high development of the embedded system, it is more urgent that the large capacity storage devices are applied to the embedded system. SSD has advantages in some way. For example, its reading and writing speed, and storage capacity are better than any other storage medium. However, on many occasions, SSD is still can't meet the requirement in speed. Therefore, it is very necessary to improve the performance of SSD.

In recent years, people have made great efforts to enhance the performance of SSD. Reference [1] studied the source, development and Present situation of SSD. Reference [2] made a comparing of SSD and Mechanical Disks. Reference [3] analyzed how to drive the SSD and how the file system work on VxWorks. Reference [4] proposed an algorithm to improve the performance of SSD. Reference [5] analyzed the characteristic of parallel storage system. They indicated that it is important and feasible to enhance the performance of SSD and they have laid the research foundation of this paper.

In this paper, we propose an algorithm called DATA (Dynamic self-Adaptation Threshold Algorithm). This algorithm is based on that the SSD has the characteristic of parallelism and the most of I/O request are not uniform. If we make full use of the free time fragment to write some of the data into the buffer, we can improve the reading and writing speed obviously. Besides, we studied the dosFs and rawFs in VxWorks. And we found that speed of I/O in rawFs is much faster than it in dosFs. Therefore, if we apply the DATA to rawFs, the reading and writing speed of SSD can be further improved a lot.

2. RAWFS

As we know, rawFs is the smallest file system which is provided by VxWorks. It only provides I/O operation of disk which is the most fundamental function. RawFs considers the whole disk as an independent file. On some occasion which has a higher requirement in reading and writing speed, rawFs can be a good choice.

The structure and the initialization of rawFs is shown in Figure 1.

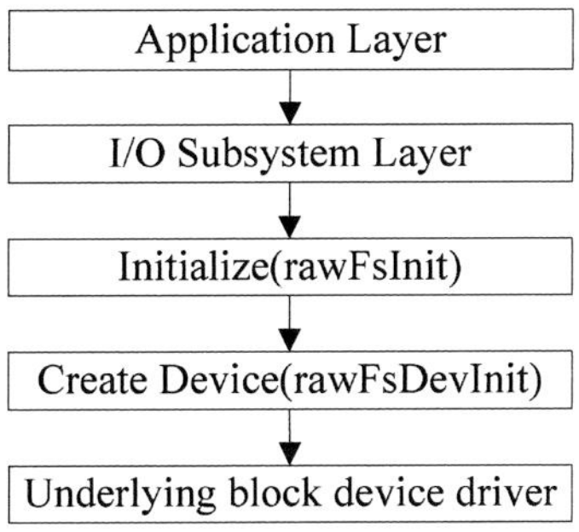

Figure 1. The structure and the initialization of rawFs.

Function rawFsInit called function iosDrvInstall which is a register function provided by I/O subsystem. It provided the intermediate drivers for I/O subsystem and build relationship between intermediate layer and upper layer. Underlying block device driver fills in the information which is needed by the rawFs in the structure named BLK_DEV, and it called function rawFsDevInit to establish relationship between intermediate layer and underlying layer.

3. DYNAMIC SELF-ADAPTATION THRESHOLD ALGORITHM

SSD has the characteristic of multi-level parallelism. For example, the channel and channel, the chip and chip, they are parallel respectively. So it is not impossible that every channel or chip is busy at the same time. We can take advantage of parallelism to write data back to the data buffer [6] in advance. Therefore, the reading and writing speed can be improved.

DATA proposed a threshold which controls the size of data written back to the data buffer in advance. When the load is relatively free and there is free resource in the SSD, we should check the threshold before writing data back to the data buffer in advance. If the size of data in data buffer is more than or equal to the threshold, there is no need to trigger the operation of writing back in advance. Otherwise, trigger the operation immediately.

There are two kinds of data node in the data buffer which applied writing back in advance. The first one is NA (Normal Area) and the other is WA (Written-back Area). They are shown in the Figure 2.

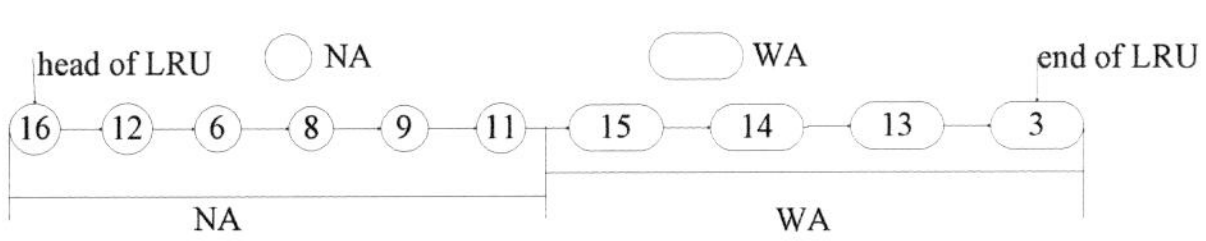

Figure 2. Two kinds of nodes in data buffer.

We can know from the Figure 2, the data buffer is made up of NA and WA. The buffer needs to maintain the order of data. Usually, there are many algorithms can do this [7]. For example, LRU, LFU, FIFO and so on [8-9]. In this paper, we take the example of LRU to explain how the DATA works. The data in the buffer are formed into a queue. The head of LRU is the data which has just been accessed. The end of the LRU is the data which has not been accessed for long time. There are four possible cases because the data buffer is divided into two areas in logical. The first case, hit the NA. Secondly, hit the WA. Thirdly, hasn't hit the data buffer and the size of WA is more than 0. Lastly, hasn't hit the data buffer and the size of WA is equal to 0. These four cases are shown in the Figure 3-6.

3.1. *Request hit the NA*

The data 9 is the requested data at the present. It is in the NA. We just have to move it to the head of LRU queue.

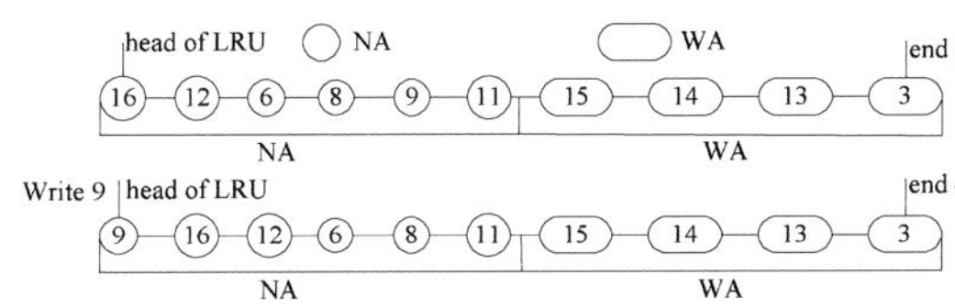

Figure 3. Request hit the NA.

3.2. *Request hit the WA*

The requested data is 13. But 13 is in the WA. We should get it from the queue of WA and then move it to the head of NA.

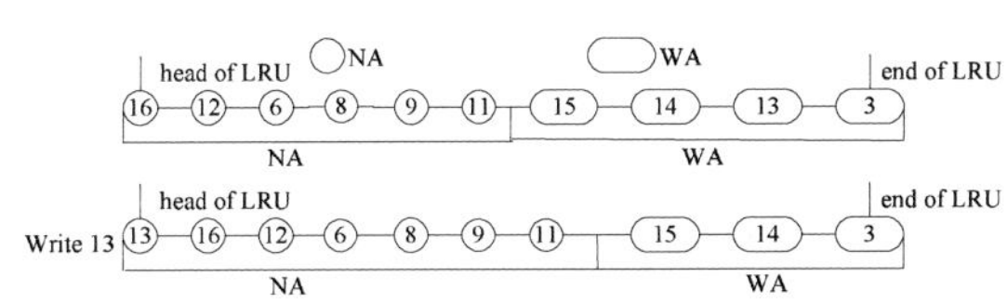

Figure 4. Request hit the WA.

3.3. *Request hasn't hit the data buffer and the size of WA is more than 0*

The request data is 2 and it isn't in the data buffer. The size of WA is not more than 0. The data 3 is in the WA and it is the end of LRU. It means it has been written to the flash before. In order to write the requested data to the head of LRU queue, we just need to discard the data 3. The size of the WA is decremented by one but the size of NA is increased by one. So we can write the requested data to the head of LRU queue.

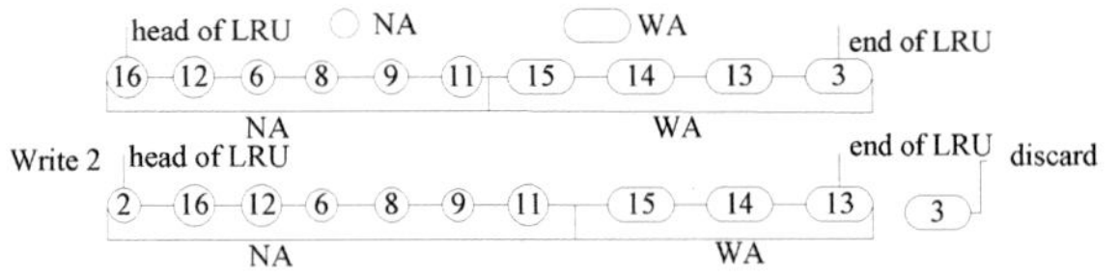

Figure 5. Request hasn't hit data buffer, and WA is more than 0.

3.4. *Request hasn't hit the data buffer and the size of WA is equal to 0*

The requested data (data 2) is not in the data buffer and the size of WA is equal to 0. Before writing the requested data into the head of LRU queue, we should write the end of LRU (data 3) into the flash and then write the data 2 into the head of LRU queue.

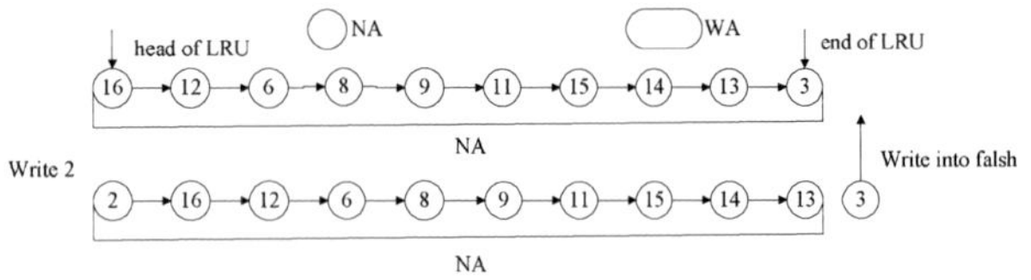

Figure 6. Request hasn't hit data buffer, and WA is equal to 0.

In order to adjust the threshold dynamically, we should make addition or subtraction on two occasions. The one is the writing operation hit the WA of data buffer. It means that there are too much data writing back in advance. Therefore, the threshold should be decreased by one. The other one is the writing operation didn't hit the WA and the size of WA is equal to 0. It means the operation of writing back in advance is not enough. The threshold should be increased by one. We can know the process of adjustment from Figure 7.

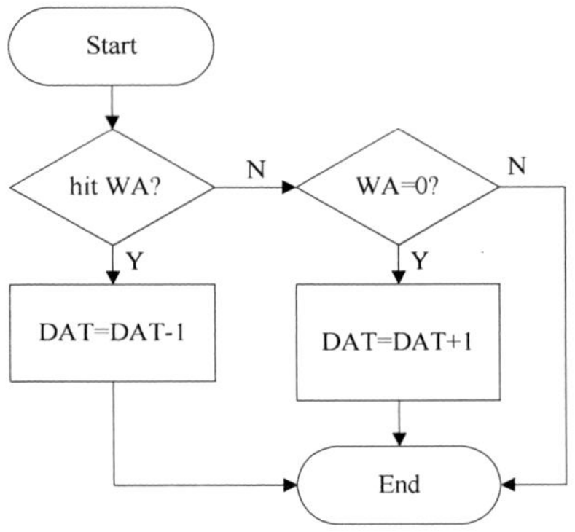

Figure 7. The adjustment of DAT.

4. EXPERIMENT AND RESULTS

4.1. *Experiment environment*

Simulation environment is made up with two parts, a PC and a computer case which is running VxWorks operating system. And the computer case is consisted of CPU, memory (4G), PCIe-SATA adapter and SSD (512G) with SATA interface. Client provide SATA interface but the host provide PCIe interface, therefore we need to use PCIe-SATA adapter to convert the interface. In this simulation, the chip of the adapter is 88SE9125. The computer case is described in more detail in the Figure 8.

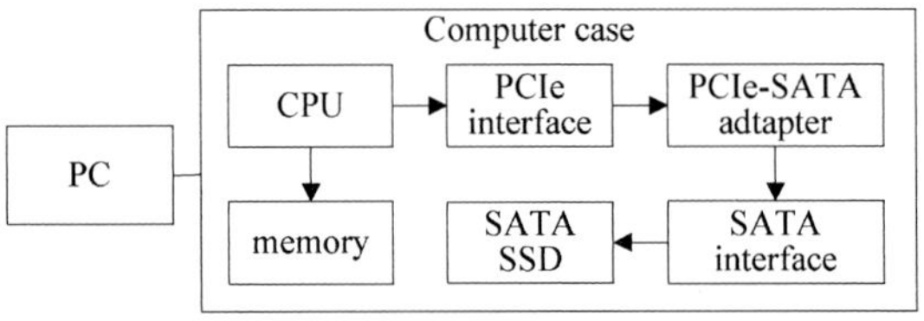

Figure 8. Components of simulation environment.

The program is compiled at the PC and then the computer case downloads the object code form PC through network interface. The computer case is connected with PC by serial. We can observe the information of SSD and the results of executing the program through hyper terminal. And we can debug our algorithm by workbench.

4.2. *The results of experiment*

We set 10 blocks as the test objects. Their size are 10M, 20M, 30M, 40M, 50M, 60M, 70M, 80M, 90M, 100M. Every block is tested 20 times. In order to avoid the random error, the average speed is regarded as the finally result.

Table 1. Read/write speed under dosFs[1].

Block Size	Reading Speed	Writing Speed
10	198	162
20	213	162
30	205	166
40	207	160
50	205	155
60	207	166
70	206	157
80	208	164
90	207	158
100	208	163

[1]The dimensions of size of block, read speed and write speed are MB, MB/Sec and MB/Sec. The data in the tables are rounded to the nearest value. The rules also apply to Table 2-3.

We can know from Table 1 that reading speed under dosFs is about 206MB/Sec and writing speed under dosFs is about 160MB/Sec.

Table 2. Read/write speed under rawFs.

Block Size	Reading Speed	Writing Speed
10	243	192
20	245	191
30	239	187
40	240	188
50	242	190
60	246	185
70	244	193
80	238	190
90	240	191
100	243	188

We can know from table 2 that reading speed under rawFs is about 242MB/Sec and writing speed under rawFs is about 190MB/Sec. The speed is almost twice under dosFs.

Table 3. Read/write speed under rawFs used DATA.

Block Size	Reading Speed	Writing Speed
10	287	242
20	286	241
30	283	240
40	281	238
50	289	239
60	290	240
70	282	243
80	285	244
90	288	245
100	289	241

After using DATA, the read/write speed is improved. Reading speed is about 286MB/Sec and writing speed is about 241MB/Sec.

The comparing of these three situations is shown in the Figure 9-10.

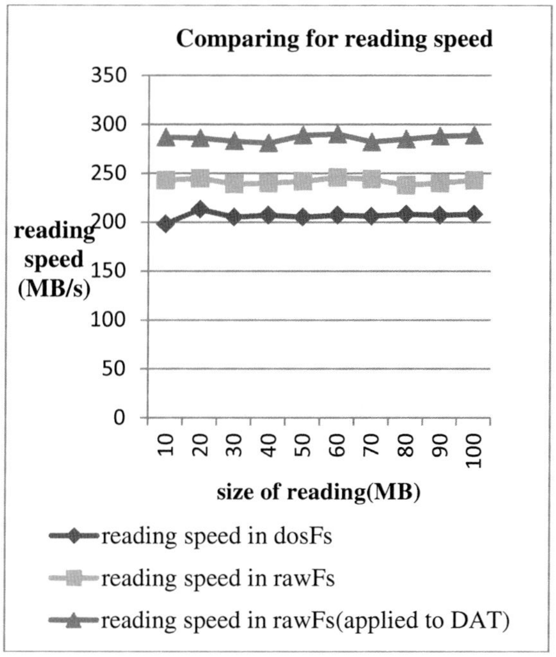

Figure 9. Comparing result of reading speed.

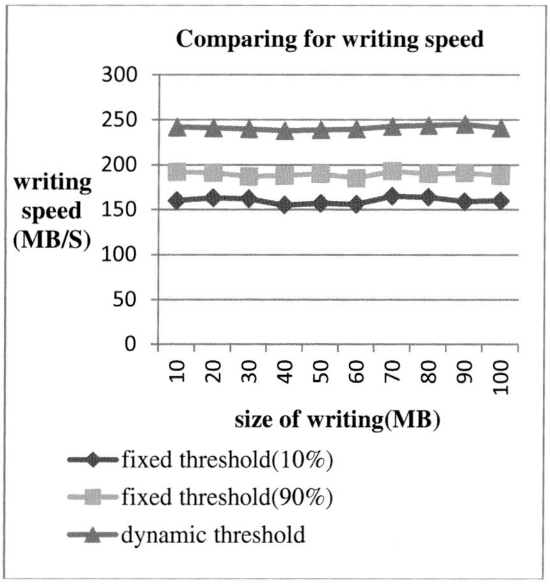

Figure 10. Comparing result of writing speed.

5. CONCLUSIONS

We can draw some conclusions from the simulation results. The reading and writing speed of SSD under rawFs is much faster than it under dosFs. And if we apply the DATA to the rawFs, we can further improve the speed. Therefore, on the occasion which has high a higher requirement, we can consider to apply DATA to rawFs, and increase the reading and writing speed in many directions. What's more, it is necessary to further study the characteristics of parallel storage system. For example, we can try to set up RAID (Redundant Array of Inexpensive Disks), and try to increase the reading and writing speed in another way [10].

REFERENCES

— [1] M - system, CR- 513 development team. Solid state disk puts flash to work Computer Design, 1994, (2): 99~ 102.

— [2] Milo Polte, Jiri Simsa, Garth Gibson. Comparing Performance of Solid State Devices and Mechanical Disks. IEEE, 2008.

— [3] Wind River Systems, Inc. VxWorks BSP Developer's Guide [M]. USA: WSR, 2002.

— [4] Seon-Yeong Park, Dawoon Jung, Jeong-Uk Kang, et al. CFLRU: A replacement algorithm for flash memory. In CASES06: Proceedings of the 2006 International Conference on Compilers, Architecture and Synthesis for Embedded Systems, New York, NY, USA, 2006. ACM: 234-241.

— [5] Watson, R.W.; Coyne, R.A., "The parallel I/O architecture of the high-performance storage system (HPSS)," Mass Storage Systems, 1995. 'Storage - At the Forefront of Information Infrastructures', Proceedings of the Fourteenth IEEE Symposium on, pp. 27, 44, 11-14 Sep 1995.

- [6] H. Kim and S. Ahn. BPLRU: A buffer management scheme for improving random writes in flash storage. In Proc. of FAST'08, 2008.
- [7] Abraham Silberschatz, Peter B. Galvin and Greg Gagne, "Memory Management Strategies" in Operating System Concept, 8th ed. Wiley Student Edition, pp. 315-417.
- [8] C.C. Kavar and S.S. Parmar, "Performance Analysis of LRU Page Replacement Algorithm with Reference to Different Data Structure," IJERA, 2013, Vol. 3, Issue 1, pp. 2070-2076.
- [9] Fei Li, "Fairness Analysis in Competitive FIFO Buffer Management," Performance, Computing and Communications Conference, 2008. IPCCC2008. IEEE International, pp. 239, 246, 7-9 Dec. 2008.
- [10] S. Im and D. Shin. Flash-Aware RAID Techniques for Dependable and High-Performance Flash Memory SSD. IEEE Transactions on Computers, 60(1):80-92, Jan. 2011.

System Architecture and Design of MDM Platform for Railway

P. Li* & T.Y. Shi
Institute of Computing Technologies, China Academy of Railway Sciences, Beijing, China
Email: liping@rails.in, ict_liping@sina.com

ABSTRACT: In order to solve information island problems and promote information sharing among multiple information systems in Chinese railway, it is necessary to improve railway master data management (MDM) to ensure the identification uniqueness, characteristics consistency of master data. At present, it is lack of planning and standard, separate collection and maintenance for MDM in railway. In this paper, the railway master data planning is given and the life cycle management of railway master data is analyzed. On this basis, the system architecture of railway MDM platform is presented and the MDM platform is designed. At last the benefits of master data management for Chinese railway are analyzed.

KEYWORDS: Master data management; System architecture; MDM planning; Railway transportation.

1. INTRODUCTION

Master data is the most important and fundamental data in China railway information chain. It can bridge the borders of the multiple business processes and serves as the link for data exchange between the various business systems. Master data for Chinese railway mainly describes the basic identity or state property, including the infrastructure, mobile devices, passengers, cargo, personnel, institutions, etc. Additionally, the master data also support the main railway information system, while the corresponding master data are considered to be the most important and fundamental data in the whole railway information chain. It can bridge the borders of the multiple business processes and serves as the link for data exchange between the various business systems. The master data with integrity and uniqueness can play a great role on data exchange between the existing information systems in the field of intelligent transport system.

Because of more than 30 railway information systems are established for each respective coding system since 1980's. Coding methods and maintenance mechanism are both not uniform. The corresponding results can lead to the following problems in the practical applications. It is including as follows:

– Information islands among business information systems are extremely serious. MDM lack overall planning, and each system separately construct, the same master data exists in multiple systems, standards of data elements and coding rules of master data are inconsistent.

– The naming, type and range of the same object in the various systems do not have the same representation. One part of the master data exist inconsistencies, inaccuracies, incomplete and other issues.

– It is lack of uniform maintenance control process. Master data extremely lack regulatory management and control, and its update source become confusion.

– China railway does not have a uniform enterprise-class master data management and maintenance platform in technology. Meanwhile, it does not formulate a complete management process and the related management system of master data.

– Master data lack historical changing record and version control, which is not conducive to the data traceability and to carry out the analysis and decision of historical data.

Currently, the China Railway Corporation has been rapidly transformed into enterprises, and it is in urgent need to unite and regulate master data from the perspective of the enterprise information technology, and accelerate the integration of railway information resources. It makes a good foundation for the interoperability, resource sharing and comprehensive benefit in business information systems. Therefore, it is already imminent to carry out the design of MDM platform of railway.

2. RESOURCE PLANNING FOR MASTER DATA IN RAILWAY

Railway master data is mainly defined by the shared and relatively static data between the various systems in the whole railway enterprise. The main data cross each business department in the railway enterprise and distribute in a plurality of different systems. Railway master data have the following characteristics.

2.1. *Identification uniqueness*

The same master data coding requires the unique identification mark in the railway enterprises (code name, feature description, etc.), to clearly distinguish the specific details of business objects, business scope and business. Unique identification information encoded in the maintenance of master data is the basis for business activities. Each business links is completely dependent on master data coding identification to define subsequent handling and processing in the business transfer process. At the latter of the business links, the main data coding identification also become the dimension of data analysis to determine the scope and direction of the analysis.

2.2. *Characteristics consistency*

Since the scope of application of the railway enterprises is expanding, the phenomenon that master data encoded in different systems overlap and cross is commonplace. As the features of the master data encoding is often used as the conditions to determine the business process and the specific dimension hierarchical of data analysis. Thus it should make sure that the key features of the master data are highly consistent with others in different applications and systems, which is a necessary condition for the integration of railway enterprise application, unified standard, and the successful implementation of the railway enterprise data warehouse.

2.3. *Transaction stability*

Master data encoding is key operational information, which is used to describe the objects of business operation. Identification information and key features in the course of business can inherit, quote and copy by generated data in the course of business transactions. Unless the characteristics of the master data coding itself change, the main attributes of the master data itself will not be modified with the process of transaction, regardless of complex and long-lasting.

2.4. *Long-term effectiveness*

The effectiveness of the master data encoding generally exist through the entire life cycle of the business object. As long as the business object that is represented by master data encoding still exist, the master data need to continue to maintain the effectiveness in the system. In addition, the measures taken by the failure of the master data coding are usually marked invalid or deletion, rather than directly physical deleted.

According to the types and characteristics of various types of railway mobile and fixed resources, railway master data resources divide into six categories: fixed facilities, mobile equipment, transportation products, personnel agencies, materials and equipment, and financial statistics.

3. LIFE CYCLE MANAGEMENT PROCESS OF RAILWAY MASTER DATA

In order to improve the quality of railway master data from accuracy, completeness, consistency, timeliness, understandability and accessibility, it need to strengthen the life cycle of railway master data of business process management. As depicted in Figure 1, the life cycle of railway master data which is composed of five steps including creation, cleaning, update, failure and release.

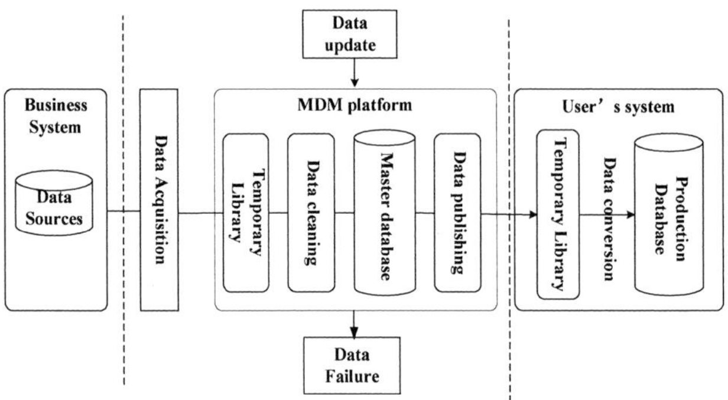

Figure 1. The lifecycle of master data.

3.1. *Creation of master data*

According to the data demand of master data and the existing standard input platform, it should be created corresponding data content. The way of master data's storage includes artificial storage and bulk import.

3.2. *Cleaning of master data*

It includes data verification by the platform and data audit from management level. After re- checking, coding rules, content and other multiple checking, the initialization of the data is confirmed by responsible departments in accordance with quality requirements of accuracy, completeness and uniqueness in the data source system.

3.3. *Updating of master data*

It should update the corresponding master data in the plat form in accordance with the provisions of the documents, and synchronize the version management of data. The updated master data are timely published on the platform.

3.4. *Master data failure*

The failure of the master data means that the main business carried by master data no longer has a factual business relationship with Railway Corporation, due to the data cleaning or actual business requirement. After the competent business department determines data failure, master data platform is modified on time and release real-time data failure notice to the relevant business systems.

3.5. *Master data release*

They are the initiative to release (push) and passive query (pull). Master data are created after check, calibration and audit. Then the master data are released to subscribed business systems. According to their different business requirement, each business system can download or invoke their own master data through the interface with master data platform or interfaces provided by master data. The released master data include the requirement of business information systems, together with the increment and completion of master data.

4. SYSTEM ARCHITECTURE OF MDM PLATFORM FOR RAILWAY

Railway MDM platform, unified management and maintenance of the railway's business information system shared master data, makes sure that the master data of unity, integrity, accuracy, consistency and authority. It can send to each railway business information system on time and provide the basis for connectivity of railway business information system and comprehensive utilization of information resources. The system architecture of Railway MDM platform is shown in figure 2. The framework is divided into user access layer, data exchange layer, application layer, data resource layer, basic operation environment layer.

4.1. *User access layer*

The user access layer provides the access platform interface for the various business information systems. Master data get the latest shared data from the platform. It includes passenger and cargo services system, transport organization field system, operation and management field system, safety management system, construction management system and integrated management system.

4.2. *Data exchange layer*

The data exchange layer provides the data transfer between different application systems and platforms on the basis of the ESB, message middleware, the universal service interface etc.

4.3. *Application layer*

The application layer has some functions such as data model management, data management, change management, data synchronization, rights management and system management. Data model management provides data object management, data element management, encoding rules management etc. Data management provides master data management, public encoding management, standard management, and so on. Change management provides the basis of the change management, change status monitoring, data distribution, version management, business system data monitoring, etc. Data synchronization provides data import, data subscription, data download and release, and other functions. Rights management provides the role configuration, user management, etc. System management provides user monitoring, data monitoring, platform monitoring, statistical analysis, data backup, log management and etc.

4.4. *Data resource layer*

The data resource layer saves utility code library, master database, standard database, database management system, as well as the historical database for version back.

4.5. *Basic operating environment layer*

The basic operating environment layer provides the basis of the hardware and software environment which is used on servers, storage, network, and middleware and database platform.

MDM platform for railway is mainly to provide the data model management, data management, change management, data synchronization, rights management, system management and other functions.

Data model management and maintenance data object classification system defines the data elements and master data contains utility based encoding rules, in order to ensure the standardization of data. The function of the model management mainly includes the data object management, data management, coding rule management.

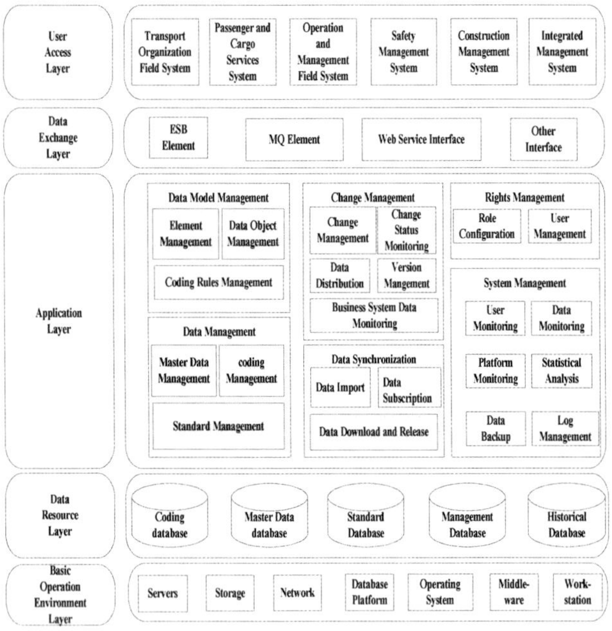

Figure 2. The system architecture of railway MDM platform.

Data management is the core of the platform functions, including the master data, common basic code and standard specification of the basic operation, such as adding, deleting, changing and checking. Among these operations, adding, deleting and changing operations change the data, so they must be approved by data management department before taking effect.

Change management is used to change the state of the master data such as add, delete, and update changes, according to provided unified management and monitoring.

Data synchronization is mainly realizing the business information systems and data synchronization between the master data platforms. On the one hand, initialized data import platform, on the other hand platform update data release to each business information system on time.

Rights configuration management functions mainly include user management and role management.

System management mainly provide users of the system monitoring, data monitoring, platform resources monitoring, statistical analysis, data backup, etc.

5. DESIGN OF MDM PLATFORM FOR RAILWAY

The design of MDM platform for railway includes five aspects: data planning, organization structure, management process, and management system and technology platform.

5.1. *Data planning*

Data are the core of MDM platform, so reasonable planning is needed before the railway MDM platform construction. The data planning includes the following aspects.

Scope of Data: Railway master data itself is not invariable but a category that development gradually along with the railway business. So the data of platform management cannot have clear quantitative data sets at the beginning. To define the scope of data should adopt qualitative and quantified way.

Data Standard: Data standard is the basic premise of information exchange and sharing. It is used to reach a consensus between data providers and users on meaning and format of the data. Data of railway MDM platform mainly includes the master data metadata standard and basic coding standard encoding rules, etc.

5.2. *Organizational structure*

Master data management requires the support of corresponding organizational structure. The structure of master data management is the division of duties and the hierarchy relationship of each management elements to complete the management work. To complete master data management tasks, each department duties need to be clarified, such as department, responsibilities, hierarchy relationship.

5.3. *Maintenance and management process*

Master data management needs to be carried out in accordance with the unified and controlled process. The master data management process is to complete the lifecycle management of master data the responsibility of different departments to complete a series of activities. Order between each activity is strictly limited. It is also specific arrangements that the content of the activities, methods, responsibilities and so on, to make the transition between different activities in different positions and roles. It is necessary to define the maintenance of master data management activities, including what operation steps, all aspects of organization involved, roles and responsibilities, and the collaboration between each link.

5.4. *Management system*

Master data management system is to ensure the right of each link in the management process. Persons who is formulated by the relevant responsible must be abided by the rules or guidelines. Management system should include the following contents: the range of master data, the functions and organizational structure, management process, master data management platform, evaluation methods and so on.

5.5. *Technology platform*

MDM platform is the support platform of railway master data management. As construction and use unified platform in the whole railway enterprise, the master data collection, update and sharing should be done depends on the platform.

6. CONCLUSION

Unified master data is foundation of the railway information system to realize information exchange and sharing, information comprehensive utilization, and information integration. Master data platform construction can produce great benefits for China railway.

REFERENCES

- [1] Jia Limin, Li Ping. 2005. System Architecture of Chinese RITS. *Proceedings of the Eastern Asia Society for Transportation Studies*, Tokyo, 1424-1432.
- [2] Du Rui. 2013. MDM Application in Tobacco Enterprise. *Science Innovation and Application*, 27:25-26.
- [3] Yu Xi, Zhang Yiqiang. 2013. Quality Control of Master Data based on Pattern Matching. *Journal of Computer Applications,* 33(S1):73-75.

Software Defect Prediction Using Fuzzy Integral and Genetic Algorithm

C. Jin* & E.M. Dong
School of Computer, Central China Normal University, Wuhan 430079, P.R. China
**Email: jincong@mail.ccnu.edu.cn*

ABSTRACT: The fuzzy classification plays an important role to predict defect of software modules. In this paper, the fuzzy measure (FM) is used to improve the predict accuracy and capability by acquiring all possible interactions among metrics and apply Choquet integral (CI) for classifying in n dimensional space and automatic searching the least misclassification rate based on distance. To implement the model, we also need to determine the unknown parameters, and which is implemented using genetic algorithm (GA) on the training data. The proposed model is tested on the four NASA software projects. The results indicate that the predict performance of proposed model is better than other predict models.

KEYWORDS: Fuzzy integral; Genetic algorithm; Software; Defect prediction.

1. INTRODUCTION

In recent decades, software defect prediction is becoming an important field in software engineering. Flawed software modules cause software failures, enhance development and maintenance costs, and reduce customer satisfaction. Studies have shown that the majority of defects are often found in only a few software modules. Accordingly, the prediction of the defect software modules can ensure software developers to focus quality assurance activities and allocate effort and resources more efficiently. Identification of defect software modules is commonly achieved through binary prediction models that classify a module into either defect or non-defect category. These prediction models almost always utilize static product metric. Classification is a procedure of constructing a mathematical model based on training set and uses the model to assign a categorical label to any new sample [1].

Many classification methods have been studied to predict defects in software. In [2], authors investigated the impact of the object-oriented metrics to predict defect modules using logistic regression. In [3], support vector machine (SVM) was used to reduce the risks of defect modules. In [4], authors proposed the AntMiner+ models of mining software to predict defect modules and applied AntMiner+ on NASA software defect datasets. The proposed method was compared with some machine learning and statistical methods. The authors found that the prediction accuracy of AntMiner+ is generally higher than other methods. In [5], authors used minimize entropy principle to build the classification model to classify modules as defect or non-defect, and found that the modified MEPA model had higher predictive accuracy. These methods have their own characteristics.

We notice that fuzzy theory [6] has brought new tools for software defect prediction [7]. In fact, software defect has qualitative characteristics rather than quantitative in nature, so it is a fuzzy concept. Moreover, the classification of software modules is often not well separated and there are no well-defined boundaries. So, to solve software defect prediction problems using fuzzy theory are very suitable undoubtedly.

Fuzzy integral (FI) has been an effective model for solving classification problems. In this paper, we studied the applicability of CI for software quality predicting, and GA was combined with CI for avoiding CI to fail into a local minimum. Unlike the existing methods, a very important property of proposed model is that the interactions among metrics, which lead the contributions from various metrics toward the classification to be non-additive, are explicitly expressed by FM.

2. PREPAREDNESS KNOWLEDGE

As FI [8] classification, FM reflects the importance of the metrics, as well as their inherent interaction, toward the discrimination of the points. A combination of the metrics may have a mutually restraining or a complementary synergy effect on their contributions toward the classification decision. So FM defined on the power set of all metrics is a proper representation of the respective importance of the metrics and the interaction among them, and a relevant nonlinear integral is a good fusion tool to aggregate the information coming from the metrics for the classification. And we discriminate the categories that estimated the classification line to separate the given data in the metrics space and the integral projection. In this section, the main principles of this technique are explained, starting with a short introduction to FM and CI.

2.1. *FM and CI*

FM is a set function used to expression the grade of fuzziness. Let $X=\{x_1, x_2, \ldots, x_n\}$ be a finite set of metrics with n metrics on information space, and denote $P(X)$ as the power set consisting of subsets of X. μ is a mapping from $P(X)$ over a set X is defined as a set function μ: $P(X)\to[0,1]$ and such that

$$\mu(\varphi)=0, \mu(X)=1 \tag{1}$$

For any E, $F\subseteq X$, if $E\subseteq F$ then $\mu(E)\leq \mu(F)$ (2)

X is a nonempty universe. The set function μ is non-additive in general, and its range is here arbitrarily chosen as the unit interval. For a finite set $A\in P(X)$ and a FM function μ, f is a nonnegative function. CI of f can be formulated as follows

$$(c)\int fd\mu = \sum_{i=1}^{N}(f(x_i') - f(x_{i-1}'))\mu(A_i) = \sum_{i-1}^{N}(\mu(A_i) - f(A_{i+1}))f(x_i) \tag{3}$$

s.t. $f(x_1') \leq f(x_2') \leq \ldots \leq f(x_{n+1}')$, $f(x_0') = 0, \mu(A_{n+1}') = 0$ (4)

Where, $\{f(x_1'), f(x_2'), \ldots, f(x_{n+1}')\}$ is the non-decreasing order of $\{f(x_1), f(x_2), \ldots, f(x_{n+1})\}$ and $A_i = \{x_i', x_{i+1}', \ldots x_n'\}$ is a non-decreasing order permutation of $(x_1, x_2, \ldots, x_n)$. When μ is a classical measure and CI possesses most properties of FI. We let CI be with respect to non-additive signed measure and the set function to take negative values and to be non-monotone. Hence, the weighted CI is expressed as

$$Y = (c)\int (a+bf)d\mu \tag{5}$$

Where, $\mu_i, i = 1,2,\ldots,2^n - 1$, denote the values of the set function on the nonempty sets in $P(A)$, is restricted to be regular $(\max_{A\subset X}|\mu(A) = 1|)$ and f denotes a given nonnegative set function, where $f(x_1),\ldots, f(x_n)$ represent the values of each metric for one observation. The parameters $a = (a_1, a_2, \ldots, a_n)$ and $b=(b_1, b_2, \ldots, b_n)$ are n dimensional vectors satisfy $a\in[0,\infty)$ with and $|b_i|\in[0, 1]$. In Eq.(5), for convenience, $\mu_1, \mu_2, \ldots, \mu_n, \mu_{12}, \mu_{13}, \ldots$ used as a substitute for $\mu(x_1)$, $\mu(x_2)$, $\ldots$, $\mu(x_n)$, $\mu(x_1, x_2)$, $\mu(x_1, x_3)$, ...In this paper, CI is as a projection tool to reduce the complexity of the classification problem in an n dimensional space.

2.2. *Nonlinear integral projection*

We denoted a point $(f(x_1), \ldots, f(x_n))$ by $(f_1, \ldots, f_n)$ for the sake of simplicity, in the metric space it can be regarded as a function f defined on X. It represents an observation of the metrics. f is projected to be $\hat{Y}$ on a real axis, the value of the virtual variable is defined through a weighted nonlinear integral. The formula is listed as

$$\hat{Y} = \int \omega f d\mu \tag{6}$$

Where, ω is the weight function of X with $\sum_{i=1}^{n}\omega(x_i)$. The projection is characterized by a set of parameters consisting of weights ω and the values of μ. Once all of these values are determined, we can calculate virtual value $\hat{Y}$ from f. The two classes of records in the training dataset will be projected to be two classes on axis L. An optimum search for the best classification boundary between the two classes under the criterion of minimizing the misclassification rate can be adopted.

We define the misclassification rate as the number of misclassified points in the training set divided by data size. In fact, the best classification boundary must be all points having possessing the lowest number of misclassified points. Thus, the classification boundary is the best classification boundaries for given μ. μ under the criterion of minimizing the corresponding misclassification rate, and then obtain an optimal classification.

2.3. *Classification based on CI*

The nonlinear CI classification with signed FM is to enhance the classification accuracy and power by capturing all possible interactions among metrics.

We suppose that the two classes are A and A'. And the class A has p sample and p' sample belonging to class A' in the learning data. Moreover, all of these sample have the same metrics, $x_1, x_2, \ldots, x_n$. Thus, the metric space is the n dimensional space R^n. The ith sample in A denoted by t_i is expressed as

$$t_i = (f_i(x_1), f_i(x_2), \ldots, f_i(x_n)), i = 1,2,\ldots,p \tag{7}$$

while the i'th data point in A' is similarly denoted by t_i, $i = 1,2,\ldots,p'$.

And then we establish a Choquet hyperplane (CH) H that is determined by

$$H : (c)\int (a+bf)d\mu - B = 0 \tag{8}$$

Where, B is an unknown real number. We let all of these unknown parameters and B be in [-1, 1]. And the natural criterion of determining these parameters optimally is to maximize the total sum of signed distances of the learning data in two classes from the respective side to the CH H. On one side of H, the signed distance d_i from a data s_i in A to H is the signed distance from the projection of s_i paralleled with H on line L to the intersection of H and L, which is equal to

$$d_i = \frac{(c)\int (a+bf)d\mu - B}{\sqrt{\mu_1^2 + \mu_2^2 + \ldots + \mu_{2^n-1}^2}}, \quad i = 1,2,\ldots,p \tag{9}$$

From the other side of H, the signed distance of a sample to H is just the signed distance from the projection of paralleled with H on line L to the intersection of H and L, which is equal to

$$d_{i'} = \frac{B - (c)\int (a+bf')d\mu}{\sqrt{\mu_1^2 + \mu_2^2 + \ldots + \mu_{2^n-1}^2}}, \quad i' = 1,2,\ldots,p' \tag{10}$$

The function $F(s) = (c)\int (a+bf)d\mu$ or $F(s) = (c)\int (a+bf')d\mu$ from the metric space to one dimensional line L can be transformation identified the projection paralleled with H onto L. That is, under this projection, any $t_i = (f_i(x_1), f_i(x_2),\ldots, f_i(x_n))$, $i = 1, 2, \ldots, p$ in the metric space has an representation by the function $(c)\int (a+bf)d\mu$, and the CH H itself has an represented by B, thus total signed Choquet distance (CD) is

$$D = \sum d_i + \sum d_{i'} = \frac{(\sum_{i=1}^{p} \int (a+bf)d\mu - B) + (B - \sum_{i'=1}^{p'} \int (a+bf')d\mu)}{\sqrt{\sum_{i=1}^{2^n-1} \mu_i^2}} \tag{11}$$

In Eq. (11), CD for the misclassified points has a negative value. As to the optimization of CH H, we expect that H should be selected to an optimal position. In this case there is an interval between classes A and A', CH H as the classifying boundary should pass through the metric space along the interval. This means that total D should be maximized. So, a criterion to determine the optimal hyperplane is suitable.

Thus, for given learning data set, the unknown parameters a, b, μ, and B can be determined by maximizing total distance D. And after determining the classifying boundary H expressed by Eq. (8). For any new sample $t_i = (f_i(x_1), f_i(x_2),\ldots, f_i(x_n))$, we can classify t into class A or A' based on the following formula

$$\begin{cases} H:(c)\int (a+bf)d\mu \geq B & \text{for all } x_i \in A \\ H:(c)\int (a+bf)d\mu < B & \text{for all } x_i \in A' \end{cases} \tag{12}$$

3. PREDICT MODEL USING CI

As software defect prediction models should be accurate and correct, we apply CI classification technique to induce a model predicting software defect module and adopt the penalty-factor to adjust the misclassification point in the optimal progress. The following is the detail of this predict model.

3.1. *Software defect predict model using CI*

CI is used to improve classification accuracy, and we let that the training data set consist of p sample belonging to the defect modules and p' sample belonging to the non-defect modules. The metrics are x_1, x_2, $\ldots$, x_n. CH H is determined by

$$H:(c)\int (a+bf)d\mu = M \tag{13}$$

where M is the unknown real number and the value is in [-1, 1]. μ is in interval [0, 1].

In the software predict progress, for optimizing CH M, the hyperplane will be pushed to the opposite side as far as possible by the points from classes defect modules and non-defect modules, i.e., M should be set in an optimal position. Since the number of defect modules is much smaller than the number of non-defect modules, which leads to the non-defect modules has more power than the defect modules such that the optimization problem has no solution. Since software managers are interested in predicting defect modules, we decided to use penalty-factor to solve this problem.

$$D = \sum d_i + \sum d_j$$
$$= \frac{(\sum_{i=1}^{p} c_i \int (a+bf)d\mu - M) + (M - \sum_{j=1}^{p'} c_j \int (a+bf')d\mu)}{\sqrt{\sum_{i=1}^{2^n-1} \mu_i^2}} \tag{14}$$

Where, c_i and c_j are penalty-factors and set the proportion of two classification sample. In this predict model, the module points is said to be separated by the hyperplane if it is separated without error and the distance between the closest points to the hyperplane is maximal. CI is to draw a linear boundary between the two classify module points, and this line that the margin space is maximized between the two classify samples. For the boundary parameter, we are to compute using training data. If the training data are linearly separable by hyperplane in the n dimensional space then there exists a function such that Eq. (13). The parameters a, b of hyperplane H as classifying boundary can be determined by maximizing the penalized total distance D in Eq. (14). After determining the classifying boundary H Eq. (13), for any new software module, we classifies into defect or non-defect modules according to Eq. (15)

$$\begin{cases} H:(c)\int (a+bf)d\mu \geq M & \text{for all } x_i \in \text{defect} \\ H:(c)\int (a+bf)d\mu < M & \text{for all } x_i \in \text{non-defect} \end{cases} \tag{15}$$

We apply GA to solve the optimization problem for CI classification. These parameters are optimally determined according the training data by GA. The each group parameter is interpreted as the chromosomes. The modules are each scored as to fitness using a fitness score based on D. The population is renewed by crossover and mutation operations, and the best fit is retained in the next generation. The components of the algorithm are outlined and explained as follows.

3.2. *Several problems about GA*

(1) Coding and decoding. The chromosome represents CI projection which contains all $\mu_1, \mu_2, \ldots,$ and the matching vectors a, b and M. The parameters $\mu_1, \mu_2, \ldots,$ matching vectors a, b and M are coded as binary genes number $g_1, g_2, \ldots, g_N$ and g_{N+1}. Where $N = 2n\text{-}1\text{+}2n$. So, each gene is a bit string. The length of the bit string depends on the required precision for the solution. For example, if the required precision of the values is 0.001, then we need 10 bits to present each gene. Once the genes are generated, they are decoded by the formula $u_i = 2(g_i - 0.5)$ for i = 1, 2,…, N; $B = 2(g_N\text{-}0.5)$, etc.

(2) Population and chromosomes. Each chromosome is a gene string $g_1, g_2, \ldots, g_{N+1}$. The length of chromosome is $10\times(N+1)$. The population P consists of a large number of chromosomes. The population size is p. The defect value of p is 50.

(3) Chromosomes' fitness. For each chromosome $g_1, g_2, \ldots, g_{N+1}$, after decoding the genes, we obtain the parameter estimation $\mu_1, \mu_2, \ldots, \mu_n$, a, b and M, which represent a hyperplane H according to Eq.(8). Then, for the given training data, the corresponding D from the training sample points in the data set to the hyperplane H can be calculated by Eq.(10). The relative fitness of this chromosome in the current population is defined by the linear enhancement of Goldberg [9], the concrete description is

$$F = \frac{(\rho-1)D_{avg}}{D_{\max}-D_{avg}}D + \frac{D_{\max}-\rho D_{avg}}{D_{\max}-D_{avg}}D_{avg} \qquad (16)$$

Where, D_{max} is the max distances correspondingly in the dataset to CH H in the current population. D_{avg} is the average distance and ρ is the constant and is set 1.2.

(4) Parent selection. Denoting the fitness of the ith chromosome in the current population by F_i, we let probability $p_i = F_i / \sum_{i=1}^{p} F(i)$ to the ith chromosome, i=1, 2,…, p. Select two chromosomes randomly from the population as the parents according to the probability distribution $\{p_i | i=1, 2, \ldots, p\}$.

(5) Produce new chromosomes. We use two-point probability distribution, and choose a genetic operation via a random switch from mutation and crossover and then produce two new chromosomes. Repeat this procedure to get p new chromosomes.

(6) Renew population. Calculate the distance of each new chromosome and add these p chromosomes to the current population. According to the distance of these $2p$ chromosomes, and then choose the best p chromosomes to generate new population.

(7) Stopping qualification. Repeat the above procedure to get the population generation by generation until the largest total signed distance. This largest distance is associated with the best chromosome in the population.

After stopping, output the best chromosome in the last population. The initial values of the population are given by uniformly distributed (on [0, 1]) random numbers and a reorder program is used to guarantee the monotonicity of parameters μ.

4. EXPERIMENTS

We applied CI on four publicly datasets of NASA software projects: PC1, PC4, KC1 and CM1. PC1 is flight software from an earth orbiting satellite that is no longer operational. It consists of 40 KLOC of C code. PC4 is flight software from an earth orbiting satellite that is currently operational. It consists of 36 KLOC of C code. KC1 is a single CSCI within a large ground system. It is made up of 43 KSLOC of C++ code. CM1 is from a science instrument. It is written in C code with approximately 20 KSLOC. Each dataset contains 21 software metrics at the module-level the associated dependent Boolean variable-defect. The number of software modules for each of these datasets and the number of defect and non-defect modules are listed in Table 1.

Table 1. Dataset properties.

	PC1	PC4	KC1	CM1
Size	1059	1347	1571	496
FP	76	178	1252	48
NFP	983	1169	319	448

4.1. *Performance measures*

The performance of prediction models for two-class problem which is defect or non-defect is typically evaluated using a confusion matrix, which is shown in Table 2. In this study, we used the commonly used prediction performance measures: accuracy, precision, recall and F-measure to evaluate and compare prediction models quality. These measures are derived from the confusion matrix.

Table 2. Confusion matrix.

		Predicted	
		Non-defect	Defect
Actual	Non-defect	TN=True Negative	FP=False Positive
	Defect	FN=False Negative	TP=True Positive

Accuracy (*Acc*), *Precision* (*P*), *Recall* (*R*) and *F-measure* (*F*) is calculated as follows respectively

$$Acc = (TP + TN)/(TP + TN + FP + FN) \tag{17}$$

$$P = TP/(TP + FP) \tag{18}$$

$$R = TP/(TP + FN) \tag{19}$$

$$F = (Precision \times Recall)/(\alpha \times R + (1-\alpha) \times p) \tag{20}$$

Where α is weight, it is set 0.5.

4.2. *Data preprocessing*

The variables are 21 metrics at the module including McCabe, Halstead, Line Count, and Branch Count. To make sure that only relevant variables are included in the datasets, we applied to wipe off the redundant variables of the needless and the repetitive metrics, which are possessed of similarity classification information in the datasets. This involves searching through all possible combinations of variables in the dataset to find which subset of variables works best for prediction. The algorithm evaluates the each subset of variables by considering the individual predictive ability of each variable along with the degree of redundancy between them. So, this way reduced the metric dimension in effective and shortens the training time. It can be adaptive adjusted the variance rate in the evolutionary process and prevent the premature of GA. Table 3 provides the resulted best subset of independent variables in each dataset.

Table 3. Metrics retained after selection for the different datasets.

Dataset	Subset of Selected
PC1	Loc, E,V(g), I, LOCodeAndComment, LOComment, LOBlank, Uniq-Op
PC4	Loc, LOComment, E, V, L, Uniq-Opnd
KC1	Loc Loc, V, D, V(g), LOCode, LOComment, LO-Blank, Uniq-Op, Uniq-Opnd
CM1	Loc, IV(g), K, I, LOComment, LoBlank

4.3. *Experiment results*

For experiments, the classification task of CI is to distinguish between erroneous and correct software modules. In order to do so, we have made an 80%/20% stratified split up of the original datasets into training and test datasets. To compare the results of proposed method, a benchmarking study is performed that includes commonly used state-of-the-art classification techniques C4.5, SVM and AntMiner+. In experiments, the penalty-factor α=0.05. The crossover probability was set to 0.9 and the mutation probability was 0.01. In experiments, the preset parameters are a=(0,0), b=(1,1), M=0.1 and FM are random data. The classifying boundaries of four projects are shown in Figure 1(a-d).

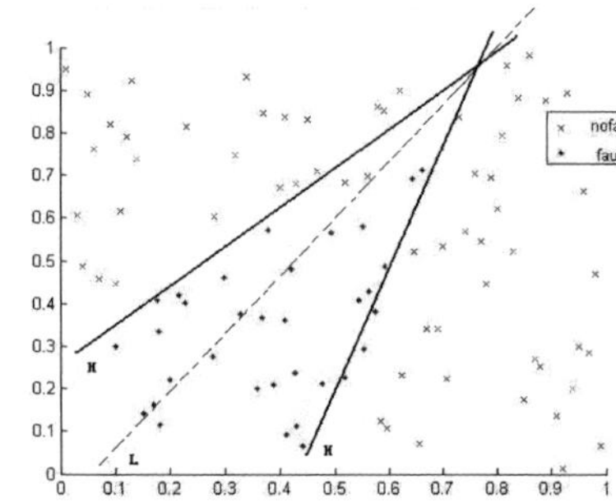

(a) PC1

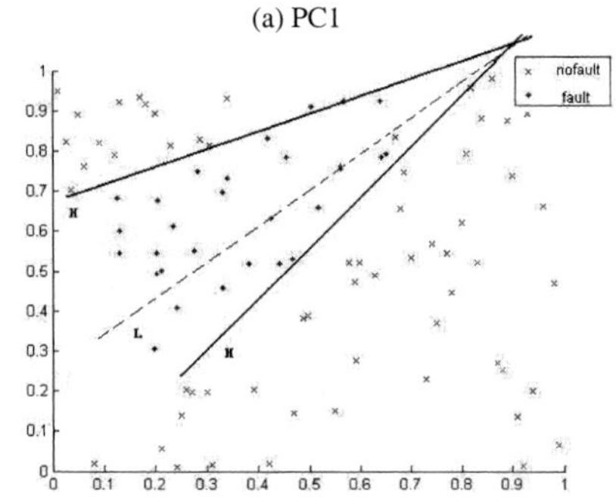

(b) KC1

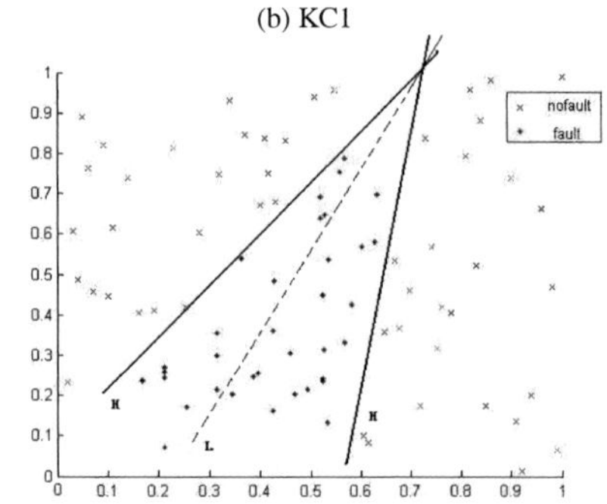

(c) PC4

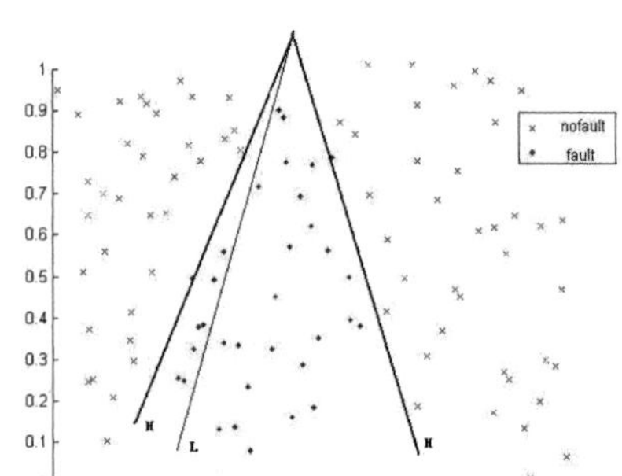

(d) CM1

Figure 1. Hyperplanes of PC1, KC1, PC4 and CM1.

Fig. 1(a-d) show the classes' boundary of the four dataset software module. It can be observed that the classes' boundary is the clearing. So we can believe CI is a good approach, and it is the effective in the software module classify. In proposed approach, we can automatic selection of the least misclassification rate, and penalize the misclassified points.

From Fig. 2(e-h), we can observe the accuracy of predict on the four dataset used in the simulation experiment where the projection line *L*, the predict accuracy is dramatically high the by nonlinear CI and the interaction of the metric, especially at the genetic evolution stabilized after 50 generations, the predict accuracy rate more than 90%, even 95%.

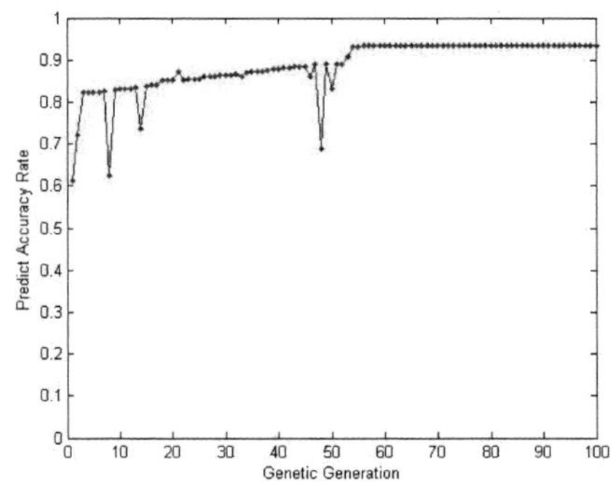

(a) PC1

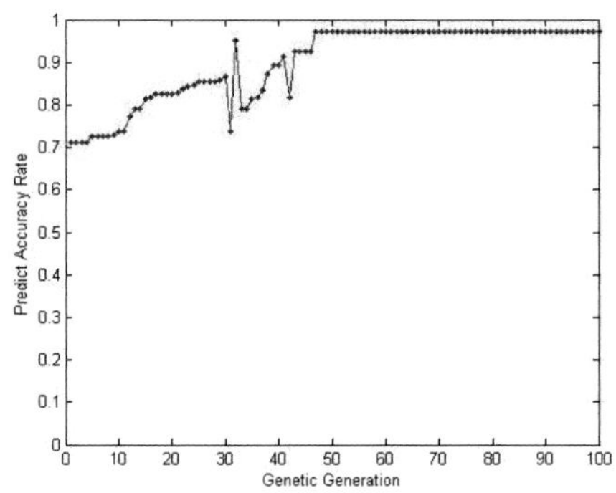

(b) KC1

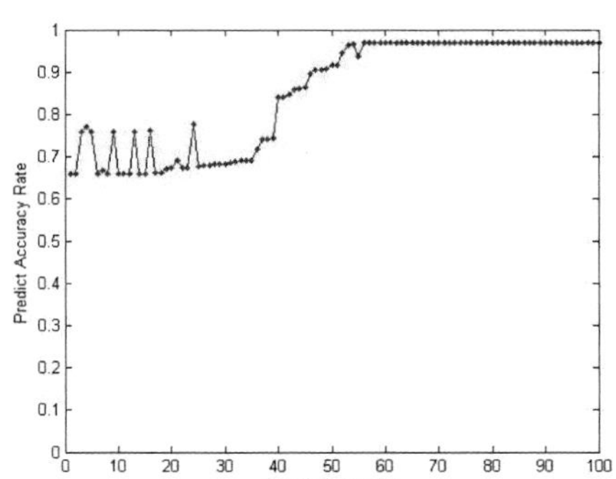

(c) PC4

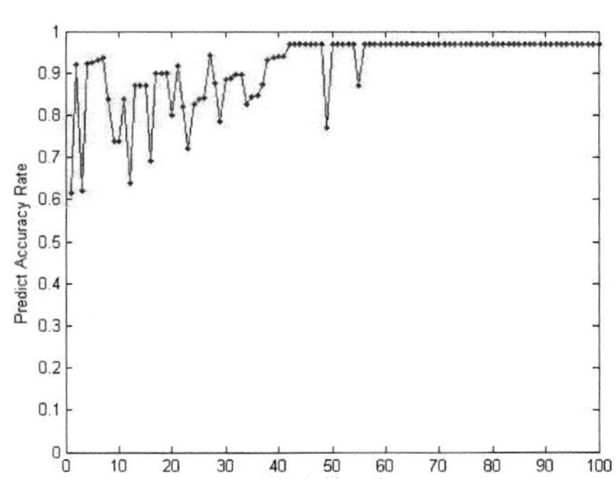

(d) CM1

Figure 2. Predict accuracy rates.

In addition, the comparison results of different predict models are listed in Table 4.

Table 4. Compared result of proposed model with other models.

Prediction model	Accuracy	Precision	Recall	*F*-measure
C4.5	79.87	77.08	71.70	71.95
SVM	84.59	84.95	97.28	96.58
AntMiner+	80.51	91.67	88.12	88.29
Proposed method	85.68	80.75	98.07	97.02

On the whole, the results indicate that proposed approach is competitive and can be regarded as one of the best software quality predict model.

5. CONCLUSIONS

In this paper, we first introduce CI classification technique for predicting software defect. This method allows automatic search for the least misclassification rate and can discriminate defect modules and non-defect modules. We can used to discover classification boundary in software modules to improve the software development quality. We run CI classifier on four software project datasets and evaluate and the performance of proposed approach with other compared models in the four datasets. The simulation results show that the prediction performance of proposed model is generally better than other models.

ACKNOWLEDGMENT

This work was supported by the science and technology research program of Wuhan of China (Grant No. 201210121023).

REFERENCES

— [1] Roberto B, Andrea P. 2010. Brain-computer evolutionary multi-objective optimization (BC-EMO): a genetic algorithm adapting to the decision maker. *IEEE Transactions on Evolutionary Computation*, 14(15), 671-687.
— [2] Basili V, Briand L, Melo W. 1996. A validation of object-oriented design metrics as quality indicators. *IEEE Transactions on Software Engineering*, 22(10), 751-761.
— [3] Karim O E, Mahmoud O E. 2008. Predicting defect-prone software modules using support vector machines. *Journal of Systems and Software*, 81(5), 649-660.
— [4] Vandecruys O, Martens D, Baesens B, Mues C, Backer M De, Haesen R. 2008. Mining software repositories for comprehensible software fault prediction models. *Journal of Systems and Software*, 81(5), 823-839.
— [5] Chen J S, Cheng C.H. 2008. Extracting classification rule of software diagnosis using modified MEPA. *Expert Systems with Applications*, 3(1), 411-418.

- [6] Zimmermann H.J. 1991. *Fuzzy Set Theory and Its Applications*, Kluwer, Boston.
- [7] Cong J, Shu-wei J. 2014. Applications of fuzzy integrals for predicting software fault-prone. *Journal of Intelligent and Fuzzy Systems*, 26(2), 721-729.
- [8] Ha M H. 1998. *Fuzzy Measure and Fuzzy Integral Theory. Beijing*, Science Press.
- [9] Kvan T. 2000. Collaborative design: what is it? *Automation in Construction*, 9(4), 409-415.

The Research on Clustering Java Program Based on Extended Jaccard Coefficient

*L.H. Zhong, X.M. Huang, J.J. Li, N.W. Zhang & M.S. Ye
College of Computer and Information Engineering, Jiangxi Normal University, Nanchang, China, 330022
**Email: 1674428@qq.com*

ABSTRACT: In order to improve the quality of the Java source code for meeting the design requirements of the "high cohesion, low coupling". This paper proposes the extended Jaccard coefficient for measuring the similarity between the class not only considering the inheritance, association etc, but also the method caller and called relationship. Also we implement a prototype system to aid software maintains by clustering several closely related classes into the same package. The tests show that the structure of java source code is the more in line with the characteristics of high cohesion and low coupling after adjustment.

KEYWORDS: Jaacard coefficient; Clustering; High cohesion; Low coupling; Software refactoring.

1. INTRODUCTION

During software engineering practice, it shows that if the structure of the software meets the "high cohesion, low coupling" design features, the ripple effect caused by the software change control can not only be varied within more smaller range, but also the cost of the software maintenance can be reduced. However, due to various reasons, for example, the programmer's coding style is not strictly in accordance with the design documentation, which may lead to the implementation not complying with the "high cohesion, low coupling" feature.

For overcoming this problem, in this paper we investigate how to improve the structure of the Java source codes to meet the features of "high cohesion, low coupling" based on our previous research [1, 2, 3]. By mapping the relation such as inheritance, association and method called etc. to the attribution and mapping class to entity, this paper proposes the extended Jaccard coefficient to define the distance between entities and use a hierarchical clustering algorithm to provide (semi) automation software support for modifying the program structure.

The remaining sections of this paper are organized as follows. Section 2 presents an overview of related work on software refactoring, Section 3 presents the extended Jaccard coefficient and its meaning. The process of clustering based on extended Jaccard coefficient with an example is presented in Section 4. Section 5 presents the evaluation of the new technique based on MQ [15]. The conclusions and future work are outlined in Section 6.

2. RELATED WORKS

Software refactoring, which is the process of changing a [object-oriented] software system in such a way that it does not alter the external behavior of the code, yet improves its internal structure [9]. In recent years, lots of methods such as data clustering had been proposed on how to implement the software refactoring, data clustering is a kind of technology that a set of physical or abstract objects could be grouped into multiple classes of similar objects [4], it can solve some problems in the domain of software refactoring. For example, S.Mancoridis analysised the extracted module dependency graph by clustering and the results are presented to user by visualizing for the clustering analysis [5]. In order to achieve the program's modularization The Marios Fokaefs proposed a metric based on Jaccard coefficient , and used a hierarchical clustering algorithm to identify the likely classes needed to be refactored, finally they given a metric indicator of evaluating program design quality [6]; Jens Dietrich constructed Java program dependence graph by using BARRIO(Eclipse plugin), and used clustering technology to analysis their implementations, then compared the cluster with program packages, thereby identified the place needs to be refactored [7]. Alkhalid used a variety of clustering algorithms to analyze the source code, and investigated how to refactoring in the case of keeping the same number of Java package or reseting the number of packages [8]. Keith Cassell developed a visualization tools named ExtC, which can help programmers use the clustering algorithms to reconstruct the program, through visual means, they can recognize the important feature of the relationship between the class members and members [11]. Simon used the virtual modeling language and the three-dimensional way to show the distance between the class members, helping programmers to choose the likely refactoring places related to the class properties and methods [12]. The Ducasse proposed the concept of relative metric and absolute metric and developed a visualization tools providing a global and relative views [13].

3. THE EXTENDED JACCARD COEFFICIENT

Before using the hierarchical clustering algorithm, firstly we need to define the similarity calculation formula among Java classes. Jaccard coefficient (also Jaccard index) [9, 10] has been widely used and great influence in the area of software modularization, the formula is given as followed:

$$\text{Jaccard}(X, Y) = \frac{|X \cap Y|}{|X \cup Y|} \quad (1)$$

The numerator represents intersections of entity X with entity Y Properties collection, denominator denote the union of entity X and entities Y Properties. However, Jaccard coefficient only be considered in the calculation of the distance between the two entities, reflecting the relative similarity between the two entities. It lacks the ability to measure the similarity between entities within the global scope; it may lead to the result that multiple strong dependency classes may not be reconstructed in the same package. For avoiding those situations, this paper gives the extended Jaccard coefficient as followed.

$$D(X, Y) = \frac{|X \cap Y|}{|M|} \quad (2)$$

In formula (2), the numerator represents the same number of elements in the set of attributes X and the set of attributes Y, denominator M is the sum of the number of all entities in the application set of attributes. The larger the value of d (x, y) described entities E (x) of the set of attributes represented by X and Y represents a set of attributes of entity E (y), the greater the similarity value and the stronger dependence, i.e. X represents a class of the attribute set C (x) and Y represents a set of attributes of the class C (y) may need to put in a package through after clustering; the value of d (x, y) turn smaller, then smaller similarity of the E (x) and E (y) and the weaker the dependence, so the C (x) and C (y) may not be required by clustering into a package; when d (x, Y) = 0, the two entities have completely not interaction, attribute do not have the same elements in the collection, that is not the same property values, clustering two attribute collections on behalf of the class may be placed in two different packages; when d (x, y) = 1, the two entities are equal and there is a relationship between the only two entities on behalf of the class in the program, and other entities are independent to each other, that is, other classes and between classes without calling relationships and dependencies between C (x) C (y), C (x) and C (y) should be placed in a package.

4. CLUSTERING BASED ON THE EXTENDED JACCARD COEFFICIENT PREPARING THE NEW FILE WITH THE CORRECT TEMPLATE

4.1. *The definition of entity and attribute set*

Definition 1 Entity: refers to the Java classes in package, represented by the symbol E (class name). For example, the class Game is denoted E (Game) in Figure 1.

Definition 2 Attribute set: for the entity E (class name), the symbol of A (class name) represents the corresponding set of attribute, which mainly can be considered under the following situation:

- If one class accesses or uses the other class's attributes and methods, the later class's attributes and methods will be included in the attribute set. For simplicity, the attribute set does not contain the API functions. That is, If Attribute a or Method f in the class B of package P is accessed by the other Class c of other packages ,then P.B.a∈A(C)or P.B.f()∈A(C).
- Consider the called class's attributes and methods. If the Attribute a or Method f of the Class C in packet P is accessed by other classes, then P.C.a∈A(C)or P.C.f()∈A(C)
- Consider the inherit relationship: if Class c inherits the Class b of Package P, then P.B∈A(C)
- Consider the aggregation relationship: if Class B in Package P belongs to Class C, then P.B∈A(C)
- Consider the association relationship: if Class C references Class B in Package P, then P.B∈A(C).

4.2. *Similarity matrix*

The similarity matrix portray the similarity between entity similarity algorithm, used in this paper are as follows:

Input: *A // A is the set of the entity and its attribute set*
Output: *smimatrix*
Program creatmatrix

```
Begin
Dim classattribute As String[][];
Dim smimatrix As Float[][] ;
Dim i As int;      Dim n,k As float;
Begin
classattribute[][]=A;
n=elementlenth(classmattribute);
// elementlenth()is used to count the number of theattributes
for i = 0 to classattribute.length;
for m = i + 1 to classattribute.length;
{
callk=getsame(i);       // get the common attribute
smimatrix[i][m]=k/n;
}
End;
```

For example, in order to calculate the similarity matrix of Figure 1, in which the five classes belong to different packages, i.e. Class entry belongs to Package P1, Class game belongs to Package P2, Class gui belongs to Packet P3, Class logik belongs to Packet P4, Class round belongs to P5. The sets of attributes of entity for each class are followed.

A(entry)={P1.entry.getActPos(),P1.entry.entry(),P1.entry.setActPos() }

A(game)={ P4.logik.logik(),P3.gui.gui(),P3.gui.setLogik(),P4.logik.setGui() }

A(gui)={P4.logic.logik(),P3.gui.Jposition,P3.gui.gui(),P2.game.main()}

A(logik)={P4.logik.setGui(),P4.logik.logik(),P5.round.round(),P5.round.setEntry(),P5.round,set,ActPos(),P5.round.entries, P5.round.nset,P3.gui.JposNr,P3.gui.Jfrage, P5.round.getEntryActPos(),P2.game.main(),P5.round.getEntryText(),P5.round.lastset,P5.round.lastsetstat,P3.gui.Jposition}

A(round)={P5.round.round(),P5.round.lastsetstat,P5.round.se-tEntry(),P5.round.setActPos(),P5.round.entries,P5.round.nset,P5.round.getEntryActPos(),P5.round.getEntryText(),P5.round.lastset }

Take the above sets of attributes as input into the code; we construct a matrix as followed with the distance between classes.

	entry	game	gui	logik	round
entry	0.0	0.0	0.0	0.0	0.09375
game	0.0	0.0	0.0625	0.03125	0.0
gui	0.0	0.0625	0.0	0.03125	0.0
logik	0.0	0.03125	0.03125	0.0	0.1875
round	0.09375	0.0	0.0	0.1875	0.0

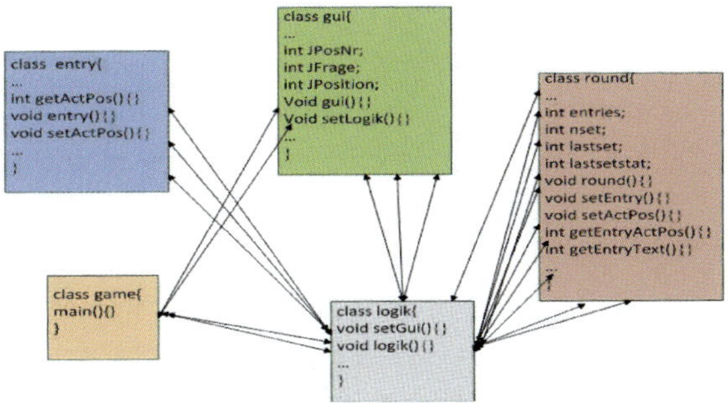

Figure 1. The class diagram of an application.

4.3. *Clustering based on similarity matrix*

Then we adopt the cohesion-type hierarchical clustering techniques [5]. That is, based on the similarity matrix above, the result is shown in Table 1.

Table 1. The compared results.

	Use the Jaccard coefficient	Use the extended Jaccard coefficient
The number of the java package before	5	5
The number of the class	5	5
The number of the java package after clustering	4	4
The index of Java Package before	1 2 3 4 5	1 2 3 4 5
The index of Java Package after clustering	1 2 2 3 4	1 2 3 4 4

The first line indicates the number of packets in the game application is 3, the second line indicates the total number of classes of the game application is 5, and the third line represents the number of desired by the user to obtain a Java package is 4, the fifth line is the original packet number corresponding the entity attribute set, the seventh line of the clustering process results correspond to the number of entities where the package should be placed in the same package. The result is presented by the set "1 2 3 4 4", where the number of four respectively correspond to the Class logi and round Figure 1 is, which means that the logik class and round class should be placed in a package, a corresponding entity Entry indicates entry class should be independent in a package, 2,3 on behalf of the game and the gui should be placed in a different package. According to the above results and with reference to Figure 1, it shows that the dependencies between the Logik class and the round class relatively stronger than the dependencies between the game class and the GUI class, so the logik class and round class relatively would be more reasonable to put into a package.

5. THE IMPLEMENTATION OF THE SYSTEM

The system is divided into three parts in figure 2: the pre-processing module based clustering algorithm, the interactive refactoring module, and the comparison module before and after.

- The preprocessing module based on clustering algorithm: this module is the basic for the java program refactoring later, it takes the program dependency model as input and stores the output in a text file, then the user can decide do an interactive refactoring or take automatically refactoring.
- The interactive refactoring module: this module is based on the results of pre-processing module and guarantee the program can be compiled successfully after refactoring without changing the external behavior Interactive means the user can join the refactoring process and the final system can be reconstructed from the database.
- The comparison module: this module users can clearly see the the reconfigurable packet structure before and after contrast chart, comparison chart can be very straightforward to know the effects before and after refactoring.

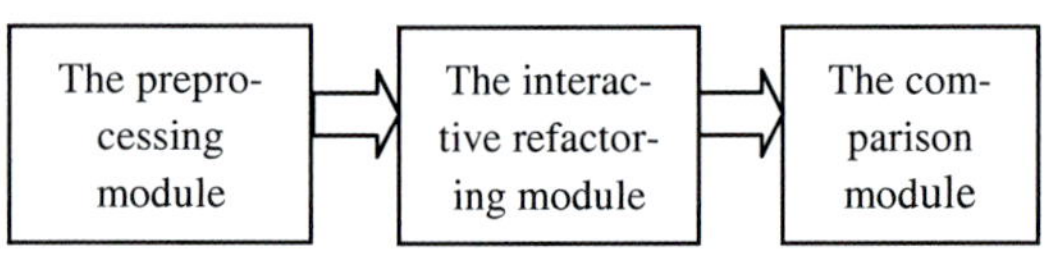

Figure 2. The system of refactoring at Java package level based on Clustering.

6. EVALUATION

In order to evaluate the quality of the clustering about the different number of the packages objectively, we selected module division quality evaluation formula MQ that proposed in literature [12], MQ is defined as follows.

$$MQ \begin{cases} \frac{1}{k}\sum_{i=1}^{k} A_i - \frac{1}{\frac{k(k-1)}{2}}\sum_{i,j=1}^{k} E_{i,j} & k>1 \\ A_1 & k=1 \end{cases}$$

Where, Ai represents the internal correlation in the ith sub-graph, the internal correlation of the ith sub-graph is decided by the N_i nodes consisted of the sub-graph and the edges correlation μ_i among the nodes; $E_{i,j}$ is the correlation between the ith sub-graph and the jth sub-graph, $E_{i,j}$ is determined by the number N_i, N_j of the nodes and the edges correlation between the ith sub-graph and the jth sub-graph. MQ is a value ranged from -1 to 1, The more larger the value MQ is, the more possibility the effect of clustering meets principle about "high cohesion, low coupling".

We take the jaccard coefficient and the extended Jaccard coefficient proposed in this paper as the similarity calculation formula respectively to cluster the Checkstyle system[1]. When the scope number of packages is from 3 to 9, the MQ about the effect of different division is shown in Table 1. We can find that when the number of the packages is 4,7,8 and 9, the division based the extended Jaccard is better than the division based Jaccard. For example, figure 3 and figure 4 shows that Checkstyle system produced different division based on the two different coefficients when the number of packages is set to 4.

Table 2. Comparsion of different MQ about checkstyle system.

	3	4	5	6	7	8	9
Jaccard	0.1507	0.16872	0.19688	0.20747	0.15921	0.13695	0.12643
extendedJaccard	0.1507	0.17804	0.19433	0.20608	0.17097	0.14285	0.12908

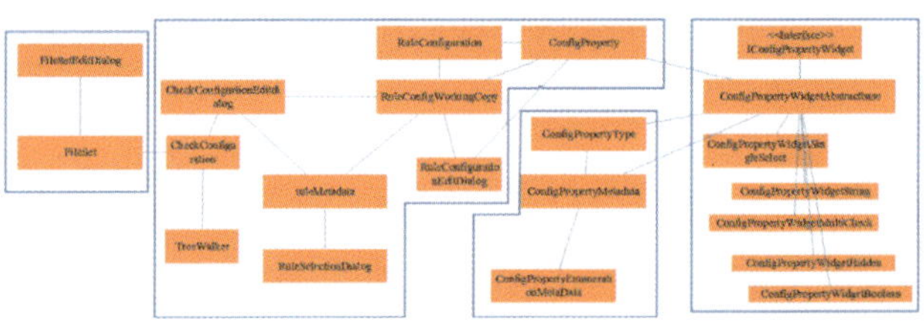

Figure 3. The division based on Jaccard when the No. of packages is 4.

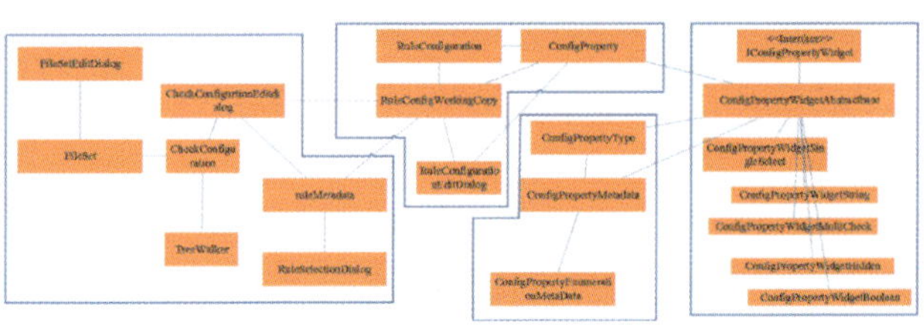

Figure 4. The division based on extended Jaccard when the No. of packages is 4.

7. CONCLUSION

Software refactoring is a way to improve the quality of software, in order to allow Java programs to meet the "high cohesion, low coupling" features in the structure, this paper presents the implementation of the Java source code based on the hierarchical clustering algorithm clustering. In this paper, we make a mapping between the elements in the Java program such as inheritance, call relationship into the entities and attributes in the cluster. Also we analysis the shortcoming of Jaccard coefficient and propose Extend Jaccard coefficient, based on which a hierarchical clustering algorithm is used to reconstruct the

[1] http://sourceforge.net/projects/checkstyle/?source=directory

Java package. the experimental results show that some problems by using our method can be more in line with the characteristics of "high cohesion, low coupling" on certain issues. Indeed Our works is Similar with the work mentioned in Reference 8, but their similarity calculation method only consider the call relationship between classes, not consider others relationship between the class and lack of the ability to measure the similarity between the entities within the global scope.

ACKNOWLEDGMENT

The article is sponsored by the National Natural Science Foundation Project (No. 61262015, No. 61462040), Jiangxi Provincial Natural Science Foundation Project (20142BAB207027, 20142BAB207011), Jiangxi science and technology support project (20142BBE50028), the Science and Technology Project of Jiangxi Provincial Education Department (GJJ13230).

REFERENCES

- [1] Zhong Lin Hui, Research on the evolution information acquisition and application in CBSE[D] Peking Univ. 2007.
- [2] Zhong Lin Hui, Xie Bing, Shao Wei-Zhong, Supporting component-based software development by extending the CDL with software configuration information Computer Research and Development, China, 2002.10
- [3] Zhong Lin-hui, Yao Xin-fan, Xu Jing, Li Hui, Research on strategy of software architecture refactoring based on clustering of component dependency relation, Application Research of Computers, 2010.8.
- [4] J. Han and M. Kamber Data Mining: Concepts and Techniques Third Edition (The Morgan Kaufmann Series in Data Management Systems) (M). ISBN 978-0-12-381479-1 Elsevier Publication, 2011.
- [5] S. Mancoridis and Mitchell, B.S, Using Automatic Clustering to Produce High-Level System Organizations of Source Code, the 6th International Workshop on Program Comprehension , Page(s): 45 – 52, 1998.
- [6] Marios Fokaefs and Tsantalis N, Decomposing Object-Oriented Class Modules Using an Agglomerative Clustering Technique, Software Maintenance, 2009. ICSM 2009. IEEE International Conference on, Pages(s): 20-26, Sept. 2009.
- [7] Jens Dietrich and Vyacheslav Yakovlev, Cluster Analysis of Java Dependency Graphs, Proceeding SoftVis '08, Proceedings of the 4th ACM symposium on Software visualization, Pages 91-94 New York, USA, 2008.
- [8] A. Alkhalid and Alshayeb M, Software refactoring at the package level using clustering techniques [J]. Software, IET June 2011, pages: 276-284.
- [9] N. Anquetil & T. Lethbridge. Experiments with Clustering as a Software Remodularization Method. Proceedings of the 6th Working Conference on Reverse Engineering, 1999.
- [10] Peter H.A. Sneath and Robert R. Sokal. Numerical Taxonomy. Series of books in biology. W.H. Freeman and Company, San Francisco, 1973.
- [11] Keith Cassell, Craig Anslow, Lindsay Groves, Peter Andreae Visualizing the Refactoring of Classes via Clustering. ACSC 2011.
- [12] Simon, F., Steinbrckner, F. & Lewerentz, C., Metrics based refactoring, Proceedings of the Fifth European Conference on Software Maintenance and Reengineering, 2001.
- [13] St´ephane Ducasse Butterflies: A Visual Approach to Characterize Packages In Proceedings of the 11th IEEE International Software Metrics Symposium 2005.
- [14] M. Fowler, Refactoring: Improving the Design of Existing Programs. Addison-Wesley, 1999.
- [15] S. Mancoridis, B. Mitchell, Y. Chen, and E. Gansner. Bunch: A clustering tool for the recovery and maintenance of software system structures. Proceedings of the 15th International Conference on Software Maintenance, 1999 P.50–59.

The Overall Architecture Design and Implementation of CET-4 Diagnostic Practice System

D.Y. Liu*, H. Zhang & M. Wu
Center of Modern Educational Technology, University of Science and Technology of China, Hefei, China
E-mail: derekwolf@163.com

ABSTRACT: Firstly, the theory and techniques of the CET4 Diagnostic Practice System were analyzed. Secondly, the architecture and development mode of the system has been determined and the main functional modules has been designed detailedly. Last, the implementation of system architecture has been elaborated on the basis of the development environment and tools. This system is a kind of deep practice and innovation on CET-4, aimed at learners can receive personalized learning guidance and targeted diagnostic evaluation according to their characteristics, thus improving the standard of English learners and learning ability, so it has a wide range of prospect and practical value.

KEYWORDS: English; Study; System; Diagnostic evaluation.

The College English Test (CET), as a national standardized teaching exam, has become one of the standards when the enterprises and institutions hire the university graduates [1]. In the process of learning English, the learners have different understanding and expression disorder due to different basal levels and learning progress, so personalized assessment of learning outcomes and periodically diagnoses of learning disabilities is the effective method of improve the standard of English learners. Diagnostic evaluation, also known as "teaching evaluation", generally refers to the prediction about the students' states, such as knowledge, skills and emotion, before the teaching activities or during the teaching process [2].

Based on this, this paper attempts to design and implement CET-4 Diagnostic Practice System, as an online learning system which takes the CET-4 as the background, provides the learners with personalized recommendations and help them enhance the English [3]. There were two versions in the development process of the system, the first one which has only the student-side and the administrator-side without the teacher-side is intended for independent learning of students without the guidance of teachers while the second one adds the teacher-side based on the first one, the student can learn English under the guidance of teachers to promote teaching at the school.

1. TECHNICAL BASIS

1.1. *MVC design pattern*

MVC, short for Model-View-Controller, is a software architecture model used to implement the user interface in the software engineering, which divides a given software into three parts-model, view, controller to separate the input, processing and output of the application [4].

The main advantages of the MVC design pattern are enhancing the reusability of the code and weakening the coupling of the code. The system is a large application, which needs complicated development, so the advantages of the MVC design pattern plays a more important role in the development process of the large-scale software.

1.2. *ASP.NET MVC framework*

ASP.NET is a Web application framework of the sever-side designed for Web developers to generate dynamic web pages, which is developed by Microsoft to provide convenience for the programmer to create dynamic websides, web applications and network services, which is essentially a development platform based on common language runtime [5].

ASP.NET MVC Framework is an open-source Web application framework, which is one of ASP.NET development model, which means using MVC design pattern for developing ASP.NET applications [6]. ASP.NET MVC framework combines the advantages of the three technologies-WebForm, MVC and agile application development, which is favored by the majority of programmers.

2. SYSTEM DESIGN

2.1. *System architecture design*

The system uses the ASP.NET MVC framework, which is divided into three parts-model, view, controller. Because the users are three roles- students, teachers and administrators and their functions are different, the Area mechanism is used to divide the system into two different subsides-the subside of students as well as the subside of teachers and administrators, each of whom has its own intact MVC directory structure. As is shown in Figure 1.

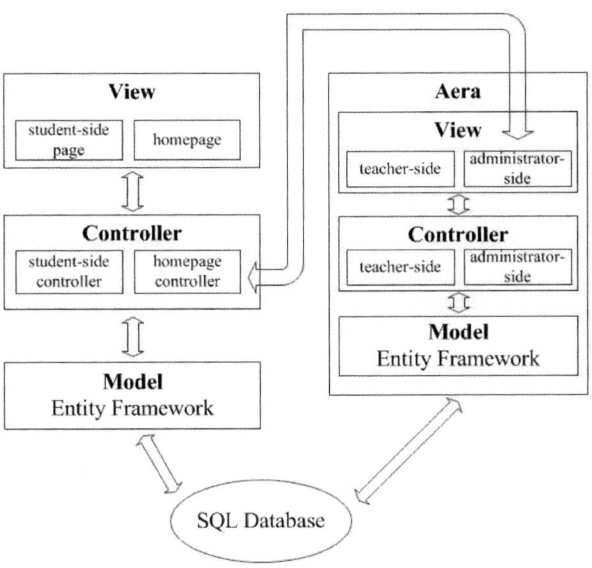

Figure 1. The system architecture diagram.

2.2. *Function module design*

The system concludes seven main modules based on features-system login, autonomous giving paper, personalized generating paper, answering papers, homework evaluation, statistical diagnosis and user management. The seven modules and the three user subsystems (the subsystem of students, the subsystem of teachers and the subsystem of administrators) are interconnected, as is shown in Figure 2.

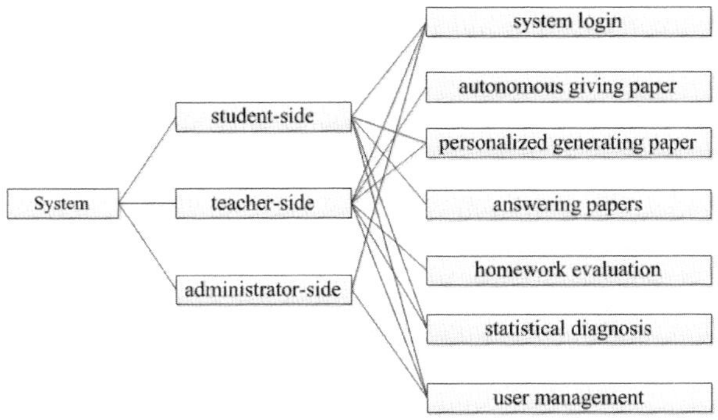

Figure 2. The function module diagram.

2.2.1. *System login*

It's to identify the users' identity and provide different functions and privileges. The types of users are students, teachers and administrators.

2.2.2. *Autonomous giving paper*

It's a unique feature of teachers, who can add a new set of questions to the system for the use of students. The teachers need to set the basic information such as title, time, score, type and question type of the papers (standard paper set provided).

2.2.3. *Personalized generating paper*

It consists of two parts-autonomous practice of students and assigning homework of teachers. In the autonomous practice of students, the system offers six training modes-random, real CET-4 papers, types of questions, knowledge points, the weakness of knowledge points and maximum score. While the teachers can assign the homework for students by choosing following three modes in the assigning homework of teachers-real CET-4 papers, types of questions and knowledge points.

2.2.4. *Answering papers*

It's only for students, which includes two parts-paper display and paper saving. Papers will display the questions by modules according to the types of them, the questions of the same type display on one page, which will jump to another page when click on the button of next question.

2.2.5. *Homework evaluation*

It's a unique feature of teachers, who can view and evaluate the homework submitted by students and put the feedback of evaluation details to the interface of student-side.

2.2.6. *Statistical diagnosis*

It shows three sections in the subsystem of students:

1. Recent test scoring rate trend chart, the system offers a test scoring rate trend chart of the student in nearly 10 times, the average scoring rate of all tests and the volatility of scoring rate in nearly 3-time practices.

2. The situation of mastering the knowledge points, the system shows a chart of the average scoring rate of all students at each knowledge point, average scoring rate of knowledge points of the cumulative tests of the student, the knowledge points that the scoring rates failed and the knowledge points that the scoring rates are lower than the overall level.

3. The scoring situation of the types of questions, which contains the scoring rates of all kinds of questions of all users and of the distribution of the scoring rates of all kinds of questions the student.

It shows two sections in the subsystem of teachers:

1. In the overall situation, the system can help teachers count the total information of four parts-the number and scoring rates of questions answered autonomously, the scoring rates of assigning homework and the average scoring rate of all the students of the specified class in the specified time as well as the detailed information of three parts-recent test scoring rate, knowledge points scoring rate and the scoring rate of the types of questions of each student.

2. In the performance details, teachers can see the scores, the highest score, the lowest score, the average score and the variance of a certain homework of all the students of a certain class and the scoring rates of knowledge points and all kinds of types of questions as well as error-prone question number and knowledge points of corresponding class in several tests.

2.2.7. *User management*

In this system, the main function of this module includes three parts: student-side allows students only to modify their personal information; teacher-side allows teachers not only to modify their personal basic information but also to manage classes; administrator-side can add and delete teachers as well as bulk-import students.

3. SYSTEM IMPLEMENTATION

The system is hierarchically designed and developed to achieve the functions of the system based on the ASP.NET MVC framework, using SQL SERVER 2008 database management tools, applying C# programming language, guided by a unified idea of software development, following the MVC design pattern [7].

3.1. *Model*

The directory structure diagram of the Models is shown in Figure 3.

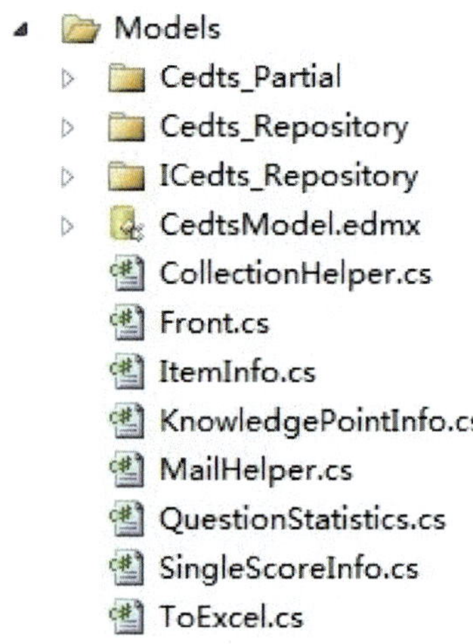

Figure 3. The directory structure diagram of the Models.

Entity Data Model is performed by files suffixed "edmx" in Visual Studio project, which can be visual edited. The method of database mapping is used to finalize the construction of the entire entity data model stored in the file named "App.config" through generating entity data models by mapping the entities and relationship models directly from existed database, excluding sensitive data from the connection string and setting in the application code and selecting the database objects included in the models-tables, views and storing procedures.

Meanwhile repository pattern is used to package entity data models in the database to create a consistent data access method to weaken coupling of modules, which can be achieved by three steps-creating interfaces related to data operation and defining methods; achieving the above interfaces; operating classes through interfaces in the controller layer.

The interfaces and classes are classified by creating an interface folder named "ICedts_Repository" and a class folder named "Cedts_Repository" for clearer program logic and more convenient maintenance. Operating system user data will be described as an example as follows.

(1) Create an user data interface named "ICedts_UserRepository", the code is shown as follows:

```
public interface ICedts_UserRepository
{
bool LogOn(string Account, string Password);
......
}
```

(2) Implement interface "ICedts_UserRepository", the code is shown as follows:

```
public class Cedts_UserRepository : ICedts_UserRepository
{
CedtsEntities db;
public Cedts_UserRepository()
{
db = new CedtsEntities();
}
bool ICedts_UserRepository.LogOn(string Account, string Password)
{
return db.CEDTS_User.Where(p => p.UserAccount == Account && p.UserPassword == Password).FirstOrDefault() != null;
}
……
}
```

(3) Achieve data access through a new class "ICedts_UserRepository" in the controller layer, the code is shown as follows:

```
public class AccountController : Controller
{
ICedts_UserRepository _userrepository;
public AccountController(ICedts_UserRepository r)
{
_userrepository = r;
}
```

3.2. *Controller*

It is responsible for handling all of the pages logical business, which is getting the data from the model layer and transferring it to the view layer. The essence of the controller is class named ending of "Controller". The controller layer of the main module created three classes-AccountController (homepage), HomeController (student-side homepage) and PaperShowController (paper display); the controller layer of Area module created five classes-AdminController (teacher-side and administrator-side homepage), AssignController (assigning homework), PaperController (autonomous giving paper), ScoreController (score statistics) and UserController (User management). PaperShowController will be described to show some Action methods as an example, the code is shown as follows:

```
[Authorize(Roles = "学生用户")]
public ActionResult PaperShow()
{
if (Continues == "1") //Paper not finished
{
ViewData["title"] = ppc.paperTotal.Title;
ViewData["Temp"] = "1";
}
Else //Paper finished
{
ViewData["title"] = pp.Title;
ViewData["Temp"] = "2";
pp.timeList = new List<int>();
}
return View();
}
```

3.3. *View*

It consists of the pages of the system, responsible for the display of the system interface. The directory structure and the controller class as well as Action methods are one-to-one correspondence in the ASP.NET MVC framework. View has two ways to obtaining data form Action:

Account/LogOn.aspx gets user account name passed over from the Controller through ViewData["Name"], the code is shown as follows:

```
<%@ Page Title="" Language="C#" Inherits="System.Web.Mvc.ViewPage<dynamic>" %>
<!DOCTYPE html>
<html>
<head runat="server">
……
</head>
<body class="index">
……
<div id="after" style="display: none;">
<span id="ViewName">
<%:ViewData["Name"] %></span><br />
<span>使用诊断练习系统</span><br />
</div>
……
</body>
</html>
```

Strongly typed view adds the names of specific classes that page needs in the page declaration, Model objects are used to have a unified representation of specific classes in the page content, Account/UserTask.aspx will be described as an example, the code is shown as follows:

```
<%@ Page Title="" Language="C#"
Inherits="System.Web.Mvc.ViewPage<PagedList<Cedts_Test.Models.AssignedTask>>" %>
<!DOCTYPE html>
<html>
<head runat="server">
……
</head>
<body>
<p class = "tasktitle">未完成作业列表</p>
<table class="tbRecords" cellspacing="0">
<thead>
<tr>
<th class="pname">作业名称</th>
<th class="ptime">发布时间</th>
……
</tr>
</thead>
<tbody>
```

```
<% foreach (var item in Model)
{ %>
<tr>
<td class="pname"><%: item.TaskName%></td>
<td class="ptime"><%: String.Format("{0:g}", item.AssignTime)%></td>
......
</tr>
<% } %>
</tbody>
</table>
</body>
```

In order to reduce the complexity of the HTML tags in the process of view development and accelerate the development of the view layer, HTML helper methods are adopted to help to generate some HTML tags and content, which is mainly used for form submission and data validation.

Master Pages are used to make a unified style of pages having similar module functions. Different page styles are set based on different user roles-student-side uses Site.Master as a master page while teacher-side and administrator-side uses Admin.Master as master pages, which makes the system both well categorized and effectively distinguished.

4. EPILOGUE

The CET-4 Diagnostic Practice System has a detailed needs analysis, specification framework design, a rational module division and correct code programming based on scientific, reliable, secure and maintainable software engineering principle, which can not only pointedly provide learners with professional diagnostic evaluation to satisfy the requirement of learners' personalized learning but also provide teachers with the functions of autonomous giving paper, assigning homework and score management to have a comprehensive and detailed grasp of learning details of learners.

REFERENCES

- [1] Xiongying Tang. CET and College English Course Evaluation [J]. Foreign Language Education, 2005, 26(1): 56-60.
- [2] Scheerens J, Glas C, Thomas S M, et al. Educational evaluation, assessment and monitoring: A systematic approach [M]. Taylor & Francis, 2003.
- [3] Yejun Jiang. The Study on the Correlation of the Item Bank of Diagnostic Exercise System [D]. Hefei: University of Science and Technology of China. 2012.
- [4] Haibo Ouyang. Design and Implementation of the Task Management and Data reporting System based on ASP.NET MVC B/S Framework [D]. Chengdu: University of Electronic Science and Technology of China. 2012.
- [5] Zhen-Jun Fan. Implementation Method of ASP. net-based the Three Layers [J]. Computer Science, 2007, 4: 080.
- [6] Baoxi Huang. ASP.NET MVC 2 Development Training [M]. Beijing: Publishing House of Electronics Industry, 2011.
- [7] Len Bass, Paul Clements, Rick Kazman. Software Architecture in Practice [M]. Addison-Wesley Professional, 2003.

Application of Improved RBAC Model in Safety Quality System of Project Construction

J.H. Li
CCCC Fourth Highway Engineering Co, Ltd, Beijing, China

S. Qian*
The College of Traffic Management Cadres, Department of Computer Science Institute, Beijing, China

C.X. Zhang
CITIC Investment Co. Beijing, China

Email: qs250@qq.com

ABSTRACT: The user's identity management which becomes increasingly burdensome can be finished and the safety and reliability of the user's identity identification of the software system can be improved in virtue of RBAC model. RBAC module shall also be properly changed and modified based on the specific software application system to better adapt to and meet the business demand. Improved RBAC module is proposed in this paper based on the demand of the project construction enterprise through the study of the actual development process of the user's identity authority management in the safety quality system of project construction and the RBAC module-based workflow management system is also analyzed. In the operation process of the actual project, improved RBAC-based workflow platform has been successfully researched and developed and put into the project construction line. It plays a vital role in connecting several business systems and realizing the safety management of the user's identity in the management safety quality management of the project.

KEYWORDS: RBAC; Workflow; Architectural design.

1. INTRODUCTION

Many enterprises have come to realize the safety in advancing the informatization. The simple data and information encryption in the most general sense can no longer satisfy the user's safety demand which is always changed. In particularly, if the safety requirements are proposed for the authority and authorization management inside the enterprise, the enterprise's information will be certainly disclosed when the personnel change their post or are dismissed through the authority control and management inside the enterprise. Therefore, the basic demand of many enterprises in advancing the informatization and construction is the configuration based on the enterprise's internal basic authority. [2][3] As the one that operates and uses all the software systems, the user is the final objective for safety and configuration. As the demand of management integration, the role itself binds the authority and is finally authorized to the user. As a result, the user's management in all the enterprise's software system shall be developed again in order to realize the integrated management of the safety control of enterprise's informatization user. [1]

2. INTRODUCTION TO RBAC

2.1. *Basic contents*

RBAC (Role_Based Access Control) technology is the main way for the authority control of the modern information communication technology in the civil safety prevention field based on the basic technical idea that the visitor will not be authorized with authority individually but with role based on the management identity and then the data and then the operation authority of data and system are bound on the role defined by the system. Such mode enjoys actual application value in the actual commerce and application since the system operation authority is not related to the specific operation in the management mode but to the organization authority of the organization. In other words, all the operation authorities are decided by the role acted by the individual itself in the organization instead of the specific individual.

According to RBAC, the authorization of the specific visitor is no longer necessary to be considered since all the safety control cores have been transformed as the role authorization and authorization retaking. It has better safety strategy and flexible treatment way in the actual execution.

2.2. *Working principle*

The working principle of RBAC is developed based on the role and it is definitely the business logic relationship added between the user and authority. The direct business authority logic relationship between the user and authority is realized through the role. The user can finish the role configuration based on the actual situation. The role directly determines the authority scope of the operation data. On the basis of such business logic model, the user carries out level-based management authority according to its management demand. In general, the top authority is mainly focused on the system administrator and the authorization transmission of the personnel at all levels is realized through the administrator's top level-based authorization, but the complete authorization mode is not allowed. As a result, RBAC is not the initiative authorization, i.e., passive authorization mode, as shown in Fig. 1.

The authorization is developed by aiming at the user in the traditional way but the system needs to release the business logic relationships between the user and the system if the organization is changed, such as the post transfer or the dismissal of the personnel, making the software system development more complicated. As the role-based control management mode is enhanced, only the logic relationship between the user and the role needs releasing in the aforesaid management activity, which makes it highly flexible and applicable to the operation mode of daily management. The flexible and dynamic management of the user's authority is thus realized.

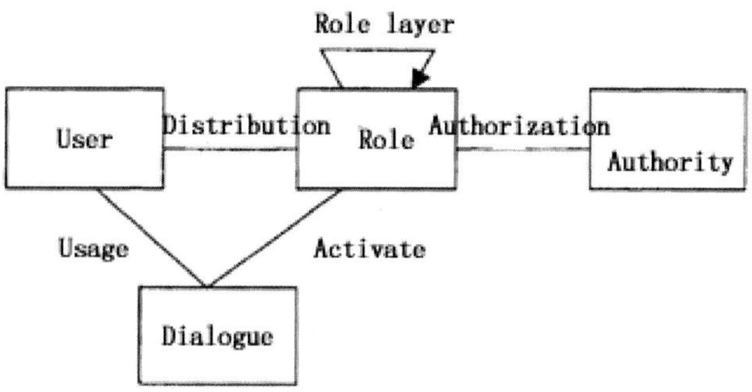

Figure 1. Basic principle diagram of RBAC model.

2.3. *Demand of RBAC model in the safety quality management of project construction enterprise*

Safety quality plays a vital role in the project construction and entails collaboration logic and single sign-on finished with the enterprise's all kinds of comprehensive project systems among the users. The planning and design of the enterprise's RBAC model-based workflow platform is the basic demand for the secondary platform development of the project construction enterprise in the future software system R & D. It generally consists of the following several points:

(1) Identification of the user's identity. The certification and recognition of the enterprise user's identity shall be finished and it is of necessity to judge if the user's identity information is correct by the RBAC-based workflow platform.

(2) Task of functional module configuration. The user's basic identity as well as the authority and operation logically associated by the identity shall be determined after such identity is successfully identified.

(3) Confirmation of user's department and identity. The department allocation after the user configuration (including the configuration of the user's group) and the configuration of special user's authority and identity identification shall be finished by RBAC-based workflow platform. The releasing of the user logic can be decided by RBAC principle and thus more flexible configuration is needed. [4]

(4) Safety management of user's login and secret key management. The safety identification prior to and during the user's login, safety identification of authority after login and the secret key encryption of critical information are finished based on RBAC-based workflow platform.

3. REALIZATION OF RBAC IN THE SAFETY QUALITY SYSTEM OF PROJECT CONSTRUCTION

3.1. *Basic architectural module*

On the basis of the safety quality system R & D of one project, this article is focused on how to realize the user's integral RBAC module control within the system. RBAC-based workflow platform generally needs to finish and realize the connection of the enterprise's safety quality system with the user's login management control and safety management function of other system platforms. [1] It includes eight main management demand functional module units, as shown in Fig. 2.

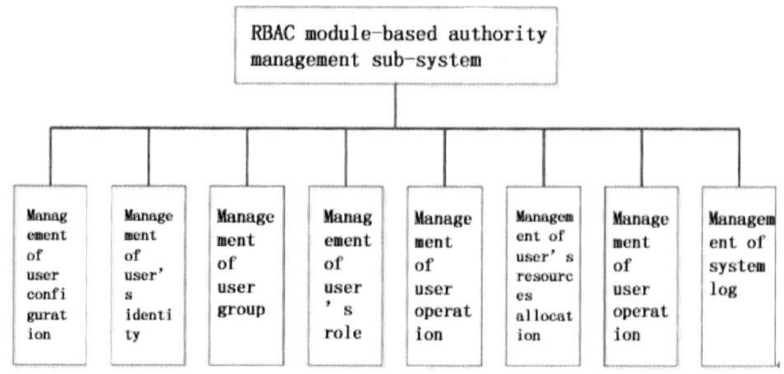

Figure 2. Main functional module units of workflow platform.

3.2. *Improved RBAC module*

On the basis of the traditional RBAC workflow module, it is discovered in this R & D that the safety quality management business flow of this project enterprise is not totally applicable to the R & D mode of the browser/server as the development mode of the traditional RBAC is generally about the client/server mode, which focus on the control in the development process and binds the specific user, role and authority through control. [5][6] In the webpage development process (browser/server), the business data are received and processed by the webpage which is not capable of analyzing the control in the specific software development process. It thus loses the business logic relevance capacity with the user's authority and role. [6][7]

As shown in Fig. 3, the most outstanding breaking point of the improved RBAC module is about the introduction of role set, which is equivalent to the specific organ (department) of one enterprise. WEB page is improved to introduce the third-party control related to the browser. The webpage user operation force and the role authorization are bound by this control in order to realize the basic design of the control front-stage interaction unit of the foundation through WEB page. [8]

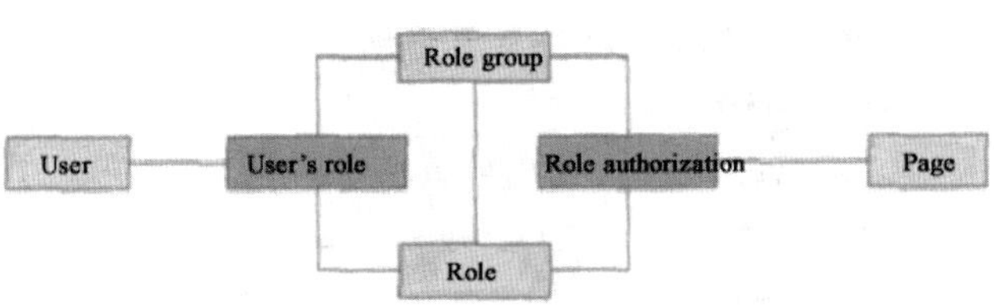

Figure 3. Basic principle diagram of improved RBAC model.

3.3. *Architectural design of RBAC module-based workflow management system*

In the R & D of this project, the architectural design of the workflow management system based on RBAC module is structurally divided into three layers, i.e., present layer, workflow management layer and database layer, as shown in Fig. 4.

(1) Presentation layer

The presentation layer is the part used by the user for the interface presentation of the front-stage operation. When analyzed from the perspective of the user, it can be divided into the process definition personnel, administrator and common user. Among them, the process definition personnel can define the workflow business logic layer through the process definition tools directly. The administrator can finish the process monitoring and management control of operation service through WEB interaction page and the user can manage the workflow lists through WEB interaction page. [10] Both the administrator and the common user manage and control the business logic through the workflow engine directly.

(2) Workflow management layer

Divided into the workflow engine and business processing logic layer, the workflow engine is the packaging middleware researched and developed individually and used for supporting WEB interaction and processing the interface relationship between the bottom layer business data. The workflow engine is divided into work item manager, operation service manager, process monitor and work list manager. The work item manager is mainly used for the management and control of the basic work item contents and is changed by the work list manager. If the common user manages the work list through WEB page, the data transmission and control of the work item manager are realized by the work list manager. The operation service manager and process monitor are mainly used for the monitoring and control management of the integral business logic layer. [9]

The business logic is the business design unit finished by the user according to the business characteristics through definition, including the process modeling module, event manager, organization structure manager, historical data manager and exception handling manager. The process modeling module is used for supporting the name of business segment and relevant property contents as determined by the process definition process. The event manager is triggered based on the event definition among the processes. The organization manager can realize the type and layer of the organization defined by the operation service manager. As the auxiliary supporting unit, historical data manager and exception handling manager can be used mainly for the exception handling and recovery of the workflow business. [8]

(3) Database and database management system

They are used for the storage and retrieval of the relevant business flow data. They are divided into the work flow business data structure and business data with the former one used for the metadata language definition of workflow engine, conceptual structure design, logistic structure design, etc. and the latter one used for saving the actual business data.

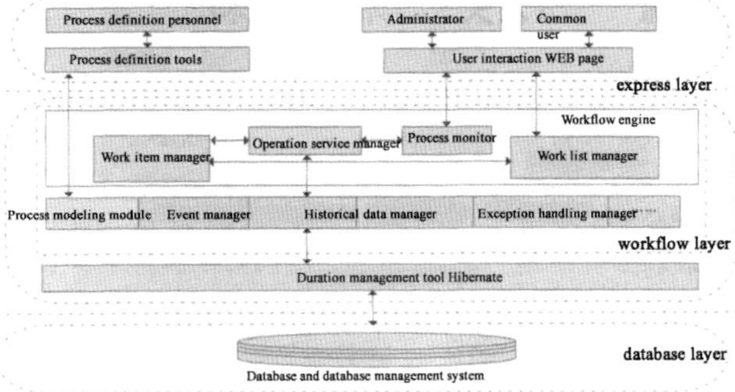

Figure 4. Architectural design of RBAC module-based workflow management system.

4. CONCLUSION

This article is focused on the summarization and organization of RBAC module-based enterprise workflow platform and the brief analysis and descriptions are made based on RBAC. On the basis of the R & D of safety quality management system in the project construction field, the improved RBAC module is proposed and the workflow management system based on RBAC module is analyzed.

In the operation process of the actual project, improved RBAC-based workflow platform has been successfully researched and developed and put into the project construction line. It plays a vital role in connecting several business systems and realizing the safety management of the user's identity in the management safety quality management of the project.

REFERENCES

- [1] Li Weiqin, Yang Yaping, Role-based Visit Control System [J], Electronic Engineer, 2000(26):16-21.
- [2] Yu Sen, Wang Yanzhang, Study on One Kind of Role Network Model-based Electronic Government System Framework and Realization [J], Computer Engineering and Application, 2003(12):31-35.
- [3] Huang Jian, Qing Hansi, Wen Hongzi, Visit Control of Role with Time Features [J], Software Journal, 2003, 14(11):1944-1954.
- [4] Wang Xinsheng, Study of RBAC Module and Realization of Its Application Framework, Master's Thesis, Jiangsu University, 2003. 4: p14-15.
- [5] An Weilian, Realization and Application of RBAC Module in J2EE Platform, Master's Thesis, Beijing University of Posts and Telecommunications, 2008. 4: p19-22.
- [6] Lei Jinmin, Study on the Workflow Technology and Realization of Workflow Engine, Master's Thesis, Wuhan University of Technology, 2008. 4:p35-36.
- [7] Li Ailing, Study and Design of Critical Technology of Workflow Platform Development [J], Research and Development, 2011. 4:p24.
- [8] Zhu Yu, Study and Realization of Workflow Engine, Master's Thesis, UESTC. 2004. 12:p43.
- [9] Cui Lei, Design and Development of RBAC-based Workflow Platform, Master's Thesis, Chengdu University of Technology, 2005. 5:p35.
- [10] Huang Mu, Design of RBAC Module-based Authority Management System, Master's Thesis, Jilin University, 2013. 5:p6.

Author Index